P. Sutherland

PAUL T. O'DONNELL

EUGENE L. MALEADY

Principles of Real Estate

W. B. SAUNDERS COMPANY

PHILADELPHIA / LONDON / TORONTO

W. B. Saunders Company: West Washington Square
Philadelphia, PA 19105

1 St. Anne's Road
Eastbourne, East Sussex BN21 3UN, England

1 Goldthorne Avenue
Toronto, Ontario M8Z 5T9, Canada

Principles of Real Estate   ISBN 0-7216-6911-5

© 1975 by W. B. Saunders Company. Copyright 1971 and 1974 by W. B. Saunders Company. Copyright under the International Copyright Union. All rights reserved. This book is protected by copyright. No part of it may be reproduced, stored in a retrieval system, or transmitted in any form or by any means, electronic, mechanical, photocopying, recording, or otherwise, without written permission from the publisher. Made in the United States of America. Press of W. B. Saunders Company. Library of Congress catalog card number 75-14863.

Last digit is the print number: 9   8   7   6   5

PREFACE

The authors have long recognized the need of the real estate profession for a single text which would cover the fundamental body of knowledge required by the professional in the field. They envisioned the development of this text as one which would provide to those interested, a single work which, when mastered, would not only prepare them for state licensing examinations, but would also expose them to the professional techniques of successful real estate practitioners with many years' experience in the field of real estate brokerage.

The first draft of this text was developed to fill this need. As the class - testing spread through some thirty odd states, the emphasis in its application changed from one of attempting to satisfy the requirements of separate state real estate licensing examinations to one of preparing the real estate practitioner to be able to function in a professional manner, and in the public interest, no matter where he might work within the country. We recognize that various state licensing laws differ in many details; nevertheless, it has become increasingly evident that, since the body of law governing the world of real estate stems from the one source, English Common Law, differences are more a matter of form than of substance.

To claim that any text, positively and for all time, has identified all essential areas of so vast a field as the profession of real estate would be presumptuous. Rather, this work is viewed as another step forward in what would seem to be an unending process of changes, additions, deletions, modifications, and refinements in future editions, necessitated by the hoped-for development of real estate into a truly professional field of endeavor.

Our effort was to analyze the basic scope of knowledge, legal and professional, required by the real estate associate, and to present a logical, sequential presentation of that requirement in a fundamental body of knowledge. We present this material not as a magic pill designed to instill knowledge painlessly, but as an effort to compress into one volume those legal requirements of which any practitioner in the field of real estate must be aware, must understand, and with which he must comply, together with a distillation of proven Listing and Closing Principles and Practices. We urge the reader to look upon this text only as a firm base on which to build further knowledge of the real estate profession.

In presenting that fundamental body of knowledge, the authors feel that the text may well serve as an introductory volume for the major in real estate or as a separate course for the major in Business Administration. From the starting point of this text, the real estate major can proceed to any of the specialized fields of real estate, and the Business Administration major can see the application of many of his other studies to this one field. Equally, many parts of the text will be pertinent to the homeowner, prospective homeowner, and the lessor and lessee.

No introduction would be complete without an expression of our appreciation to our friends and affiliates in the real estate world across the country and to the many students who have contributed so much to our education. Also, we must express our deepest gratitude to our co-workers and staff who gave so much in assistance, ideas, criticism: To Walt and Judy Hall; to Nancy Doherty who labored so patiently as editor, typist, proof-reader; to Jo O'Donnell, Ruth Brown, Jane Richter, and to all the other members of the staff.

Also, we wish to express a special note of thanks to Dr. Arthur Williams and Dr. Kenneth Lusht of Pennsylvania State University, to J. Howard Ridgway of the Community College of Philadelphia, to Professor Richard Howe of Orange Coast College, and to Professor Fred D. Veal of Miami - Dade Community College. Their invaluable critiques and suggestions assisted immeasurably in rounding out and refining the final product.

Paul T. O'Donnell
and
Eugene L. Maleady

CONTENTS
(General)

Preface

		Page
CHAPTER 1	THE REAL ESTATE PROFESSION	2
CHAPTER 2	SPECIALIZED FIELDS OF REAL ESTATE	15
CHAPTER 3	THE PRINCIPAL - AGENT RELATIONSHIP	39
CHAPTER 4	ON CONTRACTS	60
CHAPTER 5	GENESIS OF AMERICAN PROPERTY LAW	97
CHAPTER 6	FREEHOLD ESTATES AND TENANCIES	117
CHAPTER 7	NONFREEHOLD ESTATE AND TENANCIES	160
CHAPTER 8	TAXATION AND ASSESSMENT	183
CHAPTER 9	PRINCIPLES OF ECONOMICS AND REAL ESTATE APPRAISING	206
CHAPTER 10	DIGEST OF LISTING PRINCIPLES AND PRACTICES	227
CHAPTER 11	DIGEST OF CLOSING PRINCIPLES AND PRACTICES	256
CHAPTER 12	THE SALES CONTRACT	291
CHAPTER 13	REAL ESTATE FINANCING	322
CHAPTER 14	CONVEYANCING	397
CHAPTER 15	PROPERTY INSURANCE	445
CHAPTER 16	MATHEMATICS IN REAL ESTATE	478
APPENDIX A	CLOSING STATEMENTS	499
APPENDIX B	TRUTH-IN-LENDING	517
APPENDIX C	FEDERAL ANTI-DISCRIMINATION LAW	535
APPENDIX D	UNIFORM COMMERCIAL CODE	541
APPENDIX E	ADDRESSES OF REAL ESTATE LICENSE LAW OFFICIALS	545
APPENDIX F	CODE OF ETHICS NATIONAL ASSOCIATION OF REALTORS	551

Chapter 1

The Real Estate Profession

A.	EVOLVEMENT OF THE REAL ESTATE PROFESSION	2
	1. Beginnings	2
	2. End of the Frontier	2
	3. Post-Frontier Development	3
	4. Enactment of Homestead and Exemption Laws	3
	5. Land Speculation and Real Estate Brokerage	4
	6. Organized Real Estate Activities	5
	7. Regulation of Real Estate Practitioners	5
B.	THE SCOPE OF REAL ESTATE ACTIVITIES	6
	1. General	6
	2. Real Estate Today	6
	3. Scope as Correlated to Property Classification	6
	4. Scope as Correlated to Form of Employment	6
C.	REAL ESTATE AS A PROFESSION	7
	1. Definition	7
	2. The Real Estate Professional	7
	3. The Real Estate Profession	7
	a. Magnitude of the Industry	7
	b. The Profession's Fundamental Body of Knowledge	9
	4. Professional Standards and Criteria	10
	5. Inseparability of Theory from Practice	10
VISUAL AIDS		11
REVIEW QUESTIONS		13

Chapter 1
The Real Estate Profession

A. EVOLVEMENT OF THE REAL ESTATE PROFESSION

   1. <u>Beginnings</u>

The origins of the real estate brokerage business are lost somewhere in the mists of pre-history; however, since the real estate business revolves around the ownership, possession, and use of land, we have only to turn to the Bible to find innumerable references to ownership of land. Further, the museum of the University of Tennessee contains a stone tablet from Lagash, estimated to date from 2500 B.C., which contains the record of the sale of land by the king to the high priest.

In the original thirteen colonies, the chartered companies and proprietors, who were granted lands by the Kings of England through agents, sold lands and recruited settlers. With the birth of the United States and expansion to the West, newly acquired lands became public lands (federal property), were divided into parcels, and were sold or opened to homesteading, lending impetus to the development of the real estate business as we know it today.

   2. <u>End of the Frontier</u>

The settling of the fertile, well-watered and wooded regions east of the Mississippi is vividly described in J. M. Peck's "A New Guide for Emigrants to the West" (1836). Peck describes the "three classes, like the waves of the ocean" that inundated the wilderness. The pioneer, who subsisted "largely upon the natural growth of vegetation" and from the "proceeds of hunting," was the first to venture across the frontier into the wilderness. These pioneers cleared a patch of wooded area, built a crude log cabin, and moved on when they could sell their partially developed acreage to the second wave of settlers whose arrival crowded their existence and spurred their adventurous spirit. The newcomers extended the cultivated areas, cleared roads, bridged rivers and streams, planted orchards, constructed school houses and mills, and built houses of more permanence with glass windows. Civilization began to take root. Communications between settlements were established. Then, in a final wave, came men with "capital and enterprise" who erected structures of brick and stone, increased the products of agriculture above immediate needs, and sought wider markets for their surplus products. Commerce developed; diverse business enterprises emerged. Communities developed into towns. Newspapers, politicians and professional men entered the scene. At this point in our history we can sense the need for those with expertise in real property matters. The last advance carried settlers across the remaining reaches of the continent to the Pacific. This final advance began around 1840, and continued for a half a century until 1890, when the federal census declared the frontier at an end.

3. Post-Frontier Development

The frontiersman ceased to exist after his penetration of the last frontiers, the Pacific Coast - or what is now California and Oregon. Trading posts and missions sprang up; government aid was sought for the necessary irrigation projects, the transcontinental railroads, the development of mines and timber resources. The steady geographical advances westward of our forefathers kept the land problem alive. The settlers' demands generally were favored as against those who would exploit the public domain for strictly revenue purposes. Those in public office were forced by their constituents to present a suitable land policy. Heavy grants to the railroads and the passage of the Homestead Act were inevitable.

4. Enactment of the Homestead and Exemption Laws

In 1762, exactly 100 years before a Homestead Act was enacted in this country, Jean Jacques Rousseu's writings on the Social Contract were published. On real property he wrote, "In general, to establish the right of the first occupier over a plot of ground, the following conditions are necessary: first, the land must not yet be inhabited; second, a man must occupy only the amount he needs for his subsistence; and in the third place, possession must be taken, not by an empty ceremony, but by labour and cultivation, the only sign of proprietorship that should be respected by others, in default of a legal title."

Homestead and Exemption Laws in the United States were based on the belief that the public domain belonged to the people and that each head of a family was entitled to a home or farm which could not be seized for non-payment of debts. This theory was gradually developed for a half a century after 1785. We can be rather sure that brokerage in real estate was taking hold throughout the country around this time. Earlier laws were designed primarily to generate revenue for the Federal Government. Financial pressure which preceded the financial panic of 1837 was beginning to be felt at all levels of government.

In the original 13 states (and their later subdivisions) and in trans-Appalachian states of Kentucky, Tennessee, and Texas the states owned the public land within their boundaries and were not affected by federal land policy. However, in the rest of the original territory and in all the new areas annexed, land not already in private possession comprised the public domain. Faced with a financial crisis in 1835, the Federal Government sold these vast landholdings to extinguish the mounting public debt. The real estate brokerage business was established

The increasing demand for legislation to relieve the plight of tenant farmers pointed the way for the adoption of a general Homestead Law, and on May 20, 1862, The Homestead Act was enacted. This act provided that any citizen (or alien who had declared the intention of becoming a citizen) if 21 years old or head of a family, or if a veteran of at least 14 days' service in the armed forces of the United States during an actual war, and if the individual had never been engaged in a war against the United States or assisted in such a war, on payment of $10 could file a claim to not more than 160 acres of the surveyed public domain. After having "resided upon or cultivated" this land for the five subsequent years, and if by then a citizen, the settler could receive a patent on payment of additional fees.

The homestead so acquired was exempt from seizure by any creditor. Still, the difficulties experienced by the homesteaders were formidable. Transportation costs to the selected acreage, capital expenditures for housing, implements, fencing, and livestock depleted the settlers' funds and, in many instances, buried them in debt so deeply that any immediate success with crops tended to be nullified. As late as 1890, only one in three homesteaders was able to remain on his land long enough to get a deed.

During the 1860's and 1870's, certain of the major rail lines were financed by means of land grants. In some instances, these grants consisted of ten mile square blocks of land alternating on either side of the tracks as the black squares on a checkerboard. The real estate broker of today probably first appeared during this period as a land sale agent, operating on behalf of the transcontinental railroads. These railroads established land sale offices throughout the East and Middle West to sell their granted lands to farmer/settlers, frequently offering free transportation to the buyer and his family. The subsequent history of this operation was replete with scandal, and certain of our early rail barons out-rivaled the robber barons of the Middle Ages. Many an unsuspecting farmer sold his farm, paid for new land with the proceeds, and upon his arrival at the supposed new farm discovered, belatedly, that he had been swindled and was homeless and destitute, far from familiar home territory, family, and friends. Undoubtedly, some of the opprobrium which has tainted today's real estate broker stems from the scurrilous brokerage activities of this earlier era.

Despite such reprehensible practices and the enactment of the Homestead Act, the government was not dissuaded from granting large blocks and extensive acreage to the monopolist. By 1900, less than 600,000 farmers holding about 80,000,000 acres received patents. On the other hand, the railroad companies alone acquired title to 183,000,000 acres.

5. <u>Land Speculation and Real Estate Brokerage</u>

The "commutation clause" of the Homestead Act transformed many a homesteader into a speculator or agent. Only six months of settlement enabled the homesteader to purchase the land at $1.25 an acre. Acting in the capacity of real estate agents for buyers seeking huge estates, many settlers realized sizable profits without ever becoming actual homesteaders. In the 40 years between passage of The Homestead Act and the beginning of the 20th Century, only about one new farm in ten represented a free homestead. The number of real estate brokers at this period was significant enough to be the target of cities seeking additional sources of revenue. Late in the 1800's, they focused upon the idea of taxing those engaged in real estate brokerage with a license fee more akin to an occupation tax than a regulatory levy. Taxes of this nature were generally supported as they tended to eliminate, curtail, or control the practice of "Kitchen" or "Curbstone" brokerage.

6. <u>Organized Real Estate Activities</u>

At the close of the 19th Century, those leaders professionally engaged in real estate activities were attracted to each other and realized the advantages to be gained from formalized association. Local and state boards were formed across the nation and, as early as 1908, state boards joined together to form a national organization which was realized with the founding of the National Association of Real Estate Boards, NAREB - predecessor to the NATIONAL ASSOCIATION OF REALTORS (NAR) - an organization dedicated to professionalism in the real estate industry. The "Code of Ethics," drafted by NAREB in 1913, served well to define the moral conduct expected of its members. To further enable the general public to differentiate between members and non-members, NAREB, in 1916, registered the term "Realtor" (with a capital "R") to describe the professional in real estate who subscribes to the Association's Code of Ethics as a member of the national and local organization. The need for such an organization is reflected in its growth from 45 boards with about 3,000 members in 1908 to almost 1,600 boards with over 100,000 members in 1972.

7. <u>Regulation of Real Estate Practitioners</u>

The Code of Ethics of the National Association of Real Estate Boards served well to guide the activities of the organization's members, particularly in the absence of any real estate licensing law. The necessity for regulatory controls in the public interest was recognized in the early years of the 20th Century. In 1908, the prosecuting attorney for Los Angeles sought a state law to punish those selling real estate under false pretenses. The need was felt nationwide and in 1913 NAREB voted to encourage the enactment of real estate regulatory laws in every state. In 1911, the Legislature of California was the first to pass a statute regulating real estate brokers. This legislation, however, was vetoed by the Governor. In 1917, a similar act was passed, but was almost immediately challenged and subsequently held unconstitutional by the courts.

Nevertheless, the trend had been started. In February, 1919, Oregon passed a real estate license law which became effective on May 29, 1919. The first effective real estate license law became a reality. Today, real estate licensing laws are effective in all states.

B. THE SCOPE OF REAL ESTATE ACTIVITIES

1. General

Real estate activities today encompass, either directly or indirectly, a field of activity both private and public that taxes the imagination. Of itself, the term "real estate" embraces any and every estate or interest in land and the improvements thereon. An "interest" in land is further analyzed as encompassing its use, possession, and disposition, which may or may not involve ownership. An "estate" in land may be better understood as relating to one's quantity of interest in land. To further complicate our comprehension of the vast scope of real estate activities, we must consider that the elusive term "real estate" includes "real property", defined as land, buildings, minerals, and other products of the soil as well as the air space above the soil. This, however, is but a partial biopsy of but one of the two classifications of real property (i.e., corporeal property). Incorporeal property, such as easements, rights-of-way, and licenses, and any other interest in realty (real property) which cannot be considered physical and which is not readily apparent is the second consideration.

2. Real Estate Today

The real estate business has been defined as a "vocation in which real property forms the stock in trade and is bought, sold, leased, or rented." It involves those who deal for themselves, or as agents for others, or both. One can conceive that whenever the "stock in trade" includes land, buildings, minerals, and other products of the soil, the air space above the soil, easements, rights-of-way, licenses, and any other such interest, activities in real estate are involved. When we further consider that land pervades and permeates the physical, economic, social, and political aspects of society, we may begin to imagine the importance, the impact, and the implications of the real estate business.

3. Scope as Correlated to Property Classification

When viewed from the classifications assigned to properties, the spectrum of real estate activities extends from residential property at one end to investment properties at the other with the broad classification of income properties (including business, industrial, and agricultural properties) spanning the gap between the two. (Reference Paragraph C1, Chapter 2, Specialized Fields of Real Estate.)

4. Scope as Correlated to Form of Employment

Succinctly, the scope of real estate activities is embraced by the three broad types of employment normally encountered: the practitioner acting as an agent, an independent contractor, or on his own behalf. (Reference Paragraph B, Chapter 2, Specialized Fields of Real Estate).

C. REAL ESTATE AS A PROFESSION

1. Definition

The real estate profession has been aptly described by the Florida Real Estate Commission as "a calling in which skill and experience in real estate values and practices, coupled with high standards of integrity, are offered as a service to the public, and confidence in the possession and application of these qualities is invited."

We hear a great deal about the need for "professionalism" in today's competitive real estate market. The word "professionalism" is used repeatedly . . . and usually without a thorough understanding of what professionalism entails. If aspiring real estate agents are to become professional, if real estate firms are to be regarded by the public as truly professional organizations, it behooves each of us to know precisely the dimensions of our frame of reference. We should, then, dissect the word "professional", examine its component parts, put it back together again, and then determine how best to achieve or earn the appellation "professional."

2. The Real Estate Professional

Current interpretations describe a professional as one who has, through education and training, grasped the principles (i. e., theory) of his profession and proceeds to apply effectively and with wisdom these principles in practice. The word "profession," per se, suggests a position requiring a considerable amount of higher education. At one time, the term referred mainly to the three learned professions of law, medicine, and theology. Today, the term is used less exclusively and tends to give status to many other ways of earning a livelihood. Precisely used, however, the word "professional" relates to the more learned callings. Such being the case, we must consider whether or not real estate, a calling, and the fundamental body of knowledge necessary to master the intricacies of its activities are sufficiently comprehensive in both scope and depth to fall within the definition of a profession.

3. The Real Estate Profession

a. Magnitude of the Industry -

It is probably conservative to estimate that two thirds of the world's entire wealth is invested in real estate. Joseph P. Klock, a leader in the real estate industry, describes the field of real estate vividly:

> "On it is built the hospital in which we are born, the homes in which we live, our places for work and worship, and our last resting place. On land is grown the food we eat. Land cradles the water which every living thing needs to stay alive. No known force can destroy it. Since the beginning of time, land has served as the basis of wealth. Through the centuries men have warred for its possession. Men have spent their

life's strength to acquire land. From the loss of it, thrones, fortunes, and whole civilizations have fallen."

In the United States, real estate equities represent the largest indicator of value in our national economy. Real estate brokerage and counseling is a multi-billion dollar business.

The magnitude of the real estate business is such as to dwarf any other field of endeavor in the United States. Consider only one aspect: It is estimated that merely to maintain our present number of private dwellings, whether individual homes or apartments, during the decade 1970 to 1980 we will require 2,000,000 units per year to replace those which become obsolete or are destroyed.

In 1973, some 2.4 million units were produced at a mean sales price of $30,000, for a total volume of $72 billion. In the same year, Detroit's best ever, automobile sales reached $68 billion. The $72 billion figure, of course, does not include resale of existing homes, commercial and investment real estate, rental, and all the other fields of real estate.

To consider another aspect of residential sales . . . the average mortgage, reportedly, is in existence something less than eight years, and there are approximately 64 million residential units in the United States, 70% owner occupied. At a conservative estimate, based upon these figures, 5 million would be re-sold annually. Again using our mean price of $30,000, we arrive at the staggering figure of $150 billion. And we are still talking residential real estate only.

The ramifications of the industry can be clearly seen in the 1974-1975 recession, with unemployment in construction trades topping the unemployment figures, layoffs in appliance factories, in lumber companies, in manufacturing plants of such varied items as pipe, electric cable, nails, screws, septic tanks, what have you.

This vast industry is, moreover, a fragmented one. There are no big three or big ten in the real estate business. Instead, it is made up of a multitude of small firms, the "giants" among them employing a maximum of 800 to 900 employees. In most areas of the country, a real estate brokerage firm which employs 50 people would be considered "large," and there would probably not be more than one of such size in any county.

In such a fragmented industry, gathering of statistics is most difficult. Although many individuals across the country have been licensed as real estate brokers or salespersons, the actual number practicing in the field is difficult to determine. The NATIONAL ASSOCIATION of REALTORS, the professional association which dominates the field, projects a membership of 500,000 for 1975. The membership is restricted to brokers and salesmen, so the figure does not include the administrative and support staffs of the firms. Lumping together these groups with non-members would certainly make an estimate of 1,000,000 employees, in the sales end of real estate alone, a conservative figure.

The conclusion, then, is that the biggest business in the country is, in fact, a conglomeration of small businesses; however, the shape of things to come is visible. A handful of companies around the company have expanded into multi-branch operations, each branch essentially small in itself, but the whole approaching proportions never before seen in the industry. More visible, and growing more rapidly, are networks of affiliated firms, using common identifications, common advertising, common methods, and, through association, attempting to obtain the benefits of big business economies, purchasing power, and marketing ability.

b. The Profession's Fundamental Body of Knowledge -

The body of knowledge clothing this vast industry demands mastery in varying degrees of a wide range of subjects which include: building construction; architectural forms; period designs; land development and subdivision; land descriptions; interior decorating; city planning; population growth and trends; transportation factors; taxation and assessments as they relate to the acquisition, retention, and disposition of property; government impact on real estate relative to restrictions, zoning, building codes, subsidized housing programs; existing and proposed legislation; animal husbandry; agrology; agronomy; sociology; topography; psychology; investment analysis; legal ramifications of the laws of property; principal-agent relationship; conveyancing; contracts; state licensing law and applicable regulatory rules; merchandising; economics; appraising; management, to include both personnel and property; financial aspects of property sales, leases, and exchanges; accounting procedures in preparing closing statements; market analysis; environmental design; and counseling . . . to name the most important. In this frame of reference it would appear reasonable that real estate is, indeed, sufficiently demanding of a considerable amount of higher education to be classified more precisely as a profession than a business. This observation, of course, is not to infer that one engaged in real estate activities is, by such involvement, automatically projected before, and accepted by, the public as a professional. Much is yet to be accomplished before the erroneous image of the prototype shoddy real estate broker or salesman is erased from the public's mind.

4. Professional Standards and Criteria

Despite the advances made and the sophistication injected into all areas of real estate activities, almost exclusively attributable to the educational and training programs of the proprietary institutions and, in particular, the NATIONAL ASSOCIATION OF REALTORS through its educational arm, the National Institute of Real Estate Brokers (NIREB), much remains to be done. The acceleration of change in our society, spinning us almost uncontrollably into the super-technological society of the immediate future, presses the industry to intensify its education and training efforts to insure a more thorough and faster mastery of the ever increasing flood of required knowledge which is being generated at a rate which seemingly defies complete comprehension or absorption.

The real estate industry, for all its progress, historically has been fragmented and disorganized. As a consequence, it has failed, and continues to fail, in its competition with other businesses and industries to attract the money, manpower, and public trust that it is striving to deserve. Partially, but perhaps significantly, contributing to this failure is the profession's failure to clearly establish the perimeters which encompass and identify the fundamental body of real estate knowledge that should serve as the base from which future developments and progress can be measured. Lacking a clearly identifiable and acceptable fundamental body of real estate knowledge, the profession has been unable to develop, scientifically and meticulously, universally recognized professional standards (and the accompanying criteria) against which the real estate practitioner can be measured . . . not only by his peers, but by the public as well. Of necessity, professional standards and criteria must be born out of the womb of that fundamental body of knowledge.

5. Inseparability of Theory from Practice

As professional real estate standards and criteria are inseverably connected with its fundamental body of knowledge, so, too, is the acquisition of knowledge inseparable from the effective application of this knowledge in daily practice.

While absorption and understanding of required knowledge is a prerequisite to the realization of success in any endeavor, such, of itself, is insufficient if one is to be accepted as a professional.

Logical theory, coupled with effective practice, cannot be divorced from one another, if productive results are to be achieved in any sphere.

The development and utilization of standards and criteria, carefully tailored to measure not only one's absorption of the required real estate knowledge but also designed as well to measure the practitioner's effectiveness in application, will, eventually, but inevitably, purge the industry of those lacking the attributes, abilities, will, desire, and enthusiasm essential to success.

REAL ESTATE FIRSTS

1835   **FIRST PUBLIC LAND SALES**

1862   **HOMESTEAD ACT**

1908   **FIRST NATIONAL ORGANIZATION**
               NAREB

1919   **FIRST STATE LICENSE LAW**
               OREGON

SCOPE
AS CORRELATED TO
PROPERTY CLASSIFICATION

1. Residential
2. Income
3. Investment

SCOPE
AS CORRELATED TO
FORMS OF EMPLOYMENT

1. Agency
2. Independent Contractor
3. Principal Acting on Own Behalf

Chapter 1

REVIEW DEFINITIONS IN GLOSSARY OR TEXT OF FOLLOWING TERMS:

    commutation clause   NAREB
    conveyance   NIREB
    corporeal property   patent
    estate   real estate
    homestead   real property
    Homestead Laws   REALTOR
    incorporeal property   realty
    interest   speculator

REVIEW QUESTIONS:

1. At what point can we reason that real estate, as a business, had its beginning in the United States?

2. What were the Homestead and Exemption Laws based on?

3. What states were not affected by federal land policy?

4. When was the Homestead Act enacted?

5. What were the provisions of the Homestead Act?

6. When could a settler receive title to public land?

7. Could a creditor seize one's land acquired under the Homestead Act?

8. What was the "commutation clause" of the Homestead Act?

9. Which state passed the first effective real estate license law?

FOR ANSWERS TO REVIEW QUESTIONS

1.

2.

3.

4.

5.

6.

7.

8.

9.

Chapter 2

Specialized Fields of Real Estate

A.	INTRODUCTION			17
B.	FORM OF EMPLOYMENT AS FRAMEWORK OF SPECIALIZATION			17
	1.	Agency		18
		a. Factor		18
		b. Broker		18
			(1) Real Estate Broker	18
			(2) Real Estate Salesman	19
	2.	Independent Contractor		20
	3.	Master-Servant		20
	4.	Principal Acting on Own Behalf		20
C.	SPECIALIZATION UNDER AGENCY RELATIONSHIP			21
	1.	According to Property Type		21
		a. Residential Property		21
		b. Income Property		22
			(1) Commercial Property	22
			(2) Industrial Property	23
			(3) Agricultural Property	25
		c. Investment Property		25
	2.	According to Services Offered		25
		a. Property Management		25
		b. Mortgage Placement Service		26
		c. Business Opportunities or Business Chance/Sales		26
		d. Property Insurance		28

D.	\multicolumn{2}{l	}{SPECIALIZATION AS AN INDEPENDENT CONTRACTOR}	29

- D. **SPECIALIZATION AS AN INDEPENDENT CONTRACTOR** — 29
  1. <u>Appraising</u> — 29
  2. <u>Counseling</u> — 29

- E. **SPECIALIZATION AS PRINCIPAL ACTING ON OWN BEHALF** — 29
  1. <u>Land Programs</u> — 30
     - a. Land Acquired for Speculation — 30
     - b. Land Acquired for Development — 30
       - (1) Subdividing — 30
       - (2) Developing — 30
  2. <u>Building Programs</u> — 31
     - a. Speculative Building — 31
     - b. Speculative Buying — 31
     - c. Buying to Renovate and Resell — 31

- F. **MISCELLANEOUS AREAS OF SPECIALIZATION** — 32

VISUAL AIDS — 32

REVIEW QUESTIONS — 37

Chapter 2
Specialized Fields of Real Estate

A. INTRODUCTION

Unfortunately it is true that most people, interested in or entering the real estate profession, are aware only of those facets exposed to them in the listing and selling of residential properties. The diversified, specialized, and potentially lucrative opportunities which exist in income and investment properties are seldom initially brought to the attention of the neophyte. As a consequence, the attitudes, aptitudes, and attributes which often would render them adaptable to these more complex and sophisticated real estate activities are not expeditiously tapped.

The immeasurable, but undoubtedly tremendous, opportunities looming in the real estate profession as a consequence of the expected population growth, with the accompanying economic expansion, should suffice to attract the attention and stimulate the interest of an increasing number of individuals to the broad field of real estate as a career.

In an effort to divide this extensive career field into specialized categories, we must first realize that the two general areas open to investigation are the public and private areas of real estate activities. Those real estate activities associated with the various levels, departments, and agencies of the federal, state, and local governments relative to taxation, acquisition, disposal, management, control, regulation, and financing of real property, usually on a non-profit basis, comprise the public area of real estate specialties. This chapter will be channelized toward those activities which primarily come under the umbrella of the <u>private</u> real estate sector.
In an effort to dissect this sprawling area of specialization in a logical manner, the <u>form of real estate employment</u> will be adopted as the generic category under which the specialized activities will be classified.

B. FORM OF EMPLOYMENT AS FRAMEWORK OF SPECIALIZATION

Whenever an employment relationship is created between two persons, one the employer and the other a dependent worker, either actually or potentially, such relationship falls within the purview of the labor laws. The type of work is of no significance; whether the work is physical or mental is immaterial. The subordination of one individual to another in an employment relationship is the only test that need be applied. And yet, in a practical sense, discerning precisely that which differentiates the master from the servant, the servant from the independent contractor, or the agent from any of the others is not always an easy matter. The following categories and classifications are attendant upon usually accepted definitions, devoid of intricate legal interpretations.

1. Agency (Reference Chapter 3, The Principal-Agent Relationship)

Whenever a real estate associate agrees with a real estate owner to locate a buyer or tenant, or to search for real estate for a purchaser or prospective tenant, that associate is acting in the capacity of an agent. The one whom he serves is his principal. The type of property is immaterial; it may be residential, income, or investment property. Any real estate associate hired to perform specific real estate brokerage services for a commission in accordance with an agreement is automatically an agent. He may become an agent without compensation as it has been held that the absence of compensation is immaterial.

The rights and powers of the agent and the function he performs frequently classify him as either a "factor" or a "broker". While in real estate activities one is generally not concerned with the responsibilities of a factor agent, a rudimentary understanding of a "factor" may, perhaps, enable us to more clearly understand the functions of a broker. It may be well to emphasize at this point that while all brokers are agents, not all agents are brokers.

    a. Factor

        A factor, generally referred to as a commission merchant, is one who is involved in the business of receiving and selling goods for a commission. The factor has both possession and control of another's property (which is usually personal property) and has the authority to sell such property. Ordinarily, a factor has goods delivered to him with the understanding that he may sell them in his own name. A broker, on the other hand, may act only in the name of his principal.

    b. Broker

        (1) Real Estate Broker

            As specifically applied to the field of real estate, a broker is rather lengthily described in most states along such lines as "a person, partnership, association or corporation who, for another, and for a fee, commission, or other valuable consideration, or with the intention or in the expectation or upon the promise of receiving or collecting a fee, commission or other valuable consideration, sells, exchanges, purchases or leases or negotiates, offers, attempts or agrees to negotiate the sale, exchange, purchase, rental, or leasing of any real estate, or buys or offers to buy, sells or offers to sell, or otherwise deals in options on real estate, or advertises or holds himself out as engaged in the business of selling, exchanging, purchasing, renting, or leasing real estate, or assists or directs in the procuring of prospects or the negotiation or completion of any agreement or transaction which results or is intended to result in the sale, exchange, purchase, leasing, or renting of any real estate, or negotiates or offers, attempts, or agrees to negotiate a loan secured or to be secured by mortgage or other encumbrance upon real estate."

The term "real estate broker" shall also include "any person employed by or on behalf of the owner or owners of real estate at a stated salary and/or commission basis or other compensation to sell, exchange, or offer for sale such real estate or any part thereof, and who shall sell or exchange, or offer or attempt or agree to negotiate the sale or exchange of any lot or parcel of real property."

The term "brokerage" relates predominantly to the activities of one known as an agent who serves as an intermediary in the sale of commodities belonging to the seller for an agreed upon compensation usually based upon a percentage of the gross selling price of the commodities.

Today, some states also include still another activity in brokerage which a few years ago required a special license. This activity revolves around the brokerage of "business opportunities", with or without the conveyancing of title to the real property or an interest therein. A "business opportunity" is defined as meaning and including the sale or lease of a business and goodwill of an existing business enterprise or opportunity.

It is important to consider that the sale of a business opportunity involves the selling of personal property. In several states the special classification of "business opportunity license" no longer exists. In these states applicants for licensure are examined on business opportunity brokerage practices and, upon receipt of their real estate license, may legally negotiate business opportunity transactions. Just as a real estate broker is authorized in many states to act as a business opportunity broker, so, too, may a real estate salesman act as a business opportunity salesman.

(2) Real Estate Salesman

A real estate salesman, or associate, or affiliate broker, is an individual who performs any act or engages in any transaction which results or is intended to result in the sale, exchange, purchase, renting, or leasing of any real estate, or in a loan secured or to be secured by mortgage or other encumbrance upon real estate. He is employed by and is under the direction and supervision of a broker, or a regular employer engaged in the real estate business. The salesman is the agent of the broker and is responsible to his principal, the employing broker, for those obligations imposed under the Law of Principal-Agent. As such, a real estate salesman cannot be an independent contractor.

2. Independent Contractor

One may enter into a contractual employment relationship with another in one of three ways. If an individual subjects himself and his services to the disposal of another in such a manner that his actions are generally controlled by the latter, either a master-servant or an agency relationship, as previously described, is established. If, however, the contractual employment relationship reflects that the second party is to effect a specific end result and is to retain full control over the details and manner in which the work is to be conducted in bringing about the result, he is considered to be an independent contractor. Furthermore, in such a relationship, the recipient of such services is usually not responsible to third parties either in tort or in contract for the actions of the independent contractor.

3. Master-Servant

As defined by the Labor Code, an ordinary employee, or servant, is one who is employed to render personal services to his employer, other than in the pursuit of an independent calling, and who, in such service, remains entirely under the direction and control of the master. An employee (servant) works for his employer (master). An agent goes a step further in acting for and in the place of the principal in business and legal dealings with third parties. In the typical real estate office of moderate size, the secretary-receptionist or filing clerk would be an ordinary employee. Normally, a real estate broker (affiliate or associate) hired by a principal would not be classified as an employee. Nor would a real estate salesman. Both, in most states, as a matter of law, are agents of the real estate broker under whom they are licensed.

Many statutes govern the relationship between the master and the servant. In an employer-employee relationship, the employer is obliged to withhold and deposit income taxes; withhold and deposit employee's social security payment, and match such payments with an equal sum; observe wage and hour laws; observe child labor laws; make contributions to the state unemployment compensation fund; and carry workmen's compensation insurance. For the purposes of most license laws, it is of primary significance to each licensee that salesmen and affiliate or associate brokers are always agents of the employing broker and cannot function as independent contractors nor as strictly employees.

4. Principal Acting on Own Behalf

Frequently a real estate licensee will become involved in real estate transactions on his own account. The California Department of Real Estate in its Reference Book relating to real estate practices wisely cautions the licensed broker in this respect.

> "The licensed broker should be particularly careful
> in this respect, as his contacts with real estate owners
> and prospective purchasers are made largely because
> of the fact that he is a licensed agent. His office signs,
> signs on property, and printed stationery all advertise
> the fact that he is a licensed real estate broker and care
> must be taken to dispel this impression if he chooses
> to act as a principal in dealing with real property. It
> is particularly dangerous for the broker to start out on
> a transaction with the status of an agent and subse-
> quently, during the time the deal is in progress, switch
> his status to that of a principal. Various court decisions
> indicate that the burden of proof under these circum-
> stances is upon the agent to show that the person with
> whom he was dealing was fully informed of his change
> in status."

The primary objective of the principal acting on his own behalf is to realize a profit on transactions relating to the sale or purchase of real properties or interest therein.

The specialized fields of real estate may be broadly indexed under two major categories, either in accordance with the specific types of properties involved, or the specialized service offered.

C. SPECIALIZATION UNDER AGENCY RELATIONSHIP

1. According to Property Type

The classification of property as to type extends from residential property at one end of the spectrum to investment property at the other. These two specialized property types are overlapped by a third, extremely broad, classification which we will call "income property."

a. Residential Property

Residential property is generally construed to mean that property primarily acquired for use as a residence. In some parts of the country the word "residence" refers exclusively to a one-family dwelling while "residential property" implies two to four family houses, inclusive. For the purposes of isolating a specialized field of real estate, our definition focuses on the former interpretation. Residential property, therefore, used primarily as a residence or "private home" forms the backbone of most real estate operations, and very often during the early phases of expansion into other specializations, the activity and profits generated from this "bread and butter" activity subsidize the more glamorous aspects of the industry. In the field of residential real estate we first detect the development of a fundamental body of real estate knowledge representing the theory and practice of real estate, as applied during the course of the practitioner's daily activities. This is often the training area and the breeding ground for those with the special abilities and attributes which cause them to be absorbed into the more intricate, complex, and sophisticated areas of specialization. Even within the classification of residential property, one can readily recognize the probable need for further specialization in one of the following sub-classifications of residential property:

> Existing homes
> New homes
> Second homes
> House lots or sites
> Bulk land for residential developments
> Condominiums and Cooperatives.

b. Income Property

Income property is a broad classification of property which produces income directly (e. g., rental property) or as a factor in the production of income (e. g., commercial property used in one's trade or business). Because of the distinctive considerations attached to the various types of properties which may be acquired primarily for investment and the associated areas of competency demanded of those involved in such transactions, investment properties are considered as a separate classification.

The sub-classifications under income property may be identified as commercial, industrial, and agricultural properties.

(1) Commercial Property. This type of income property, as distinguished from industrial or agricultural properties, is normally zoned for business purposes. It would include parking lots, lofts, warehouses, gasoline stations, shopping centers, resort property, and stores and shops of all descriptions. Property held for the production of income through rental to one or more tenants is also included in the sub-classification of commercial properties. Office buildings, motels, hotels, apartment complexes, et cetera, are examples of commercial properties used to generate rental income. Obviously, specialists involved in transactions relating to these types of property must be well grounded in accounting, finance, economics, and appraising.

Migration to the suburbs has had a most significant effect on society in the development of the suburban or exurban shopping centers. With the population spillage into suburbia, in-town shops, particularly department stores, were quick to follow the flow. Around every city or metropolitan area during the past twenty years we have witnessed the consolidation and transformation of small, rural communities into large suburbs housing a mobile population which leaves its area of residence daily to commute to the city or to the suburban industrial/business area.

This movement has led to the establishment of real estate firms whose associates specialize entirely in the field of developing shopping centers or malls; others specialize in drive-in theaters; still others in locating, acquiring and developing sites for franchise-type food operations. The list is virtually endless, and each requires an expertise peculiar to its own field.

Concurrently, this flight to the suburbs has created a new field of real estate specialization within the central city relating to commercial real estate brokerage expertise in redevelopment within the inner city. Atlantic City and Sacramento are prime examples of the trend in this direction.

The urban mall, comprising a mix of office buildings, department stores, specialty shops, restaurants, hotels, and frequently apartment houses, creates a multiplicity of opportunities for a wide variety of specialists within the real estate profession.

Opportunities for the associate specializing in office buildings are almost limitless. The types of office buildings are myriad, ranging from the inner city skyscrapers to the sprawling suburban office parks or the small professional buildings which dot the suburban towns. Although other types of business activities are steadily fleeing to the suburbs, financial institutions, investment houses, and specialized businesses (e. g., insurance) give rise to a host of inter-dependent business activities which not only keep parts of the inner cities alive and active, but generate a continuing demand for office space. Similarly, the imaginative real estate professionals who can refurbish and convert the old, classical structures to suit modern demands have a fertile field to sow and harvest.

(2) Industrial Property. Industrial property, as described by the American Institute of Real Estate Appraisers, is "a combination of land, improvements, and machinery which has been adjusted, synchronized, and perfected into a functioning unit intended for the assembling, processing, and manufacturing of finished or partially finished products from raw materials or fabricated parts . . . industrial property includes property used for the production of natural resources, such as, minerals and oil."

Historically, industrial development has been guided by several important considerations which are decisive when determining the probability of expansion and profitable growth. Heavy industry in its quest for continued development requires an acceptable combination of raw material source, labor supply, transportation network, and favorable political and economic climates. The steel industry presents us with the classic example of the meshing of these important factors with iron ore being transported by truck, ship, barge, or rail to the proximity of the coal supply necessary for fabrication. Labor then concentrated in the area where opportunities for employment emerged. Rail, water, and road networks mushroomed to move the finished products to far-flung markets. The textile industry developed in similar fashion. Cotton was moved by ship to New England coastal areas where, initially, water-powered mills, serviced by skilled immigrant workers, fabricated the finished products which were then transported by ship and rail to market.

Light industry, which was not saddled with the heavy transportation costs for raw materials, tended to concentrate in the vicinity of heavy industry or city areas where the concentrated pool of labor could be tapped. Hence, the phenomenal growth of such great industrial centers as Pittsburgh, Detroit, and Chicago. Today, although heavy industry is still pressured by the same high transportation costs, improved means of transportation such as the present day huge ocean and lake going bulk carriers have, to a degree, helped keep costs within reason. Heavy industries, consequently, tend to remain fixed in areas where they were established.

Light industry, however, appears to be following the overall trend towards decentralization which is evidenced by the population flight to suburbia, with the additional spur to industry in the development of the national, interstate highway system. The same phenomenon which has led to urban sprawl and megalopolis, with the accompanying atrophy and decay of the inner cities, has given birth to the industrial park, situated beside the interstate highway over which goods can move expeditiously to markets anywhere within the country, or to ports for overseas shipment.

Yet another factor seen increasingly prominent in the development of light industry is the growth of area industries with companion and complementary businesses locating in the same area. This flight to the suburbs has created a diversity of exciting opportunities for the real estate associate. Specialists in land sales in metropolitan area suburbs today have extensive opportunities to fuse land packages not only for individual homes, apartment complexes, or shopping centers, but for industrial parks as well. Marginal lands, unsuited for residential purposes, may well be adapted for light industry, truck terminals which tend to follow industry, warehouses, or distribution centers. Obviously, the specialist in this highly technical area of real estate would be expected to be familiar in areas of construction, financing, land use, taxation, zoning, market and economic trends, transportation considerations, and the availability and cost of labor and raw materials. Specialization in this area would require at least a rudimentary knowledge of the manufacturing process, cost accounting, material handling and storage.

    (3)   Agricultural Property. Land devoted to, and especially suited for, the raising of crops or livestock falls within this sub-classification of income property. The legal rules and principles of real property law applicable to the ownership and disposition of this type of property are sufficiently extensive to warrant specialization. The differentiation of crops as "fructus naturales" or "fructus industrialis", for example, is an area singularly associated with agricultural property. The Doctrine of Emblements, the Contract of Agistment, state control of diseased animals, and the nature and use of cattle, railroad, and partition fences are areas generally foreign to one's real estate involvement in other property classifications.

  c. Investment Property

Investment property as distinguished from income property is real property acquired for the specific purpose of realizing a profitable return at some future date. It is property which is not held (as is income property) for the immediate and continuing production of income. Such property generally consists of unimproved real estate held for the purpose of capital growth through increases in real estate prices. The ability to counsel buyers and sellers in this sophisticated area of real estate requires long years of experience supplemented by accumulated knowledge of the specific market areas where such property is located. How, what, when, where to buy and sell investment properties, the dangers of speculation, the application of economic principles, how best to financially acquire and legally take title, determining the right price, understanding and anticipating the fluctuation in land value . . . all are areas of knowledge which assume special significance in investment property. Theodore Roosevelt has stated, "Every person who invests in well selected real estate in a growing section of a prosperous community adopts the surest and the safest method of becoming independent, for real estate is the basis of wealth." Individuals specializing in investment properties project and represent themselves as being competent to advise buyers in the proper selection of property for investment.

2.   <u>According to Services Offered</u>

    a.   Property Management. Property management involves the licensee acting in the capacity of an agent for his principal (the property owner) as a business manager responsible for the diverse duties inherent in that title. The principal/owner is usually interested in realizing the highest return with the least amount of personal inconvenience or involvement from his property commensurate with its highest and best use over the economic life of the property. In fulfilling his responsibilities, the property manager must be proficient in the areas of advertising, merchandising, property maintenance, property preservation, personnel qualification and supervision, showing techniques, employment application preparation and processing, leasing practices - to include cost accounting practices, property insurance, tax implications, as well as the political, social, and economic problems which invariably arise.

The property manager, as an agent, stands in a fiduciary relationship with his principal and is governed by and subject to the law of agency. He is obliged to be obedient, loyal, and faithful to his principal. He must exercise judgment, prudence, and skill and perform his duties diligently. He must keep his principal fully advised and even suggest the disposition of the property if, in his judgment, such serves the best interest of the property owner.

For guidance and direction in legal, tax, fiscal, and other matters where he lacks the knowledge or expertise, the property manager must be sufficiently prudent to engage the services of competent experts. As a manager of income property, his field of specialization would embrace the manifold property classifications reflected in Paragraph C 1b, above.

b. Mortgage Placement Service. The purchaser of real estate who can pay in cash the full purchase price of the property is rare indeed. Most transactions involving the transfer of title to real property require some degree of financing. It has even been suggested that "selling real estate is usually selling down payment and credit terms." Moderate to large size real estate firms are often deluged with loan applications. The broker may wish to exploit this source of business activity by creating either a special loan department or a subsidiary mortgage company and become a loan agent of a mortgage lending institution. In most states, when one acts for a compensation in negotiating a new loan, or for selling an existing mortgage note, he is required to be licensed as a real estate broker or salesman.

c. Business Opportunities or Business Chance/Sales. A "business opportunity" or "business chance" is defined as meaning and including the sale or lease of the business and goodwill of an existing business enterprise or opportunity. A business opportunity or business chance broker includes all persons, firms, corporations and associations that engage directly or indirectly in the business of buying, selling, or dealing in any established business or business opportunity, or goodwill or interest therein, or who, for a profit, compensation, or commission, engage in the business of offering to establish others in business or who declare to the public that they are engaged in the business of buying, selling, or dealing in established businesses or business opportunities. In many states the special classification of business opportunity license no longer exists. Statutes in these states have merged business opportunity and real estate licenses.

Business opportunity brokerage is indeed a sophisticated specialization, taxing not only the licensee's persuasive abilities but his technical knowledge as well. To explore a sampling of these areas of required knowledge, we may cite the broker's duty to determine the existence of any pending citations or violations from governmental agencies against the business and/or the owner that would prevent the selling or transferring of any license or permit. Matters relating to the employees must be thoroughly examined to include the number of personnel involved, health and welfare programs, insurance, paid vacations, the terms of a union contract if one is in force, business hours, business days, et cetera. All items reflected on the firm's balance sheet and operating statement should be meticulously checked. Payment of business taxes should be insured and, wherever applicable, the sale and use tax law must be complied with where retail sales of tangible personal property are made. The broker must advise his client of the necessity to certify, where necessary, the working condition of all equipment used in the operation of the business. The required clearance from appropriate governmental agencies to legally effect the business transfer must be secured. If a lease exists, it must be circumspectly studied to include the right of the seller to assign his interest therein.

The broker's skill in estimating value will be summoned into play in arriving at a competitive list price. His deliberation must enable him to properly value physical stock, furniture, fixtures, supplies, and equipment. Additionally, he may be called upon to establish a value on that intangible expectation of continued public patronage known as "goodwill". Furthermore, under the Uniform Commercial Code pertaining to bulk transfers of goods, the broker should see that the seller and buyer observe the statutory provisions designed to alert the transferor's creditors of the impending transfer so that they may obtain payment of their claim, or protection of their rights, before the business assets are disposed of or encumbered.

The business opportunity broker, in handling the sales of businesses, will encounter forms and documents peculiar to the transfer or financing of personal property. These would include bills of sale, chattel mortgages, conditional sales contracts, written documents of assignment. Other documents relating to financing transactions involving security interests in personal property are likely to be employed.

Business opportunity brokerage is enmeshed in specialized contractual documents, forms, and reports. Clauses relative to representations and warranties should be included in the agreements of sale. Some businesses involve the transfer of a license, franchise, or distributorship requiring compliance with regulations of governmental agencies. Where a seller is disposing of a going business, the buyer may seek assurances that the seller will not subsequently compete by insisting on protective covenants. Assignment of accounts receivable, assignment of existing lease, stock with the business, and compliance with zoning laws, building codes, and other government regulations must be areas of concern for the broker. Chattel security problems and compliance with the applicable provisions of the Universal Commercial Code require his constant vigilance.

In short, the business opportunity broker must protect the seller by adequate security whenever the sale is on the installment basis or for credit. He must insure that the buyer is getting what he pays for, and he must ascertain that all applicable laws are being complied with by all parties to the transaction.

d. Property Insurance. Conceptually, property insurance brokerage is not a specialized field of real estate. Nevertheless, property insurance is a natural adjunct of real estate brokerage much akin to that of mortgage financing and property management and can be a lucrative source of additional business income for the progressive real estate firm.

In order to provide full service to clients and customers, many real estate brokers represent insurance underwriters in the capacity of insurance agents. Property Insurance is a branch of business requiring a high degree of specialization. In most states, separate licensing laws govern the licensure of insurance brokers. The responsibilities of an insurance broker would include the analysis of the client's insurance needs and the development of complete schedules reflecting the types and amount of insurance coverage required. Property insurance would include the two broad categories of fire insurance and liability insurance. Included in the latter would be policies covering owners', landlords', and tenants' liability; sprinkler leakage insurance, steam boiler insurance; glass insurance; consequential losses from fire other than the direct loss to the property of the insured. This would include rent, leasehold and demolition insurance. Workmen's Compensation Insurance would also be considered.

D. SPECIALIZATION AS AN INDEPENDENT CONTRACTOR

   1. Appraising

   An appraiser may be described as a person who is engaged in the procedures of estimating the value of property. This description includes the professional appraiser who devotes the bulk of his time to real estate appraising, either as a fee appraiser or as an employee of some agency. We will concern ourselves in this paragraph with the fee appraiser acting in the capacity of an independent contractor.

   The appraiser is required to be intimately familiar with the "tools of valuation" and, of course, with appraisal terminology. He must be thoroughly cognizant of the deeper meanings of "value" and "market value". He must be adept in determining what information must be collected (and from whom), collated, analyzed, and integrated in estimating such value, and how to gather and use the collected data. Certainly he is expected to have an in-depth knowledge of the various appraisal approaches to establishing estimated values and the methods and techniques developed for applying them. Finally, he must be able to completely and accurately prepare the appraisal report.

   The potential clientele of a real estate appraiser is substantial. It includes governmental agencies at all levels, business and industrial organizations acquiring business plant sites or disposing of their existing holdings, non-profit organizations buying or selling real properties or having a need for a determination of present holdings, and lending institutions of all types. The volume of appraisal business from these and many other sources is continually increasing and presages a lucrative and satisfying field of specialization for those so inclined.

   2. Counseling

   The myriad approaches and considerations involved in the acquisition or conveyance of title to real property may reach a degree of complexity and sophistication, particularly in transactions involving income or investment properties, which justifies the services of the real estate counselor. These professionals have acquired a special expertise in the diverse areas which surround most real estate transactions. Methods of appraising, merchandising, financing, taxation, and a plethora of related political, social, and economic data fall within the specialized field of knowledge required of the real estate counselor. His services are sought after by lending institutions, governmental agencies, business and industrial organizations, investors, owners, builders, and developers. Usually, the real estate counselor is employed as an independent contractor for an agreed fee. The need is constant for increasing numbers of these specialists who can dissect the real estate transaction, evaluate alternatives available to both clients and customers, and suggest the wisest course of action to each.

E. SPECIALIZATION AS PRINCIPAL ACTING ON OWN BEHALF

   Many real estate organizations establish within their structures, or create as subsidiary organizations, administrative and operational units which enable them to engage in real estate activities as principals for the purpose of producing autonomous areas of profit separate from agency activities or fee services as independent contractors. Generally, these activities may be categorized as land programs and building programs.

1. Land Programs

Those operators involved in land programs acquire real property speculatively for resale or for development and resale.

   a. Land Acquired for Speculation. Such land usually changes ownership quickly. The speculator is not to be regarded as an investor. He buys prudently and expects a rapid and significant rise in value. His profit is realized upon securing a ready purchaser who will pay the appreciated value.

   b. Land Acquired for Development. The terms "subdividing" and "developing" are often used inter-changeably. There is a fine, but significant, difference which should be made at the outset. Each term relates to a distinct real estate activity lending itself to specialization. A subdivider may generally be described as one who buys undeveloped acreage wholesale, segments it into smaller parcels, and sells it retail. A subdivider is usually not interested in extending his involvement into the intricacies and complexities of land development. In the development program subdivision looms as the first important phase.

      (1) Subdividing. A subdivision is a tract of land divided into lots which are suitable for home-building purposes. Frequently, if the operator's intent is simply to subdivide, his expenses are limited to the purchase price and those relative to surveying and marking and for the preparation and submittance of the surveyor's plat for governmental approval. Subdividing in this manner does not alter the physical characteristics of the land. It is merely a "paper" subdivision, and when the plat is approved and accepted, by placing it on public record it serves as notice of intent to change the area to urban, suburban, or even rur-urban site utilization as reflected on the plat or record. Frequently, the operator's profit is realized when the entire "paper" subdivision is purchased.

      (2) Developing. Land developing is far more extensive in scope than subdividing and involves far greater expenditures. As a rule of thumb, the selling price of a site in the average development may be three to four times the cost of the "raw" land. The expenses borne by the land developer would include the cost of water mains, sanitary sewers, street

grading and asphalt, curbs and gutters, earth moving and filling when necessary, and other miscellaneous expenses such as, survey, legal filing, brokerage, and overhead. These expenses, when added to the cost of raw land, still would not reflect the developer's profit which would reasonably approximate ten percent. These observations assume that the cost for installing sidewalks, for the extension of electric, gas, or telephone utilities, and for providing public or recreational facilities are not carried by the developer.

Those specializing in this area are usually persons with extensive real estate experience. They have the wisdom to seek out those possessing the required expertise in the highly complex area of land utilization. Developers are intimately acquainted with the space requirements of a community; they are abreast of population and market trends, and certainly they are aware of community growth and patterns of expansion. Finally, they must be attuned to the absorption rate at which building sites in newly developed areas can profitably be sold.

2. Building Programs

Real estate operators specializing in building programs designed for profitable sales may become involved in any of three areas: speculative building; speculative buying; and buying with a view to altering, remodeling, modernizing, or renovating prior to resale. Building programs concern the operator with improvements to the real property as well as the real property, per se.

   a. Speculative Building: Normally the speculative builder will purchase building lots and construct buildings thereon with the expectation of selling both the land and the structure at a profit.

   b. Speculative Buying: The real estate operator active in speculative buying of buildings equates to a degree with the land speculator who expects a rapid and significant increase in the value of his speculative investment.

   c. Buying to Renovate and Resell: This particular area of specialization often enables one to acquire property at a comparatively low price because of its physical deterioration, economic obsolescence, or functional obsolescence. In these cases, the builder is concerned with the renovation and modernization of an existing structure rather than with the construction of a new one. His profit, of course, is realized when the property is sold at a price reasonably in excess of cost and expenses which will insure an acceptable percentage of profit.

F. MISCELLANEOUS AREAS OF SPECIALIZATION

The foregoing paragraphs investigate those specialized activities generally acknowledged as being embraced by private real estate practices as differentiated from public real estate activities. The activities cited certainly are not all inclusive. So diverse and so ever-changing and expanding is the entire spectrum of real estate that a current all-encompassing enumeration of activities would be impractical, if not impossible. Nevertheless, we must acknowledge the exciting areas of syndication for the acquisition of real estate and for the marketing of real estate securities. Research and development programs relating to the physical, economic, social, and political aspects of our society as they affect real estate values are absolutely necessary.

Closely tied to research and development is the continuing and increasing demand for in-depth educational and training programs required to keep the real estate practitioner abreast of the accelerated changes remolding the real estate profession in line with the technological advances touching all phases of our daily lives. These areas, and undoubtedly many others, add color and substance to the incomplete picture of real estate that this chapter has attempted to sketch and frame.

FRAMEWORK OF SPECIALIZATION

FORMS OF EMPLOYMENT

1.   Agency

2.   Independent Contractor

3.   Master-Servant

4.   Principal Acting on Own Behalf

SPECIALIZATION UNDER AGENCY RELATIONSHIP

1. **According to Property Type**

2. **According to Services Offered**

SPECIALIZATION UNDER AGENCY RELATIONSHIP

1. **According to Property Type:**

    a. **Residential Property**
    b. **Income Property**
    c. **Investment Property**

DEFINITIONS

a. **Residential Property:**
real property primarily acquired for use as a residence

b. **Income Property:**
real property acquired for the **immediate and continuing** production of income either directly or indirectly

c. **Investment Property:**
real property acquired for the specific purpose of realizing a profitable return **at some future date**

TYPES OF INCOME PROPERTY

COMMERCIAL

INDUSTRIAL

AGRICULTURAL

SPECIALIZATION
UNDER AGENCY RELATIONSHIP

2. **According to Services Offered:**

    a. Property Management
    b. Mortgage Placement Service
    c. Business Opportunities Sales
  *d. Property Insurance

*Conceptually not a specialized field of real estate

SPECIALIZATION
AS AN
INDEPENDENT CONTRACTOR

1. Appraising

2. Counseling

SPECIALIZATION AS PRINCIPAL ACTING ON OWN BEHALF

1. **Land Programs**
    a. **Speculation**
    b. **Development**
        (1) Subdividing
        (2) Developing

2. **Building Programs**
    a. **Speculative Building**
    b. **Speculative Buying**
    c. **Buying to Renovate and Resell**

Chapter 2

REVIEW DEFINITIONS IN GLOSSARY OR TEXT OF FOLLOWING TERMS:

affiliate broker	investment property
agricultural property	public real estate activities
appraiser	residential property
business chance	rural
business opportunity	rur-urban
commercial property	servant
fiduciary relation	suburban
goodwill	subdivider
income property	subdivision
industrial property	urban

REVIEW QUESTIONS:

1. Is an agent in the principal/agent relationship subject to the control of his principal?

2. Is compensation a requirement for one to act as an agent?

3. What are the three broad classifications of property according to property type?

4. Name three sub-classifications of "income property".

5. How is investment property distinguished from income property?

6. Does property management usually involve a principal/agent relationship?

7. Name two real estate activities which fall within the sphere of services under the principal/agent relationship.

8. Name the two categories which embrace real estate specialization under the agency relationship.

9. What specific forms of employment serve as a framework of specialization relative to real estate activities?

10. Name two areas wherein a principal, acting in his own behalf, may specialize in real estate activities.

FOR ANSWERS TO REVIEW QUESTIONS:

1.

2.

3.

4.

5.

6.

7.

8.

9.

Chapter 3

The Principal-Agent Relationship

A.	THE AGENCY	43
	1. What Is an Agency?	43
	2. Importance of the Agency Relationship	43
	3. Effects of an Agency Relationship	43
	4. Agency As Distinguished from Other Relationships	43
B.	THE PRINCIPAL	44
	1. Definition	44
	2. Who May Be a Principal?	44
	3. Kinds of Principals	44
	a. Disclosed Principal	44
	b. Undisclosed Principal	44
	c. Partially Disclosed Principal	44
C.	THE AGENT	44
	1. Definition	44
	2. Who May Be an Agent?	45
	3. Kinds of Agents	45
	a. Classified According to Scope of Authority	45
	(1) General Agent	45
	(2) Special Agent	45
	(3) Factor and Del Credere Agent	45
	b. Classified According to Manner of Appointment	45
	(1) Actual Agent	45
	(2) Ostensible Agent	45
D.	HOW THE AGENCY RELATIONSHIP IS CREATED	45
	1. Introduction	45
	2. Creation of the Agency Relationship	46

	a.	Express Agency		46
	b.	Implied Agency		46
	c.	Agency By Necessity		46
	d.	Agency By Statute		46
	e.	Agency By Estoppel (Ostensible Agency)		46

E. AGENT'S OBLIGATIONS, RIGHTS, LIABILITIES, AND AUTHORITY — 47

    1. <u>Agent's Obligations to Principal</u> — 47

        a. Obedience — 47
        b. Loyalty — 47
        c. Good Faith — 47
        d. Judgment, Prudence, and Skill — 47
        e. Duty to Account — 47
        f. Duty to Personally Perform — 48
        g. Duty to Give Notice — 48

    2. <u>Agent's Rights</u> — 48

        a. Against His Principal — 48
        b. Against Third Party — 48

            (1) On Contracts — 48
            (2) On Negotiable Instruments — 48
            (3) In Tort — 48

    3. <u>Agent's Liability to Third Party</u> — 49

        a. Disclosed Principal — 49
        b. Undisclosed Principal — 49

            (1) On Contracts — 49
            (2) On Negotiable Instruments — 49
            (3) For Money Received — 49
            (4) In Tort — 49

        c. Agent's Warranties — 49

            (1) Warranty of Authority — 49
            (2) Warranty of Principal's Competency — 49

    4. <u>Agent's Authority</u> — 49

        a. Introduction — 49
        b. Types of Authority — 50

		(1)	Express Authority	50
		(2)	Implied Authority	50
		(3)	Necessary Authority	50
		(4)	Statutory Authority	50
		(5)	Apparent Authority	

F. PRINCIPAL'S OBLIGATIONS, RIGHTS, AND LIABILITIES 51

    1. <u>Principal's Obligations</u> 51

        a. To Agent 51

            (1) To Compensate 51
            (2) To Reimburse 51
            (3) To Indemnify 51

        b. To Third Party 51

            (1) For Acts of Agent 51
            (2) For Torts of His Agent 52

    2. <u>Principal's Rights</u> 52

        a. Against His Agent 52
        b. Against Third Party 52

            (1) On Contracts 52
            (2) On Negotiable Instruments 52
            (3) In Torts 52

    3. <u>Principal's Liabilities</u> 52

        a. On Contracts 52
        b. On Negotiable Instruments 52
        c. In Torts 53

            (1) Negligent Acts 53
            (2) Willful Acts 53

        d. For Agent's Crimes 53

G. THIRD PARTY'S OBLIGATIONS AND LIABILITIES 53

    1. <u>Obligations to Principal</u> 53
    2. <u>Liabilities to Agent</u> 53

		a.	On Contracts	53
			(1) Disclosed Principal	53
			(2) Undisclosed Principal	53
		b.	In Tort	54

H. TERMINATION OF THE AGENCY … 54

    1. <u>By Acts of the Parties</u> … 54

        a. Performance … 54
        b. Mutual Agreement … 54
        c. Discharge of Agent by Principal … 54
        d. Breach by the Agent … 54

    2. <u>By Operation of the Law</u> … 54

        a. Death … 54
        b. Insanity … 54
        c. Bankruptcy … 54
        d. Change of Law … 55
        e. Destruction of Subject Matter … 55

    3. <u>Notice of Termination to Third Parties</u> … 55

        a. When Terminated by Acts of Parties … 55
        b. When Terminated by Operation of Law … 55

VISUAL AIDS … 55

REVIEW QUESTIONS … 58

Chapter 3
The Principal-Agent Relationship

A. THE AGENCY

1. <u>What Is an Agency</u>? - - Generally, an agency is that relationship created by employment. Specifically, it is that relationship between one party, known as the principal, who authorizes another, known as the agent, to represent him in business dealings. In the real estate business we must become familiar with the laws governing principal and agent since a broker's employment by a property owner to represent him in contractual relations with potential buyers falls within the principal-agent relationship.

The American Law Institute has prepared a <u>Restatement of Agency</u> which defines "agency" as "the fiduciary relation which results from the manifestation of consent by one person to another that the other shall act on his behalf and <u>subject to his control</u>, and consent by the other so to act." A commentary on the foregoing statement says that "the relation of agency is created as the result of conduct by two parties manifesting that one of them is willing for the other to act for him <u>subject to his control</u>, and that the other consents so to act." The principal must in some manner indicate that the agent is to act for him, and the agent must act or agree to act on the principal's behalf and subject to his control. Generally, and traditionally, the term "agency" has been defined as the legal fiduciary relationship that exists when one individual (the principal) authorizes another (the agent) to create, modify, or terminate contractual relations involving the principal and third parties.

2. <u>Importance of the Agency Relationship:</u> - - When an agency relationship is created, specific obligations, rights, and liabilities emerge which relate to the principal, the agent, and the third party (the person with whom the agent deals). Moreover, these obligations, rights, and liabilities are peculiar to the principal-agent relationship as distinguished from other types of employer-employee associations.

3. <u>Effects of an Agency Relationship:</u> - - The principal in an agency relationship is bound by the acts of his agent when the latter is operating within the scope of his authority. It is as if the principal had performed the acts himself. Obviously, when the principal delegates to another the authority to act in his behalf, legal risks are created. Instances have arisen where the principal has been held liable for torts committed by his agent against third persons while the agent was representing him and acting within the terms of his employment.

4. <u>Agency As Distinguished from Other Relationships:</u> - - In the usual employer-employee relationship, the employee simply does what he is instructed to do; he does not deal with third parties. An agent, on the other hand, deals with third

parties as the principal's representative. Furthermore, in the exercise of his authority, the agent is expected to use his discretion and judgment in protecting and promoting the interests of his principal. There are situations where an individual may function both as an employee and as an agent alternately, but not simultaneously during the same employment period. The clerk in a market while stocking shelves is acting in the capacity of an employee. However, if asked by his employer to wait on customers, this same clerk becomes an agent. It is to be noted that in an agency relationship the agent acts for and in behalf of another (his principal) and is subject to his employer's control.

An independent contractor, however, is not subject to the control of the person with whom he has contracted. An independent contractor contracts for certain end results and retains complete control over the procedures employed to obtain such results.

B.   THE PRINCIPAL

1. <u>Definition</u>: - - A principal in an agency relationship is one who employs another (called an agent) to represent him in legal or business dealings with third persons.

2. <u>Who May Be a Principal</u>? - - Any person who is legally capable of acting on his own behalf may appoint an agent to act for him. (See Chapter 4. Paragraph E.)

3. <u>Kinds of Principals:</u> - - There are three kinds of principals - disclosed, undisclosed, or partially disclosed.

    a. Disclosed Principal. A disclosed principal is one whose identity in an agency relationship is made known to third persons dealing through the agent.

    b. Undisclosed Principal. A principal is undisclosed when an agent, in dealing with third persons, does not reveal the existence of an agency relationship or the identity of the principal, but appears to act in his own behalf rather than for another.

    c. Partially Disclosed Principal. A principal is considered partially disclosed when the agent, in his dealings with third persons, reveals the existence of an agency relationship but does not divulge the identity of his principal.

C.   THE AGENT

1. <u>Definition</u>: - - An agent in an agency relationship is one employed by and under the control of another, known as the principal, to represent said principal in business and legal dealings with third persons.

2. <u>Who May Be an Agent?</u> - - Anyone so appointed by the principal may be an agent. Even a minor or one mentally ill may be agent, because the acts of such persons are deemed to be those of the principal. Obviously, the principal should exercise care in his appointment of an agent, as he may be ultimately held responsible for his agent's acts.

3. <u>Kinds of Agents</u>

   a. Classified According to Scope of Authority

      (1) General Agent. A general agent is one given broad authority to act on behalf of his principal in a number of acts.

      (2) <u>Special Agent</u>. A special agent is one whose authority to act is confined to a particular job or a specific task. A real estate broker employed to sell a house is a special agent in that his agency authority is restricted to only those acts necessary to simply sell his principal's property.

      (3) Factor and Del Credere Agent. An agent working more or less independently as, for example, a middleman or commission merchant with whom customers deal directly and to whom they look for satisfaction is called a factor. If the "factor" guarantees the credit of a third person to his principal, he is known as a "del credere" agent.

   b. Classified According to Manner of Appointment

      (1) Actual Agent. An actual agent is one acting under an express or implied agency by the voluntary act of the principal. (A real estate broker hired by a property owner to represent him in the sale of his property is an actual agent).

      (2) Ostensible Agent. An ostensible agent is one acting under the apparent authority of his principal as opposed to express or implied authority. An ostensible agent is appointed by force of law and without the voluntary assent of his principal.

D. HOW THE AGENCY RELATIONSHIP IS CREATED

1. <u>Introduction:</u> - - How an agency relationship is created determines the classification of the agency. No agency is ever created without some action or conduct on the part of the principal. A would-be agent cannot by his conduct alone or by any statement he might make establish an agency relationship. It, therefore, behooves third parties when dealing with an agent to determine the nature and extent of the agent's authority. Third persons dealing with an agent do so at their own peril.

2. <u>Creation of the Agency Relationship</u>: - - An agency relationship generally may be created in five ways: by express agreement (i. e., appointment), by implication (including ratification), by necessity, by statute, or by estoppel (known as ostensible agency).

    a. <u>Express Agency</u>. An express agency is created <u>voluntarily</u> through <u>contractual agreement</u> between the principal and the agent. The contract establishing an express agency <u>may be oral or written</u>, such as with a power of attorney. Note, however, that in consonance with the Statute of Frauds (see Chapter 5) if the agency contract cannot be performed within a year from the time the contract is entered into, it must be reduced to writing. Consequently, if, by the terms of the agreement, the agency will extend beyond a year, the agreement, to be enforceable, must be in writing.

    b. <u>Implied Agency</u>. An implied agency is created <u>voluntarily</u> by the <u>conduct and acts of the principal and agent</u> which reflect the intent to create an agency relationship even though such intent is not expressed orally or in writing. An implied agency is also created by ratification if the principal, with full knowledge of all the facts, accepts the benefits of his agent's unauthorized acts.

    c. Agency By Necessity. An agency by necessity does not require the voluntary consent of the principal or the agent for the creation of the agency. It is created by force of law when circumstances make such an agency necessary. If, for example, a broker contracts for the repair of burst water pipes in the absence of the principal whose property he has been employed to sell, it would be held that an <u>agency by necessity was created in order to prevent loss to the principal</u>.

    d. Agency By Statute. Agency by statute is usually created by state statute on individuals (or legal entities) to facilitate the service of process when such service otherwise would be difficult or impossible.

    e. Agency By Estoppel (Ostensible Agency). An agency by estoppel, like the agency by necessity, does not require the voluntary consent of either the principal or the agent. Such an agency is created by force of law to prevent (estop) the principal from denying its existence. An agency by estoppel is created when all of the following conditions exist:

        (1) The principal willfully or negligently gives the false impression that another is his agent.

        (2) A third person, in reliance of the false impression, deals with the alleged agent.

(3) The third person is damaged by the fact that an actual agency relationship did not exist.

The conduct of the agent alone cannot create an ostensible agency. No agency is ever created without some action or conduct on the part of the principal. The third person can only rely on the principal's representations. Note, too, that an agency by estoppel (ostensible agency) may be created by a principal's silence when there is a duty to speak.

E. AGENT'S OBLIGATIONS, RIGHTS, LIABILITIES, AND AUTHORITY

1. Agent's Obligations to Principal

   a. Obedience. An agent must obey all instructions issued by his principal which relate to the contract of employment, whether or not he is acting with compensation. In obeying the instruction of his principal, the agent is duty-bound to remain within the scope of the authority conferred upon him.

   b. Loyalty. The duty of an agent to be loyal to his principal supersedes and yet encompasses all of his other obligations to the principal. An agent cannot engage in any activity that competes or interferes in any degree with the business of his principal. Because of the loyalty demanded of an agent, a real estate broker may not represent both seller and buyer in the same transaction unless both have been informed and consent to his acting in the dual role. Loyalty also requires that confidential information acquired by the agent may not be used to advance his own interest at the expense of the principal, e. g., using for personal gain knowledge that his principal's property has increased in value.

   c. Good Faith. The relationship between an agent and his principal is one of highest trust and confidence known as a fiduciary relationship. For example, if a real estate broker sells his principal's property for a price higher than that authorized by the principal, the additional profit belongs to the principal and not the agent.

   d. Judgment, Prudence, and Skill. An agent in performing his duties must exercise reasonable judgment, prudence, and skill. In agreeing to perform within the terms of the agency, the agent implies that he possesses the required knowledge, training, and skill to properly perform and to do so in a professional manner.

   e. Duty to Account. An agent must maintain proper records which will enable him to account to the principal for all money or property entrusted to him. Money collected by the agent must not be mingled with his own. If deposited in a bank, it must be deposited in a separate account and so identified that a trust is apparent. Failure to keep such funds separate is known as commingling and may be cause for revocation of a broker's license.

f. Duty to Personally Perform. An agency relationship is usually one involving a contract for personal services. In the absence of authority to do so, an agent may not delegate his duties unless such duties are purely mechanical in nature requiring no particular knowledge, training, skill, or responsibility.

g. Duty to Give Notice. The agent, in his fiduciary relationship with the principal, is duty bound to keep the principal fully informed of all facts which materially affect the subject matter of the agency and which come to the agent's attention within the scope of his employment. This rule imposes on the agent the duty to relay all information which might materially affect the interest of the principal. If, for example, a real estate broker in his capacity of agent for the seller gains knowledge of facts which will materially increase the value of his principal's property over and above the price asked by the principal, he is obligated to communicate such information to the principal.

2. Agent's Rights

   a. Against His Principal. An agent's rights against his principal correlate to the obligation of the principal to the agent - i. e., compensation, reimbursement, and indemnification. (See Paragraph F 1a below).

   b. Against Third Party

   (1) On Contracts. An agent can bring suit against the third party for non-performance whenever the agent is bound by the contract as in the case of contracts he enters into for his undisclosed principal. An agent can also enforce contracts against third persons when his commission or compensation is predicated on the performance of the contract.

   (2) On Negotiable Instruments. The agent can enforce a negotiable instrument made by a third party as payable to the agent if the principal's name does not appear anywhere on the instrument.

   (3) In Tort. The third party is always liable for his torts against an agent regardless of the agency relationship.

3. Agent's Liability to Third Party

   a. Disclosed Principal. When an agent advises a third party that he is acting as an agent and discloses the identity of his principal, he assumes no liability as to the resulting contractual obligations if he has acted within the scope of his authority.

   b. Undisclosed Principal.

   (1) On Contracts. When an agent contracts with a third party without disclosing the existence of an agency relationship or the identity of his principal, or when the agent contracts for a fictitious or non-existent principal, he may be held liable on the contract to the third party.

   (2) On Negotiable Instruments. The agent may be held liable on a negotiable instrument to a third party, unless the principal's name appears somewhere on the instrument.

   (3) For Money Received. An agent receiving money from a third party for the benefit of his principal is under no obligation to account to the third party.

   (4) In Tort. An agent is always liable for torts he commits against third persons.

   c. Agent's Warranties

   (1) Warranty of Authority. When acting in a representative capacity for his principal with a third party, the agent implies that he has authority to so act in the particular transaction. If, when dealing with a third party, the agent knows he has no authority, he is guilty of fraud.

   (2) Warranty of Principal's Competency. An agent warrants that his principal is capable of being bound. Therefore, an agent who represents a principal who is a minor may be held liable for non-performance by his principal.

4. Agent's Authority

   a. Introduction. In every instance it is important to determine the scope of the agent's authority, for an agent while working within such scope binds his principal. Furthermore, the principal's liability is determined by the agent's acting within the scope of his authority.

b. Types of Authority. There are, generally, five types of authority that an agent may have. These are determined by the method by which such authority is conferred.

   (1) Express Authority. Express authority is that authority which is explicitly set forth as instructions by the principal in the agency agreement. It is voluntarily conferred on the agent by his principal and is sometimes referred to as an actual authority.

   (2) Implied Authority. That additional authority ordinarily required by an agent to carry out the express authority is implied authority. Implied authority is usually in accordance with the usual authority of similar agents by usage and custom of the business under similar circumstances.

   Generally, an agent does not have the authority to delegate his authority to a sub-agent. But a real estate broker has the implied authority to delegate his authority to his salesmen. This implied authority of the real estate broker arises out of custom and usage, because the nature of his business is such that it is presumed that the principal (seller) contemplated that the authority given to the agent (broker) would be exercised through sub-agents (salesmen).

   (3) Necessary Authority. Necessary authority is conferred on an agent by force of law when an emergency or unusual situation develops which cannot be communicated to the principal to obtain approval and when action is necessary by the agent to protect or promote the best interests of his principal.

   (4) Statutory Authority. Statutory authority is that conferred on an agent by statute. (Reference D 2e above).

   (5) Apparent Authority. Apparent authority is that conferred on an agent as a matter of law without the voluntary assent of either the principal or his agent but necessitated for the protection of innocent third parties who rely on the impression created by the principal's words, acts, or conduct that appropriate authority has been conferred on his agent. Note: it is necessary that there be some conduct on the principal's part on which the third party can rely (even if such action is negative, such as a failure to disavow responsibility for the actions of the agent).

F. PRINCIPAL'S OBLIGATIONS, RIGHTS, AND LIABILITIES

1. Principal's Obligations

    a. To Agent

        (1) To compensate. The principal is obligated to compensate his agent for his services, unless, of course, the agent agrees to perform gratuitously. The amount of compensation is usually set forth in the agency agreement. In the absence of an express agreement to the contrary, a real estate broker earns his commission the moment he presents the seller with a buyer who is ready, willing, and able to meet the seller's terms. The commission is also earned by the broker the moment the seller contracts with the buyer, even though such buyer may later be unable to meet the seller's terms.

        (2) To reimburse. The principal is obligated to reimburse the agent for expenses incurred while acting on his principal's behalf and within the scope of his authority.

        In the ordinary real estate agency situation, the principal has no such duty to reimburse the broker. By the terms of the usual listing agreement and also by custom, the broker's sole compensation is a percentage of the selling price, and it is understood that the real estate broker will pay his expenses out of his commission.

        (3) To indemnify. The principal is obligated to secure his agent against any loss or damage (indemnify) suffered as a consequence of the agent following his principal's instructions under the agency relationship.

    b. To Third Party

        (1) For Acts of Agent. The principal is obligated to honor all contractual agreements entered into by the agent in the principal's name, while the agent is acting within the scope of his actual or apparent authority. It is irrelevant whether or not the third party knows he is dealing with an agent. If the agent has actual authority, he is authorized to make a binding contract in his principal's name. When an agent, however, acts beyond the scope of his actual authority, a determination must be made whether or not the principal has clothed the agent with the apparent authority to so act.

(2) For Torts of His Agent. A principal is liable for his agent's torts if they are committed while the agent is doing what he is intructed to do. If, for example, in the course of his employment an agent makes fraudulent statements to a third party which were not authorized by the principal, the principal would be liable for any damages caused by the willful or negligent acts of his agent which the agent engaged in while promoting the interests of his principal.

2. Principal's Rights

   a. Against His Agent. The principal's rights against his agent are a correlation of the obligations which his agent owes to him in their agency relationship.

   b. Against Third Party

      (1) On Contracts. The principal can enforce against the third party any contract between the third party and the agent which has been authorized or ratified by the principal. This holds true even in those instances where the principal is undisclosed and where the third party would not have entered into the contract had he known the identity of the principal.

      (2) On Negotiable Instruments. The principal always has the right to enforce negotiable instruments against the third party who delivers such to the principal or his agent. Note, however, that when the third party makes the instrument payable to the agent, and the principal is undisclosed, many states prevent the principal from enforcing the instrument against the third person.

      (3) In Torts. A third party is liable for those torts he commits against the principal.

3. Principal's Liabilities

   a. On Contracts. The principal is bound by the provisions of a contract with the third party when such contract was entered into by the agent while acting with express, implied, or apparent authority.

   b. On Negotiable Instruments. A principal is liable on negotiable instruments only when his name appears somewhere on the instrument. Only a person whose name appears on a negotiable instrument is liable on it.

c. In Torts

    (1) Negligent Acts. The principal is liable to third parties for damages suffered as a consequence of the actions of the agent so long as the agent was complying with the principal's instructions, or so long as the agent was acting within the scope of his authority and on his principal's behalf.

    (2) Willful Acts. The principal is not liable for the willful or intentional torts of his agent against third parties, unless, of course, the agent was seeking to further his principal's interest.

d. For Agent's Crimes. The principal ordinarily is not liable for his agent's crimes, unless he actually aids or participates in their commission. Most states, however, have enacted statutes which hold a principal liable for certain crimes committed by his agents ... e. g., the sale of liquor to a minor by a salesman without the knowledge and consent of the proprietor.

Note: The above discussion of the duties and responsibilities of the principal to the agent and of the agent to the principal applies to the real estate salesman as well as to the broker. The broker is the agent of the property owner (although occasionally he is the agent for the buyer); the salesman is the agent of the broker.

G. THIRD PARTY'S OBLIGATIONS AND LIABILITIES

1. Obligations to Principal

In effect, the third party dealing through an agent is contracting with the principal. It is recognized that during the stages of negotiation the agent is the go-between; nevertheless, once the contract has been entered into, the agent is no longer involved. The obligations which follow are those of the principal and the third party. It is the obligation of the third party to live up to the terms of his agreement.

2. Liabilities to Agent

a. On Contracts

    (1) Disclosed Principal. The third party ordinarily owes no contractual duty to the agent representing a disclosed principal simply because the contractual agreement only exists between the third party and the principal.

    (2) Undisclosed Principal. The third party is liable for suit by the agent of an undisclosed principal since such an agent

binds himself to the third party.

  b. In Tort. Torts committed by third parties generally give cause of action by the agent regardless of the type of agency.

H. TERMINATION OF THE AGENCY

 1. By Acts of the Parties

  a. Performance. Since most agencies are based on contracts, the rules applicable to the termination of contracts apply to the agency relationship. When the purpose for which the agency was created is achieved, the agency is terminated. If an agent is appointed for a specific period of time, lapse of that time terminates the agency. In short, when the terms of the contract have been performed, the agency terminates. When it is possible for one of several agents to perform, such as selling a house on an open listing, it is held that the performance by the first agent terminates the authority of the others.

  b. Mutual Agreement. Any agency relationship may be terminated by mutual agreement.

  c. Discharge of Agent by Principal. The principal at any time has the power to terminate the agent (except where the agent has an interest in the subject matter). If such discharge is in violation of the agency contract, the principal will be liable for his breach. Regardless of what may ensue as the result of legal action, the principal-agency relationship is terminated.

  d. Breach by the Agent. The agent may simply quit, thereby terminating the agency. Wrongful termination, however, may subject the agent to a suit for damages by the principal. Nevertheless, one cannot be forced to work against his will.

 2. By Operation of the Law

  a. Death. The death of the principal or the agent generally will automatically cancel the agency relationship. Notice of the death of one party to the agency by the other party is not required.

  b. Insanity. The insanity of either party to the agency generally will automatically terminate the relationship. Again, notice to the principal or the agent of the other's insanity is not required.

  c. Bankruptcy. By the general rule, the bankruptcy of either party will terminate the agency, except in the case where the bankruptcy has no effect upon the agency or its purpose. In a real estate agency, bankruptcy of the owner terminates the agency, because the title to the property passes to the trustee in bankruptcy.

   d. Change of Law. A change of law causing the purpose of the agency to become illegal will cancel the relationship. An agency to sell liquor in an area which passes a dry law will automatically be terminated.

   e. Destruction of Subject Matter. The destruction or loss of the subject matter of the agency will automatically end the agency. The destruction of a house by fire terminates the real estate broker's agency to sell the property.

3. Notice of Termination to Third Parties

   a. When Terminated by Acts of Parties. The principal is responsible for notifying third parties who were aware of the agency relationship.

   b. When Terminated by Operation of Law. No duty to notify third parties devolves upon the principal.

CLASSIFICATION
BY TYPES

PRINCIPAL

Disclosed
Undisclosed
Partially Disclosed

AGENT

General
Special

THE PRINCIPAL-AGENT RELATIONSHIP

CREATION OF AGENCY RELATIONSHIP

1. Express
2. Implied
3. By Necessity
4. By Statute
5. By Estoppel

AGENT'S AUTHORITY

1. Express
2. Implied
3. Necessary
4. Statutory
5. Apparent

THE PRINCIPAL-AGENT RELATIONSHIP

AGENT'S OBLIGATIONS TO PRINCIPAL

1. Obedience
2. Loyalty
3. Good Faith
4. Judgment, Skill
5. To Account
6. Personally Perform
7. Give Notice

PRINCIPAL'S OBLIGATIONS TO AGENT

1. Compensate
2. Reimburse
3. Indemnify

COMMISSIONS

YOU **EARN** YOUR COMMISSION WHEN YOU:

1. Produce a buyer who is ready, willing, and able
   ... or
2. When the seller contracts with the buyer.

THE PRINCIPAL-AGENT RELATIONSHIP

TERMINATION OF THE AGENCY

BY ACTS OF PARTIES	BY OPERATION OF LAW
1. Performance	1. Death
2. Mutual Agreement	2. Insanity
3. Discharge of Agent	3. Bankruptcy
4. Breach by Agent	4. Change of Law
	5. Destruction of Subject Matter

Chapter 3

REVIEW DEFINITIONS IN GLOSSARY OR TEXT OF FOLLOWING TERMS:

    actual agent
    agency
    agency by necessity
    agent
    disclosed principal
    express agency
    fiduciary
    general agent

    implied agency
    indemnity
    ostensible agency
    partially disclosed principal
    principal
    special agent
    tort
    undisclosed principal

REVIEW QUESTIONS:

1. How is an agency relationship distinguished from that of an independent contractor?

2. Name five ways that an agency relationship can be created.

3. What type of agency is created when a real estate broker contracts for the repair of burst water pipes in the absence of the principal whose property the broker has been engaged to sell?

4. What are the agent's obligations to his principal?

5. Name five types of agent's authority.

6. What are the principal's obligations to the agent?

7. When does the real estate agent earn his commission?

8. Name four ways an agency can be terminated by the acts of the parties.

9. What warranties are made by the agent to the third parties?

10. May a minor be appointed by the principal as his agent?

11. When may an agent be held liable on a contract to a third party?

12. Is an agent liable to account to the third party for money received from the third party for the benefit of his principal?

FOR ANSWERS TO REVIEW QUESTIONS:

1.

2.

3.

4.

5.

6.

7.

8.

9.

10.

11.

12.

Chapter 4

On Contracts

A.	INTRODUCTION		65
	1. General		65
	2. Basis of Contracts		65
	3. Categories of Contracts		65
		a. Formal	65
		b. Informal	66
	4. Types of Contracts		66
		a. Express	66
		b. Implied	66
		c. Bilateral	66
		d. Unilateral	66
		e. Executed	66
		f. Executory	66
		g. Void	66
		h. Voidable	66
		i. Unenforceable	66
B.	PREREQUISITES OF AN INFORMAL CONTRACT		67
	1. Mutual Assent		67
	2. Legal Consideration		67
	3. Competent Parties		67
	4. Legal Purpose		67
	5. Legal Form		67
C.	MUTUAL ASSENT		67
	1. The Offer		67
		a. General	68
		b. The Offer Must Be Intentional	68
		c. The Offer Must Be Definite	
		(1) As to Time	68
		(2) As to Price	68
		(3) As to Property	68

	d.	The Offer Must Be Communicated			68
	e.	Options			69
	f.	Termination of the Offer			69

              (1) General   69
              (2) By Rejection   69
              (3) By Counter Offer   69
              (4) By Lapse of Specified Time   69
              (5) By Express Revocation   69
              (6) By Death of Offeror or Offeree   70

    2. <u>The Acceptance</u>   70

        a. General   70
        b. Who May Accept ?   70
        c. Terms of Acceptance   70
        d. Communication of Acceptance   70

D. CONSIDERATION   71

    1. <u>Definition</u>   71
    2. <u>Consideration on Sealed Instruments</u>   71
    3. <u>Adequacy of Consideration</u>   71
    4. <u>Types of Consideration</u>   71
    5. <u>Cancellation Clauses</u>   71

E. CAPACITY OF PARTIES   72

    1. <u>General</u>   72
    2. <u>Infants</u>   72
    3. <u>Insane Persons</u>   72

        a. Under Guardianship   72
        b. Not Under Guardianship   72

    4. <u>Drunkards</u>   72
    5. <u>Married Women</u>   73
    6. <u>Convicts</u>   73
    7. <u>Spendthrifts and Aged Persons</u>   73
    8. <u>Corporations</u>   73

F. LEGAL PURPOSE   73

    1. <u>General</u>   73
    2. <u>Illegal Contracts</u>   73
    3. <u>Sunday Contracts</u>   73
    4. <u>Effects of Illegality</u>   74

G.		LEGAL FORM	74
	1.	General	74
	2.	Advantages of Written Contracts	74
H.		THE STATUTE OF FRAUDS	74
	1.	Purpose of Statute of Frauds	74
	2.	Form and Content of the Memorandum	74
	3.	Application of the Statute of Frauds	75
	4	Contracts for the Sale of Interests in Land	75

      a. Definition of Land — 75
      b. Agency Contracts for Sale of Land — 76
      c. Contracts Involving a License — 76
      d. Contracts Concerning Boundaries — 76
      e. Leases — 76

  5. Contracts for the Sale of Goods — 76

      a. General — 76
      b. Meaning of Goods — 76

  6. Contracts Not Performable Within a Year — 77
  7. Oral Executory Agreements Concerning Land — 77
  8. As Defense to Third Parties — 77

I. CONTRACT INDUCED BY FRAUD, DURESS, OR MISTAKE — 77

  1. General — 77
  2. Fraudulent Misrepresentation — 78

      a. Misstatement — 78
      b. Failure to Disclose — 78

          (1) Fiduciary Relationship — 78
          (2) Correction of Misrepresentation — 78
          (3) Dangerous Defects — 78

      c. Material Fact — 78
      d. Reliance on Misstatement — 79
      e. Resulting Damage — 79
      f. Unintentional Misstatement — 79
      g. Effects of Fraud — 79

	3.	Duress	79
		a. General	79
		b. Effects of Duress	80
	4.	Mistake	80
		a. General	80
		b. Bilateral Mistake	80
		c. Unilateral Mistake	80
		(1) Mistake As To Identity	80
		(2) Mistake As To Transmission of Figures	80
		d. Effect of Mistake	80
J.	DISCHARGE OF CONTRACT	81
	1.	General	81
	2.	Discharge by Performance	81
	3.	Discharge by Release	81
	4.	Discharge by Accord and Satisfaction	81
	5.	Discharge by Novation	81
	6.	Discharge by Alteration	81
	7.	Discharge by Statute of Limitations	81
	8.	Discharge by Bankruptcy	82
		a. Voluntary Bankruptcy	82
		b. Involuntary Bankruptcy	82
K.	BREACH OF CONTRACT	82
	1.	General	82
	2.	Conditions for Performance	82
		a. Conditions Precedent	82
		b. Conditions Concurrent	82
		c. Conditions Subsequent	83
	3.	Time As a Condition	83
		a. Extended Delays	83
		b. When "Time Is of the Essence"	83

	4.	Remedies for Breach of Contract	83

        a. Excuse from Performance — 83
        b. Specific Performance — 83
        c. Damages — 84

    5. Anticipatory Breach — 84

        a. Definition — 84
        b. Remedy for Anticipatory Breach — 84

    6. Liquidated Damages — 84

L. EXCUSES FOR NON-PERFORMANCE — 84

    1. General — 84
    2. Destruction of Subject Matter — 84
    3. Death or Illness — 85
    4. Mistake — 85
    5. Hardship — 85
    6. Prevention — 85
    7. Frustration of Purpose — 85

VISUAL AIDS — 85

REVIEW QUESTIONS — 93

Chapter 4
On Contracts

A. INTRODUCTION

1. General:-- A contract is a promise or an agreement between competent parties who have a legal duty to perform or subject themselves to action at law for breach of their contractual obligations. A contract is a type of property which has value and which may be sold. The law of contracts pervades almost every business transaction. In the field of real estate the broker or salesman is involved during the course of his daily activities with a variety of contracts. He may enter a contract of association with the principal of the firm which he has joined. He will enter into a contractual agreement when he is hired as an agent to represent a property owner desirous of selling or leasing his property. In the course of such representation the real estate broker will become involved with options, offers, acceptances, purchase and sale agreements between seller and buyer, "step" contracts between builder or contractor and buyer, bills of sale, lease agreements, deeds, mortgage notes, and perhaps several others - all having as their basis the law of contracts. Whether for the sale of property or services, the contract is the principal method by which business is conducted. Everyone engaged in business should be familiar with this law. For the real estate associate, it is essential that his knowledge of the law of contracts be far more intimate.

2. Basis of Contracts: -- The promise is the basis of the contract. Without a promise there can be no contract.

3. Categories of Contracts: --

    a. Formal. Formal contracts are --

        (1) Written contracts under seal, or

        (2) Those following the forms of negotiable instruments, e. g., checks and promissory notes.

The formality of the contract does not relate to its written form but from the attachment of the seal or from the wording. Formal contracts, under certain conditions, are enforced where informal contracts are not.

b. Informal. Informal (simple) contracts are those oral or written contracts which are categorized from the nature of the transaction, not from the form in which they are drawn. Oral contracts have the same validity as informal written contracts except where the Statute of Frauds requires the contract to be evidenced by a written memorandum.

4. Types of Contracts: - -

   a. Express. An express contract is one wherein the terms are expressly or specifically stated by the parties. It may be oral or written.

   b. Implied. An implied contract is one wherein the terms are not stated but are implied from the conduct of the parties.

   c. Bilateral. A bilateral contract is one wherein a promise is exchanged for a promise.

   d. Unilateral. A unilateral contract is one wherein a promise is exchanged for an act.

   e. Executed. An executed contract is one wherein both parties have fully met their contractual obligations; it is fully executed.

   f. Executory. An executory contract is one wherein something still remains to be done by one or both of the parties.

   g. Void. A void contract is no contract at all. It is a nullity. An illegal contract, for example, is a void contract. The parties to a void contract can neither enforce it nor make it valid by agreement.

   h. Voidable. A voidable contract is valid and will be enforced. Its distinguishing feature is that one of the parties may elect to be bound or may avoid its consequences. He has the option to do either, and until the party with the option elects to avoid the contract, it remains valid. Contracts of infants, for example, are voidable contracts.

   i. Unenforceable. Unenforceable contracts are valid contracts but will not be enforced usually because of a barrier imposed by law. Contracts barred by the Statute of Limitations and those failing to meet the requirements of the Statute of Frauds are unenforceable contracts. Unenforceable contracts are not voidable since the obligation to perform still exists, but it will not be protected. In a voidable contract the obligation is destroyed.

Note: Quasi Contracts. Quasi contracts (also known as "contracts implied in law") are implied contracts which do not have a promise as their base. Relief is given under the law to prevent one party from being unjustly enriched at the expense of the other.

B. PREREQUISITES OF AN INFORMAL CONTRACT

1. <u>Mutual Assent</u>: - - The agreement or willingness to contract must be evidenced by the words or the acts of the contracting parties. This mutual agreement to enter into contractual relationship is evidenced by the offer made by one party (the offeror) and an acceptance made by the other (the offeree). At the moment the offer is properly accepted, an agreement results. (Reference Paragraph C, infra).

2. <u>Legal Consideration</u>: - - There must be legal consideration to form a valid contract. Consideration originally was intended to serve as evidence that parties to the contract were willing to be bound by the legal consequences of their acts or conduct. No informal contract is valid, and no informal contract will be enforced , without consideration. (Reference Paragraph D, infra).

3. <u>Competent Parties</u>: - - Parties to a contract must have the legal capacity to contract. Legal capacity is differentiated from either physical or mental capacity. (Reference Paragraph E, infra).

4. <u>Legal Purpose</u>: - - Contracts without legal purpose are generally void. Contracts which by their formation or performance involve torts or are against public policy are illegal and preclude any of the parties thereto from acquiring rights under the agreement. (Reference Paragraph F, infra).

5. <u>Legal Form</u>: - - If a contract is to be under seal, or if it is such as to fall under the Statute of Frauds, it must be in writing. Otherwise, a contract normally need not be reduced to writing in order to be enforceable under the law.

C. MUTUAL ASSENT

1. <u>The Offer</u>

   a. General. An offer is a proposal made by the offeror to the offeree reflecting a willingness to do or refrain from doing something on condition that the offeree in return does or refrains from doing something . Mutual assent is prerequisite to the formation of a contract. This assent is sometimes referred to as "a meeting of the minds". It is also known as the "offer and acceptance". To be valid, an offer must be:

(1) Intentional

(2) Definite

(3) Communicated.

b. The Offer Must Be Intentional. The person making the offer must intend to be legally bound if the offer is accepted. Mere inquiries as to price and terms are not offers to buy. Advertisements, even when the price is stated, are not regarded as offers, nor is information contained in booklets or catalogues. Why? Simply because the intention to be legally bound in an enforceable obligation upon acceptance is non-existent.

c. The Offer Must Be Definite. To be binding, any agreement must be sufficiently definite and precise to be enforced, if necessary, by the court. The courts are not prone to declare an agreement void if it is possible to interpret the words and acts of the parties. The contract must be definite --

(1) As to Time. If no time for performance is stipulated, the courts will assume that reasonable time is intended. If it is not possible for the courts to make such a determination, the agreement will fail for indefiniteness.

(2) As to Price. If no price is reflected, the courts will assume, as in the case of time, that a reasonable price was intended. A contract, however, calling for the "division of commission on a liberal basis" would be too indefinite, and the contract would fail for indefiniteness.

(3) As to Property. If the property to be sold or exchanged is too indefinitely described, the agreement may fail. If, for example, a seller who has two properties on Elm Street places "the house on Elm Street" on the market, and if one house is later purchased without being described more specifically, the contract would be held to be too indefinite.

d. The Offer Must Be Communicated. Not only must the offer be made by the offeror to the offeree, the offeree must know of the offer at the time he accepts. An unexpressed desire to enter into an agreement cannot constitute an offer. Furthermore, an offer can only be communicated by the offeror or his authorized agent. If an offeree learns of an offer from some other party or source, no offer results.

e. Options. An option is a binding promise under seal or a promise for which consideration is given to hold an offer open for an agreed period of time. An option prevents the person giving the option (the offeror or optionor) from revoking the offer or giving it to another party. Frequently the one receiving the option (the offeree or optionee) pays or promises to pay money to keep the offer open; however, anything of value may serve as consideration. It is significant to note that an option transforms an offer into a binding contract because of the consideration furnished by the offeree. This contract of option is irrevocable for the period of the option, even by death. In the absence of an option, an offer may be revoked at any time before acceptance - even though there may be an agreement to keep the offer open for a definite time. Option contracts are usually assignable.

f. Termination of the Offer.

   (1) General. Once the offer is terminated, no contract can result from subsequent acceptance. An offer may be terminated in several ways.

   (2) By Rejection. Rejection by the offeree terminates the offer even if the offer was to have remained open for a longer period. Once rejected, an offeree cannot change his mind and accept. Acceptance following rejection constitutes a new offer which must then be accepted by the original offeror who now becomes the offeree.

   (3) By Counter-Offer. A counter-offer is a rejection of the original offer by an attempted acceptance which departs from the terms of the offer. An acceptance must be in the terms of the original offer. Any variation is, in effect, a rejection of the original offer because of the implication that the offeree considers the original terms unacceptable.

   (4) By Lapse of Specified Time. When a time for acceptance is stipulated, the offer is terminated automatically on the expiration of the specified time. When no time is specified, acceptance must be made within a reasonable time.

   (5) By Express Revocation. The offer may be revoked by the offeror at any time before acceptance by communication to the offeree of his intention to revoke. Any statement which conveys an unwillingness to contract is sufficient revocation. Even if the offeror promised to hold his offer open for a specific period and is ethically and morally obligated to do so, the right to revoke remains. A revoca-

tion must be communicated to the offeree, and it must be received by the offeree or have reached a location where it would have been available to him. Knowledge of the revocation by the offeree from any source terminates the offer.

(6) By Death of Offeror or Offeree. Death revokes an offer. If the offeree is unaware of the death of the offeror, the offer is still terminated. An offeror cannot continue to make an offer after his death, nor can an offeree accept after death.

2. <u>The Acceptance</u>

a. General. An acceptance is an indication by some word or act of willingness to be bound by the terms of an offer. Together with the offer, an acceptance is evidence of mutual assent which is a prerequisite in the formation of a contract. Silence is generally not interpreted as acceptance.

b. Who May Accept? Acceptance of an offer can be made only by the person or persons to whom the offer is extended. Offers are not assignable.

c. Terms of Acceptance. The acceptance must conform to the terms of the offer. Any new terms or conditions set forth in the acceptance - or any deviation - become in effect a counter offer and, as such, a rejection of the original offer. Any instructions given by the offeror in the offer relative to time of acceptance, place of acceptance, or manner of acceptance must be strictly complied with by the offeree.

(1) A unilateral offer is not accepted until the requested act is completed, and the offeror may revoke his offer at any time before substantial performance is completed.

(2) A bilateral offer is accepted by a promise to do what is requested in the offer. Formal procedures are not required by the laws of acceptance. A nod of the head may suffice.

d. Communication of Acceptance. An acceptance must be communicated for a contract to result. However, while an offer is not effective unless the offeree knows of the offer, an acceptance may be valid even though the offeror does not know of the acceptance. For example, an acceptance of a bilateral offer (received by mail) becomes effective when it is communicated to the offeror by depositing the acceptance in the mail if it is properly addressed and stamped.

D. CONSIDERATION

   1. <u>Definition</u>: - - Consideration may be defined as an exchange of promises whereby each promisor undertakes to do or to refrain from doing some act which will be detrimental to the promisor or beneficial to the promisee. The words "benefit" and "detriment" are misleading in that they refer to legal benefit and detriment and not actual benefit or detriment. The key idea of consideration is the surrender of or the promise to surrender a legal right at the request of another. It may be an act, or a failure to act, or a promise to act or to refrain from acting. If each party to the contract is obligated and each receives what he bargained for, consideration is present.

   2. <u>Consideration on Sealed Instruments:</u> - - The law governing the necessity of consideration for the validity of informal contracts does not apply to formal contracts or written contracts under seal. The seal originally was a wax impression made with a signet ring or similar device. At the present time statutes in many states have modified the rules relative to sealing. The word "seal" or the initials "L.S." for "locus sigilli" (meaning "place of the seal") may be adequate. Today, any extraneous material which can be attached to an instrument may serve as a seal. The act of sealing was considered a sufficient guarantee of the promisor's intent to enter into a binding agreement. Moreover, the validity of sealed instruments had been established a long time before the doctrine of consideration emerged.

   3. <u>Adequacy of Consideration</u>: - - The value of the consideration given is generally held to be unimportant unless there is some evidence of fraud. There is no requirement under the law that the consideration exchanged be of equal value or of even approximately equal value. The usual dollar consideration reflected in deeds and other instruments or the surrender of a document with no value is sufficient consideration. There is only one exception where the courts will enforce the adequacy of consideration . . . that is when there is a promise to pay a sum of money for a larger sum when both promises are to be performed at the same time.

   4. <u>Types of Consideration</u>: - - Consideration in support of a contract must be "valuable". The courts differentiate between "good" consideration and "valuable" consideration. A promise based on friendship for which the promisor receives only personal satisfaction in return is called "good" consideration and is insufficient. "Good", "meritorious", and "moral" considerations are all insufficient since the promisee gives nothing in return.

   5. <u>Cancellation Clauses</u>: - - A contract which allows either or both parties to avoid the contract at any time without notice is void because of lack of consideration. In such contracts neither party is bound to anything.

E. CAPACITY OF PARTIES

1. <u>General</u>: - - By capacity (or competency) is meant legal competency or capacity as distinguished from either physical or mental. Presumably, all persons are competent to contract without restriction except infants, insane persons, drunkards, married women, convicts, spendthrifts or aged persons, and corporations. Contracts entered into by those lacking competency are voidable by the incompetent party.

2. <u>Infants</u>: - - An infant, in the eyes of the law, is one who has not reached the age of majority. In most states the age of majority has been reduced to 18 years of age. Some states provide that a woman reaches majority upon marriage, regardless of age. Contracts between an adult and an infant are voidable only by the infant. The adult's obligation is enforceable unless the infant disaffirms. An infant's contracts for the necessaries of life (i. e., food, clothing, shelter, medical attention, and a certain amount of education) are exceptions to the rule. Such contracts are voidable by the infant, but the infant is liable for the fair value of the benefit received as differentiated from the contract price, after the infant's station in life is duly considered. Upon reaching majority, the infant must elect either to be bound by the contract made during his minority or to avoid it. Ratification will be assumed, unless by some act it is unequivocally indicated that he chose to avoid the contract.
Note: A minor cannot disaffirm a sale of his real estate until he reaches his majority. Prior to disaffirmance, however, he may enter into possession, assume management of the property, and appropriate the income from such property while title rests with the adult.

3. <u>Insane Persons:</u> - - Contracts involving insane persons must consider whether or not a guardian has been appointed.

    a. Under Guardianship. Contracts of an insane person under guardianship are void, not merely voidable.

    b. Not Under Guardianship. Where no guardian has been appointed, contracts made during periods of insanity are voidable like those of an infant. However, if an insane person who has no guardian enters into a contract during a lucid period, the contract is not voidable. Like the infant in contract, the insane person is liable for the fair value of necessaries. Similar to contracts involving infants, an insane person may either ratify or avoid his contract upon return to normalcy.

4. <u>Drunkards:</u> - - Intoxication of itself does not invalidate a contract made in such a state. Only if such intoxication is to such an extent as to render one incapable of understanding the effects of his action are his contracts voidable. There is a differ-

ence, however, between the contracts of a drunkard and those of an infant or insane person. Contracts of one incapacitated by intoxication cannot be disaffirmed if by such disaffirmance a third party would be injured who had subsequently purchased the property involved. Drunkards, like infants, are liable in contracts for the necessaries of life.

5. Married Women: - - All states have removed the Old Common Law restrictions on married women so that they may now make contracts as though they were single, and without the concurrence of their husbands. A few states declare, however, that a contract between a married woman and her husband is void.

6. Convicts: - - In many states statutes have been enacted which view a felon as civilly dead, or that his rights and powers are suspended during the period of imprisonment. Provisions, however, are usually made for the administration of his estate by a committee or by trustees.

7. Spendthrifts and Aged Persons: - - If a guardian is appointed, contracts made by a spendthrift or aged person are void.

8. Corporations: - - The contractual powers of a corporation are limited by its charter.

F. LEGAL PURPOSE

1. General: - - A contract must be legal in its purpose and in the method provided for its performance. It cannot violate any law or infringe upon the legal rights of others. Agreements whose object or the manner in which they are to be performed are contrary to the law or public policy are illegal and as such unenforceable in court.

2. Illegal Contracts: - - Any contract is illegal if it is, by its formation or performance, criminal, involves a tort, or is against public policy. Such contracts are usually void. Some specific types of illegal contracts are those in restraint of trade, wagering contracts, usurious contracts, contracts obstructing the administration of justice, and Sunday contracts.

3. Sunday Contracts: - - Whether or not contracts entered into on Sunday or to be performed on Sunday are illegal depends upon the law of the particular state where the contracts are made. In some states such contracts are legal. In Arizona and in Illinois, for example, a contract signed or a deed delivered on a Sunday or legal holiday is valid and enforceable. Furthermore, in Illinois, when the last day for execution of a contract or deed falls on a Sunday or holiday, the document may be executed on the next business day. In other states, however, Sunday contracts are illegal. Statutes which declare Sunday contracts illegal and void do not apply to preliminary contractual negotiations. An offer may be made on a Sunday and accepted on a weekday without violation of the Sunday law. Conversely, however, acceptance on a Sunday of an offer presented on a weekday would result in an illegal contract. Formal contracts, such as deeds and negotiable instruments, do not become effective until delivered. Consequently,

a promissory note or a deed signed on a Sunday but delivered on a weekday is not in violation of the Sunday law. Where contracts call for performance at a future date which accidently falls on a Sunday, the contract is not illegal and will be performable on the following day.

    4.   <u>Effects of Illegality</u>: - - A party to an illegal contract normally cannot recover money paid under the terms of the contract. Neither can he recover damages for breach of the contract nor fair value of the services rendered.

G. LEGAL FORM

    1.   <u>General</u>: - - There is no requirement that a contract be in writing unless it is to be under seal or falls within the Statute of Frauds.

    2.   <u>Advantages of Written Contracts</u>

        a.   It proves the existence of a contract.

        b.   Disputes as to nature and terms of contract are minimized.

        c.   In legal proceedings the written terms cannot be contradicted.

        d.   If under seal, the requirement of consideration is satisfied.

        e.   If under seal, the period within which suit can be brought is extended in most states from six to twenty years.

H. THE STATUTE OF FRAUDS

    1.   <u>Purpose of Statute of Frauds</u>

An Act for Prevention of Frauds and Perjuries was enacted in 1677 by the British Parliament to prevent perjuries and frauds often perpetrated by claims based on non-existent oral contracts. This celebrated English statute has been adopted, in a more or less modified form, in every state. The chief characteristic of the Statute of Frauds, as it is commonly designated, is the provision that no suit or action shall be maintained on certain classes of contracts, unless there shall be a note or a memorandum thereof in writing, signed by the party to be charged or by his authorized agent. The present day statutes are substantially the same as the originals except for considerable modernization under the Uniform Commercial Code, particularly relating to the sale of goods (Section 17 of the original Statute). (Reference Appendix D.)

    2.   <u>Form and Content of the Memorandum</u>

Under the Statute of Frauds a memorandum is required to render the contract enforceable, and it must meet the following requisites:

a. It must be in writing.

b. It must be signed by the person to be charged or bound.

c. It must describe the parties.

d. It must describe the subject matter of the contract.

e. It must reflect the price, terms, and conditions of the contract.

No particular form is required. A letter may prove sufficient, or a memorandum may be comprised of several writings, if all are signed and attached or cross-referenced to each other. It is not necessary that the memorandum be drawn at the same time the contract is made. The memorandum may be made at any time.

3. Application of the Statute of Frauds

The Statute of Frauds holds that the following types of express contracts must be evidenced in writing in order to be enforceable:

a. Contracts for the sale of land or any interest in or concerning land.

b. Contracts for the sale of goods and certain other personal property over $500 in value.

c. Contracts not to be performed within one year.

d. Contracts by executors or administrators to pay estate claims out of their own funds.

e. Contracts wherein the consideration is marriage and the promise given in return is other than a promise to marry.

f. Contracts where one person promises to answer for the debt, default, or wrong of another.

4. Contracts for the Sale of Interests in Land

a. Definition of Land. Land includes soil and everything attached to it. Within the Statute of Frauds, land includes more than just earth. It includes also contracts for the transfer of rights in land such as mortgages, easements, or the sale of mineral rights and timber. Contracts for the sale of real property or interests therein are within the Statute of Frauds and are unenforceable unless evidenced in writing and signed by the party to be charged. A contract for the sale of products of the land (e. g., fruits, vegetables, growing trees) falls within the Statute of Frauds, if ownership is to be transferred before these products are severed from the land. If ownership passes after severance from the land, the Statute of Frauds does not apply.

b. Agency Contracts for Sale of Land. When a property owner orally promises to pay a real estate broker a commission if the broker finds a buyer and negotiates the sale, such agreement is one of employment and does not fall within the Statute of Frauds. In this instance, the sale of real property is only the condition, the performance of which entitles the broker to his commission under the contract of service.

c. Contracts Involving a License. There is in law a distinction between an interest in land and a mere license. An interest involves either an ownership in the land, an easement, or a right to take products of the land. A license, on the other hand, simply allows a person to use the land of another. Contracts involving licenses do not fall within the Statute of Frauds and are valid even though they are oral.

d. Contracts Concerning Boundaries. Contracts concerning land boundaries involve an interest in land and do fall within the Statute of Frauds. An oral agreement, therefore, to fix a boundary is not enforceable.

e. Leases. Generally, leases need not be in writing unless the contractual period is such that it comes under the Statute of Frauds. In certain states, however, any estate or interest in land involving landlord and tenant which is not in writing and signed by the landlord has the force and effect of a tenancy at will.

A lease, in most states, for a period of more than one year must be in the form of a written contract to be enforceable. In Ohio, all leases must be in writing. In Pennsylvania, California, and Indiana, leases for a period of more than three years must be in writing. On the other hand, in Louisiana and Delaware, there is no requirement for a lease to be in writing in order to be enforceable.

5. Contracts for the Sale of Goods

   a. General. In all states contracts for the sale of goods whose value is $500 or more fall within the Statute and are unenforceable if not in writing unless . . .

   (1) The buyer has made partial payment, or

   (2) The buyer receives and accepts all or part of the goods.

   b. Meaning of Goods. Contracts involving the sale of intangibles such as shares of stocks, accounts receivable and the like are viewed as sales of goods and fall within the Statute. Contracts for the sale of fruits, vegetables, trees, and other products of the land are treated as sales of goods only if ownership is to pass after severance from the land.

6. Contracts Not Performable Within a Year

In most states, contracts which cannot possibly be performed by both parties within one year from the date of the contract fall within the Statute of Frauds, and must be evidenced in writing to be enforceable. In North Carolina, Louisiana, and Pennsylvania there is no such requirement. In Mississippi the term is 15 months. In all other states if, even theoretically, it is possible to perform the contract within a year, the Statute does not apply. The year is figured from the time the contract is made, not from the time performance is commenced. Therefore, a contract for one year, commencing the day after the contract is made, falls within the Statute. If performance is to commence on the same day the contract is made, it does not fall within the Statute of Frauds.

7. Oral Executory Agreements Concerning Land

The courts, in effect, disregard the Statute of Frauds in cases where a purchaser has made valuable and substantial improvement on land conveyed to him in an oral agreement. It is held that the seller who refuses to convey because the contract was oral is attempting to use the Statute of Frauds to perpetrate a fraud.

8. As Defense to Third Parties

Third parties cannot use the Statute of Frauds as a defense that a contract is unenforceable because it is not evidenced in writing. Only the parties directly involved in the contract can avail themselves of such a defense. Assume, for example, that A orally agrees to purchase B's house, and C, aware of A's oral contract with B, signs a written agreement with B for the purchase of the same house. A's rights were unenforceable.

I. CONTRACTS INDUCED BY FRAUD, DURESS, OR MISTAKE

1. General: - - In the making of contracts, the law requires the contracting parties to conduct themselves with a certain degree of fairness. As a minimum standard, a contracting party shall not induce others to contract by employing fraudulent misrepresentations. Nor will a contracting party knowingly conceal matters which if exposed might prevent the contract from being formed. The use of force or pressure to induce another to contract is prohibited. The effect of failure to meet the minimum standards of conduct may void the contract or completely nullify it, and in some instances damages may be recovered.

2. <u>Fraudulent Misrepresentation</u>: -- Fraud and misrepresentation in most respects are similar. An intentional misstatement of an existing material fact which induces another to act thereon to his damage is fraud. Misrepresentation is identical in all respects except the first. Intention to mislead is not an essential element of misrepresentation. An unintentional misstatement of fact made honestly and in good faith allows the injured party remedies identical with those arising in the case of fraud with but one exception. (Reference sub Paragraph 2f following).

    a. Misstatement. The basis of fraud or misrepresentation is an untrue statement. Even a partial truth becomes an untruth when information is requested and the partial truth given in response is designed to create a false impression and, in fact, does.

    b. Failure to Disclose. One party to a contract is under no duty to the other to inform him of special facts or circumstances that vitally affect the subject matter and which are known only to him. "Caveat emptor", Latin for "let the buyer beware," is the appropriate maxim which summarizes the rule that the buyer takes the risk as to the quality of goods in a contract of sale where the buyer has an opportunity of examining goods before purchase. Silence, of itself, is not a misstatement and does not constitute fraud. There are, however, three situations in which one party is duty bound to disclose to the other party facts of which the latter is unaware.

        (1) Fiduciary Relationship. A person in a fiduciary relationship as in the case of a real estate broker with the property owner he represents is under a duty to make full disclosure of all material facts.

        (2) Correction of Misrepresentation When one party innocently misrepresents a fact to the other party and later learns of the falsity of his statement, he is obligated to correct his misrepresentation.

        (3) Dangerous Defects. A seller who knows that defects in an article make it dangerous to life or property is duty bound to disclose the defects to the buyer who is unaware of them.

    c. Material Fact. The misstatement must relate to a material existing fact to constitute fraud. To be "material" it must have a definite moving influence upon the conduct of the contracting party. If an expert, who by his experience or position is better qualified to judge than others, intentionally misstates his opinion, his opinion may be interpreted by the courts as fact. Many courts have held that all persons who intentionally misstate their opinion are guilty of fraud.
Note: An intentional misrepresentation of existing local or state law gives no basis for rescission since the law is presumably a matter of common knowledge and open to all.

d. Reliance on Misstatement. Most states hold that if all the information is readily available to determine the truth of statements made, reliance upon the misrepresentation is not justified since the party is said to be negligent in not taking advantage of the courses open to him to confirm the truth of the statements made.

e. Resulting Damage. To establish fraud the party relying upon the misstatement must prove that such reliance resulted in damage. Such damage may simply be evidence which indicates that the contract would have been more valuable had the statements been true.

f. Unintentional Misstatement. An unintentional misstatement is misrepresentation, not fraud. "Intent" is the key word which differentiates one from the other. Nevertheless, a contracting party may be injured as much as though the statement had been made intentionally. Rescission in such case is the remedy. In the absence of intent, the right to sue and recover damages for misrepresentation is usually denied.

g. Effect of Fraud. The injured party in fraudulent contracts has several remedies:

(1) Executory Contract. The injured party may plead fraud as a defense for non-performance.

(2) Executed Contracts. The injured party may ask for a rescission and a return of his consideration for which he will return the consideration received. To rescind, the injured party must act with reasonable promptness or forfeit this course of action.

(3) The injured party may abide by the terms of the contract and bring a tort action of deceit to recover damages suffered as a result of the fraud.

3. Duress

a. General. Duress exists whenever an act deprives the party under duress from exercising his free will and forces him to involuntarily assent to a contract. In essence, duress is the inability to voluntarily exercise one's will at the time of the formation of an agreement because of fear which is usually the result of some misconduct by the other party. Examples of duress are assault and battery, confinement, threats of personal violence, threats of destruction of property, any of which results in the performance of an act by the other as a consequence of the threat.

b. Effects of Duress. A contract made as the result of duress is voidable by the person imposed upon.

4. Mistake

   a. General. A mistake is the misunderstanding of a fact. Mistakes occur when one or both parties to a contract form an untrue conclusion about an important part of the contract. Mistakes generally fall into two well defined categories: bilateral mistakes and unilateral mistakes.

   b. Bilateral Mistake. A bilateral mistake arises when there is a mutual assumption that a material fact exists when it does not. There are two types of bilateral mistakes:

   (1) When there is no "meeting of the minds", and

   (2) When the agreement is more burdensome for one of the parties.

   In the first instance there is no contract. In the second instance the contract is voidable by the injured party.

   c. Unilateral Mistake. When only one of the contracting parties makes a mistake there is usually no basis of relief since it is held that such mistakes are the result of carelessness by the injured party and should not affect the rights of the other party. A party makes a mistake at his own peril, and the other contracting party is under no obligation to correct the error. There are two well recognized exceptions: mistake as to the identity of persons - and mistake relating to the transmission of figures which form the basis of a contract.

   (1) Mistake As to Identity. When one party erroneously believes he is contracting with a certain person, but, in fact, is dealing with a different person, the contract is invalid, since one will not be forced to contract with another against his will.

   (2) Mistake As to Transmission of Figures. When figures form the basis of a contract (as in the case of a contractor submitting his estimates for a bid), and incorrect figures were submitted which to the offeree were obviously incorrect, then the offeror may be relieved of his contractual obligation.

   d. Effect of Mistake. A mistake can render a contract void or voidable, as indicated above, on the ground that the necessary element of mutual assent is lacking.

J. DISCHARGE OF CONTRACT

   1. <u>General</u>: - - Discharge of a contract terminates the contract. A contract is discharged whenever the duty to perform has been terminated. There are several ways by which a contract may be discharged, most of which are discussed below.

   2. <u>Discharge by Performance</u>: - - Usually a contract is discharged by the complete performance of all contractual terms by both parties to the contract.

   3. <u>Discharge by Release</u>: - - Executory agreements which have not been performed by either party may be discharged by mutual agreement since the release by one provides the necessary consideration for the release of the other. However, executory agreements which have been fully performed by only one party cannot be so discharged without the release taking the form of a written instrument under seal or a written instrument which is supported by consideration reflecting that the party's obligations to perform are discharged.

   4. <u>Discharge by Accord and Satisfaction</u>: - - The parties to a contract may agree to give and receive a substitute for the promised performance. The "accord" is the agreement of the contracting parties whereby one is to do something other than what is stipulated in the terms of the contract. "Satisfaction" results when the new terms are fully performed. Both the accord and the satisfaction must take place before the old obligation is discharged unless, of course, the new agreement stipulates that it is rescinding and replacing the old.

   5. <u>Discharge by Novation</u>: - - Novation is the substitution by agreement of parties to a contract. In effect, a novation is a substituted contract which discharges the old contract by changing the parties to the contract rather than their obligations. To be effective, a novation must be under seal or supported by consideration. Such an agreement may be express or implied.

   6. <u>Discharge by Alteration</u>: - - If made with fraudulent intent, a material alteration of the written evidence of an agreement by either party to the agreement discharges the duty of the other party to perform. An alteration of the date, amount, time and place of performance, or rate of interest may be a material alteration. Innocent alterations and those made by other than the contracting parties do not affect the rights of the contracting parties and are viewed as though no alteration has been made.

   7. <u>Discharge by Statute of Limitations</u>: - - The Statute of Limitations sets a time limit within which a suit must be started. The time limit varies among states, and some states distinguish between oral and written contracts. Contract action must be initiated within the prescribed time limit after the obligation matures or after the

cause for action arises. Otherwise, such obligation will be discharged.

    8. <u>Discharge by Bankruptcy</u>: - - Under the National Bankruptcy Act one may be discharged from his obligations under certain conditions. Bankruptcy may be either voluntary or involuntary.

        a. Voluntary Bankruptcy. The voluntary filing of a petition in bankruptcy is usually all that is required for the federal court to take control of all property involved to satisfy, as far as possible, the claims of creditors.

        b. Involuntary Bankruptcy. Involuntary bankruptcy may be brought about if the debtor owes at least $1,000. If twelve or more creditors exist, at least three must sign the petition. Otherwise, the signature of only one is required.

K.   BREACH OF CONTRACT

    1. <u>General</u>: - - Breach of contract is the unexcused non-performance of the contract. A breach of contract occurs when one party to the contract - -

        a. Fails to perform in whole or in part,

        b. Gives advance notice that he does not intend to perform (anticipatory breach), or

        c. Renders performance impossible for himself or the other party.

    2. <u>Conditions for Performance</u>: - - Most contracts require the performance of a contract which is conditioned upon the occurrence or non-occurrence of a particular happening. These conditions fall into three categories: conditions precedent, conditions concurrent, and conditions subsequent, all of which may be express or implied.

        a. Conditions Precedent. Contracts which require one of the parties to perform some duty before he gains a right against the other party are called conditions precedent. When the condition precedent has been performed, the promisee becomes obligated to perform.

        b. Conditions Concurrent. When parties to a contractual agreement must act simultaneously, conditions concurrent are said to exist. An agreement, for example, which calls for the conveyance of title to real estate upon payment of a specified amount is illustrative of a condition concurrent.

c. Conditions Subsequent. A condition subsequent is a contractual provision which excuses a duty to perform a promise after the duty has arisen. A sale giving the buyer the opportunity to return the goods if he is dissatisfied includes a condition subsequent.

3. <u>Time As a Condition</u>: - - When the precise time for performance of a contract involves primarily the expenditure of labor and material, or the production of a product of little value to other than the contracting party, time is not usually considered to be of major significance. For example, the failure of a builder to complete construction of a house by the stipulated date in the contract would not give cause for the buyer to rescind the contract, although he may recover damages if such resulted from the delay. There are exceptions.

a. Extended Delays. An extended delay which becomes material relative to performance may justify rescission. In those instances where no specific date for performance is stipulated, a reasonable time is implied.

b. When "Time Is of the Essence." A condition precedent may be established by including in the contract a clause which states that time is of the essence in this agreement. In this case, failure to perform on time gives grounds for rescission.

4. <u>Remedies for Breach of Contract</u>: - - There are generally three remedies offered to a party aggrieved by a breach of the contract by the other party: the aggrieved party may be excused from performance; he may obtain a decree for specific performance; he may recover damages suffered. The law in most instances allows only damages for a breach of contract. In some cases, however, a choice of damages or a decree for specific performance is offered.

a. Excuse from Performance. Breach by one party relieves the other from any requirement to fulfill the contract.

b. Specific Performance. A decree for specific performance is a court order which directs a promisor to perform specifically as provided in the contract. It normally will be granted only when the thing contracted for is unique and cannot be replaced or reproduced adequately . . . or bought on the open market. Land is considered unique since no parcel is like any other, and the parcel contracted for cannot be purchased on the open market. A decree for specific performance would be appropriate. Specific performance will not be granted in every instance where damages are inadequate. Specific performance will not be granted to require personal services to be rendered, or when undue hardship would be inflicted on the defendant . . . or when the contractual terms are uncertain, or if effective enforcement is unreasonably difficult. In short, a decree for specific performance is discretionary with the court.

c. Damages. Damages in a breach of contract normally are limited to the amount of actual loss. Litigation expenses between the contracting parties cannot be recovered. However, such expenses between the promisee and third parties are recoverable. Damages for mental anguish are not recoverable for breach of business contracts. In general, the law holds that parties must minimize their loss. An agreement providing for liquidated damages will not be enforced if the amount set is disproportionate to the probable loss, and if it involves a penalty.

5. Anticipatory Breach

   a. Definition. Anticipatory breach is the repudiation by one party to a contract agreement of a contract obligation before the duty to perform arises. Such repudiation may be made by a definite statement or by an act which makes it impossible for him to perform.

   b. Remedy for Anticipatory Breach. The promisee is justified in immediately filing suit for breach of contract without waiting for the stipulated time for performance. A repudiation may be withdrawn before the promisee brings suit or changes his position, but not thereafter.

6. Liquidated Damages

Many contracts, and especially those for the purchase of real estate, provide that, in the event of default by the buyer, any deposit made by him will be retained by the seller (or divided between seller and real estate agent) to compensate for damages suffered by the seller (whose property was taken off the market) and the agent (for expenditure of his time, advertising, et cetera).

L. EXCUSES FOR NON-PERFORMANCE

1. General: -- Parties to a contract are expected to perform on their contractual promises or pay damages. The law does not usually recognize excuses for non-performance. Unforeseen circumstances, in some instances, may allow for the nullification or rescission of the contract whereby all parties are excused from performance and relieved of liability.

2. Destruction of Subject Matter: -- Destruction of any specific subject matter essential to the completion of the contract relieves all parties from their contractual obligations and results in a rescission of the contract.

3. <u>Death or Illness</u>: - - Death or illness of a contracting party will normally not result in rescission unless the contract calls for the personal services of the disabled party. Contracts, for example, for the sale of property are unaffected by the death or illness of either or both of the parties. In the event of death it is assumed that the provisions of the contract will be carried out by the estate of the deceased.

4. <u>Mistake</u>: - - Only in those instances of mutual mistake as to the nature or existence of the subject matter which precludes a meeting of the minds will a contract be rescinded.

5. <u>Hardship</u>: - - To be effective, provisions must be made in the contract for unusual circumstances which later could develop if such developments are to be effective as an excuse for non-performance. Otherwise, hardship will not excuse a contracting party from performance.

6. <u>Prevention</u>: - - It is implied in every contractual agreement that the parties thereto will do nothing which would interfere with the performance of the other party. If such interference results, the party attempting to perform is relieved of his obligation and may initiate action to recover damages because of the breach of the implied condition.

7. <u>Frustration of Purpose</u>: - - When parties understandingly enter into an agreement whereby the thing contracted for is for a particular purpose, the development of circumstances without the fault of either party, which makes it impossible to accomplish the purpose, results in the rescission of the contract.

CATEGORIES OF CONTRACT

1. FORMAL
(Relate to form of the instrument)
  a. Written contracts under seal
  b. Negotiable instruments

2. INFORMAL
(Relate to nature of transaction)

TYPES OF CONTRACTS

1. Express
2. Implied
3. Bilateral
4. Unilateral
5. Executed
6. Executory
7. Void
8. Voidable
9. Unenforceable

PREREQUISITES OF INFORMAL CONTRACTS

1. **MUTUAL ASSENT:**
    a. Offer
    b. Acceptance
2. **LEGAL CONSIDERATION**
3. **COMPETENT PARTIES**
4. **LEGAL PURPOSE**
5. **LEGAL FORM**

1. **MUTUAL ASSENT**

    a. **OFFER:**
    - (1) Intentional
    - (2) Definite:
        - (a) Time
        - (b) Price
        - (c) Property
    - (1) Communicated

    b. **ACCEPTANCE:**
    - (1) By offeree
    - (2) Conform to terms of offer
    - (3) Communicated

TERMINATION OF THE OFFER

1. **Rejection**
2. **Counter offer**
3. **Lapse of time**
4. **Express revocation**
5. **Death of offeror - ee**

CAPACITY OF PARTIES

1. **Infants**
2. **Insane Persons:**
   a. **Under Guardianship**
   b. **Not Under Guardianship**
3. **Drunkards**
4. **Married Women**
5. **Convicts**
6. **Spendthrifts and Aged Persons**
7. **Corporations**

TYPES OF CONSIDERATION

1. GOOD

2. VALUABLE

STATUTE OF FRAUDS

Form of Memorandum

1. Written
2. Signed
3. Parties described
4. Subject described
5. Price, terms, conditions noted

STATUTE OF FRAUDS

1. Contracts for sale of land or interests therein.
2. Contracts for sale of goods over $500.
3. Contracts not to be performed within one year.
4. Contracts by executors or administrators to pay estate claims from own funds.
5. Contracts of marriage wherein promise of one is other than a promise to marry.
6. Contracts where one promises to answer for debt, default, or wrong of another.

FRAUD

1. Intentional
2. Misstatement
3. Material fact
4. Reliance
5. Resulting damage

DUTY TO DISCLOSE

1. Fiduciary relationship
2. Correct misrepresentation
3. Dangerous defects

EFFECTS OF FRAUD

Injured party may seek:
1. **Non-performance**
2. **Rescission**
3. **Damages**

DISCHARGE OF CONTRACT

Performance
Release
Accord and satisfaction
Novation
Alteration
Statute of Limitation
Bankruptcy

BREACH OF CONTRACT

(remedies)

1. Excuse from performance
2. Specific performance
3. Damages

EXCUSES FOR NON-PERFORMANCE

1. Destruction of Subject Matter
2. Death or Illness
3. Mistake
4. Hardship
5. Prevention
6. Frustration of Purpose

Chapter 4

REVIEW DEFINITIONS IN GLOSSARY OR TEXT OF THE FOLLOWING TERMS:

administrator	improvement
accord and satisfaction	interest
anticipatory breach	land
bilateral contract	license
breach of contract	misrepresentation
capacity	novation
contract	option
counter-offer	quasi-contract
emblements	seal
estate	specific performance
executed contract	Statute of Frauds
executor	Statute of Limitations
executory contract	surety bond
express contract	unenforceable contract
fraud	unilateral contract
illegal contract	void contract
implied contract	voidable contract

REVIEW QUESTIONS:

1. What is the basis of a contract?

2. Name two types of formal contracts.

3. What are the prerequisites of an informal contract?

4. What criteria must a valid offer meet?

5. Name five ways by which an offer can be terminated.

6. Must the acceptance of an offer be communicated?

7. What is the key idea of "consideration?"

8. Are contracts of an infant void or voidable?

9. Are contracts of insane persons under guardianship void or voidable?

10. Does intoxication of itself invalidate a contract?

11. What are the advantages of a written contract?

12. What purpose does the Statute of Frauds serve?

13. What requisites must a memorandum meet under the Statute of Frauds to render a contract enforceable?

14. Name five types of express contracts which must be evidenced in writing to be enforceable.

15. What is the difference between an interest in land and a license?

16. When determining whether or not a contract comes under the Statute of Frauds with respect to its being performed within a year, is the year figured from the time the contract is made or from the time performance is commenced?

17. Can third parties use the Statute of Frauds as a defense?

18. What is the difference between fraud and misrepresentation?

19. May silence of itself constitute fraud?

20. Name three situations where one party is duty-bound to disclose to the other party facts of which the latter is unaware.

21. The relationship between a broker and the property owner he represents is known as what type of relationship?

22. What are the remedies for a breach of contract?

23. Name two excuses for non-performance.

24. Will death normally result in rescission of the contract?

FOR ANSWERS TO REVIEW QUESTIONS:

1.

2.

3.

4.

5.

6.

7.

8.

9.

10.

11.

12.

13.

14.

15.

16.

17.

18.

19.

20.

21.

22.

23.

24.

Chapter 5

Genesis of American Property Law

A.	THE UNITY OF PROPERTY AND LAW		99
	1. Historical Concepts		99
		a. Rousseau	99
		b. Smith	99
		c. Cicero	99
		d. Bentham	99
	2. On the Nature of Property		99
		a. General	99
		b. Economic Importance	100
		c. Political Implication	100
	3. The Meaning of Property		100
		a. General	100
		b. Things	100
		c. Relationships	100
	4. Property as Things		101
		a. General	101
		b. Physical Property	101
		(1) Derivation of "Property"	101
		(2) Real Property	102
		(3) Personal Property	102
		c. Physical Things Relating to Property	102
		(1) General	102
		(2) Corporeal Property	103
		(3) Tangible Property	103

	5.		Property as Relationships	103
		a.	General	103
		b.	Incorporeal Property	103
		c.	Intangible Property	104
	6.		The Total Concept of Property	104
	7.		Historical Reference	104

B. THE DOCTRINE OF TENURES 105

    1. Free Tenures 105

        a. Military Tenure — 106
        b. Socage Tenure — 106
        c. Sergeanty Tenure — 106
        d. Frankalmoign Tenure — 106

    2. Unfree Tenures 107

        a. Villein Tenure — 108
        b. Copyhold — 108
        c. Customary Freehold — 108

    3. Incidents of Tenure 109

        a. During Tenant's Lifetime — 109

            (1) Homage — 109
            (2) Fealty — 109
            (3) Aids — 109

        b. Upon Tenant's Death — 110

            (1) Wardship — 110
            (2) Relief — 110
            (3) Escheat — 110
            (4) Marriage — 110

C. THE DOCTRINE OF ESTATES 110

D. CONCLUSIONS 111

VISUAL AIDS 111

REVIEW QUESTIONS 115

Chapter 5
Genesis of American Property Law

A. THE UNITY OF PROPERTY AND LAW

1. <u>Historical Concepts</u>

   a. Rousseau writes, "The first man who, having enclosed a piece of ground, bethought himself of saying '<u>this is mine</u>' and found people simple enough to believe him, was the real founder of civil society.

   "Such was, or may well have been, the origin of society and law which bound new fetters on the poor and gave new powers to the rich which irretrievably destroyed natural liberty, eternally fixed the law of property and inequality, converted clever usurpation into unalterable right, and, for the advantage of a few ambitious individuals, subjected all mankind to perpetual labor, slavery, and wretchedness."

   b. Adam Smith, on this point, does not seem to disagree. He writes, "Where there is no property . . . civil government is not so necessary."

   c. Cicero's view seems in consonance with those later expressed by Rousseau and Smith when he states:

   "Let the civil law be once abandoned, or but negligently guarded, not to say oppressed, and there is nothing that any man can be sure to receive from his ancestors or leave to his children."

   d. Jeremy Bentham states, "Property and law are born together and die together. Before laws were made there was no property; take away laws and property ceases."

2. <u>On the Nature of Property</u>

   a. General. Practically everything one does during the course of his daily activities revolves around, and is affected by, property. And yet, the term "property" often connotes different things to different people at different times. In business generally, and in the field of real estate brokerage specifically, it is necessary when dealing in the sphere of property law that we understand precisely the definitions of property in its various applications, its history, its nature, and its function.

b. Economic Importance. Property is the very essence of economic activity. Property is a measure of wealth; economics is a study of wealth. A country's ecomomic structure is a reflection of its concepts of property. In a true socialistic society, while some private ownership of property is tolerated, communal property, nevertheless, predominates, and individual interests are subordinated to the interests of the state or the group. In the yet-to-emerge communist state, the entire concept of the private ownership of property is repudiated. Marx and Engles in "The Communist Manifesto" rather emphatically state that . . . "the theory of the Communists may be summed up in a single sentence: abolition of private property." In a capitalistic society, individualism prevails, private property predominates, and group interests are subordinated to those of the individual. Regardless of the economic structure, property can exist only in an ordered society.

c. Political Implication. Private property is protected and secured by those laws which protect the person, property, and liberty of the individual. The right to ownership of private property and the freedom to contract formed the basis in Anglo-American law of the economic and political philosophy of western civilization. Today, despite all the controls and restrictions which envelop it, private property, particularly in land, continues to be a vital institution of the United States' legal system and the "American Way of Life," and it is generally regarded as an indispensable element of any free society. With such vast importance attached to the various concepts of property, it is of paramount importance that we understand the different meanings associated with the term "property."

3. The Meaning of Property

a. General. From the early days of English law throughout the course of history, the term "property" has been viewed from two basic concepts; one concept views property as things, the other concept views property as relationships.

b. Things. Within the concept of property as "things" we include not only the physical property itself, but also those physical things which relate to the property - such as, contracts, notes, deeds, et cetera.

c. Relationships. Within the concept of property as "relationships" we mean specifically the relationships between property (viewed as things) and persons. In the area of property law, the term property itself is meaningless. It assumes a meaning only upon association with an individual.

4. Property as Things

    a. General. Since the term "property" in property law is meaningless of itself, it is necessary to further qualify the term with some preciseness if we are to have a "meeting of the minds" in our dealings as professional real estate associates with our employers, prospects, bankers, attorneys, and others. When we previously dissected the term "property as things" we found included therein the physical property itself and those physical things relating to the property. Our attention is thus focused initially on some consideration of physical property, per se.

    b. Physical Property

        (1) Derivation of "Property." The first concept of property was developed by pre-agricultural societies - the hunters and nomadic tribes - at a time when the hunter's weapons or the herder's cattle were the primary elements of property. Personal property, therefore, was the first type of property known. When hunters and herdsmen, with the evolution of society, became agriculturalists with an interest in the cultivation of a particular piece of land, the concept of real property was developed. Primitive man, having poured his labor into the clearing and plowing of his land, coupled with the sowing and harvesting of the crops from his land, had created a new concept of property which did not relate to the weapons or tools that he could carry with him or to the domestic animals which he could drive before him. This new concept of property related instead to a piece of ground, immovable as it was, from which, at the expense of his labor and sweat, he could derive personal profits in the form of crops.

        The term used today to define the two major types of property (i. e., real and personal) have existed since pre-historic times, but derive their present definition from the Latin which is the basis for some two-thirds of our English language.

        The injured party, who had suffered the loss of an item of personal property, such as a pig which had been slaughtered and consumed by the guilty parties, could not appeal for the restoration of the no longer existent pig. Instead, he had to sue before the rulers of the community for a substitute for the loss, whether in terms of a replacement animal or the equivalent in the current medium of exchange. His suit was consequently directed against the individual responsible and was called a suit "in personam." Hence the term personal as it relates to property.

        The person deprived of his right or interest in land (including the soil with its agricultural crops or the minerals contained within the land) did not plead for a substitute item or value which perhaps no longer existed. Rather, such a person sought the retrieval of the still existent thing (in Latin called "res") of which he had been deprived. (In Old French, the word for "thing" was "real," hence the term in use today - real). The specific action for recovery of the land was called an action "in rem" (the accusative case form in the Latin of the noun "res").

It becomes evident, therefore, that the terms "personal property" (sometimes referred to as "personalty") and "real property" (sometimes referred to as "realty") evolved from the particular types of legal remedies developed to secure an individual's property rights.

(2) Real Property. Today, real property is that which is fixed, immovable, indestructible, unique in character as it relates to one separate, distinct area of land with the improvements on it, the minerals under it, the products of the soil from it, and the air space above it.

(3) Personal Property. In the early days of our civilization - and in the civilizations of many undeveloped countries today - the most notable movable thing among a man's personal possessions was his cattle which, among other things, served as a significant medium of exchange because of its mobility. In the Old French, the word for cattle was "chatel" from which we derive the word "chattel." Today, "chattel" is defined as any <u>tangible</u> movable or immovable <u>personal</u> property.

In a broad sense, personal property includes that property which is not a part of or attached to the land. More specifically, personal property is comprised of those <u>tangible and intangible</u> things which are not real property but which are capable of ownership. While the term "chattel" relates to only tangible personal property, "personal property" encompasses both tangible and intangible concepts.

c. Physical Things Relating to Property

(1) General. We have been concerned to this point with the actual physical property itself - both land (real property) and chattel (a part of personal property). Any exposition of physical property is incomplete without consideration of those physical things which <u>relate</u> to property, both real and personal. If such physical things relate to real property, they are referred to as "corporeal property." If such physical things relate to personal property, they are referred to as "tangible property."

(2) Corporeal Property. The word "corporeal" is derived from both the Old French (corporel) and the Latin (corporalis) meaning belonging to the body (corpo) thing (relis). The Latin "relis" relates to land. Those physical things such as light, air, and water which touch or are directly concerned with the land cannot be garnered - they cannot be fixed to the land. Nevertheless, an owner, by an easement, may acquire a right to have light over his land by the imposition of a duty on an adjacent property owner to refrain from blocking such light. Similarly, an owner may acquire air rights. By agreement, an owner, likewise, may acquire rights in running water. Such then is the nature of physical things relating to land (real property). We observe, therefore, that corporeal property embodies the actual land itself <u>together with</u> the physical things (i. e., light, air, water) which <u>relate to the real property</u>.

(3) Tangible Property. The word "tangible" comes from the Latin "tangere," meaning "to touch," and is the term in property law relating to personal property and the physical things relating to (or representative of) personal property. Business and commercial transactions today necessitate the use of forms and negotiable instruments which serve as evidence of the existence or transfer of personal property. Such forms and instruments are reflections of the actual personal property and are viewed as physical things that relate to personal property.

5. Property as Relationships

a. General. It has been pointed out in Paragraph 3, supra, that the broadest view of the term "property" would include the two basic concepts, one viewing property as "things" (see Paragraph 4, supra) and the other viewing property as "relationships" between the physical "thing" and the individual. The "relationships" (note the plural form) can be very specifically dissected into components. These components are the individual's "rights," "powers," "privileges," and "immunities." When viewed collectively, these components are referred to in property law as "interests." Therefore, we may conclude that "property as relationships" are concerned with an individual's "interest" in the property. It is well to note that the property, per se, is not associated with the word "interest." "Interest" relates only to <u>the individual</u> with respect to property. The adjectives used to describe "property as relationships" are "incorporeal" when used in connection with <u>real property</u> and "intangible" when used in connection with <u>personal property</u>.

b. Incorporeal Property. Any interest in land other than physical is incorporeal property. Examples would include easements, rights of way, and licenses.

c. Intangible Property. Any interest in personal property is intangible property. Examples include patents, trademarks, copyrights, and royalties.

6. The Total Concept of Property

In the previous paragraphs of this section, property as "things" and property as "relationships" have been explored. The concept of "relationship brought into association the property with an individual. The relationship between an individual and a property was determined to be the individual's interest in the property. For one to "have" property infers that one has an "interest" - a degree of ownership - in that property. He may have a totality of interest (or ownership) to encompass all rights, powers, privileges, and immunities, or his interest may be considerably less. The quality of interest as well as the quantity of interest must be considered. When we speak of the quantity or duration of one's interest in land, we refer to his "estate." When we speak of the quality of his interest in land, we refer to his "tenancy." Chapter 6 - "Freehold Estates and Tenancies" - and Chapter 7 - "Nonfreehold Estate and Tenancies" - further develop these terms.

7. Historical Reference

The real estate business of today is inextricably enmeshed in property and, to a certain but measurable degree, property law.

The roots of our present day laws extend back over a thousand years to the time when England was an isolated and exposed province of the deteriorating and disintegrating Roman Empire which for over four hundred years had superimposed over the island its sophisticated culture and its tightly structured governmental organizations. With the onslaught of the invading hordes of barbarians and their eventual subjugation of the island, civilization slid into the Dark Ages. This period was aptly described by Winston Churchill in his History of the English Speaking Peoples. He wrote, "England was once again a barbarian island. It had been Christian; it was now heathen. Its inhabitants had rejoiced in well planned cities with temples, markets, academies. They had nourished craftsmen and merchants, professors of literature and rhetoric. For four hundred years there had been law and order, respect for property and a widening culture. All had vanished. The buildings, such as they were, were of wood, not stone. The people had lost entirely the art of writing. Some miserable runic scribblings were the only means by which they could convey their thoughts or wishes to one another at a distance. Barbarism reigned in its rags without even the stern military principles which had animated and preserved the Germanic tribes. The confusion and conflict of petty ruffians sometimes called Kings racked the land. There was nothing worthy of the name nationhood, or even tribalism."

Government disintegrated and, with it, the security of its laws. Marauding bands roamed the countryside and confiscated lands by right of force. Leaders of these bands would reward their followers for past and anticipated services with parcels of the plundered land, and thus emerged the nascent feudal political structure with its roots imbedded in the land. Landowners lived in constant fear of having their property expropriated by lawless invaders. Their only security was to seek an alliance with a chieftain who could afford protection and to pay whatever price that might be demanded for such protection. This, then, was the plight of the property owner and the prevailing mode of society in England in the year 1066, which chronicled the emergence of property law as we know it today in the United States.

The Norman Invasion in the Fall of 1066 was the turning point. William the Bastard landed at Pevensey Bay on the southeast coast of England on September twenty-eighth of that year. A few weeks later, on the afternoon of October fourteenth, the Norman Invaders under William engaged the defenders led by King Harold in a fierce battle at Hastings, a seaside town of Sussex, England. During this engagement King Harold was killed by a stray arrow. His leaderless forces battled on gallantly until dusk. As darkness fell, however, the crushed English forces scattered, leaving William the conqueror and victor of one of the most daring military gambles in history. On Christmas Day, William the Conqueror was crowned King of England at Westminster.

B. THE DOCTRINE OF TENURES

From the moment of his coronation William became vested in title to all of the conquered land. From this circumstance evolved the theory still held to this day that in England all land is owned by the Crown and that while subjects may hold land of the Crown as tenants, they cannot own it. The very foundation of the English Doctrine of Tenures emerges from the theory that there is no allodial land (land held in absolute independence) in England. The Doctrine of Tenures defines the relationship between two parties, whereas the Doctrine of Estates defines the relationship of the parties to the land.

At this time a money economy was non-existent. Land and the rents and profits derived from the land constituted almost all of the tangible wealth of the country. The entire social structure was erected upon tenants holding land from a lord in return for services they would render. Eventually the myriad services rendered became somewhat standardized. Each category of service became known as a tenure and reflected how the land was held. The tenures themselves were classified further as free tenures and unfree tenures. The free tenures extended down through the feudal pyramid to, but not including, the workers of the field. These tillers of the soil, the "villeins", were bound to the land by an unfree tenure in return for the security emanating from the power of the lord. From the outset, feudalism and its law of the feuds served not only as a method of holding property but also as a system of government as well. The association of property and law was thus established.

1. Free Tenures

The extensive land holdings of the defeated Saxon nobility were confiscated as prizes of war and were subsequently granted by William to his followers as rewards for their past loyalty and to insure their future support. The grants by William conveyed land to be held by the Barons (tenants holding immediately of the King) rather than being owned by them. In return was the obligation of the Barons (sometimes referred to as Tenants-in-Chief) to perform specific services for the King.

The Tenants-in-Chief who were responsive directly to the King enjoyed the highest social positions in the feudal aristocracy. These land barons, however, also had needs to be satisfied not unlike those of the King. Thus was perpetuated by the process of "subinfeudation", the system of feudal tenure which extended from the Crown to the actual possessor of the land and tiller of the soil. In between this long feudal chain may have been many links in the form of mesne (intermediate) lords who were themselves vassals of their superiors, yet lords to their subordinates.

The primary problem following the conquest of England was securing the peace and suppressing all existing opposition. This required military might. The immediate specific service demanded by the King of his Barons, therefore, was the furnishing of Knights and Yeomen for his army.

    a.   Military Tenure

The agreement between the King and Baron was known as a tenure, from the Latin "tenere", to hold. When the arrangement was such that a Baron would hold land in return for providing a certain quota of Knights for the King's army (the number being determined by the size of the grant), such a tenure was called a military tenure. The land held by the Baron was called his "fief" or "feud". In today's law the word has evolved to "fee" meaning, simply, land and/or an interest in land. More aptly, perhaps, the word "fee" described an estate of inheritance.

    b.   Socage Tenure

In addition to security, there were other fundamental services or needs required by the King. Land, therefore, was doled out to secure these services. Products of the soil essential for life, for example, were furnished annually by tenants who held land of the King under a socage tenure.

    c.   Sergeanty Tenure

The luxurious pomp, splendor, and ceremony, necessitated by medieval aristocracy, gave rise to still another type of tenure whereby the landholder would provide services, ranging from those of a ceremonial nature through services as butlers, cooks, and a wide assortment of petty services, to the ridiculous extreme of an individual whose service was that of holding the King's head during channel crossings should he become sick. Sergeanty tenure was the name given to the holding of land by providing such services. The word "sergeanty" derives from the medieval Latin word "serientia", meaning service. Sergeanty tenure was further subdivided into grand sergeanty and petty sergeanty. Grand sergeanty was usually restricted to tenants-in-chief and obligated them in person to perform some ceremonial or honorable service for the King. In petty sergeanty the service to the King was of a nonpersonal nature.

    d.   Frankalmoign Tenure

This was a tenure peculiar to the clergy and religious groups. The word "frankalmoign" means "free alms"; a Frankalmoign Tenure assured the grantor and his heirs those services of a religious nature, such as prayers and masses for their souls in return for the grant of land.

2. <u>Unfree Tenures</u>

The essence of the unfree tenure was that, although the tenant's services were specifically identified as to quantity (e. g., so many hours per day, per week), they were indefinite as to quality. This allowed the lord to assign to the tenant whatever type work he wished. The two types of unfree tenures were the Villein Tenure (later called copyhold) and Customary Freehold.

    a. Villein Tenure

As previously noted, the relationship between the King and his tenants-in-chief was but the beginning of the feudal chain of tenures. The tenants-in-chief, in effect, were a reflection on a smaller scale of the royal establishment. As land barons, these tenants-in-chief required a diversity of services and subsistence. To satisfy these needs, the tenants-in-chief would grant a portion of their holdings to others in return for the type of tenure sought. Thus was created the "subtenure" representing the relationship between the tenant-in-chief and his tenant. After the necessary grants to sub-tenants had been made, the choicest land retained by the tenant-in-chief became the site of his castle or manor. The manorial lands were tilled by peasants of the lowest social position known as villeins, or non-freemen. These villeins lived and worked under the arbitrary rule of the lord in return for the lord's protection, shelter, and perhaps a small parcel of land for the villein's own needs. This, then, formed the basis of the medieval custom of villeinage, restricted to those who actually worked the land in a state of modified servitude, since their services were obligatory. Villeinage is a medieval term describing a person's conditions as being intermediate between freedom and slavery. Their position was precarious. On the one hand, the villein was assumed to be a person free by birth, and yet, everyone born of villein stock belonged to his master and was bound to undertake any service which might be imposed on him by his master's command. During this early period, the royal courts refused to entertain suits of villeins against their lords. In criminal, political, and even civil matters, however, the villeins' rights were viewed as those of the general body of citizens. The <u>tenure</u> held by the villein mirrored his restricted status in relation to his lord. While the villein could <u>hold</u> land of the lord, he could not freely dispose of such land. This, then, was the essence of villein tenure . . . <u>the holding of land by a villein of which he cannot dispose freely.</u>

b. Copyhold

Copyhold tenure grew out of the old custom of villeinage. The struggle of the villeins to obtain greater freedom persisted. In time, they secured a commutation of their service obligations for payment in kind. Their condition gradually improved as well as their precarious tenure of land. The villeins were not members of the court baron like the freeholders. In relation to the tenants in villeinage, the court baron was called the customary court. The records of this customary court constituted the title of the villein tenant, held by a copy of the court roll ... hence the term "copyhold." The real property law as it applied to the villein tenant was specifically that as was recorded in the court roll which reflected the customs of the manor.

The word "copyhold" includes in its definition the word "tenure." Copyhold, in English law, was an ancient form of land tenure legally defined as "holding at the will of the lord according to the custom of the manor." At this point, only the freeholder of manoral lands could be a member of the "court baron." In relation to the tenants in villeinage, this court baron was called the customary court. The villein's title was that taken from the court records, and the real property law relating to this title emerged from the "customs of the manor." The detecable difference between villein tenure and copyhold emerges. The villein tenant held at the will of the lord ... period. The copyholder held at the will of the lord and according to the customs of the manor. In the time of the Domesday Survey, manorial lands were granted in part to free tenants (thus, freehold estates) and in part reserved by the lord himself for his own uses. It was this latter land that the villeins held of the lord. Originally, the occupation and cultivation of the land was at the pleasure (will) of the lord. Later, however, it grew into an occupation by right, recognized first of all by custom of the manor, and later by law.

c. Customary Freehold

Customary Freehold is a species of tenure resembling copyhold. It was also known as "privileged copyhold" or "copyhold by frank tenure." Like ordinary copyhold, the land was held by copy of court roll. However, instead of being expressed to be held "at the will of the lord," the land was expressed to be held only "according to the custom of the manor." This land could be conveyed by the villein.

The court roll of the manor represented the evidence of title as well as a record of the special laws as to fines, heriots, quit rents, et cetera, existing in the manor. Feudal obligations peculiar to the copyhold tenure obviously were inequitable. As an example, the obligation revolving around "heriot" entitled the lord of the manor to seize the tenant's finest beast or other chattel upon the tenant's death. In time, however, the villeins' status gradually improved and their precarious tenure of land, rather than being subject arbitrarily "at the will of the lord," was held "according to the custom of the manor," and the tenant's title therein could be conveyed by an ordinary conveyance. Thus evolved the "customary freehold," a variety of the copyhold tenure and in theory as well as practice an unfree tenure, until in England the Law of Property Act, 1922, abolished the tenure as from January 1, 1926, converting all customary freeholds into ordinary freeholds. In the United States, the customary freehold of pre-1926 was the forerunner of today's leasehold.

3. Incidents of Tenure

The four characteristic free tenures ... military, socage, sergeanty, and frankalmoign ... provided the lord with services relating to security, subsistence, splendor, and spirit, respectively.

Additionally, however, there were other obligations owed to the lord by the tenant incidental to the tenant's right in holding the land from his lord. These obligations, known as incidents of tenure, attended to each type of free tenure and generally were broken down into two categories: those incurred during the tenant's lifetime; and those incurred after his death.

    a. During Tenant's Lifetime

The obligations incurred during the lifetime of the tenant revolve around the personal relationship existing between the lord and tenant. This category of obligations included homage, fealty, and aids.

(1) Homage was the ceremony by which the tenant acknowledged himself the vassal of the lord. During this ceremony the tenant knelt on both knees before the lord who was seated. The tenant, whose clasped hands were held between the hands of the lord, would intone, "I become your man from this day forward of life and limb and of earthly worship, and unto you shall be true and faithful, and bear to you faith for the tenements that I claim to hold of you, saving the faith that I owe unto your sovereign lord, the King." The ceremony concluded with the lord kissing the tenant.

(2) Fealty was the oath taken by the tenant in which he promised his complete loyalty. Breach of this oath was a serious felony akin to treason which resulted in the forfeiture of land held by the offender.

(3) Aids encompassed those financial contributions of the tenant to his lord during times of stress. These would

include ransoming the lord in the event of his capture, contributing to defray the expense of knighting the lord's eldest son, and giving to the lord's eldest daughter upon her marriage.

b. Upon Tenant's Death

The category of obligations incurred upon death of the tenant well might be considered the forerunner of present day inheritance problems. They revolve around wardship, relief, escheat, and marriage.

(1) Wardship. The incident of wardship arose when the tenant died leaving a minor as his heir. In such instances, the lord was entitled to all of the profits from the land held by the tenant until his heir became of age.

(2) Relief. Upon reaching majority, the ward was compelled to sue for possession and, additionally, pay for the privilege of gaining such possession. This payment to the lord by the heir for the privilege of succeeding to his ancestor's land was called "relief" and may be likened to the inheritance tax of today.

(3) Escheat. If the tenant died without leaving heirs, there was no problem. The land simply reverted or "escheated" to the lord, the owner.

(4) Marriage. The incident of marriage was the consequence of the intense rivalry between the land barons of England. It was theoretically possible for a minor tenant through marriage to form an alliance with a family hostile to the lord. Through this vehicle of the incident of marriage, the lord had the right to arrange a suitable marriage for his ward.

C. THE DOCTRINE OF ESTATES

We have seen that the Doctrine of Tenures explores the feudal relationship between the lord and vassal. As the decades passed following the Norman Conquest, the Norman feudalistic structure, which was superimposed on the existing feudal structure of the land, gradually gave way under the inexorable pressures of an ever-changing society. The final period of medieval feudalism was increasingly punctuated by difficulties arising from a conflict of opposing positions between the lord and tenant. Out of the widening split emerged the Doctrine of Estates which charted the development of our modern landholding concepts.

The Doctrine of Estates defined the relationship of the parties to the land, the person to the thing as opposed to the person-to-person relationship reflected by the Doctrine of Tenures. The Doctrine of Estates addressed itself to the length of time for which land was held in contrast to "how" it was held under the Doctrine of Tenures. The basis of the Doctrine of Tenures was the theory that all land is owned by the Crown and only held by the subjects of the crown as tenants. The concept of one's abstract ownership of interests in the land rather than the actual ownership of the corporeal land was a singularly distinctive contribution of early English legal thought to the law of real property. This "interest" that one has in land is referred to as his "estate". An individual's estate in land relates to time (i. e., how long). Consequently, an "estate in land" more specifically is interpreted as "time in land" and measures the quantity of interest (time-wise) rather than the quality of interest (tenancy-wise).

D. CONCLUSIONS

American property law in general, and the laws of real property in particular, were born without significant mutilation of the two English doctrines of estates and tenures.

Our modern concept of estates and tenancies is inseparably linked with the feudal structure of medieval England.

A proper appreciation of the historical beginnings of property law best assures us of a clearer understanding of what we have inherited and of what we may bequeath.

PROPERTY

1. REAL:
a. Corporeal (Things)
b. Incorporeal (Relationships)

2. PERSONAL:
a. Tangible (Things - Chattels)
b. Intangible (Relationships)

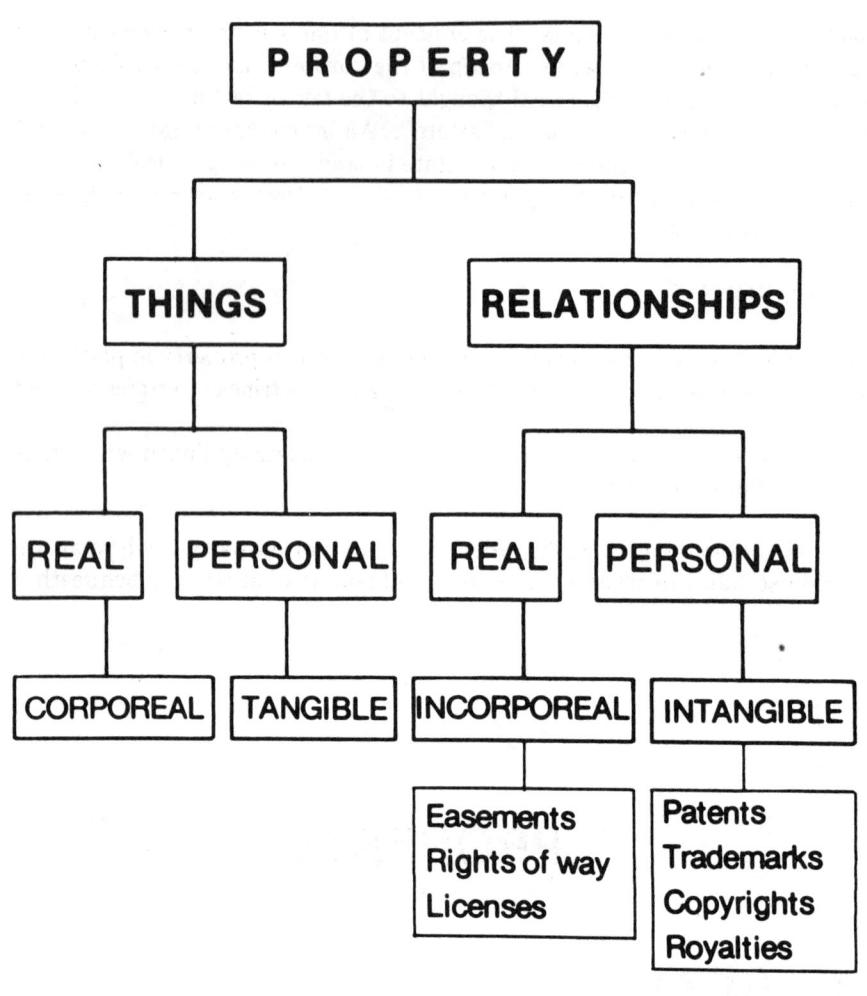

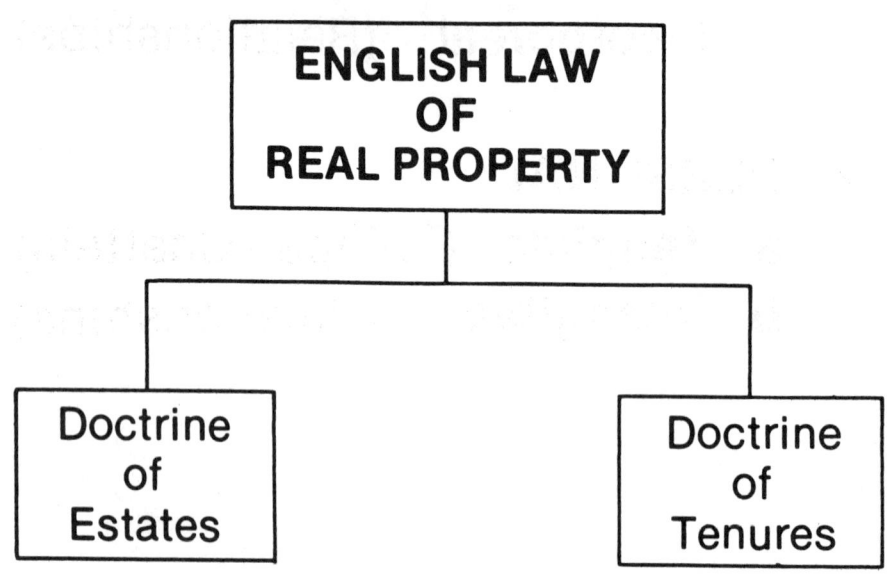

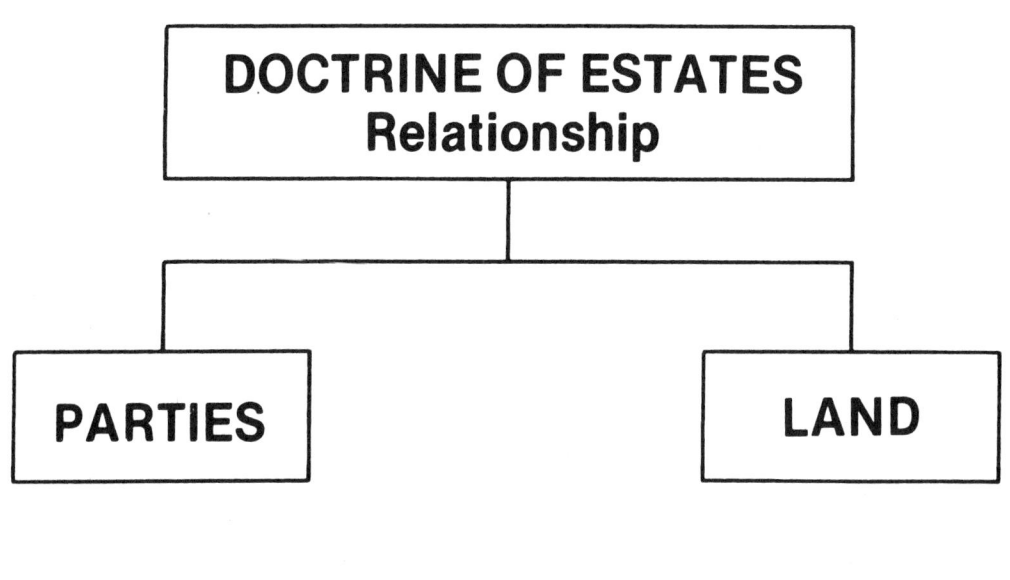

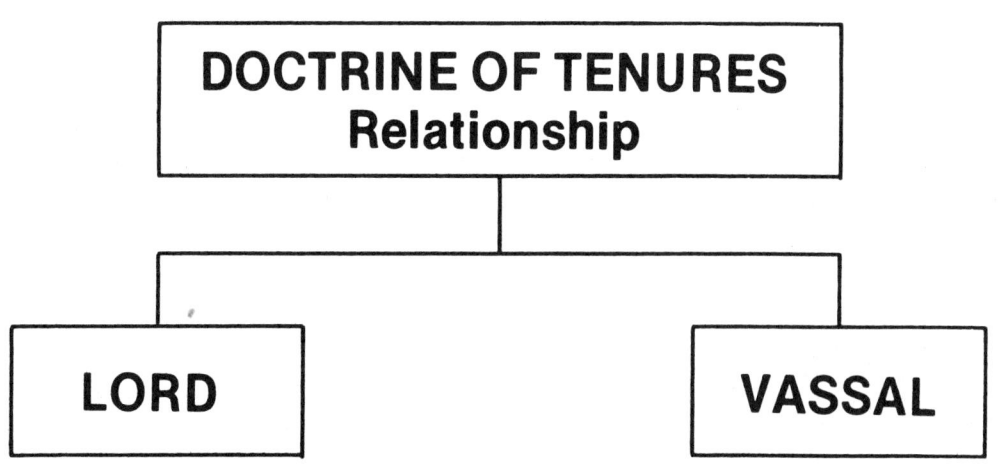

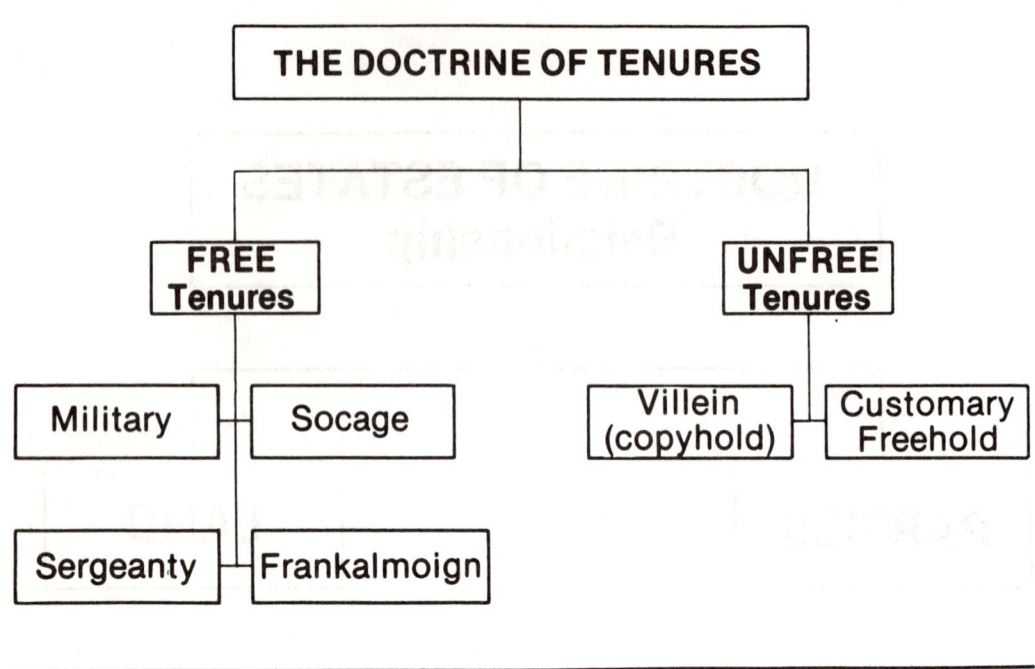
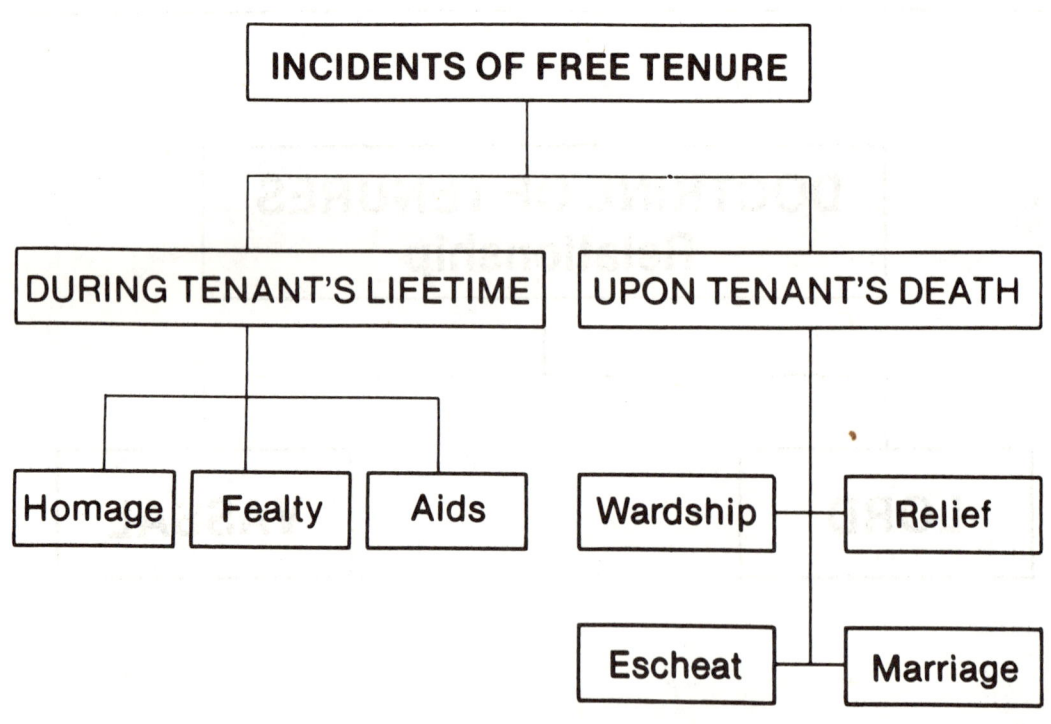

Chapter 5

REVIEW DEFINITIONS IN GLOSSARY OR TEXT OF FOLLOWING TERMS:

aids	military tenure
baron	personal property
chattel	personalty
chose in action	real property
corporeal property	realty
Doctrine of Estates	relief
Doctrine of Tenures	sergeanty tenure
fealty	socage tenure
frankalmoign tenure	subinfeudation
free tenure	tangible property
homage	tenure
incidents of tenure	unfree tenure
incorporeal	vassal
intangible	villein
lord	wardship

REVIEW QUESTIONS:

1. The term "property" historically has been viewed from two basic concepts; one concept views property as things. How does the other concept view property ?

2. In property law, what are the four components incorporated in the term "interests" ?

3. What are the two specific doctrines under the English law of real property ?

4. Name the four types of free tenure.

5. Name the two types of unfree tenure.

6. What are the incidents of tenure incurred during the tenant's lifetime ?

7. What are the incidents of tenure which arise upon a tenant's death ?

8. Which doctrine explores the feudal relationship between the lord and vassal ?

9. Which doctrine defines the relationship of the parties to the land ?

FOR ANSWERS TO REVIEW QUESTIONS:

1.

2.

3.

4.

5.

6.

7.

8.

9.

Chapter 6

Freehold Estates & Tenancies

A.	ESTATES AND TENANCIES - INTRODUCTION			121
B.	FREEHOLD ESTATES:			123
	1.	Inheritable Fee Estates		123
		a.	Fee Simple	123
			(1) Fee Simple Absolute	123
			(2) Fee Simple Qualified	123
			(a) Fee Simple Determinable	123
			(b) Fee Simple Subject to a Condition Subsequent	124
			(c) Fee Simple Subject to an Executory Interest	125
		b.	Conditional Fee	125
		c.	Fee Tail	126
	2.	Noninheritable Life Estates		127
		a.	Act of Parties (Conventional Life Estates)	127
			(1) Ordinary Life Estate	127
			(2) Estate Pur Autre Vie	127
		b.	Operation of the Law (Legal Life Estates)	128
			(1) Life Estate by Fee Tail after Possibility of Issue Extinct	128
			(2) Life Estate by the Marital Right	128
			(3) Life Estate by Curtesy	129
			(a) Life Estate by Curtesy Initiate	129
			(b) Life Estate by Curtesy Consummate	129
			(4) Life Estate by Dower	129
			(a) Inchoate Dower	130
			(b) Consummate Dower	130

   (5) Right of Homestead   131

     (a) Probate Homestead   131
     (b) Statutory Homestead   131
     (c) The United States Public Lands Homestead   132

C. CONCURRENT TENANCIES: 132

  1. <u>Tenancy by the Entirety</u>   133
  2. <u>Joint Tenancy</u>   133
  3. <u>Tenancy in Common</u>   134
  4. <u>Tenancy in Coparcenary</u>   135
  5. <u>Tenancy in Partnership</u>   135
  6. <u>Community Property</u>   135

D. HOW ESTATES ARE CREATED: 136

  1. <u>General</u>   136
  2. <u>By Original Entry</u>   137
  3. <u>By Involuntary Transfer</u>   137

    a. Judicial Sale   137
    b. Tax Sale   137
    c. Mortgage Foreclosure Sale   137

  4. <u>By Voluntary Transfer Through Owner</u>   137
  5. <u>By Adverse Possession</u>   137
  6. <u>By Accretion</u>   138

    a. Alluvion   138
    b. Reliction   138

  7. <u>By Will</u>   139
  8. <u>By Descent</u>   139

E. INTERESTS AND ESTATES IN LAND: 139

  1. <u>Interest in Land</u>   139

    a. Rights   139
    b. Power   139
    c. Privileges   139
    d. Immunities   139

  2. <u>Estate in Land</u>   139

    a. When Estate Is Involved   140

			(1)	Freehold Estate	140
			(2)	Nonfreehold Estate	140

        b.   When No Estate Is Involved   140

             (1)   Lease   140
             (2)   License   140

    3.   <u>Bundle of Rights</u>   140
    4.   <u>The Rights of Possession and Control</u>   140
    5.   <u>Right of Quiet Enjoyment</u>   141
    6.   <u>Right of Disposition</u>   141

F.   LIMITATIONS ON ESTATES: 141

    1.   <u>General</u>   141
    2.   <u>Limitations Imposed by Operation of the Law</u>   141

        a.   Eminent Domain   141
        b.   Zoning Laws   141

             (1)   Enforcement of Ordinances   141
             (2)   Nonconforming Uses   141
             (3)   Variances   142
             (4)   Spot Zoning   142

        c.   Police Power   142
        d.   Escheat   142
        e.   Adverse Possession   142
        f.   Water Rights   142
        g.   Air Rights   142

    3.   <u>Limitations Created by the Owner</u>   143

        a.   Restrictions in the Deed   143
        b.   Easements   143

             (1)   By Deed   143
             (2)   By Necessity   143
             (3)   By Prescription   143

        c.   License   143
        d.   Profit   144

    4.   <u>Limitations Imposed by Creditors</u>   144

        a.   Voluntary Liens   144
        b.   Involuntary Liens   144

		(1)	Common-law Liens	144
		(2)	Equitable Liens	144
		(3)	Statutory Liens	145
	c.	General Liens		145
		(1)	Lien of Judgment in Personam	145
		(2)	Federal and State Tax Lien	145
		(3)	Decedent's Debts Lien	145
	d.	Specific Liens		145
		(1)	Lien of Judgment in Rem	145
		(2)	Mortgage Lien	146
		(3)	Tax Lien	146
		(4)	Assessments	146
		(5)	Vendee's Lien	146
		(6)	Vendor's Lien	146
		(7)	Mechanic's Lien	146
		(8)	Attachments	146
	e.	Judgments		147

VISUAL AIDS   149

REVIEW QUESTIONS   156

Chapter 6
Freehold Estates & Tenancies

A. ESTATES AND TENANCIES - INTRODUCTION

The law on real property of all the states in the United States except Louisiana (whose legal system was based upon the Code Napoleon) was derived principally from the common law of England. In the English law of real property there are two specific doctrines: the doctrine of estates and the doctrine of tenures. (See Chapter 5). The two main estates were the "fee simple" which endured as long as the tenant or any of his heirs survived (whether his descendants or not), and the "life estate" which terminated with the tenant's death. In the year 1285 another estate was created called a "fee tail" which endured as long as the tenant or any of his descendants lived. These three estates exemplified the central principle under English law of real property that, while a subject could not own the land itself, he could enjoy a certain status in relationship to the land with certain interests resulting therefrom. Thus evolved the idea in early English legal thought of an individual's "ownership" in an abstract "estate" (from the Old French "estat" and the Latin "status" - to stand) rather than in the physical (corporeal) land.

The English doctrine of estates in land was adopted in the United States with few changes even though the English doctrine, when it was transplanted in this country, included many relics of feudalism which had no relationship to conditions in America. The English classification of estates as either "freehold" or "nonfreehold" was also adopted. Under this classification, the term "real property" relates specifically to freehold interests in land. Nonfreehold interest in land is considered in the category of "personal property" with the result that, even today, leaseholds (nonfreehold interests in land held under leases) are considered as personal property. Today, freehold estates in land are for the most part confined to three types: the fee simple, the fee tail, and the life estate.

The licensee, working in the field of real estate in any of the fifty states, must have sufficient knowledge of estates and tenancies to insure that, when he accepts a listing,or attempts to negotiate a purchase for a buyer, the owners of the properties involved actually have the legal right to sell the properties. One of the oldest cliches in the business world is, "If it can happen, it will happen." Over the course of a career in real estate it will happen: the widow who has only a life estate will, from lack of knowledge, attempt to sell it; the two spinster sisters will innocently attempt to sell the family property without the agreement of the brother in the next state who, although he is agreeable to relinquishing his third, has never been asked to do so formally; and so on.

The prudent licensee will examine the deed to any property with which he is involved. If he finds that it deviates from the norm and that any of the conditions explained herein is present to complicate the transaction, it is not his province to render a legal interpretation. Rather, he should be alerted that legal assistance may be required to remedy or remove any obstructions which might prevent the transfer of the property. Hence, he should be familiar with law and usage in his area. Any deviation from the standard should be a warning light for him.

In brief, he should insure that:

1. The property is a fee simple absolute.

2. The tenancy is such that he is assured that all owners are agreeable to the proposed sale.

3. If it is not in accord with both 1 and 2 above, the sellers should be queried on their knowledge, or lack of knowledge, of the complicating factors. They should be advised to obtain legal advice on their right to sell and any steps which might be necessary for them to take in order to insure the legality of their move.

With the above in mind, the licensee then must be aware that:

1. A fee simple absolute estate, meaning no conditions are attached, may be transferred without legal problems.

2. The fee tail, although it still exists on the statute books of four states, is not a bar to conveyancing.

3. A life estate may not be sold by the tenant without the waiver of the remaindermen or those with a reversionary interest.

4. That a tenant in severalty is a sole owner and that, so long as he is legally competent, he may transfer his property.

5. That tenants by the entirety must both concur in the sale of the property.

6. That all joint tenants and all tenants in common must concur in the sale of the property.

7. That, in those states following the community property formula, individual state law will govern on the ability of one partner to sell a property and that he must be aware of the law in his state.

8. That the best rule is "better safe than sorry" and that in any instance where a party to a transaction is married, regardless of tenancy, because of the ramifications of such laws as those governing dower, curtesy, and homestead, the signatures of both spouses should be obtained on any transaction as an indication that the non-owning spouse is waiving his/her rights.

B. FREEHOLD ESTATES

1. Inheritable Fee Estates

   a. Fee Simple

   A "fee simple" is an estate (interest) in land reflecting complete ownership without limitation, and of potentially infinite duration. The word "fee" is derived from the old Anglo-Saxon word "feoh", meaning cattle or property. This usage arose from cattle being used in early times as a medium of exchange or payment . . . and property consisting chiefly of cattle. Today, the word "fee" indicates an <u>estate of inheritance</u>. The word "simple" as used in English Ecclesiastical Law means "<u>one with no jurisdiction annexed to it</u>." Today, the word "simple" signifies that there are no restrictions with respect to the inheritable characteristics of the estate. A fee simple (also known as "fee simple absolute" or "fee") is an estate in land without limitation which is inheritable without restrictions by the heirs of the owner. A fee simple may be either absolute or qualified.

   (1) Fee Simple Absolute. A fee simple absolute is also known as a "fee" or as a "fee simple". It is the largest estate known to the law.

   At common law, the only way a fee simple estate could be created was by the inclusion of the words of inheritance, "and their heirs" or "and his heir". Under modern statutes, such words of inheritance are no longer required. Unless the grantor specifically describes a lesser estate, it is presumed that the grantee receives a fee simple estate.

   (2) <u>Fee Simple Qualified</u>. A fee simple qualified is also known as a "base fee" or a "defeasible fee". Although the duration of the fee is potentially unlimited, it may become finite by the occurrence or non-occurrence of some event specified in the instrument creating the estate. There are three types of fee simple qualified estates: the fee simple determinable; the fee simple subject to a condition subsequent; and the fee simple subject to an executory limitation.

   (a) <u>Fee Simple Determinable</u>. A fee simple absolute normally expires <u>only</u> upon the death of the fee owner who dies intestate and leaves no heirs. In such circumstances the estate reverts or escheats to the state which is presumed to occupy and hold the rights of the feudal lord. A fee simple determinable, however, is also limited to expire automatically, upon the occurrence or non-occurrence of some event specified in the instrument creating the estate. Nevertheless, a fee simple determinable estate is, indeed, a fee simple estate in that it <u>may</u> last forever. It is not a fee simple absolute because it <u>can</u> end. As a general rule, the words "<u>so long as</u>", "<u>until</u>", "<u>during</u>", "<u>while</u>", et cetera, denote a fee simple determinable. Mr. Teetotaler, for example, sells his estate of fee simple absolute in his property to Mr. Boozer and his heirs <u>so long</u> as the premises are not used for the sale of alcoholic beverages. Mr. Boozer has received a fee simple determinable in the property. Mr. Boozer's fee (or time in the land) is not of infinite duration. It could terminate <u>automatically,</u> if the premises are used for the sale of liquor. Similarly, Mr. Goldfarb may devise his estate in fee simple absolute to Miss Lovelace and her heirs <u>until</u> she marries. Miss Lovelace has a fee simple determinable estate in the property.

[margin note: fee back to grantor]

Owners of a fee simple determinable estate enjoy the same "bundle of rights" as the fee simple absolute owners. The determinable quality of the estate, however, follows the transfer to subsequent owners who hold the estate subject to the determinable features specified by the original grantor. It is important to note that the intent of the person transferring the estate in this manner (i. e., fee simple determinable) is for the estate to expire <u>automatically</u> upon the happening or non-happening of the stated event. It does <u>not</u> require an affirmative act by the grantor or his heirs to terminate it.

(b) <u>Fee Simple Subject to a Condition Subsequent.</u> The fee simple subject to a condition subsequent is a fee simple with a provision that the conveyor or his successor in interest has the <u>power to terminate</u> the estate granted upon the occurrence of a stated event. The estate is not automatically terminated as in the fee simple determinable. While similar to the fee determinable, there are significant differences. Upon the happening of a specified event, the fee simple <u>determinable</u> requires no affirmative action on the part of the grantor; the estate automatically expires. In a fee simple <u>subject to a condition subsequent</u> the estate does <u>not</u> end ipso facto upon the happening of a specified event. An affirmative act of re-entry by the conveyor or his successor is required before the estate can revert to the grantor.

As a general rule, the words "on condition", "on the condition that", "upon express condition that", "provided that", usually coupled with a provision that, if a specified event happens, the conveyor or his successor "may re-enter and repossess the premises", signify a fee simple subject to a condition subsequent.

If, for example, Mr. Teetotaler conveys to Mr. Boozer and
his heirs "on the condition that" if the premises are used to
sell alcoholic beverages, Mr. Teetotaler or his heirs shall have
a right to re-enter and possess the land as of his former estate,
Mr. Boozer has an estate in fee simple subject to a condition
subsequent. Mr. Goldfarb, similarly, may devise his estate to
Miss Lovelace and her heirs, provided that Miss Lovelace remains single. Should Miss Lovelace marry, the grantor or his
heirs may re-enter and repossess the premises. In these examples, the grantor would retain a future interest called
either a <u>right of entry for condition broken</u>, or <u>a power of
termination</u>.

It is important to note that upon the happening of the stated
event, in a fee simple subject to a condition subsequent, the
granted estate continues in existence despite the breach of
the condition. The granted estate will continue until the
grantor effectively exercises his right of entry, or power to
terminate, by bringing an action to recover the land. This is
the distinguishing characteristic of a fee simple subject to a
condition subsequent when compared with a fee simple determinable which ceases automatically upon the breach of
the stated condition.

(c) <u>Fee Simple Subject to an Executory Interest</u>. The fee simple
subject to an executory interest was not recognized in law
until the passage of the Statute of Uses in 1536. This type of
fee simple provides that upon the happening of a named event,
ownership shall pass <u>automatically</u> (unlike the fee simple subject to a condition subsequent) from the grantee to some <u>third</u>
person (not the grantor, as in the fee simple determinable). For
example, Mr. Teetotaler, an owner in a fee simple absolute,
transfers his interests to Mr. Boozer and his heirs "so long as
the premises are not used for the sale of alcoholic beverages,
then to Mr. Abstainer and his heirs." Mr. Boozer has an estate in fee simple subject to an executory limitation.

b. Conditional Fee

The "conditional fee" is also known as "fee simple conditional" and
is easily confused with "fee simple subject to a condition subsequent".
The "conditional fee" dates back to early English common law when,
in feudal England, the landed gentry understandably were desirous of
keeping land within the family for as long as the family existed. In an
effort to keep their lands intact, conveyances were often confined to
a specific grantee and <u>heirs of his body</u>. In this manner, the estate
could exist as long as there were lineal descendants of the grantee.
When the lineal descendants ran out, the land would revert to the

original grantor or his heirs. Thus, the early courts held that in a conveyance "A to B, and the heirs of his body" the grantee acquired a conditional fee. The condition, of course, was the birth of issue capable of inheriting the estate. The intent of the conveyor was to ensure that the estate would pass only to the heirs of the body of the grantee and of the body of successive owners, thereby keeping the land in the "biological family" until the line of descent became extinct. This intent, however, could be thwarted simply upon birth of issue. After such birth, for all intents and purposes, the grantee's conditional fee was enlarged to a fee simple absolute when the condition of birth was met.

The Statute De Donis Conditionalibus, passed in 1285, was designed to satisfy the intent of the grantor to prevent the depletion of family lands. With the passage of this famous statute, an estate in "fee tail" emerged to replace the conditional fee. Not all states, however, adopted the Statute De Donis Conditionalibus as part of their common law. As a consequence, the old English common law version of the conditional fee is recognized today in Iowa, Oregon, and South Carolina only.

c. Fee Tail

The "fee tail" estate was created in 1285, with the passage of the Statute De Donis Conditionalibus. This statute eliminated the "conditional fee". In effect, the fee tail tenant owned a freehold inheritable estate, but with some limitations. While he could use the estate during his lifetime, he could not dispose of it in any manner which would prevent its descending to his bodily heirs, if any, or to prevent its reverting to the grantor if there were no bodily heirs. The same rights and limitation passed to each succeeding fee tail tenant. Such an estate could be an estate in <u>tail male</u> or an estate in <u>tail female</u>. Either one could be a fee tail <u>general</u> or a fee tail <u>special</u>. A grant to a man and the male heirs of his body created a fee tail male. A grant to a man and the female heirs of his body created a fee tail female. A grant to a man and the heirs of his body by a particular spouse created a fee tail special. If no particular spouse was designated, a fee tail general resulted.

Inevitably, techniques were developed to defeat the intent of the grantors. The American colonists basically rejected the idea of entailed estates and primogeniture which smacked of the landed gentry. Early state constitutions and statutes rejected this early English statute. Currently, only four states recognize the fee tail estate: Delaware, Massachusetts, Rhode Island, and Maine. Even in these states, one in possession of the land in fee tail can convey a fee simple absolute estate by an ordinary deed, and thereby cut off the "entail". Still other states such as Illinois and Colorado give A, the first grantee, a life estate, and his issue a remainder in fee simple. There are many variations among the states, and the student would be well advised to study the applicable statutes.

2. <u>Noninheritable Life Estates</u>

When the life estate is created, provision is usually made for the designation of the person to whom the estate passes upon termination of the life estate. The estate that is left at the termination of the life estate is called a "remainder" which is an estate in fee simple. The person designated to receive the remainder estate is known as the "remainderman". The remainderman may be <u>known</u> when the life estate is created, thereby giving rise to a "choate" interest, or he may be <u>unknown</u> or even unborn, giving rise to an "inchoate" interest. The known remainderman's interest is known as a "vested" interest. If not known or not yet living, the remainder is known as a "contingent" interest. A remainder interest may be disposed of in the same manner as any other interest in property.

If, upon termination of the life estate, the estate is to revert to the original owner, it is called reversion. If the original owner of the estate is dead, the reversion is to his heirs. As with a remainder interest, a reversionary interest may be sold, mortgaged, or otherwise disposed of in the same manner as any other interest in real property.

Like the fee simple, the life estate may be determinable, subject to a condition subsequent, or subject to executory limitation. The life estate is neither devisable nor inheritable. It may be created by an act of the parties, by deed, or by will (conventional life estate), or by operation of the law (legal life estate) arising out of the marital relationship.

    a. Act of Parties (Conventional Life Estate)

Conventional life estates are subdivided into ordinary life estates and estates <u>pur autre vie</u> <u>(for the life of another)</u>.

(1) Ordinary Life Estate. An estate which is measured by the life of the grantee is called an ordinary life estate, or simply a life estate. No special words are required to establish a life estate, so long as the grantor's intent is clear. A conveyance "to B during his life" or "to B for his lifetime" would convey an ordinary life estate.

(2) Estate Pur Autre Vie. An estate measured by the life of one other than the grantee creates an estate pur autre vie. A conveyance, for example, "to A for the life of B" creates such an estate. B takes nothing from the grant and is known as the <u>cestui</u> <u>que</u> <u>vie</u> ("he whose life" is the measure of the duration of an estate). An estate pur autre vie may be created with more than one measuring life.

b. Operation of the Law (Legal Life Estates)

Legal life estates arose from the marital relationship. They can be classified as : fee tail after possibility of issue extinct; estate by the marital right; curtesy; and dower. While each will be discussed generally, all have been either abolished by statute or modified significantly. Students are cautioned to consult the most current applicable legislation. The fee tail today has been completely abolished in all but a few jurisdictions. Consequently, a life estate resulting from a tenancy in tail after possibility of issue extinct is seldom found. The estate by the marital right has been abolished by statutes in all states. Dower has enveloped curtesy in many states, and even dower has been modified by statute in all states. Nevertheless, the skeleton of property law would be incomplete without mention of these noninheritable legal life estates.

(1) Life Estate by Fee Tail after Possibility of Issue Extinct. This type of life estate resulted when the spouse of a tenant in fee tail special died without issue. A fee tail special resulted from a grant to a man and the heirs of his body by a particular spouse. For example, a conveyance to H and the heirs of his body by his wife, W, created a fee tail special. W dies, leaving no issue. On H's death, the land, by virtue of the Statute De Donis, reverts to the grantor. During his life, H enjoys a life estate. If, however, the original conveyance created a fee tail general (i. e., with no particular spouse designated) this type of life estate could not be created.

(2) Life Estate by the Marital Right. At early common law, a husband and wife were viewed as one. The wife's identity was lost in her husband's. After marriage, the wife was incapable of acquiring or disposing of property in her own name. The husband acquired the possession, use, and profits of his wife's property, both real and personal. This interest, acquired as a result of marriage, was known as an estate in the right of the wife (jure uxoris), or, more commonly, as an estate by the marital right. This estate continued only during the time of the marriage and until the birth of issue capable of inheriting the land. This type of an estate is also known as a life estate by and during coverture. During coverture and until issue was born of the marriage, the husband's full control of his wife's property extended to land in which his wife had a fee, fee tail, or life estate. The husband's coverture estate continued until the marriage was dissolved by death or divorce, or until issue was born alive of the marriage. If either husband or wife died before the birth of issue, such control

terminated, and the land returned either to the wife, if surviving, or her heirs. The enactment in the nineteenth century in all states of the Married Women's Property Acts, giving married women the right to manage their separate estates, has practically eliminated the estate by the marital right.

(3) Life Estate by Curtesy. Curtesy existed solely for the right of the husband. For curtesy to obtain, four requisites were essential: 1) a legal marriage must have existed, 2) the wife must have been actually seized of the land with an inheritable fee (i. e., fee simple or fee tail), 3) the wife must have had issue born alive and capable of inheriting, and 4) the wife must have predeceased the husband. Estate by curtesy was further subdivided into an estate by curtesy "initiate" and an estate by curtesy "consummate".

(a) Life Estate by Curtesy Initiate. This type of estate emerged from, and replaced, the husband's life estate by the marital right. It came into being at the moment of birth of issue capable of inheriting the land. The husband's life estate by curtesy initiate has been abolished by statutes in all states. Today, the husband, after birth of issue, but before the death of his wife, acquires only the possibility of an estate by curtesy in those states where curtesy still exists. Only in the event that the husband survives his wife can he acquire an actual estate in his wife's property.

(b) Life Estate by Curtesy Consummate. Upon the death of the wife, the husband's life estate by curtesy initiate was immediately transformed into a life estate by curtesy consummate. Only at this point did the husband actually realize an estate in his wife's freehold estates of inheritance. Curtesy consummate has been abolished today in most states. In such jurisdictions, the husband is usually given a statutory distribution of the wife's estate. In the few states where remnants of curtesy survive, statutes have modified the common law so as to render the common law version of curtesy almost non-existent.

(4) Life Estate by Dower. The rights of a wife in the lands of her husband are known as dower rights. In common law, if at any time during marriage a husband was seized of a freehold estate of inheritance, his surviving widow was entitled to dower which is a life estate in one-third of his land. Three

requisites were essential for dower to be created: 1) a legal marriage must have existed, 2) the husband must have been seized of freehold estates of inheritance, 3) the husband must have predeceased his wife. The widow's life estate by dower was further subdivided into an "inchoate" (contingent dower) and a "consummate" (completed) dower.

(a) Inchoate Dower. While her husband lived, the wife had a protected expectancy in her husband's land which could not be defeated by any conveyance by her husband or by will. This expectancy was based on her survival of her husband, and during his lifetime her interest was based on this contingency, therefore the term "inchoate". In most states, this interest has been abolished. As recently as January 1, 1972, the inchoate right of dower was abolished in Illinois.

(b) Consummate Dower. The wife's inchoate (rudimentary) dower became completed or consummate upon the death of her husband. The wife, at this point, became a dowager entitled to the actual division of one-third of the lands to which her dower attached, if she so elected. Once assigned the property to which she was entitled, the dowager became a tenant in dower with a life estate in the assigned land.

NOTE: Dower and Curtesy have been abolished in most states, and have been substantially modified in the others. Modern statutes usually give two rights to the surviving wife which did not exist under the common law. First, if the husband dies without leaving a will (intestate), his wife, as an heir, is usually given one-half of his estate if there is no issue, and one-third if there is issue. Second, if the husband dies leaving a will which does not sufficiently provide for the wife, the wife may renounce the will and take her statutory share of his estate which usually equates with her intestate share. (See D. 8. below)

It is important to note that estates of dower and curtesy are <u>life estates</u> carved out of the property of a <u>deceased</u> spouse, and designed to give certain rights to each spouse, as a consequence of their marriage, in the inheritable freehold property of the other. While dower and curtesy have had roots in early English law, eight jurisdictions (Arizona, California, Idaho, Louisiana, Nevada, New Mexico, Texas, and Washington) have embraced traditions in this particular regard from the civil law of Spain and France. These eight states have adopted the doctrine of "community property".

While community property theory develops rights of both husband and wife as a result of marriage, it pertains to the equal sharing of that property acquired by their joint efforts during marriage. Appropriately, then, the subject of community property is explored under CONCURRENT TENANCIES (Paragraph C below).

(5) Right of Homestead. The majority of states have established an artificial life estate in land initially designed to allow the spouse and minor children to occupy the decedent's property. Such an estate is unknown at common law and appears to be uniquely of American origin. Many writers are reluctant to elevate a homestead to the dignity of an estate. Nevertheless, some states, such as Illinois, refer to an "estate of homestead" in their Act. Today, the homestead technically extends beyond the marital interest, since it is available to the head of a family, whether or not this individual is married. The interpretations of the homestead laws are myriad. Some states acknowledge a homestead by the mere occupancy of real property as a home. Texas even provides the exemption for land used for business purposes.

Generally, there are three recognized types of homestead: the probate homestead; the statutory homestead; and the United States public land homestead.

(a) Probate Homestead. The basic purpose of the probate homestead is <u>to provide</u> for the surviving spouse and minor children out of the decedent's lands.

(b) Statutory Homestead. The statutory homestead is variously known as the <u>declared</u> homestead, the <u>voluntary</u> homestead, or the <u>constitutional</u> homestead. The basic purpose of the statutory homestead is <u>to exempt</u>, or <u>to immunize</u>, the real property of individuals, married or single, occupied as their homes, from seizure under legal process, and to restrict the conveyance and encumbrance of such real property. In Illinois, for example, the homestead has a $10,000 exemption from claims of creditors. The exemption continues for the benefit of the surviving spouse as long as the land is used by said spouse as a homestead, and for the benefit of surviving children under 21 years of age, as long as they occupy the homestead. In many states, including Illinois, homestead exemption rights can be waived only in a written conveyance. The spouse's signature is required for the release of homestead rights, and all signatures must be acknowledged.

In those states where homestead exemptions prevail, it is apparent that the homestead right must be properly waived at the time of mortgage or sale to ensure that purchasers and mortgagees are not faced with legalities revolving about these interests at some future date.

To create a statutory homestead, it is usually necessary to execute and have acknowledged a written instrument called a "declaration of homestead" in which specifically described property is to be set aside as a homestead. The instrument does not become effective until it is recorded in the office of the recorder of the county in which the land is located.

This type of <u>state</u> homestead exemption should be distinguished from those homesteads allowed under <u>Federal</u> homestead legislation designed to allow a claimant to acquire title to unappropriated public lands.

(c) The United States Public Lands Homestead. This type of homestead was to encourage the settlement of the public land of the United States. (See Chapter 1, The Real Estate Profession . . . re: Enactment of the Homestead and Exemption Laws).

C. CONCURRENT TENANCIES

In the field of professional real estate brokerage, there is generally some confusion surrounding the word "tenancy". This confusion results, perhaps, from the fact that the word itself assumes two entirely different meanings. When used in relation to "Freehold Estates" the word "tenancy" takes on the legal meaning of "a holding, or a mode of holding, an estate". "Tenancy", therefore, as used in this section relates to <u>how</u> the estate in land is held. It has no relationship to <u>time</u> as is the case when the word "tenancy" is used in relation to "nonfreehold estates" (i. e., leaseholds) where the word relates to "the <u>period</u> of a tenant's occupancy or possession". In freehold estates, ownership interests (tenancies) may be held by one person (tenancy in severalty) or by two or more persons owning the property concurrently, in common, or jointly.

In the examples given in paragraph A, above, Mr. Teetotaler, Mr. Boozer, Mr. Goldfarb, and Miss Lovelace all were <u>tenants in severalty</u> in that they shared the estate with no others, and their right of possession was individually enjoyed, i. e., severed from all others. Common law, however, recognizes that two or more persons may have simultaneous or concurrent interest in the same property, rather than successive interest, as in the examples given. At common law, four types of concurrent estates were recognized: tenancy by the entirety, joint tenancy, tenancy in coparcenary, and tenancy in common. Two other types of concurrent estates emerged in American property law, called tenancy in partnership, and community property. All will be discussed in this section.

1. <u>Tenancy by the Entirety</u>

This is a form of concurrent ownership based upon the common law precept that the husband and wife were one . . . and that "one" was the husband. In many states, therefore, a conveyance of land to a husband and wife, in the absence of words to the contrary, creates an estate called a "tenancy by the entirety". It is limited to husbands and wives. Upon the death of either, the survivor takes the entire estate; the heirs are entitled to nothing. The husband or wife may not convey any part of the realty without the other spouse joining in the deed. This type of tenancy is essentially a joint tenancy with the added feature that <u>the husband has control of the property during the marriage</u>. As in a joint tenancy, each spouse owns the entire estate and not a fractional part. Also, as in a joint tenancy, the doctrine of survivorship obtains. Tenancy by the entirety is created by deed or will; it is never created by descent. This tenancy cannot be destroyed unilaterally by either spouse. Collectively, the spouses own the entire interest; individually, they own nothing. Consequently, both must consent to a partition. The essential unity of person is demolished by divorce, which also destroys the tenancy by the entirety, and the divorced persons become tenants in common.

Five unities are requisite to a tenancy by the entirety: time, title, interest, possession, and person. The latter embraces the common law concept that husband and wife are united as one.

In the majority of states, the tenancy by the entirety has no significance, and a conveyance to a husband and wife creates a joint tenancy, or a tenancy in common, depending upon the language used. Illinois falls into this category. In other states, such as Massachusetts, tenancy by the entirety survives in all its glory, unaffected by changing times. In Arizona, California, Idaho, Louisiana, Nevada, New Mexico, Texas, and Washington, the community property statutes are recognized in lieu of tenancy by the entirety.

2. <u>Joint Tenancy</u>

A joint tenancy is a type of concurrent ownership whereby two or more persons are each regarded as owner of the whole estate, <u>as well as an undivided part</u>. Since the joint tenants each own an undivided part, as well as the whole, each may destroy the joint tenancy by partition or by conveyance inter vivos (during their lifetime). If one joint tenant conveys his share to a non-tenant, the new party becomes a tenant in common with the remaining original joint tenants, while the latter will still be joint tenants with respect to each other. The outstanding feature of the tenancy is the <u>right of survivorship</u>, by which the entire tenancy, on the decease of any one tenant, remains to the survivors, and at length to the last survivor. A severance of the joint tenancy can never be made by will, because survivorship is prior to and defeats the effect of a will. The joint tenancy is always created by deed or will and never by descent. At common law joint tenancy was preferred over tenancy in common. Under modern codes, the reverse is true. Today, a joint tenancy can be created only by a specific statement in the granting clause of the deed. In the absence of such statement, grantees are tenants in common. If the grantor wishes to create a joint tenancy, his intent should be clearly stated, as "to A and B as joint tenants and not as tenants in common."

A joint tenancy, according to common law, requires four unities for its creation and survival: time, title, interest, and possession. "Time" means that all tenants acquire their interest simultaneously. "Title" means that all tenants acquire their interest from the same conveying instrument (deed, will, et cetera). "Interest" means that all tenants have identical interest of the same type and duration in the property (i. e., fee simple, fee tail, life estate, et cetera). "Possession" means that each tenant is entitled to the possession, use, and enjoyment of the whole property subject to the rights of his co-tenants. In some states, such as Colorado and Illinois, statutes allow a grantor to convey to himself and others as joint tenants and not as tenants in common, thus creating a joint tenancy notwithstanding the absence of the common law unities of time and title.

3. Tenancy in Common

A tenancy in common is a type of concurrent ownership whereby two or more persons each owns an undivided part (which need not be equal) of the whole, but none own the whole (as in a joint tenancy). This type of tenancy may be created by deed, will, or by operation of the law. There is no provision for survivorship, and, upon death, title passes to the decedent's heirs who become tenants in common with the surviving tenants in common.

Each tenant may dispose of his undivided part or any portion thereof, either by deed or by will. A tenancy in common may be shattered by partition or merger. Only the unity of possession is required, and each tenant must have the right to occupy the whole in common with his co-tenants.

Even though a tenant in common is entitled to the possession of the premises, such possession is subject to the rights of the other tenants in common. Each tenant has an obligation to the others. Each is entitled to an accounting of rents and profits, and each to a contribution and reimbursement of sums spent for necessary repairs, and for the payment of taxes, liens, and insurance premiums. One tenant cannot commit waste, such as the removal of timber or other products of the land to the detriment and exclusion of the others. A tenant in common may force the sale of the interest of the others. This is accomplished through the medium of a partition suit. Such suit is brought, either by one tenant against the others, or by several tenants against only one. Upon the filing of the suit, a referee is appointed who is charged with the duty of effecting a partition of the premises. His first duty is to divide the property, if possible, but if this cannot be done, the court will direct the referee to sell the premises. Such sale is made at a public auction to the highest bidder. Any co-tenant may be a purchaser at such sale, as well as anyone who is a stranger to the title. Following the sale, confirmation is made by the court, a property conveyance is delivered to the purchaser, and the proceeds of the sale, less court costs and incidental expenses, are distributed to the sellers in conformance with the orders of the court. Where there is a physical partition into unequal shares, the court may order the favored co-tenant to compensate the others by a payment in money called "owelty".

NOTE: It may be noted that joint tenants as well as tenants in common, as part of their interest in the property, have the right of disposition. Each such owner, by such right, also has a right of partition which provides for the division of lands held concurrently with co-tenants into distinct portions, so that they may hold them as tenants in severalty.

4. Tenancy in Coparcenary

In the United States, for all intents and purposes, those holding an interest by tenancy in coparcenary are regarded as tenants in common, and the law relating to tenancy in common applies to tenancy in coparcenary.

A tenancy in coparcenary was created by the law of inheritance. It arose as a corollary to primogeniture, which prevailed in England and allowed only the eldest male the right of inheritance. The purpose of tenancy in coparcenary was to allow daughters to share equally as heirs when there were no sons. The daughters, as co-tenants (coparceners or sometimes just parceners), were considered collectively as a single heir acquiring a single estate. The rule of primogeniture never took root in this country, and, in nearly all states, as a consequence, tenancy in coparcenary was never fully recognized.

In a tenancy in coparcenary, each tenant (coparcener or parcener) owns an undivided part of the whole, and each tenant can dispose of his undivided share or portion thereof by deed or by will. The tenancy may be terminated by conveyance by one parcener, by partition, or by the whole vesting or descending in one parcener. The feature of survivorship does not exist. Upon death, heirs inherit the undivided interest of the deceased parcener. All of these features equate with those of a tenancy in common. However, as in a joint tenancy, coparceners have a single estate, and one parcener could convey her share by a release to her co-tenant.

This type of tenancy at common law required the unity of time, title, and possession. The interest of the coparceners could be unequal.

5. Tenancy in Partnership

Tenancy in partnership is a type of concurrent ownership in which the partners, as co-owners, hold specific partnership assets, both real and personal. This form of tenancy was created by the Uniform Partnership Act which was drafted in 1914. Subsequently, the Act has been adopted in most states.

6. Community Property

Community property is a type of concurrent ownership existing between husband and wife during their marriage. It is a system of marital property rights emerging from French and Spanish civil law just after the decline of the Roman Empire. Today, it exists in eight states: Arizona, California, Idaho, Louisiana, Nevada, New Mexico, Texas, and Washington. None of these states, interestingly enough, recognizes either dower or curtesy, although all have enacted the homestead exemption.

Under this system, husband and wife become equal and concurrent co-owners of all property (real and personal) acquired during marriage (which itself is considered a "community") by their joint effort. Either spouse may own separate property. Separate property may be defined as 1) that property which was owned by either spouse prior to marriage, or 2) acquired by gift, inheritance or will during marriage, together with the income, rents, profits, et cetera, from either type. Such separate property is subject to the control of the spouse concerned. The spouses may, by mutual consent, convert community property into the separate property of either. A presumption will be made that all property of a married couple is community property. If one is to rebut this presumption, careful records relative to acquisition should be maintained.

Upon death, the decedent can devise his one-half of the community property; the remaining half remains vested in the surviving spouse. If the decedent leaves no will (i. e., dies intestate) some statutes give all to the survivor. The statutes vary widely, however, and each should be studied carefully as applicable.

It may be of interest to note that, prior to enactment of the Revenue Act of 1948, six states (Michigan, Nebraska, Oklahoma, Oregon, Pennsylvania, and Hawaii) passed community property legislation to afford their citizens a favorable tax position. Subsequent to enactment of the Revenue Act which extended the right of all married couples to split their income, five of the states repealed their community property acts, while the Supreme Court of Pennsylvania held its statute unconstitutional.

D.   HOW ESTATES ARE CREATED

1.   General: - - Estates are created and title to real property may be acquired in the following ways:

        a.   By original entry (called title by occupancy).
        b.   By involuntary transfer (e. g., judicial sale, tax sale, mortgage foreclosure sale).
        c.   By voluntary transfer through the owner (e. g., gift or sale).
        d.   By adverse possession.
        e.   By accretion.
        f.   By will.
        g.   By descent, regulated by statute.

2. **By Original Entry:** - - Title to all land in the United States was derived from the United States Government with a few exceptions where titles derived from grants of sovereigns who took possession by settlement or conquest. Individuals who occupied land for the time prescribed by federal statute and in accordance with conditions established by law acquired title <u>by patent</u> from the federal government.

3. <u>By Involuntary Transfer</u>

   a. Judicial Sale. It is sometimes necessary to sell the property of a defendant in order to secure the money required to pay a judgment to a successful plaintiff. The sale is conducted under the jurisdiction of a court, by a sheriff or other authorized official.

   b. Tax Sale. A tax sale is a public sale of a delinquent taxpayer's land. The purchaser acquires a "tax title".

   c. Mortgage Foreclosure Sale. This is a type of judicial sale by which a mortgagee (the lender) secures the money to repay the debt.

4. <u>By Voluntary Transfer Through Owner:</u> - - Voluntary alienation may occur by gift or sale. Examples of such transfers are: a sale of real estate under a contract consummated by delivery of a deed, or transfer of title by a deed of trust or mortgage as security for the payment of a note. This right of alienation (i. e., the right to transfer ownership of real property to another) is one of the important rights of real estate ownership.

5. <u>By Adverse Possession:</u> - - Title by adverse possession is acquired when one enters into actual physical possession of the land of another, and remains on it exclusively, openly, and notoriously for a continuous period of time as prescribed by statute. Such adverse possession entitles one to legal title even though another has paper title. Actual knowledge by the true owner that his land is so occupied is not essential. The possession must be of such nature that a reasonably diligent owner would have knowledge of the adverse claim. The adverse claimant must, however, actually make a claim of ownership to gain title by adverse possession.

(See Table Next Page)

Statutory Time Requirement of Occupancy to Claim Title by Adverse Possession (Years)

State	Years	State	Years	State	Years
Alabama	20	Kentucky	7	North Dakota	20
Alaska	7	Louisiana	30	Ohio	21
Arizona	10	Maine	20	Oklahoma	15
Arkansas	7	Maryland	20	Oregon	10
California	5	Massachusetts	20	Pennsylvania	21
Colorado	18	Michigan	15	Rhode Island	10
Connecticut	15	Minnesota	15	South Carolina	10
Delaware	20	Mississippi	10	South Dakota	20
D. C.	15	Missouri	10	Tennessee	20
Florida	7	Montana	5	Texas	25
Georgia	20	Nebraska	10	Utah	7
Hawaii	10	Nevada	5	Vermont	15
Idaho	5	New Hampshire	20	Virginia	15
Illinois	20	New Jersey	20	Washington	10
Indiana	10	New Mexico	10	West Virginia	10
Iowa	10	New York	10	Wisconsin	20
Kansas	15	North Carolina	20	Wyoming	10

With some claim of title, a lesser period of time may be required to claim title. In Illinois, for example, only seven years of adverse possession is required with some claim of title. Particular statutes must be checked to determine modification of these statutory time requirements.

6. <u>By Accretion</u>: -- Accretion is the gradual accumulation of land to that of a property owner by the action of water through natural causes (as opposed to "avulsion" which is the sudden, perceptible removal of land from the estate of one person to another, as by a sudden change in the course of a river).

    a.   Alluvion. When land is added by imperceptible, gradual deposits by water which extend the shore or bank, such increase is called "alluvion".

    b.   Reliction. When land is gradually increased by the receding of water, such increase is called "reliction".

Any slow and gradual increase in land by alluvion or reliction belongs to the owner of the land to which the newly formed land has been added. The rights accruing to those who own property on the banks of a river or stream, including the right of accretion, are called "riparian rights". Such property is referred to as "riparian property", and such an owner is known as "riparian proprietor". Distinguished from <u>riparian</u> property, which is situated on the banks of rivers and streams, is <u>littoral</u> property which is real property situated on the shore of a lake, sea, or ocean. In some states, such as Arizona, the common law doctrine of riparian water rights has been eliminated.

7. By Will: - - Disposition of one's property after death may be affected by an instrument in writing called a will. When real property is being transferred, the will is often called a "devise" and the beneficiary a "devisee." (When personal property is transferred, the word "testament" is used, and the beneficiary is called a "legatee"). When one dies leaving a will, he is said to have died "testate," and, after death, he is referred to as the testator. The provisions of the testator's will are carried out by a person known as an "executor."

8. By Descent: - - When a person dies without leaving a will, he is said to have died "intestate." His real property passes to his heirs or those so entitled according to the Statute of Descent of the state. This Statute or Law of Descent provides for distribution of the property to widows, children, surviving parents, brothers and sisters, et cetera, according to carefully designed steps. Individual state law must be consulted in each case. The person who probates the estate of one who dies intestate is called an "administrator."

E. INTERESTS AND ESTATES IN LAND

1. Interest in Land: - - It is important to differentiate between an "interest" in land and an "estate" in land. While all estates involve an interest, not all interests involve an estate. Interests in land are comprised of varying aggregates of legal rights, powers, privileges, and immunities, or a portion of any one of them.

   a. Rights. A property owner's right to ownership, possession, and use of his property imposes a duty on all others not to deny or interfere with his rights.

   b. Power. A property owner has the power to dispose of his property and thus change his legal relation to the land.

   c. Privileges. A property owner has the privilege (or legal freedom) to control his property as he deems fit. He enjoys, for example, the privilege of having his property maintained, renovated, remodeled, et cetera, and no one has a right to interfere with this privilege.

   d. Immunities. A property owner is immune to having his legal relation to his property altered by another. If, for example, a property owner owes money secured by a mortgage and subsequently pays off the mortgage, he is immune from any legal rights of the mortgagee to foreclose.

2. Estate in Land: - - For an estate in land to prevail, three elements must be included: use, possession, and disposition. The Statute of Frauds in all states holds that a contract for the sale of land or any interest in or concerning land must be in writing in order to be enforceable. Determining if an interest is involved is a responsibility of the real estate agent.

a. When Estate Is Involved

   (1) Freehold Estate. A freehold estate involves an <u>estate</u> since the following rights are included:

   (a) Use
   (b) Possession
   (c) Disposition
   (d) Ownership

   (2) Nonfreehold Estate. A nonfreehold estate (known also as a "leasehold" or "tenancy for years") involves an estate since the following minimum essential rights are included:

   (a) Use
   (b) Possession
   (c) Disposition

b. When No Estate Is Involved

   (1) Lease. When a lease is for other than for a definite and certain period of time (as in a tenancy at will), an interest, but not an estate, may be involved, since only the following rights are included:

   (a) Use
   (b) Possession

   (2) License. A license does <u>not</u> involve even an interest, since only the <u>use</u> of land is involved.

3. <u>Bundle of Rights:</u> - - The interests projected above have become known as the owner's "bundle of rights." He may sell any or all of them. In summary, there are four basic rights that are inherent in the ownership of land and included in the "bundle of rights."

   a. Possession
   b. Control
   c. Quiet Enjoyment
   d. Disposition

4. <u>The Rights of Possession and Control:</u> - - Possession includes not only physical control or the power to have physical control, but also legal sanctions to enforce such control. Possession is distinguished from mere custody. Custody is limited to physical control, free of any interest in the property adverse to the owner. Possession is the link between physical control and the owner's personal relationship to the property.

5. Right of Quiet Enjoyment: - - "Quiet Enjoyment" means freedom from troubles or disturbances caused by defects in the title. "Quiet Enjoyment" does not mean freedom from noise, confusion or turmoil. It is evidenced by a clause inserted in a warranty deed or a lease that gives the grantee or tenant the right of possession without disturbance.

6. Right of Disposition: - - The right of disposition includes a property owner's right to sell his property, give it away, leave it to his heirs when he dies, lease the property, or grant an easement over it.

F. LIMITATIONS ON ESTATES

1. General: - - There are certain limitations which the owner of realty may be required to recognize. These limitations generally fall into three categories:

    a. Limitations imposed by operation of the law.
    b. Limitations created by the owner.
    c. Limitations imposed by creditors.

2. Limitations Imposed by Operation of the Law

    a. Eminent Domain. The right of the Federal Government, the state, or any subdivision thereof to take private land for a public purpose upon just compensation is called the right of "eminent domain". Under this right, private land can be taken for such things as public buildings, schools, highways, power projects, housing projects, and many other public uses. When this right is exercised, commissioners are appointed to appraise the property which is taken in condemnation proceedings. The appraised value is paid to the owner. Each state provides avenues of appeal on compensation for owners whose property is condemned. Consult local statutes.

    b. Zoning Laws. Cities, towns, even villages, have the right to pass zoning ordinances. These are regulations by which communities restrict the use of certain land areas and control the type, density, and volume of building construction in such areas.

        (1) Enforcement of Ordinances. Where zoning ordinances have been passed, it is generally necessary to submit plans and specifications when applying for a building permit. A board examines the plans to ensure that there is no violation of the zoning laws before a permit is granted.

        (2) Nonconforming Uses. Even though an area is zoned for a different purpose, zoning ordinances usually allow existing structures to continue in use. However, replacing or rebuilding such structures may be prohibited.

(3) Variances. A variance is an exception to existing zoning laws and may be allowed by a special board of appeals in the event of unusual hardship or special circumstances.

(4) Spot Zoning. Spot zoning may be allowed in areas which are being transformed from one general use to another. In such instances, a different zoning status may be applied for certain property from that given to the surrounding area.

c. Police Power. Police power is that which state and local governments impose by legislation to protect the property, life, health, safety, and morals of their citizens. Such ordinances may include fire-prevention laws, require minimum standards of plumbing, electric wiring, heating equipment, construction, et cetera. The closer people live together, the more regulations of this kind can be anticipated. The extent of police power is limited by the state constitution and by the Fourteenth Amendment to the Constitution of the United States which protects personal liberties and freedoms.

d. Escheat. Escheat is the return of real or personal property to the state when an owner dies without legal heirs.

e. Adverse Possession. Adverse possession is the holding and use of real (or personal) property without legal title and without consent of the owner. To secure ownership by adverse possession, possesion generally must be hostile, actual, notorious, exclusive, continuous, and under claim of title. The period of such possession varies in different states. (Reference paragraph D. 5., above).

f. Water Rights. Water rights are the rights of an owner of land adjoining a stream, which is not navigable, to use the stream to a reasonable extent. Such use must not diminish or interfere with the right of use of others who may be further down the stream. The owner of such adjoining land does not have title to the water. His title is to the soil to the middle of the stream. When the water freezes, the ice is considered part of the land; and, therefore, it belongs to the owner of the bed of the stream.

g. Air Rights. At the present time, it is generally acknowledged that the owner of land does not, as was formerly thought, own "up to the sky". The upper air space is freely navigable. Air rights are limited by Federal Statute, such as the statutes permitting construction of condominiums, and by zoning laws.

3. <u>Limitations Created by the Owner</u>

   a. Restrictions in the Deed. An owner may write into the deed restrictions on the use of the land being conveyed. In effect, such restrictions are similar to zoning laws.

   b. Easements. An easement is an interest in land which gives the owner of the easement (the dominant owner) the right to make some use of the land belonging to another (the servient owner). The most common easements are: the right of way over the grantor's land; the right of drainage; the right to erect poles and suspend power lines over the land; the right to lay pipelines or sewage systems beneath the surface.

   An easement is an interest in real property which, once established, cannot be terminated without the consent of the owner of the right. The easement attaches to the land forever and passes to successive owners. It is an encumbrance against the property. Easements may be created:

   (1) By Deed. Generally, an easement is expressly granted in a deed conveying the property. In such cases, it is referred to as an "easement appurtenant", and it must be accepted by future purchasers of the land. In some instances, the easement is made by a separate contract which is binding only on the parties to the agreement. This type of an easement is called a "personal easement".

   (2) By Necessity. An easement by necessity (sometimes known as an implied easement) may be created by operation of the law, where the easement is necessary, and where its prior use has been obvious and continuous.

   (3) By Prescription. Prescription is a means of acquiring an easement through the open, continuous, adverse trespass upon real property for a specified period of time. The time required is usually the same as that necessary to obtain title by adverse possession.

   c. License. A license, relative to real property, is a right granted, either in writing <u>or orally</u>, whereby one acquires the authority to use another's land for a particular purpose, but does not acquire any permanent interest in the land. A license differs from an easement in that . . .

   (1) It is personal and can only be used by the person granted the privilege. It does not run with the land.

(2) It may be revoked at any time.

(3) It carries no interest in the land and, therefore need not be in writing.

d. Profit. A profit is a right to take something from the land of another. For example, the right to take water from the well on another's land is a "profit".

4. Limitations Imposed by Creditors

The right, given by law to a creditor, to have a debt, obligation, duty, tie, claim, or charge satisfied out of the property belonging to another is called a lien. A lien is not a property in or a right to the thing to which it relates. It is a right to enforce a charge upon another's property in payment or satisfaction of some claim. While all liens are limitations or encumbrances, all encumbrances are not necessarily liens (e. g., incorporeal rights such as easements, rights of way, et cetera).

Whether or not a charge for services is a lien on real property can be determined easily by asking the question, "Can the real property be sold to satisfy the charge?" If the answer is "no", then the charge cannot be a lien. A typical example is a water bill. Since no levy can be made against the property to effect a forced sale to satisfy the charge, such charges are not liens. The term "lien" is a generic term. Standing alone, it includes voluntary and involuntary liens, general liens, and specific liens.

a. Voluntary Liens. Voluntary liens arise out of contractual relations. The usual type of voluntary lien against real property is the mortgage. The borrower (mortgagor) gives the lender (mortgagee) a lien upon real property to secure the mortgage loan.

b. Involuntary Liens. Involuntary liens are liens created by operation of the law. Such liens arise where the law itself, without stipulation of the parties, raises a lien as a legal consequence from the relations of the parties or the circumstances of their dealings. This species of liens may be further categorized as "common-law liens", "equitable liens", or "statutory liens".

(1) Common-law Liens. As the term implies, common-law liens arise under the rule of common law. Such liens include the right extended to one person to retain that which is in his possession but belongs to another, until the demand on the charge of the person in possession is paid or otherwise satisfied.

(2) Equitable Liens. The equitable lien differs essentially from a common-law lien, in that in the equitable lien possession remains with the debtor or person who holds proprietary

interest. An equitable lien is a right by which a creditor is entitled to obtain satisfaction from the debtor of his debt by resort to specified property belonging to the debtor. It is not a right in the land itself, but a personal right against the owner of the property. Equitable liens arise either from a written contract which indicates an intention to charge some particular property with a debt or obligation (e. g., voluntary liens), or is implied and declared by a court of equity from considerations of right and justice as applied to relations of the parties or the circumstances of their dealings.

(3) Statutory Liens. Statutory liens are those created or defined by a statute. Mechanic's liens, vendor's liens, and vendee's liens are examples of statutory liens.

c. General Liens. A general lien is one's right to detain all of a debtor's real and/or personal property until a debt is satisfied. Such a lien depends entirely upon an express or implied contract. Examples of such liens are judgment liens in personam, tax liens (federal and state), and decedent's debt liens.

(1) Lien of Judgment in Personam. A judgment in personam is one against a particular person. Most judgments are judgments in personam.

(2) Federal and State Tax Lien. Tax liens falling within the definition of a general lien are those statutory liens existing in favor of the federal or state government against a particular person and attending to his property, both real and personal.

(3) Decedent's Debts Lien. Upon death, all who have debt claims against the deceased may establish liens on his property.

d. Specific Liens. A specific lien is a lien upon a specific parcel of real property which the holder can enforce only as security for the performance of a particular act or obligation. A specific lien is also known as a particular lien because it attaches and binds only to a particular piece of property, unlike a general lien which is levied against all of one's assets. A specific lien creates a right in one person to retain something of value belonging to another as compensation for labor, material, or money expended in that person's behalf. Examples of such liens are: judgment liens in rem; mortgage liens; tax liens; assessments; vendor's liens; vendee's liens; and mechanic's liens (i. e. statutory liens).

(1) Lien of Judgment in Rem. A judgment in rem is a decision against a thing - real or personal. It is conclusive on all persons. Tax liens, mechanic's liens, assessments for street improvements are judgments in rem, when adjudicated, as

they bind a particular piece of property.

(2) Mortgage Lien. A mortgage lien is an equitable lien binding the specific property pledged as security for repayment of a debt.

(3) Tax Lien. Tax liens falling within the definition of a special lien are those imposed by constitution or statute as security for payment of a tax. The tax lien is levied <u>against the property</u> itself, <u>not</u> on the interest of the <u>person assessed</u>, and allows the collecting body to allow the property to be taken or sold for non-payment of taxes.

(4) Assessments. Assessments are charges made upon specific real property which has been especially benefited by a local improvement. Assessments do not recur regularly as do taxes. They are not apportioned according to the value of the property affected, but according to the benefits received. It is assumed that the land receives all the benefits. Buildings, consequently, are not considered in apportioning assessments. Improvements, such as roads, sidewalks, sewage, et cetera, which are done by the government and which add to the value of the land are called "betterments".

(5) Vendee's Lien. Upon default by the seller (vendor), the buyer (vendee) may attach a vendee's lien on the property for expenses incurred by the seller's failure to perform.

(6) Vendor's Lien. If the buyer (vendee) fails to pay the full purchase price, the seller has a vendor's lien for the unpaid balance.

(7) Mechanic's Lien. Any person who performs labor on real property, or furnishes materials for the improvement of the property, has the right under law to claim a "mechanic's lien" for the amount due against the specified real property to which he has added value. For the protection of third parties, the law requires the lien to be recorded promptly.

(8) Attachments. An attachment is a lien which the plaintiff gets <u>before</u> entry of judgment, to assure him of the availability of defendant's property for eventual execution in satisfaction of his claim - assuming the plaintiff gets the judgment. An attachment is the <u>process</u> by which real or personal property of a defendant in a law suit is seized and retained in the custody of the law as security for satisfaction of the judgment which <u>the plaintiff hopes to obtain</u> in the

pending litigation. In some jurisdictions, such as Colorado, the plaintiff obtaining the attachment must file a bond to protect the defendant against any loss caused by the attachment in the event the plaintiff loses the case.

Many states will allow the filing of an attachment only when it is believed that the defendant will flee from the state with his property, or when the defendant is not a resident of the state where the action is being brought. Thus, it is possible in some cases to have frozen some of the defendant's assets even before the start of a law suit simply by asking the court to issue a writ of attachment on all or part of the defendant's property. In such instances it is possible for the debtor to release the property from the attachment by putting up a counter bond. An attachment is filed in the registry which holds the property in anticipation of a judgment against the debtor. Attachments, and the procedures associated with their use, are governed by state statutes which vary considerably. If the plaintiff receives a judgment against the defendant, the attached property may be sold to satisfy the judgment.

e. Judgments. A judgment is the <u>final</u> determination of the rights of the parties to an action or proceeding by a court of competent jurisdiction. A judgment does not automatically create a lien. It first must be properly recorded. Once recorded, a judgment encumbers the property to which it is attached. If the party against whom the judgment is rendered appeals to a higher court, "execution" of the judgment is "stayed" pending the higher court's decision. If the lower court's decision is not appealed, the decision of that court becomes final when the time provided for a review of its decision has expired. In most cases the losing party will voluntarily comply with the decision of the court and satisfy the judgment. In some instances, however, the assistance of the court is required to enforce the final decision of the court. If, for example, a judgment for dollar damages is not paid by the judgment debtor, the judgment creditor may apply for a "writ of execution" which directs the sheriff to seize <u>personal</u> property of the judgment debtor and to sell enough of such <u>personal</u> property to cover the costs and expenses of the sale. Such a writ of execution authorizes the sheriff to seize both tangible and intangible personal property.

If the judgment debtor's <u>personal</u> property which is seized and sold by the sheriff does not provide adequate funds to pay the judgment, the writ of execution is returned to the court with a statement of the extent to which the judgment is left unsatisfied. When such an execution is returned unsatisfied in whole or in part, the judgment then becomes a lien on any _real_ property owned by the judgment debtor within the jurisdiction of the court which issued the writ of execution. When a judgment creditor obtains a judicial lien on real estate of a judgment debtor, the creditor is entitled to have the real estate sold at a judicial sale and to have the net proceeds of the sale applied against the judgment.

A judgment creditor with an unsatisfied writ of execution not only has a lien on the judgment debtor's _real property_ owned at the time the judgment becomes final, he also has a judicial lien on any _real property_ acquired by the judgment debtor during the life of the judgment. Such judgment life is prescribed by statute and during such life a judgment debtor cannot convey clear title to real estate as long as the judicial lien is unsatisfied. When a title search is made, and a judgment against an individual has been entered, such judgment constitutes a "cloud on the title" of the judgment debtor.

A judgment creditor is entitled to as many writs of execution as may be necessary to satisfy the judgment of the court. While a writ of execution is not the sole method of enforcing a judgment, it is almost always used to ensure that there will be a judicial lien on any real estate owned by the judgment debtor.

Judgments may be classified as either _judgments in personam_ or _judgments in rem_.

(1) Judgment in Personam. A judgment in personam is a judgment against a particular _person_ as distinguished from a judgment against a thing, right, or status (judgment in rem). A judgment in personam is a general lien which binds all the judgment debtor's freehold interest in real property as well as his personal property.

(2) Judgment in Rem. A judgment in rem is an adjudication pronounced on the _status_ of some particular thing or subject matter. It is a specific lien which operates directly upon the property, and the adjudicated status of the property is binding upon _all_ persons in so far as their interests in the property are concerned.

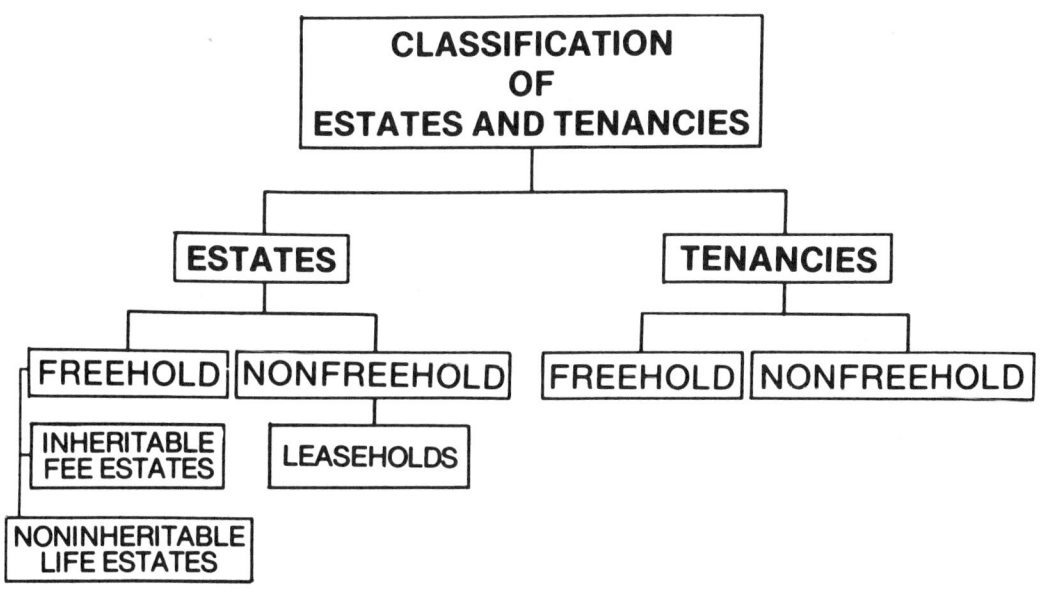

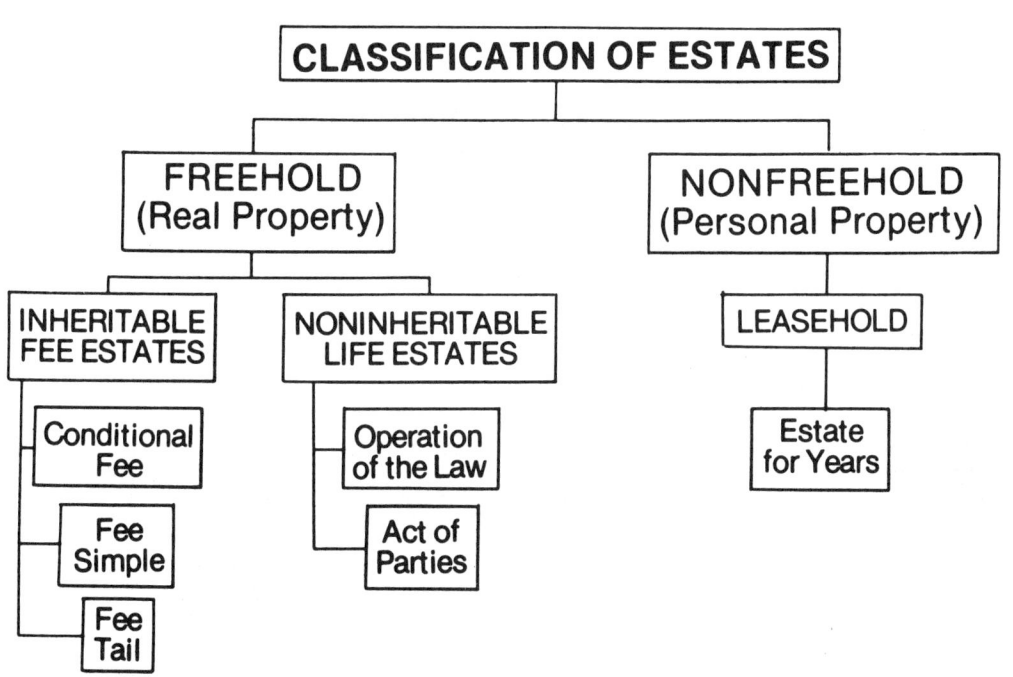

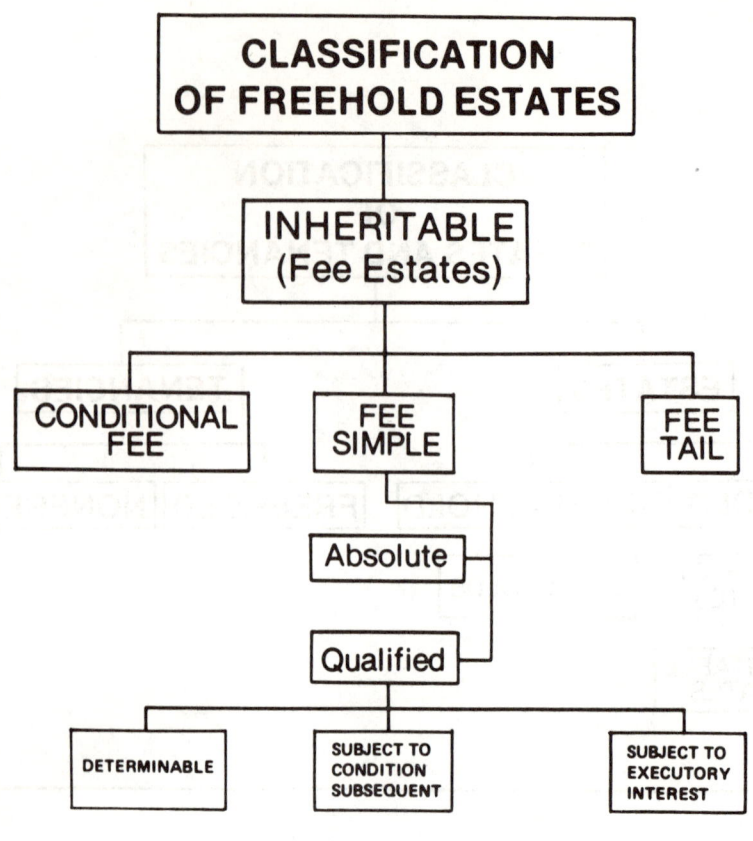
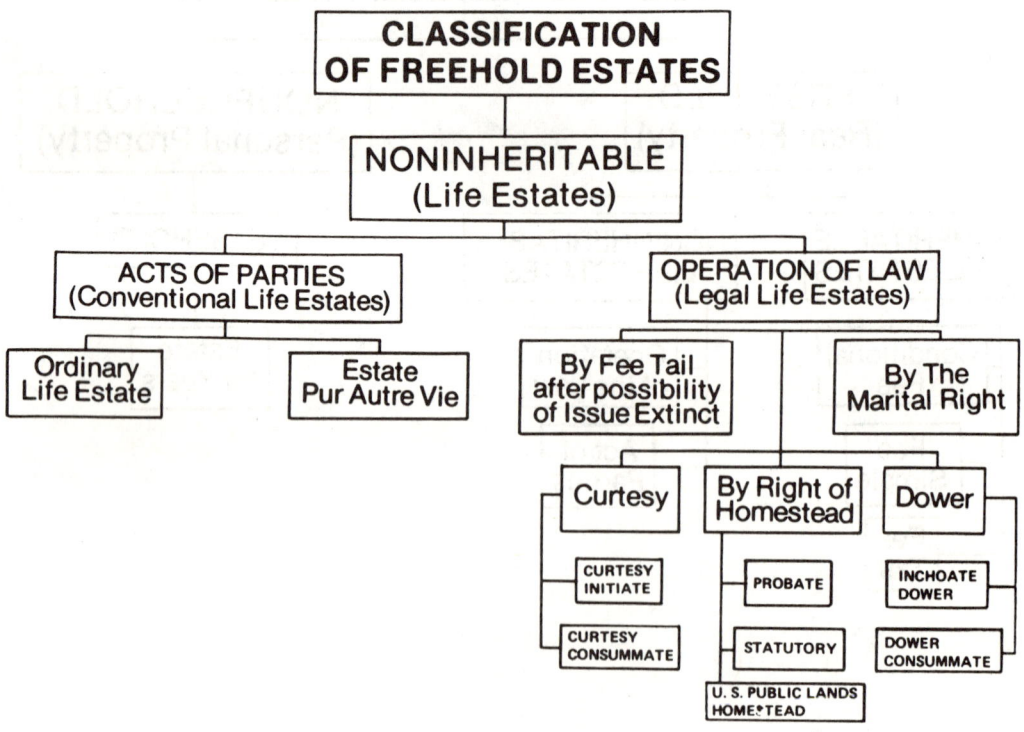

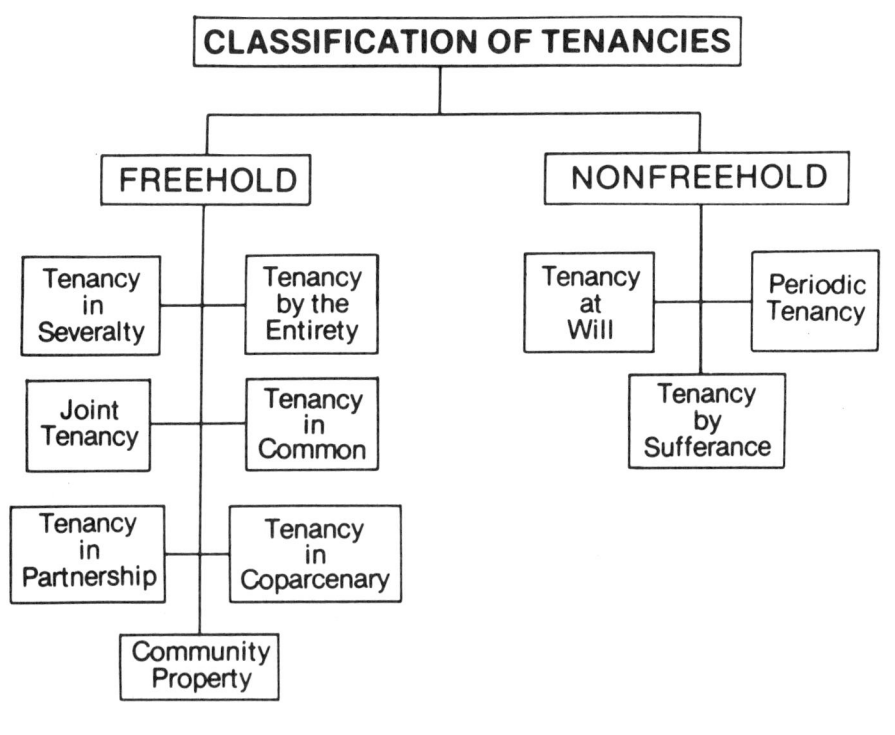

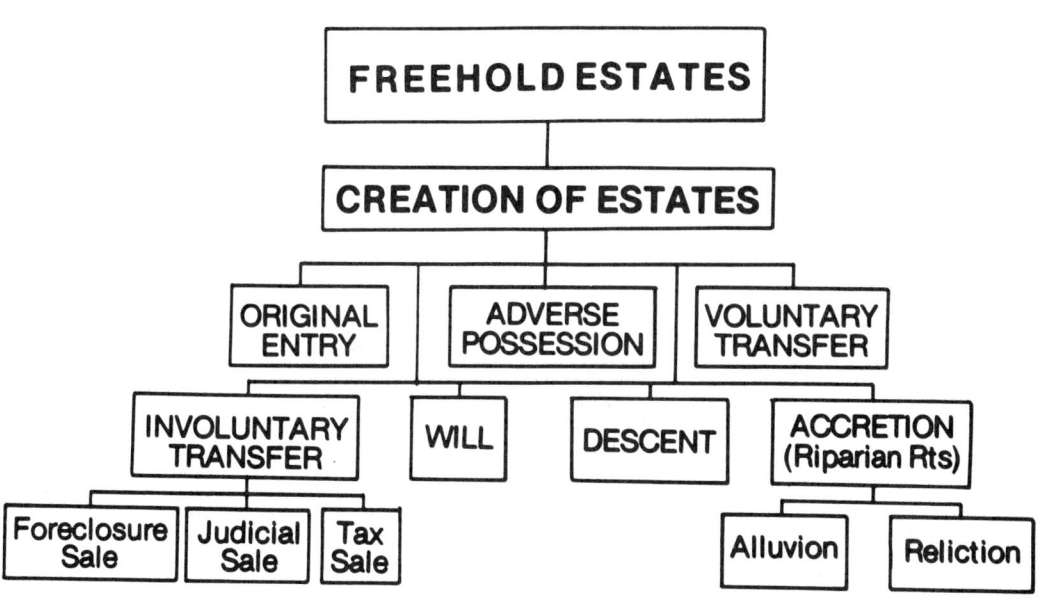

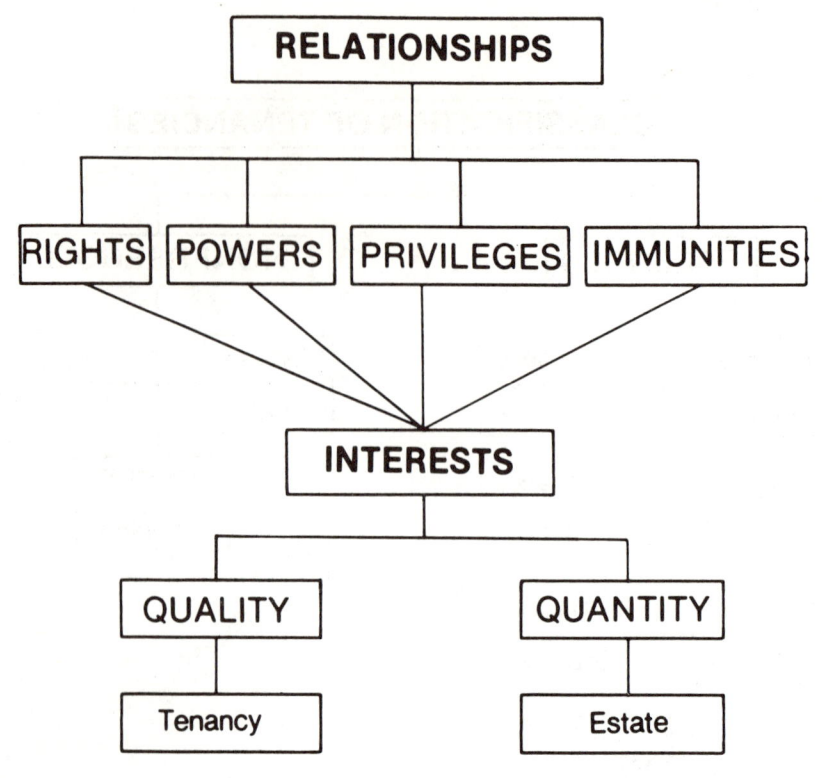

ESTATES IN REALTY

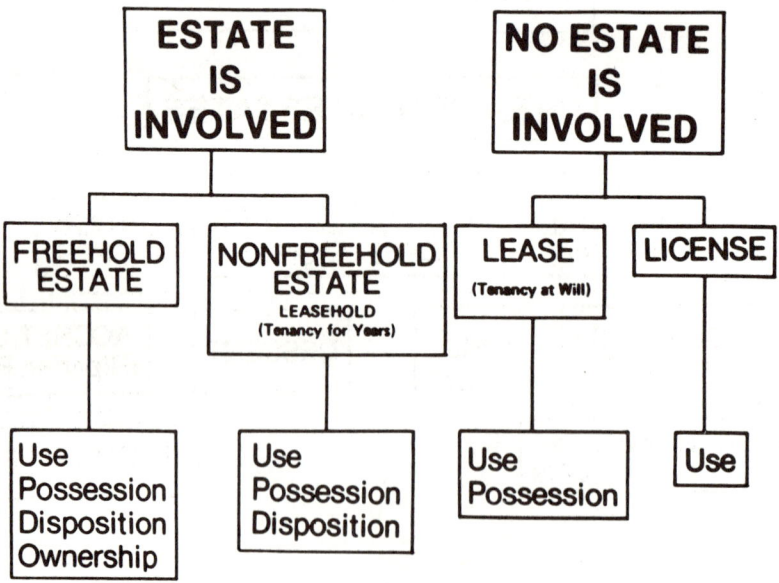

FREEHOLD ESTATES

BUNDLE OF RIGHTS

1. **Possession**
2. **Control**
3. **Quiet Enjoyment**
4. **Disposition**

FREEHOLD ESTATES

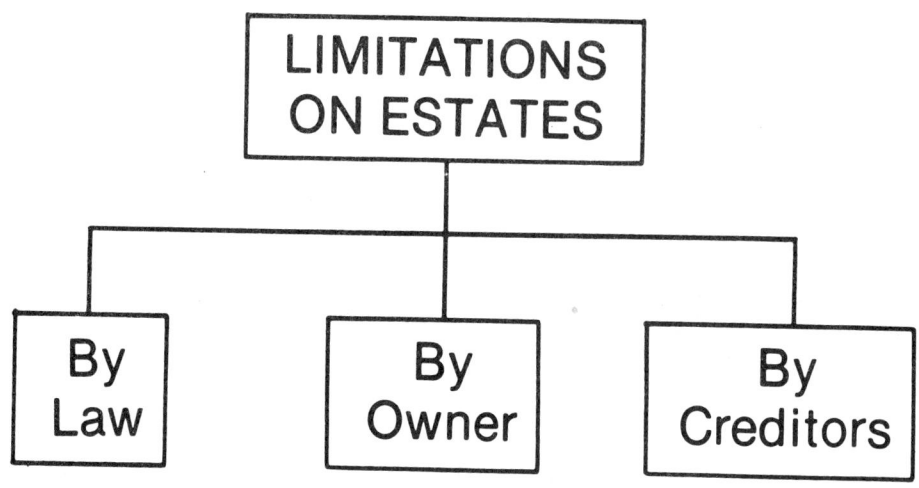

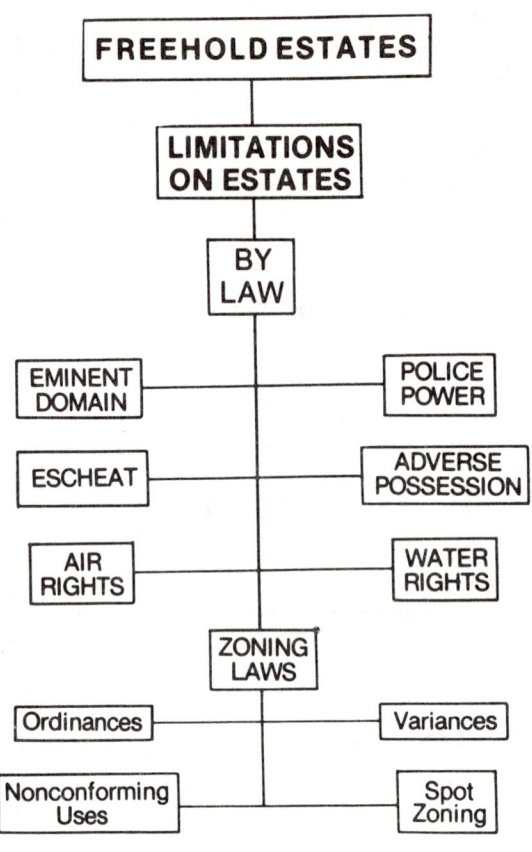

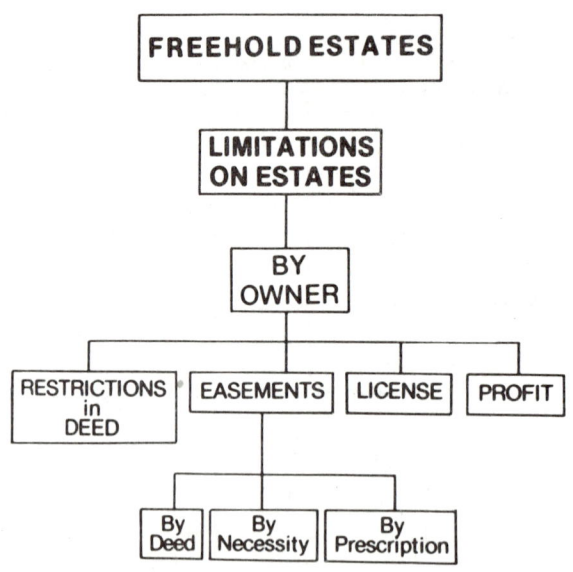

154

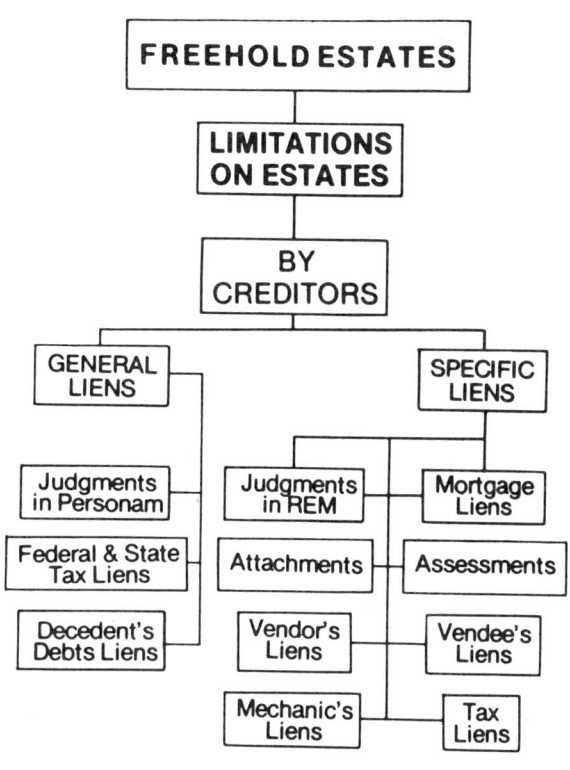

FREEHOLD ESTATES AND TENANCIES

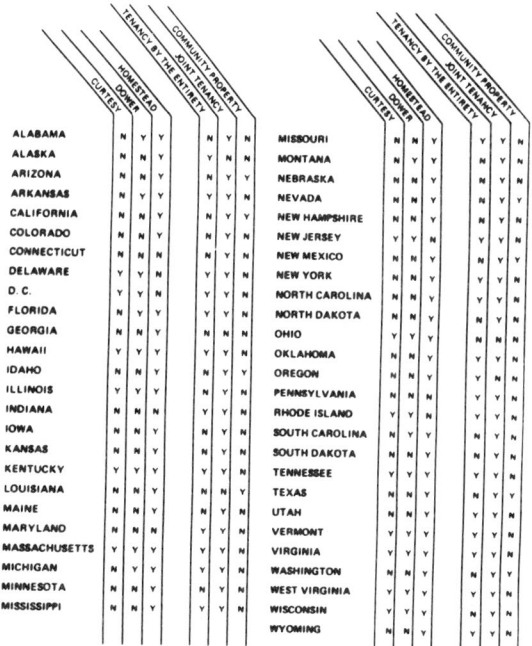

Chapter 6

REVIEW DEFINITIONS IN GLOSSARY OR TEXT OF FOLLOWING TERMS:

abutting	inchoate
accretion	intestate
adverse possession	joint tenancy
air rights	judgment
allodial	judicial sale
alluvion	legatee
assessment	license
attachment	lien
bundle of rights	life estate
curtesy	prescription
decedent's debt lien	profit
devise	reliction
devisee	remainder
dower	remainderman
easements	reversion
easement appurtenant	riparian rights
easement by necessity	tax sale
eminent domain	tenancy
escheat	tenancy by entirety
executor	tenancy in common
fee simple	tenancy in severalty
fee simple absolute	testate
fee simple determinable	testator
fee simple qualified	variance
fee tail	vendee
fee upon condition	vendor
foreclosure	water rights
immunities	

REVIEW QUESTIONS:

1. Name the two broad classifications of freehold estates in land.

2. Can a life estate be sold or mortgaged?

3. What type of tenancy is limited to husband and wife?

4. What type of tenancy makes no provision for survivorship?

5. In what type of estate do all parties own the entire undivided interest in the estate?

6. Name four ways by which an estate can be created.

7. What four basic rights are included in the bundle of rights ?

8. What does "quiet enjoyment" mean ?

9. Name four limitations on estates which are imposed by operation of the law.

10. What are "zoning laws" or "zoning ordinances" ?

11. What is "police power" ?

12. Name three limitations on estates which are created by owners.

13. Name three ways by which easements are created.

14. What is an "easement by prescription" ?

15. Name four limitations on estates which are imposed by creditors.

16. What is an attachment ?

17. What is a judgment ?

FOR ANSWERS TO REVIEW QUESTIONS:

1.

2.

3.

4.

5.

6.

7.

8.

9.

10.

11.

12.

13.

14.

15.

16.

17.

Chapter 7

Nonfreehold Estate & Tenancies

A.	CREATING THE NONFREEHOLD ESTATE	163
	1. Introduction	163
	2. The Landlord-Tenant Relationship	164
B.	TYPES OF INTERESTS:	165
	1. General	165
	2. Estate for Years	165
	3. Tenancy at Will	166
	4. Periodic Tenancy	166
	5. Tenancy by Sufferance	167
C.	DIFFERENCE BETWEEN A LEASE AND A LICENSE	168
D.	FORM AND CONTENTS OF A LEASE	168
	1. Form	168
	2. Contents in General	168
	3. General Covenants and Conditions	168
E.	RIGHTS AND DUTIES OF THE LANDLORD	169
	1. Rent	169
	a. Date of Payment	169
	b. When Due	169
	2. Security Deposit	169
	3. Repossession	170
	4. Renewal of Lease	170
	5. Holdover	170
	6. Fire Clause	170
	7. Fixtures	170
	8. Right to Enter Premises	171
	9. Repairs	171
	10. Unhealthy Conditions	171

F.	RIGHTS AND DUTIES OF THE TENANT			171
	1.	Right to Possession and Use		171
	2.	Right to Quiet Enjoyment		172
		a. Eviction		172
			(1) Actual Eviction	172
			(2) Constructive Eviction	172
		b. Dispossession		173
	3.	Duty to Redeliver		173
	4.	Duty to Repair Premises		173
	5.	Waste		173
		a. Voluntary Waste		174
		b. Permissive Waste		174
	6.	Right of Assignment and Sub-lease		174
		a. Assignment and Sub-lease Differentiated		174
		b. Restricting Clause		174
		c. Assignment		174
		d. Sub-lease		175
	7.	Renting to Roomers		175
G.	TYPES OF LEASES			175
	1.	Gross Lease		175
	2.	Net Lease		175
	3.	Percentage Lease		175
	4.	Step Lease		175
	5.	Ground Lease		175
	6.	Leaseback		176
	7.	Renewal Lease		176
	8.	Revaluation Lease		176
	9.	Index Lease		176
	10.	Sandwich Lease		176
	11.	Lease-Option		176
	12.	Farm Lease		176
	13.	Rooftop Lease		176
H.	EFFECT OF TRANSFER OF OWNERSHIP ON LEASE			176

I.	REMEDY FOR RECOVERY OF RENT		176
	1. General		176
	2. Distrain for Rent		177
	3. Replevin		177
	4. Landlord's Lien		177
J.	TERMINATION OF THE LEASE		177
	1. Surrender		177
		a. By Mutual Agreement	177
		b. By Operation of Law	177
	2. By Breach of Covenants		177
	3. By Destruction of Premises		177

VISUAL AIDS   178

REVIEW QUESTIONS   180

Chapter 7
Nonfreehold Estate & Tenancies

A. CREATING THE NONFREEHOLD ESTATE

1. Introduction

The strict technical meaning at common law of an "estate" was a freehold in lands. Interests in land of less than freehold were not regarded at common law as any part of the ownership, but merely as hirings of the land. These latter nonfreehold interests were classified as 1) leaseholds (the hiring of land for a definite time), 2) tenancies at will (the hiring of land at the will of the lessor), and 3) tenancies at sufferance (continued possession of land after lawful possession had expired). Under the English Property Act of 1925, a definite distinction was made between a legal estate and an interest in land. The only two estates which can exist at law today, in England, are a fee simple absolute in possession and a term of years absolute. Additionally, only five classes of interest in land can now exist under English law, the most important being rent charges, easements, and similar rights. Unfortunately, no such clear cut distinction between estate, interest, or tenancy has been made in the United States, resulting in loose usage of such terms which serves only to confuse the serious student. For example, the Statute of Frauds in every state holds that contracts for the sale of land or any interest in or concerning the land must be evidenced in writing in order to be enforceable. Obviously, real estate practitioners should understand precisely what is embraced by the term "interest" to fully protect their clients and customers. In most states, a tenancy at will is not required to be in writing. When considered in conjunction with the Statute of Frauds, it would appear, then, that a tenancy at will does not involve an interest, yet, obviously, the tenant does enjoy a possessory interest.

Many states, in considering interests of less than freehold, regard such interests as estates. Thus, we have in these states reference to estates for years, estates at will, estates at sufferance, periodic estates, et cetera. Many other states do not regard nonfreehold interests as estates, but rather as tenancies. In these latter states, then, the reference is to tenancies, e. g., tenancies for years, at will, sufferance, et cetera. A few states adopt a middle position and consider a leasehold for a certain and definite time as an estate, while all other nonfreehold interests are regarded as tenancies. The reader is advised, however, that the terms "estates" and "tenancies", when describing nonfreehold interests, are used, unfortunately, interchangeably and often consecutively, in the same passages, by many legal writers. Some clarification seems in order if the reader, during his introduction to nonfreehold estates and tenancies, is to avoid utter confusion.

"Estates" are interests in land, but, while all estates are interests in land, not all interests in land are estates. Historically, as stated above, the term "estate" related only to freehold interest. Later, the term was extended to include an interest in land that was for a definite and certain duration (i. e., a leasehold or tenancy for years). Today, the term has been further extended to embrace a diversity of interests, such as mortgage rights and rights of creditors. Technically, an "interest in land" is a right in, or to, property that is less than ownership or title. Modern law classifies estates as freehold and nonfreehold. A freehold estate endures for an indeterminable length, while the duration of a nonfreehold estate is capable of determination. Such nonfreehold estates are in the nature of a leasehold interest. Interests in land which do not lend themselves to a precise determination of their duration in this text will be regarded not as estates, but as tenancies.

A tenancy, which is a possessory interest, involves a continuing relationship between the lessor and the lessee, unlike the conveyance of a freehold estate of inheritance which normally severs all contacts between the grantor and the grantee once the deed is delivered. Tenancy relates to the holding of another's land as differentiated from the ownership of land.

Generally, the power to grant a tenancy is coincident with the general power to make dispositions of land. Consequently, any owner of an estate in land may grant a valid tenancy for any interest less than his own. No tenancy can arise, however, unless the tenant obtains the right of exclusive possession of the land. If the land owner remains in general control, no tenancy has been granted, only a mere license, as when one is a resident in a hotel, motel, or lodging house.

The English Doctrine of Tenures (Chapter 5) defines the relationship between the parties, not the relationship of the parties to the land as in the Doctrine of Estates. In modern English law, the relationship of the landlord and tenant is confined to instances where one person, known as the lessee or tenant, holds from another person, known as the lessor or landlord, an interest in land under a lease or tenancy which is less than a freehold. The law of landlord and tenant in the United States developed from the English law and is essentially identical (except for more modern statutory modifications in England). Therefore, the English classification of estates as freehold and nonfreehold was adopted in the United States. Leasehold estates, as in England, are considered personal property, designated by the ambiguous term "chattels real", and are treated for many purposes as chattels rather than land.

2. The Landlord-Tenant Relationship

The relationship between a landlord and a tenant is created by a lease. A lease is a contract, express or implied, oral or written, between the owner of real property (called the landlord or lessor) and a tenant (called the lessee) for the possession and use of lands, and the improvements thereon, in return for the payment of rent. The language of the lease must be adequate to reflect an intent by the landlord to divest himself of possession and to vest possession in the tenant. (The granting of an estate by lease is called a "demise"). The lease generally need not be reduced to writing, unless the period of time involved places it under the Statute of Frauds.

In most states, any estate in land created without a written instrument signed by the landlord has the force and effect of tenancy at will only.

Technically, in a lease, the owner (lessor) has divested himself of one of his rights from his "bundle of rights". This is the right of possession in exchange for rent. For the term of the lease the lessee becomes the owner (in the sense of possessor), and, unless he commits waste, has the right of "quiet enjoyment".

Today, the lease falls within two major areas of the substantive law - - the law of property and the law of contract. A lease is a conveyance of property for a fixed period of time, and it is also a contract between the landlord and tenant defining respective rights for the period of the lease.

B. TYPES OF INTERESTS

1. General

The term "tenancy", as used in relation to a "freehold" estate (Chapter 6), describes how land was held. In this chapter, however, the word "tenancy", as it relates to "nonfreehold" estates generally, describes how long the estate (interest) is held by the tenant. If the period of time that the tenancy is held, as reflected in the lease, is certain and definite, a "leasehold estate" is created which is also known as an "estate for years" or a "tenancy for years". All other types of tenancies, where no definite period of possession is stated, may be regarded as tenancies at will.

2. Estate for Years

The term "estate for years" is somewhat misleading. An estate for years is a tenancy for a fixed period of time. It may be for one day, a week, a month, a year, or one hundred years. (NOTE: some states have set limits on lease terms). It is not limited to "years", and therein lies the basis for confusion.

An estate for years is evidenced by a lease for a fixed period and, for that matter, is sometimes more appropriately referred to as a "lease for a fixed period". This type of tenancy is commonly referred to as a "leasehold". A leasehold is an estate held under a lease for a definite and certain period of time. An "estate" is an interest or right in the 1) possession, 2) use, and 3) disposition of land. Where, in the lease agreement, the "landlord" grants exclusive possession to the tenant for a certain and definite period of time, it is implied that within that period of time the tenant's right of possession includes the inherent right of physical control and dominion over the leased property which, in turn, infers the right of disposition within the period of time reflected by the lease. In short, a leasehold gives the tenant the right to possess, use, and dispose of (e. g., assign, sublet, or leave by will) the leased property. On the other hand, a lease for an uncertain and indefinite period of time confers no such right of disposition. Such a lease allows only for the possession and use of the land, but not that third essential element - "disposition".

Like an estate in fee simple, or a life estate, an estate for years may be subject to a special limitation, or a condition subsequent, or an executory limitation. Most leaseholds creating an estate for years are, in fact, subject to a condition subsequent, giving the lessor a right of re-entry, or the power of termination, on breach of any of the specified contractual conditions by the lessee.

Termination notice is not required in an estate for years because the expiration date is fixed and certain. Notice, however, may become a consideration, if the lease provides for automatic renewal. In New York, a statute provides that an <u>automatic renewal</u> clause is not binding on the tenant unless the landlord first notifies the tenant of its existence in the lease, at least 15 and not more than 30 days before the time within which the tenant is required to give such notice of termination. Unless expressly provided for in the lease, the death of the tenant does not terminate the lease.

Since leases, other than those creating leaseholds (i. e., leases for definite terms), do not contract for the transfer of interests in land, they generally need not be in writing. Conversely, a lease for a definite term is a leasehold and must be in writing regardless of the terms, because an <u>interest</u> in land is involved. A leasehold is personal property. Because the leaseholder can dispose of his interest, a leasehold estate passes to the personal representative of the lessee upon his death. Technically, and historically, a tenant for years (leaseholder) <u>owns</u> the property for the time specified in the lease, and, even though this view is frequently altered by statute or contractual agreements, it still is the basic concept in an <u>estate for years</u>. Keep this concept in mind, as it will later aid in the understanding of some of the unusual provisions in a lease and, further, will serve as a warning to reduce to writing all the terms of the lease agreement. Failure to heed this precaution may find the tenant bound to the responsibilities of owning a piece of property when he only intended to rent it.

3. <u>Tenancy at Will</u>

A tenancy at will is created whenever parties enter into a lease for an <u>indefinite</u> period of time. The tenancy is at the will of either party and can be terminated by either party unilaterally by giving only such notice as is required by statute. Such a lease may be express or implied. <u>The tenant has no right to dispose of the property</u>. Death of either the landlord or tenant terminates such tenancy.

At common law, the tenancy at will could be terminated by either party without any notice. This characteristic has been softened by statutes in some states which require a notice of termination equal to the rent-paying period, or a specific period of time, such as 30 days. For all practical purposes, such statutes convert the tenancy at will to something very much like a periodic tenancy. Obviously, the tenancy at will is a fragile sort of interest in land, since it can be shattered by the will of either party unilaterally.

4. <u>Periodic Tenancy</u>

The periodic tenancy evolved as a means of alleviating the harshness of a tenancy at will, where either the landlord or the tenant could terminate the tenancy, unilaterally, without notice. It is important to realize the distinction between a periodic tenancy and an estate for years. In an estate for years, termination notice is not required, because the expiration date is fixed and certain. Not so with a periodic tenancy ! A series of separate tenancies is not involved; the original tenancy continues until terminated by proper notice.

A periodic tenancy (also known as a tenancy from year to year or a tenancy from period to period) is a daily, weekly, monthly, yearly, or other periodic tenancy which continues indefinitely, from period to period, until ended by a notice to quit by either landlord or tenant. Do not confuse a "tenancy from year to year" with a "tenancy for years". A "tenancy from year to year" is a periodic tenancy and not one for a fixed period of time as is a "tenancy for years". The period of time in a periodic tenancy is defined for the specific period (a month or a year), but remains uncertain as a termination date is not specified. Thus, if A agrees to lease B's property for $200 per month, payable monthly, a periodic tenancy is created. The tenancy is indefinite in that it continues from period to period upon payment of the rent until proper notice is given. If, on the other hand, A agrees to lease B's property for only one month, beginning on a specified date, at $200 per month, an estate for years (i. e., tenancy for years) is created. When a tenant for years (leaseholder) holds over after the termination of a lease for a definite period, and the landlord accepts rent, a periodic tenancy or a tenancy at will is created.

5. Tenancy by Sufferance

A tenancy by sufferance is a form of tenancy whereby the landlord permits (suffers) the tenant to occupy the property. This type of tenancy is created where a tenant holds over, without right, after the expiration of a definite period. Also, if the tenant's original entry was wrongful and other than by lease, and if, at the landlord's option, such tenant is allowed to continue in possession, a tenancy by sufferance is created. Note particularly that in this type of tenancy there is no obligation on the tenant's part to pay rent or on the landlord's part to permit occupancy. If the landlord accepts the payment of rent normally due after the expiration of a term, the acceptance is evidence of his intent to regard the person in possession as a tenant. Such an act creates a periodic tenancy. A tenancy at sufferance normally may be terminated at any time by the landlord, although some states require the giving of some notice.

A tenant at sufferance, at most, has only a possessory interest in the land. If a tenant does not vacate the premises at the termination of the lease or notice period, he assumes the position of a trespasser who is entitled to no more consideration than a wrongdoer. The identification of this type of tenancy as an estate at sufferance is prevalent in many jurisdictions and may tend to confuse the reader who is not aware that the term in this usage is a misnomer.

C. DIFFERENCE BETWEEN A LEASE AND A LICENSE

The law recognizes a distinction between a lease and a license. A lease is, in part, a contractual agreement for the possession and use of the landlord's property in return for the payment of rent. A license is merely a privilege granted by one person (licensor) to another (licensee) to use his land for a particular purpose without the licensor transferring any interest in the land. A license simply gives one the privilege of going on another's land without committing trespass. As an example, the permission granted to erect a billboard on one's property is a license. Also, A contracts to use the conference room in B's hotel. The contract involves a license. Similarly, the relationship between a landlord and tenant differs from that of a boarding house keeper and boarder. A tenant has the exclusive possession of the premises leased, while a boarder or lodger simply enjoys the use of the premises subject to the control and supervision of the boarding house keeper. Also, a landlord has no lien on a tenant's belongings, while a boarding house keeper does.

D. FORM AND CONTENTS OF A LEASE

1. Form: - - Typical lease forms are available, pre-printed, from a variety of sources. With minor modification it is the lease form used for tenancies of houses and apartment dwellings. There is no required form for a lease. It may be implied or expressed in any words which indicate clearly the intentions of the parties. Many terms found in a lease are insertions by the landlord to make the tenant think that he has obligated himself in certain ways. Even though such terms are agreed to by the tenant, many cannot be enforced by the landlord. Leasehold agreements must be in writing to protect the interests of all parties. Duplicates are usually prepared, each an original, one being retained by the lessor, the other by the lessee. The lease need not be under seal, and it need not be acknowledged, if it is not going to be registered.

2. Contents in General: - - A properly prepared lease should contain: 1) a description of the property; 2) the term or the length of time the lease is to run (if a leasehold agreement, the duration must be definite and certain as to commencement and termination); 3) the amount of the rent; 4) when the rent is to be paid; and 5) commencement date; 6) signatures of the parties. In addition, the specific rights and obligations of the parties should be set forth in clauses of the lease. Those clauses are technically known as "covenants" or conditions.

3. General Covenants and Conditions: - - A covenant is an agreement to do or refrain from doing a certain act. It is legal terminology for the provisions of a contract. Not all covenants or conditions are expressed in a lease. Some are implied by law. Basically, the landlord is entitled to his rent and to the return of the property to his possession at the end of the term in good condition. The tenant, on the other hand, is entitled to possession and continued occupancy free from interference. All leases contain general covenants providing for these. Some of the other rights, duties, and liabilities are categorized below as pertaining either to the landlord or the tenant.

E.   RIGHTS AND DUTIES OF THE LANDLORD

1. <u>Rent</u>: - - Generally, a total rental sum is indicated which is divided into monthly installments. Usually, the rent clause states that in the event the tenant violates any of the covenants in the lease, the entire sum becomes due and payable. As a rule, such a clause is not enforceable. There are restrictions on the amount that the landlord can recover on a breach of covenant. This amount is generally limited to the actual damages suffered by the landlord. If a tenant vacates his lease, some clauses state he will have to pay the entire balance of the rent for the unexpired term of the lease. The landlord, however, is entitled only to the actual amount of the loss suffered. Furthermore, the landlord must make an honest effort to rent the premises before he can collect anything.

> a.   Date of Payment. Most leases call for rent payment in advance of the lease period. If no date is specified, the rent is due on the last day of the period for which it pertains. Theoretically, if rent is payable, according to the terms of the lease, on the first day of the rental period, the landlord may evict the tenant for non-payment of rent if such provision is not met. Practically, however, to carry out eviction proceedings in such a case may be quite difficult, if not impossible, unless the tenant was considerably in arrears of his rent.
>
> b.   When Due. Under the law, rent is due the landlord for the tenant's use of the leased premises. In the absence of any contrary agreement, the tenant pays the rent when use of the premises has been enjoyed, i. e., at the end of the rental period, not at the beginning. Rent falling due on a Sunday is payable on the following day; if rent falls due on a holiday, in most states it is due on that day. If the tenant fails to pay his rent when it is due, the landlord is entitled to bring action to recover the premises through a summary proceeding known as "dispossess".

2. <u>Security Deposit</u>: - - A common provision in leases provides that the tenant pay the landlord a deposit as security for the tenant's performance of the lease. Usually, this deposit takes the form of a payment equivalent to one or more months' rent and is paid to the landlord in advance of the tenant's occupation of the leased premises. The security deposit clause often provides that the deposit will be applied to the last month(s) of the term. Many clauses also provide that the deposit will be forfeited as "liquidated damages" in the event that the tenant breaches any condition of the lease. As stated in the preceding sub-paragraph, such a clause would be unenforceable, since the landlord can recover only damages actually suffered. Any amount over that actually suffered as damages by the landlord is construed to be an absolute <u>penalty</u> for non-performance and, as such, is not retainable. The landlord is only a trustee of the security deposit. He cannot use it for any purpose other than that for which it is provided. Consequently, if a security deposit is required, the lease should clearly state the specific use to which the deposit is to be put. (Certain states have enacted legislation which requires a landlord to pay interest, at a specific rate, on any security deposit required from a tenant.)

3. <u>Repossession</u>: - - The landlord has the right to repossess the premises at the end of the term of a lease. The landlord may also repossess, if the tenant refuses to pay the rent due and abandons the premises. If the tenant commits waste (see paragraph F 5) or becomes a nuisance to other tenants because of his conduct, the landlord may also repossess.

4. <u>Renewal of Lease</u>: - - Generally, the lease agreements include automatic renewal clauses to the effect that, unless the tenant notifies the landlord in writing, by a certain period before the expiration of the lease, that the tenant does not intend to renew, the landlord shall have the right to regard the lease as automatically renewed for a like period to the original term. Tenants who neglect to carefully read their leases may find themselves bound for another term. Some states require the landlord to give the tenant notification, prior to the termination of the lease, that it contains an automatic renewal clause.

5. <u>Holdover</u>: - - When the tenant continues in possession after the expiration of the term of the lease, he is a holdover. If circumstances exist which are beyond the control of the tenant, such as illness, he is generally not considered a holdover. The landlord may elect to evict the holdover tenant; often, however, the tenant continues in possession and continues to pay rent. At common law the tenant was viewed as a tenant at sufferance. The courts today take varying views. Some say he is a tenant at sufferance, others suggest a periodic tenancy is created based on the rent period. To be safe, the parties to the lease should provide for this contingency and clearly state what effect holding over shall have. Generally, it is difficult to regain possession of premises when a tenant holds over. The courts are inclined to be lenient and tend to allow the holdover tenant considerable time to find new premises.

6. <u>Fire Clause</u>: - - A lease usually provides that the tenant will immediately notify the landlord in event of any fire, and that the landlord must repair the damages as soon as possible. If the damage is not such as would require the tenant to move, the rent continues regardless of the fire. If, however, damage is to such an extent as to cause the tenant to relocate, the rent ceases until the landlord restores the property to its former condition. In leases where the subject matter is the land with improvements thereon (as differentiated from a lease of a part of a building), the lessee remains liable under the lease and is obligated to pay rent even though the improvements are destroyed by fire, flood, or other calamity, unless there is a covenant to the contrary in the lease, or a statute exists which provides remedies to the lessee.

7. <u>Fixtures</u>: - - Improvements in the leased premises, made by the tenant, which are attached in such a manner that subsequent removal would cause substantial injury to the premises, are considered "fixtures" and become part of the realty. In the absence of lease provisions to the contrary, fixtures become the property of the landlord, unless they were erected for the specific purpose of carrying on a trade. Even so, trade fixtures, or fixtures mutually agreed upon to be regarded as the tenant's personal property and removable by him, must be so removed by the tenant <u>prior</u> to expiration of the term of the lease or they become the property of the landlord.

8. Right to Enter Premises: -- In the absence of a provision in the lease to the contrary, the lessee has the sole and exclusive right to the occupancy and control of the premises. Most leases, however, provide that the landlord may enter the premises to place "for rent" or "to let" signs thereon or to show the premises to prospective tenants, if the tenant has notified the landlord of intent to leave at the end of the term of the lease. Even without such provisions, the landlord has the right to enter the premises to make a demand for rent due. The landlord also has the right to enter premises which have been abandoned by the tenant in order that the property may be cared for. Caution in this instance must be exercised. If the landlord accepts the abandoned premises without protest, the tenant is relieved of loss should the landlord fail to locate a new tenant; the lease is viewed as being terminated by mutual agreement of the parties.

9. Repairs: -- The landlord is under no obligation to repair the leased premises in the absence of an agreement to do so. The lessee takes possession of the property as leased and cannot hold the landlord for repairs without his consent. Even a promise by the landlord to repair the premises after the lease is executed cannot be enforced because consideration is lacking. Reference paragraph B 2, where it was pointed out that technically and historically a tenant for years owns the property for the time specified in the lease. As temporary owner, it should not be viewed as surprising that the tenant and not the landlord is responsible for repairs. The landlord, nevertheless, is responsible for substantial repairs . . . such as restoration of the electrical or plumbing systems or the replacement of the roof. He is also responsible for those areas referred to as "common passageways" and for exercising reasonable care in maintaining them, with respect to safety, in the condition they were in at the time of letting. Local statute may place other requirements on the landlord to execute certain repairs and should be consulted. In Illinois, for example, a House Bill held void every lease provision exempting the lessor from liability for damages or injuries to persons or property resulting from negligence of the lessor, his agents, servants, or employees in the maintenance or operating of the leased premises.

10. Unhealthy Conditions: -- The landlord is duty-bound to notify the lessee of any unhealthful conditions existing on the premises arising from latent defects. Failure to so notify constitutes fraud and gives the tenant the right to abandon the premises.

F. RIGHTS AND DUTIES OF THE TENANT

1. Right to Possession and Use: -- The lessee is the absolute owner of the premises for the period of the lease and for the purposes for which the lease was created. While the tenant is in possession, the landlord has no right to enter the leased premises or interfere in any manner with the lessee's possession or use of the premises. It has been held also that an employee of the landlord has no right to enter the leased premises for the purpose of making repairs without the consent of the lessee. This also means that a landlord cannot bar access to one's apartment through public areas of the premises.

2. <u>Right to Quiet Enjoyment</u>: - - There is in every lease an implied covenant that the landlord will do nothing by his own act, <u>or by the act of any successor</u> to him in ownership of the property, to disturb the "quiet enjoyment" of the tenant. This imposes a duty on the landlord to evict tenants who interfere with another tenant's right to quiet enjoyment, but does not imply that the landlord must evict anyone already in the premises at the time the lease was signed.

    a. Eviction. Originally, an eviction was understood to be a dispossession of the tenant by some act of his landlord. Of late, it has come to include any <u>wrongful</u> act of the landlord which may result in an interference with the tenant's possession. As pointed out above, one of the covenants in a lease, whether express or implied, is the assurance by the landlord that the tenant will enjoy undisturbed possession of the premises. Any breach of this covenant by the landlord is called an "eviction". An eviction has the legal effect of terminating the lease. The tenant may rightfully cease paying rent and may, in addition, bring an action against the landlord for breach of the covenant of quiet enjoyment of the premises. There are two types of eviction: actual and constructive.

        (1) Actual Eviction. An actual eviction is involved if the lessor, or one acting with his consent, interferes with the <u>possession of the land</u> by the lessee. It may consist of ousting the tenant from all or a portion of the leased premises. It may be by legal action or physical force. Note: in an ordinary lease, the landlord has no right to evict for non-payment of rent. Actual eviction, for example, occurs when the leased premises are blocked by the landlord. Statutory dispossess proceedings are quite restrictive and make it difficult for a landlord to evict his tenants.

        (2) Constructive Eviction. Constructive eviction occurs when the landlord permits certain conditions to exist which substantially make it undesirable or impossible for the tenant to use the premises, or which interferes with the lessee's <u>enjoyment</u> of the leased land. Thus, if a landlord fails to provide essential services, such as heat and hot water, the tenant may vacate the premises, stop paying rent, and sue the landlord for damages on the theory that he has been evicted just as surely as if the landlord had thrown him out bodily. It is important to note that there can be no eviction <u>until the tenant vacates the premises</u>. If he remains in possession, he must continue to pay rent, and he has no right to damages. When the landlord fails to

obey local ordinances requiring certain actions to be performed on the premises, this may also constitute constructive eviction, depending on the extent and seriousness of the landlord's delinquency. Usually constructive eviction cannot be claimed by the lessee, unless the lessor was advised of the condition and afforded the opportunity to take remedial action.

b. Dispossession. Dispossession is the result of a summary proceeding (dispossess) on a legal action brought by the landlord against the tenant to exclude him from occupancy of real property for failure to pay rent or for breach of the conditions of the lease. Dispossession differs from eviction, which may infer a violation by the landlord of an important provision of the lease amounting to an interference with the tenant's useful and peaceful enjoyment of the premises (constructive eviction).

Note: Television Antennas and Wires. The law in the United States as generally interpreted holds that the area on the outside of the house or apartment is the exclusive property of the landlord and is not considered part of the leased premises. Unless specifically authorized in the lease, the tenant is accorded no such rights outside the leased area. The law has been strictly applied in this specific regard. Where the tenant lacks permission, the landlord may remove antennas and wires at will or get an injunction to prevent installation.

3. <u>Duty to Redeliver</u>: - - Every lease contains an implied covenant that, at the end of the term, the tenant will redeliver the premises to the landlord in the same condition as when he received possession. The lessee is not bound to make payment for ordinary wear and tear as a consequence of reasonable use - or for actual destruction beyond his control. Anything more than ordinary wear and tear is called "waste". If guilty of waste, the tenant must pay the landlord for the damages done. (Reference sub paragraph 5, below).

4. <u>Duty to Repair Premises</u>: - - The tenant has the duty, in the absence of agreement to the contrary, to keep the premises maintained by making ordinary or minor repairs necessary to keep the premises from deteriorating and depreciating unduly. The tenant is not obligated to make major repairs, nor is he liable to make repairs required at the time he took possession.

5. <u>Waste</u>: - - The tenant is liable in damages for any unreasonable or improper use, abuse, mismanagement, or omission of duty relating to the leased premises which results in its substantial injury. There are two types of waste: voluntary and permissive.

    a.   Voluntary Waste. Any positive act by the tenant, of an unreasonable nature, which causes injury to the leased property and results in damage, is called voluntary waste.

    b.   Permissive Waste. Omission or failure to act to prevent injury to the leased property which results in damage is permissive waste.

6. Right of Assignment and Sub-lease

    a.   Assignment and Sub-lease Differentiated. By assignment, a lessee (assignor) transfers his <u>entire interest</u> to an assignee. When the lessee sublets, he transfers to the sub-lessee only a <u>part of his interest</u>. In the absence of clauses in the lease to the contrary, the lessee has the right to assign or sub-lease his interest in the leased premises.

    b.   Restricting Clause. Many leases for a definite term have restricting clauses which unqualifiedly forbid the tenant from assigning or subletting the premises. Since such restrictions constitute a restraint upon the lessee's right of alienation, they are not favored. Consequently, while conditions and covenants prohibiting assigning or subletting are sanctioned, they are subject to strict interpretation by the courts to protect the tenant and to avoid the forfeiture of the lease because the lessee was in violation of the restrictive covenant.

        Where the covenant has been qualified by the use of the words "which consent (to assign or sublet) shall not be unreasonably withheld," the landlord's right to refuse consent has generally been upheld. When the lease contains such a qualified covenant, the landlord must consent unless he has good reason not to do so. If the tenant in such a case assigns or sublets the premises without the landlord's permission, the landlord has two alternatives: he may accept the new tenant, or he may terminate the lease. This general rule, however, varies in some states. Local rules should be examined before taking measures contrary to the terms of the lease.

    c.   Assignment. An assignment of a <u>leasehold</u> (i. e., a lease for a definite and certain term) is a transfer by the lessee (assignor) of ALL the unexpired interest he holds at the time of the assignment. The assignee takes the leased premises on the same terms as those expressed in the original lease (head lease) between the landlord and tenant. By the assignment of all his interests the lessee-assignor divests himself of "privity of contract". "Privity" is a legal term reflecting a mutual relationship to a property right. A "privity of estate" is that which exists because of the landlord's and the tenant's mutual interest in the same property. Because of the lease agreement between the landlord and the tenant, a "privity of contract" also exists. When the lessee assigns all his interests in the leased property to another (assignee), the assignee succeeds to the rights of the lessee and is in privity of estate with the lessor (landlord). The assignee may become liable to the lessor (landlord) for performance of the lessee's covenants that run with the leasehold.

    d.   Sub-lease. A sub-lease of a leasehold is a transfer by the lessee of only a PART of his interest to another (sub-lessee) at the time of subletting. In a sub-lease, the lessee retains some interest. The sub-lease grants to the sub-lessee only a part of the estate (interest) held by the lessee under the head lease. (The head lease is varyingly referred to as the original lease, the main lease, the master lease, and the underlying lease). The interest or part retained by the lessee may be a portion of the term of the original lease or a particular portion of the premises. Unless a lease provides otherwise, a tenant may sublet. A prohibition against subletting will not prevent an assignment, nor will the prohibition against assignment prevent subletting. The only limitation to assigning and subletting, when the lease does not preclude same, is that the premises must be used for the same purpose for which the tenant rented them.

7. Renting to Roomers: - - Taking in roomers does not constitute either an assignment or a subletting. The relationship between the tenant and the roomer is that of a license, and, unless there is a specific clause in the lease to the contrary, a tenant has the right to take in roomers.

G. TYPES OF LEASES:

    1. Gross Lease: - - All operating expenses, taxes, and insurance are paid by the landlord.

    2. Net Lease: - - Part or all of the maintenance and operational costs of the property, in addition to rent, are paid by the tenant.

    3. Percentage Lease: - - A "percentage lease" relates to rent paid by a commercial tenant based on a percentage of the tenant's gross sales.

    4. Step Lease: - - A step lease allows for the increase or decrease of rent payments at fixed intervals in accordance with the terms of the lease contract. A step lease is also known as a "graded" lease or a "graduated" lease.

    5. Ground Lease: - - Only the land is leased.

6. <u>Leaseback</u>: - - A "leaseback" is a simultaneous sale of property and lease back to the former seller by the buyer who becomes the landlord (lessor). It is sometimes referred to as a "sales-leaseback".

7. <u>Renewal Lease</u>: - - Provides at time of negotiation for an extension. If the clause is an "option to renew", the option rests with the lessee. If an "automatic renewal", both parties retain the right to make a decision.

8. <u>Revaluation or Re-appraisal Lease</u>: - - The amount of rent is recalculated periodically on the basis of an appraisal.

9. <u>Index or Escalator Lease</u>: - - A lease in which the amount of rent is tied to national indices, such as the cost of living index or value of the dollar.

10. <u>Sandwich Lease</u>: - - Essentially, the subletting of a leased property in which the lessee lets to another party and becomes both lessor and lessee. Unless prohibited by the terms of the instrument, a lessee may assign or sublet his lease.

11. <u>Lease-Option</u>: - - A lease containing an option to permit the lessee to purchase the property at a fixed price or a negotiated price, or a price to be established by neutral appraisers.

12. <u>Farm Lease</u>: - - A lease used in rural areas. Usually provides for a flat annual rental, a share of the crops, or both.

13. <u>Rooftop Lease</u>: - - A frequently used instrument to lease space for the erection of display or advertising signs.

H. EFFECT OF TRANSFER OF OWNERSHIP ON LEASE

A lease executed by one owner with a tenant is generally binding upon the new owner when the property is sold. There is an exception, however. If a lease endures for more than a certain term of years (varying from state to state) from the date it was made, or if its term can be extended to more than the statutory period, it must be acknowledged, and <u>notice</u> of the lease (not necessarily the lease itself) must be recorded at the Registry of Deeds by either the lessor or the lessee, if it is to be binding on bona fide purchasers.

I. REMEDY FOR RECOVERY OF RENT

1. <u>General</u>: - - The right to rent generally accompanies the owner's reversionary interest. Rent which is associated with this reversionary interest is called "rent service". When one person possesses the reversionary interest, while another owns the right to rent, the rent is either a "rent charge" or a "rent seck".

2. <u>Distrain for Rent</u>: -- Under common law, where the lessor had a reversionary interest, the payment of rent due could be enforced by seizing chattels located on the leased premises belonging to the lessee or to third parties. This right is referred to as the right to "distrain for rent". The action at law pursued by the landlord to recover for rent is called "distress for rent". If the right to the rent is in one other than the reversionary owner, there is no right to distrain for rent unless this right was specifically expressed in the rental agreement. When such right is expressed, a "rent charge" is involved. When not expressed, a "rent seck" is involved.

In some states, statutes have abolished this common law remedy. In others, it has been adopted with modifications. Usually, all of the tenant's personal property which is not perishable is subject to be "distrained" for rent; only the property on the premises can be distrained (i. e., taken for rent).

3. <u>Replevin</u>: -- The word "replevin" means a redelivery to the owner of a thing taken in distress. It is a personal action brought to recover the possession of goods which were taken. Generally, replevin applies to the recovery of goods distrained for rent. To recover possession of personal property taken, the owner may bring suit to replevin the things. If the owner prevails, the court will issue an order called a "writ of replevin" which directs the sheriff to recover the goods.

4. <u>Landlord's Lien</u>: -- At common law, a landlord has no lien upon a tenant's property for unpaid rent. In many jurisdictions, such a lien has been expressly given the landlord by statute. The landlord and the tenant may, by express provision in the lease, provide that the landlord be given a lien upon the tenant's personal property present in the leased premises.

J. TERMINATION OF THE LEASE

The contractual aspects of a lease, like any other contractual agreement, terminate at the expiration of the period specified in the agreement. Death of either the landlord or the tenant does not ordinarily terminate the contract. Leases are also terminated by:

1. <u>Surrender</u>

A surrender is the giving up of the interest, terminating its further obligations. It may be:

    a. By mutual agreement of the parties, or

    b. By operation of the law, where they do something inconsistent with the continuance of the original agreement causing an estoppel, as when the landlord assumes unqualified possession or gives a new lease.

2. <u>By breach of the covenants by either party.</u>

3. <u>By destruction of the premises if there is no covenant to repair.</u>

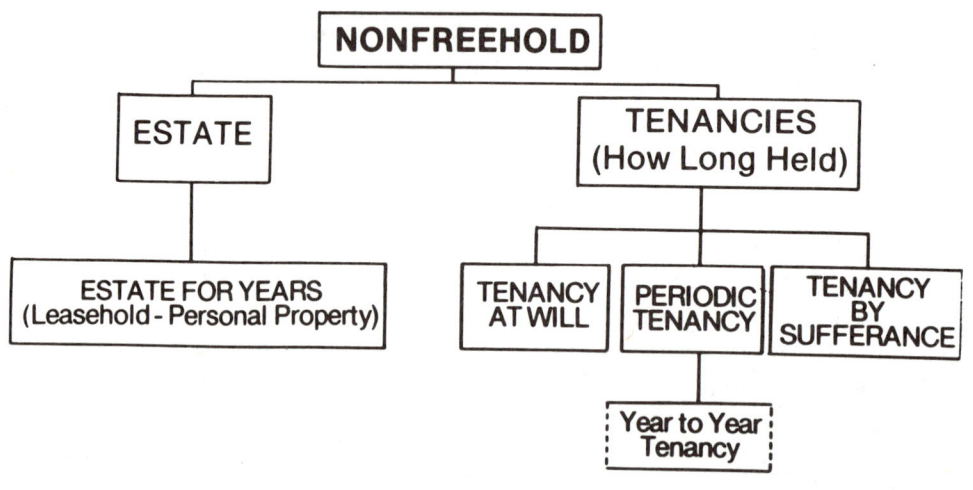

CLASSIFICATION OF ESTATES AND TENANCIES

- NONFREEHOLD
  - ESTATE
    - ESTATE FOR YEARS (Leasehold - Personal Property)
  - TENANCIES (How Long Held)
    - TENANCY AT WILL
    - PERIODIC TENANCY
      - Year to Year Tenancy
    - TENANCY BY SUFFERANCE

RIGHTS & DUTIES OF

LANDLORD

DUTIES:
  Relinquish possession
  Ensure quiet enjoyment
  Make major repairs

RIGHTS:
  Repossess at end of term
  Receive rent
  Recover for damages

TENANT

RIGHTS:
  Exclusive possession
  Unrestrained use
  Disposition:
      Assign
      Sublet
      Bequeath

DUTIES:
  Redeliver at end of term
  Pay rent
  Prevent waste:
      Voluntary
      Permissive
      Equitable

THE LEASE

1. **FORM**
2. **CONTENTS**
   a. **Description**
   b. **Term**
   c. **Rent**
      (1) Commencement Date
      (2) Payment Date
   d. **Signatures**
3. **COVENANTS AND CONDITIONS**
   a. **Security Deposit**
   b. **Repossession**
   c. **Renewal**
   d. **Holdover**
   e. **Fire Clause**
   f. **Fixtures**
   g. **Right to Enter**
   h. **Repairs**
   i. **Unhealthful Conditions**

ASSIGNMENT AND SUB-LEASE DIFFERENTIATED

ASSIGNMENT:

A transfer by the lessee (assignor) of **ALL** the unexpired interest he holds at the time of the assignment.

SUB-LEASE:

A transfer by the lessee of only a part of his interest to another (sub-lessee) at the time of the sub-letting.

Chapter 7

REVIEW DEFINITIONS IN GLOSSARY OR TEXT OF FOLLOWING TERMS:

actual eviction
assignee
assignment
assignor
constructive eviction
covenant
demise
dispossess
distrain
eviction
gross lease
ground lease
landlord
lease
leaseback
leasehold

lessee
lessor
net lease
percentage lease
periodic tenancy
permissive waste
privity
rent
repossess
step lease
sub-lease
tenancy at will
tenancy for years
tenant
terre-tenant
voluntary waste
waste

REVIEW QUESTIONS:

1. Name the three general categories of tenancies which relate to nonfreehold interests.

2. The word "tenancy", as used in nonfreehold interests, generally relates to what ?

3. Is a "leasehold estate" identical to a "tenancy for years" ?

4. Is a "tenancy for a fixed period" the same as a "tenancy for years" ?

5. Does a "lease for an indefinite period" confer an "interest" in land ?

6. Is a leasehold considered real or personal property ?

7. Does death of either the landlord or tenant normally terminate a tenancy at will ?

8. What is a "tenancy from period to period" ?

9. What is the difference between a "tenancy for years" and a "tenancy from year to year" ?

10. What is the difference between a lease and a license ?

11. What terms are synonymous with "headlease"?

12. What is meant by "distrain for rent"?

FOR ANSWERS TO REVIEW QUESTIONS:

1.

2.

3.

4.

5.

6.

7.

8.

9.

10.

11.

12.

Chapter 8

Taxation & Assessments

A.	THE RIGHT TO TAX	185
B.	TAXES AS A SOURCE OF REVENUE	185
C.	TAXES AS AN INSTRUMENT OF NATIONAL ECONOMIC POLICY	185
D.	HISTORICAL REFERENCE	186
E.	CRITERIA FOR TAX POLICY	187

    1. Social Equity — 187

        a. Benefit Principle — 187
        b. Ability to Pay Principle — 187

    2. Consistency with Economic Goals — 188
    3. Ease of Administration and Compliance — 188
    4. Revenue Adequacy — 188

F. THE PROCESS OF TAXATION — 189

    1. Budget — 189
    2. Appropriation — 189
    3. Levy — 189
    4. Assessment — 189
    5. Computation — 190
    6. Collection — 190

G. GENERAL CLASSIFICATION OF TAXES — 192

    1. According to Effective Rate Structure — 192

        a. Progressive Tax — 192
        b. Proportional Tax — 192
        c. Regressive Tax — 192

    2. According to Who Bears the Final Burden — 192

        a. Direct Taxes — 192
        b. Indirect Taxes — 192

    3. According to Specific Measurement/Quantity or Value — 192

		a. Specific Tax	192
		b. Ad Valorem Tax	192
	4.	According to Base	192
		a. Income Tax	193
		b. Consumptive Tax	193
		c. Business Tax	193
		d. Property Tax	193
H.	PROPERTY TAXES		193
	1.	Property Taxes in General	193
	2.	Real Estate Taxes Specifically	194
I.	TYPES OF REAL ESTATE TAXES		194
	1.	General	194
	2.	Real Property Taxes	195
	3.	Capital Gain Taxes	195
	4.	Income Taxes	195
J.	TAX CLASSIFICATION OF REAL ESTATE		195
	1.	General	195
	2.	Real Estate Held as Personal Residence	195
	3.	Real Estate Held for Investment	196
	4.	Real Estate Held for Sale to Customers	196
	5.	Real Estate Held for the Production of Income	196
	6.	Real Estate Held for Use in Trade or Business	197
K.	TAX EFFECTS OF REAL ESTATE TRANSACTIONS		197
L.	TAX ADVANTAGE OF HOME OWNERSHIP		197
M.	DIVERSITY OF TAX SYSTEMS		198
VISUAL AIDS			199
REVIEW QUESTIONS			203

Chapter 8
Taxation & Assessments

A. THE RIGHT TO TAX

A state's right to levy taxes for the support of governmental functions designed to safeguard the health, welfare, law, and morality of its citizenry is of paramount importance. The government's growth, progress, and strength is dependent upon its power to tax and upon its ability to tax wisely. Imprudent tax policies by government may be tantamount to social, economic, or political exploitation. For these reasons, our Founding Fathers had the foresight to weave into our constitution various safeguards designed specifically to protect the property owner.

B. TAXES AS A SOURCE OF REVENUE

Our economic structure, our political system, and the individualism underlying the American way of life impose basic obligations of citizenship on each of us. As the population expands, controls become more complex, as does society itself. The demands we levy upon our government become awesome. We expect security at the local and national levels; we demand equal educational opportunities throughout our society; we seek unemployment insurance, welfare payments, adequate housing, sufficient benefits for our senior citizens which will allow them to live out their years with dignity; public health facilities; and, perhaps, even guaranteed employment, with a guaranteed minimum income. Enjoyment of these governmental services depends upon all citizens meeting their obligations. Perhaps the most fundamental obligation of the citizen is that of paying those compulsory levies imposed by governmental taxing bodies on private sources to raise the revenue required for the performance of various public functions. Our next most important obligation is to obey those laws adopted by the representatives we have freely elected to positions at every level of government.

Existing tax laws were developed by representatives of the majority of our electors. If we are to continue to build and sustain a strong nation built upon law with a society that respects and obeys all laws until they are modified or changed in the peaceful, orderly, and prescribed manner, then we, as individual citizens, must meet our obligations and fulfill the duties our government places upon us.

C. TAXES AS AN INSTRUMENT OF NATIONAL ECONOMIC POLICY

Although the tendency is to regard taxes almost exclusively as a source of revenue, they must also be recognized as an important instrument of national economic policy. During inflationary periods, such as war, nations initiate tax increases to stabilize the economy. Conversely, in periods of depression tax reductions are granted to stimulate commerce. When government spending equals a significant percentage of the national product, taxes play a critical role as a balance wheel in a nation's economy.

D.   HISTORICAL REFERENCE

Equitable taxation, with the consent of the governed, as a major source of governmental revenue is a rather recent phenomenon in human history. For centuries, the chief source of public revenue was in the public domain. Taxation was comprised chiefly of excises on domestic consumption, and custom duties on foreign trade. Practically all revenue requirements in ancient Greece and Rome were met with income from mines, taxes on consumption and trade, gifts from wealthy citizens, and tributes from subjugated countries. Direct taxes on income and wealth were virtually unknown.

In the feudal hierarchy of the middle ages the King, Duke, Count, and Baron derived income from the land they held directly and from dues imposed upon others who held land at their pleasure. Slowly, from the 14th century on, such revenues were replaced by taxes as the feudal system disintegrated with the growth and progress of industry and commerce, coupled with the more centralized functions of government. During this period, land, which was the primary source of wealth, became the major source of taxation. Initially, land taxes in England were based on area. Later, annual rental value was substituted as the base.

Arbitrary and oppressive approaches by governments were not unknown, and rebellion against such approaches played a key role in modern tax history. The Magna Charta of 1215 and the Bill of Rights of 1689 conceded the principle of consent and representation relative to taxation, and failure on the part of Great Britain to apply this principle to the Colonies gave birth to the American Revolution. The Pilgrims broadened the British basis of land tax into a property tax which embraced not only real property but also personal property and, in addition, the rated earning capacity of an individual's trade or profession. In the 19th Century, with ever expanding sources of wealth, the property tax concept adopted by the Pilgrims was further broadened to include taxes on incomes and inheritances. Uniformity and equity replaced arbitrariness and oppression. Taxation policies became sophisticated and complex.

In the United States, World War I marked the period of the effective use of both income and inheritance (death) taxes. Prior to that time, the bulk of federal revenue was realized from customs, excises on liquor and tobacco, and land sales. At state and local levels, the general property tax furnished most of the needed revenues. It was during World War I that estate, corporate, and individual income taxes were initiated by the federal government. At state levels, gasoline taxes, retail sales taxes, motor vehicle levies, and taxes on net income provided the major source of revenue, while the property tax was largely abandoned - only to be adopted by the various taxing bodies at the local level.

E. CRITERIA FOR TAX POLICY

In establishing today's criteria for the overall tax policy of the United States, the maxims set forth by Adam Smith in "Wealth of Nations" (1776) serve as the traditional point of departure. In this writing, Smith develops the tests of equity, certainty, convenience, and economy as follows:

I. The subjects of every state ought to contribute towards the support of the government, as nearly as possible in proportion to their respective abilities - that is, in proportion to the revenue which they respectively enjoy under the protection of the state . . .

II. The tax which each individual is bound to pay ought to be certain and not arbitrary. The time of payment, the manner of payment, the quantity to be paid, all ought to be clear and plain to the contributor and to every other person . . .

III. Every tax ought to be levied at the time, or in the manner, in which it is most likely to be convenient for the contributor to pay it . . .

IV. Every tax ought to be so contrived as both to take out and keep out of the pockets of the people as little as possible.

As these maxims are tailored to modern society, they may be analyzed under four categories: social equity; consistency with economic goals; ease of administration and compliance; and revenue adequacy.

1. Social Equity

It is a self-evident first principle of taxation that taxes should be impartial and equitable. Social justice dictates that taxes meet the "equity" test by being impartial in their application and also meet the "equality" test by reducing economic inequalities. In determining social equity relative to taxation, two principles are involved; the "benefit" principle and the "ability to pay" principle.

a. Benefit Principle. Where benefits received from government can be identified and measured, the benefit principle can be applied. Gasoline taxes and social security employment taxes are viewed as justifiable, since the benefits accruing to the taxpayer are more or less in direct proportion to his payments.

b. Ability to Pay Principle. While a person's net income is generally recognized as the best measure of his ability to pay, it is only one element considered in determining the measurement of ability. Also to be considered are family obligations, marital status, dependency responsibilities, and whether income is "earned" or "unearned". Generally, both Adam Smith and John Ramsey McCulloch,

British Economist and Statistician, (writing nearly 75 years after Smith) held that taxes should be proportional to income rather than progressive or regressive. The predominant view today is reflected by Frank William Taussig (1859 - 1940), U. S. Economist, who, contrary to Smith and McCulloch, asserted that only through progression could democratic ideals of justice in taxation be achieved. The progressive view was recognized 3,000 years ago by the Indian sage, Manu, the author of the "Code of Manu" (A.D. 1000), a compilation of laws reflecting Hindu thought. He wrote, "To make the burden of taxes equal . . . is not effected by a mere numerical proportion. The man who is taxed to the amount of one-tenth . . . of an income of 100 rupees per anum . . . is taxed far more severely than the man who is taxed an equal proportion of an income of 1,000 rupees . . . "

2. Consistency with Economic Goals: - - The concept of using taxes to promote a stable economy, in conjunction with maximum use of resources, was popularized only toward the mid-20th Century. Taxes became recognized as not only affecting the spending power of taxpayers in their roles as producers and consumers, but also as affecting incentives and initiatives in their roles as workers, managers, and investors. Relative to these economic effects, the ideal tax structure would limit or restrict private spending during inflationary periods and increase or expand private spending during periods of depression. Furthermore, such a tax structure would minimize interference with incentives and initiatives.

3. Ease of Administration and Compliance: - - The desirability of social equity and consistency with economic goals in any tax program is necessarily altered by considerations as to the efficiency of the administration of the program by the government and the ease of compliance by the taxpayer. The tax program must lend itself to effective administration at reasonable cost to the government. Similarly, the tax program must reduce to a minimum illegal evasion as well as avoidance through subterfuges and legal loopholes which, if allowed to persist in excess, would render any program unjust and unworkable - no matter how laudatory its social or economic objectives.

4. Revenue Adequacy: - - Revenue to the government must be adequate to provide the collective services required of its citizenry. Traditionally, it was expected that taxes alone would be adequate to balance the annual budget. This position has been modified to tolerate deficits in lean years, provided they were offset by surpluses in good years. In essence, the concept of a balanced annual budget gave way to a cyclically balanced budget. Some modern economists have repudiated the idea of a balanced fiscal budget for the central government and aim, instead, for a balanced economic budget for the nation. In this sense, revenue adequacy is not determined by the fact that government expenditures are covered, but, rather, that required funds can be raised (without borrowing, if necessary) to realize full and stable employment.

F.   THE PROCESS OF TAXATION

   1.   Budget

   As commonly understood, the budget is the forecast by a government of all the expenditures that it will have to cover during a financial year and of the revenue that it will have to raise, after considering and allowing for governmental borrowing. In practice, each department, division, or branch of the government develops and submits its estimates of appropriations for the appropriate fiscal period. After analysis and integration, usually followed by some modification, the estimates are collated. The total reflects the amount of money to be appropriated, after deductions have been made of revenues derived from sources other than from taxation. This amount represents the sum that must be realized by taxation. In the United States there are at least three levels of government, each with its own tax powers: federal, state, and local. States are typically divided into counties, and counties into towns or townships. In turn, these may be further divided into school districts. Taxes for separate districts, such as, school, fire, port, sanitary, and irrigation are usually based upon budgets approved by the respective governing body. Sometimes, incorporated cities and villages replace or are added to these subdivisions. Nevertheless, all have independent or delegated tax powers to meet their budgetary requirements.

   2.   Appropriation

   Upon submission of budgets by the various offices of government, they are circumspectly examined, approved, and then funneled to the body responsible for drafting the appropriation proposal for final debate and enactment into law. Appropriation is the decision of the taxing authority formally enacted into law to meet the expenditures forecast in the budget. The appropriation additionally identifies and itemizes the specific purpose of each expenditure, the amount to be expended for each purpose, and the specific source from which the revenue is to be raised.

   3.   Levy

   The imposition of a tax by the legislative body on a specific source, for a specific amount, for a specific purpose, is known as a tax levy. Taxes may be levied by the federal government, the state, county, city and town, school district, and highway commissioner. They may be levied directly upon real property and personal property, or they may be levied upon income, purchasing power, et cetera. The date of the levy will vary from state to state. In Illinois, for example, general taxes are levied annually, based on the calendar year. They become a lien on January 1 of the tax year and are payable the following year.

   4.   Assessment

   An assessment is the act of assessing, or the specific amount or value assessed. Assessed valuation is the value placed upon real or personal property for taxation purposes by the appropriate governmental authority. Such value may or may not be an indication of the property's market value. Uniformity is the key, and, provided the assessments are uniform and equitable, such valuation serves as a guide to the relative values of similar property in the same assessment jurisdiction. In Illinois, the county assessor must recompute the assessed value on each parcel within his county every four years. Methods of assessing vary considerably. Generally, however, two methods are employed: property is assigned a high assessment value accompanied by a low tax rate, or assigned a low assessment value with a correspondingly higher tax rate. The assessor is an elected official who evaluates property for the purpose of taxation. The assessor's duties are to list all property, and the owners thereof, subject to taxation. This listing is called the assessment roll or the tax list which is completed by the assessor when he places an assessed valuation on each parcel listed. Most states have established boards of taxation which supervise, to some extent, the work of the assessor. This board usually is appointed by the governor. In a few states, however, the board is elected, as in Illinois, where it is called the Board of Equalization. The purpose of such boards is to equalize the assessments of the various taxing jurisdictions rather than handle individual complaints. Individual complaints of the taxpayers are submitted in the form of an appeal. Appeals are provided for by statute and specify boards of commissioners, or supervisors, or courts where the taxpayer may protest the amount assessed. When a taxpayer, upon protest to the taxing officials, is unsuccessful in securing relief, he may appeal to the courts which will review the action of the tax officials. During these proceedings (proceedings "a certiorari"), the tax officials produce their records and certify them to the court in order that the court may render a determination relative to the legality of the taxation process.

5. <u>Computation</u>

To determine the amount of tax to be levied against a specific property, a tax rate must be first established. In establishing this tax rate, the total amount of money to be raised is considered in conjunction with the total assessed value of all taxable property within the taxing district. The amount to be raised is divided by the total assessed value to arrive at the tax rate. This rate is then applied to the assessed value of any particular parcel of land to arrive at the specific tax levy for that parcel. Assume, for example, that the budget figure (after deducting revenues from areas other than real estate) amounts to $500,000, and the assessed value of all property within the taxing district to be $20,000,000. We would determine the tax rate by dividing the $20,000,000 into the $500,000, arriving at a rate of .025 per $1.00, or $25 per $1,000 of assessed valuation. The rate expressed as a decimal (.025) is known as the millage rate. A mill is one-thousandth of one dollar.

The tax thus computed is then entered on the tax books, and, in most instances, becomes a lien on the land until paid. Tax laws usually state that tax liens are superior and take precedence over all other liens, even those that antedate the tax lien.

6. <u>Collection</u>

   a. General

   Tax calendars are usually set by statute. Dates established coordinate with the compilation of the assessment roll (tax list) and the tax computation. Billing and collection procedures vary among the states. In many states, taxes are due when billed, although in most jurisdictions a grace period is allowed during which taxes may be paid without incurring a penalty. Payment of the tax at the proper time, to the appropriate official, discharges the lien. In some states, general taxes are payable in equal installments over the course of the year; in others, one annual payment is required.

b. Discounts

Declining discounts are offered by some states, ranging from four to one percent, if taxes are promptly paid.

c. Penalties

A penalty is the "interest" charged for non-payment of taxes on or before the due date (penalty date). The interest is computed on the amount of taxes unpaid and is usually accumulated as a certain percentage monthly. In Oregon, for example, interest on unpaid taxes accumulates at the rate of two thirds of 1% per month on each quarterly installment from its due date until paid. A fraction of a month is considered as a full month. In Illinois, any amount unpaid after the penalty date (due date) is subject to a one percent a month penalty.

d. Enforcement of Delinquent Taxes

Since taxes become a first lien on the taxed property, normally when billed, non-payment can result in foreclosure proceedings when the statutory period has elapsed from the date of the delinquency. For example, in Illinois tax sales in some counties are held in October, and in other counties in January or February. The owner or other interested persons may redeem real estate sold for delinquent taxes within two years of the date of the sale. After the two year redemption period, the tax sale purchaser is required to notify the delinquent owner and interested parties if he desires to establish ownership. Following such notification, the purchaser may apply for a tax deed. Unsold property subject to delinquent taxes is forfeited to the State and a 12 percent per annum penalty is added.

G. GENERAL CLASSIFICATION OF TAXES

1. <u>According to Effective Rate Structure</u>

Taxes classified according to effective rate structure are known as progressive, proportional, or regressive. The differentiation depends upon the ratio of tax liability to net income or net worth.

   a. Progressive Tax. If the tax takes a greater percentage of one's income as that income increases, the tax is progressive.

   b. Proportional Tax. If the ratio of tax liability to net income or net worth is constant, the tax is known as proportional.

   c. Regressive Tax. If the ratio declines as the income increases, the tax is regressive.

2. <u>According to Who Bears the Final Burden</u>

Taxes may be classified as either direct or indirect depending upon who bears the final liability.

   a. Direct Taxes. Generally, direct taxes are those borne by the persons upon whom the government levies the taxes. Such direct taxes include those levied on net income, net worth, death, gift, and real property.

   b. Indirect Taxes. Consumptive taxes, many business taxes, and payroll taxes are ordinarily considered to be indirect taxes.

3. <u>According to Specific Physical Measurement/Quantity or Value</u>

   a. Specific Tax. A tax or duty is specific when it is based on a physical measurement or quantity, e. g., per ton, per foot, per gallon.

   b. Ad Valorem Tax. A tax or duty is classified as ad valorem (i. e., according to value) when it is based on value and levied as a percentage of that value, e. g., 30 mills per dollar (3.0%) of property value.

4. <u>According to Base</u>

As the American economy matured, new sources of income and wealth were discovered and investigated by legislators and tax planners. Foremost among the taxes which emerged were those classified as income, property, consumptive, and business taxes.

a. Income Tax. The breadth and versatility of income as a tax base can best be pictured if one observes the variety of taxes to which income may be subjected as it flows through a corporation. As income enters the corporate structure, gross receipts or gross income may be taxed; net profits realized after deduction of expenses from gross income may be taxed; excess profit similarly may be subject to taxes. As income flows out of the corporation as dividends, it may be taxed as distributed profit. The dividend, when received by the stockholder, may be taxed as a progressive personal income tax, or perhaps a schedular income tax, whereby different rates are applied to different sources of income. So we see that income may be further subdivided, for tax purposes, into that which is produced and that which is received.

b. Consumptive Tax. Consumptive taxes are those "hidden" taxes passed on to the consumers and are reflected in higher product prices, even though they initially were levied on the producers and distributors.

c. Business Tax. Business taxes generally encompass all taxes resulting from the ownership and operation of businesses. Such taxes bear no relationship to the personal status of the business owner.

d. Property Tax. In the United States, the general property tax is the broadest based of all taxes. It is an impersonal levy which focuses on both personal and real property. The property tax is determined by the property's exchange value and is levied against the property owners. The right to tax <u>real</u> property in the United States falls exclusively within the authority of the individual states. The U. S. Government has no authority to tax real property. Property may be subject to tax, if it is either owned or transferred. Transfers of wealth as a consequence of death are taxed under both estate taxes, which apply to the decedent's estate as a whole, and inheritance, succession, or legacy taxes, which are levied on the heirs' distributive shares. Transfers of wealth by gift are similarly taxed. Our attention now will focus on a more detailed examination of the property tax.

H. PROPERTY TAXES

1. Property Taxes in General

In Colonial days, property taxes had their beginnings as levies on specific forms of property with emphasis on land and houses. While taxes were levied on capital value, as opposed to rental value, such levies were often arbitrarily imposed. Land might be classified as arable, pasture, or woodland, and the value per acre would apply equally within a specific classification. Houses were valued according to the number of windows, doors, or chimneys. Various classes of personal property were also subject to taxation. Thus, the general property tax reflects a levy on all property, real (corporeal and incorporeal) and personal (tangible and intangible). Following the Civil War, various classes of property were withdrawn from the general property tax category simply because of the increasing difficulty in placing levies on personal property, particularly intangible personal property. Intangible personal property so regularly evaded assessment that in many states the applicable tax is only nominal. Tangible personal property, likewise, eludes assessment. Used household furniture and clothing, et cetera, realistically have little or no real market value. Moreover, such items may easily be concealed from assessors who venture across the threshold. As a consequence, personal property, both tangible and intangible, has lost its importance as a tax base to the extent that in many states only real estate remains subject to the property tax.

2. Real Estate Taxes Specifically

Real estate is both immobile (with the exception of mobile homes and houseboats) and visible. Consequently, the brunt of property tax levies are borne by real property. Unfortunately, much hardship is endured by property taxpayers as a result of inequalities in the real property taxes. Valuation of real estate is a task calling for considerable expertise, and local assessors have not always been selected for their technical competence. Coupled with political pressures, serious inequalities in the distribution of the property tax burden have evolved. Property owners, therefore, have continuously sought protection from arbitrary and excessive taxes through state legislation - which fixes the maximum rate that can be levied by local authorities. While such limits have been broadly adopted, they, too, have often proved arbitrary and have resulted in unbalanced local budgets which, in turn, have adversely affected local government services.

In striving to develop a criterion for a real estate tax policy which embraces social equity, consistency with economic goals, ease of administration, and revenue adequacy, we become involved in the process which frames the real estate tax program. This process relates to budget, appropriation, levy, assessment, computation, and collection.

I. TYPES OF REAL ESTATE TAXES

1. General

Adam Smith, writing on the sources of revenue reflects . . . "the private revenue of individuals . . . arises ultimately from three different sources: Rent, Profit, and Wages. Every tax must finally be paid from someone or the other of those three different sorts of revenue, or from all of them indifferently." Rent (more accurately, economic rent) is the income derived from the ownership of land. Profit is the income received by the owners of capital (i. e., all the "produced" instruments of production - to include factories, structures, equipment, raw materials, finished products, trade facilities, et cetera). Wages are the form of payment for the use of labor. Land, labor, and capital are factors in production without which production could not take place. Real estate taxes relate to the income generated through two of these factors - land and capital. These taxes include real property taxes, capital gain taxes, and income taxes.

2. Real Property Taxes

Real property taxes do not fall within the realm of the federal government. They are direct taxes levied against individuals parcels of land by the city, town, county, or village.

3. Capital Gain Taxes

Capital Gain Taxes are those applied to gain or profit realized on the sale or exchange of capital assets. The principal capital assets are properties held for investment or for personal use.

4. Income Taxes

Income Taxes relative to real estate are those taxes applied to the net income realized from the management and ownership of real property.

J. TAX CLASSIFICATION OF REAL ESTATE

1. General

In order to predict the probable tax consequence of a proposed real estate transaction, it is necessary for the taxpayer to determine specifically the nature of his holding of the property. Proper identification of the precise type may control the incidence of federal income, estate, and gift taxes. As an example, the sale of real estate held for investment may result in a gain which is subject to a capital gain tax. The sale of this same real estate held for resale will be taxed as ordinary income. Generally, real estate can be categorized into the following five types of holdings for tax consideration:

      a. Real estate held as a personal residence;
      b. Real estate held for investment;
      c. Real estate held for sale to customers;
      d. Real estate held for the production of income;
      e. Real estate held for use in trade or business.

2. Real Estate Held as Personal Residence

Residence is defined as that property used as the taxpayer's principal residence. It may be a houseboat or a trailer. If the taxpayer lives in and is a stockholder in a cooperative apartment corporation, his stock would qualify. So, too, would a condominium.

Expenses incurred for personal, living, family purposes, repair and maintenance, are non-deductible on real estate held as a personal residence. Nor is depreciation allowed as a deduction. Any loss incurred as a consequence of sale is nondeductible... yet a gain is taxed as a capital gain. On the other hand, however, interest paid on a mortgage loan and real property taxes are deductible. The owner of a personal residence may, in certain instances, defer any gain realized on the sale of such property, provided he purchases a new home at a price at least equaling the proceeds realized from the sale. The special treatment applies, if the taxpayer -

a. buys a new residence and uses it as his principal residence within one year before or after he sells his old residence, or

b. he starts to build a new residence before or within a year after he sells the old residence and uses the new property as his principal residence within 18 months after he sells his old residence.

If the taxpayer meets either test, gain is recognized only to the extent that the adjusted sales price of the old residence exceeds the cost of the new residence.

3. Real Estate Held for Investment

This type of real estate holding is usually limited to unimproved real estate held for the purpose of capital growth through increases in real estate prices. Owners of such property are entitled to deduct all expenses incurred for conservation and maintenance. Taxes and carrying charges on unimproved investment property may be capitalized or deducted at the owner's option. Gains and losses resulting from either sales or exchanges are taxed as capital transactions.

4. Real Estate Held for Sale to Customers

The owner of real estate held for sale to customers in the ordinary course of the owner's trade or business is entitled to deduct all expenses incurred relative to the property, to include repairs, maintenance, casualty losses, interest and taxes. Deduction for depreciation is not allowed. Sales of such property are regarded as ordinary income transactions, not capital transactions. Any gain realized is taxed as ordinary income, and any loss suffered is deductible as an ordinary loss.

5. Real Estate Held for the Production of Income

Real estate held for the production of income, but not used in the trade or business of the taxpayer, is a capital asset similar to real estate held for investment. However, the owner of property held for the production of income is entitled to deduct an allowance for depreciation. Whether or not such property actually produced income is immaterial. The owner need only establish the fact that such property was held during the taxable year for such purpose.

6. Real Estate Held for Use in Trade or Business

This particular type of holding is given the most favorable treatment under the tax laws. Since depreciable property used in trade or business is not a capital asset by definition, gains and losses from its sale or exchange normally would be ordinary. A special rule, however, allows the taxpayer the advantage of treating certain gains as capital gains and certain losses as ordinary losses when such property is held over six months. This is known as "Section 1231" treatment. Since losses incurred in sales or exchanges occurred in the taxpayer's trade or business, he is entitled to treat such loss as a part of his net operating loss for the purpose of carryover, if the loss is not entirely absorbed in the year suffered.

K. TAX EFFECTS OF REAL ESTATE TRANSACTIONS

As reflected above, every real estate transaction alters the financial status of the contracting parties. Real estate brokers have a responsibility to their selling clients and buying customers to insure that they receive competent legal and financial advice relative to their altered status. Buyers and sellers in most real estate transactions have alternative methods of acquiring and disposing of real property. Each method normally will reflect varying advantages and disadvantages, and invariably one specific method will prove financially most beneficial to one or both parties. As a consequence of the many ways in which one's tax return can be affected by a real estate transaction, it behooves all real estate brokers, in fulfilling their responsibilities to their clients and customers, to insure that they receive expert counseling relative to the tax consequences of a transaction.

L. TAX ADVANTAGE OF HOME OWNERSHIP

The competent real estate broker will be aware of his responsibilities to advise his buying customers of the tax impact of their real estate investment. The following figures illustrate the actual financial implications as they affect the purchaser of a $40,000 home.

We will assume this taxpayer files the long form 1040 and itemizes his expense deductions on Schedule A.

If our purchaser secures a conventional 80% mortgage loan of $32,000 (80% of $40,000), his cash investment (down payment) will be $8,000 (20% of $40,000). Supposing his loan extends for 25 years at a 7½% interest . . . we arrive at a figure of $236.48, representing the combined monthly principal and interest payment, exclusive of the tax.

The purchaser's first monthly payment reflects a $200 interest payment and $36.48 applied to the reduction of the principal. The real estate broker must not fail to consider the inevitable tax payment, assumed in this example to be $130 per month, and an insurance premium payment of $20 per month. Thus, total monthly outlay to enjoy home ownership would appear to total $386.48. At the close of the tax year, however, our purchaser's financial posture is not quite so bleak.

On Schedule A., Form 1040, this taxpayer may deduct for the entire year his total loan interest payments as well as his total property tax payment. Should this purchaser be in the 40% bracket, he is entitled to deduct 40% of the interest and tax payment or $132 (Interest, $200 and Tax, $130 x .40). In effect, his monthly payment as a homeowner, because of the compensating tax aspect, is reduced from $386.48 to a more palatable $254.48. Furthermore, the monthly principal payment of $36.48 is actually a savings representing our purchaser's equity in the purchased property.

As a consequence of his investment, this taxpayer's actual cost of home ownership is $218 per month - rather than the $386.48, which appears to be the cost when accepted without further analysis.

M. DIVERSITY OF TAX SYSTEMS

There are as many local and state tax systems in the United States as there are states. The states may venture into practically every area at the disposal of the federal government for taxation purposes. The only major restriction is that states may not tax interstate commerce. Thus, only customs duties are not available to state authorities. Local subdivisions are delegated tax powers by the state. Such tax powers of the smaller units of government, however, are usually confined to the property tax - which accounts for the major part of their revenues.

Although the systems are so diverse, generally they will follow a pattern.

1. The assessor(s) place a valuation on a property, as a whole or divided between the value of the land and the value of the improvements thereon.

The homeowner has the right to protest an excessive assessment to the assessor(s) and, if unsuccessful, to the courts.

2. The tax bill is forwarded to the property owner. The rate may be expressed in mills (thousandths of a dollar - .050), or in dollars per hundred - $5.00, or in dollars per thousand - $50.

At this point, the taxpayer may request a reduction or "abatement of taxes" from municipal authorities; again, if unsuccessful, he may appeal to the courts.

CRITERIA FOR TAX POLICY

1. Social Equity

2. Consistency with Economic Goals

3. Ease of Administration and Compliance

4. Revenue Adequacy

THE PROCESS OF TAXATION

1. Budget
2. Appropriation
3. Levy
4. Assessment
5. Computation
6. Collection

GENERAL CLASSIFICATION OF TAXES

1. According to Effective Rate Structure

2. According to Who Bears the Final Burden

3. According to Specific Quantity or Value

4. According to Base

CLASSIFICATION OF TAXES ACCORDING TO EFFECTIVE RATE STRUCTURE

1. Progressive Tax
2. Proportional Tax
3. Regressive Tax

CLASSIFICATION OF TAXES
ACCORDING TO
WHO BEARS THE FINAL BURDEN

1. Direct Taxes
2. Indirect Taxes

CLASSIFICATION OF TAXES
ACCORDING TO
SPECIFIC MEASUREMENT, QUANTITY OR VALUE

1. Specific Tax
2. Ad Valorem Tax

CLASSIFICATION OF TAXES
ACCORDING TO
BASE

1. Income Tax
2. Consumptive Tax
3. Business Tax
4. Property Tax

TAX CLASSIFICATION OF REAL ESTATE

REAL ESTATE HELD FOR:

1. Personal Residence
2. Investment
3. Sale to Customers
4. Production of Income
5. Use in Trade or Business

TYPES OF REAL ESTATE TAXES

1. Real Property Taxes
2. Capital Gain Taxes
3. Income Taxes

Chapter 8

REVIEW DEFINITIONS IN GLOSSARY OR TEXT OF FOLLOWING TERMS:

"ability to pay" principle
ad valorem
appeal
appropriation
assessed valuation
assessment
assessment roll
assessor
"benefit" principle
board of equalization
budget
business tax
capital gains
capital gain tax
consumptive tax
direct tax
fiscal

income tax
indirect tax
levy
mill
penalty
proceeding "a certiorari"
progressive tax
property tax
proportional tax
real estate tax
real property tax
regressive tax
revenue
specific tax
tax
tax list

REVIEW QUESTIONS:

1. As citizens, what are our most important obligations to the government in return for services demanded of it?

2. What new taxes came into being during World War I?

3. What taxes are levied at state level?

4. What is the first principle of taxation?

5. What are the considerations in regard to the "ability to pay" principle?

6. What determines the amount of money to be realized by taxation?

7. Name three levels of government which have their own tax power.

8. What are the two methods employed in assessing?

9. How is a tax rate established?

10. Name the five types of real estate holdings for tax consideration.

11. What is Section 1231 ?

12. What are the only taxes not available to state governments ?

FOR ANSWERS TO REVIEW QUESTIONS:

1.

2.

3.

4.

5.

6.

7.

8.

9.

10.

11.

12.

Chapter 9

Principles of Economics and Real Estate Appraising

A.	ECONOMICS IN REAL ESTATE	209
B.	ON VALUE IN GENERAL	209

    1. What Is Value   209
    2. The Two Meanings of Value   209
    3. Elements of Value   210

        a. Utility   210
        b. Scarcity   210
        c. Demand   210
        d. Transferability   210

    4. Types of Value   210

C. COST AND PRICE IN RELATION TO VALUE   211

    1. Cost   211
    2. Price   211
    3. Value   211

D. FORCES INFLUENCING VALUE   211

    1. General   211
    2. Physical Forces   211
    3. Economic Forces   211
    4. Social Forces   211
    5. Political Forces   211

E. ECONOMIC PRINCIPLES AFFECTING VALUE   212

    1. Principle of Supply   212
    2. Principle of Demand   212
    3. Principle of Progression   212
    4. Principle of Regression   212
    5. Principle of Conformity   212
    6. Principle of Change   213
    7. Principle of Substitution   213
    8. Principle of Highest and Best Use   213
    9. Principle of Diminishing Returns   213

F.	FACTORS IN PRODUCTION WHICH AFFECT VALUE		213
	1. General		213
	2. Land		213
	3. Labor		213
	4. Capital		213
G.	REAL ESTATE APPRAISALS - GENERAL		214
	1. What Is An Appraisal?		214
	2. Purpose of An Appraisal		214
	3. Functions of An Appraisal		214
	4. Market Value Defined		214
	5. The Appraisal Process		214
	6. Appraisal Approaches		215
		a. Market Data Approach	215
		b. Cost Approach	215
		c. Income Approach	215
H.	THE APPRAISAL PROCESS		215
	1. General		215
	2. Defining the Problem		215
	3. Developing the Overall Plan of Action		215
	4. Initiating the Collection Effort		216
		a. General Data	216
		b. Specific Data	216
	5. Processing the Data Collected		216
	6. Applying Processed Data to Appraisal Approaches		217
	7. Arriving at Final Estimate of Value		217
	8. Finalizing the Appraisal Report		217
I.	MARKET DATA APPROACH IN APPRAISING		217
J.	COST APPROACH IN APPRAISING		218
	1. General		218
	2. Accrued Depreciation		218
		a. Physical Deterioration	218
		b. Functional Obsolescence	218
		c. Economic Obsolescence	218

	3.	Methods of Estimating Reproduction Cost		218
		a.	Quantity-Survey Method	218
		b.	Unit-in-Place Method	219
		c.	Comparative Method	219
	4.	Reproduction Cost and Replacement Cost Differentiated		219
		a.	Reproduction Cost	219
		b.	Replacement Cost	219
K.	INCOME APPROACH IN APPRAISING			219
	1.	General		219
	2.	Gross Rent Multiplier (Conversion Factor)		220

VISUAL AIDS 220

REVIEW QUESTIONS 224

Chapter 9
Principles of Economics
and
Real Estate Appraising

A. ECONOMICS IN REAL ESTATE

The REALTORS' Code of Ethics, as amended at the 1974 Annual Convention, in describing the REALTORS' relations to the public, describes the REALTOR as one who " . . . should keep himself informed on matters affecting real estate in his community, the state, and the nation, so that he may be able to contribute responsibly to public thinking on such matters." The same code states, "In justice to those who place their interest in his care, the REALTOR should endeavor always to be informed regarding laws, proposed legislation, governmental regulations, public policies, and current market conditions in order to be in a position to advise his clients properly."

To be so informed on matters affecting real estate and current market conditions, and to be able to ascertain what facts are pertinent relative to the properties for which he accepts the agency - infers that the REALTOR must have some knowledge of the principles of economics and a general idea of the appraisal process. So important is such knowledge to every real estate broker and salesman that proof of such knowledge, at a rudimentary level at least, has been made a requirement for licensing in most states.

B. ON VALUE IN GENERAL

1. <u>What Is Value</u>: - - Value in real estate, as in other capital goods, is the present worth of anticipated future benefits from ownership. Value is described in many ways. It is the capacity of an economic good to command other goods in exchange. It represents that price at which supply and demand coincide on the market. Value, then, is determined by the intersection of supply and demand.

2. The Two Meanings of Value: - - The word value, according to Adam Smith, has two different meanings. When used to express the utility of some particular object, it is called "value in use". When used to express the power of a commodity in purchasing other goods, it is called "value in exchange." "The things which have the greatest value in use," according to Smith, "have frequently little or no value in exchange; and, on the contrary, those which have the greatest value in exchange frequently have little or no value in use. Nothing is more useful than water, but it will purchase scarcely anything; scarcely anything can be had in exchange for it. A diamond, on the contrary, has limited value in use, but a very great quantity of other goods may frequently be had in exchange for it." "Value in use"

is sometimes referred to as subjective value. "Value in exchange" is more commonly known as "market value" and is sometimes referred to as objective value.

3. Elements of Value: - - Value is a composite of four elements:

    a. Utility - While a commodity may be scarce, if it lacks utility, there will be no demand.

    b. Scarcity - Air, for example, has unquestioned utility and demand, but is so plentiful that it has little value in commerce.

    c. Demand - Demand follows utility. To be effective, however, demand must be supported by purchasing power.

    d. Transferability - To have value in the market, a commodity, or title to the commodity must be transferable.

All are essential elements; none alone suffices to create value.

4. Types of Value: - - There are, of course, other concepts of value used in the real estate business which are included here for identification purposes and because one of these types of values may be required in an appraisal assignment.

    a. Assessed Value. The valuation placed on property by local or county assessors for property taxation purposes.

    b. Investment Value. Value in use based on the productivity of real estate.

    c. Book Value. Value of assets as reflected on the books of a business. It bears no relation to market value.

    d. Insurable Value. Fire insurance value used as a base to calculate the amount of insurance that should be carried on destructible portions of realty.

    e. Reasonable Value. Amount a purchaser would be justified in paying for a particular property under current market conditions.

    f. Rental Value. The rental that a property would command on the open market at a specific time.

    g. Salvage Value. Price obtainable for all or parts of a building upon removal from the site and use or assemblage elsewhere.

    h. Scrap Value. Price obtainable for materials in a dismantled structure to be sold for scrap.

Additionally, there are many other references to value, such as par value, tax value, cash value, capital value, speculative value, true value, exchange value, reproduction value, replacement value, and cost value.

C. COST AND PRICE IN RELATION TO VALUE

General - The terms cost, price, and value are frequently used by the general public interchangeably; however, to the economist, each has its specific, individual meaning.

1. <u>Cost</u>: - - Cost relates to <u>past</u> expenditures (money, material, labor, etc.) to produce or acquire a commodity.

2. <u>Price</u>: - - Price is the amount <u>presently</u> asked for a commodity. Price infers that the commodity is for sale.

3. <u>Value</u>: - - Value relates to <u>present</u> worth and <u>future</u> anticipated benefits. While cost may affect value, neither cost nor price are synonymous with value.

D. FORCES INFLUENCING VALUE

1. <u>General</u>: - - In Chapter 7 - ON THE NATURE OF PROPERTY, it was stated that in the area of property law the term property itself is meaningless. It assumes a meaning only upon association with an individual. The relationship is inseparable. What affects one will affect the other. Those same forces which affect the growth, development, and progress of man also affect property and all aspects of property including its value. These forces may be categorized as:

    a. Physical
    b. Economic
    c. Social
    d. Political

2. <u>Physical Forces</u>: - - Physical forces, some wrought by nature - others created by man - create, preserve, modify, and sometimes destroy value. Temperature, precipitation, soil, topography, drainage, mineral resources, pests, natural boundaries, maintenance or lack thereof, et cetera, all have an effect on the value of property.

3. <u>Economic Forces</u>: - - Economic forces have a marked effect on property value. These include: natural resources, business, commercial, and industrial trends. Everything that relates to the economic health of a community is an economic force which influences value.

4. <u>Social Forces</u>: - - Customs, traditions, attitudes, instincts, and desires of a people are factors exerting social forces which influence property values. Man has been described as a social animal. Factors which relate to the society he moves in would include: fluctuations in population size; rates of marriage, divorce, births, and deaths; grouping by ethnic background, stratification by sex and age grouping; religious, philosophical, educational, cultural, recreational, and other social and aesthetic considerations. These factors make up the social forces which also influence the value of property.

5. <u>Political Forces</u>: - - Political forces which relate to property values would include: zoning ordinances; building codes; administration of health, safety,

and welfare systems and programs; availability of government housing; government insured or guaranteed loans; rent controls; and fiscal policies relating to the availability of money and credit.

All of these forces are in a constant state of fluctuation and change. All are interwoven and interdependent. All influence value trends and must be understood and considered by professional real estate brokers.

E.   ECONOMIC PRINCIPLES AFFECTING VALUE

An understanding of the following economic principles affecting value is essential for real estate agents to clearly grasp an insight into why, when, and how changes take place in their market area. Many of these principles are inseverably connected. Some are interrelated; others are interdependent. For example, scarcity diminishes supply which accentuates demand which influences price and increases profits which stimulate competition in a free society. Competition tends to relieve scarcity by increasing supply which satisfies demand, thereby moderating prices and consequently reducing profits which dilutes demand and once again diminishes supply. Thus, the cyclical effect of these principles is seen as they play themselves out in any given market area. It then becomes the real estate agent's responsibility not only to understand each principle independently, but also to recognize what cyclical position the applicable principles have reached and what course is developing in his market area.

1.   <u>Principle of Supply</u>: - - The principle of supply holds that the greater the supply of a commodity, the lower its value. Scarcity influences supply and, conversely, increases value. If demand is constant, an increase in supply will almost certainly reduce price and increase the quantity bought and sold. The results of a decrease in supply are the opposite.

2.   <u>Principle of Demand</u>: - - The principle of demand holds that the greater the demand for a commodity, the higher its value. Generally, if demand is constant, an increase in demand will raise price. With less certainty, perhaps, it will also increase the quantity bought and sold. Similarly, a decrease in demand has the opposite effect.

3.   <u>Principle of Progression</u>: - - The principle of progression holds that properties of higher value will enhance the value of a lower value property in their proximity.

4.   <u>Principle of Regression</u>: - - The principle of regression holds that properties of lower value will adversely affect the value of a better property in their proximity.

5.   <u>Principle of Conformity</u>: - - The principle of conformity holds that property reaches and maintains its highest value when its utilization conforms with essential and permissible land uses.

6. **Principle of Change:** -- The principle of change holds that everything is in a state of continuous movement and change, of continuous renewal and development, where something is always arising and developing, and something is always decaying and disintegrating. Individual properties, neighborhoods, areas, districts, towns, and cities are continually affected by this principle. In considering the value of property, that which must be considered primary is not what is apparently durable but is, in fact, in a state of decline. Rather consider those values which are improving and developing . . . even if at a given moment they may not appear to be durable.

7. **Principle of Substitution:** -- The principle of substitution holds that the maximum value of a property is determined, to a considerable extent, by the cost of the timely acquisition of a substitute property.

8. **Principle of Highest and Best Use:** -- This principle maintains that the value of property is greatest when it is adapted to that use which, at a given time, will yield the highest return and continue in demand in the foreseeable future.

9. **Principle of Diminishing Returns:** -- More appropriately referred to as the "law of diminishing returns", this principle holds that an increase in some inputs (relating to the factors in production, i.e., land, labor, capital), as these inputs relate to other fixed inputs, will cause the total output of a commodity, which the inputs help produce, to increase until a point is reached when the extra output resulting from similar additions of extra inputs is likely to become less and less.

F. FACTORS IN PRODUCTION WHICH AFFECT VALUE

1. **General:** -- The factors (sometimes called "agents") in production are a necessary condition for production; without these factors, production could not take place at all. Productive factors are generally classified into three groups:

    a. Land
    b. Labor
    c. Capital

2. **Land:** -- Land represents a resource which is limited in supply when compared to demand. Land cannot be increased as the result of production. The income derived from ownership of land is called economic rent.

3. **Labor:** -- Labor represents all the productive resources that can be applied only at the cost of human effort. Wages or salary are the payment for the use of labor.

4. **Capital:** -- Capital is the complex factor in production. Simply stated, capital refers to all the "produced" instruments of production. These would include investment in factories, structures, equipment, raw material, finished products, trade facilities, et cetera. The owners of capital receive their income in many forms; profits and interest are the usual ones.

G. REAL ESTATE APPRAISALS - GENERAL

1. What Is An Appraisal ? An appraisal is an <u>estimate</u> and <u>opinion</u> of the value of a property <u>as of a specific date</u>. More specifically, it is a conclusion of value logically based upon a careful study of general and specific data. A formal appraisal is a written estimate of value certified by one **represented as an expert because of** training, experience, and expertise.

2. <u>Purpose of An Appraisal</u>: - - The purpose of any appraisal is to render an estimate of the value being sought. We have seen from foregoing paragraphs that there are many different classifications of value, any of which may be desired for a particular purpose. By far the most common purpose of an appraisal is for the estimation of a property's <u>market</u> <u>value</u>.

3. <u>Functions of An Appraisal</u>: - - The function of an appraisal is the specific use to which the estimate of value will be put. Use varies considerably and the appraisal may be conducted in order to:

   a. Establish a selling price.
   b. Establish a bid or offering price.
   c. Establish a basis for **property exchange**.
   d. Establish a price for condemnation **proceedings**.
   e. Assist courts in foreclosure proceeding.
   f. Establish basis for assessments.
   g. Establish basis for property insurance.
   h. Establish basis for inheritance taxes.
   i. Assist in investment decisions.
   j. Establish depreciation schedules.
   k. Assist in arriving at book value.
   l. Aid in setting rents.
   m. Assist in settling damage claims.
   n. Establish cost estimates.
   o. Aid in distribution of estate assets.
   p. Establish credit standing.

4. <u>Market Value Defined</u>: - - Market value is the highest **price** estimated in terms of money for which a property will sell in a competitive market at a particular time by a seller to a buyer, each acting prudently and without obligation to act, with knowledge of the uses to which the property can be adapted, and for which it is capable of being used.

5. <u>The Appraisal Process:</u> - - The techniques used by the appraiser to arrive at his estimate of value have been standardized to a significant **degree.** The collection, recording, evaluation, interpretation, and reporting procedures have been approached scientifically. The entire system, from defining the appraisal problem to the arrival at the final estimate of value, is known as **The Appraisal Process** and is more fully explored in Paragraph H of this chapter.

6. <u>Appraisal Approaches</u>: - - There are three generally accepted approaches (methods) in arriving at an estimate of value:

   a. Market Data Approach. (Also known as the Sales Approach, the Comparison Approach, or the Direct Sales Comparison Approach). This method compares the property with similar properties which have been sold recently or are currently on the market in the same area or in competing areas. (See Paragraph I, below.)

   b. Cost Approach. (Also known as the Replacement Cost Approach and the Reproduction Cost Approach). This approach adds to the value of the land the cost of all improvements minus depreciation. (See Paragraph J, below.)

   c. Income Approach. (Also known as the Capitalization Approach and the Gross Rent Multiplier Approach). The estimate of value is established by considering the present and anticipated income from the property. (See Paragraph K, below.)

H. THE APPRAISAL PROCESS

1. <u>General</u>: - - The Appraisal Process is a systematic procedure of defining the problem of the appraisal and then developing the plan for collecting, recording, evaluating, interpreting, and reporting the data required to solve the problem. The appraisal process may be broken down into the following steps:

   a. Defining the problem.
   b. Developing the overall plan of action.
   c. Initiating the collection effort.
   d. Processing the data collected.
   e. Applying the processed data to the appraisal approaches.
   f. Arriving at a final estimate of value.
   g. Finalizing the appraisal report.

2. <u>Defining the Problem</u>: - - Before the appraiser can proceed to collect and process any data he must first determine precisely what he is required to do and why. In defining an appraisal problem the following factors must be considered:

   a. Establish the effective date of the appraisal.
   b. Identify the real estate (corporeal and incorporeal)
   c. Establish the purpose of the appraisal.
   d. Advise the client of estimated time required and cost.

3. <u>Developing the Overall Plan of Action</u>: - - A carefully developed plan of action is necessary if the appraisal is to be complete and accurate, timely, and economic. In the overall development of the plan the following elements relating to both the quantity and quality of the appraisal must be incorporated:

a. Identify pertinent supply and demand factors.
b. Identify data requirements.
c. Identify and develop sources of information.
d. Determine best approaches to employ.
e. Develop detailed research program.
f. Outline the appraisal report.
g. Schedule the work program, and
h. Assign priorities.

4. <u>Initiating the Collection Effort</u>: -- The appraiser's final estimate of value can be neither better nor more complete than the information from which it is derived. The timely collection of complete, accurate, and pertinent information is, perhaps, the most difficult and time-consuming step in the appraisal process. The required appraisal data may be classified as <u>general</u> and <u>specific.</u>

   a. General Data. General data encompasses regional, city, and neighborhood information and takes into consideration those forces (i.e., physical, economic, social, and political) and principles (supply, demand, et cetera) which influence and affect value.

   b. Specific Data. Specific data relates to the site and to the property itself. It includes the following information: title information, type of ownership, physical description of land and improvements, services and utilities, tax information, and highest and best use.

5. <u>Processing the Data Collected</u>: -- Processing the data collected logically consists of three analytical operations: recording, evaluation, and interpretation. Normally, information will be processed in accordance with its importance.

   a. Recording. Recording is reducing the collected data to writing or some form of graphical representation and then grouping related items together. Recording makes subsequent interpretation easier, more accurate, and facilitates the final preparation of the appraisal report by having together all available information on a specific facet of the appraisal in a convenient form.

   b. Evaluation. Evaluation is a critical appraisal of the data collected as a basis for its subsequent interpretation. It includes:

      (1) Pertinence of the information.
      (2) Reliability of the <u>source</u> of the information.
      (3) Accuracy of the information.

   c. Interpretation. Interpretation determines the significance of the information with respect to what is already known. It develops probable meaning of evaluated information. Interpretation is the result of critical judgment and involves two stages:

(1) Analysis. Analysis is the taking apart or the sifting and sorting of evaluated information.

(2) Integration. Integration is the putting back together, or the combination of those elements isolated in analysis to form a logical picture.

6. <u>Applying Processed Data to Appraisal Approaches</u>: - - There are potentially three appraisal approaches which can be employed to arrive at a final estimate of value. Initially, the appraiser should <u>consider</u> all approaches. In some instances all three may be used; in other cases circumstances may suggest that only one approach may be feasible.

7. <u>Arriving at Final Estimate of Value</u>: - - The entire procedure and the results of the appraisal procedure should now be reviewed by the appraiser. Most appraisal assignments call for an indication of the most probable market value figure or the <u>range</u> within which the market value most probably falls. This figure, because it is an <u>estimate</u>, should be appropriate and rounded off to preclude any criticism that the <u>estimate</u> makes claim to an unwarranted degree of precision. The correlation of the values indicated in the approaches used is not an arithmetical average but an overall determination based on the appraiser's knowledge, experience, judgment, and analysis of <u>all</u> the information collected and processed.

8. <u>Finalizing the Appraisal Report</u>: - - The final written appraisal report should reflect the procedures followed by the appraiser and should communicate convincingly the logic employed in arriving at his final estimate of value. The report should be sufficiently complete to stand alone.

I. MARKET DATA APPROACH IN APPRAISING

The market data approach is especially applicable in appraising residential properties in an active market where, as the name suggests, the market data on sales of comparable properties give an indication of what the appraised property may sell for under specific market conditions at a particular time. The basic economic principle relating to this approach is the Principle of Substitution. It is important when using this approach that the properties selected for comparison be carefully selected. In addition, the appraiser must be alert to conditions and circumstances attending the properties selected. Considerations not always clearly evident may substantially affect the selling price or current market price. Some of these considerations are the length of time the property sold remained on the market and the terms and conditions of sale enjoyed by the buyer, which, if lenient and favorable, would have a tendency to result in a higher sales price. Personal property accompanying the sale or the inclusion of additional property rights would have a similar effect. Whether or not major repairs and improvements have been made, or if modern fixtures have been installed, would be considerations affecting price and would explain substantial variance in price. Comparative sales should be as recent as possible.

J. COST APPROACH IN APPRAISING

1. <u>General</u>: - - Cost Approach (sometimes known as the Summation Approach) is based on the cost of production and tends to give the <u>upper limit</u> of a property's value. This approach is especially useful when market activity is insufficient to provide meaningful comparables or where the uniqueness of the appraised property or its special purpose affords little comparable sales information. It is a useful approach in appraising new or proposed construction. Employing the Cost Approach, the appraiser must first estimate the value of the land by viewing it as if it were vacant and available to be put to its highest and best use. The appraiser would then determine the estimated reproduction cost of the building and other improvements. It will then be necessary to calculate the accrued depreciation suffered by the building and other improvement and then deduct this depreciation from the reproduction cost new in order to estimate the present worth of the buildings and improvements. The estimated present worth of the building and improvements would then be added to the estimated value of the land to arrive at an indication of the market value of the appraised property via the Cost Approach. The estimation of accrued depreciation is a difficult task and presents the appraiser with one of his more serious problems. This approach requires a higher degree of training and ability than either of the other methods.

2. <u>Accrued Depreciation</u>: - - Accrued depreciation need be estimated only in the Cost Approach. Accrued depreciation is the aggregate of all depreciation which has accumulated as of the date of the appraisal. There are three causes of depreciation:

   a. Physical Deterioration. Any impairment of the physical condition of the property through age, use, and action of the elements.

   b. Functional Obsolescence. Functional obsolescence is inherent in the property and is manifested by <u>internal</u> deficiencies such as over-capacity, inadequacy, inefficient design, et cetera.

   c. Economic Obsolescence. Economic obsolescence is the result of <u>external</u> causes such as restrictive zoning, changes in the character of the area, et cetera.

3. <u>Methods of Estimating Reproduction Cost</u>: - - In estimating the reproduction cost new of all improvements on the property, the methods of estimation are:

   a. The Quantity-Survey Method. This method is used primarily by cost estimators and contractors. It necessitates taking inventory of all materials and equipment of which the property is composed and applying to this inventory the current price of such material and equipment, labor costs, overhead costs and fees necessary to construct a suitable replacement. Special knowledge, which few appraisers have, is required to use this method. Normally, this method would not be economically feasible.

b. Unit-in-Place Method. The unit in place method requires pricing, on a linear or square foot basis, the different units of the structure (e. g., walls, floors, roof covering, et cetera) and using installed costs on doors, windows, plumbing fixtures, electrical outlets, et cetera. This is a modification of the Quantity-Survey Method.

c. Comparative Method. In this method, building costs are estimated by comparison of the property being appraised with similar newly constructed buildings whose costs are known and have been reduced to units per square foot of floor area of living space - or per cubic foot of the building content.

4. Reproduction Cost and Replacement Cost Differentiated: - - Reproduction is a term which relates to the physical property while replacement relates to the use of the property.

a. Reproduction Cost. Reproduction cost is generally accepted as being the cost to reproduce an exact replica of the property. Generally, this would be impractical because of outmoded construction practices, unavailability of materials, et cetera. This approach, consequently, would be more appropriately called the "replacement cost approach". Some appraisals, nevertheless, are made to determine the reproduction costs, such as those involving insurance claims.

b. Replacement Cost. Replacement cost is the current cost of replacing a new property having the equivalent utility of the property being appraised.

K. INCOME APPROACH IN APPRAISING

1. General: - - The Income Approach is the valuation of real estate based on the anticipated income the real estate will earn. This approach is especially applicable in the evaluation of income-producing property, although it is seldom used as the only method in determining the value of such property. Where residential properties are in an area where such properties are rented in significant numbers, the Income Approach may be used quite effectively as there is a tendency for the ratio between the sales price of the property and the gross monthly unfurnished rental to be rather consistent for the same type of property in the same market at the same time. In some neighborhoods the number of residential properties in a rental status may be too meager to justify the use of the Income Approach. When that approach is employed, it is important that reasonably similar properties be used for comparison. It is important, also, that the property rent used is "economic rent" which is the rent actually being received. Before the Income Approach (sometimes referred to as the Capitalization Approach

or the Gross Rent Multiplier Approach) can be used as a method in determining the market value of the property being appraised, it is necessary to ascertain the "Gross Rent Multiplier" of the unfurnished rental properties which are to be used as comparables.

2. <u>Gross Rent Multiplier (Conversion Factor)</u>: - - The "gross rent multiplier" is the number which reflects the ratio between the sales price of a residential property and its monthly <u>unfurnished</u> rental. The gross rent multiplier is also called the "conversion factor". It is determined by simply dividing the selling price of a property by the amount of the monthly rental. If, for example, a comparable residential property which rented for $200 per month sold for $20,000, the gross rent multiplier (or conversion factor) would be 100 ($20,000 ÷ $200). To apply this gross rent multiplier the economic rent of subject property would be determined and then multiplied by the gross rent multiplier to arrive at an estimated market value. If subject property could command a monthly rent of $225, this figure would be multiplied by the conversion factor for the neighborhood of 100 (gross rent multiplier) which would indicate an estimated market value of $22,500 for subject property.

THE TWO MEANINGS OF VALUE

1. VALUE IN USE:
Subjective value

2. VALUE IN EXCHANGE:
Objective value (mkt. value)

ELEMENTS OF VALUE

1. **Utility**
2. **Scarcity**
3. **Demand**
4. **Transferability**

COST AND PRICE IN RELATION TO VALUE

COST: Past expenditures to produce or acquire a commodity.

PRICE: Amount **presently** asked for a commodity.

VALUE: Present and **future** anticipated benefits.

FORCES INFLUENCING VALUE

1. PHYSICAL
2. ECONOMIC
3. SOCIAL
4. POLITICAL

ECONOMIC PRINCIPLES AFFECTING VALUE

PRINCIPLE OF **SUPPLY**
PRINCIPLE OF **DEMAND**
PRINCIPLE OF **PROGRESSION**
PRINCIPLE OF **REGRESSION**
PRINCIPLE OF **CONFORMITY**
PRINCIPLE OF **CHANGE**
PRINCIPLE OF **SUBSTITUTION**
PRINCIPLE OF **HIGHEST & BEST USE**
PRINCIPLE OF **DIMINISHING RETURNS**

FACTORS IN PRODUCTION AFFECTING VALUE

1. Land
2. Labor
3. Capital

APPRAISAL APPROACHES

1. **MARKET DATA:**
   Sales Approach
   Comparison Approach
   Direct Sales Comparison Approach

2. **COST:**
   Summation Approach
   Replacement Cost Approach
   Reproduction Cost Approach

3. **INCOME:**
   Capitalization Approach
   Gross Rent Multiplier Approach

REAL ESTATE APPRAISING

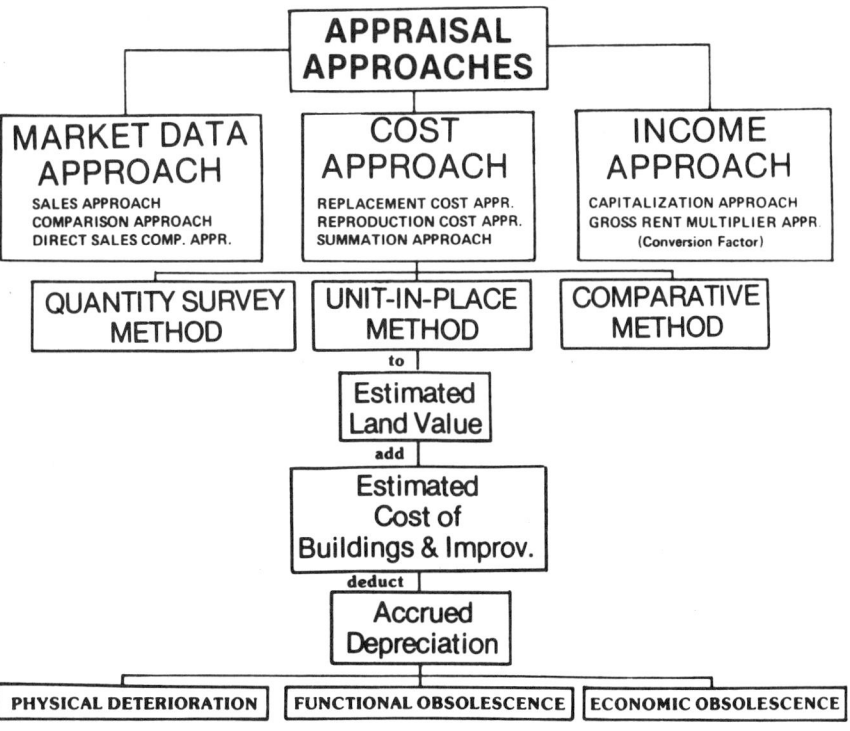

Chapter 9

REVIEW DEFINITIONS IN GLOSSARY OR TEXT OF FOLLOWING TERMS:

accrue	hundred percent location
accrued depreciation	income approach
acre	land
appraisal	market data approach
capitalization	market price
capitalization approach	market value
comparison approach	net
cost	objective value
cost approach	obsolescence
cubage	over-improvements
cubic content	percolation test
depreciation	physical deterioration
direct sales comparison approach	price
economic life	purchase
economic obsolescence	remaining economic life
economic rent	replacement cost
face value	replacement cost approach
front foot	reproduction cost
functional obsolescence	sales approach
gross income	subjective value
gross rent multiplier	unearned increment
gross rent multiplier approach	value
ground rent	value in exchange
highest and best use	value in use

REVIEW QUESTIONS:

1. What are the two meanings of value?

2. What are the <u>elements</u> of value?

3. What are the forces that influence value?

4. Name six economic principles affecting value.

5. What are the factors in production affecting value?

6. Name five uses to which an appraisal can be put.

7. What is the "appraisal process"?

8. What are the three causes of depreciation?

9. What are the three methods of cost estimation?

10. What is the "gross rent multiplier"?

11. What is the difference between "Market Price" and "Market Value"?

FOR ANSWERS TO REVIEW QUESTIONS:

1.

2.

3.

4.

5.

6.

7.

8.

9.

10.

11.

Chapter 10

Digest of Listing Principles and Practices

A.	LISTINGS - THE BEGINNING OF THE END		230
	1.	Recognize Your Employer	230
	2.	Understand Your Employment Relationship	230
		a. Agency	230
		b. Agent	231
		c. Real Estate Salesman	231
		d. Independent Contractor	231
		e. Cooperating Broker	231
	3.	Review Your Employment Obligations	232
	4.	Know Your Product	232
	5.	Service Your Clients	232
	6.	Protect and Promote Your Clients' Interests	233
	7.	Accept the Consequences	233
		a. Shoddy Practice	233
		b. Average Involvement	233
		c. Total Commitment	233
	8.	Commit Yourself to Your Sellers	234
		a. The Sellers Are Your Clients	234
		b. Sellers Are a Major Source of Referrals	234
		c. Listings Alone Generate Business Activity	234
B.	SOURCES OF LISTINGS		234
	1.	The Key to Your Personal Success	234
	2.	Listings Acquired by Your Company	234
		a. Unsolicited Listings	234
		b. Solicited Listings	235
	3.	Listings Acquired by You	235
		a. Unsolicited Listings	235
		b. Solicited Listings	235

227

C.	PROFESSIONAL LISTING PROCEDURE		235
	1. Introduction		235
	2. Listing Objectives		236
		a. Enlist the Property Owner	236
		b. List the Property Exclusively	236
	3. Achieving Your Objectives		236
		a. WHO Should Take the Listing?	236
		b. WHAT Pre-Planning Is Necessary?	236
	4. The Pre-listing Appointment Phase		237
		a. Initiation of the Collection Effort	237
		b. Recording the Information Collected	237
	5. The First Appointment Phase		237
		a. Objectives	237
		b. Fixtures	238
	6. The Second Appointment Phase		238
	7. The Post-listing or Servicing Phase		239
D.	SECURING THE ELUSIVE EXCLUSIVE		240
	1. Introduction		240
		a. Types of Listings	240
		(1) Open Listing	240
		(2) Exclusive Listing	240
		(a) Exclusive Agency	240
		(b) Exclusive Right to Sell	240
		b. Exclusive Listings Versus Open Listings	241
	2. The Sellers' Objectives		241
	3. The Sellers' Alternatives		241
	4. Your Objectives		242
		a. General Objectives	242
		(1) Enlist the Property Owners	242
		(2) List Their Property	242

		b.	Specific Objectives		242
			(1) Convince Sellers to Employ Professional Assistance		242
			(2) Convince Sellers to Hire Your Services Exclusively		242
	5.	Overcoming Sellers' Resistance to Employing Professional Assistance			242
		a.	Diagnose the Malady		242
		b.	Prescribe the Remedy		243
	6.	Overcoming Sellers' Resistance to List Exclusively with You			243
		a.	Objections		243
		b.	Rebuttals		243
	7.	Achieve Your Primary Objective			245
E.	SERVICING YOUR SELLERS				245
	1.	Service Is Your Only Product			245
	2.	Professionally Service Your Sellers. AIM to Please.			245
		a.	Advise Fully		245
		b.	Inform Continually		245
		c.	Make Timely Recommendations		246
	3.	Your Single Most Important Responsibility			246
F.	THE EMPLOYMENT CONTRACT				246
	1.	General			246
	2.	Ready, Willing, and Able Buyer			246
	3.	Efficient and Procuring Cause			247
	4.	Seller's Acceptance of Buyer			247
	5.	Associate Must Be Licensed and Hired			247
G.	COMMISSION DISBURSEMENTS				247
	1.	General			247
	2.	Associate's Listing - Associate's Sale			248
	3.	Associate's Listing - Company Sale			248
	4.	Associate's Listing - Cooperative Sale			248
	5.	Company Listing - Associate's Sale			248
	6.	Cooperative Listing - Associate's Sale			249

VISUAL AIDS   249

REVIEW QUESTIONS   254

Chapter 10
Digest of
Listing Principles and Practices

A. LISTINGS - THE BEGINNING OF THE END

  1. Recognize Your Employer

    Traditionally, and almost universally, the time, attention, and thrust of activity of residential real estate agents have been devoted to romancing buyers to the exclusion, and at the expense, of their clients, the sellers.

    The real estate profession itself has consistently indoctrinated its members subliminally on the importance of catering to the customers (the buyers) without compensatory emphasis on the legal requirement to service the sellers. In virtually all residential real estate transactions your clients are your sellers. It should be clear that your image and reputation as real estate practitioners will be reflected by your clients and potential clients, who will measure your professionalism by the amount of service you render them. Your professional performance, obviously, is judged most critically by those who pay for your services. Almost without exception the property owner (the seller) pays the commission to the real estate broker in a residential transaction.

  2. Understand Your Employment Relationship

    The majority of employing real estate brokers regard their salesmen as independent contractors and few salesmen care to contest this view. Similarly, a great many real estate licensees do not clearly understand the difference between a "client" or a "customer", or between a "co-broker" and a "sub-agent". This general, widespread confusion, with the resultant misplaced loyalties and misguided efforts, has been a major deterrent to the professionalization of the real estate industry and probably the principal reason why, in the minds of the general public, the image of the prototypical real estate agent is somewhat less than flattering. At the outset, then, it behooves us to clarify our terms to ensure that what is read, interpreted, and understood by the reader equates with the intentions of the author.

    a. Agency. "Agency" is defined by the American Law Institute as "the fiduciary relation which results from the manifestation of consent by one person to another that the other shall act on his behalf and subject to his control, and consent by the other to so act." Whenever a real estate broker agrees with a real property owner to locate a buyer or tenant, or to search for real estate for a purchaser or prospective tenant, that broker is acting in the capacity of an agent.

b. Agent. The agent in an agency relationship is one employed by and <u>under the control of another</u>, known as the principal, to represent said principal in business and legal dealings <u>with third persons</u>.

c. Real Estate Salesman. The term "real estate salesman" generally means any person employed or engaged by or on behalf of and under the <u>direction</u>, <u>control</u>, and <u>supervision</u> of a licensed real estate broker to do or deal in any activity of a real estate broker. Real estate salesmen are agents <u>of the employing broker</u> and are responsible to their principal (i. e., the employing broker) for those obligations imposed under the Law of Principal-Agent.

d. Independent Contractor. Independent contractors are those who are responsible to their employers only as to the result of their work. The use of the term "independent contractor" is confused by the different interpretations of the term as employed by the Internal Revenue Service and as employed by the various Real Estate Commissions. In some states, such as California, the <u>sales man's</u> position is decisively clarified by the California Department of Real Estate in its Reference Book which states: "For the purpose of the license law . . . <u>salesmen</u> are always <u>agents</u> of the broker and <u>cannot be independent contractors</u>." In other states, a licensed <u>broker</u> may work with another broker as an "affiliate" or "associate" broker and function as an independent contractor. In still other states, even those holding broker's licenses, if employed by another broker, are considered as "salesmen" and agents of the employing broker and not independent contractors.

e. Cooperating Broker. The term "<u>co-broker</u>" is, in its usual application, a misnomer. Its common misuse and the erroneous inferences drawn by the application of this term have encouraged practices which are morally unsound, if indeed not illegal.

Incorrect usage of the term "co-broke" has aggravated an already abrasive situation. "<u>Co-broker</u>" is a term generally <u>interpreted as one who jointly, equally, reciprocally, or mutually shares the same authority as a directly appointed agent of the principal.</u>

The general rule in real estate practice prohibits listing agents from establishing new principal-agent relationships between their own principals and other brokers who may be cooperating in the transaction.

Most listing contracts now in common use across the country appear to permit the listing brokers to delegate much of the work of procuring buyers to their own associates and to cooperating brokers, all of whom would be considered as AGENTS OF THE LISTING BROKER and not agents of the seller, bound by the obligations of an agent to the principal in consonance with the Laws of Agency.

3. Review Your Employment Obligations

Real estate brokers, and those agents employed by them, owe a very special allegiance to their clients. The law specifically prohibits them from profiting personally by virtue of their agency relationship. The fiduciary character of this relationship envelops the brokers throughout the course of their business association with their clients. This fiduciary relationship is manifested by a completely frank and candid exchange of trust and confidence which the courts have viewed in the same manner, and with almost the same strictness, as applied to the relationship of trustee and beneficiary. In this regard, then, agents are duty bound to act with the highest respect towards their principals. Agents may not obtain any advantage therein over their principals by the slightest misrepresentation, concealment, duress, or adverse pressure of any kind. Agents may not use the influence which their position gives them to obtain any advantage from their principals. With this basic understanding of the nature of the fiduciary relationship between the principal and the broker, we can more readily understand why the law will not force one to work against one's will in an agency relationship as either principal or agent. It would be paradoxical to expect of a reluctant principal or agent the full exchange of confidence and trust so necessary to the fiduciary character of the agency relationship. (Reference Chapter 3, The Principal-Agent Relationship).

4. Know Your Product

You do not sell real estate. You neither possess nor control real estate. Your product is SERVICE. Your ability to service your clients (and your customers) professionally can be measured accurately by the amount of pertinent knowledge you possess and apply effectively, in practice, with will, desire, and enthusiasm. As professionals, you offer your services to your clients; you proffer your knowledge, training, experience, judgment, prudence, and skill to further their aims and to protect and promote their interests.

The professional in real estate realizes the obvious truth that full service to clients infers an executed contract, one which assures the client a combination of the best price, on the most favorable terms and conditions, in the shortest period of time, with the least amount of inconvenience. The thrust in education and training should focus attention on full service to your clients which would automatically ensure well-balanced and professional attention to prospective buyers without which full service would not be possible.

5. Service Your Clients

In the field of residential real estate, the property owners (who are nearly always your clients) and their property are the hub of all real estate activity.

Your success will be entirely dependent upon your ability to win the confidence of property owners in your market area, to attract from among these property owners well-motivated sellers, to procure from these sellers competitively priced listings, on exclusive contracts, and to subsequently provide these property owners (turned sellers - turned clients) with continuing professional SERVICE. And the service we refer to infers the fulfillment of all of your legal obligations . . . and then some. This "and then some" is that indispensable ingredient for success which can best be identified as SACRIFICE.

6. Protect and Promote Your Clients' Interests

It is possible to protect and promote your clients' interests only when you are able to isolate, analyze, and understand those interests. The final determination of whether or not your association with your clients will equate with that of an inept amateur or a well-tempered professional will depend upon your ability to elicit from your clients all the pertinent information necessary to enable you to discover their desires, concerns, motivations, and interests.

7. Accept the Consequences

   a. Shoddy Practice. If your protection and promotion of your clients' interests are slovenly or shoddy, you may be certain that your dissatisfied sellers, wittingly or unwittingly, will broadcast your deficiencies indiscriminately.

   b. Average Involvement. If your involvement with your clients' problems is average, there is most assuredly a complete absence of sacrifice, and most probably a repudiation in some degree of your obligations. The average real estate agent is a mediocre real estate agent, and mediocrity in anything equates with the worst of the good and the best of the bad. In today's competitive market, no tangible benefits are likely to result.

   c. Total Commitment. If, however, you have totally committed yourself and your talents to the interests of your client, fulfillment of your responsibilities is assured, especially when a measure of sacrifice is also programmed. As a consequence of professional service (which always reflects a commitment surpassing duty) you may be certain that you, by name, will be recommended voluntarily, enthusiastically, and continually by your sellers to all in their spheres of influence who may now, or in the future, require the services of a professionally competent, personally interested, and committed real estate agent. When you have, with diligence, protected and promoted your sellers' interests as their agent, they will, in turn, serve as your agents . . . your publicity agents, voluntarily and without compensation.

8. <u>Commit Yourself to Your Sellers</u>

There are three reasons why your primary concern as a residential real estate agent must be your sellers.

   a. The Sellers Are Your Clients. First, the sellers are your employers. They are the source of your commission: directly, if you serve as their exclusive agent, and indirectly, if you serve as the cooperating sub-agent responsible for introducing buyers for their property.

   b. Sellers Are a Major Source of Referrals. Your success in the real estate business, as evidenced by the fun and profit you derive from it, will depend on the quality and quantity of your personal referral business. As noted previously, the major sources of your personal referral business are the <u>property owners in your market area,</u> in general, and, specifically, those property owners whom you have successfully represented in the sale of their homes . . . i. e., your sellers.

   c. Listings Alone Generate Business Activity. Listings generate business activity. The more listings, the greater the activity. And remember this . . . the associates who have not contributed their share of listings . . . <u>regardless of their sales record</u> . . . have done nothing to contribute to the growth and progress of their firm.

B. SOURCES OF LISTINGS

1. <u>The Key to Your Personal Success</u>

   The continuing acquisition of qualified listings is the key to your personal success and the foundation upon which is built the development and progress of your firm. Associates who do not continually contribute their share of qualified listings - we repeat - regardless of their sales record - have done nothing to contribute to the growth of their firm or their own personal referral business. Cultivating property owners, acquiring qualified listings and providing professional service to your clients are your most important daily activities as a real estate agent. Accept this as a hard fact and an accepted truism. A PROGRESSIVE REAL ESTATE FIRM CANNOT AFFORD TO SHELTER A LISTLESS ASSOCIATE.

2. <u>Listings Acquired by Your Company</u>

   a. <u>Unsolicited Listings</u>. In the real estate business generally, and in the area of listing specifically, reputations are built and sustained primarily on the quality of SERVICE promised and delivered. Sales naturally follow service, and the firm with an established record of professional service will always have a ready and continuing source of property owners soliciting the firm's services.

In the area of unsolicited listing the majority of business flows to your firm as a direct consequence of its reputation and the number of "sold" signs displayed throughout your market area. (Note: some areas prohibit the display of real estate signs. For example, several municipalities in Illinois, including Chicago, have enacted a "no-sign" ordinance which makes it unlawful for real estate brokers to display "For Sale" signs in residential areas. Such ordinances would cover "Sold", "Open House", "New Homes", et cetera).

b. Solicited Listings. There are two methods generally recognized by real estate firms as effective means of soliciting listings. These are direct mailing to specific locations within the market area and advertising.

3. Listings Acquired by You

a. Unsolicited Listings. The sources of listings available to the individual associate are so diverse and so numerous that it is difficult to imagine how it would not be possible for all associates to achieve their monthly listing objective consistently. This is particularly true if listing activity - both acquisition and servicing - has been integrated into each associate's daily program, EVERY DAY. In the analysis of listings acquired by you, we find that these listings, like those acquired by the firm, fall into two general categories - solicited and unsolicited. As unsolicited listings are attracted to your firm as a result of its reputation and as a consequence of property owners fully serviced, so, too, are unsolicited listings referred directly to you.

b. Solicited Listings. To acquire qualified listings, you must ultimately establish contact with sellers or potential sellers and then convince them to list their property with you exclusively. There are three obvious listing sources that fall into the classification of "sellers". They are identified by the "For Sale by Owner" sign placed on their property, the "For Sale by Owner" advertisement, and the expired multiple listing of a competing broker.

C. PROFESSIONAL LISTING PROCEDURE

1. Introduction

Listings activate and perpetuate the entire selling cycle. The selling cycle is about to begin. You are about to meet the most lucrative source of personal referrals in the real estate business. Are you prepared, mentally, physically, and emotionally, to meet your client ? Are you prepared to fulfill your legal and moral obligations to your client ? Are you prepared to go still one step further - are you willing to sacrifice for your client ?

2. Listing Objectives

Your listing objectives are twofold: one related to the property owner, the other related to the property.

   a. Enlist the Property Owner. As your primary objective, you want to transform the property owner into your agent, your publicity agent . . . voluntarily and without compensation . . . for your firm and yourself, as a consequence of your professional service.

   b. List the Property Exclusively. As your secondary objective, you wish to add a salable, well-listed property to your firm's inventory. You are aware that a salable listing is a competitively priced property, secured on a long term exclusive contract, from a seriously motivated seller.

3. Achieving Your Objectives

There are two areas of consideration which bear directly on the probability of achieving the two listing objectives. WHO should enlist the property owners and list the property, and WHAT pre-planning is necessary?

   a. WHO Should Take the Listing? Should inexperienced or mediocre associates serve in the capacity of purchasing agents or buyers for their firm?

   The answer is obvious. Only highly qualified, thoroughly trained, experienced professional associates should be given this responsibility.

   Those associates who have not yet attained such status should, whenever feasible, be given every opportunity to accompany the professional lister . . . to observe, learn, and acquire the knowledge, professional skill, approaches, and techniques employed in winning the trust and confidence of the seller, and of properly pricing, marketing, and servicing the listing.

   b. WHAT Pre-planning Is Necessary? "Proper prior planning precludes pitifully poor performance." Nowhere is this expression more apropos than in the listing process. Professional listing planning procedures cover four distinct phases:

   (1) The pre-listing phase,
   (2) The first appointment phase,
   (3) The second appointment phase, and
   (4) The post-listing, or service phase.

4. The Pre-listing Appointment Phase

   a. Initiation of the Collection Effort. The pre-listing appointment phase commences the appraisal process. The required appraisal data may be classified general and specific. During the pre-listing appointment phase of the listing procedures, we are involved in the collection and recording, on a Competitive Properties Report, of general data which encompasses regional, city or town, and neighborhood information, and takes into consideration those forces (i. e., physical, economic, social, and political) which influence value.

   b. Recording the Information Collected. During the pre-listing appointment phase, the listing agent will commence preparation of the Competitive Properties Report. In effect, the listing agent, by use of this reporting form, is employing one of the three generally accepted approaches (methods) in arriving at an estimate of value. This approach is called the "Market Data" Approach. The other two approaches are the "Cost Approach" and the "Income Approach." (Reference Chapter 11, Principles of Economics and Real Estate Appraising).

5. The First Appointment Phase

   a. Objectives. When you initially spoke with your sellers, you arranged, tentatively, an appointment at their home, during the evening or at some other appropriate time when both sellers (husband and wife) would be available in a relaxed atmosphere, free of interruptions or disturbances. You also arranged with one of your sellers for an earlier opportunity to inspect the property and to record the available physical data required on your listing sheet. This preliminary visit would not require the presence of, or consultation with, both owners. You have requested the sellers to have ready for you, during the preliminary visit, those papers and documents that will be necessary to complete the listing. These will include plot plans, deed, tax statements, mortgage statements, and any other documents or papers such as liens, attachments, et cetera, which affect the status of title.

   You are now ready for the first appointment phase. It is also time to reflect for just a moment on what your specific objectives are during this important listing phase. You have four objectives:

   (1) Establish rapport with your sellers,
   (2) Collect specific property data by inspecting the property and preparing the listing sheet,
   (3) Determine clients' motivation,
   (4) Prepare sellers for the second appointment phase.

b. Fixtures. During the collection of specific property data, much difficulty has arisen because of insufficient attention given by real estate agents to those items of personal property that have become so attached to the real property as to become realty and which will pass with the property. Such items are called "fixtures". A fixture is an item of personal property that has lost its identity as such, and, through its attachment or association with real estate, becomes real property. Distinguishing between real and personal property is not always an easy task. The courts have developed the following tests which enable us to determine whether property attached to realty has become part of the realty. These tests fall into three areas: annexation, adaptation, and intention.

(1) Annexation. The test of annexation alone is inadequate. Many things annexed to the land or buildings may or may not be fixtures. Furniture and equipment, physically annexed, may be easily removed and, although substantially fastened, are not necessarily fixtures. Other items such as doors, windows, shades, storm windows, et cetera, are readily detached, but are usually regarded as fixtures because they are an integral part of the building; moreover, they pertain to its function. The method of attachment, and whether or not removal will materially damage the article or the building and the land, are other considerations. Portability, therefore, is another consideration to be weighed in subjecting the property to the annexation test.

(2) Adaptation. Adaptation relates to the use to which an article is put in promoting the purpose for which the land or the improvement is used. Thus, if an article improves the property, makes it more valuable, and extends its use, it is a fixture. Rarely, however, are articles so placed except to advance the purpose for which the land is to be used. This test alone, consequently, is not adequate.

(3) Intention. The test of intention is more inclusive. Annexation and adaptation give evidence of an intention to make an item of personal property a fixture.

An article which does not lose its identity upon annexation, and removal of which will not materially injure it or the real property, may continue after annexation to be considered personal property by the agreement of the parties. The time and place for the broker to determine which of those questionable articles are fixtures or personal property is when the listing is being taken at the sellers' property.

6. The Second Appointment Phase

Remember, your listing objectives are to enlist the property owners and to list their property. Of these two objectives, your primary thrust is to **enlist the property owner** to be your publicity agent. Hopefully, if this paramount objective is realized, your personal referral business will be enhanced.

Your reputation and that of your firm will depend upon your ability to service the listing professionally. If the sellers insist on placing insurmountable obstacles in your path which, in your judgment, will make a satisfactory sale improbable, it is far wiser to reject the listing. Your image will not be damaged. Your sincere concern will be respected. Eventually, your rejected sellers will most probably be forced, by the turn of events, to belatedly acknowledge the wisdom of your advice and the folly of their unreasonable demands. Even in extreme situations such as these, you may well have achieved indirectly your principal objectives . . . the enlistment of a willing press agent.

During the second appointment phase of the listing procedure, the following eight specific areas demand your attention and concern:

a. Establish rapport once again (with husband and/or wife) if you have not yet met both.

b. Analyze the market and explain the Competitive Properties Report in preparation for reaching an agreement on the matter of the selling price.

c. Explain your firm's services.

d. Prepare your clients for the closing process.

e. Exploit clients' leads and contacts.

f. Recheck everything; satisfy all queries.

g. Verify the accuracy and completeness of the Listing Sheet with your clients' initials.

h. Secure the listing, exclusively, on a long term contract.

This well-listed property will enhance the growth, development, and progress of your firm, and your personal referral business. Your listing will give added impetus to, and will infuse new life, interest, and activity into, the operational business cycle of your firm. The close of this real estate transaction has begun.

7. The Post-Listing or Servicing Phase

You have not yet met your two listing objectives. While you have presumably secured a competitively priced property, from a well-motivated seller, on a long term exclusive listing, much yet remains to be done to completely enlist the property owner. Your success in achieving this final, yet most important, objective will depend from this moment on upon the frequency and quality of the service you render for the term of the exclusive listing contract.

D. SECURING THE ELUSIVE EXCLUSIVE

1. Introduction

In order for real estate brokers to be <u>entitled</u> to their commissions, they must be employed by their clients, and they must be the <u>efficient and procuring cause</u> of the sale. Real estate brokers <u>earn</u> their commission when they produce a buyer who is <u>ready</u> to meet the sellers' terms and conditions when the sale is to take place, <u>willing</u> to enter into the necessary contractual relationships, and financially <u>able</u> to close the transaction when title is conveyed. Consequently, it is generally accepted that, as soon as real estate brokers become the "efficient and procuring cause" by producing buyers who are ready, willing, and able to meet the terms and conditions stipulated by the sellers, they earn their commission.

    a. Types of Listings. There are generally two categories of "hiring" contracts: the "open" listings and the "exclusive" listings. The "exclusive" listings may be further classified as either "exclusive agency" or "exclusive right to sell." The listing employment contract is an agreement between the property owners, as principals, and the real estate brokers, as their special agents, hired to represent the owners. The listing employment contract is not a contract for the sale or purchase of real estate; it is simply a contract for SERVICES, the real estate agents' only product.

    (1) <u>Open Listing</u>. An open listing is the listing of <u>property by the seller with one or more brokers</u>. Any broker with whom the property is listed may sell the property and be entitled to the commission. The owners, too, may sell the property themselves without obligation to any of the brokers to whom this listing was given.

    (2) Exclusive Listing.

        (a) <u>Exclusive Agency</u>. An exclusive agency is a binding bilateral (i.e., exchange of promises) contract whereby <u>one broker</u> is given the exclusive right to find a buyer. <u>Under such contracts, the sellers reserve the right to find their own buyers without paying the listing broker a commission</u>. However, the sellers are not free to list the property with any other brokers.

        (b) Exclusive Right to Sell. An exclusive right to sell is a binding bilateral contract whereby <u>only</u> the broker to whom this listing is given has the right to sell. This type of listing contract excludes even the sellers, and, if the sellers do sell on their own behalf, they are obligated to pay a commission to the broker to whom the exclusive right was given.

    b.   Exclusive Listings Versus Open Listings. Erroneously, many sellers are of the opinion that they are tying up their properties and themselves by signing an exclusive listing contract. Actually, the opposite is true. It is the task of the professional associate to enlighten the homeowners accordingly.

An open listing is simply an authorization given to brokers by property owners to act as one of any number of agents for the sale of their property. The owners list and offer their properties for sale with as many brokers as they wish. They are free to revoke such listings with any one, or all of them, or they may sell the property themselves. Nevertheless, while this listing is in effect, the fiduciary relationship between principal and agent prevails.

Professional brokerage service is discouraged under such circumstances. Considerable time and expense must be put forth, if a property is to be professionally listed, effectively merchandised, competently serviced, and, hopefully, sold. An open listing does not provide the professional associate with sufficient protection to justify the required investment to procure a buyer.

2. The Sellers' Objectives

Your understanding of the sellers, their objectives, apprehensions, and points of resistance is essential, if you are to be successful in earning their trust, their confidence, and their listing . . . exclusively. What are the sellers' objectives? There are four primary objectives:

    a.   The Best Price,
    b.   With the Most Favorable Terms and Conditions,
    c.   In the Shortest Period of Time,
    d.   With the Least Amount of Inconvenience.

If you can convince a seller of your ability to provide the type of service which will ensure the realization of these objectives, you will be able to convert that seller into your seller exclusively. To do so, you will have to convince the reluctant owner with logic, advanced with a great deal of tact and understanding.

3. The Sellers' Alternatives

The mere fact that property owners have reached a decision to sell their property identifies them as sellers. As such, they now become prime targets for the professional real estate associate. Once, however, the decision to sell is reached, these property owners are faced with three alternatives: <u>should they attempt to sell their own property without benefit of professional real estate services; should they retain the professional services of several real estate firms; or should they list exclusively with just one agency</u>? As a real estate agent, you, too, must concern yourself with these alternatives, because the reasons sellers select one alternative over the others, and the objections they offer to support their rejection of the other alternatives, must be clearly understood.

4. <u>Your Objectives</u>

Your present and continuing concern is to focus clearly on both your general, overall listing objectives and your specific, immediate listing objectives.

    a. General Objectives

        (1) Enlist the Property Owners
        (2) List Their Property

    b. Specific Objectives

        (1) Convince Sellers to Employ Professional Assistance
        (2) Convince Sellers to Hire Your Services Exclusively

Now is the time to consider specifically the resistance that can be expected from property owners who have decided to sell their property without professional assistance.

5. <u>Overcoming Sellers' Resistance to Employing Professional Assistance</u>

    a. <u>Diagnose the Malady</u>. Some of the reasons why property owners choose to sell their property themselves have been previously discussed. When you attempt to solicit their listings, you may be confronted with one, or a combination, of the following or similar rebuffs:

        (1) "We'll try to sell it ourselves first."
        (2) "We have always sold our property without brokers."
        (3) "We'll think it over and let you know later."
        (4) "We've already placed an ad, and we're getting great response."

The sellers you approach for their listing will only be swayed by being shown the services and benefits which will accrue to them through association with a real estate agency and which they cannot realize on their own. What, then, can truly professional real estate associates do for these apprehensive sellers that they cannot do as well for themselves?

b. Prescribe the Remedy

    (1) Pricing the Property
    (2) Avoiding Legal Entanglements
    (3) Negotiating
    (4) Merchandising the Property
    (5) Qualifying the Buying Suspects
    (6) Arranging Financing
    (7) Minimizing Inconveniences
    (8) Insuring the Safety of the Sellers' Family and Property

These are a few of the reasons which may induce the property owners to abandon their intention of selling their own property. There is not a knowledgeable broker who would advise his own wife or mother otherwise. If this one point can be imparted with sincerity to the sellers, you may well have earned their trust and confidence . . . and their exclusive listing.

6. Overcoming Sellers' Resistance to List Exclusively with You

Assuming that you have convinced the sellers to abandon their idea of acting on their own behalf, it now behooves you to induce them to give you the exclusive listing contract. You may once again be faced with resistance. As a professional, however, you have the advantage of experience and sound brokerage knowledge which must now be put into play.

Most often the resistance you meet will be disguised as a statement. These statements from the owners should not be regarded as insurmountable obstacles. View them, rather, as questions which beg for reasonable answers.

Let's consider a few of the most typically encountered views of apprehensive owners.

a. Objections

    (1) "Another agency will list for more."
    (2) "We can't accept your suggested selling price."
    (3) "We have a friend in the business."
    (4) "We don't want to tie up our property."
    (5) "You can handle it for a month."

b. Rebuttals

    (1) When you thoroughly explain your appraisal method and outline precisely how together, you and the sellers will arrive at a suggested market price, supporting your conclusions with facts and figures, the sellers cannot help but

be impressed with your logic and professional approach.
As to the agency up the street which has promised to list
the property for $3,000 more than your Competitive
Properties Report (CPR) reflects, you need simply ask
the sellers to show you the competitor's CPR to support
and justify its appraisal.

(2) Unfortunately, most homeowners feel that they must allow
a few thousand dollars buffer for negotiations, unaware
that just these "surplus" thousands project the property
out of the competitive market. Advise these sellers that
your reputation and the reputation of your firm rests on
your ability to competitively price property. Assure your
sellers that your CPR will reflect current market conditions
and that it will be continually updated as new competitive
properties come on the market and existing ones are removed. Convince them also that your CPR will be shown
and explained to all qualified and interested buyers to
squelch at the outset any buyer tendency to bargain.

And finally, to assuage your wary sellers, show them the
record of success your firm enjoys in concluding transactions precisely at or very close to the list price dictated
by your CPR's.

(3) The owners should realize that their primary obligation is
to their family, not to the friend. Since you, as a professional
associate, have done your homework, you will have carefully
and fully prepared your Competitive Properties Report.

If, however, the sellers remain adamant, their obligation to
their friend can be thoroughly satisfied by simply extending
the right of sale to this friend, a special provision in the exclusive listing contract. There should be no further resistance
on this point.

(4) All the points covered in Paragraph 1b, above, relate to
the rebuttal of this objection. Perhaps the best counter to
the reluctance of the sellers to "tie up" their property is the
"Law of Agency" which holds that no person will be compelled to act as either principal or agent against his will. Consequently, the sellers may fire their agent at any time the
agent fails to fulfill his obligations to the sellers. Professional
real estate agents would be reluctant to divert their valuable
time and effort from their exclusive clients to merchandise
and fully service an open listing where they have absolutely
no assurance that the owners, or some other competing

broker, will not thwart all of their endeavors by selling the property.

(5) Sellers attuned to the mechanics of merchandising property would not expect professional service in such a short time. It is the associate's job to explain the process to the owner.

Surveys in specific parts of the country indicate that it takes an average of 97 days to sell the average house at the current market price. Your professional analysis of your market will enable you to determine the average time span between listing and contractual agreement. Present the sellers with these facts.

7. Achieve Your Primary Objective

Your immediate and continuing concern must be cultivation of all property owners in your market area to transform them into your press agents. Regardless of the outcome of your efforts to secure from these property owners a competitively priced listing on a long-term exclusive contract, you have endeavored to convince them that you are sincerely interested in their problem. Should these sellers, despite your overtures, decide not to seek professional assistance, or should they decide not to list with you exclusively, there is a natural tendency to lose sight of your primary objective of enlisting the property owner to your cause . . . whether or not you are able to secure an exclusive listing from these potential sellers has little bearing on achieving your primary objective. Since they are still property owners, your task is to enlist them in your cause.

E. SERVICING YOUR SELLERS

1. Service Is Your Only Product

SERVICE . . . As a real estate associate, that is your only product . . . SERVICE. Your motivation in any real estate transaction must spring from a spirit of SERVICE . . . not monetary gain. A successful career in this business can be yours in no other manner.

2. Professionally Service Your Sellers. AIM to Please.

a. Advise Fully. Initially, it is your responsibility to ADVISE your sellers fully of precisely what services both you and your firm (who) are pledged to perform, and why these services and functions are necessary.

b. Inform Continually. Secondly, it is your responsibility to continually INFORM your sellers when these services are to be extended, how they are to be extended and where results are to be realized.

c. Make Timely Recommendations. Finally, it is your responsibility to MAKE TIMELY RECOMMENDATIONS to your sellers for actions or decisions required of them which will best enable you to represent their interests in obtaining the highest price, realizing the best terms and conditions, negotiating the sale in the shortest time, while subjecting your sellers to the least amount of inconvenience.

3. Your Single Most Important Responsibility

The single most important responsibility the lister assumes, after initially acquiring the listing, is to maintain CONSTANT COMMUNICATION with the sellers, reinforced with FREQUENT PERSONAL CONTACT to keep them apprised of all developments which affect their interest . . . positive or negative.

AIM to please the sellers. As your relationship continues, you will have won their trust, deserved their confidence, and earned their reliance on your professional judgment and recommendations.

AIM to please your sellers, and as their agent you will have achieved your paramount objective. You will have ultimately transformed them into your agents, your voluntary and enthusiastic press agents . . . whether or not you or associates from your firm consummated the sale.

F. THE EMPLOYMENT CONTRACT

1. General

When a seller hires the services of a real estate broker to represent him in the sale of his property, a fiduciary relationship is created which places the associate in a position of trust and confidence with his employer, the seller. The relationship thus established is one of principal and agent - which is more fully explained in Chapter 3. The Principal-Agent Relationship is something which should be continually reviewed. Under this employment contract, the associate earns his commission for his services at either one of two times:

a. When he produces a buyer who is ready, willing, and able to meet the sellers' terms, or

b. When the seller contracts with the buyer.

In some states (e. g., Arizona) the employment agreement must be in writing. In others (e. g., Illinois) there is no such requirement.

2. Ready, Willing, and Able Buyer: - - As soon as the associate becomes the "efficient and procuring cause" by producing a buyer who is ready, willing, and able to meet the terms and conditions stipulated by the seller, he earns his commission.

The associate is not required to consummate the sale. The seller cannot rob the agent of his compensation by refusing to deal with a ready, willing, and able prospect or by withdrawing the property from the market. He cannot terminate the agency and later negotiate with the associate's prospect. The fee or commission is earned when it can be shown that the associate is the efficient and procuring cause of the sale.

    3.   <u>Efficient and Procuring Cause</u>: - - The legal difficulties in determining who was the efficient and procuring cause of a sale usually arise when more than one associate becomes involved in a real estate transaction. An associate must be the inducing cause of a sale to be entitled to compensation for his services. Generally, the associate who consummates the sale is entitled to the commission, and the burden of proof in determining "efficient and procuring cause" rests upon the contesting associate.

    4.   <u>Seller's Acceptance of Buyer</u>: - - The real estate associate earns his commission if the seller enters into a contractual relationship with the buyer. By so doing, the seller, by implication, accepts the buyer as ready, willing, and <u>able</u>. He relieves the associate of the responsibility of proving the same. In this instance, the associate earned his commission by producing a buyer who was acceptable to the seller.

    5.   <u>Associate Must Be Licensed and Hired</u>: - - Regardless of the amount of time, expense, or energies expended by an associate to produce a qualified buyer, he will be unable to claim any compensation for his efforts unless he was licensed and specifically hired by the seller. The hiring (listing) contract is an essential element upon which the associate's compensation rests.

G.   COMMISSION DISBURSEMENTS

    1.   <u>General</u>

    The amount of the commission paid by the seller to the associate is determined by <u>mutual agreement</u> and made a part of the hiring contract. Generally, the commission is a percentage of the selling price of the property and may vary widely from area to area and in accordance with the particular type of property sold. For example, the brokerage commission on re-sale residential property may be 6%; land, 10%; new homes by builders, 5%; et cetera. Usually associates are not principals but are associated with brokerage firms - each firm with its own internal policies relative to commission breakdowns. It is not unusual for a brokerage firm to require 50% of the gross commission for administrative costs, operational expenses, and growth plans. The remaining amount of the commission is then disbursed, per established policy, between the listing associate and the selling associate. The percentage distribution varies widely and often depends upon the type of listing. Normally, however, the listing associate's percentage is applied directly to the selling price of the property. Usually, the lister is not penalized by circumstances of a sale which may diminish gross commission received. There are generally five situations involving commission considerations affecting the associate:

a.	Associate's Listing	-	Associate's Sale
b.	Associate's Listing	-	Company Sale
c.	Associate's Listing	-	Co-brokerage Sale (Competitive Firm)
d.	Company Listing	-	Associate's Sale
e.	Co-brokerage Listing	-	Associate's Sale

2. <u>Associate's Listing - Associate's Sale</u>: - - <u>In this instance the listing associate found a buyer for his seller's property and consummated the sale without assistance from his office associates or those of competing firms.</u> We will assume that the firm's policy has established 50% of the gross commission goes to the firm, with the balance being distributed to the listing and selling associates. If the property sold for $20,000, and the commission on the sale was 6%, the gross commission would be $1,200. Half of this amount would go to the firm, and the remaining $600 would be distributed to the listing and selling associates. In this instance, the $600 would go to the associate who was fortunate enough to sell his own listing.

3. <u>Associate's Listing - Company Sale</u>: - - We will, in this example, assume that the associate's $20,000 listing was sold at that price by a company associate. The commission on the sale is 6%, or $1,200. As in our first example (Paragraph 2, above), the company receives 50% of the gross commission, or $600. We will assume that the remaining 50% (or $600) will be split in the following manner between the listing associate and the selling associate:

<u>Listing Associate</u>	-	25% of the gross commission - $300
<u>Sales Associate</u>	-	Balance of the $600 after deduction of $300 for Listing Associate - $300.

4. <u>Associate's Listing - Cooperative Sale</u>: - - In this particular type arrangement, <u>two brokerage firms are involved</u>, and the distribution of the commission between the firms is our first consideration. The agreed-upon split between the listing firm and the selling firm varies widely throughout the country and even within a state. We will assume that the listing firm and the selling firm share evenly in the commission. In our example of the $20,000 property carrying a 6% or $1,200 commission, we can see that the listing associate's firm receives the entire commission ($1,200) from the seller and then disburses half ($600) to the selling firm. The listing associate, as in the previous examples receives his 25% of the gross commission, or $300. The selling firm compensates its selling associate.

5. <u>Company Listing - Associate's Sale</u>: - - In this situation, the associate <u>sold a property listed by a company associate</u>. Using the same $20,000 property as our example, we determine that the gross commission is $1,200 (6% of $20,000). The firm retains 50% (or $600) with the remaining $600 being disbursed to the listing and selling associates. In our example, the listing associate receives, as usual, his 25% of the gross commission ($300), and our selling associate receives the remaining amount of $300.

6. <u>Cooperative Listing - Associate's Sale:</u> - - In this example, as is the case in Paragraph 4, above, <u>two brokerage firms</u> are involved. We will assume that these firms agree to split the 6% commission on the $20,000 property 50/50. The competitive firm which listed the property will be paid the entire 6% ($1,200) by the seller they represent. This firm will subsequently send our associate's firm a check for its 50% share of the gross commission (50% of $1,200, or $600). In this instance, it is usual practice for the firm to retain 50% of the $600, or $300, and give the selling associate the remaining 50%, or $300.

THE PRINCIPAL-AGENT RELATIONSHIP

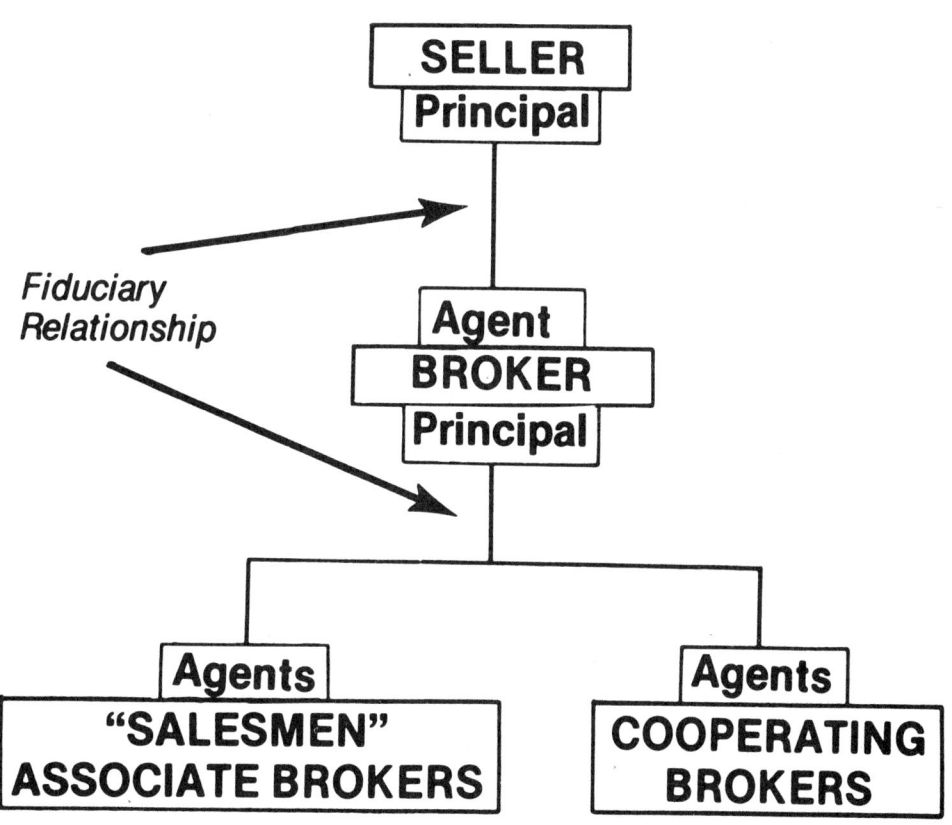

ON SACRIFICE

SACRIFICE is the one condition necessary to render service.

SACRIFICE is the distinguishing feature between duty and service.

SACRIFICE is the one indispensable ingredient for success.

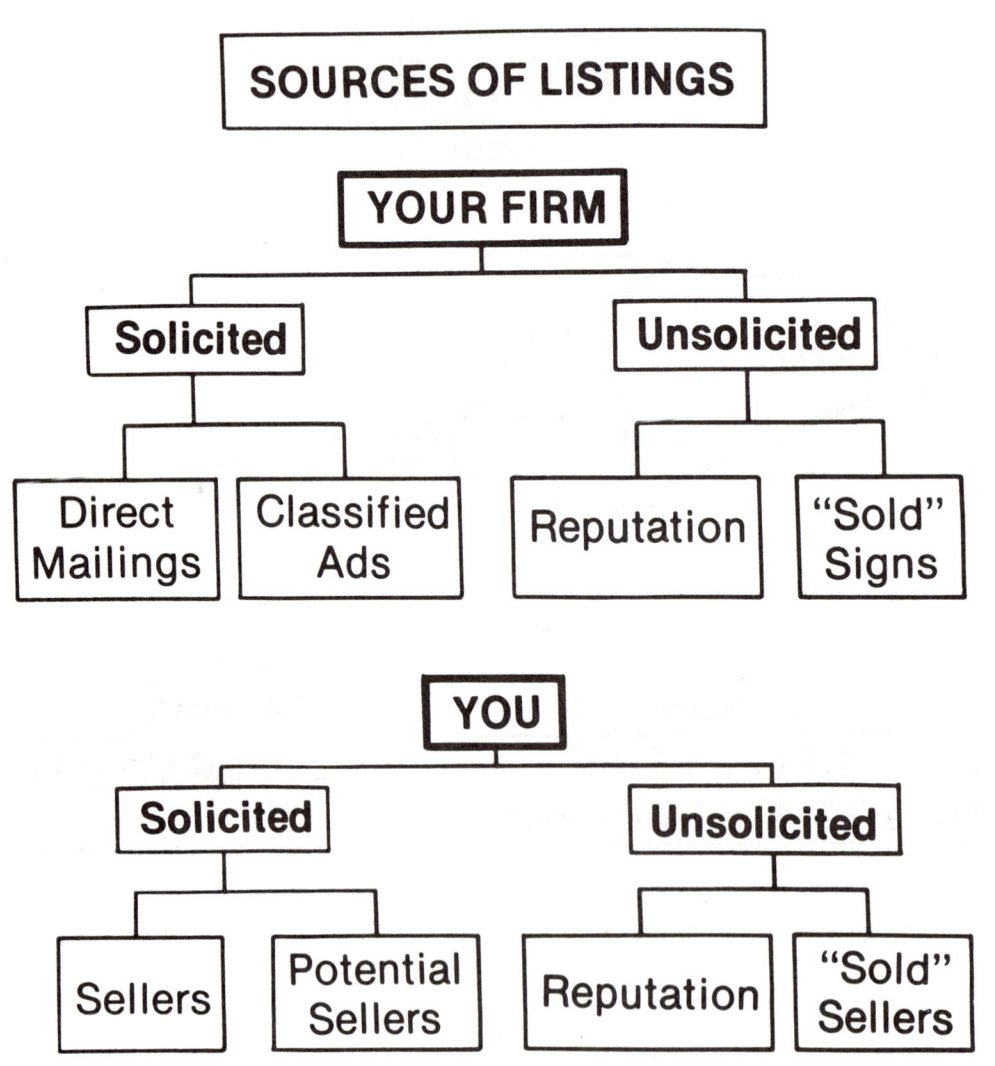

250

LISTING OBJECTIVES

1. **Enlist the Property Owners**
2. **List Their Property Exclusively**

LISTING PLANNING PROCEDURE

1. **The pre-listing appointment phase**
2. **The first appointment phase**
3. **The second appointment phase**
4. **The post-listing or servicing phase**

TYPES OF LISTINGS

1. **OPEN**

2. **EXCLUSIVE:**
   a. Exclusive Agency
   b. Exclusive Right of Sale

FIXTURES

The three tests in determining if personal property has become realty:

ANNEXATION
ADAPTATION
INTENTION

YOUR OBJECTIVES

1. GENERAL:

a. Enlist the Property Owners
b. List Their Properties

2. SPECIFIC:

a. Convince Sellers to Employ Professional Help
b. Convince Sellers to Hire Your Services Exclusively

THE POST-LISTING OR SERVICING PHASE

A. • Advise Fully
  I. • Inform Continually
   M. • Make Timely Recommendations

The Professionals **A.I.M.** to please

Chapter 10

REVIEW DEFINITIONS IN GLOSSARY OR TEXT OF FOLLOWING TERMS:

"able" independent contractor
appraisal market data approach
cooperating broker open listing
exclusive agency "ready"
exclusive right to sell "willing"
fixture

REVIEW QUESTIONS:

1. What are your two listing objectives?

2. Who should take the listing?

3. How many phases are there in the listing planning procedure?

4. Name three types of listing employment contracts.

5. What is the difference between an "exclusive agency" and an "exclusive right to sell?"

6. What tests have been developed by the courts to determine whether property attached to realty is a fixture?

7. What are the sellers' objectives?

8. Name three reasons why property owners should seek professional brokerage service in the sale of their property.

9. Name three reasons why property owners should list their property exclusively with one broker.

10. Name the three prerequisites a real estate associate must meet to be entitled to his commission.

11. Name the two circumstances when an associate earns his commission.

12. What is your only product as a professional real estate agent?

13. After acquiring the listing, what is your single and most important responsibility?

FOR ANSWERS TO REVIEW QUESTIONS:

1.

2.

3.

4.

5.

6.

7.

8.

9.

10.

11.

12.

13.

Chapter 11

Digest of Closing Principles and Practices

A.	UNDERSTANDING YOUR CUSTOMERS	261
	1. Analysis of a Buyer	261
	2. Suggested Treatment	261
	3. The Anatomy of a Real Estate Transaction	262
B.	PROFESSIONAL TELEPHONE TECHNIQUES	263
	1. Grasp the Opportunity	263
	a. The Importance of Classified Advertising	263
	b. The Objectives of Classified Advertising	264
	c. The Cost of Classified Advertising	264
	2. The Importance of Floor Time	264
	3. When Customers Call	265
	a. Determine Their Objective	265
	b. Set Your Objectives	265
	c. Achieve Your Objectives	265
	(1) Control the Conversation	265
	(2) Guide Your Suspects Through Each Psychological Stage	266
	4. Create Confidence	266
	a. Put a Smile in Your Voice	266
	b. Refer to Caller Continually by Name	266
	c. Assume the Toll Charges	266
	5. Attract Attention	266
	a. Know Your Properties	266
	b. Determine Motivational Urge	267
	6. Rouse Interest	267
	a. Discuss Comparable Properties	267
	b. Appeal to Motivational Urge	267

	7.	Establish Want	267
C.		PROFESSIONAL QUALIFICATION TECHNIQUES	268
	1.	S. E. R. V. E. Your Customers	268

- 7. Establish Want — 267
- C. PROFESSIONAL QUALIFICATION TECHNIQUES — 268
  - 1. S. E. R. V. E. Your Customers — 268
    - a. Organize Your Time — 268
    - b. Professionally Serve — 268
  - 2. Secure the Appointment — 268
    - a. Time — 268
    - b. Place — 268
  - 3. Establish Rapport — 269
    - a. Create Confidence — 269
      - (1) Be Punctual — 269
      - (2) Identify Areas of Mutual Interest — 269
    - b. Introduce Your Blank Forms and Agreements — 269
    - c. Explain That All Properties on the Market Are Available Through You — 269
    - d. Determine Emotional Reasons for Buying — 269
    - e. Explain the Qualification Process — 269
    - f. Check Your Empathy and Ego Drive — 270
  - 4. Render Professional Service — 270
    - a. Who? — 270
    - b. What? — 270
    - c. Where? — 270
    - d. Why? — 271
  - 5. Verify Customers' Readiness, Willingness, and Financial Ability — 271
    - a. When? — 271
    - b. How? — 271
      - (1) How Much Is a Comfortable Monthly Investment? — 271
      - (2) How Much Is Available for Down Payment? — 271
  - 6. Enjoy the Hunt — 272
- D. PROFESSIONAL SHOWING TECHNIQUES — 272
  - 1. Home Hunting . . . A Rare Experience — 272

2. Are You Ready? 273

    a. Mentally? 273

        (1) Know Your Clients 273
        (2) Know Your Customers 273
        (3) Know Your Properties 273
        (4) Know Your Market Area 274
        (5) Know Yourself 274

    b. Physically? 274
    c. Emotionally? 274

3. Get Set 274

    a. Your Clients 274
    b. Your Customers 275
    c. Your Office 275
    d. Your Supplies and Forms 275
    e. Your Listing Books 275
    f. Your Selected Listings 275
    g. Your Vehicle 275
    h. Your Itinerary 275
    i. Yourself 276

4. Go 276
5. Stop 276
6. Look 276

    a. First Things First 276
    b. Accentuate the Positive 277
    c. Eliminate the Negative 277
    d. Latch on to the Affirmative 277

7. Listen 277

    a. Analyze Customers' Negative Reactions 277
    b. Capitalize on Customers' Positive Reactions 277

8. Is Your Slip . . . Showing? 278

    a. Follow Through 278
    b. Advise Your Clients 278
    c. Secure the Signatures 278

E. PROFESSIONAL CLOSING TECHNIQUES 278

    1. Introduction 278

	2.	What Buyers Expect of You	279
		a. Decisiveness	279
		b. Calm Assurances	279
		c. Professional Confidence	279
		d. The Opportunity to Buy	279
		e. Timely Humor	279
	3.	When to Close	279
		a. It's Never Too Early	279
		b. It's Never Too Late	279
		c. The Process Is Continuing	280
	4.	Where to Close	280
	5.	How to Close	280
		a. The "Affirmative" Technique	280
		b. The "Assumptive" Technique	280
		c. The "Closing Question" Technique	280
		d. The "Defensive Persuasion" Technique	281
		e. The "Direct Approach" Technique	281
F.		PRESENTING THE OFFER - CONVEYING THE ACCEPTANCE	281
	1.	Review Your Objectives	281
	2.	Meet Your Objectives	281
		a. Time Is of the Essence	281
		b. Solicit Listing Associates' Assistance	282
		c. Offer Must Be Personally Presented	282
		d. Recall the Acronym C. A. R. E. S.	282
	3.	Create Confidence	282
		a. Control the Circumstances	282
		b. Listen to Sellers' Objections	282
		c. Counter Each Valid Objection	282
		d. Proceed with Caution	283
	4.	Attract Attention	283
		a. Dissect the Difference	283
		b. Emphasize the Benefits	283
	5.	Rouse Interest	283
		a. Reiterate the Benefits	283
		b. Encourage Decisiveness	283

6. <u>Establish Want</u> 283

    a. Keep the Negotiations Open 283
    b. Elicit a Counter-offer 284
    c. Analyze the Counter-offer 284
    d. Timing Can Be Crucial 284

7. <u>Secure the Signatures</u> 284
8. <u>Service Is Success</u> 284

VISUAL AIDS 285

REVIEW QUESTIONS 289

Chapter 11
Digest of Closing Principles and Practices

A. UNDERSTANDING YOUR CUSTOMERS

   1. Analysis of a Buyer

   Full service to your clients presupposes your ability to search for, find, and thoroughly qualify a specific buyer who is "ready" to meet your client's terms and conditions when the sale is to take place, "willing" to enter into a contractual relationship with your client, and "able" to financially close the transaction when your client's title is to be conveyed. Without buyers, there are no efficient and procuring causes of sales, and without consummated sales, there are no commissions.

   Buyers often entertain a preconceived notion of a proto-typical real estate agent as either a hard-sell, objectionable, cigar-smoking huckster, or a frilly, flighty female out to make a fast dollar at their expense. They generally sense that either the sellers' interests or yours are primary and that they somehow will pay the price. Over the years, buyers have, unwittingly perhaps, been subliminally indoctrinated to distrust real estate agents. They are justifiably concerned when they, for example, read about state legislative committees on government regulations filing bills to set up recovery funds "for the victims of real estate brokers". Buyers are indecision personified, yet they are motivated to buy, usually as a result of changing conditions or pressures. As "problems in motion", buyers today demand that they be professionally served. There is an increasing tendency by courts and legislatures to establish measures for the protection of the public against any undue advantage exercised by real estate agents by virtue of their experience, expertise, economic strength or position, specialization, or practical control in a business transaction in behalf of their selling clients. Furthermore, buyers are tools of your profession, and, as with any skilled professional, your ability to respect the tools of your profession and to work with those tools efficiently and effectively to achieve your objective is the measure of your personal success. Perhaps most important is the fact that buyers are potential sellers. Buyers who buy in your market area, whether or not they seek out your services are, at the moment of conveyance, immediately transformed into property owners, and, thus, potential sellers.

   2. Suggested Treatment

   a. Convince Buyers You Are Their Sincere Friend. In almost all social or business exchanges there is an inherent reluctance to reveal too much about oneself, or give too much of oneself, except to those with whom one is thoroughly familiar.

Mutual confidence must be created before your offer of professional services will be eagerly accepted. Then you can proceed to determine if your buying suspects are ready, willing, and able buying prospects.

"If you would win a man to your cause," said Abraham Lincoln, "first convince him that you are his sincere friend."

b. Present Your References. One effective method of gaining your buyers' confidence is to give them the names of several satisfied clients whom you have serviced in previous transactions. Your prospects will seldom call these references, but they will appreciate your subtle and diplomatic acknowledgement of their apprehension.

c. Determine Their Need. In your association with your buyers, a most important consideration is to determine their need and then help them satisfy that need. Few buyers are thoroughly knowledgeable about the many facets related to houses. How many buyers are cognizant of the advantages and disadvantages of each selection they think they want ? How many buyers know enough to observe beyond the obvious or search behind the superficial ? Not many. Why ? It's not their job. It's YOUR job.

d. Accumulate Property Data. Presumably you, as a professional, are constantly striving to enrich your own knowledge of the tools of your profession. There is no escape from the fact that, to be professional and enjoy the success that professionalism commands in the real estate business, you must continually accumulate pertinent facts and data relating to the properties you deal with.

e. Invest Your Time Wisely. No matter how diligently you work, you cannot earn more time. The time that you have cannot be hoarded. It cannot be placed in reserve. In the field of real estate activities, perhaps the greatest amount of time is wasted by the inept or the inexperienced in their capacity as tour director for sightseers.

f. Qualify Your Buyers Professionally. As a professional, you have very definite obligations. You must sift, screen, cull, and discard all those who do not qualify as prospective buyers, for they are the thieves of your time and dissipators of your energies. Furthermore, they distract you from your primary responsibility of promoting the interests of your sellers.

3. The Anatomy of a Real Estate Transaction

For decades neophyte salespeople in practically all fields of selling have been introduced early in their careers to the A. I. D. A. It represents what is called the psychological approach to the selling process. The letters stand for "attention", "interest", "desire", and "action". They relate to the various stages through which each customer must be guided in an unvarying pattern by the professional salesperson.

After much analysis and critical observation, The Hall Institute has determined that virtually all real estate transactions, from inception to culmination, proceed, in sequence, through similar points of progress without disturbing or rearranging the A. I. D. A. pattern. While these stages are associated with the psychological processes experienced by buyers and sellers as they progress from one level to another, they also mirror the anatomy of most real estate transactions. With slight modification, therefore, and with the inclusion of a vital initial phase, The Hall Institute has adopted this pattern.

However, emphasis, rather than being placed on the noun, has been placed on the action word, the verb. One added phase, indispensable in all real estate transactions, is that of "creating confidence". When combined, these phases expose the anatomy of all real estate transactions. To repeat, each phase is inseparably fused with the phase which precedes or follows it. In servicing your clients and customers, before you can secure that all important signature on the contract, you must establish a need, a desire, a want. You know that this "want" must first be preceded by an "interest" which must be roused in your buyers. You know, too, that before you can even commence to excite interest you must first attract your buyers' attention . . . that very necessary psychological process of "winning their ear". However, before your buyers become amenable to any of these processes, you, as an individual, must be acceptable to them. You must be able to initially establish that rapport, that vital harmonious relation, from which confidence is created.

In reverse order, these psychological processes can be remembered by recalling the acronym C. A. R. E. S.

        Create Confidence
        Attract Attention
        Rouse Interest
        Establish Want
        Secure the Signatures

There is no shortcut to success. Success is earned by the professional who C. A. R. E. S.

B.   PROFESSIONAL TELEPHONE TECHNIQUES

    1.   Grasp the Opportunity

        a.   The Importance of Classified Advertising. It is probably conservative to estimate that one third of all buyers' inquiries to your firm are traceable to classifed ads. When statistics suggest that it takes between 25 to 30 calls on classified ads to produce one caller who eventually buys, our concern is long overdue.

    b. The Objectives of Classified Advertising

        (1) Ad Writer's Objective. The ad writer's classified advertising objective is to make the telephone ring.

        (2) Your Objective. There is only one objective of classified advertising from your point of view as a real estate associate. That objective is to give you the opportunity to <u>arrange appointments</u> with potential buyers who call in response to a specific ad. Emphatically, your objective is NOT, repeat NOT, to sell the callers the specific homes they call on.

    c. The Cost of Classified Advertising. After salaries, advertising costs represent <u>the</u> highest single expense of most real estate firms. Despite this hard, cold fact, there is ample evidence that few firms have developed the necessary training programs to educate their associates in the proper techniques of handling resultant inquiries from their classified ads.

    A great deal of time, energy, and money is allocated to the careful selection of properties to be advertised, to the studied preparation of ad copy, to the choice of media, and to the frequency of projection. It is illogical that, after committing this effort, most firms leave the rest to chance. As a consequence, in the great majority of cases, the primary objective of classified advertising is thwarted by non-trained, ill-trained, inept or lackadaisical associates who simply cannot or do not have the knowledge, ability, or desire to fully exploit the costly opportunities literally placed in their hands when they pick up the telephone receiver to answer a prospect's inquiries.

2. <u>The Importance of Floor Time</u>

If your firm has been in business for any considerable length of time, it is probable that thousands of dollars have been spent in a great number of areas to build its reputation and to project a professional image in the market area to attract potential clients and customers. By accepting floor time, you are able to reap the benefits of your firm's sizable investment at no expense to yourself.

The importance, then, of carefully selecting the associates who can recover these heavy expenses by exploiting the purpose of their expenditure for advantage and profit comes clearly into focus.

Company policy should clearly and emphatically require of all associates, through training and testing, a demonstrated proficiency in handling telephone inquiries on ads BEFORE they are given the privilege of assigned floor time.

3. When Customers Call

a. Determine Their Objective. When buying suspects call on a specific ad, it is likely that they are still engaged in the process of elimination and selection. People inquiring on specific ads do so for amplification of information included in the ad, or for information omitted. Obviously, then, the calls are prompted because the callers want more information. Furnishing too much information in your ads may decrease the number of inquiries you receive. Furnishing too little information may fail to attract the readers' interest sufficiently to prompt them to call.

Obviously, as floor associate, if you simply answer the callers' questions, their curiosity will soon be satisfied, and their elimination and selection process will continue. Whatever opportunity you had for determining their objectives and achieving your own is lost. Your best clue in determining your callers' objectives is hidden in the ad which prompted their inquiry. What specific point in the ad stopped their roving eyes? Your clue is there.

b. Set Your Objectives. When the telephone rings in response to your classified ads, all the weapons in your arsenal should be loaded and aimed at your objectives. There are two . . . your immediate objective and your ultimate, major objective.

Your immediate objective is to secure the caller's name, address, and telephone number. With this essential information, you can pursue your major objective of arranging an appointment even if the caller should unilaterally and peremptorily terminate the conversation.

Your major, as well as ultimate, objective is, of course, to arrange an appointment with your callers. Efforts, however, to meet either of your objectives are likely to prove fruitless without first establishing that all important rapport with your callers.

c. Achieve Your Objectives

(1) Control the Conversation. To meet your objectives, it is essential that YOU control the telephonic conversation. The interrogator is always in control. When the telephone rings, however, the callers, after specifying why they called, most often are likely to commence asking a series of questions. At this point, you may either maintain control or relinquish it . . . depending upon your knowledge and skill. Obviously, you eventually must answer many of the callers' questions. To

maintain control, however, simply remember that you must ask more questions than the callers. This is done by following every question you answer with probing questions of your own. If you develop the conscious habit of immediately following your answer to a caller's question with one or more questions of your own, you will discover how surprisingly easy it is to control the conversation . . . a necessary first step in meeting your objectives.

(2) Guide Your Suspects Through Each Psychological Stage. Your telephonic approach is essentially the same as your personal approach. The psychological stages through which each suspect must be guided remain the same. We have covered these stages in some detail in Chapter 12. The acronym C. A. R. E. will guide you in your approach. In short, you must first Create confidence, then Attract attention . . . and sustain it until you can Rouse interest and Establish want.

4. Create Confidence

   a. Put a Smile in Your Voice. The caller's first impression of you will be based on the sound of your voice, your selection of words and phrases, your courtesy, and your enthusiasm, all of which can easily be detected by the caller from your voice tone and inflections.

   b. Refer to Caller Continually by Name. Securing the caller's name and using it often throughout the conversation is an excellent way of maintaining a semblance of rapport. If you are unsuccessful during your initial attempt to secure their identification, try continuously to win them over by your helpfulness, courtesy, honesty, and sincere interest. However, when you do secure their name, use it continually throughout the conversation.

   c. Assume the Toll Charges. You might try engaging the callers in light conversation before abruptly getting down to business. Ask the callers if they are on a toll call. Suggest that you call back and assume the charges. (This will often give you their name and number at the outset). In any event, they will appreciate the gesture and your concern.

5. Attract Attention

   a. Know Your Properties. You know that your ad has already attracted the callers' attention to a degree. What you don't know is whether it specifically was the information furnished or the information omitted. It is reasonable to assume that the callers' attention probably can be sustained only until their reasons for calling have been satisfied.

At this point, another of your tools comes into play, i. e., your knowledge of property. You must know your inventory. You should know of every available piece of property in your market area. You must know these properties by price, location, size, style, and <u>emotional impact</u>.

    b.   Determine Motivational Urge. If, for example, the heading of your ad read "Blueberries", you have an inkling as to the motivational urge which caused the reader to call. Logically, the well prepared floor associate would have scanned all available listings for identical or at least similar properties which featured "<u>blueberries</u>", not the rational specifications such as three bedrooms, bath and a half, et cetera.

6.   <u>Rouse Interest</u>

    a.   Discuss Comparable Properties. Your ad attracted the callers' attention. Your questioning sustained that attention and, additionally, enabled you to explore the callers' motivational urge. We know that interest is roused when the possibility exists that the object capable of satisfying the callers' need or solving their problems is available . . . and attainable.

        It behooves you, therefore, to elicit from these callers those requirements and specifications they <u>think</u> are essential, and then to advise them of the available properties comparable to the one they called on which might well satisfy their need.

    b.   Appeal to Motivational Urge. Additionally, as previously suggested, the professional associates will have at their disposal the full particulars of a comparable list of properties in the same price range and appealing to the same motivational urge as the property advertised. When the callers are made aware that many other properties are available which may meet their demands, you are well prepared to lead them to the next psychological stage. This stage, you will recall, is the establishment of "want".

7.   <u>Establish Want</u>

        It has been often stated that the most important secret of salesmanship in any field is to find out what the customers really want, and then help them find the best way to satisfy their want. Through skillful and persistent questioning, conducted courteously, coupled with patient, attentive listening, you will control the conversation and, to a reasonable degree, determine what the callers <u>ostensibly</u> want. If you have been able to engage the callers thus far, securing an appointment as the first step in satisfying their wants will be largely a matter of form.

C. PROFESSIONAL QUALIFICATION TECHNIQUES

1. S. E. R. V. E. Your Customers

    a. Organize Your Time. In the real estate business, the demands on your time, if you approach and attach your responsibilities scientifically, will not allow you to waste a moment. You must quickly differentiate between the buying suspect and the buying prospect.

    A few wisely scheduled hours spent qualifying your buying prospects BEFORE any showings may save you hours, days, and even weeks of your precious time.

    This, then, is our purpose, i. e., to swiftly guide you, with a minimum expenditure of time, in your effort to professionally qualify your customers . . . to quickly cull the suspects, thus enabling you to serve your bona fide prospects diligently.

    b. Professionally Serve. Your immediate task is to channel all of your energies and talents to professionally S. E. R. V. E. your customers by . . .

    (1) Securing the Appointment
    (2) Establishing Rapport
    (3) Rendering Professional Service
    (4) Verifying Customers' Readiness, Willingness, and Financial Ability . . . Before You Commence . . .
    (5) Enjoying the Hunt.

2. Secure the Appointment

    a. Time. Timing is vitally important in everything you do. There is always a best time to do anything. The best time to arrange an appointment with your buying prospects will normally be when both husband and wife can be interviewed simultaneously, with a minimum of distractions, and in an atmosphere of calm which is conducive to leisurely and pleasant conversation.

    b. Place. Ideally, the qualifying interview should be conducted at the customers' home, where they are at ease and where their manner of living can be observed. Much can be learned by the astute associate from the customers' neighborhood, their home, their selection of furnishings, their figurines, paintings, collections, decorative articles, books, or even magazines. All these reflect tastes, interests, style of living. These clues are available to you for the asking . . . for the asking for an appointment at their home and at their convenience.

3. Establish Rapport

   a. Create Confidence

      (1) Be Punctual. Your punctuality in meeting your appointment will not go unnoticed. Lateness will cause frowns. A few moments early is the norm. But ringing your customers' bell precisely at the appointed time will surprise and please most customers.

      (2) Identify Areas of Mutual Interest. Most people naturally exercise a good deal of restraint when dealing with strangers ... particularly in revealing their financial status and innermost feelings ... when they can see no obvious need for such revelations. Invariably, some subject of mutual interest can be discovered. It may be an avocation, a hobby, a sport, an author ... perhaps just children or pets. You may share a similar political view. Once you discover that "something" you have in common and commence to exchange views, you are no longer a stranger.

   b. Introduce Your Blank Forms and Agreements. Provide your customers with blank copies of your "offer" forms, deposit receipts, and your Purchase and Sale Agreement for their familiarization. Later, when use of these forms becomes necessary, the psychological resistance or usual apprehensiveness may be negated by your foresightedness.

   c. Explain That All Properties on the Market Are Available Through You. Clearly explain that any property they might see on the market is obtainable through you at no extra expense. Soon you will have your customers calling you in regard to your competitors' ads or signs that might interest them.

   d. Determine Emotional Reasons for Buying. J. P. Morgan once said, "A man generally has two reasons for doing a thing: one that sounds good, and the real one." Specific requirements, such as the number of bedrooms, baths, family room, garage, et cetera ... these are your customers' rational reasons ... they sound good. You'll have no difficulty extracting this information. The information you require will not be provided so easily. You're seeking the all important <u>emotional</u> reasons. These will have to be elicited with patience and skill.

   e. Explain the Qualification Process. As professional real estate advisor to your customers, you are required to have this family and financial data if you are to do your job properly. With it you will be able to eliminate certain homes beyond their reach. Conversely, their financial status may well enable them to buy into a price range of homes they now only dream about. These explanations, without delving into specific details or figures at this moment, will prepare your buyers for the probing questions you must now commence to ask if you are to properly serve their interests.

    f. Check Your Empathy and Ego-Drive. Empathy and ego-drive require delicate balancing. Excessive ego-drive destroys your sensitivity. The "high pressure" associate is excessive ego-drive personified. Too much empathy and you suffer. Excessive empathy turns to sympathy. At that stage, the administration of professional service becomes impossible. Check your empathy and ego-drive frequently, as you would your gas and oil. Psyche yourself to "top" both of them off . . . then zero in on your objectives and relentlessly maintain your focus.

4. Render Professional Service

The quality of service you are able to provide your customers, and your ultimate success in determining their needs and satisfying their rational specifications and their emotional desires, will depend upon your ability to collect and analyze the pertinent information which bears on their problems. The type and extent of the information you elicit will relate directly to the type questions you ask and the manner in which you ask them.

Consistent, intelligent, and relevant questions which answer the four interrogatives WHO, WHAT, WHERE, and WHY should enable you to collect all the necessary property and personal data. The additional two interrogatives, WHEN and HOW, will be discussed in Paragraph 5, following.

    a. Who ? Family composition and related information is collected with the use of the interrogative "who". You must ascertain the family makeup by number, ages, and sex. Mental, physical, and emotional health of each member is often significant and should be determined. Pets, too, should be considered.

    b. What ? The interrogative "what" relates primarily to your customers' past and present housing and their future housing needs.

    c. Where ? Location, because of its immediate effect on all members of the family, is an area that should be explored thoroughly. Accessibility to rivers, mountains, shore or lake areas, shopping facilities, or major transportation routes or facilities may well be important, but heretofore unstated, requirements.

d. Why ? Undoubtedly your most important interviewing aid is the interrogative "why". The other five are indispensable in eliciting from your customers their rational requirements. "Why" digs beneath the superficial. It probes for reasons and relates to <u>emotions</u>. It zeros in on the real, rather than the ostensible, reasons, and delves deeply for those all important <u>motivational</u> urges.

5. Verify Customers' Readiness, Willingness, and Financial Ability

Qualification procedures, when properly followed, will enable you to define more accurately the rational specifications and the emotional desires of your customers. Additionally, these procedures will enable you to verify their readiness, willingness, and financial ability to buy. In probing for this type of information, you have at your disposal two more question words known for their value in dislodging answers from the reticent. These questions are "when" and "how".

a. When ? The interrogative "when" pertains to time. The "readiness" and the "willingness" of your buyers also pertain to time. Even more significant, however, is the fact that time is also the measure of urgency.

b. How ?

(1) How Much Is a Comfortable Monthly Investment ?

Usually, the first indication of your customers' need for your guidance is their revelation of the maximum price they are willing to pay for a house. This immediately tells you that they have given insufficient consideration to the tax factor. Your concern is not what they <u>think</u> they want to pay for a home, but what you <u>know</u> they can afford to pay. To make this determination, you must know the <u>maximum amount they can comfortably invest monthly</u>. Once this figure is obtained, you will advise them that together you will study this important statistic and verify their ability to make that monthly investment. Better now than after they have found a property which they have set their hearts on owning, only to discover that a lending institution does not view their position as optimistically as they do.

(2) How Much Is Available for Down Payment ?

You require two figures from your customers in order to determine how much they can afford to invest in a home and where this home probably will be located. The first figure is what they consider as a comfortable monthly investment. The second figure is the amount of money they have available for a down payment. With these two figures, together with your knowledge of the tax picture in the various sections of your market area, you will be able to guide your customers to homes within their price range. Too often, real estate agents bluntly ask for the price home their customers are seeking, assuming erroneously that their buyers are cognizant of the varying tax rates in the surrounding towns and taking for granted that buyers are aware of the diverse methods of purchasing and the interest rates and perhaps "points" charged, depending upon the method of purchase chosen.

6. Enjoy the Hunt

At the conclusion of your qualification process, it will become apparent to all that your efforts were an effective adjunct to the selection and showing process. While seated in the comfort and safety of your customers' home, you have been able to eliminate many properties which would be beyond their abilities to purchase . . . many of which would be shown by the less experienced associate to the eventual disappointment of both sellers and buyers.

You have satisfied yourself that you are now fully informed, and your customers are fully advised and confident that they have the capacity to purchase in the price range established and still stay within bounds of the comfortable, maximum monthly figure determined. Now you can sit back with justifiable pride, knowing that a most difficult part of your job is done and that your professionalism has helped your customers considerably in their preparation for searching for and selecting a home. This, then, is the next stage you enter into with your PROSPECTS.

ENJOY the HUNT !

D. PROFESSIONAL SHOWING TECHNIQUES

1. Home Hunting . . . A Rare Experience . . .

Home hunting is a rare experience, and, because it is, you should make it as enjoyable as possible for your buyers. As in every hunt, the expectation, the anticipation, the preparation, all combine to become memorable aspects of this singular experience. Your customers are about to embark on a wonderful shopping spree. They are out to buy happiness. This day should be filled with adventure and excitement. You play the indispensable role in this safari as the professional guide. You have already made certain that your buyers are well equipped for the trophy they're after. Your job now is to lead them to the hunting grounds, search with them for the quarry, caution them along the way, advise them whenever necessary, and suggest when it's time to load, take aim, and fire. During your thorough qualification procedures, you have won the buyers' trust and confidence. On this day, they will come to rely on your judgment and will seek your recommendations. You're the professional. You have every expectation of leading a successful hunt. You have the interests of your buyers at heart. Your quarry is out there somewhere. You know your buyers are ready, willing, and able to take it. Furthermore, you have every confidence in your own professionalism. There is no reason why you all should not enjoy the hunt.

Your excellence in qualification and closing are worthless skills if not complimented by a thorough knowledge of showing techniques which logically bridges the gap between start and finish of prospect relations.

As in all other areas of practical real estate activities, the selection and showing of homes should not be a haphazard undertaking, but one guided by logic and scientific precision.

2. Are You Ready?

    a. Mentally?

        (1) Know Your Clients. It's not possible for you to know your sellers, if you meet them for the first time with your buying prospect. Nor is this any way to impress your clients with your professionalism. Pre-inspection of the homes you intend to show is a professional must. In many instances it will be your first opportunity to meet the sellers. But, even more important, it affords you the opportunity of briefing them on precisely what they should do in order to present their home to its best advantage.

        The advantages of pre-inspecting all homes to be shown negate any rationalizations not to. The sellers will be impressed with your thoroughness (be sure to leave your card). Your buyers' confidence in you will be immeasurably increased by your demonstrated proficiency, and you will have gained considerably more confidence in your own preparedness.

        (2) Know Your Customers. Time alters all circumstances. Customers will modify some of their specific desires and eliminate others, as the urgency of their situation intensifies. Remember, nothing remains fixed or unchangeable. You must remain flexible and adaptable to changing situations.

        (3) Know Your Properties. Know your merchandise. Perhaps nothing will shatter your customers' confidence in you more than your inability to match most of their specifications to properties you've selected to show them. Most

associates, at one time or another, have been criticized for showing homes to customers with just those features their buyers did not want.

    (4)   Know Your Market Area. The location of property frequently is more important to homebuyers than the property itself. There may be certain amenities associated with a particular area which will entice buyers to decide on a home less desirable than one in an area which does not appeal to them. Knowing pertinent facts about your market area is as important as knowing your specific properties and the advantages and disadvantages of property features.

    (5)   Know Yourself. Don't prejudge. Included in your selection of properties to show are several designed to psychologically prepare your buyers for the home YOU THINK most fills their needs. Be alert, however, and be prepared to sell <u>every</u> home you select. Remember, one man's prison is another man's castle, and no matter how undesirable a home may be to your taste, it may be precisely what your buyers are looking for.

    b.   Physically? Your knowledge can be applied in practice to the extent of your physical capabilities. A weak body deters a strong mind. Your success in the real estate profession, as in any other, will be hindered just as disastrously by physical deficiencies as by mental laziness or lack of preparation. Physical fitness and mental alertness are inseparable. Both are essential, if you are to exploit your showing skills fully.

    c.   Emotionally? Confidence, aplomb, poise, savoir faire, self assurance, self possession . . . all involve a conviction of your own worth or an unself-conscious certainty of succeeding at whatever you attempt, unhampered by doubt, hesitation, or fear. If you know yourself and the tools of your profession . . . PEOPLE and PROPERTY . . . you should have no reason to be doubtful, hesitant, or fearful, and every good cause to exude confidence. And confidence in yourself is essential if you are to control, direct, and guide your clients to their desired objectives.

3.   <u>Get Set</u>

You are ready . . . mentally, physically, and emotionally. But before you GO, there are a few details demanding your attention. Let's check them out.

    a.   Your Clients. Make certain that the sellers have been advised of the time you expect to arrive. Make every effort to arrive on time

. . . not too early, and never too late, without first calling ahead to advise the sellers of changes in original schedules.

b. Your Customers. Presumably, you have finalized arrangements to meet your buyers at a specific location and at a definite time. Last minute verification of these arrangements is always in order.

c. Your Office. If your buyers are meeting you at your office, their impression of you will be enhanced by every indication of organization you can project. Attention to detail. Remember, you're not a run-of-the-mill agent . . . you're a professional.

d. Your Supplies and Forms. Since you intend to finalize a contractual agreement at the conclusion of your showings, you had better double check the inventory of forms and supplies to take with you. This would include Offer Forms, Purchase and Sale Agreements, Cash Receipts, carbon paper, blank notes, and any other form required by your company.

e. Your Listing Books. Along the route, your buyers might be attracted to homes that are on the market which you identify either from your personal knowledge or by "For Sale" signs on the property. Make sure your listings and those in M. L. S. are complete and current. Leave nothing to chance. Be prepared for any and every eventuality . . . and every opportunity.

f. Your Selected Listings. What to select and when to show . . . these are always problems that tax your talents and test your ingenuity. Your selection of listings should be the result of meticulously analyzing all you know about your buyers. Your choices must be as nearly compatible as possible to their rational specifications and their emotional desires.

g. Your Vehicle. Your vehicle is your mobile office and should reflect the same degree of cleanliness and orderliness as your office. All necessary preparation for a comfortable, safe, and relaxing drive should have been made. In inclement weather, make certain you have the equipment necessary for the welfare, safety, and convenience of your buyers. Snow tires and an umbrella are must items when warranted by weather conditions.

h. Your Itinerary. Your itinerary will be dictated by the homes you select to show, the order in which selected, and the routes of approach decided upon. As in every aspect of real estate, attention to detail is very important.

i. Yourself. Meticulous attention must be paid to your attire, your grooming, your manners, and personal habits. Carelessness about yourself will be interpreted by your buyers as a character fault which carries over to your work. Being careless is much like being pregnant . . . either you are or you're not.

4. <u>Go</u>

It's time to get on with the showings. Everything to this point has been checked and double checked. You should firmly, but tactfully, convince your buyers to ride in your car. The time spent on your showings is precious and should not be wasted by your buyers asking directions, or by you giving them. This is the appropriate time to talk about anything BUT the houses you are to show. Your planned itinerary should take you by areas of beauty or interest to your buyers. Point out houses along the way which have recently been sold or which are currently on the market. Educate your passengers as to community facts. Listen carefully to their questions, which often reflect their interests. Finally, if drawn into converation about the property you are about to show, confine your comments to the obvious deficiencies which require some attention. The mind is made of such fragile stuff that even words leave their impression. Make certain your buyer's actual impression by observation erases your verbal description of the deficiencies.

5. <u>Stop</u>

Now, precisely, is the moment to apply the formula C. A. R. E. S. Your buyers have developed confidence in you by this time, hopefully. Pay particular attention once again to every detail. It takes only a few moments to take a Polaroid shot of the house for your buyer. They'll look at it long after the showing, and it may well serve as a reminder of the benefits they otherwise might soon forget. Choose the best entrance; every home has more than one, many have three or more. Select the entrance which will present to your buyers the best first impression on entering. If the sellers are unavoidably at home, proper introductions are appropriate. Exchanging pleasantries should be the extent of the conversation. As soon as grace and good form permit, take charge and proceed with the showing, remembering always to relax your customers in order that they may "enjoy the hunt."

If you have fully won the confidence of your buyers, they will want you to explore, investigate, uncover and discover with them. Accede, however, to their preference. Let your buyers relax and enjoy this singular experience. Your job, you will recall, is to serve . . . not sell. You know the property. Guide them delicately . . . control them subtly.

6. <u>Look</u>

a. First Things First. Guide your buyers towards the appealing areas of the home first. Allow them to discover items of interest before uncovering defects or deficiencies. Psychologically, if their first impressions are of areas or objects which are abrasive or distasteful, they may close their minds to the more beneficial and favorable aspects.

b. Accentuate the Positive. Lead your buyers to think positively. Ask questions during the showing which are not only legitimate questions, but those which will elicit a "yes" answer. If your buyers discover a benefit . . . accentuate it with an appropriate question or remark. <u>Repetition is an aid to memory</u>. Amplify, magnify, accentuate the positive aspects repeatedly . . . but tactfully.

c. Eliminate the Negative. It's a natural defensive technique, unwittingly employed by buyers, to express real or imagined objections. When objections or negative comments are aired . . . IGNORE THEM. Remember, repetition is an aid to memory. IGNORE THEM.

If, however, the buyers repeat their objection or negative comment . . . LISTEN, and LISTEN WELL. Then tackle the objection. Air it. Expose it. Minimize it logically. Then dispose of it.

d. Latch on to the Affirmative. If you have empathized effectively with your buyers, and if you have correctly anticipated their needs and identified their motivational urge, you will recognize when a property satisfies their wants and should be purchased by them.

If, in your considered opinion, this particular house comes closest to satisfying their wants, it is your responsibility to advise them accordingly. You are looking after their interests in gently persuading them to act decisively and affirmatively.

7. <u>Listen</u>

a. Analyze Customers' Negative Reactions. You have made your selection of homes for your buyers after careful qualification and interpretation of their overt and covert desires. You have placed yourself in their position and concluded that the homes you chose to show them would most probably stimulate interest. If, after your first showing, you find yourself to be in obvious error, now is the time for full and frank two-way communications with your buyers before valuable time is wasted in continued showings of similar properties.

b. Capitalize on Customers' Positive Reactions. As you proceed to your next showing, confident that you are on the right track, you must discipline yourself to patiently listen to your buyers' post mortem on the property you've just left. Pay particular attention to what pleased them. Was it a significant physical feature, or a seemingly insignificant emotional experience? Herein may be buried the motivational key to your buyers' problem.

8. <u>Is Your Slip . . . Showing?</u>

   a. Follow Through. In many instances, homes are purchased on the same day they are shown. If such fortune is not yours, and you sincerely believe your buyers have found the right home, it is up to you to take the offensive and systematically follow through.

   b. Advise Your Clients. Your sellers are on "pins and needles". Report back to them as soon as possible . . . the same day if possible. Telephonically, if necessary . . . personally, if you can. Advise them fully and candidly, but with sufficient sensitivity to avoid embarrassment to them. Many times, at this stage, the sellers will voluntarily offer to negotiate price or consider more favorable terms. These factors may be precisely what you need in your follow through with your buyers.

   c. Secure the Signatures. You have served your buyers professionally . . . to this point. You have not professionally served them completely until you have met their objective. Their objective is to purchase a home. They can't purchase a home without signing an Offer to Purchase or a Purchase and Sale Agreement. You believe that you have found the right home. You sense that your buyers want it, but are indecisive and hesitant. It is understandable that your buyers are indecisive and hesitant. It is inexcusable if you are.

E. PROFESSIONAL CLOSING TECHNIQUES

   1. <u>Introduction</u>

   Your buyers came to you for one primary purpose . . . to assist them in finding a suitable home to buy. They came to you because of your general knowledge of the market, and because of your specific knowledge of properties, territories, and financial considerations. They came to you to be professionally served. If you have served them well, you will not have to sell them anything. You need only advise and recommend. Your buyers will buy. In order to buy, however, they must first make an offer on the property they have selected. At this stage of development, that is your objective . . . obtaining the <u>full-price</u> offer from your buyers.

2. <u>What Your Buyers Expect of You</u>

   a. Decisiveness. Now is the time to recall Emmette T. Gatewood's definition of a buyer, "... a demand in human form ... an indecision personified ... a mass of confused molecules looking for a catalytic agent to make him into a compound of decision." You are that catalytic agent. The time for decision is now. Take out that blank Purchase and Sale Agreement or your Earnest Money Deposit Receipt, and assume the closing posture.

   b. Calm Assurances. Your buyers will look to you for support and strength. They will need your reassurances to stabilize their mental anxieties, indecisions and general unrest. This is the time for you to display contagious enthusiasm and a calm sureness of manner in coping firmly but courteously with all developments.

   c. Professional Confidence. Your buyers will subconsciously look to you to help eliminate their indecisions, to support their positive observations, and to minimize or eliminate their anxieties and uneasiness. Don't let them down.

   d. The Opportunity to Buy. Your buyers want to buy. They do not want to be sold. The decision to act must be theirs. It should not be imposed on them. Your job is to clear the path for their progress towards these ends.

   e. Timely Humor. Nothing adds lightness or buoyancy to any such emotionally charged atmosphere as does the right amount of levity. As a professional, it again falls on you to do all in your power to make the entire transaction an enjoyable and satisfying experience. You are the island of calm in a sea of turbulence. At all times you must remain in complete control of your customers as well as the circumstances. Levity is often effective when all else fails.

3. <u>When to Close</u>

   a. It's Never Too Early. You started to close your buyers during your first qualifying interview at their home. At that time, you strengthened their confidence in you by your announcement that together ... sooner or later ... by joint efforts, you fully expected to find the home they are looking for.

   b. It's Never Too Late. If all your knowledge and experience convince you that the buyers have found the best available home in the market area of their preference, and in the time available to them, you would be shirking your responsibilities to cease your services after the first "no". It's easy for you to take "no" as final. You accept their decision as final. You would <u>if</u> you were a mediocre agent. You will not as a professional associate. Your true mettle as a professional in closing your buyers begins with their first "no".

    c.   The Process Is Continuing. Closing is a continuing process. Everything you do, everything you say, should be channelled towards that climactic moment when your buyers sign the contract.

4.   Where to Close

The time separation between the decision to buy and the execution of the contract may be long enough for the fires of your buyers' desires to die out. Close in the sellers' home when conditions permit, in your car, if appropriate, or back at your office, if you must. Your buyers' home should be the last choice for obvious psychological reasons.

5.   How to Close

It is important to realize that "closing procedures" or "testing techniques" are a poor substitute for the professional qualification of your customers. When your buyers have been qualified, using the acronym S. E. R. V. E. as your guide, you know, and they know, when their home is found and you will simultaneously share the joy of discovery. Testing techniques are superfluous in such circumstances. Nevertheless, occasions will arise when proper qualification is not possible before showing. In these rare instances, testing techniques must be employed. The following approaches are recommended:

    a.   The "Affirmative" Technique. This technique psychologically conditions your buyers to dwell on the positive aspects of a property. Simply stated, you carefully phrase questions designed and guaranteed to produce a "yes" answer, an affirmative nod, a silent acquiescence, or an inferred acceptance. You can practice this technique on your spouse, can't you? You see the logic behind this approach, don't you? Give it a try, won't you?

    b.   The "Assumptive" Technique. This is a technique where the associate assumes the sale and proceeds with questions which normally would follow the vital one, had it been asked.

    c.   The "Closing Question" Technique. This technique is perhaps one of the most effective techniques because it is quite direct. When employing this technique, the associate asks any question, the answer to which may be entered on the offer form, deposit receipt, or purchase and sale agreement. Such questions are,

"When would you prefer conveyance, Mr. and Mrs. Buyer ?", or, "What is your full name, Mr. Buyer ?" In some sales circles, this technique is referred to as "the order blank close".

    d.   The "Defensive Persuasion" Technique. A relatively new technique which is proving quite effective is the "defensive persuasion" technique. This is the clever art of turning any question the buyers ask into a closing question of your own. If, for example, your buyers should ask, "Do the hall runners go with the house ?" . . . you, in replying, would ask, "Do you want the hall runners to go with the house ?"

    e.   The "Direct Approach" Technique. This is the most professional and most effective closing technique. When you have won your buyers' complete trust and confidence, when they know you are looking after their interests as their sincere friend, when they rely on your judgment, and when you know that this is the house they should buy . . . SAY SO and ask for their approval on the purchase agreement.

F. PRESENTING THE OFFER - CONVEYING THE ACCEPTANCE

1. Review Your Objectives

You have fulfilled your obligations to your sellers when, through your professional services, you have obtained for them the best possible price for their property while realizing for them the most favorable terms and conditions. Furthermore, you have negotiated the transaction in the shortest time possible, with a minimum amount of inconvenience.

You have obligations to your customers also. These obligations are met when you have, through professional service, identified their rational desires and emotional needs and have then satisfied those desires and needs.

Your personal reputation and financial success will depend upon your ability to professionally service <u>both</u> sellers and buyers to their mutual benefit and satisfaction.

2. Meet Your Objectives

    a.   Time Is of the Essence. Time is of the essence in presenting all offers and counter-offers. Remember, your buyers, even after submitting an offer, are probably still apprehensive, still cautious, still subject to vacillation. Until the sellers accept your buyers' offer, the property remains on the market. Buyers can experience a change of heart. You must move quickly while their enthusiasm is running high and while their anxieties continue to stimulate their interest.

b. Solicit Listing Associates' Assistance. If the listing is another associate's, solicit his assistance. If the situation were reversed, you most certainly would insist that all negotiations be processed through you. The listing associates cannot fully service their clients if they are not intimately involved in this critical phase of developments. Moreover, their support of your offer can be invaluable and is often the deciding factor in successfully concluding negotiations.

c. Offer Must Be Personally Presented. A cardinal rule must be followed at this point. The offer must be presented in person to the sellers, both the husband and wife, simultaneously. Discussion of the offer must not be conducted over the telephone. It is almost impossible for you to avoid becoming enmeshed in the details of the offer, if you initially telephone the sellers to arrange for an appointment. Consequently, you will request the listing associates to arrange the personal interview with you. If the lister is not immediately accessible, ask the office secretary or another associate to set up the appointment.

d. Recall the Acronym C. A. R. E. S. Continually recall the acronym C. A. R. E. S. This will provide you with your blue print for action. In presenting your offer, you must first create confidence, attract attention, rouse interest, establish want . . . before you finally . . . secure the signatures.

3. Create Confidence

a. Control the Circumstances. The atmosphere may be volatile and emotionally charged. You are expected to be that "island of calm in a sea of turbulence." It is your job to control the circumstances as they develop rather than allowing yourself to be controlled by them. Even under the most favorable circumstances, emotional reactions in varying degrees of intensity should be expected and anticipated . . . particularly when offers are presented which are less than the listed price.

b. Listen to Sellers' Objections. Allow the sellers time to fully vent their objections to the offer. Don't interrupt. Encourage them to completely expose their every objection. Listen. Listen. Remember that soup is not always eaten as hot as it is served. Allow time for your sellers to cool down.

c. Counter Each Valid Objection. Reflect the picture of patience and professionalism; then, calmly and firmly counter all valid objections (most of which should have been anticipated) with facts and logic.

d. Proceed with Caution. Proceed with due caution. Buyers are winning a home. Sellers, in many instances, are losing memories. Even with a full price offer and the most favorable terms and conditions, emotional problems can, and often do, arise. Tact, diplomacy, sensitivity, and compassionate understanding are continually required.

4. Attract Attention

   a. Dissect the Difference. Above all, focus your attention on the difference between the list price and the amount of the offer. Dissect this difference. Analyze it thoroughly.

   b. Emphasize the Benefits. Market activity relates directly to property pricing and the subsequent fluctuations in such pricing. Discuss this market activity, or lack of it, with the sellers. Keep continually in mind the time element and educate the sellers as to the indeterminable time necessary to find other well-qualified buyers and the related cost in anxieties and frustrations which must be suffered by the sellers. Certainly discuss the favorable aspects of the offer, e. g., quick conveyance, large down payment, absence of contingencies, et cetera.

5. Rouse Interest

   a. Reiterate the Benefits. Once again, explain the immediate benefits to be enjoyed by acceptance of the offer. Continued anxieties are considerably minimized. Further inconveniences are eliminated, uncertainties are negated, future plans can now be formulated. Once again the sellers can enjoy some semblance of normal home life and that peace of mind which normally follows decisive action.

   b. Encourage Decisiveness. Explain to the sellers the position of the buyers, who are involved in a sizeable financial transaction. The buyers are timid, defensive, apprehensive, and may, at that very moment, be vacillating and subconsciously looking for a way out. Time is of the essence. The buyers may withdraw their offer at any moment prior to acceptance by the sellers. Any change of the offer by the sellers negates the buyers' offer. Unqualified acceptance of the offer, on the other hand, solves the major problems of the sellers and affords them, once again, that mental tranquillity they so earnestly desire.

6. Establish Want

   a. Keep the Negotiations Open. You will be faced with situations where your sellers firmly reject the offer. Your immediate task now is to keep the negotiations open. Prepare the ground for a reasonable counter-offer. Review market activity in general and that activity on the sellers' property specifically.

b. Elicit a Counter-offer. Your next course of action is to obtain from your sellers a counter-offer. Exact from them the lowest price that they would be willing to accept.

c. Analyze the Counter-offer. This procedure tends to lend greater force and substance to all of your previous arguments supporting your buyers' offer. Point out the needless loss of time, the continued anxieties, the expected frustrations, and the disruption of normal family life which must be endured still further. Ask, once more, for their acceptance of the offer.

d. Timing Can Be Crucial. Minor, inconsequential changes must be discouraged. Much can transpire during the time interval necessary to secure ratification of the changes and to secure the required signatures.

7. Secure the Signatures

Once the offer is accepted by the sellers, or the counter-offer is accepted by the buyers, the acceptance must be communicated for a binding contract to result. It is imperative to realize that all changes to the contract, no matter how trivial, should be dated and must be initialed by all parties concerned. Be certain that all parties are in receipt of properly initialed and signed contracts. It would be prudent, where changes, corrections, deletions, or additions are numerous, that the contract be redrafted and finalized to avoid subsequent misinterpretations or misunderstandings.

8. Service Is Success

You sold your product - SERVICE. Negotiations have been completed. Contracts have been executed. Title has been conveyed. You have fulfilled your legal and moral obligations to your selling clients and your buying customers. For both parties your professional knowledge and skill have enabled you to negotiate the best price, at the most favorable terms, in the shortest period of time, with the least amount of inconvenience. You have fully promoted and protected the interests of your clients and, simultaneously, have identified, isolated, examined, and satisfied the rational desires and emotional needs of your customers. You have rendered a vital social service to your fellow man !

As a consequence of your professional service, your former clients will shout your praises to their spheres of influence who remain in your market area long after they themselves depart. Your new property owners will be certain to reinforce your professional image and reputation to all they embrace within their new circle of contacts. All this is your reward for the sacrifices you made while coddling your clients and captivating your customers.

ANATOMY OF A REAL ESTATE TRANSACTION

- C. • Create Confidence
- A. • Attract Attention
- R. • Rouse Interest
- E. • Establish Want
- S. • Secure the Signatures

The Professional Associate C.A.R.E.S.

THE TRANSFORMATION OF CUSTOMER TO POTENTIAL CLIENT

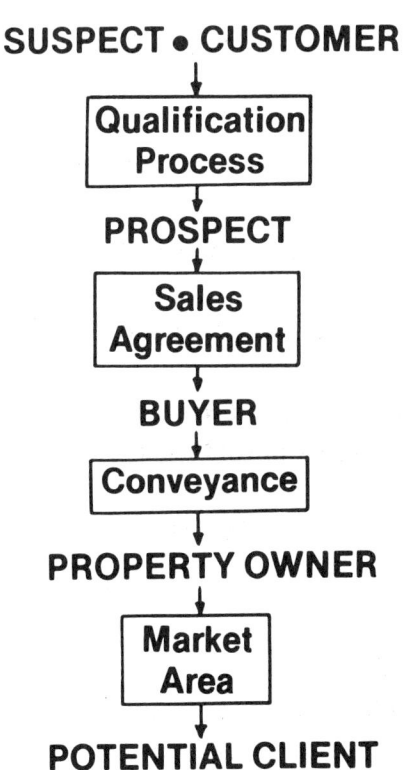

SUSPECT • CUSTOMER
↓
[Qualification Process]
↓
PROSPECT
↓
[Sales Agreement]
↓
BUYER
↓
[Conveyance]
↓
PROPERTY OWNER
↓
[Market Area]
↓
POTENTIAL CLIENT

OBJECTIVES WHEN THE TELEPHONE RINGS

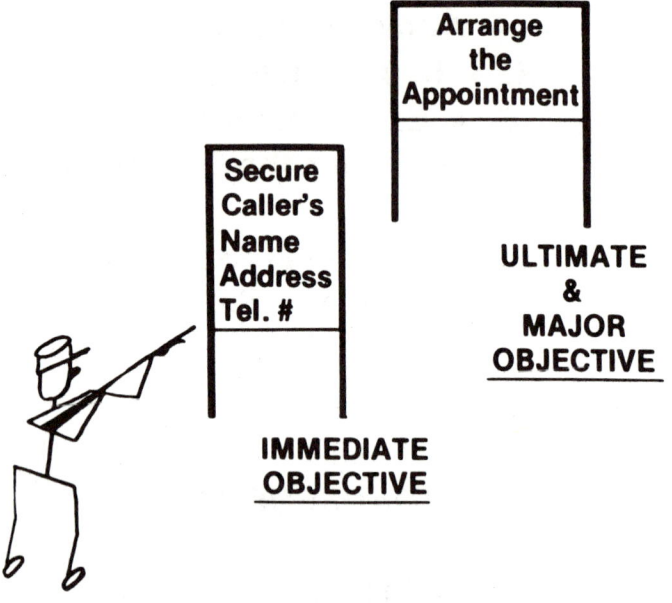

SERVE YOUR CUSTOMERS

S. • Secure the Appointment

E. • Establish Rapport

R. • Render Professional Service

V. • Verify Readiness, Willingness and Financial Ability

E. • Enjoy the Hunt

**The Professional Associates
S.E.R.V.E.**

RENDER PROFESSIONAL SERVICE

1. WHO?
 a. Family composition
 b. Ages and sex
 c. Mental, physical, emotional health
 d. Pets

2. WHAT?
 a. Past Housing
 b. Present Housing
 c. Future Needs

3. WHERE?
Location - Location - Location

4. WHY?
 a. Emotional Desires
 b. Motivational Urges
 c. Rational Specifications

VERIFY BUYERS'
- **Readiness**
  - **Willingness**
    - **Financial Ability**

1. WHEN?
 a. **'When'** relates to **'Time'**
 b. **'Time'** relates to **'Urgency'**
 c. **'Urgency'** relates to **'Motivation'**
 d. **'Motivation'** relates to **'Price'**

2. HOW?
 a. How much is a comfortable monthly investment?
 b. How much is available for the down payment?

IS YOUR SLIP . . . SHOWING?

1. Follow Through
2. Advise Your Clients
3. Secure the Signatures

TESTING TECHNIQUES

1. The **AFFIRMATIVE** Technique

2. The **ASSUMPTIVE** Technique

3. The **CLOSING** Technique

4. The **DEFENSIVE PERSUASION** Technique

5. The **DIRECT APPROACH** Technique

Chapter 11

REVIEW QUESTIONS:

1. What psychological selling processes does the acronym C. A. R. E. S. stand for?

2. From the associate's point of view, what is the objective of classified advertising?

3. Is floor time a right which is coincidental with association or a privilege?

4. When the telephone rings in response to your classified ad, what is your immediate objective at the beginning of your telephone conversation?

5. Where would be the ideal location to qualify your customers?

6. When would be the ideal time to qualify your customers?

7. Which are more significant, the buyers' rational specifications or their emotional (motivational) needs?

8. When must closing techniques be employed to test your buyers?

9. What does the acronym S. E. R. V. E. stand for?

10. In qualifying your customers relative to their financial ability, what two questions are asked with the interrogative "HOW"?

11. In the interests of time, is it advisable to present offers telephonically?

12. How should an offer be presented?

13. What is your immediate task when the sellers firmly reject the offer?

14. Must the acceptance of an offer be communicated to the buyers before a binding contract results?

FOR ANSWERS TO REVIEW QUESTIONS:

1.

2.

3.

4.

5.

6.

7.

8.

9.

10.

11.

12.

13.

14.

Chapter 12

The Sales Contract

A.	THE PURCHASE AND SALE AGREEMENT	294
	1. Introduction	294
	2. Importance	294
B.	ESSENTIAL ELEMENTS OF A PURCHASE AND SALE AGREEMENT	296
	1. Mutual Assent	297
	a. Description - General	297
	(1) Definiteness	297
	(2) Buildings, Structures, Improvements, Fixtures	297
	(3) Personal Property	297
	(4) Effect of the Words "About" and "More or Less"	298
	b. Description - Specific	298
	(1) The Metes and Bounds System	298
	(a) Metes and Bounds	298
	(b) Courses and Distances	298
	(2) The Rectangular Survey System	299
	(a) General	299
	(b) Checks	299
	(c) Ranges	299
	(d) Townships	301
	(e) Sections	302
	(f) Description	303
	(3) The Plat System	305
	2. Consideration	305
	3. Competent Parties	305
	4. Legal Purpose	306
	5. Legal Form	306

C.	PURCHASE PRICE	306
	1. General	306
	2. Ballooning the Purchase Price	306
D.	TERMS AND CONDITIONS	307
	1. Down Payment	307
	a. Additional Deposits	307
	b. Promissory Notes as Down Payment	307
	c. Safeguarding Deposits	307
	2. Time and Place for Performance	308
	3. Conditions Affecting Title	308
	4. Adjustments	308
	5. Broker's Commission	308
	6. Insurance Clause	308
	7. Condition of Property at Conveyance	309
	8. Provisions for Perfecting Title	309
	9. Acceptance of Deed as Full Performance	309
E.	EXECUTION OF THE SALES CONTRACT	309
	1. General	309
	2. Partial Execution	309
	3. Authority of Broker to Sign for Sellers	309
	4. The Transfer of Equitable Title	310
F.	ACKNOWLEDGEMENT OF THE SALES CONTRACT	310
G.	RECORDING THE SALES CONTRACT	310
H.	EXTENSION OF THE AGREEMENT	310
I.	CHANGES TO THE AGREEMENT	311
J.	PURCHASE BY MORTGAGE TAKEOVER	311
	1. General	311
	a. Assumption of the Mortgage	311
	b. Subject to the Mortgage	312
	2. Inclusion of Takeover in the Agreement	312

K.	OPTION TO PURCHASE		312
	1. General		312
	2. Advantages		313
		a. To the Buyer	313
		b. To the Seller	313
L.	SPECIFIC PERFORMANCE CONTRACT		313
	1. General		313
	2. Advantages		314
		a. To the Buyer	314
		b. To the Seller	314

VISUAL AIDS   315

REVIEW QUESTIONS   318

Chapter 12
The Sales Contract

A.   THE PURCHASE AND SALE AGREEMENT

    1.   Introduction

Real estate agents and attorneys often loosely refer to a binding contract as an "offer to purchase" even after the offer has been accepted and communicated. Once accepted, the offer to purchase becomes a binding contract; subsequent documents are merely formalities stemming from that contract. After acceptance of an offer by the seller, the ensuing contract would better be called a "binder contract" to reflect that the parties are bound by it. Or, perhaps, a "preliminary contract" might be a proper description to show that a more formal deed or long-term contract is yet to be executed. The term "interim contract" is often used to suggest that the period covered extends to a point in time when the transaction is to be formally closed. Perhaps most widely used are the terms "purchase contract," "sales contract," or "purchase and sales contract" to show that it is a contract by which one has agreed to sell and the other has agreed to purchase. All of these terms mean substantially the same. All are in common enough usage so that real estate agents should clearly understand their meaning. Regardless of the name, any agreement in writing whereby one person, for consideration, agrees to sell to another a specific piece of property, under certain terms and conditions, is a valid and enforceable contract which is subject to all the ordinary requirements of a contract as reflected in Chapter 4 - - - ON CONTRACTS.

    2.   Importance

There is little doubt that the practice of real estate brokerage brushes closely, and sometimes abrasively, with the practice of law. The preparation, for example, of the sales agreement by the real estate agent for his client magnifies the overlapping tendency. Real estate brokers and practicing attorneys jealously guard their field of endeavor. In some states, the Supreme Court has been asked to rule whether or not real estate brokers should be enjoined from preparing certain legal documents relating to and affecting real estate, and the title thereto, such as: receipts and options for purchase, contracts for sale, deeds, deeds of trust, leases, and from giving advice to the parties to such documents as to the legal effect of the documents.

In addressing itself to this problem, the Colorado Supreme Court said: "The first question to be determined is: Does the preparation of receipts and options, deeds, promissory notes, deeds of trust, mortgages, releases of encumbrance, leases, notices terminating tenancies, demands to pay rent or vacate, by completing standard and approved printed forms, coupled with the giving of explanation or advice as to the legal effect thereof, constitute the practice of law ?

"This question we answer in the affirmative.

"The remaining and most difficult question to be determined is:

"Should the defendants, as licensed real estate brokers (none of whom are licensed attorneys), be enjoined from preparing in the regular course of their business the instruments enumerated above, at the requests of their customers and only in connection with transactions involving sales of real estate, loans on real estate or the leasing of real estate, which transactions are being handled by them ?

"This question we answer in the negative . . . "   (Conway-Bogue Investment Company v Denver Bar Association)

The court further explained . . .

"We feel that to grant the injunctive relief requested, thereby denying to the public the right to conduct real estate transactions in the manner in which they have been transacted for over half a century, with apparent satisfaction, and requiring all such transactions to be conducted through lawyers, would not be in the public interest; that the advantages, if any, to be derived by such limitation are outweighed by the conveniences now enjoyed by the public in being permitted to choose whether their brokers or their lawyers shall do the acts or render the service which plaintiffs seek to enjoin . . . "

In 1966, the Illinois Supreme Court ruled that a real estate broker is authorized to fill in the blanks on a printed form of a sales contract commonly in use in the community where he does business. He may also supply factual information to enable the contract to be completed for signatures. However, it has been ruled that the preparation or completion of any subsequent document necessary to implement the terms of the sales contract is prohibited and falls within the prohibited area of "practicing law without a license."

In some states, real estate brokers are prohibited from preparing contractual agreements, for their principals, which involve third parties. In other sections of the country, the real estate broker may even prepare the deed.

In general, however, real estate brokers are allowed to prepare the usual legal documents, on standard and approved forms, by filling in the blanks, at the request of their clients and customers, with information obtained from the usual sources in transactions relating to their brokerage practice, when no compensation for such preparations are realized other than their ordinary commission.

All real estate agents are cautioned to exercise great care in the preparation of sales contracts to ensure that the public interest continues to be served and that those courts, which have ruled favorably for brokers, will not have reason in the future to change their opinions.

The purchase and sale agreement is the culmination of all the associate's efforts in a particular transaction. Execution of the contract for the sale of land provides the time for the buyer to examine the seller's title prior to actual conveyancing. The contract does not give the buyer possession; it gives him a right (equitable title) to receive the property at a specified date and imposes a duty on the seller to deed the property (convey legal title) to the buyer on the date so specified. In some respects, the purchase and sale agreement is the most important document the associate prepares. Indeed, the contents of the deed, to a certain extent, are based on information contained in the purchase and sale agreement. State licensing laws specifically require both brokers and salesmen to prove their understanding of real estate agreements. Thus, when drawing this vital agreement, the real estate broker must be fully aware of the responsibilities he undertakes. A poorly drawn agreement may lead to general dissatisfaction of the parties involved, which often deteriorates into open controversy and failure to perform. Expensive litigation is courted by improperly drawn agreements. Furthermore, an associate may subject himself to license suspension or revocation because of incompetency. It behooves the professional real estate practitioner to make certain that all parties to the contract clearly and fully understand all the provisions in the contract and their rights and duties relating to those provisions. Presumably (if professional brokerage practices were followed), the sellers were previously exposed to a blank purchase and sale agreement to familiarize them with its contents and to dispel any fear of the form at the critical moment of execution. Similarly, the buyers, ideally, would have been given a copy of the blank contract for their familiarization during the first qualification interview. In any event, before the associate can be assured that the parties to the contract understand its terms and conditions, it holds that he, too, must be intimately familiar with the form and content of this very important instrument.

B. ESSENTIAL ELEMENTS OF A PURCHASE AND SALE AGREEMENT

The Purchase and Sale Agreement, being a sales contract, must incorporate all the essentials of a contract to be valid. These are:

   a. Mutual Assent

      (1) Offer

         (a) Intentional
         (b) Definite

            1. Time
            2. Price
            3. Property (Legal Description)

         (c) Communicated

      (2) Acceptance

      b.   Consideration
      c.   Competent Parties
      d.   Legal Purpose
      e.   Legal Form

1. <u>Mutual Assent - Reference Chapter 4</u>
   Paragraph B. 1.

   The agreement or willingness to contract must be clearly evidenced in the agreement by the words of the contracting parties. This mutual agreement to enter into contractual relationship is usually contained in that paragraph of the purchase and sale agreement identifying the contracting parties, e. g., "JONES, hereinafter called the SELLER, <u>agrees to SELL</u> (the offer) and SMITH, hereinafter called the BUYER, <u>agrees to BUY</u> (the acceptance) upon the terms hereinafter set forth ... et cetera." Note that mutual assent is comprised of an offer and an acceptance, and we further note that one of the three prerequisites of an offer is that it be definite as to the description of the property involved. If the property to be sold or exchanged is too indefinitely described, the agreement may fail. It behooves one, therefore, to be familiar with the various systems employed to provide a legal description of real property.

   a. Description - General

       (1)   Definiteness. As indicated above, any contract must precisely describe the property involved if the agreement is not to fail because of indefiniteness. The description should generally identify the precise location, the shape, and the size of the property. Ideally, the description in the sales contract should be the same as that given in the seller's deed. The mere street address of a property is, of itself, insufficient and does not satisfy the requirements of the law.

       (2)   Buildings, Structures, Improvements, Fixtures. A description of the land infers the inclusion of all buildings, structures, and improvements thereon, and these need not be, but usually are, specifically included in the agreement. Controversy often arises relative to what personal property is considered as a fixture and passes with the land. A properly drawn agreement will leave nothing to chance, but will specifically identify all fixtures included in the sale.

       (3)   Personal Property. Any agreement for the purchase and sale of personal property should be separate and distinct from the purchase and sales agreement and should be evidenced by a bill of sale.

(4) Effect of the Words "About" and "More or Less". In the description of a parcel of real estate, the adjectives "about" and "more or less" are often encountered to modify courses, distances, and area. Legally, the word "about" is regarded as having no effect on the term it is used to modify. Quantity is the most uncertain element in land descriptions. When the quantity of land is modified with the words "by any and all measurements and contents more or less" or simply as "more or less", it must be consistent generally with the controlling quantity determined through use and application of monuments, courses, and distances.

b. Description - Specific

Generally, real property is described by using one of the following three major systems: the Metes and Bounds System, the Rectangular Survey System, and the Plat System.

(1) The Metes and Bounds System. A description by metes and bounds frequently starts with a monument from which is determined the distance and the angle of the line to the next monument, continuing thusly until the tract is completely enclosed and thoroughly described. In this application a monument may be some sort of a structure or stone or other permanent object which serves to mark a boundary. When used, the center of the monument is the boundary reference. If the monuments are permanently fixed and unequivocally identified, their use in land description is satisfactory.

(a) Metes and Bounds. Metes are lineal measurements (e. g., inches, feet, yards); bounds are artificial and natural boundaries. While "metes" determine the quantity of land, the "bounds" contain the land within fixed limits. Such a description must, of course, have a <u>definite</u> starting point and <u>definite</u> terminal point.

(b) Courses and Distances. Application of the metes and bounds system varies among surveyors. Because of this variance, the law of metes and bounds has created an order of precedence. Course (or angles) will control over distances when a discrepancy arises. It is presumed that lines connect the monuments, if the angle is correct. Some metes and bounds descriptions use only courses and distances starting from a known point. It is important to note the differentiation between the terms "courses" and "distances". A course is an angle. It is the compass direction of a boundary line with respect to true North or magnetic North. Distances are the specific measurements between terminal points of the boundary.

(2) The Rectangular Survey System

(a) General. After the Revolutionary War had ended and new areas were added to the public domain, it became apparent that a plan had to be developed for locating lands in the new western territory for subsequent sale. Thomas Jefferson devised the plan which is known today as the Rectangular Survey System. This plan was adopted by Congress on May 20, 1785. Ohio became the testing ground for the new system of land description. Much was gained from the Ohio experience, and some changes in the law were made. The second such survey was initiated in Indiana about 1810. Since that time, all the land west of the Mississippi River has been surveyed in this manner, with the exception of Texas. The system today has been adopted by thirty states because of its practicality, where the metes and bounds system may not be appropriate or acceptable because of the susceptibility of monuments to destruction, shifting, or removal.

(b) Checks. The objective of this survey system was to create a checkerboard of squares of the same size covering a given area. The largest unit of measure is called a "quadrangle" or a "check" measuring 24 miles on each side. Each quadrangle or check is further divided into 16 squares called "townships" whose four boundaries each measure six miles. Each township is further divided into 36 one-mile square sections which in turn can be further subdivided into halves and quarters.

(c) Ranges. In commencing any survey, however, a starting point must be established. This starting point, moreover, must be specifically located by geographical coordinates (i. e., latitude and longitude). By an act of Congress, on the order of the Secretary of the Interior, the General Land Office of the Government was instructed to mark and establish specific parallels of latitude called "baselines" and specific meridians of longitude, called "principal meridians". The system, as it evolved, established 35 north-south lines of longitude (principal meridians) which follow no specific pattern. These principal meridians are identified by either a number (e. g., Fifth Principal Meridian) or a name (e. g., Salt Lake Meridian). Each parcel of land under this system is described in conjunction with only one specific principal meridian which is not necessarily the nearest principal meridian. Similarly, east-west (parallels) lines of latitude called "baselines" have been established. The location of a particular property is identified with respect to the eastward or westward direction from the north-south principal meridians, and then with respect to the northward or southward direction from the east-west base line. The specific distance to the particular property is first measured eastward or westward from a specific principal meridian in six-mile strips. These six-mile wide columns or strips run northward and southward and are called "ranges." Ranges are numbered beginning with number 1 immediately followed by the directional indicator east or west of the specific principal meridian. This procedure furnishes one of the two necessary coordinates.

(d) Townships. A second requirement is to locate the property in conjunction to its specific north or south distance with a range, measured from the applicable base line. This distance from the base line is also measured in increments of six miles. Each six-mile increment north or south of the base line cuts the column of ranges into squares measuring six miles. The resulting squares are called "townships." An east-west row of townships is called a "tier."

Townships are numbered, beginning with number 1, further identified as either north or south, depending upon its direction from the baseline. A description of a township would read, for example, "Township 4 north, range 4 east of the _____ Principal Meridian. The 36 square mile township thus formed by the intersection of the range lines by the tier (or township) lines is the basic unit in the Rectangular Survey System.

(e) Sections. Each township (measuring 36 square miles) is divided into 36 one-mile square (640 acres) sections. These sections are numbered 1 through 36, always beginning in the upper right hand corner (northeast corner), then proceeding westward to the last section in the tier (number 6), then eastward along the next lower tier, et cetera. The last section in the lower right corner (southeast corner) of the township is always number 36. As a matter of interest, each section number 16 was set aside for school purposes by law. The proceeds from the lease or sale of this "school section" were available to the township for school purposes.

6	5	4	3	2	1
7	8	9	10	11	12
18	17	16	15	14	13
19	20	21	22	23	24
30	29	28	27	26	25
31	32	33	34	35	36

TOWNSHIP (36 Square Miles)
Divided into 36 Sections each one mile square

Each square-mile section (640 acres) may also be further subdivided into quarters, called the northwest, northeast, southwest, or southeast quarter.

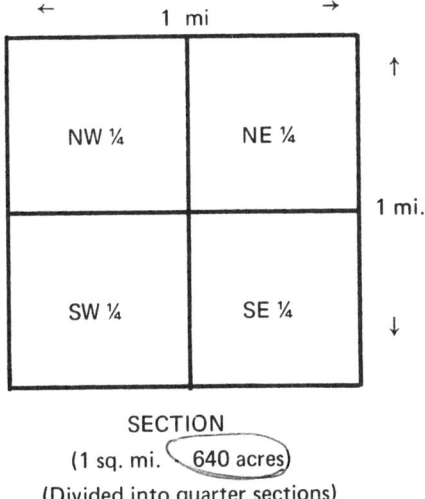

SECTION
(1 sq. mi. 640 acres)
(Divided into quarter sections)

These quarters may be further subdivided into quarters or halves which can be further subdivided.

NW QUARTER SECTION
Further Subdivided

(f) Description. To describe the northwest quarter of the above quarter section, the description would be written as: the NW¼ of NW¼ of Section _____ (the words "of" are not necessary).

Incorporating this portion of a description with a full description we would have: NW¼, NW¼, Section 1, Township 4 north, range 4 east of the _____ Principal Meridian. (The word "sector" may assist the reader in remembering the order in which the description is written, i. e., section, township, range).

Thus, it may be seen that the Rectangular Survey System (also known as the Congressional Survey System or the Government Survey System) provides a comprehensive and accurate system for the expeditious location of any land in an area.

6th PRINCIPAL MERIDIAN

6	5	4	3	2	1			
7	8	9	10	11	12	36 sq. miles		
18	17	16	15	14	13			
19	20	21	22	23	24			
Township 4 North Range 4 West				35	25 36	TOWNSHIP 4 NORTH RANGE 3 WEST	TOWNSHIP 4 NORTH RANGE 2 WEST	TOWNSHIP 4 NORTH RANGE 1 WEST
TOWNSHIP 3 NORTH RANGE 4 WEST						TOWNSHIP 3 NORTH RANGE 3 WEST	TOWNSHIP 3 NORTH RANGE 2 WEST	TOWNSHIP 3 NORTH RANGE 1 WEST
TOWNSHIP 2 NORTH RANGE 4 WEST						TOWNSHIP 2 NORTH RANGE 3 WEST	TOWNSHIP 2 NORTH RANGE 2 WEST	TOWNSHIP 2 NORTH RANGE 1 WEST
TOWNSHIP 1 NORTH RANGE 4 WEST						TOWNSHIP 1 NORTH RANGE 3 WEST	TOWNSHIP 1 NORTH RANGE 2 WEST	TOWNSHIP 1 NORTH RANGE 1 WEST

BASE LINE

The above illustrates the subdivision of one full 24 mile square check or quadrangle with the 6th Principal Meridian acting as the point of departure. The check is further subdivided into 16 six-mile square townships, with the township in the upper left corner subdivided into 36 one-mile square sections. Section 6 (upper left hand corner of the subdivided township) is divided into quarters with the lower right hand quarter further subdivided into quarters. To describe the location of this latter quarter of a quarter section, we would write:

SE¼, SE¼, SECTION 6, TOWNSHIP 4 NORTH, RANGE 4 WEST of the 6th PRINCIPAL MERIDIAN.

NOTE: Because the earth is an oblate spheroid, the meridians of longitude converge as they extend towards the poles. To correct the error caused by this curvature, the area between the intersecting base lines and meridians of longitude are further divided into quadrangles (checks) described above. In order to keep the townships as nearly 6 miles square as possible, a "correction line" or jog is made at every check as the meridian lines continue toward the pole.

> (3) The Plat System. Using the plat system, a tract of land described by the metes and bounds system or the rectangular survey system is divided into streets, blocks, and lots. Maps or plans of real property indicating their subdivision into smaller lots or parcels which contain streets, blocks, and lot numbers are filed by a subdivider or developer with appropriate office of record for the area in which the property is located. These maps or plans are called "plats". A "plat book" is a record maintained by the aforementioned office showing the location, size, and name of the owners of each plot of real property in a given area. The land may subsequently be described in relation to the recorded plat simply by giving the lot number, block, and subdivision name. For example, Lot 7, in Block 3 of Joe Hughes' Subdivision in the Town of Marshfield, Massachusetts, might describe real property located in that area.
>
> NOTE: Similarly, a description of a parcel of land may be made by reference to a plan or to another deed. When a description by such a reference is used, all the details identifying and determining the location, shape, and size of the land in the reference are to be regarded as having been expressly set forth in the agreement. Description by reference usually is reflected in the agreement as "Being the same premises conveyed to the Seller by deed recorded with the _____ office of record in Book _____, Page _____."

2. Consideration: - - Reference Chapter 4 - - Most sales contracts cite that the agreement is under seal. If such is the case, no consideration need pass between the contracting parties. Generally, however, sufficient consideration exists in the concurrent mutual promises of the contracting parties.

3. Competent Parties: - - Reference Chapter 4 - - The full name of all parties to the contract should be entered. If the sellers are husband and wife, the full name of each should be reflected, e. g., John A. SELLA, husband, and Mary E. SELLA, wife.

It is good business practice to capitalize the family name for two reasons. First, in many instances foreign names pose difficulty in differentiating the given name from the family name - and a male from a female name. Furthermore, in some cultures it is not customary for a wife to assume the family name of the husband. Particular attention should be given to precise spelling of all names. The sellers and the buyers must be identified. The words seller and vendor are used synonymously, as are the words buyer, purchaser, and vendee.

    4. <u>Legal Purpose</u>: - - Reference Chapter 4 - - <u>Legal purpose</u> must be considered at the outset. Whether or not contracts entered into on Sunday are illegal depends upon the law of the particular state where the contracts are made. As stated in Chapter 4, (Sunday Contracts), statutes which declare Sunday contracts illegal and void do not apply to preliminary contractual negotiations. An offer may be made on a Sunday and executed on a weekday without violation of the Sunday law. Conversely, however, acceptance on a Sunday of an offer presented on a weekday would result in an illegal contract. Formal contracts, such as deeds, do not become effective until delivered.

    5. <u>Legal Form</u>: - - Reference Chapter 4 - - A contract for the sale of real estate, in order to be enforceable, <u>must be in writing</u>. No particular form is required for a sales agreement as long as the written memorandum names the parties, sufficiently describes the property, states the price, terms, and conditions, and is signed by the person to be charged. (Reference Chapter 5).

C.   PURCHASE PRICE

    1.   <u>General</u>: - - The agreed upon purchase price of the property should be <u>accurately reflected in the agreement</u>. Provisions should be made in the contract that the purchase price be paid in <u>cash</u> or <u>certified check</u>. Terms of the purchase may call for the "<u>takeover</u>" or the "<u>assumption</u>" of the seller's existing mortgage by the buyer. Such provisions must be clearly reflected in the sales agreement. (Reference Paragraph J, infra). The legitimate purchase price of the property is perhaps the closest figure to a true appraisal. Many lending institutions base the amount of money they will loan on a property as a percentage of the purchase price. Banks must allow themselves a margin of safety to safeguard the funds entrusted to them.

    2.   <u>Ballooning the Purchase Price</u>: - - Unfortunately, there are some brokers who, in their efforts to hold together a sale which might otherwise fall apart, will inflate the purchase price on the sales contract to agree with that falsely entered on a loan application. If, for example, the legitimate purchase price on the property is $20,000, and the bank will loan 80% of the purchase price or $16,000, in order for the sale to go through, the buyer is obliged to make a down payment of $4,000. However, we will assume that the buyer can only accumulate $2,000. The unscrupulous broker will inflate (hence, "balloon") the purchase price on paper only to $22,500. Knowing the bank's policy will allow them to loan 80% of the "purchase price" (falsified to $22,500) or $18,000, combining the buyer's $2,000 with the bank's loan of $18,000 gives the seller his full asking price of $20,000. The consequence of this

type of activity should be clearly understood. When a loan application containing an inflated purchase price is submitted to any lending institution, misrepresentation is committed. The mere submission of the falsified application is the crime of uttering and forgery. The fact that the broker does not sign the loan application does not relieve him from liability. The crime of conspiracy to defraud is committed, and all who knowingly participated are liable.

D. TERMS AND CONDITIONS

1. Down Payment: -- An adequate deposit, which the buyers would not be inclined to forfeit, strengthens the finality of their decision to buy. It takes them out of the market. Additionally, it protects the broker for his labors and the sellers for removing their property from the market. Furthermore, it may compensate the sellers who have gone on record as accepting a lower price than agreed upon when the property was initially listed with the broker. The amount of the purchase price and the lapse of time agreed upon before transferring title are factors to be considered in determining what an adequate deposit would be. Ten percent of the purchase price - or, as a minimum, an amount sufficient to satisfy the associate's commission, is usually considered adequate. Some listing contracts provide that all deposits made and forfeited by the buyer shall first be used to satisfy the broker's commission, and the balance, if any, shall belong to the seller. Perhaps a more equitable arrangement would provide that all monies paid on account, if forfeited by the buyer, shall be divided equally between the seller and the broker, but on no account shall the sum paid to the broker exceed the commission agreed upon.

   a. Additional Deposits. If the buyers upon signing the sales contract have insufficient money to make an adequate deposit, provisions should be made that the buyer agrees to pay specific additional sums at definite dates. This provision should further state that the date is of the essence of the agreement.

   b. Promissory Notes as Down Payment. If part of the down payment is in the form of a promissory note, it is essential that the sales contract reflect this fact. It is the broker's fiduciary obligation to his principals, the sellers, to advise them accordingly.

   c. Safeguarding Deposits. Where the broker has an exclusive contract with the sellers, the contract should provide that all deposits made by the buyer are to be held by the broker, as agent for the seller, subject to the terms of the agreement and to be duly accounted for at the time for performance. Most states, either by law or by the rules and regulations of the licensing commission, require that all monies of whatever kind and nature belonging to others and accepted by the broker, shall be deposited in a separate bank account maintained by the broker as a depository for funds belonging to others.

2. Time and Place for Performance: - - A definite time and place for performance should be written into the agreement. If no date is specified, the agreement will not fail for indefiniteness, as the courts will generally assume that the parties intended a reasonable time. If either party to the agreement insists upon a specific closing date, to which they will hold the other party absolutely, then the agreement should read as follows after the time and date: "which time and date are of the essence of this agreement."

The time of closing the transaction and the time that possession of the premises are to be given to the buyer may not be the same. In the absence of agreement between the seller and the buyer, the right to possession follows the legal title. The contract should express and specify as to delivery of possession to the purchaser, and should definitely fix the date of such possession.

3. Conditions Affecting Title: - - The broker should make certain, after scrutinizing the owner's deed, that there are no problems in the title which will affect the transferability of the property. Reference is made to mineral rights, mining rights, easements, building restrictions, et cetera. The agreement should be written subject to grants, rights, easements, covenants, and restrictions of record. Normally, the type of deed by which the premises are to be conveyed is specified.

4. Adjustments: - - Provisions should be made for proration between sellers and buyers of any collected rents, mortgage interest, prepaid premiums on insurance if assigned, water and sewage use charges, fuel, taxes, and any other charges which may be involved.

5. Broker's Commission: - - Generally, the commission clause in the sales contract provides for payment by the seller to the broker of either a specific amount or a rate. In some instances reference to the commission to be paid is made to "the customary rate charged in the _____ area." Since such information is included in the "hiring" or "listing" contract, it is not necessary to include it in the sales contract. In some circumstances, it may be preferable to omit the commission clause.

6. Insurance Clause: - - In the event of complete destruction of the property by fire prior to passing of papers, the legal owner of the property generally assumes the loss. If the buyer does not wish to buy, he can recover all deposits. However, many agreements contain a clause which obliges the buyer to take title, even if the structures on the land were completely destroyed by fire. This clause states as follows: "the building shall, until the performance of the agreement, be kept insured by the seller in an agreed amount and that in case of any loss all sums recovered or recoverable on account of said insurance shall be paid to or assigned on delivery of the deed to the buyer." For this reason, it is vitally important to make certain that the building is fully and properly insured. It is also possible to include another clause which would give the buyer an option to carry on or withdraw from the contract in the event of complete destruction.

7. Condition of Property at Conveyance: - - Usually, a clause is inserted in the agreement providing that full possession of the premises is to be delivered at the time of the delivery of the deed, in the same condition as they are at the time the agreement is signed, reasonable use and wear excepted. The agreement may also obligate the buyer, if there is damage caused by circumstances over which the seller had no control.

8. Provisions for Perfecting Title: - - Generally, provisions are made in the agreement for extension of the time for performance for either the seller or buyer, or both, as provided in the clause, to remove any defects in the title. Frequently, provisions are also included which authorize the seller to use the purchase money, or any portion of it, to clear the title of any or all encumbrances or interests.

9. Acceptance of Deed as Full Performance: - - Most purchase and sale agreements provide that the acceptance of the deed by the buyer (or his nominee) shall be deemed to be a full performance and discharge of every agreement and obligation in the contract. Without this provision, if the seller was unable to convey a good title, the buyer has the option of accepting conveyance of all the rights the seller has, with adjustment for the proper abatement in the purchase price for whatever losses or damages the buyer suffers.

E. EXECUTION OF THE SALES CONTRACT

1. General: - - When the agreement is signed by all parties concerned (legally called the execution), the associate, at that moment, is generally entitled to his commission. When the contract is executed, the broker is no longer concerned as to the purchasers' financial ability to buy. The sellers' acceptance of the buyers, as evidenced by their mutual assent to the contract, relieves the associate of that concern. In dower states, it is important to obtain the signature of the seller's wife. In such instances, if a spouse does not join in the agreement, he or she cannot be forced in any way to join the deed. In many contracts a clause is inserted whereby the seller's spouse agrees to join in the deed and to release and convey all statutory and other rights and interests in the premises. When all signatures are secured, the broker affixes his signature and gives one copy of the executed contract to each of the parties. Failure to do so is a violation of the license law in many states.

2. Partial Execution: - - When an agreement has been executed by only one of the contracting parties, it is not binding on that party. Until executed by all parties, the agreement is incomplete and cannot take effect as a valid contract.

3. Authority of Broker to Sign for Sellers: - - Ordinarily, a real estate broker has no authority to execute the purchase and sale agreement for the sellers simply because of the principal-agent relationship formed in the employment contract. The listing employment contract establishes the broker as a special agent as opposed to a general agent. (Reference Chapter 3, Paragraph C). Where the broker is specifically given this authority, the appointment to execute a binding contract must be in writing,

since the sales contract is required to be in writing. Such appointment gives the broker what is known as "power of attorney", and the broker becomes an "attorney in fact".

4. The Transfer of Equitable Title: - - When the sales agreement is fully executed, equitable title in the property is transferred to the vendee (purchaser). The equitable title owner is one who has a present title which will ripen into a legal title upon the performance of the condition subsequent (conveyancing).

F. ACKNOWLEDGEMENT OF THE SALES CONTRACT

An acknowledgement for a sales agreement is a statement made by the seller that he signed the agreement of his own volition, without any coercion, duress, or undue influence. In many jurisdictions such acknowledgement must be made before a notary, a justice of the peace, or two witnesses (the broker may serve as one) who make affidavit that they were present and witnessed the signatures being affixed. Normally, it is not necessary to have a sales agreement acknowledged. Acknowledgement, however, permits the agreement to be recorded and, in effect, places a cloud on the sellers' title, thus protecting the buyer - particularly if considerable time is to elapse between the contract signing and conveyancing. Transferring title at the conveyance normally removes this cloud.

G. RECORDING THE SALES CONTRACT

Recording the sales contract is not required, but normally is permitted by statute if the agreement is acknowledged. The entire agreement need not be recorded; a memorandum (also acknowledged) will suffice if the parties are identified and the real estate is sufficiently described.

H. EXTENSION OF THE AGREEMENT

If the clause in the sales agreement providing for the time and place of performance makes no reference to time being of the essence, the extension of this type of an agreement for a reasonable length of time does not require the execution of a formal agreement to extend. Performance on time, however, may be made a condition precedent by adding a clause that "time is of the essence in the agreement." In this manner, the parties to the agreement have stipulated time to be of importance when normally it is not so considered. In this instance, if it appears probable that the contract cannot be performed at the time and date specified, it is sound practice to execute the formal extension to avoid the possibility of legalities. If such an extension is not executed when required in contracts stipulating that time is of the essence, failure of either party to perform on time affords ground for rescission, unless the court construes that the time clause is a penalty provision. In such a case, the court may rule that specific clause to be unenforceable.

I. CHANGES TO THE AGREEMENT

Once the sales agreement has been executed, the broker must not change or modify the contract in any way unless he obtains the agreement of both parties in writing.

J. PURCHASE BY MORTGAGE TAKEOVER

1. General: - - Frequently, the seller may agree to allow the buyer to "takeover" the existing mortgage as part of the terms and conditions of the sale. A "takeover" is precisely what the term implies. It is a transfer of title to a new buyer, subject to the payment by the buyer of the seller's existing mortgage at the rate of interest prevailing on the existing mortgage. As a standard practice, the agreement of sale on these terms would be predicated on the seller's acceptance of the credit statement ordered on the buyer by the listing broker. If there is a reasonable spread between the purchase price and the seller's existing mortgage balance, and the buyer's credit report shows a sound credit rating, then a good, solid sale can usually be consummated. A takeover is generally a fast way to sell property for the highest price with less than the usual closing costs. The only problem that could develop for the seller would be if the buyer defaulted on the seller's mortgage payment, and the property is sold at foreclosure at a bid price falling short of covering the amount due on the mortgage plus costs. As a practical matter, the chances of this happening are rather remote. In such an eventuality, the sellers can take back the mortgage by reassuming the responsibility of making the mortgage payments. The balance of the mortgage will, in all probability, have been reduced somewhat, and the sellers can resell the property, very likely for an additional profit. The purchaser can take over the mortgage in one of two ways: he may "assume the mortgage" or may take deed to the property "subject to the mortgage". The distinction between these two terms is subtle, but important.

    a.   Assumption of the Mortgage. When the purchaser "assumes" the seller's mortgage, he promises to pay to the mortgagee for the seller any deficiency resulting from a foreclosure by the mortgagee (the lender). The purchaser, in other words, has entered into a contract with the seller for the benefit of a third party (the mortgagee). Thus, in an assumption of the seller's mortgage by the purchaser, the mortgagee, upon foreclosure, may collect any deficiency from the purchaser. If the purchaser cannot pay, the mortgagee may then seek payment from the mortgagor (seller) on the mortgage note or bond which continues to hold the seller liable to the mortgagee.

        In some instances, when there is an assumption clause in a deed, both the purchaser and the seller sign the deed, as contrasted to the normal case when only the grantor signs the deed. This is justified by virtue of the fact that with the assumption clause the parties enter into a written contract in addition to a deed conveying title to the property. In some states, however, the courts have held that the contract wherein the purchaser agrees to "assume" the seller's mortgage may be entered in evidence as proof to that effect against the purchaser.

In some states, such as Massachusetts, the mortgagee, on default of payment, can sue only the seller for payment and not the purchaser. It is important to note that should the mortgagee, at some later date, enter into any sort of an agreement which affects the terms of the mortgage with the purchaser who has assumed such mortgage, such agreement relieves the seller (mortgagor) of all liability to the mortgagee.

    b.   Subject to the Mortgage. When the purchaser buys "subject to" the mortgage, he is not liable for any deficiency in the event of foreclosure by the mortgagee. The most the purchaser can lose is any equity he may have built up in the property. In this instance, the seller remains primarily liable to the mortgagee. When a purchaser buys a property "subject to" the mortgage, he promises nothing; he simply acknowledges the existence of the mortgage. Any agreement affecting the mortgage made between the mortgagee and the purchaser has no effect on the seller's (mortgagor's) liability to the bank. The seller remains fully liable - unlike the seller who allows his mortgage to be assumed.

2.   <u>Inclusion of Takeover in the Agreement</u>: - - When the seller agrees to allow the buyer to take over the existing mortgage, details of the takeover should be included in that provision of the agreement which reflects the manner in which the purchase price is satisfied. The following is an example:

> The agreed price for said premises is $30,000, of which $2,000 have been paid as a deposit this day.
>
> The balance of the purchase price is to be paid by assumption by the buyer of the seller's existing first mortgage with the Friendly Savings Bank adjusted to the balance outstanding at the time of passing, plus whatever cash is required which, together with the deposit made, will total the full purchase price of $30,000.

K.   OPTION TO PURCHASE

    1.   <u>General</u>

An "option to purchase," sometimes called a "receipt and option contract," or simply an "option", is an agreement whereby the buyer purchases the exclusive right to buy the seller's property at a stated price at any time during the period fixed by the option. While the option is a contract, it is not specifically a contract to purchase. It develops into a contract of purchase only when the buyer duly "exercises" his option to purchase in accordance with the terms of the agreement. The consideration for the option is the earnest money paid by the purchaser for the time set aside as the period within which the option must be exercised.

2. Advantages

   a. To the Buyer

   (1) The buyer has the choice of exercising his option and receiving delivery of the property, or

   (2) The buyer may elect to refuse to consummate the transaction and forfeit his deposit without further concern of being compelled to specifically perform.

   (3) Under such an option agreement, the risk, in the event the property is destroyed, remains with the seller until the transaction is consummated.

   (4) The seller cannot compel the purchaser to "specifically perform" by accepting and making full payment for the property.

   (5) The buyer, when exercising his option, can compel the seller to convey in an action for specific performance. The seller, however, must be content with the liquidated damages, the earnest money posted by the buyer.

   b. To the Seller

   (1) If the prospective purchaser fails to exercise his option to purchase according to the terms of the option contract, the seller may immediately declare a forfeiture of the earnest money, which becomes liquidated damages without further litigation.

   (2) When a purchaser allows his option to expire, the seller's property may be placed on the market immediately without necessity for a time consuming lawsuit.

   (3) When properly employed, the option to purchase adequately compensates the seller for taking his property off the market for the time agreed.

L. SPECIFIC PERFORMANCE CONTRACT

1. General

When something as unique as land, which cannot be adequately reproduced or replaced, is involved, a decree for specific performance may be ordered by the court. This order directs the defaulting party to a contract to perform exactly and specifically in accordance with the terms of the agreement. In most jurisdictions, where a contract allows either party the right to enforce specific performance, the buyer is considered to be the owner of the property, and, although he does not have legal title, he has "equitable title." This equitable title allows the purchaser to legally force the seller to convey legal title. Similarly, the seller can compel the buyer to accept legal title and perform as agreed. This right is called "specific performance," and the parties lose this right only if they waive it in the contract.

2. <u>Advantages</u>

    a. To the Buyer

        The buyer, upon default, can be compelled to specifically perform by the seller only after completion of a sometimes costly lawsuit. Moreover, a recorded specific performance contract and a lawsuit may render the property unsalable for months, or even years, which prompts the seller all too often to satisfy himself with an insufficient deposit which the buyer would forfeit.

    b. To the Seller

        If a "specific performance" type contract is carefully drawn, the seller, upon default by the purchaser, would be able to compel the purchaser, through court action, to accept the property and pay for it. The seller does not have this remedy with an option to purchase agreement.

THE SALES CONTRACT

ESSENTIAL ELEMENTS:

1. **Offer and acceptance**
2. **Names of competent sellers and buyers**
3. **Consideration**
4. **Legal purpose**
5. **Legal form**
6. **Legal description of real estate**

LEGAL DESCRIPTION OF REAL ESTATE

1. **Metes and Bounds System**
2. **Rectangular Survey System**
3. **Plat System**

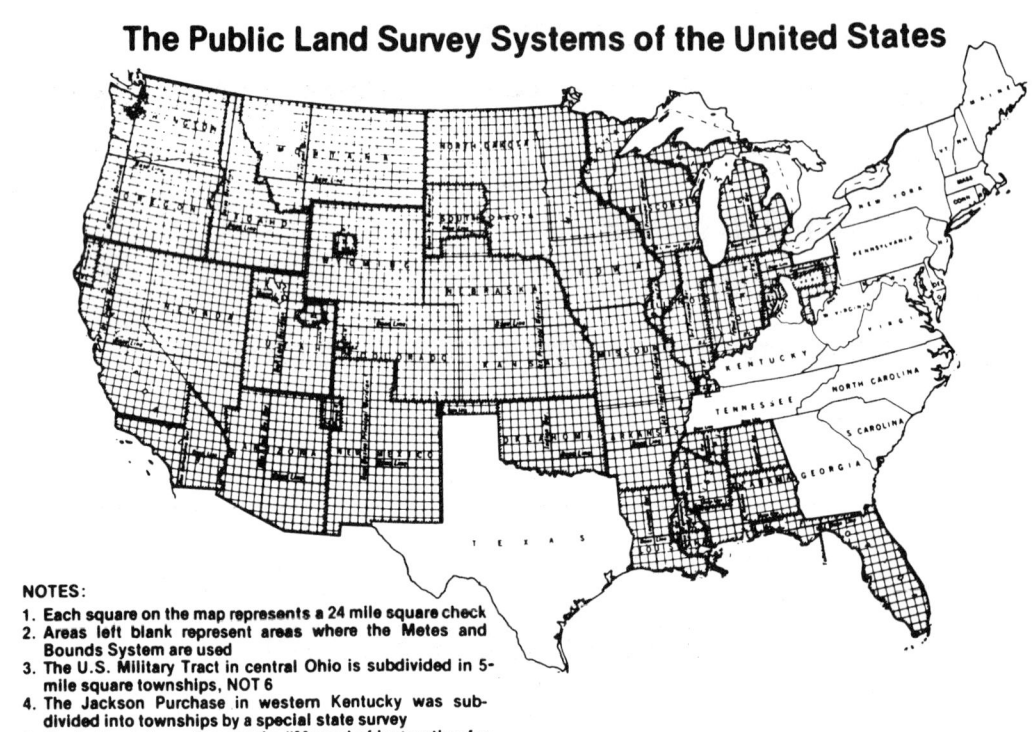

The Public Land Survey Systems of the United States

NOTES:
1. Each square on the map represents a 24 mile square check
2. Areas left blank represent areas where the Metes and Bounds System are used
3. The U.S. Military Tract in central Ohio is subdivided in 5-mile square townships, NOT 6
4. The Jackson Purchase in western Kentucky was subdivided into townships by a special state survey
5. For further information see the "Manual of Instruction for Public Land Surveys" issued by the General Land Office of the Dept. of Interior

THE SALES CONTRACT

MORTGAGE TAKEOVER

1. ASSUMPTION OF THE MORTGAGE: Subsequent agreement between mortgagee and buyer relieves seller of liability to mortgagee.

2. SUBJECT TO THE MORTGAGE: Seller remains liable.

Chapter 12

REVIEW DEFINITIONS IN GLOSSARY OR TEXT OF FOLLOWING TERMS:

bank draft	et ux
base line	frontage
bench mark	liquidated damages
betterments	metes
bill of sale	monument
binder	principal meridian
bounds	promissory note
certified check	purchase
commingling	purchase and sale agreement
commission	range
course	recording
distance	section
earnest money	security deposit
encumbrances	time is of the essence
equitable ownership	township
et al	vendee
	vendor

REVIEW QUESTIONS:

1. What are the essential elements of a purchase and sale agreement?

2. What must the legal description of the real estate include?

3. What is the legal effect of the word "about"?

4. What is the most uncertain element in land description?

5. Name three methods of providing a legal definition of a parcel of land.

6. What legal form is required for the purchase and sale agreement?

7. What is the effect of ballooning the purchase price?

8. How must deposits be safeguarded?

9. What amount is considered as an adequate deposit?

10. What is the significance of the words "time is of the essence" in an agreement?

11. Name five adjustments to be considered in drawing up the purchase and sale agreement.

12. Is it necessary that the broker gives a copy of the purchase and sale agreement to both buyer and seller?

13. Does the real estate associate normally have authority to sign the purchase and sale agreement for his principal, the seller?

14. What type of ownership is transferred to the vendee when the sales agreement is fully executed?

15. Is recording of the agreement required?

16. What is a "mortgage takeover"?

17. What is the difference between an "assumption of the mortgage" and a "subject to the mortgage"?

18. How large is a "check"?

19. How many townships are in a "check"?

20. What is the area of a township?

21. How many sections are there in a township?

22. What is the area of a section?

FOR ANSWERS TO REVIEW QUESTIONS:

1.

2.

3.

4.

5.

6.

7.

8.

9.

10.

11.

12.

13.

14.

15.

16.

17.

18.

19.

20.

21.

22.

Chapter 13

Real Estate Financing

A.	SOURCES OF LOANS		329
	1. <u>Introduction</u>		329
		a. General	329
		b. Historical Development	329
	2. <u>Institutional (Conventional) Lenders</u>		330
		a. Savings and Loan Associations	330
		(1) Federal Savings and Loan Associations	331
		(2) State Savings and Loan Associations	332
		(3) Maximum Loan and Terms - Summary	332
		(4) Prepayment Penalties	333
		(5) Acceleration Clause	333
		(6) Housing Opportunity Allowance Program	333
		b. Commercial Banks	333
		(1) Maximum Loan and Terms - Summary	334
		(2) Acceleration Clause	335
		c. Mutual Savings Banks	335
		d. Life Insurance Companies	335
		(1) Maximum Loan and Terms - Summary	336
		(2) Prepayment Penalties	336
		(3) Acceleration Clause	336
	3. <u>Noninstitutional Lenders</u>		337
		a. Mortgage Companies	337
		b. Individual and Nonfinancial Organizations	337
B.	FINANCING THE REAL ESTATE TRANSACTION		338
	1. <u>Obtaining the Loan</u>		338

	a.			The Promissory Note	338
		(1)		Essential Elements	339
			(a)	The Promise	339
			(b)	A Sum Certain in Money	339
			(c)	Fixed or Determinable Time	339
			(d)	The Payee	340
			(e)	The Signature	340
		(2)		Suggested Elements	340
			(a)	Date Signed	340
			(b)	Prepayment Privileges or Penalties	340
			(c)	Acceleration Clause	341
			(d)	Witnesses	341
			(e)	Endorsers	341
			(f)	Guaranty	341
			(g)	Reference to Security Given	342
	b.			Termination of the Notes	342
		(1)		General	342
		(2)		Satisfaction Piece	342

2. Securing the Loan ... 342

	a.	Mortgage	343
	b.	Trust Deed	343

C. QUALIFYING FOR THE LOAN ... 343

1. Application ... 343

	a.		The Loan Request	343
	b.		Borrower Information	343
		(1)	Employer	343
		(2)	Other Income	343
		(3)	Dependents	344
		(4)	Living Expenses	344
		(5)	Insurance	344
		(6)	Relationship to the Lender	344
		(7)	References and Reports	344
	c.		Property Information	344
		(1)	Identification	344

			(2)	Preliminary Title Information	344
			(3)	Improvements	344
			(4)	Economic Data	345
			(5)	Appraisal	345
			(6)	Repayment Ability	345
	2.	Credit Analysis			345
	3.	Processing			345
		a.	Personal Interview		345
			(1)	Application Accuracy	345
			(2)	Is the Loan Workable?	345
			(3)	Collateral Review	345
			(4)	Loan Costs	346
		b.	Appraisal Report		346
		c.	Credit Analysis		346
		d.	Loan Committee		346
	4.	Closing the Loan			346
D.	THE REAL ESTATE MORTGAGE DEED				347
	1.	Historical Background			347
	2.	The Three Theories of Real Estate Mortgages			347
		a.	Lien Theory		348
		b.	Title Theory		348
		c.	Combination Theory		349
	3.	Form and Content			349
		a.	The Conveyance		349
			(1)	Quitclaim or Limited Covenants	349
			(2)	Mortgage Covenants	349
			(3)	Statutory Power of Sale	350
		b.	The Defeasance Clause		350
	4.	Types of Real Estate Mortgages			351
		a.	Balloon Mortgage		351
		b.	Blanket Mortgage		351
		c.	Budget Mortgage		351
		d.	Closed Mortgage		351
		e.	Construction Loan Mortgage		351

		f.	Conventional Mortgage	352
		g.	Demand Mortgage	352
		h.	Direct Reduction Mortgage	352
		i.	FHA Mortgage	352
		j.	Industrial Property Mortgage	352
		k.	Installment Mortgage	352
		l.	Junior Mortgage	352
		m.	Leasehold Mortgage	352
		n.	Limited Reduction Mortgage	352
		o.	Open End Mortgage	352
		p.	Open Mortgage	352
		q.	Package Mortgage	353
		r.	Purchase Money Mortgage	353
		s.	Term or Straight Mortgage	353
		t.	VA Mortgage	353
		u.	Variable Rate Mortgage	353
		v.	Wrap-around Mortgage	353
	5.	Rights and Liabilities of the Mortgagor		353
		a.	Rights of the Mortgagor	353
		b.	Liabilities of the Mortgagor	354
	6.	Rights of the Mortgagee		354
	7.	Recording of the Mortgage Deed		354
	8.	Redemption and Foreclosure		354
		a.	Redemption	354
			(1) Before Foreclosure Sale	354
			(2) After Foreclosure Sale	355
		b.	Foreclosure	355
			(1) Foreclosure by Suit in Equity	355
			(2) Foreclosure by Exercise of Power of Sale	355
			(3) Foreclosure by Entry and Writ of Entry	356
			(4) Strict Foreclosure	356
	9.	Deficiency Decree		356
E.	THE TRUST DEED			356
	1.	General		356
	2.	Purpose		356
	3.	Parties to a Trust Deed		357
	4.	Who May Act as Trustee		357
	5.	Trust Deed as Security for Note		357

	6.	Assignment	357
	7.	Payments	357
	8.	Request for Reconveyance	358
	9.	Default	358
	10.	Foreclosure	358
	11.	Reinstatement	358

F. TRUST DEEDS AND MORTGAGE DEEDS COMPARED 359

    1. Parties 359
    2. Title 359
    3. Statute of Limitations 359
    4. Remedy 359
    5. Redemption 359
    6. Satisfaction 360

G. ALTERNATE METHODS OF FINANCING 360

    1. Installment Land Contracts 360
    2. Collateral Loans 361
    3. Syndications and Joint Ventures 361
    4. Real Estate Investment Trusts 362
    5. Sale and Lease-backs 362
    6. Exchanges 363
    7. Guaranteed Trade-ins 363

H. GOVERNMENT INVOLVEMENT IN REAL ESTATE FINANCING 364

    1. Historical Background 364
    2. Governmental Agencies and Organizations 364

        a. Federal Reserve System 364
        b. Veterans' Administration (VA) 365
        c. Federal Home Loan Bank System 365
        d. Federal Savings and Loan Insurance Corporation 365
        e. Federal Deposit Insurance Corporation 365
        f. Federal Housing Administration (FHA) 365
        g. United States Housing Authority 366
        h. Federal Public Housing Authority 366
        i. National Housing Agency 366
        j. Housing and Home Finance Agency 366
        k. Public Housing Administration 366
        l. Federal National Mortgage Association (FNMA - - "Fannie May") 367
        m. Government National Mortgage Association (GNMA - - "Ginnie May") 367
        n. Federal Home Loan Mortgage Corporation (FHLMC - - "Freddie Mac") 367

	o.	Department of Housing and Urban Development (HUD)	367

I. VETERANS' ADMINISTRATION (VA) GUARANTEED LOANS ... 368

    1. Introduction ... 368
    2. Eligibility ... 368
    3. Certificate of Eligibility ... 369
    4. Guaranteed Home Loans ... 370

        a. Limitation ... 370
        b. Lender ... 370
        c. Procedures ... 370
        d. Maximum Loan and Term ... 370
        e. Prepayment Privileges ... 371
        f. Mortgage Takeover ... 371
        g. Mortgage Discounts (Points) ... 371

    5. Direct Home Loans ... 371

        a. General ... 371
        b. Procedures ... 371
        c. Maximum Loan ... 372

    6. General ... 372

J. FEDERAL HOUSING ADMINISTRATION (FHA) INSURED LOANS ... 373

    1. General ... 373
    2. Organization ... 374
    3. Purpose ... 374
    4. Operations ... 374
    5. Financing ... 374
    6. Activities ... 374

        a. Mutual Mortgage Insurance (MMI) System ... 374
        b. Evaluation of Materials and Methods ... 375

    7. Title I - National Housing Act (Non-residential) ... 375
    8. Title II - National Housing Act (Home Mortgage Insurance) ... 376
    9. Mortgage Risk Rating System ... 377

        a. General ... 377
        b. Determining Economic Soundness ... 378
        c. Architectural Analysis ... 379
        d. Valuation Estimates ... 379

		(1)	Application	379
		(2)	Value Defined	379
		(3)	Analysis of Value	380
	e.	Mortgage Credit Analysis		380
		(1)	General	380
		(2)	Required Estimates	381
			(a) Income	381
			(b) Monthly Housing Expense	381
10.	Payment of FHA Insured Mortgage			382
11.	Mortgage Insurance Premium			383
12.	Section 203 (b), Title II - National Housing Act (Sales Housing)			383
	a.	General		383
	b.	Procedures		383
	c.	FHA Maximum Limits for Residential Loans		383
	d.	Basis of Making the Loan		383
	e.	Amortization Periods		384

NOTE: PRIVATE MORTGAGE INSURANCE

384

VISUAL AIDS   385

REVIEW QUESTIONS   394

Chapter 13
Real Estate Financing

A. SOURCES OF LOANS

1. Introduction

    a. General

    Rarely does the average buyer of property have the full purchase price to buy a property outright. In order to make the purchase, the buyer usually seeks to obtain the necessary amount of money from some lending source. The buyer's ability to obtain the money required to purchase the desired property is often the prerequisite to the culmination of the real estate transaction. In most instances, the real estate agent plays an important role in assisting his customer, the buyer, in his efforts to obtain the necessary financing. For this reason, a rudimentary knowledge of real estate financing is essential.

    b. Historical Development

    In 1890, only 36.9% of the families in the United States had title to their property. Since that time, more has been done in this country to promote home ownership through liberal financing arrangements than in any country in the world. Practically anyone with a small cash investment who enjoys a good employment record and firm credit standing can purchase a home through mortgage financing. Today, close to 70% of American families either own or are buying their own homes.

    Prior to 1930, most financing for the purchase of homes was of the short term loan type usually extending from five to fifteen years. Most of these loans required a significant down payment, often as high as 50%. Obviously, few young couples could enjoy home ownership. With the enactment of the National Housing Act in 1934, which created the Federal Housing Administration (FHA), the picture changed dramatically. The very purpose of the creation of the FHA was to stimulate home ownership by enticing lending institutions to liberalize their financing policies. This was accomplished by the FHA <u>insuring</u> lending institutions against certain losses which they might suffer as a consequence of their making specific types of real estate loans. Furthermore, by insuring lending institutions against loss, lower down payments and interest rates were made possible as well as the extension of the loan period to twenty, thirty, and even forty years. These advances resulted in lower monthly payments and enabled many more families to enjoy home ownership.

Practically all residential financing today revolves around conventional loans (i. e., loans which are neither insured nor guaranteed by the government), FHA insured loans, and Veterans' Administration (VA) guaranteed loans. Each of these will be considered more fully in subsequent sections of this chapter.

The field of financing, at the time of writing, is entering another period of change bordering on the revolutionary. Because of high interest rates, tight money, inflation, and governmental actions, the financing of real estate is in the most critical period since the depression of the 1930's. At the moment, a proposed bill is before Congress which would raise the maximum loan under the FHA program for single family homes from $33,000 to $45,000 and would increase the maximum loan limit for Federal Savings and Loan Associations on private residences from $45,000 to $55,000. Further action can be expected in the next Congress with some indications that the minimum deposit standard under FHA may be reduced and additional Federal funds provided to stimulate construction. The reader is advised to treat maximum or minimum figures in this chapter with care and to check for latest developments in the field.

2. Institutional (Conventional) Lenders

Generally, mortgage money markets are categorized as either primary or secondary markets. The primary mortgage money market is made up of all lenders who supply funds directly to the consumer (borrower) and who, as a rule, hold the promissory note until the obligation is discharged. The secondary mortgage money market is where existing notes are bought, sold, and borrowed against. Lenders or investors in the secondary mortgage money market purchase mortgages as long-term investments in competition with other types of securities.

The vast majority of all real estate loans are made by institutional (financial and nonfinancial) lenders, comprised primarily of savings and loan associations, commercial banks, mutual savings banks and life insurance companies.

The characteristics of the lenders in the primary mortgage money market are summarized below. The reader, however, is advised that the loan making policies of institutional lenders are subject to continuing changes as dictated by the supply and demand cycles of the economy.

    a. Savings and Loan Associations

Savings and Loan Associations are the largest single source of residential mortgage financing. Nationally, they account for approximately 45%

of all non-farm mortgage recordings. Savings and Loan Associations are also known as building and loan associations, cooperative banks, and homestead associations. All accept savings chiefly through the sale of shares of stock. Funds obtained are reinvested primarily in first mortgage loans on homes. The majority of these loans are conventional loans secured by residential real estate. While authorized to make FHA insured loans and VA guaranteed loans, savings and loan associations are not permitted to make consumer and business loans. Because they specialize in real estate financing, these associations are usually quite liberal in their conventional lending policies, particularly with regard to their appraisal and qualification requirements. Since their interest rates paid to depositors are based on the interest charged to borrowers, interest on loans is usually higher than banks or insurance companies.

The principal functions of the savings and loan associations are 1) to promote thrift by providing a convenient place for people to save and invest money, and 2) to provide for the sound and economical financing of homes.

There are two types of savings and loan associations: Federal chartered, and State chartered. Although Federal and State regulatory agencies establish the maximum loan-to-value ratios, amortization periods, et cetera, the individual policies of each association will be set within that regulatory framework by each board of directors.

(1) Federal Savings and Loan Associations

Savings and loan associations chartered by the Federal Government must affix the word "Federal" to their names. These associations are governed by regulations of the Federal Home Loan Bank Board. Under Federal Home Loan Bank regulations, federally chartered savings and loan associations may make home mortgage loans (other than FHA or VA) on owner-occupied single family dwelling units, up to 90% of the lesser of the appraised value or of the selling price of the home offered as security, providing the loan does not exceed $45,000. As of 1972, federal associations can make 95% loans up to $36,000. Individual units in a planned unit development, condominium, cooperative apartment, or cluster development qualify under the definition of an owner-occupied single family dwelling. No other liens are permitted, and provision must be made for insurance and tax payments.

Conventional loans for federal associations are generally restricted to an area of 100 miles from their home offices or branch offices, provided that they are not made beyond the state limits of the state of incorporation.

Loans in excess of $45,000 and beyond the area limits stated above may be made on homes and on income-producing property providing such loans do not exceed 20% of the total assets of the savings and loan association.

While savings and loan associations are permitted to make the FHA insured or VA guaranteed loan, throughout the nation, less than 30% of all mortgages recorded are either FHA insured or VA guaranteed.

(2) State Savings and Loan Associations

Savings and loan associations chartered by the individual states are governed by regulations of a specifically designated supervisory body, such as a state savings and loan commissioner, superintendent of banks, et cetera. State associations are also permitted to make the same type of 90% loans. Under certain circumstances, state savings and loan associations may also make loans in an amount equal to 95% of the lesser of the appraised value or the purchase price of the home offered as security. No other liens are permitted, and provisions must be made for insurance and tax impounds.

(3) Maximum Loan and Terms -- Summary

    (a) Single Family Dwellings

        Maximum loan:
            95% of appraised value up to $36,000
            90% of appraised value up to $45,000
        Maximum term: 30 years

    (b) Two to Four Dwelling Units

        Maximum loan: 80% of appraised value
        Maximum term: 30 years

    (c) Five or More Dwelling Units

        Maximum loan: 75% of appraised value
        Maximum term: 25 years

    (d) Commercial Property

        Maximum loan: 75% of appraised value
        Maximum term: 25 years

(e) Developed Building Lots

   Maximum loan: 75% of lot value
   Maximum term:
      Individuals - 5 years
      Builders   - 3 years

(f) Mobile Homes

   Maximum loan:
      New - 110% of manufacturer's invoice price
      Used - 100% of wholesale value
   Maximum term:
      New - 12 years
      Used - 8 years

(4) Prepayment Penalties

Savings and loan associations traditionally charge penalties for prepayment unless the purchaser places a new loan with the lender.

(5) Acceleration Clause

Savings and loan notes and mortgages usually contain an acceleration (alienation or due-on-sale) clause which allows them to approve or disapprove the purchaser, to demand an increase in interest rate, or to charge assumption fees.

(6) Housing Opportunity Allowance Program

Savings and loan associations may make loans under the Federal Home Loan Bank System's Housing Opportunity Allowance Program. Such loans may be for the lowest of three alternatives: 1) the fair market value (provided that 90% of such value is covered by mortgage guarantee insurance), 2) the purchase price of the property, or 3) $25,000. The terms are 30 years on single family dwellings, and 25 years for all other residential loans.

b. Commercial Banks

Activities of state chartered banks are covered by state banking laws. National banks are governed by the National Bank Act. All national banks are required to be members of the Federal Reserve System. State banks are members by their own choice. There is no great difference between real estate loans which state and national banks may make. National banks are somewhat restricted with regard to loans on unimproved property. These banks tend towards conservative appraisal and lending practices and generally restrict their loans to current or prospective depositors. Loan interest rates are usually competitive with insurance companies but less than savings and loan associations.

Commercial banks are "general purpose" lenders. In general, their real estate financing activities may be grouped into the following four classifications:

1) Long term mortgage loans for the purchase of real estate already improved or to be improved.
2) Construction loans to finance the construction of land improvements.
3) Interim financing of mortgage companies (i. e., business loans to mortgage companies to conduct their mortgage brokerage operations).
4) Home improvement loans for repairing and modernizing existing improvements.

The term commercial bank embraces institutions ranging from the local neighborhood bank to the huge metropolitan institutions or wide-spread organizations with hundreds of branches. Although their activities may vary widely, the one feature which commercial banks have in common which distinguishes them from savings banks, savings and loan associations, and other financial institutions is the holding of deposits against which checks are drawn for use as a means of payment.

(1) Maximum Loan and Terms - Summary

    (a) Fully Amortized Conventional Real Estate Loans:

        Maximum Loan: 90% of appraised value
        Maximum Term: 30 years

    (b) Unamortized Loans:

        Maximum Loan:
           State Banks - 60% of appraised value
           National Banks - 50% of appraised value
        Maximum Term:
           State Banks - 10 years
           National Banks - 5 years

(c) Construction Loans:

> Maximum Loan: 85% of appraised value
> Maximum Term: 5 years

(d) FHA and VA Loans:

> Commercial banks are an important source for FHA and VA financing. Such loans are accepted at government-allowed loan-to-value ratios and loan periods, provided the demand for available loan funds, competitive interest rates, government fiscal policy, and bank operations make the extension of such loans feasible and profitable.

(2) Acceleration Clause

Commercial banks normally have acceleration (alienation) clauses in their mortgages or trust deeds which allow them to approve or disapprove a purchaser, to charge assumption fees, or to demand an increase in interest rates.

c. Mutual Savings Banks

Mutual savings banks are nonprofit thrift organizations operated solely for the benefit of their depositors. They come under the supervision of state banking commissions. Unlike savings and loan associations, mutual savings banks do not issue shares of stock. Funds are advanced by their organizers. These funds are repaid gradually from earnings. Depositors, even though they are creditors, do not receive a fixed interest rate on their deposits. Instead, they receive interest dividends at a rate set by the trustees of the bank based on current earnings. Mutual savings banks are located mainly in the northeastern states. Over half are located in Massachusetts and New York, with over 45% of all deposits in 1966 held in New York City banks. Mutual savings banks have an impressive record of safety. Over half of their total assets are invested in one to four family residential mortgages. Since state laws governing the investments of mutual savings banks permit them to make FHA insured or VA guaranteed loans anywhere in the United States, they are an important source of funds to mortgage companies across the country. The preponderance of real estate loans outside of the home state of these institutions are made up of FHA and VA loans.

d. Life Insurance Companies

Although the primary objective of life insurance companies is not investment, during the course of their business, substantial funds are accumulated which must be invested. For this reason, life insurance companies are classified as institutional investors. They make conventional loans on all types of properties and supply most of the loans on properties where large loans are required. Many also invest substantial amounts of their funds in FHA and VA mortgages. Loans from insurance companies usually run for 25 years. For total mortgage investments, life insurance companies for years have ranked first among institutional lenders. In the recent competitive loan market, however, they are running closely with the eastern savings banks and savings and loan associations. It is anticipated that life insurance companies will become more diversified in lending policies relative to commercial properties in the future. Their operations are governed by the state in which the company is located and by the state in which they are incorporated. State charters under which insurance companies are authorized to make real estate loans establish statutory limitations on such loans. Generally, they are required to be more selective than the savings and loan associations. By law, most insurance companies cannot make loans in excess of 75% of the appraised value, which means that substantially higher down payments are required. The interest rate, however, is often less than competing conventional sources. Most insurance companies work through real estate brokers or loan correspondents to place their loans. These brokers represent the insurance companies and collect fees (origination fees) for originating new loans.

(1) Maximum Loan and Terms - Summary

The term, ratio of loan, and rate of interest are affected by many market conditions: the age of the property, quality of construction, qualifications of the borrower, amount and term of the loan, as well as the neighborhood. The policy of one company, which may change from time to time, may differ from that of another company operating in the same area.

(2) Prepayment Penalties

In some instances, the loan cannot be paid off at all for a specific number of years. When prepayment is allowed, the penalty is usually quite high, especially during the initial years of the loan.

(3) Acceleration Clause

Since, in most instances, insurance companies are represented by loan correspondents, the processing of loans forwarded to the insurance companies would consume too much time, if acceleration (alienation) clauses were included in the note and security instrument. Consequently, insurance loans usually do not require acceleration clauses, which makes it possible for a buyer to take over such property, subject to such loans, without the necessity of obtaining the lender's approval and without assumption fees or increased interest charges.

3. Noninstitutional Lenders

Noninstitutional lenders include individuals, universities, colleges, or other endowed institutions, pension funds, trust departments of banks, title companies, mortgage companies, executors, real estate brokers, and some government agencies. They hold about one fourth of the total amount of loans on real estate in the nation.

a. Mortgage Companies

Foremost, perhaps, among noninstitutional lenders are the mortgage companies. As defined in the constitution of the Mortgage Bankers' Association of America, a 'mortgage company' is: "Any person, firm, or corporation . . . engaged in the business of lending money on the security of improved real estate . . . " Mortgage companies are organized under state laws. Their operations, therefore, vary to some extent from state to state. They are, however, subject to minimum supervision as financial institutions. They have wide latitude of powers. Many obtain their funds from commercial banks, by obtaining lines of credit and by arranging for advances from banks against mortgage documents while such loans are in the process of being sold to the ultimate purchaser of the paper.

Most companies operate primarily as mortgage loan correspondents of life insurance companies, mutual savings banks, pension funds, and other financial institutions. They make loans on homes, income property, and under FHA and VA.

The companies are generally free of lending limitations such as are placed on institutional lenders and, except for inspections by an examiner in conformity with state laws, assume entire responsibility and make all decisions about their mortgage lending operations and their servicing of these loans. Generally, mortgage companies restrict their conventional loans to selected residential and business risks, and to loans in price ranges suitable to the needs of investment firms which comprise the secondary mortgage market.

Mortgage companies throughout the country have occupied a significant role in helping large numbers of individuals and institutions to finance the purchase of real estate. Acting as mortgage loan correspondents for various companies and institutions, mortgage companies do a major share of the residential and income property financing in this country.

b. Individual and Nonfinancial Organizations

This group of lenders makes more individual mortgages from month to month than any other class of mortgagees. They rank second as a source of prime mortgage funds, and are by far the largest source of junior mortgage loans. The great majority of these loans are those made on one- to four- dwelling unit properties.

Individuals follow no uniform lending practices and, in general, are not subject to national or state licensing laws or the requirement of other regulatory bodies. As a result, individual and other noninstitutional lenders can take greater risks in their investments and charge higher interest rates.

As a rule, the individual cannot compete with institutional lenders in securing prime mortgages. Due to large scale operations, the institutions can supply funds at lower costs, and hence lower interest rates, than the individual typically can offer.

B. FINANCING THE REAL ESTATE TRANSACTION

In financing a real estate transaction, two stages are involved. First, the loan is obtained in exchange for a promissory note, and, second, the necessary security is pledged for the loan, as evidenced by the preparation of the mortgage deed or the trust deed.

1. Obtaining the Loan

At the time a buyer locates a source of money and obtains from this source the amount required to purchase a property, he must sign a promissory note wherein he promises to repay to the lender the money borrowed with interest as stipulated. When this promissory note is under seal, it is called a bond. The promissory note given to the lender is often referred to as the mortgage note. This note is the primary obligation to the lender; it is evidence of the debt. The concurrent security instrument prepared by the borrower may be either a mortgage deed or a trust deed. This deed represents the secondary obligation.

a. The Promissory Note

A promissory note is defined as a promise or engagement, in writing, to pay a specified sum at a time therein specified, or on demand, or at sight, to a person therein named, or to his order, or bearer. The promissory note given in exchange for borrowed funds for the purchase of real property is almost universally prepared to meet the requirements of a negotiable instrument.

By the Uniform Negotiable Instruments Act, a negotiable promissory note is defined as an unconditional promise, in writing, made by one person to another, signed by the maker, engaging to pay on demand, or at a fixed or determinable future time, a sum certain in money, to order or to bearer.

(1) Essential Elements

A negotiable promissory note must conform to the following requirements:

(a) The Promise. <u>The note must contain an unconditional promise or order to pay a sum certain in money.</u> The word "promise" need not be used. Any words which convey the idea that the maker undertakes a binding obligation to pay are sufficient. Words such as, "I will pay" or "I undertake to pay" are acceptable. In most states, the letters I. O. U. are an insufficient promise. Furthermore, the promise must be unconditional. Payment must not be conditioned expressly or by implication on the existence, non-existence, occurrence, or non-occurrence of a collateral matter. Where there is more than one maker, the promise will be that they will pay "jointly and severally," which allows them to be sued either together or separately for the entire amount due.

(b) A Sum Certain in Money. The second important requirement for negotiability is that <u>the sum payable must be a sum certain in money.</u> The sum payable is sufficiently certain although it is to be paid . . .

1. With interest; or
2. By stated installments; or
3. By stated installments with a provision that upon default in payment of any installment or of interest, the whole shall become due; or
4. With exchange, whether at a fixed rate or at the current rate; or
5. With costs of collection or an attorney's fee, in case payment is not made at maturity.

(c) Fixed or Determinable Time. To be negotiable, <u>the note must be payable at a fixed or determinable future time.</u> A note is payable at a fixed or determinable future time, if it is expressed to be payable . . .

1. On demand or on sight; or
2. On a fixed date; or
3. At a fixed period after date or sight; or
4. On or before a fixed or determinable future time specified therein; or
5. On or at a fixed period after occurrence of a specified event, <u>which is certain to happen</u>, though the time of happening is uncertain.

(d) The Payee. <u>The note must be payable to order or to bearer</u>. The payee must be described in the instrument with reasonable certainty. A negotiable promissory note is made payable to a third person. However, it may be made payable to the holder of a temporary or permanent office. Thus, a note made payable to the "Vice President of the Hanover Savings Bank" is negotiable. A note made payable to two or more payees, in the alternative or jointly, is negotiable.

A note may be made payable to bearer or it may be made payable in the alternative to a person named in the instrument or to the bearer. Thus, an instrument payable to "Jo Hughes or bearer" is negotiable. A note may be made payable to a name which does not purport to be the name of any person. Thus, a note may be made payable to "Cash." In such case, the instrument is payable to the bearer of the note or to any person to whom the bearer delivers the note.

The note must contain the important words of negotiability. Thus, the note, in summary, must be payable to "order" or "bearer" or to a name that does not purport to be the name of any person. A note which recites, "I promise to pay to John Brown," is not negotiable, because words of negotiability have been omitted. If the note were made payable to "Brown or order" or to the "order of Brown" or to "Brown's order" or to "bearer" or to "Brown or bearer" or to "cash," it would contain words of negotiability. When a trust deed is used as the security instrument, the notes are usually payable to "bearer."

(e) The Signature. <u>The note must be in writing and signed by the maker</u>. Any mark which a maker intends as his signature is sufficient. Often, the property given as security for the note is in the name of both husband and wife. In such instances, both must sign the note.

(2) Suggested Elements

(a) Date Signed. The date the note is signed, while not essential, is important, as it may serve to clarify the basis for calculating the time referenced elsewhere in the note.

(b) Prepayment Privileges or Penalties. When payment in full is due <u>on</u> a specified date (maturity date) or in a fixed number of months or years, the payee may refuse anticipatory payments of principal unless a penalty is paid. When the time for full payment specifies "on or before" a fixed date, or within a fixed period, the maker may make anticipatory payments of principal. The language of the note should clearly reflect whether or not anticipatory payment of principal is permitted, or when full payment will be accepted without penalty. If a penalty is to be imposed for anticipatory payments, it should be clearly stated.

(c) Acceleration Clause. The term "acceleration clause" relates to a provision in a note, mortgage deed, or trust deed, requiring immediate payment of the entire unpaid balance or principal and interest upon the happening of a specified event. Acceleration clauses may cover two circumstances. One relates to default by the maker, the other type of acceleration clause is sometimes referred to as the "alienation clause," the "due-on-sale clause," or the "assumption clause." The first, which is contained in most notes, makes the entire amount of unpaid principal and interest immediately due and payable upon default, at the lender's option. The others make the entire amount of unpaid principal and interest due and payable immediately upon the sale, transfer, and, sometimes, of further encumbrance of the property pledged as security, at the option of the lender. Without an acceleration clause, the lender would be required to foreclose the debt every time a payment was overdue, and without an acceleration clause the lender cannot accelerate the obligation upon default or transfer.

The "due-on-sale" or "alienation" clause enables the lender to approve or disapprove a buyer wishing to assume the loan. Furthermore, the lender can charge an assumption fee, or demand an increase in interest rate.

(d) Witnesses. Witnesses to the signature on a note allow suit on the note in the event of default within <u>twenty</u> years of the default. Without witnesses, the time limit to bring suit is generally <u>six</u> years. The time period may vary from state to state.

(e) Endorsers. An endorser is sometimes required by the lender when, for example, the ability of the borrower to make payments on the loan is subject to question. When a party signs the note as an endorser for the accommodation of the maker, he becomes liable to the payee for payment in event of default by the maker.

(f) Guaranty. A guaranty of a note is a <u>separate contractual agreement</u>, for which consideration is paid, wherein the guarantor agrees to assume responsibility for performance by a third party of the provisions of the note. The guarantor of the payment or performance of another is not liable until the failure of the latter to pay or perform on the due date. A guaranty is often preferred by the lender, rather than an endorsement.

(g) Reference to Security Given. The note usually contains a marginal reference to the mortgage given as security by reflecting the location of the pledged property. The note is valid without this reference, however. If the note is also secured by a "security agreement" (a chattel mortgage), covering personal property at the premises, an appropriate reference is also made on the margin of the note.

b. Termination of the Notes

(1) General

A note or bond is terminated by payment of the entire debt in accordance with the terms. Unless specifically allowed by provisions in the mortgage note, a tender of the principal by the mortgagor before the due date does not terminate the note because the lender cannot be forced to lose his investment before maturity.

(2) Satisfaction Piece

When the debt is paid, the borrower should secure from the lender a release which is called a "satisfaction piece," sometimes referred to as a "discharge." The satisfaction piece is a certificate issued by the mortgagee or trustee when the note is paid in full, describing the mortgage or trust deed, where it is recorded, and certifying that it has been paid and that the lender is willing to have it <u>discharged</u> of record. The satisfaction piece should be recorded in <u>order to</u> clear the borrower's title to the property. A satisfaction piece always carries an acknowledgement by some authorized person. The party paying the note should make certain that the acknowledgement in the satisfaction piece conforms with the laws of the state wherein the property is located.

2. Securing the Loan

When large sums of money are involved, the lender almost always insists on additional security to ensure that the borrower repays the loan. In most instances, the property being purchased with the money being borrowed serves as the required security. While there are several security devices used for this purpose, the two most commonly used are the mortgage and the trust deed (deed of trust).

a. Mortgage. A mortgage is a written document used in the financing of real property, evidencing the fact that the real property is pledged as security for repayment of the loan. The person buying the property, who prepares and gives the mortgage as security, is called the mortgagor. The lender, to whom the mortgage is given, is called the mortgagee.

b. Trust Deed. The trust deed, or deed of trust, is similarly used as a security device wherein the borrower, known as the trustor, conveys title to the property being pledged as security to a third party, known as the trustee, who holds such property for the benefit of the lender, known as the beneficiary, who acquires the status of a secured lender, pending fulfillment of an obligation, which is ordinarily repayment of a loan.

C. QUALIFYING FOR THE LOAN

The Reference Book (Vol. 1) published by the California Department of Real Estate categorizes the process of financing real estate into four steps: 1) application, 2) analysis, 3) processing, and 4) closing. A closer look at each of these four steps may prove beneficial to the real estate agent in the qualification of his customers.

1. Application

The majority of loan application forms have similar sections, usually consisting of the loan request, borrower information, property or collateral information, credit analysis, lender's action (approval or disapproval), and a processing checklist.

a. The Loan Request

This is the written request by the prospective borrower reflecting his name, amount, and terms of the requested loan, purpose of the loan, and how and when it will be repaid.

b. Borrower Information

This information enables the lender to determine the borrower's ability and willingness to repay the loan. Some of the usual items of information sought include:

(1) Employer. . . Type of Employment and Length of Time Employed. If under two years, or if the type of employment is unstable, further investigation is required.

(2) Other Income. What other sources of income are available to borrower? Does wife work: how old is she, how long on the job, and how stable the job? Young wives are often not em-

ployed too long because of the possibility of children. What about rents, annuities, royalties, et cetera? How much and how stable? Other sources of income are often not fully considered, because they are usually less stable than full-time jobs.

(3) Dependents. What dependents must be supported by the borrower and, approximately, for how much longer? Children help stabilize a borrower in one way, but, if they are young, they also add considerably to the financial burden. This, of course, affects the funds available to repay the loan.

(4) Living Expenses. What are the borrower's living expenses? How much of his gross income is available for loan payments, taxes, and insurance?

(5) Insurance. What happens to the loan in the event the borrower becomes disabled or dies? Is there sufficient insurance to provide for repayment of the loan?

(6) Relationship to the Lender. Does the borrower now do business with the lender? What kind and how important? What previous experience has the lender had with him? What business could the borrower do with the lender if the loan were granted?

(7) References and Reports. What kind of credit and character references does the borrower have? Many lenders rely heavily on their judgments on credit reporting services.

c. Property Information

Such information is necessary to determine how much security for the loan is offered. If the loan is granted, the lender will have to live with his decision for an extended period. For this reason, the lender is very much interested in the trend of the collateral's value and not just its current status. This section will include the following types of information:

(1) Identification. Specific identification of the property . . . usually the legal description.

(2) Preliminary Title Information. Existence of all claims, encumbrances, liens, mortgages, et cetera.

(3) Improvements. Description of land and improvements, including work done within the last 90 days that might be subject to mechanics' liens.

(4) Economic Data. Taxes, zoning, assessments, original price and terms, date purchased, operating income and expenses for several years if income property, et cetera.

(5) Appraisal. Present value, trends, et cetera. The appraisal by the lender is usually made after interview with the borrower.

(6) Repayment Ability. If income property, what is its reasonable ability to repay the loan?

2. Credit Analysis

This analysis is made on the basis of information contained in the application, plus supporting documents; information developed by the lender in checking the credit and character of the prospective borrower; and results of a personal interview. It is, fundamentally, a summary of the lender's judgment as to the ability and willingness of the borrower, or the ability of the property, to repay the requested loan.

3. Processing

If the loan request is approved, the lender often has a checklist of steps necessary for the completion of the processing of the loan. This checklist is frequently contained in the application form which now becomes the working document for the processing of the loan.

a. Personal Interview

Most lenders regard a personal interview with the prospective borrower as an initial necessity. The reasons are as follows:

(1) Application Accuracy. It gives the loan officer of the lending institution time to review the application with the prospective borrower, to determine the accuracy of the application, and to clear up any discrepancies or ambiguities. It also enables the loan officer to make a personal judgment of the borrower based on his long experience as a judge of people.

(2) Is the Loan Workable? Is it a sound loan for the borrower to carry? If it is not sound for the borrower, it is not sound for the lender.

(3) Collateral Review. The personal interview often reveals information about the collateral that the application will not disclose. Is the collateral sound enough to secure the loan? Will it continue to be?

(4) Loan Costs. The prospective borrower often does not realize the various costs involved in obtaining a loan. The interview enables him to discuss loan costs and to seek other information. Loan costs include loan escrow, notary, recording and legal fees, title, credit and appraisal reports, insurance, initiation fees, points, et cetera.

b. Appraisal Report

The appraisal of the property is concerned with establishing present value and the value trend. It may be done by a staff member of the lender or by an outside appraiser.

c. Credit Analysis

Armed with all the information on the prospective borrower and the property, the loan officer is now prepared to make an analysis of the requested loan. As mentioned previously, this analysis is keyed toward determination of the borrower's ability and willingness to repay.

Many lenders have established a standard of ability to repay. These various standards are usually tied to the borrower's income. In addition to the ability to pay, the question of willingness to pay is a central point in credit analysis. A check of the prospective borrower's pay habits to others who have granted him credit is most helpful in making this determination.

d. Loan Committee

Most lenders operate with a Loan Committee of experienced senior officers who analyze the loan applications recommended to them by loan officers who have screened them with borrower interviews, appraisal reports, and credit analyses. Officially, the decision as to whether or not to make a loan rests with this committee. Occasionally, the committee will be influenced by a senior officer who may be particularly familiar with the applicant for a proposed loan. If the committee approves the loan application, the file then goes to the Loan Escrow Department, where the mechanics of the actual granting of the loan are concluded.

4. Closing the Loan

The mechanics of completing the placement of a loan (closing) are normally the responsibility of an escrow holder (where utilized) or the bank's attorney when such funds are not placed in escrow.

D. THE REAL ESTATE MORTGAGE DEED

1. Historical Background

A real estate mortgage deed is an instrument evidencing the pledge of real estate as security, usually for the repayment of money borrowed. The word "mortgage" derives from the old French "mort" meaning dead and "gage" meaning pledge. In common law, the property owner often lost his land, if he was unable to repay even a small loan on the due date. The sometimes wide difference between the money borrowed and the value of the land forfeited was of no consequence. In order to avoid the inequities of this law, courts of equity began to allow the mortgagor to redeem his land after he defaulted on his payment. This right, first allowed by a court of equity, is called the mortgagor's "equity of redemption." This equity of redemption, however, now imposed a hardship on the mortgagee who may have seized the land upon default of payment. The mortgagee experienced difficulty disposing of the forfeited property simply because the purchasers were never sure that the original owner would not exercise his right of redemption. The courts once again took measures to relieve this inequity. Upon default by the mortgagor, the mortgagee, by a process called a bill to foreclose the mortgage, asked the court to set a date within which time the mortgagor must exercise his right to redeem his land. If the mortgagor failed to redeem within this fixed time, the property became the absolute property of the mortgagee to do with as he pleased. Regardless of the theory (title, lien, or combination) prevailing in a particular state, the mortgagor is generally regarded as the real owner of the land with the right to exercise all the powers of an owner, subject, of course, to the limitations contained in the mortgage. The distinguishing feature which differentiates a mortgage deed from other non-security type deeds is the fact that the mortgagor normally holds and enjoys the mortgaged premises until default.

2. The Three Theories of Real Estate Mortgages

The varying concepts relative to real estate mortgages are the consequence of two distinct influences which date back to early English law. In origin and form, the mortgage evolved from, and is associated with, common law. The restrictions by which the mortgage has been specifically tailored to fit the needs of a security device evolved from, and is associated with, the decrees of the Chancellor, who was usually a noted churchman delegated the authority to rule on such matters by the king. The bodies over which these Chancellors presided were called the chancery courts or courts of equity.

The common law concept held that the mortgagee (lender) was the owner of the property conveyed in the mortgage. At common law, the lender was considered as being vested with the legal estate so long as the debt secured by the mortgage was outstanding. As mentioned above, upon failure of payment, common law viewed the land as belonging absolutely to the mortgagee.

During the first quarter of the 17th Century, in the reign of James I, the courts of equity (chancery courts) decreed that the borrower (mortgagor) had the right to redeem after forfeiture. At first, this "equity of redemption" was considered as simply a right of the debtor. As time passed, this "right" became embedded in the law of property as an <u>estate in land</u> which was inheritable.

In English law, in spite of the terms of the mortgage which might define a particular deed as either a conveyance or a mortgage, the courts, in deciding, will look at all the circumstances of the case, and will treat the deed as a mortgage when it was the real intention of the parties that it should operate as a security only.

In this country, the colonists adopted the dual view of the mortgage, and our early courts of equity intervened to prevent the forfeiture of the debtor's equity of redemption, insisting that foreclosure should only be made by judicial sale. Resisting this view, many states permit the mortgagee to reserve in the mortgage a "power of sale" which he may exercise without the intervention of the court.

In a number of states, the common law mortgage no longer exists. In other states, it still prevails, and, in still others, a residue of both the common law concept and the court of equity treatment survive.

Today, in the United States, three legal theories prevail concerning the technical nature of real estate mortgages. They are commonly referred to as the lien theory, the title theory, and the combination theory. Regardless of the theory, the minimum requirement for the creation of mortgage deeds are the same in all states. There must be an agreement that specific real property shall be security for the payment of an obligation, and, in order to satisfy the Statute of Frauds, the agreement must be in writing.

    a.   Lien Theory

        In many states a real estate mortgage deed is not viewed as a conveyance of legal title as security, but rather as the creation of a lien upon the property mortgaged. The lien theory (sometimes called the equitable theory) prevails in Arizona, California, Colorado, Florida, Georgia, Idaho, Indiana, Kansas, Michigan, Minnesota, Montana, New York, North Dakota, South Carolina, South Dakota, Utah, Washington, and Wisconsin. These are known as the lien theory states.

    b.   Title Theory

        In some states, the view prevails that a mortgage is actually the conveyance of the legal title to the property subject to a condition, called a "defeasance clause," which provides for the automatic revestment (return) of the title to the mortgagor (borrower) upon payment of the loan secured by the mortgage. The title theory has been embraced in Alabama, Arkansas, Connecticut, Illinois, Maine, Massachusetts, New Hampshire, North Carolina, Ohio, Pennsylvania, Rhode Island, Tennessee, and Virginia. These are known as the title theory states.

c. Combination Theory

   In a few states such as, Delaware, Illinois, Mississippi, Missouri, New Jersey, and Vermont a theory exists which involves a combination of title theory and the lien theory. These are known as the intermediate states.

3. Form and Content

The form of the mortgage instrument in common use still reflects the title theory. Actually, the mortgage deed is a particular form of deed which states that it conveys the property to the mortgagee subject to the conditions set forth in the mortgage deed. The mortgage deed is comprised of two parts, the conveyance of the property and the defeasance clause.

   a. The Conveyance

      Such a conveyance of real property must be in writing, under seal, and executed (signed, acknowledged, delivered, accepted, and recorded) with all the formalities of a deed. To eliminate much of the legal verbiage formerly required in such formal documents, the full meaning of certain very important terms are, by statute in many states, (The Short Forms Act), incorporated into the mortgage simply by use of the terms without need for further amplification. The following three such terms often used in the conveyance section of mortgage deeds should be thoroughly understood in their full meaning:

      (1) Quitclaim or Limited Covenants. In a conveyance of real estate, the words "quitclaim covenants" or the words "limited covenants" shall have the full force, meaning, and effect of the following words: The grantor, for himself, his heirs, executors, administrators, and successors, covenants with the grantee, his heirs, successors, and assigns, that the granted premises are free from all encumbrances made by the grantor, and that he will, and his heirs, executors, administrators, and successors shall, warrant and defend the same to the grantee and his heirs, successors and assigns forever against the lawful claims and demands of all persons claiming by, through, or under the grantor, but against none other.

      (2) Mortgage Covenants. In a conveyance of real estate the words "mortgage covenants" shall have the full force, meaning, and effect of the following words, and shall be applied and construed accordingly: The mortgagor, for himself, his heirs, executors, administrators, and successors, covenants with the mortgagee and his heirs, successors, and assigns, that he is lawfully seized in fee simple of the granted premises; that they are free from all encumbrances; that the mortgagor has good right to sell and convey the same; and that he will,

and his heirs, executors, administrators, and successors shall, warrant and defend the same to the mortgagee and his heirs, successors and assigns forever against the lawful claims and demands of all persons; and that the mortgagor and his heirs, successors, or assigns, in case a sale shall be made under the power of sale, will upon request, execute, acknowledge, and deliver to the purchaser or purchasers a deed or deeds of release confirming such sale; and that the mortgagee and his heirs, executors, administrators, successors, and assigns are appointed and constituted the attorney or attorneys irrevocable of the said mortgagor to execute and deliver to the said purchaser a full transfer of all policies of insurance on the buildings upon the land covered by the mortgage at the time of such sale.

(3) Statutory Power of Sale. When used in the mortgage deed, the words "statutory power of sale" mean that upon default by the mortgagor of any of the provisions of the mortgage deed, the mortgagee may sell the mortgaged premises or such portion thereof together with the improvements thereon by public auction on or near the mortgaged premises, and such sale shall bar forever the mortgagor and all persons claiming under him from all right and interest in the mortgaged premises.

b. The Defeasance Clause

A "defeasance," per se, is a collateral deed made at the same time as a conveyance, containing certain conditions, upon the performance of which the estate created by the conveyance may be defeated or totally undone.

When the "defeasance" is incorporated in the same conveyancing instrument, it is called a "condition." The clause which reflects this condition in the same conveyancing instrument is known as the "defeasance clause."

By statute in many states, the full meaning of this "condition" is inferred by simply using the term "statutory condition." For this reason, the full meaning and short form use of the term "statutory condition" should be fully understood. The full meaning of the term follows:

Provided, nevertheless, except as otherwise specifically stated in the mortgage, that if the mortgagor, his heirs, executors, administrators, successors or assigns shall pay unto the mortgagee or his executors, administrators, or assigns the principal and interest secured by the mortgage, and shall perform any obligation secured by the mortgage, and shall perform any obligation secured at the time provided in the note, mortgage, or other instrument, or any extension thereof, and shall perform the conditions of any prior mortgage, and until such payment and performance shall pay when due and payable all taxes, charges, and assessments to whomsoever and whenever laid or assessed, whether on the mortgaged premises or on any interest therein or on the debt or obligation secured thereby; shall keep the buildings on said premises insured against fire in a sum not less than the amounts secured by the mortgage or as otherwise provided therein for insurance for the benefit of the mortgagee and his executors, administrators, and assigns, in such form and at such insurance offices as they shall approve, and at least two days before the expiration of any policy on said premises shall deliver to him or them a new and sufficient policy to take the place of the one so expiring, and shall not commit or suffer any strip or waste of the mortgaged premises or any breach of any covenant contained in the mortgage or in any prior mortgage, then the mortgage deed, as also the mortgage note or notes, shall be void.

4. Types of Real Estate Mortgages

Classification of types of mortgages vary widely from region to region. Some mortgages may fall into two or more classifications determined by whether the loan is conventional, government insured or guaranteed, or, perhaps, by the specific purpose of the loan, method of payment, time of payment, security pledged, type of interest, or relation to other mortgages. The following types of real estate mortgages include those most commonly encountered:

a. Balloon Mortgage. One which requires a lump sum payment at the end of the term of the mortgage.

b. Blanket Mortgage. One covering more than one parcel of real estate. The mortgagee is entitled to payment of the mortgage in full and to hold as security all the parcels until that time.

c. Budget Mortgage. Payment includes in addition to principal and interest at least one other payment, such as taxes and/or insurance.

d. Closed Mortgage. One which cannot be paid off before maturity. The mortgagee can accept payment before maturity only if he so desires. Some lending institutions will accept prepayment upon payment of a premium by the mortgagor.

e. Construction Loan Mortgage. One made for building construction on the mortgaged land. Installment advances, given as specific portions of construction are completed, are made by the mortgagee to the mortgagor as construction progresses.

f. Conventional Mortgage. One that is neither insured by the Federal Housing Administration (FHA), nor guaranteed by the Veterans' Administration (VA).

g. Demand Mortgage. One in which repayment is at the demand of the mortgagee.

h. Direct Reduction Mortgage. One requiring constant, periodic payments of both principal and interest that will pay off the principal sum loaned in full by the maturity date of the loan. (This process of gradually extinguishing a debt by a series of periodic payments is called "amortization").

i. FHA Mortgage. One whereby the Federal Housing Administration insures the lending institution against loss as a result of the mortgagor's failure to meet payments.

j. Industrial Property Mortgage. One covering not only the real estate but the fixtures and equipment contained therein as well.

k. Installment Mortgage. One which calls for periodic payments on the principal, such payments being separate from the interest payments.

l. Junior Mortgage. One which is legally subordinate to the first mortgage, such as a second mortgage.

m. Leasehold Mortgage. A mortgage of the lessee's interest under a lease; normally obtainable only from insurance companies.

n. Limited Reduction Mortgage. One providing for only a limited amount of principal reduction prior to the expiration date of the loan. The principal balance remaining at the expiration date is satisfied with a balloon payment.

o. Open End Mortgage. Not to be confused with an open mortgage. An open end mortgage is one which may be increased by subsequent advances of principal which, combined, do not exceed the amount of the loan amortized.

p. Open Mortgage. An open mortgage is one which may be repaid at any time. Building and Loan Associations usually permit such prepayment privileges.

NOTE: A mortgage which is still outstanding after its maturity date is also referred to as an "open" mortgage, or "on demand."

q. Package Mortgage. One covering both the real property and the personal property on the mortgaged premises.

r. Purchase Money Mortgage. One given at the time the property is purchased by the buyer (mortgagor) to the seller (mortgagee) as part of the purchase price.

s. Term or Straight Mortgage. One that matures at a stipulated future date with no amortization of the principal. Interest payments on term loans are usually required semi-annually.

t. VA Mortgage. (Sometimes referred to as a GI Mortgage). This type of mortgage is one wherein repayment of the loan is guaranteed by the Veterans' Administration.

u. Variable Rate Mortgage. Lending institutions are presently experimenting with VRM's to provide some guarantee to the lender that his loan, when repaid, will not be paid in devalued dollars and that interest rates will reflect current market rates, particularly in periods such as the present when such rates are rising rapidly. A favorite approach to solving this problem is "Indexing," tying the amount of the loan to an index, such as the Federal Government Cost of Living Index. It can be expected that use of VRM's will expand rapidly in the near future.

v. Wrap-around Mortgage. A mortgage in which the mortgagee assumes the payment of the existing mortgage and gives a new, increased mortgage to the borrower at a higher interest rate. As defined by its name, the new mortgage "wraps around" the original mortgage. A wrap-around would more commonly be given by a seller who continues to be responsible for his mortgage and takes a second from the buyer for the total amount at a higher rate.

NOTE: In no other area of real estate is there as much difference in nomenclature as within the field of financing. The same term may be used to define different types of loans between neighboring states or even in different parts of one state. The definitions contained herein are those most commonly used by specialists in the field; however, the student is advised, when discussing the types of mortgages, to insure common understanding of terms.

5. Rights and Liabilities of the Mortgagor

   a. Rights of the Mortgagor

   Prior to default in performance of the mortgage note, the mortgagor is entitled to the possession, control, rents, and profits of the mortgaged property. The mortgagor may dispose of the property by sale, lease, assignment, will, or gift, as long as the rights of the mortgagee against the property and against the mortgagor are not interfered with. The mortgagor, at any time after default, but before the sale of the property on foreclosure, may exercise his right of redemption - unless this right has been barred by a period of time specified by the statute. In about half the states the mortgagor has been given a statutory right of redemption which extends for a period <u>after</u> foreclosure sale. (Reference chart at end of chapter.)

    b. Liabilities of the Mortgagor

Real estate mortgage deeds usually provide that the mortgagor will pay all money obligations secured by the mortgage deed (e. g., principal and interest), insure the premises for the benefit of the mortgagee, pay taxes and assessments, and keep the premises in good repair.

6. Rights of the Mortgagee

The rights of the mortgagee are correlative to the liabilities of the mortgagor. In general, the mortgagee has the right to protect his security. He may require the mortgagor to repay the principal and interest in accordance with the terms of the note, insure the property, pay all taxes and special assessments, and keep the property in good repair. The mortgagee may also sell or transfer the mortgage note or bond to a third party. Lastly, the mortgagee has the right to foreclose on the mortgage upon breach of the conditions of the mortgage.

7. Recording the Mortgage Deed

The mortgage deed must be recorded in the designated office of record for the county or district in which the land lies in order that the mortgagee may give notice to third parties that he has an interest in the property covered by the mortgage deed. This procedure protects the mortgagee against subsequent bona fide purchasers from taking the land free from the mortgage. It should be recalled that before the mortgage deed can be recorded, it must be acknowledged by the grantor before a notary public or a justice of the peace.

8. Redemption and Foreclosure

    a. Redemption

        (1) Before Foreclosure Sale

At any time after default but before the sale of the land on foreclosure, the mortgagor may exercise his right to redeem, unless as previously indicated this right has been barred by a period of time specified by statute. <u>Note:</u> Any person having an interest in the mortgaged property is entitled to redeem if first he pays the entire mortgage debt with interest and all other costs to which the mortgagee may be entitled.

(2) After Foreclosure Sale

In most states, by statute, any person with an interest in the property either through or under the mortgagor may, within a specified period of time <u>after</u> the foreclosure sale, redeem the property sold by paying to the appropriate party the sum of money plus interest and costs for which the premises were sold or bid off. The period allowed for redemption after foreclosure sale varies greatly from state to state. In some states, however, (e. g., New York) the right of redemption <u>does not</u> survive the foreclosure sale.

b. Foreclosure

The right to foreclose accrues to the mortgagee upon breach of the conditions of the mortgage by the mortgagor. Statutes of the various states set forth the procedures by which mortgage deeds are foreclosed. Generally, there are four types of foreclosure proceedings; foreclosure by suit in equity, foreclosure by exercise of the power of sale, foreclosure by entry and writ of entry, and strict foreclosure.

(1) Foreclosure by Suit in Equity

This is the usual procedure in foreclosing. A bill for foreclosure is filed in a court of equity. The bill reflects the mortgagee's rights as provided in the mortgage deed and delineates the mortgage covenants which were breached. The court then issues a certificate of sale authorizing an officer of the court to sell the land at public auction. Following the sale, the officer of the court gives the purchaser a deed to the land. Note that in many states statutes provide a short period of time after the foreclosure sale within which the mortgagor or other persons with interests are entitled to redeem the property. Under such circumstances, the purchaser is not entitled to his deed until after the expiration of the statutory period.

(2) Foreclosure by Exercise of Power of Sale

This method is often provided for in the provisions of the mortgage and makes the mortgagee the agent of the mortgagor to sell the land. In some states, this method of foreclosure is forbidden by statute. The mortgagee, acting in his capacity as agent for the mortgagor, is not allowed to purchase at the sale.

(3) Foreclosure by Entry and Writ of Entry

A few states allow the mortgagee to foreclose after the mortgagor defaults either by entry upon the land after publication of notice and advertisement, and in the presence of witnesses, or by possession of the premises for a period of time. If the mortgagor fails to redeem within the specified time, the foreclosure is completed, and the title passes to the mortgagee.

(4) Strict Foreclosure

This procedure is usually authorized only when the mortgaged property is obviously not worth the indebtedness, the mortgagor is insolvent, and the mortgagee accepts the property in full satisfaction of the indebtedness. After the date set in the foreclosure decree, the mortgagee gets the land free from the right of redemption and free from the rights of junior mortgages and lien holders.

9. Deficiency Decree

Bear in mind that the mortgage deed is evidence only of the security pledged by the mortgagor for a debt represented by the mortgage note or bond for which the mortgagor is personally liable. If, upon sale of the pledged property at foreclosure, the amount realized is insufficient to pay the indebtedness evidenced by the mortgage note or bond, the court, in most states, may enter a deficiency decree for that part of the unsatisifed debt. Furthermore, this decree serves as a judgment against the mortgagor, and his other property may be levied on to satisfy the judgment.

E. THE TRUST DEED

1. General

A trust deed, or deed of trust in some states, is a security resembling a mortgage since it conveys land to a trustee to secure the payment of a debt, with a power of sale upon default, and upon a trust to apply the net proceeds to paying the debt and to turn over the surplus to the grantor. In many states, the trust deed takes the place and serves the uses of a common-law mortgage. Its form differs from a mortgage, but essentially it is a security device. A trust deed or deed of trust is also called a Trust Indenture and a Long Term Escrow. The trust deed is finding widespread acceptance in the United States. Today, approximately half the states have enacted legislation authorizing the use of this type of security instrument.

2. Purpose

Trust deeds are given to secure loans on real estate obtained by the borrower on his promissory note. They perform the same function as a real estate mortgage differing only in form, terms used, methods of handling, and in foreclosure.

3. Parties to a Trust Deed

A trust deed involves three parties, the Trustor (borrower), the Trustee (to whom the property is conveyed as security for the note), and the Beneficiary (lender). The note which is secured by the trust deed is given by the borrower (trustor) to the lender (beneficiary) in the same manner as in a mortgage transaction. The trustee is not involved with the note. Normally, in filling out the trust deed, the property owner and his wife will be named as "Trustor," a title insurance company or other eligible party would be named as "Trustee," and the lender would be named as "Beneficiary."

4. Who May Act as Trustee

States which have enacted a trust deed act specify who may act in the capacity of a trustee. Some states, such as Colorado, provide for the creation of the office of public trustee. Others provide that only attorneys admitted to the State Bar, banks, trust companies, savings and loan associations, title insurance companies, licensed real estate brokers, et cetera, can act as Trustee. Normally, it is usual for the title insurance company which writes the title insurance to be named as trustee in the trust deed. The trustee and the beneficiary, however, must be two different persons or corporations. They cannot be the same, since the purpose of the trust deed is to have a disinterested party control the security.

5. Trust Deed as Security for Note

The trust deed secures a promissory note made payable by the borrower (trustor) to the lender (beneficiary). The deed is recorded in mortgage records identifying the trustor as the mortgagor and the beneficiary as the mortgagee. The beneficiary (lender) holds both the trust deed and the note until: 1) the obligation is paid, 2) the trustor is in default and the property must be foreclosed by trustee's sale, or 3) the trust deed is assigned.

6. Assignment

If the trust deed is assigned by the beneficiary, a printed form is usually prepared. An "Assignment of Trust Deed by Beneficiary" or similar form is filled out, signed, acknowledged, and recorded in the same manner as an assignment of a mortgage. No notice to the trustee is required other than by the recording of the assignment in the mortgage records. The note is endorsed and delivered by the beneficiary (assignor) to the assignee together with the trust deed.

7. Payments

Payments on the note are made by the borrower (trustor) to the lender (beneficiary). Under most Trust Deed Acts, no active duty is imposed on the trustee, except to execute a reconveyance upon written request of a beneficiary, unless there has been a default and the trustee is requested to commence foreclosure proceedings.

8. Request for Reconveyance

When the indebtedness is paid in full, the beneficiary (or assignee) completes and signs the "request for Full Reconveyance," which usually appears on the trust deed form. The beneficiary then delivers the trust deed and the cancelled note (or notes) to the trustee, with any other papers, such as fire insurance policies, which are to be returned to the borrowers. The trustee, upon payment of a nominal fee, will execute a "Trustee's Deed of Reconveyance," and deliver it to the parties named by the beneficiary in the Request for Full Reconveyance. The recording of the Deed of Reconveyance prepared by the trustee will clear the title of the property from the lien of the trust deed. This equates with a "satisfaction piece" used in connection with the release of a mortgage. For his protection, the trustee will retain the original cancelled note and trust deed in his file as his authority for executing the reconveyance to the trustor. If trustors desire copies, they must procure them from the trustee.

9. Default

If a default occurs, the beneficiary prepares a "Beneficiary's Notice of Default and Election to Sell." The form and name of such notification may differ from state to state. The notice will include a description of the trust deed and the property, advising that a default has occurred, that the beneficiary has declared the entire obligation due and payable, and sets out the sums owing. Notice is given that the property will be sold by the trustee at a time and place specified.

The trustee must mail notice of sale to the proper parties before the sale in accordance with statutory provisions. Similarly, notice of the sale must be published in accordance with time specified in statutory regulations, and notice must be personally served on the occupants of the property or posted on the property if it is unoccupied.

10. Foreclosure

At the time and place set by the trustee, the property is sold to the highest bidder who is given a "Trustee's Deed." In this sale, there is no court proceeding, no period of redemption, and generally no deficiency judgment against the borrowers (trustors).

Foreclosure of a trust deed by advertisement and sale, or by judicial procedure, shall be commenced normally within the time limits for mortgages.

11. Reinstatement

Usually, the Trust Deed Act allows the trustor, or a subordinate lien holder, at any time between default and the sale, to pay the amount of the delinquency due, plus the beneficiary's costs and expenses, together with trustee's and attorney's expenses, in order to have the trust deed reinstated.

F. TRUST DEEDS AND MORTGAGE DEEDS COMPARED

Trust deeds and mortgages differ generally with reference to parties, title, statute of limitations, remedy, redemption, and deficiency judgment.

1. Parties

    a. Trust Deed. In a trust deed, there are three parties: the trustor (borrower), the beneficiary (lender), and the trustee.

    b. Mortgage. There are two parties to a mortgage: the mortgagor (borrower) and the mortgagee (lender).

2. Title

    a. Trust Deed. In a trust deed, the trustor conveys title to the trustee, not the lender, as security for an obligation owed to the lender (beneficiary). The title is reconveyed to the trustor when he fulfills his obligation to the beneficiary.

    b. Mortgage. In other than "title theory" states, a mortgage is an instrument which pledges property without delivery of title or possession (i. e., hypothecates) to the lender (mortgagee) as specific security for a debt or obligation. Generally, a mortgage does not convey title; it creates a lien.

3. Statute of Limitations

    a. Trust Deed. In a trust deed, the rights of creditors against the property are not terminated when the statute has run out on the note. Since the trustee has title to the security, he can still sell it to satisfy the debts.

    b. Mortgage. When the Statute of Limitations has run out on the principal obligation (the note), an action to foreclose on the mortgage deed (the secondary obligation) is barred.

4. Remedy

    a. Trust Deed. Upon default in a trust deed, two alternatives are available: either foreclosure or a trustee's sale is allowed.

    b. Mortgage. The only remedy in a mortgage for the mortgagee is foreclosure, unless the mortgage deed contains a power of sale.

5. Redemption

    a. Trust Deed. Under a trust deed, the debtor has no right of redemption after sale. After default the trustor has a limited right of reinstatement before the sale. The sale, under a trust deed, is final and absolute.

b. Mortgage. Under a mortgage that has been foreclosed by court action, a right to redeem may exist for a statutory period after sale.

6. Satisfaction

a. Trust Deed. Under a trust deed, the trustor, after final payment, should procure the note, trust deed, and a request for full reconveyance from the beneficiary. These instruments (the note, deed, and request) are then given to the trustee and a reconveyance obtained upon payment of the trustee's fee.

b. Mortgage. Upon satisfaction of a mortgage, the mortgagee, on demand of the mortgagor, must execute and deliver to him a certificate that the mortgage has been discharged or satisfied in a form sufficient to permit it to be recorded.

G. ALTERNATE METHODS OF FINANCING

1. Installment Land Contracts

Installment land contracts are also known as "installment contracts," "land contracts," "land contracts for sale," "contracts for deed," et cetera. Under such a contract, legal title is not conveyed by the seller until an agreed upon amount has been paid by the borrower. Normally, the financial clause of such contracts specifies the times and amounts of installments with payments being first applied to accumulated interest and accrued charges, and, finally, to payments of the outstanding balance of the purchase price.

To adequately protect the seller, the contract should also provide that, in the event of default by the purchaser, the contract is to be cancelled and all amounts paid by the purchaser be considered as rent for the period of time he was in possession. The usual forfeiture clause permits the seller to either foreclose or to sue for payments when each payment becomes due. The seller cannot elect both. Thus, upon default, the seller usually keeps the money he has collected and forecloses to repossess his property.

Installment land contracts are practical when the purchaser has insufficient funds for an adequate down payment, when mortgage financing is unavailable, or when perhaps the purchase on other terms is not desirable. Under most installment land contracts, the purchaser is entitled to a deed when he has paid a sufficient amount to qualify for and obtain a mortgage loan to pay the seller the balance due on the contract.

Under this type of contract, since legal title remains with the seller while the contract is in effect, it is considered a method of financing the purchase of real estate and is not viewed as a mortgage. The purchaser, of course, holds equitable title.

It is interesting to note that while the seller under an installment land contract holds legal title, his contractual interest is considered as personal property and in the event of his death his contractual interest would be treated as personal property.

When used, the installment land contract should be viewed as a conveyance in that the buyer may and should demand evidence of title even though such title is not to be delivered until the buyer complies with the provisions of the contract.

In such contracts, the purchaser assumes the risk of loss during the period of the contract. The escrow provision is, therefore, absolutely essential because of the usual lapse of several years between execution of the contract and delivery of the deed. With such a provision, payments by the purchaser are made to an escrow agent who is responsible for being continually aware of the status of the contract.

2. Collateral Loans

Many times, the buyer cannot pay the difference between the purchase price of the property and the balance of the existing mortgage. In such an instance, an agreement is entered into between the seller and the lender. In this agreement, the seller agrees to place in a savings account with the lending institution a specific amount of money from the cash proceeds he will receive from the sale. The existing first mortgage is increased by this amount when the seller pledges it to the institution. When the purchaser has reduced his loan to the amount approved by the lender, the savings institution will release to the seller the savings that were pledged. This method of financing is often acceptable when the seller is reluctant to carry back a second or subordinate purchase money mortgage and has no immediate need for the cash proceeds from the sale.

3. Syndications and Joint Ventures

When real estate is purchased primarily for investment purposes, one person often does not have sufficient capital to conclude the transactions. In these circumstances, several persons may join in the purchase and take title in common. A cooperative effort of this nature enables persons of limited financial means to combine their funds to effect a purchase and then share in the profits of their investment.

a. Syndication

A syndication, specifically, is a combination of persons or firms united for the purpose of enterprises too large for individuals to undertake. It is merely a combined venture without partnership or corporate designation. A syndication is usually formed for a limited period of time, normally of short-term duration. While similar to a joint venture, it is not identical to a joint venture.

b. Joint Venture

   A joint venture is the combination of two or more people to carry out a specific business venture. If more than one or two separate business transactions are involved, the association is no longer considered a joint venture but a partnership. Like syndication, the joint venture is of limited duration.

4. Real Estate Investment Trusts (REIT)

   Real estate investment trusts are types of associations or unincorporated trusts which have been authorized by federal statute to encourage the pooling of small savings by exempting the trust from paying a corporate income tax. The title to the property is placed in the name of one or more trustees. The beneficial ownership, however, must be in the hands of 100 or more shareholders. While the shares are transferable, no five persons may own directly or indirectly more than 50% of the trust. To avoid paying corporate income tax, the trust must engage only in real estate investment and not be in the "business" of buying and selling except in the normal course of exercising the duties of a trustee. A disadvantage is the strict federal and state regulatory requirements as to the type of investments that can be made. When such trusts have shareholders in more than one state, they are also subject to Security and Exchange Commission regulations.

5. Sale and Lease-backs

   A sale and lease-back has become a popular method among highly rated companies with excellent credit. The process contains two steps which are taken simultaneously, even though they appear to be separate and distinct transactions. First, an institution, such as a college or university, a life insurance company, or any institution with funds to invest, purchases real estate owned and used by a well established business organization. Then the property is leased back to the seller by the purchaser. This form of transaction is also known as a purchase lease, sale-lease, lease-purchase, and leaseback.

   a. Advantages to Seller-Lessee

      In a sale and lease-back, the seller's working capital is not tied up in fixed assets. Since such leases are not considered long-term liabilities, rent is 100% tax deductible. Lease term is often much longer than a mortgage term on the same property. As a consequence, the firm's balance sheet reflects better, and credit is considerably enhanced. This type of transaction also allows the seller to raise more cash than is realized by borrowing. Since the land portion of the property cannot be depreciated by the owner, the writing off of 100% of the lease payments is a singularly favorable advantage. Finally, for companies working under government contracts that call for cost plus a fixed fee, rent is an allowable expense item, but mortgage interest is not.

For this reason alone, many aircraft, electronic, and other defense related plants are leased rather than owned.

    b.   Advantages to Buyer-Lessor

This type of transaction allows the buyer to purchase a long-term, care-free investment and benefit from the appreciation of value of the property. The yield on investment is usually higher than that of a mortgage and when the lease payment pays off the original investment, the lessor will still have title to the property. Furthermore, the investment will not be paid off prematurely. The cost to the investor is often less to service one large investment than it is to service many small mortgages. Finally, the lease terms often give the lessor a claim against other assets of the lessee in the event of a default, which is better security protection than a trust deed affords.

6.   Exchanges

The trading or exchanging of properties may be considered an alternative to mortgage financing even though many properties involved in exchanges are already mortgaged. An exchange of real estate is a transaction in which two or more properties are traded, either at equal value, or when a sum of money is used to balance the exchange. Both principals to this type of transaction are simultaneously buyers and sellers. In recent years, this form of transaction has become increasingly popular because of the capital gains tax benefits it affords, which allow for an indefinite deferment of tax obligations.

7.   Guaranteed Trade-ins

Frequently, a buyer wishes to purchase a piece of real property but has insufficient funds to effect the purchase without first realizing the cash proceeds from the sale of another piece of real property that he owns. If the buyer's equity in his present property is adequate to purchase the desired property, it may be to the real estate broker's advantage, as well as the potential purchaser's advantage, for the broker to enter into an agreement with the buyer guaranteeing the buyer's equity under certain conditions which may include the following:

    a.   The potential buyer agrees to list his present property with the broker on an exclusive right of sale basis.

    b.   The real estate agent agrees to purchase the buyer's present property for cash, at a set net price, at the owner's option, at any time after a specified period, but during a specific period from the date of the Guarantee Agreement.

    c.   The real estate agent agrees to advance to the property owner certain sums needed for the purchase of the property to be acquired.

The guaranteed price is normally a safe percentage below the fair market value of the property to ensure that, in most instances, the property is sold before the expiration of the guarantee period.

H. GOVERNMENT INVOLVEMENT IN REAL ESTATE FINANCING

1. Historical Background

The Federal Government, prior to the economic crisis of 1929 - 1933, was not substantially involved in the control operations of the national economy. As previously noted (Chapter 8), it was not until as late as World War I that the Federal Government even conceived of estate, corporate, or individual income taxes. During the early part of this century, real estate financing was unstructured, haphazard, for all practical purposes unavailable to the masses, and unrealistic to the few who might qualify. With required down payments frequently as high as 50%, and loan balance payable usually within 15 years, obviously home ownership was within the province of only a fortunate few. During and following the Great Depression, with the enactment of the National Housing Act of 1934, the Federal Government became inextricably enmeshed in the workings of the national economy in general, and, for our purposes, specifically involved in real estate financing. The Federal Government's involvement commenced almost imperceptibly back in 1913, with the establishment of the Federal Reserve System. The multitude of programs which have surfaced relative to housing and financing are the products of intricate governmental structures, which over the years have undergone innumerable organizational changes. Today, one primary organization, the Department of Housing and Urban Development (HUD), encompasses many of the programs once administered by departments and agencies whose origins are remote and practically undiscernible. Nevertheless, the professional in real estate should at least be introduced to and become familiar with the more important manifestations of governmental involvement in real estate, especially as this involvement relates directly or indirectly with real estate financing.

2. Governmental Agencies and Organizations

a. Federal Reserve System

The Federal Reserve System was established pursuant to the Federal Reserve Act of December 23, 1913. The purposes of the act are "to provide for the establishment of Federal Reserve Banks, to furnish an elastic currency, to afford means of rediscounting commercial paper, to establish a more effective supervision of banking in the United States, and for other purposes."

The Federal Reserve Bank concerns itself with <u>commercial</u> banks rather than savings and loan associations, which come under the Federal Home Loan Bank Board. It has the authority and power to significantly influence the flow of money and credit in the United States through the various activities of its Board, such as bank reserve and discount rules, installment buying regulations, et cetera.

b. Veterans' Administration (VA)

The VA was created by Executive Order, dated July 21, 1930. It is an independent agency of the United States Government charged with administering benefits created by law for U. S. veterans and their families. On June 22, 1944, the G. I. Bill of Rights was enacted under which eligible veterans could receive education and training at government expense, readjustment allowances for unemployment, and guaranteed or insured loans for homes, farms, and businesses. Administration of much of this bill fell to the Veterans' Administration. (Reference Paragraph I, following).

c. Federal Home Loan Bank System

The Federal Home Loan Bank System was created by authority of the Federal Home Loan Bank Act, approved July 22, 1932, to provide a credit reserve for savings and home financing institutions. It governs the operation of all member savings and loan associations. All federally chartered associations, plus many state licensed associations, are members. It functions in much the same manner as the Federal Reserve System in its relation to commercial banks.

d. Federal Savings and Loan Insurance Corporation

This corporation was created under the National Housing Act and approved on June 27, 1934, to insure the safety of savings in thrift and home financing institutions.

e. Federal Deposit Insurance Corporation

The Federal Deposit Insurance Corporation was organized under authority of the Federal Reserve Act, and approved on June 16, 1933. The chief purpose of the Corporation is to insure the deposits of all banks which are entitled to the benefits of insurance under the law. The major function of the Corporation is to pay off the depositors of insured banks closed without adequate provision having been made to pay claims of their depositors. In effect, it functions as a parallel agency to the Federal Savings and Loan Insurance Corporation, except it is for commercial banks.

f. Federal Housing Administration (FHA)

The Federal Housing Administration was created in 1934, with the enactment of the National Housing Act. The FHA was organized primarily to insure loans made by approved lenders against specified losses they might realize as a result of their making specific types of real estate loans.

(Reference Paragraph J, following).

g. United States Housing Authority

The United States Housing Authority of the Department of the Interior was created by the United States Housing Act of September 1, 1937. Its purpose was to assist states in remedying unsafe and unsanitary housing conditions, and the acute shortage of decent, safe, and sanitary dwellings for families of low income. This agency was transferred, in 1939, to the Federal Works Agency and again, in 1942, to the Federal Public Housing Authority of the National Housing Agency.

h. Federal Public Housing Authority

This office was established in February, 1942, to administer public housing programs. Functions pertaining to public housing previously performed by the Federal Works Agency were assumed upon its creation. In 1947, the functions of this authority were transferred to the Public Housing Administration.

i. National Housing Agency

The National Housing Agency was established, on February 24, 1942, to consolidate housing functions relating to the following agencies, among others:

> Federal Home Loan Bank Board
> Federal Home Loan Bank System
> Federal Savings and Loan Insurance Corporation
> United States Housing Authority
> Federal Housing Administration (FHA)

The agency was dissolved upon creation of the Housing and Home Finance Agency in 1947.

j. Housing and Home Finance Agency. The Housing and Home Finance Agency was established, effective July 27, 1947, to provide a single permanent agency responsible for the principal housing programs and functions of the Federal Government.

k. Public Housing Administration. The Public Housing Administration was established as a constitutent agency of the Housing and Home Finance Agency, effective July 27, 1947. It is the successor of two agencies: the Federal Public Housing Authority and the United States Housing Authority. The purpose of the administration is to administer the federally aided, low-rent, public housing program authorized by the U. S. Housing Act of 1937.

l. Federal National Mortgage Association (FNMA - "Fannie May"). This association, originally chartered in 1938, under the National Housing Act, was rechartered under the Housing Act of 1954, and made a consitutent agency of the Housing and Home Finance Agency. Among other functions, FNMA is authorized to function as a secondary mortgage market by providing supplementary assistance to the secondary market for home mortgages by providing a degree of liquidity for mortgage investments. It was authorized to buy FHA and VA mortgages from private lending institutions, and to sell seasoned mortgages and trust deeds to individual investors and financial institutions.

Under the Housing Act of 1968, "Fannie May" was converted into a quasi-private corporation with all the elements of a private corporate entity. While still required to carry out the national real estate financial and housing policy by maintaining a secondary mortgage market in FHA and VA insured and guaranteed mortgages, it is not currently a federal bureau. In 1970, Congress passed the Emergency Home Finance Act, which allowed FNMA to buy uninsured, or "conventional" mortgages.

m. Government National Mortgage Association (GNMA - "Ginnie May"). Under the Housing Act of 1968, the then existing Federal National Mortgage Association ("Fannie May") was split into two separate corporations. The new creation, "Ginnie May", (which is still a federal agency) operates the special assistance functions for federally aided housing programs, and has the management and liquidating functions of the old "Fannie May." "Fannie May" is authorized to issue and sell securities backed by a portion of its mortgage portfolio. "Ginnie May" borrows money from the U. S. Treasury to buy FHA and VA mortgages and then resells them.

n. Federal Home Loan Mortgage Corporation (FHLMC - "Freddie Mac"). In 1970, Congress empowered the Home Loan Bank Board to establish "Freddie Mac" (an agency of the Board) to provide Savings and Loan Associations with the liquidity offered by a secondary mortgage market. "Freddie Mac" sells its own government-insured bonds and buys either insured or conventional mortgages from federally insured savings institutions.

o. Department of Housing and Urban Development (HUD). This federal agency came into existence on November 9, 1965. It absorbed all of the programs formerly administered by the Housing and Home Finance Agency and its constitutents. Its structural organization consists of seven regional offices throughout the United States and Puerto Rico, and almost 80 local offices. It administers programs which include:

(1) Large scale urban renewal efforts to eliminate slum and blight by making loans and grants to communities to tear down or rehabilitate housing and other buildings.

(2) Granting funds for building recreational and service centers, beautification projects, playgrounds, parks, et cetera.

(3) Colleges may borrow from HUD to erect student housing, dining halls, and other facilities.

(4) Helping people buy homes by insuring loans through the Federal Housing Administration (FHA).

(5) Helping banks and other lending institutions get more money to loan by buying up some of the mortgages they hold through the Federal National Mortgage Association.

(6) HUD's Model Cities Program is a direct step to solve ghetto conditions and related city problems.

(7) HUD also strives to bring equal opportunity to all Americans by eliminating all discrimination in housing.

I. VETERANS' ADMINISTRATION (VA) GUARANTEED LOANS

1. Introduction

The Veterans' Administration (VA) is an independent agency of the United States Government which is charged with administering benefits created by law for U. S. veterans and their families. The VA was created by Executive Order (No. 5398), dated July 21, 1930. On June 22, 1944, Public Law 346, 78th Congress, commonly known as the G. I. Bill of Rights, was enacted which had far-reaching effects. Under this law, eligible veterans could receive education and training at government expense, readjustment allowances for unemployment, and guaranteed or insured loans for homes, farms, and businesses.

2. Eligibility

a. A veteran who served at any time between September 16, 1940, and July 25, 1947, and was discharged under conditions other than dishonorable after at least 90 days' active service (or for service-incurred disability in less than 90 days).

b. A veteran whose entitlement was derived from active service between June 27, 1950, and January 31, 1955, inclusive. The minimum term of active service for veterans of the Korean conflict is the same as that required for World War II veterans, i. e., 90 days or discharge by reason of a service-incurred disability.

c. Veterans who served on active duty for 181 days or more, any part of which occurred after January 31, 1955, and who were discharged or released under conditions other than dishonorable, or were discharged or released from active duty after such date for a service-connected disability.

d. Unremarried widows of men who served during either of the periods referred to above and who died as a result of service.

e. Any member of the Women's Army Auxiliary Corps who served for at least 90 days and who was honorably discharged therefrom for disability incurred in the line of duty rendering her physically unfit to perform further service in the Women's Army Auxiliary Corps or in the Women's Army Corps. (This applies only to persons so discharged from the Women's Army Auxiliary Corps prior to the integration of that corps into the Women's Army Corps, pursuant to Public Law 110, 78th Congress).

f. Certain United States citizens who served in the Armed Forces of a Government allied with the United States in World War II.

g. Servicemen who have served at least 181 days in active duty status, even though not discharged, while their service continues without a break.

3. Certificate of Eligibility

If the veteran does not have a current Certificate of Eligibility, he may request a VA Form 26-1880, "Request for Determination of Eligibility and Available Loan Guaranty Entitlement," from the VA Regional Office or from a lender, such as a bank, savings and loan association, mortgage broker, et cetera, or County Service Officer. The completed form should be sent to the VA Office, together with all service and separation papers which will be returned to the veteran after the eligibility determination is made.

It is important that the veteran obtain a Certificate of Eligibility so that, if he is applying to a lender for a guaranteed loan, the lender will know he is eligible.

If the veteran sells his house and the loan has been paid in full, his eligibility may be restored.

Legislation enacted in 1970 eliminated the expiration date of the entitlement and it is now available until used.

4. Guaranteed Home Loans

   a. Limitation

      (1) Amount of Loan - No limitation

      (2) Amount of Guarantee - The maximum guaranty is $17,500, and the VA will guarantee 60% of the loan or $17,500, whichever is less. The VA does not require a down payment by the borrower.

   b. Lender

   Loan is made by a lending institution, such as a bank, savings and loan association, insurance company, mortgage company, public and private lending agencies, or individuals who are in a position to look after the loan properly. If the veteran qualifies, the VA guarantees the loan up to a certain amount, so the lender will not suffer any loss in case of failure to repay the loan.

   c. Procedures

      (1) Obtain earnest money receipt or land sales contract if existing property; have three sets of plans and specifications on proposed new construction, also firm bid on construction cost and earnest money receipt if land is purchased separately.

      (2) Locate lender who will make GI loan at a rate of interest not in excess of the maximum rate.

      (3) Ask lender to send in VA Form 26-1805, Request for Determination of Reasonable Value.

      (4) The lender and VA will process the case from this point.

   d. Maximum Loan and Term

   There is no limitation on the amount of a loan eligible for guarantee. The limitation is upon the amount of the guaranty that can be issued upon the loan. The term of years may be up to 30 years under the law for one to four family dwellings and up to 40 years for farm loans. Loans, specifically for home purposes (i.e., purchase, construction, alteration, improvement, or repair), may be guaranteed up to a maximum of $17,500. Although the amount of the GI home loan for guarantee purposes may not exceed the reasonable value determined by the VA (as evidenced by its Certificate of Reasonable Value), the eligible veteran may pay the difference between such reasonable value and the selling price from his own resources.

e. Prepayment Privilege

There is no prepayment penalty if the guaranteed loan is partially or fully prepaid.

f. Mortgage Takeover

VA loans may be assumed by any purchaser; the person assuming the loan need not be a veteran. Approval by the VA or the lending institution is not necessary.

g. Mortgage Discounts (Points)

A mortgage discount (also called points, loan brokerage fee, or new loan fee) is the loan processing fee paid by a mortgagor-borrower to a lender solely for the use of money. It represents the difference between the principal amount of a mortgage and the amount it sells for. The Federal Government fixes the interest rate on FHA and VA loans. When these rates are lower, and therefore less desirable, than other investments, the only way to obtain a loan is to discount the mortgage and raise the effective yield to the final investors (i. e., insurance companies, savings and loan associations, et cetera). As a practical matter, the lender will charge a fee (called a discount or points) for taking a mortgage. A "point" is usually one percent of the mortgage loan. During tight money markets, as high as 14 points have been charged. On VA (and FHA) loans, the seller must pay the charge, since government regulations prohibit the buyer from doing so. If the purchaser were to pay the discount, it would, in effect, be a contravention of the law which limits the effective interest rate to be charged by lender. The buyer does pay a one percent loan origination fee, but this is used to cover the expense of obtaining governmental approval; it is in no way connected to the discount points.

5. Direct Home Loans

a. General

A VA Regional Office may make direct loans to veterans for housing in housing credit shortage areas designated by the Administrator. These areas are generally rural areas and small cities and towns not near the metropolitan area of large cities. The currently eligible direct loan designated areas can be obtained from the VA Regional Office.

b. Procedures

(1) Obtain earnest money receipt or three sets of plans and specifications as in guaranteed loans.

(2) Have veteran write to the VA Regional Office, requesting direct loan, giving brief description of property, its selling price and amount of loan desired to finance the purchase or construction, including land, if any, to be purchased.

(3) Send Certificate of Eligibility with request for direct loan application. If Certificate is not available, complete VA Form 26-1880 and forward same to the Regional Office along with discharge or separation papers which show dates of entry into and discharge from active service. Direct Loan Application Form will be sent, if veteran is eligible.

(4) The veteran should be alerted to be ready to send in $50.00 with his loan application as instructed when he receives the blank application form from the VA and to be ready to pay certain closing costs assessed to him, plus tax and insurance reserves at the time of loan closing. The VA charges an origination fee of $50.00 or one percent of the loan, whichever is greater (two percent if the direct loan is used to finance the construction of the home and if stage payments are necessary . . . one percent if stage payments are not required). The credit report, appraisal fee, and the loan closer's fee are paid out of this origination fee.

(5) VA will process from here on. If the veteran and REALTOR express written desire, all letters and forms may be mailed to the veteran in care of his REALTOR.

c. Maximum Loan

The maximum direct loan which the VA can make the veteran, if he has not used any of his entitlement, is $21,000.

6. General

a. In both types of loans, guaranteed and direct, the parties should draw up earnest money receipts in such manner as to expressly provide for return of deposit and cancellation of earnest money receipt, if for any reason the type of loan desired cannot be advanced.

b. To qualify for a loan, the law requires that the contemplated terms of payment of the loan bear a proper relation to the veteran's present and anticipated income and expenses and that he be a satisfactory credit risk. He must have sufficient income to repay the loan, all other obligations , and have enough remaining for his family's support.

c. The law requires that the amount of the GI guaranteed or direct loan may not exceed the reasonable value of the property, as determined by the VA. If the price the veteran agrees to pay for the home is more than such reasonable value, the veteran must pay the difference in cash from his own resources.

d. The veteran must certify in his loan application that he now occupies, or will occupy, the property as his home within a reasonable period of time after completion of the loan.

e. When a veteran is selling his home, he should be counseled that he remains liable on his VA loan, but can make application to the VA for release of personal liability. This release will be granted by the VA, if the purchaser assumes all of the veteran's liability, and if it is determined that he qualifies as a good credit risk.

f. Farm loans to purchase a farm and farm residence, which is to be occupied by the veteran personally as his home, are eligible for guaranty when made by a lender. These loans, which are not limited in amount except that they may not exceed the established reasonable value of the property, may be guaranteed up to a specified maximum. Real estate loans for farm purposes only, and not for residential occupancy by the veteran, although not limited in amount, may be guaranteed up to a specified maximum.

g. Direct loans are available only for housing and include purchase of a farm on which there is a farm residence to be owned and occupied by the veteran as his home. Direct loans are also available to build on land owned by the veteran a farm residence to be occupied by him as his home.

h. A guaranteed or direct loan may be partially or fully prepaid at any time without penalty premium or fee.

i. The VA Regional Office will answer any questions regarding the Veterans' Administration Program.

J. FEDERAL HOUSING ADMINISTRATION (FHA) INSURED LOANS

1. General

The FHA was created to provide a system of mutual mortgage insurance, applicable to mortgage loans financing the purchase of both new and existing one- to four-family structures and to afford protection on repair and modernization loans for housing. The FHA does not build homes, nor does it make loans. It is an insuring agency operating on a self-sustaining basis by means of the insurance premiums paid by each mortgagor in his monthly remittance. The premium is based on the approximate annual rate of one half of one percent of the mortgage amount. Another significant purpose of the FHA program was to establish and promote sound minimum standards of construction, design, location, and neighborhood for housing for families of moderate means.

2. Organization

The Federal Housing Administration has been in business since 1934. It was established under the provisions of the National Housing Act, approved June 27, 1934. It now functions as a part of the Department of Housing and Urban Development (HUD).

3. Purpose

The preamble to the National Housing Act states that the purpose of the Act is "to encourage improvement in housing standards and conditions, to provide a system of mutual mortgage insurance, and for other purposes." The FHA operates under authority of Titles I, II, VII, VIII, IX, X, and XI of the Act. These titles provide for FHA insurance against loss on loans for alterations, repairs, and improvements to homes and other real property; insurance of mortgages on homes; insurance of mortgages on multi-family rental projects; insurance of loans for land development and new communities; and insurance of group practice facilities.

4. Operations

The FHA works in cooperation with private industry to make better housing available to the American people. About 40 million families have benefited through FHA insured loans.

Through the insurance programs of the FHA, the average family is enabled to finance a home on reasonable terms.

Owners of homes and other properties can borrow money needed for repairs and improvements. Cooperative and condominium groups can take advantage of the economies and other benefits of housing acquired through joint effort. Families in urban renewal areas can improve their housing conditions, and those providing facilities for housing of senior citizens, for mobile courts, and for nursing homes may qualify for desirable financing with FHA mortgage insurance. The supply of other multi-family housing at reasonable rents is increased, and essential housing for the Armed Forces is provided. The construction of group practice facilities is also encouraged. These facilities can be used for the practice of medicine, optometry, or dentistry.

5. Financing

The FHA operates without cost to taxpayers except for the rent supplement and payment subsidy programs. Its income from fees, premiums, and interest on investments has been sufficient to pay its operating costs, insurance losses, and related expenses, and to build up substantial reserves.

6. Activities

    a. Mutual Mortgage Insurance (MMI) System

        The mutual mortgage insurance system, with provisions for minimum property standards, low down payments, and amortization of the debt by monthly payments suited to the borrower's income, grew out of recognition of the need for a sound method of home financing. It has brought home ownership within the reach of many families who could not otherwise afford it, and at the same time has helped industry to maintain a high level of home construction.

Besides playing an influential part in the revision of mortgage lending practices, the mutual mortgage insurance system has other accomplishments to its credit. By providing a standardized mortgage instrument, it has made possible the purchase and sale of insured mortgages on a national scale. It has also contributed materially to improvement in housing standards through the establishment of minimum property standards, careful architectural analysis, construction inspection, and the establishment of methods of planning and developing subdivisions. Moreover, FHA analysis of local housing markets has helped to avert overbuilding in specific areas and price ranges.

 b. Evaluation of Materials and Methods

Another activity that is extremely important to the success of the FHA's mortgage insurance business is the study and evaluation of new materials, new combinations of old materials, and new or improved methods of construction and land development. FHA cannot sanction experimentation with the homeowner's money by accepting unproved materials or methods. On the other hand, it does not want to block progress by rejecting products or ideas only because they are too new to reflect long experience.

7. Title I - National Housing Act (Non-residential)

FHA insures lenders against loss in connection with more than 25 different segments of the various titles. Title I of the Act authorized the FHA to insure lending institutions against loss on loans made to finance alterations, repairs and improvements to existing structures and the building of new structures for non-residential use. About 20 billion dollars have been advanced to property owners under the Title I program. FHA liability is limited to 90% of the loss on an individual loan and to 10% of the total amount of Title I loans made by the institution. The loans are made, without FHA processing, by approved lending institutions to borrowers with satisfactory incomes and credit records. The borrower must have a fee title or life estate interest in the property, or a lease expiring not less than six months beyond the maturity of the loan, or be purchasing the property on contract.

A loan to improve a single family home, or to build a new non-residential, non-agricultural structure may be in any amount up to $5,000. It may be repaid in equal monthly installments over a period of from six months up to seven years and 32 days. A loan to repair or convert a multi-family structure which is not owned by a corporation may be as much as $15,000, or an average of $2,500 per family unit, whichever is less, and may have a maturity up to seven years and 32 days. A loan to build a new structure for agricultural use may be as much as $5,000 and may be repaid over a period of seven years or up to 15 years if the loan is secured by a first lien. A loan of $5,000, repayable in seven years and 32 days, may be had to build a new commercial structure. FHA may insure loans, up to the maximum amount of $10,000, to be repaid in 12 years and 32 days, financing the retail sale of mobile home units.

Under the Title I Program, loans are usually personal type rather than loans where collateral is pledged. FHA specifies the broad lending policies used by lenders in processing and making improvement loans.

8. Title II - National Housing Act (Home Mortgage Insurance)

Title II of the National Housing Act sets up a permanent program of mortgage insurance. Generally, the Title II Program authorized the FHA to insure individual mortgage loans to include the following purposes:

   a. Section 203 - To finance the construction or purchase of one- to four- family dwellings, single family dwellings for victims of a major disaster, and low cost single family homes in suburban and outlying areas.

   b. Section 207 - To finance the construction of large scale rental housing projects, seasonal homes, loans to certain veterans, and for trailer parks.

   c. Section 213 - To finance the construction of nonprofit cooperatives of the management or sales type, and the purchase of individual mortgages released from a sales type project mortgage.

   d. Section 220 - To finance the rehabilitation of existing dwellings and the construction of new dwellings in designated urban renewal areas.

   e. Section 221 - To finance low cost new or rehabilitated housing for the relocation of families displaced by slum clearance projects or other governmental action.

   f. Section 222 - To finance the purchase or construction of dwellings by servicemen on active duty with the Armed Forces, including the Coast Guard.

   g. Section 225 - To finance additional advances under an open-end mortgage for repairs or improvements to one- to four-family dwellings.

h. Section 231 - To finance the construction or rehabilitation of rental housing projects designed specifically for elderly persons.

i. Section 232 - To finance the construction of facilities for skilled nursing care, convalescents, and others who do not need hospital treatment.

j. Section 233 - To finance single and multi-family units where the design and/or material used is of a nature to be considered experimental.

k. Section 234 - To finance the purchase or construction of multi-family structures where the individual purchases the unit and is given deed to same, along with undivided interest in common areas and facilities. This section is known as the Condominium Housing Program.

l. Section 235 - To provide home ownership assistance in the form of periodic payments by the FHA to mortgagees, which would reduce interest costs to the purchaser on market rate home mortgages and on the share of a cooperative association mortgage.

m. Section 236 - To provide assistance to tenants and cooperators in the form of periodic interest reduction payments by FHA to the mortgagee for rental and cooperative housing projects serving low income families.

n. Section 237 - To finance home ownership for certain lower income families who cannot qualify under normal standards because of their poor credit records, but who can meet mortgage payments with appropriate budget and financial counseling.

o. Section 242 - To finance new and rehabilitated (modernized) hospitals, including major removable equipment to be used in the operation of them. The hospital must be owned and operated by one or more corporations or associations, eligibility of which is determined by the Public Health Service.

9. Mortgage Risk Rating System

a. General

Pursuant to the requirements of prudent business practice and the legal requirements of the National Housing Act, and in the interests of impartiality, uniformity, and consistency, the Federal Housing Administration has formulated a system of mortgage risk rating. A mortgage risk rating is the act of analyzing the elements which produce mortgage risk and ascribing a rating, based on the risk characteristics of individual mortgages. The purpose of the system is to determine whether or not a particular mortgage transaction has a reasonable promise of success. The rating thus derived, in the FHA risk-rating system, is called Rating of Mortgagor.

One of the requirements dealing with the insurance of mortgages under Section 203 (b), which is the principal activity of FHA, is that "no mortgage shall be accepted for insurance under this section, unless the Commissioner finds that the project, with respect to which the mortgage is executed, is economically sound." Economic soundness is lacking if the mortgagor is not an acceptable credit risk, even though the property is adequate security for the mortgage, and, contrarywise, it is lacking if the mortgagor is an acceptable credit risk but the property is not adequate security for the loan. Loss to the mortgagee can occur only in the event the mortgaged property cannot be sold in a reasonable time for an amount sufficient to discharge the mortgagor's total obligation under the mortgage, including the expenses and carrying charges incurred by the mortgagee up to the date of the sale. Obviously, then, the aim of mortgage lending policy and practice should be to avoid, if possible, recourse to forcing a sale of the mortgaged property in order to satisfy the debt of a defaulted mortgagor. Since this contingency can occur only upon default by the mortgagor, good practice and economic soundness demand not only that the mortgagor be an acceptable credit risk, but also that the mortgaged property be adequate security for the loan. Therefore, the degree of risk characterizing any mortgage loan depends upon the relationships between the present and prospective characteristics of the borrower and the property, and the amount and term of the loan.

b. Determining Economic Soundness

The FHA risk-rating system provides a method by which the economic soundness of any particular mortgage transaction can be rated by analyzing its relative degree of risk. Analysis in mortgage credit leads to a conclusion as to the borrower's past, present, and probable future willingness and ability to meet his obligations. Analysis of the real estate elements, which relate to the property and its location, leads to conclusions as to the value of the property at the time of the mortgage transaction and as to the probable future marketability of the property should its sale become necessary to discharge the outstanding obligation of the borrower to the mortgagee. The third group of elements analyzed are the amount, repayment plan, and the term of the loan.

The FHA risk-rating system is not a formula. It is a guide to judgment which is intended to bring about a maximum possible degree of accuracy and consistency in evaluating risk in mortgage transactions.

c. Architectural Analysis

The architectural analysis relates to the building improvements on a property submitted for mortgage insurance. This analysis is made to determine the eligibility and acceptability of the physical security for insurance. It also provides conclusions essential to the determination of the value of the real estate, through analysis of the physical elements of the property from the viewpoint of its quality as mortgage security. Inspections of construction of the physical security for the mortgage to be insured is in acceptable compliance with the terms of the insurance commitment and sound construction practices.

d. Valuation Estimates

(1) Application

In the FHA system, valuation estimates are required to assist in making decisions with respect to the eligibility of loans for mortgage insurance. A percentage of the estimate of value establishes:

(a) The maximum amount beyond which the National Housing Act does not permit a loan to be insured.

(b) The minimum amount of cash investment required of the mortgagor; and

(c) The ratio of loan-to-value used in risk rating.

Valuation estimates are used in FHA's mortgage insurance operations to disclose the capability of the property to secure the loan. There are two ways in which real properties constitute security for a mortgage. The first is the borrower's desire to retain ownership of a property because of the future usefulness and benefits to be derived. The second is the amount obtainable at a sale, if the mortgage is foreclosed and the property sold.

(2) Value Defined

The word "value" is defined as: "The price which typical buyers would be warranted in paying for the property for long-term use or investment, if they were well informed, acted intelligently, voluntarily, and without necessity." The National Housing Act requires that the value FHA ascribes to a property be made known to any purchaser who will use FHA mortgage insurance to finance the purchase. Where FHA value was not furnished the purchaser prior to the signing of an agreement to purchase, such agreements must be amended to place the purchaser in the same position he was in prior to entering into the agreement.

(3) Analysis of Value

Analysis of value includes not only the physical improvements, but also the manner in which value is affected by reason of its location. Further steps in the valuation analysis include an estimate of replacement cost of the property, estimate of available market price, estimate of capitalized income, and, finally, an estimate of value. The benefits, or returns, derived from ownership of a dwelling property may be in the form of amenities or satisfactions, or in the form of money. The valuation analysis gives consideration to these returns by a prescribed method of capitalization of income. A capitalization of rental income method is used when the anticipated returns are primarily monetary.

e. Mortgage Credit Analysis

(1) General

The mortgage credit risk in a mortgage loan transaction is the probability of the failure of the mortgagor to fulfill his promise of future payments in accordance with the terms of the mortgage transaction. The purpose of mortgage credit analysis is to determine the degree of mortgage credit risk in mortgage transactions to be insured and to limit the probabilities of foreclosure or collection difficulties through the application of predetermined standards with respect to acceptable risks. Mortgage credit analysis does not contemplate forced sale of the mortgage security to accomplish liquidation or to avoid loss. In some transactions there may be sufficient assurance that loss to the mortgagee or to FHA can be avoided through forced sale of the mortgage security, but to predicate the making of mortgage loans on this basis would not be in the best interests of mortgagors. A mortgage lending policy, to be sound from all points of view, must be based upon the probability that mortgagors will be able and willing to protect their ownership of mortgaged properties.

Giving proper weight to the prospective homeowner's ability to meet the terms of his mortgage is a highly important part of the FHA insured mortgage system. It is a vital factor in the economic soundness of the transaction from the point of view of the government's insurance risk. It is an important aspect of the homeowner's enjoyment and satisfaction with his purchase. It is a stabilizing influence on the whole home building field and allied industries.

(2) Required Estimates

To gauge the risk introduced into a mortgage transaction by the borrower's ability to meet monthly payments, three estimates must be made. The first is an estimate of the prospective mortgagor's dependable, continuing income, termed "effective income" by FHA. The second is an estimate of the cost of occupancy of the property, which FHA calls "prospective monthly housing expense." Third, all debts, living costs, and other financial demands are considered. All these factors are then related to judge the feasibility of the loan.

(a) Income

It is seldom possible to make a really reliable estimate of an individual's anticipated income over a period of 15 to 30 years. However, the first years of a mortgage loan are the period of greatest risk, and a forecast of a prospective borrower's income during this early period can be made with some degree of certainty. For practical purposes, this early period of risk may be assumed to be approximately one third the term of the mortgage.

In making a realistic estimate of dependable income, FHA screens out all except that of a continuing nature. Dependable, stable, continuing income after deducting federal income tax is called "net effective income" by FHA. It represents the amount of money with which the borrower can confidently expect to meet his household and other expenses. A person's income from overtime work, employment of members of the family other than a steadily employed wife (if the family pattern has been established as including her employment), return on capital investment, the renting of a room, or the rendering of occasional personal services cannot be viewed realistically as dependable continuing income.

(b) Monthly Housing Expense

In estimating the prospective monthly housing expense, the following are taken into consideration: mortgage principal and interest, mortgage insurance premium, hazard insurance premium, taxes, special assessments, maintenance, repairs, heat, and utilities. The estimate of prospective housing expense is then compared with the housing expense the borrower is accustomed to paying. If the prospective expense is greater than that previously paid, and if the applicant has been unable to build up a financial reserve while paying the lesser amount, a greater degree of risk must be recognized. When the housing expense is increased without corresponding increase in income, downward adjustments in other living standards are difficult to make. Charts portraying the relationship between prospective housing expense and net effective income are available at FHA insuring offices.

Other analyses are made to determine that past credit experience with the applicant has been acceptable, that the prospective mortgagor's income is stable, and that he has the funds necessary to make the down payment and the deposits to reserves without resorting to unacceptable secondary financing. In connection with the latter, prior to mortgage insurance endorsement, mortgagors must certify that they will not have outstanding any other unpaid obligations contracted in connection with the mortgage transaction or purchase of the property, except obligations which are secured by property or collateral owned by the mortgagors independently of the mortgaged property. FHA does not feel that furniture, trade tools, or automobiles which an applicant uses in his employment or business would be acceptable security for loans to supplement the insured mortgage.

10. Payment of FHA Insured Mortgage

An FHA insured mortgage can be held in full, without an adjusted premium becoming due, under the following circumstances:

a. No more than 15% of the original amount is prepaid on the principal in any calendar year.

b. The loan is refinanced with another FHA loan.

c. The loan is retired by payments as originally scheduled.

d. Prepayment takes place on or after the 120th scheduled payment.

The adjusted premium charge, now eliminated, was a maximum of one percent of the original amount of the mortgage or the amount of mortgage insurance premiums which would be paid through the 120th scheduled payment.

As of May 1, 1972, FHA amended its regulations to suspend the prepayment penalty for borrowers who wish to pay off their loans early.

11. Mortgage Insurance Premium

The Mortgage Insurance Premium is one half of one percent, except for Title X. The term of the mortgages, for the most part, may not exceed three fourths of FHA estimate of remaining economic life, or 30 years (35 years, if proposed construction is involved and the purchaser cannot qualify with a 30 year term), except that certain mortgages under Section 221 may be for 40 years. The FHA examination fee is $50 for proposed construction and $40 for existing or under construction properties.

12. Section 203 (b), Title II - National Housing Act (Sales Housing)

   a. General

   The largest and most important activity of the Federal Housing Administration is the insurance, under Section 203 (b) of Title II, of mortgages on one- to four-family homes. Under this section, FHA insures mortgages on both new and existing homes generally on the same liberal basis.

   b. Procedures

   When listing a property for sale, the real estate associate makes a determination as to whether or not the property would most probably be financed under the FHA program. If affirmative, he will apply for an appraisal of the property by the FHA. The nominal appraisal fee, which may vary from area to area, will accompany the application and is paid by the seller. Should the property meet the FHA standards following the appraisal, a "conditional commitment to insure" is issued with a statement of value, indicating the amount on which the loan could be based. When a purchaser is subsequently found, another form is prepared which includes the purchaser's credit, financial status, employment and personal background. While the FHA operates under several code sections, you, as a real estate broker or salesman, will be concerned primarily with Title II, Loans, Section 203 B, which relates to residential property under the normal lending program.

   c. FHA Maximum Limits for Residential Loans

   (1) Single family dwelling units - owner occupied $45,000
   (2) Two or three family units - owner occupied $48,750
   (3) Four family units - owner occupied $56,000

   d. Basis of Making the Loan

   (1) Single family unit (owner occupied) built under FHA inspection

(or not built under FHA inspection but over a year old), the basis of making the loan is as follows:

   (a)   3% down payment on first $25,000 of appraised valuation.
   (b)   10% of next $10,000 of appraised valuation.
   (c)   20% of excess over $35,000 to maximum loan permitted (in this case, $45,000).

(2) Owner occupied dwellings, less than a year old, not built under FHA inspection, the basis of making the loan is as follows:

   (a)   10% down payment on first $25,000 of appraised valuation.
   (b)   20% of the excess to the maximum insurable loan.

e. Amortization Periods

Maximum amortization periods of new FHA loans may run for either 30 or 35 years. For a 35 year loan, the property must have been built under FHA inspection originally or be a new home built under current FHA inspection. All others extend to 30 years.

NOTE: PRIVATE MORTGAGE INSURANCE

A number of privately owned companies are now insuring real estate loans in a manner similar to that of the FHA. With such mortgage insurance, lending institutions will make higher percentage loans than normal or conventional loans which are not so insured. Loans which are insured by these private mortgage insurance companies can be disbursed with more latitude and more broadly than government insured loans, since buyer and property qualification standards may be less rigid.

SOURCES OF LOANS

1. **CONVENTIONAL LENDERS:**
   Savings and Loan Associations
   Commercial Banks
   Mutual Savings Banks
   Life Insurance Companies

2. **NONINSTITUTIONAL LENDERS:**
   Mortgage Companies
   Individuals
   Nonfinancial Organizations

FINANCING THE REAL ESTATE TRANSACTION

TWO STAGES

1. **OBTAINING THE LOAN**
   PROMISSORY NOTE - **Primary** obligation

2. **SECURING THE LOAN**
   MORTGAGE DEED } **Secondary** obligation
   TRUST DEED

THE PROMISSORY NOTE

ESSENTIAL ELEMENTS

1. The Promise
2. A Sum in Money
3. Fixed or Determinable Time
4. The Payee
5. The Signature

THE PROMISSORY NOTE

SUGGESTED ELEMENTS

1. Date Signed
2. Prepayment Privileges or Penalties
3. Acceleration Clause
4. Witnesses
5. Endorsers
6. Guaranty
7. Reference to Security Given

THE REAL ESTATE MORTGAGE DEED

FORM AND CONTENT

1. **THE CONVEYANCE**
   - Quitclaim or Limited Covenants
   - Mortgage Covenants
   - Statutory Power of Sale

2. **THE DEFEASANCE CLAUSE**

STATUTORY RIGHT OF REDEMPTION

The chart below shows the time allowed to the mortgagor, after foreclosure sale, to exercise his right of redemption. Where no period is indicated, no right of redemption is allowed after foreclosure sale.

STATE	REDEMPTION PERIOD	STATE	REDEMPTION PERIOD
ALABAMA	2 yrs	MISSOURI	–
ALASKA	1 yr	MONTANA	–
ARIZONA	6 mos	NEBRASKA	Until sale is confirmed
ARKANSAS	1 yr	NEVADA	1 yr
CALIFORNIA	1 yr	NEW HAMPSHIRE	1 yr
COLORADO	6 mos	NEW JERSEY	–
CONNECTICUT	–	NEW MEXICO	9 mos
DELAWARE	–	NEW YORK	–
D.C.	–	NORTH CAROLINA	–
FLORIDA	–	NORTH DAKOTA	1 yr
GEORGIA	–	OHIO	Until sale is confirmed
HAWAII	–	OKLAHOMA	–
IDAHO	1 yr	OREGON	–
ILLINOIS	6 mos	PENNSYLVANIA	–
INDIANA	1 yr	RHODE ISLAND	–
IOWA	1 yr	SOUTH CAROLINA	–
KANSAS	18 mos	SOUTH DAKOTA	1 yr
KENTUCKY	1 yr *	TENNESSEE	2 yrs
LOUISIANA	–	TEXAS	2 yrs
MAINE	1 yr	UTAH	6 mos
MARYLAND	–	VERMONT	6 mos
MASSACHUSETTS	–	VIRGINIA	–
MICHIGAN	6 mos	WASHINGTON	1 yr
MINNESOTA	6 mos	WEST VIRGINIA	–
MISSISSIPPI	No right of redemption	WISCONSIN	–
		WYOMING	6 mos

* Only if property is sold for less than two-thirds of appraised value

THE THREE THEORIES OF REAL ESTATE MORTGAGES

1. **TITLE THEORY**
   Legal title conveyed subject to "defeasance clause."

2. **LIEN THEORY**
   Lien created upon mortgaged property.

3. **COMBINATION**

PARTIES TO THE MORTGAGE DEED

1. **MORTGAGOR** - BORROWER

2. **MORTGAGEE** - LENDER

PARTIES TO THE TRUST DEED

1. **Trustor -** Borrower
2. **Trustee -** One to whom property is conveyed in trust
3. **Beneficiary -** Lender

ALTERNATE METHODS OF FINANCING

1. Installment Land Contracts
2. Collateral Loans
3. Syndications and Joint Ventures
4. Real Estate Investment Trusts
5. Sale and Lease-Backs
6. Exchanges
7. Guaranteed Trade-Ins

VA GUARANTEED LOANS

MAXIMUM TERM:
Up to 30 years under the law.

MAXIMUM LOAN:
No limitation on amount of loan eligible for guaranty.

MAXIMUM GUARANTY:
For home purposes - $17,500

FHA INSURED LOANS

MAXIMUM LIMITS FOR RESIDENTIAL LOANS:	Owner Occupied
Single family dwelling	$45,000
2-3 family units	$48,750
4-family units	$56,000

AMORTIZATION PERIODS:	
Built under FHA inspection	35 years
All others	30 years

BASIS OF MAKING FHA INSURED LOANS
(Owner Occupied)

1. **Single-family unit built under FHA inspection or not inspected but over one [1] year old:**

   a. 3% down on first $25,000 of appraised valuation.
   b. 10% of next $10,000.
   c. 20% of excess over $35,000 to maximum.

BASIS OF MAKING FHA INSURED LOANS
(Continued)

2. **Owner-occupied dwellings, less than one year old, not built under FHA inspection:**
   a. 10% down on first $25,000 of appraised valuation.
   b. 20% of excess to maximum insurable loan.

Chapter 13

REVIEW DEFINITIONS IN GLOSSARY OR TEXT OF FOLLOWING TERMS:

acceleration clause	leasehold mortgage
accommodation party	maker
beneficiary	mortgage deed
blanket mortgage	mortgagee
bond	mortgage note
closed mortgage	mortgagor
construction mortgage	open end mortgage
conventional mortgage	open mortgage
deed of trust	package mortgage
defeasance clause	payee
deficiency decree	points (mortgage discounts)
demand mortgage	principal note
direct reduction mortgage	purchase money mortgage
equity of redemption	satisfaction piece
F. H. A. mortgage	security
foreclosure	trustee
guaranty	trustor
junior mortgage	V. A. mortgage

REVIEW QUESTIONS:

1. What is a promissory note under seal called?

2. Which is the primary obligation, the note or the mortgage/trust deed?

3. What are the essential elements of the promissory note?

4. What is the "title theory?"

5. What is the "lien theory?"

6. What are the two general parts of a mortgage deed?

7. Name three types of lending institutions.

8. Does the FHA make loans?

9. Does the FHA guarantee loans?

10. Does the VA customarily make loans?

11. Does the VA insure loans?

12. Who are the parties to a mortgage deed?

13. Who are the parties to a trust deed?

FOR ANSWERS TO REVIEW QUESTIONS:

1.

2.

3.

4.

5.

6.

7.

8.

9.

10.

11.

12.

13.

Chapter 14　　　　　　　　　Conveyancing

A. HISTORICAL DEVELOPMENT — 402

   1. General — 402
   2. Definition of Conveyancing — 402

      a. Investigation of Title — 402
      b. Drafting of the Conveyance — 403

   3. Types of Transfers — 403

      a. Voluntary Transfers — 403
      b. Involuntary Transfers — 403

   4. The Instrument of Conveyance — 403

B. DEEDS - GENERAL — 404

   1. Definition — 404
   2. Elements of a Valid Deed — 404

      a. The Premises — 404
      b. The Habendum — 404
      c. The Execution Clause — 405
      d. The Acknowledgement — 405

   3. Execution of the Deed — 405
   4. Classification of Deeds — 405

      a. Warranty Deeds — 405
      b. Quitclaim Deeds — 406

   5. Kinds of Deeds — 406

      a. Administrator's Deed — 406
      b. Bargain and Sale Deed — 406
      c. Cession Deed — 406
      d. Committee Deed — 406
      e. County Deed — 406
      f. Deed in Trust — 406

        g.   Deed of Trust (Trust Deed) 407
        h.   Deed of Confirmation (Correction Deed) 407
        i.   Deed in Lieu of Foreclosure 407
        j.   Deed of Partition 407
        k.   Deed of Release 407
        l.   Deed of Surrender 407
        m.   Executor's Deed 407
        n.   Gift Deed 407
        o.   Grant Deed 407
        p.   Guardian Deed 408
        q.   Mineral Deed 408
        r.   Reconveyance Deed 408
        s.   Referee's Deed in Foreclosure 408
        t.   Referee's Deed in Partition 408
        u.   Sheriff's Deed 408
        v.   Support Deed 408
        w.   Trustee's Deed 408

    6.   **Forms of Deeds** 408

        a.   Statutory 408
        b.   Non-statutory 409

C. **DEEDS OF PARTICULAR CONCERN TO THE REAL ESTATE AGENT** 409

    1.   <u>Warranty Deeds</u> 409

        a.   General Warranty Deed 409

            (1) Present Covenants 409

                (a) Covenant of Seisin 409
                (b) Covenant of Right to Convey 410
                (c) Covenant Against Encumbrances 410

            (2) Future Covenants 410

                (a) Covenant of Further Assurance 410
                (b) Covenant of Quiet Enjoyment 410
                (c) Covenant of Warranty 410

        b.   Special Warranty Deed 410

    2.   <u>Quitclaim Deeds</u> 411

        a.   Quitclaim Deed With Covenants 411
        b.   Quitclaim Deed Without Covenants 411

	3.	Bargain and Sale Deeds	411
		a. Bargain and Sale Deed With Covenants Against Grantor's Acts	412
		b. Bargain and Sale Deed Without Covenants Against Grantor's Acts	412
D.	THE INVESTIGATION OF TITLE		412
	1.	Assuring the Marketability of Title	412
		a. Marketable Title	412
		b. Evidences of Title	413
	2.	The Recording System	413
		a. General	413
		b. Systems of Indexing	414
		(1) The Tract System	414
		(2) The Grantor - Grantee System	414
		c. The Abstract of Title	414
		(1) Abstractor's and Attorney's Liability	415
		(2) Risks Involved	416
	3.	Title Insurance	416
		a. General	416
		b. Title Insurance Coverage	416
		c. Exclusions	416
		d. Owner's and Mortgagee's Policies	417
	4.	The Torrens System of Title Registration	417
		a. General	417
		b. Methods of Registration	418
		c. Transferring Title	418
E.	DRAFTING OF THE CONVEYANCE		418
	1.	The Premises	418
		a. Names of the Grantor and Grantee	418
		b. Operative Words of Conveyance	419
		c. Consideration	420
		d. Legal Description	420

2. The Habendum 421

   Description of Estate to be Taken 421

   a. Encumbrances 421
   b. Restrictive Covenants 422

3. The Execution Clause 422

   a. Date 422
   b. Signatures 422
   c. Seal 423
   d. Witnesses 423

4. The Acknowledgement 423

F. CONVEYING THE TITLE 424

   1. Escrow 424

      a. Definition 424
      b. Essential Elements of a Valid Escrow 424
      c. Basic Steps in the Escrow Process 425
      d. Advantages of Escrow as a Closing Device 425
      e. Who May Act as Escrow Agent (Holder)? 425
      f. Duties of the Escrow Agent 426
      g. Who Should Designate the Escrow Agent? 427
      h. The Escrow Agreement 427

   2. Matters of Concern At Closing 428
   3. Preparation by Seller 428
   4. Preparation by Buyer 429
   5. Documents to be Obtained by Seller 430
   6. Documents to be Obtained by Buyer 430
   7. Examination of Instruments 431
   8. Delivery and Acceptance of the Deed 431
   9. The Closing Statements 432

      a. Credits Due Seller 432
      b. Credits Due Buyer 432

   10. Matters of Concern After Closing 433

G.	RECORDING		433
	1. General		433
	2. Real Estate Transfer Revenue Stamp Tax		433

VISUAL AIDS 434

REVIEW QUESTIONS 442

Chapter 14
Conveyancing

A. HISTORICAL DEVELOPMENT

1. General

Charles DeMontesquieu (1689 - 1755) wrote . . . "among us goods are divided into real estates, purchases, dowries, paraphernalia, paternal and maternal inheritances; movables of different kinds; estates held in fee simple, or in tail; acquired by descent or conveyance; allodial, or held by socage; ground rents; or annuities. Each sort of goods is subject to particular rules, which must be complied with in the disposal of them."

In the early days of history in feudal England, the formalities of conveying real property required the buyer and seller, accompanied by witnesses, to go onto the land to be transferred. The seller would make a symbolic delivery of the land (called a "feoffment") by digging up a clod of earth from the ground, or breaking off a twig from a tree growing in the ground should the ground be frozen, and handing it to the buyer. This transfer of possession was called "livery of seizin." The word "livery" comes from the French verb "livrer" meaning "to deliver," while the word "seizin" comes from the old French verb "seisir" meaning "to effect legal possession." Obviously, this method of transferring title had its drawbacks, since proof of the transfer depended upon the memory and honesty of the parties and their witnesses. By the time the American Colonies were established, deeds in England had generally supplanted the ancient feudal formalities for conveying real property. In America, the rule that title to land must be transferred by the execution of a deed was established at an early date. The form of the deed, whether warranty, quitclaim, or other, served as the modern counterpart of the common law conveyance by livery of seisin described above. All states have passed legislative acts which rule on the manner in which interests in real estate may be disposed of or transferred.

2. Definition of Conveyancing

Conveyancing is the art, or science, of creating and transferring interests in property, especially land. The two main divisions of the subject of conveyancing are investigation of title and drafting.

    a. Investigation of Title. Before a purchase of real property is completed, or before a loan secured by real property is made, the purchaser or the mortgagee must be assured that the seller or the mortgagor is able to convey clear title or mortgage the land. Title to the land, therefore, must be investigated; documents of title must be searched and examined and any necessary investigation be made to clarify any questions of title. Drafting of the conveyance is undertaken only when the results of the investigation are satisfactory.

    b. Drafting of the Conveyance. In the area of drafting the conveyance, great reliance is placed on well tried precedents which may be found in books of model forms which have been collected and published since printing became common.

3. Types of Transfers

Ownership or interest in real estate may be passed from one person to another in a number of ways. A closer inspection of the methods of transfer support two major classifications, voluntary and involuntary transfers.

    a. Voluntary Transfers

        (1) Sale
        (2) Mortgage
        (3) Lease
        (4) Gift

    b. Involuntary Transfers

        (1) Bankruptcy
        (2) Adverse Possession
        (3) Accession
        (4) Accretion
        (5) Death

            (a) Will
            (b) Descent

Real Estate Agents are principally concerned with voluntary transfers. In this chapter, our focus will center specifically on voluntary transfers by sale.

4. The Instrument of Conveyance

The most common method of conveying title to real estate is by a sealed (formal) instrument in writing known as a "deed." The complete transaction involving the sale of land, however, brings into play two and possibly three legal documents: the contract to sell, the deed, and the escrow agreement (when used). Additionally, the trust deed or the mortgage may be other documents to be considered. In the entire transaction, the contract is the most important instrument, as it serves as the blueprint for the others. Drafting of the contract was covered in Chapter 14, The Sales Agreement. The mortgage deed and the trust deed are subjects of the previous chapter on

Real Estate Financing. This chapter will concern itself with the other documents relating to the conveying process . . . the escrow agreement and the instrument of conveyance called the deed.

B. DEEDS - GENERAL

1. Definition

In law, a deed is a sealed instrument in writing, duly executed and delivered, containing some transfer, bargain, or contract. Loosely defined, it is also such an instrument before it has been given effect by delivery. In its broadest or most general sense, a deed properly includes every such instrument, but it is often used specifically to describe an instrument conveying a fee in land, as distinguished from a lease, mortgage, or other instrument under seal. A will, although under seal, is not a deed because it does not require delivery or acceptance. In common usage today, a deed is a <u>formal</u> written document by which title to real property is conveyed from one person to another, and it is frequently referred to as a "conveyance." The deed should be distinguished from a contract of sale or the purchase and sale agreement, which is simply the agreement to convey title in the future. A deed is the actual conveyance. The person conveying the property is known as the "grantor"; the person to whom the property is conveyed is the "grantee."

2. Elements of a Valid Deed

A deed of conveyance must be in writing to comply with the requirements of the Statute of Frauds. The wording of the deed is immaterial; it need not follow any prescribed form as long as the intent to convey is clearly expressed. Certain requirements, however, must be met, and these requirements are traditionally embraced by one of the four major parts of the usual deed: the premises, the habendum, the execution clause, and the acknowledgement.

    a. The Premises

        (1) Name of the grantor and grantee
        (2) Explanatory facts of the transaction
        (3) Operative words of conveyance (i. e., granting clause) which may include designation of quantity of <u>present</u> interest transferred.
        (4) Consideration
        (5) Legal description of the premises

    b. The Habendum (to have and to hold clause)

        (1) Description of estate to be taken (i. e., fee simple, life estate, etc.)
        (2) Declaration of trust, if any
        (3) Conditions or powers affecting the grant
        (4) Covenants of title, when necessary to state them

c. The Execution Clause (Testimonium)

   (1) Date
   (2) Signatures of the grantor(s) (and spouse where required)
   (3) Seal (if required)
   (4) Signature of witnesses (if required)

d. The Acknowledgement

   The attestation by a public officer adds authenticity to the deed and, while not necessary to the conveyance of title, is often a prerequisite to recording.

Most deeds today contain these traditional parts, yet a conveyance may still be sustained if it is in writing and contains the identification of competent grantor(s) and grantee(s) the words of conveyance, a description of the land, consideration, and the signature of the grantor(s). These six items then comprise the essential element of a valid deed. Delivery and acceptance complete the conveyance.

3. Execution of the Deed

"Execution" has often been summed up in the words "signed, sealed, and delivered." Delivery is essential to conveyance. Without it, the entire transaction is without meaning. Title does not pass until the deed is delivered. This is the final act by which the grantor signifies his intention that the instrument shall operate as his deed. It is one of the most important steps in the transfer of real property, and it must be intentional and voluntary. A delivery may be effected by acts without words, or by words without acts, or by both words and acts. Delivery is a matter of intent. Any distinct act or word by the grantor, with intent to pass title to the grantee, by transferring the deed to him, or to another for his benefit, may be construed as a delivery. Furthermore, to be complete and effective, the deed, upon delivery, must be accepted by the grantee. The law prescribes no specific formality for either delivery or acceptance, excepting that both must be the concurrent acts of the grantor and grantee, respectively.

4. Classification of Deeds

There are two basic classifications of deeds ... warranty and quitclaim. Either is sufficient to transfer such interest as a grantor presently has. Each of these major classifications may be further subdivided as follows:

a. Warranty Deeds

   (1) General Warranty Deeds
   (2) Special Warranty Deeds

b. Quitclaim Deeds

   (1) Quitclaim Deeds With Covenant
   (2) Quitclaim Deeds Without Covenant (Release Deed)

The warranty deed is traditionally used by grantors who purport to convey an indefeasible fee simple. The quitclaim deed is used by the grantor to surrender any interest he might happen to have. If the warranty deed contains the six usual covenants, it is called a general warranty deed; with less than the six covenants, it is called a special warranty deed. If a quitclaim deed covenants that the grantor has done nothing to impair the title since he became connected with the land, it is called a quitclaim deed with covenant. A quitclaim deed without covenant (sometimes called a release deed) warrants nothing. Each of these will be explored in subsequent paragraphs.

5. Kinds of Deeds

Various kinds of deeds are drafted and used for specific purposes. They may be either warranty or quitclaim in form. Another grouping may be the indenture and the deed poll. The identure is executed by all parties, while the deed poll is executed by the grantor only. Today, practically all real property deeds are deed polls. The grantee need not sign, since he becomes bound by the terms of the deed by his acceptance. Some of the more frequently encountered kinds of deeds are noted below.

   a. Administrator's Deed. A kind of deed used by the administrator of an estate to convey property of one who has died intestate.

   b. Bargain and Sale Deed. Such a deed carries with it an implied covenant that the grantor has possession and substantial title.

   c. Cession Deed. A deed used to convey street rights of privately owned property to a municipality.

   d. Committee Deed. A committee deed is used when the property of an incompetent is to be conveyed. A committee is appointed, and court approval must be obtained, before the transfer can be made.

   e. County Deed. A deed used when county-owned property is conveyed.

   f. Deed in Trust. This is a form of deed which conveys real estate to a trustee, usually to establish a land trust, which is a method employed for secret ownership. In Illinois, for example, where land trusts are authorized, statutes allow beneficiaries to retain and enjoy all the benefits of ownership, but with the record title appearing in the name(s) of others. Each beneficial interest is viewed as personal property and, as such, is not subject to any of the restrictions (such as dower rights) which are applicable to real estate. Such deeds provide other benefits, as well, to the beneficiaries. Land is not tied up in the event of an owner's death. Land would not be subject to forced sale under partition proceedings. Furthermore, it is an ideal method for several people to own title together, because the title is unaffected by judgments levied against any of them. In Illinois, the trustee is required by law to disclose the name of every owner or beneficiary of the property within ten days of receiving official complaint of a violation of building laws or ordinances.

g. Deed of Trust (Trust Deed). A deed of trust (as opposed to a deed in trust) is used in some areas of the country as a security instrument in much the same manner as a mortgage. The deed is placed in trust with a third party to insure payment of the indebtedness, or to assure that some other condition of the transaction is met. This form of deed is also known as a trust deed, a trust indenture, and a long-term escrow.

h. Deed of Confirmation. This kind of deed is used to correct mechanical errors in another deed. Also known as a correction deed.

i. Deed in Lieu of Foreclosure. This deed is used by a mortgagor to convey title to the mortgagee to eliminate the necessity for foreclosure of the property.

j. Deed of Partition. The deed of partition (partition deed) is used when concurrent owners divide land so that each can individually own specified portions.

k. Deed of Release. This kind of deed is used to release property or a portion of it from the lien of a mortgage or from a trust deed. It is most frequently used when a mortgage covers more than one parcel.

l. Deed of Surrender. This deed is used to convey an Estate for Life or an Estate for Years to a remainderman or to one who will receive it in reversion.

m. Executor's Deed. This type of deed conveys title to a testator's property.

n. Gift Deed. A grantor may make a gift of the property to the grantee and use a grant deed form or a quitclaim deed form for the purpose. Such a deed is valid unless made to defraud creditors, in which event it may be voided by them.

o. Grant Deed. This kind of deed is used extensively in California. It warrants that the property is free of encumbrances made by the grantor or anyone claiming under him, during the time the grantor was the owner of the property. It also guarantees any further right to the property that the grantor may acquire.

- p. Guardian Deed. A deed used to convey the property of an incompetent. The selection of a guardian, and the transfer of the property, must meet court approval.

- q. Mineral Deed. A deed which severs the mineral rights to one's property.

- r. Reconveyance Deed. An instrument conveying title to property from a trustee to the trustor upon termination of the trust.

- s. Referee's Deed in Foreclosure. A deed prepared by an official of the court which foreclosed the mortgage on a property and temporarily conveys the title to the referee.

- t. Referee's Deed in Partition. This deed is similar in content to a referee's deed in foreclosure. It conveys title to property when co-owners decide to divide their interest. The manner of division is determined by the court-appointed referee.

- u. Sheriff's Deed. A sheriff's deed is one given to a party upon the foreclosure of property. The title conveyed is only that acquired by the state or the sheriff under the foreclosure and carries no warranties or representations whatsoever.

- v. Support Deed. This deed is used when property is conveyed, with the consideration being that the grantee will support the grantor for the rest of his life. If such support ceases, a court may disavow the deed.

- w. Trustee's Deed. A deed of conveyance executed by a trustee. It is usually used when a trustee sells or conveys title of the trust real estate out of the trust. The instrument reflects the fact that the trustee executes the deed in accordance with the authority and powers granted to him by the trust agreement or by the deed in trust.

6. Forms of Deeds

Deeds may be further categorized according to their form. Being a very formal document, a deed for centuries was a lengthy, confusing instrument, composed of perplexing legal terminology. In most states, statutes have been enacted which set forth a condensed version of the deed in which all covenants or warranties mentioned in short form carry, by implication, the same meaning, weight, and force as though they were written out in full. As a consequence of such statutes, deeds may be grouped as either statutory (short form) or non-statutory.

- a. Statutory. The statutory or short form deed is used normally for general warranty deeds, quitclaim deeds, bargain and sale deeds, grant deeds, and those deeds executed pursuant to court order, to include administrator's deeds, executor's deeds, referee's deeds, et cetera.

b. Non-statutory. Non-statutory deeds would normally include guardian's deeds, committee's deeds, cession deeds, deeds of trust (trust deeds), deeds of confirmation, deeds of surrender, deeds of release, et cetera.

Both the form and content of deeds will vary according to the interest being conveyed and the purpose of the conveyance. As indicated above, state laws and statutory provisions relating to the conveyance of real property may also influence the particular form employed. Nonetheless, the essential elements of a deed are substantially the same in all states.

C. DEEDS OF PARTICULAR CONCERN TO THE REAL ESTATE AGENT

Of the many classifications and kinds of deeds in use, the real estate agent is particularly exposed to warranty deeds, quitclaim deeds, bargain and sale deeds, mortgage deeds, and trust deeds. The latter are viewed as security instruments, rather than strict instruments of conveyance transferring indefeasible estates. They have been previously examined in Chapter 15. A more detailed examination of the remaining three types of deeds is warranted here.

1. Warranty Deeds

Warranty deeds are those which contain covenants of warranty. Whether a warranty deed is a general or special warranty deed is determined by the covenants incorporated within the deed. If all six generally recognized covenants are included, the deed is a general warranty deed. The warranty deed gives the grantee every possible future guarantee by providing that the grantor gives full covenants and warranties. These covenants and warranties are generally implied in the statutory deed. When enumerated, they are inserted in, or immediately following, the habendum clause. The warranty deed gives the grantee the greatest degree of protection. The operative words in a warranty deed would include: "convey and warrant," "grant, bargain, and sell," and "warrant general."

a. General Warranty Deed

The general warranty deed contains six covenants: seisin, right to convey, against encumbrances, further assurance, quiet enjoyment, and warranty. The first three are called present (in praesenti) covenants because, if at all breached, they are breached at the moment the deed is delivered and accepted. The last three are called future (in future) covenants, because they may be breached at a future date.

(1) Present Covenants

(a) Covenant of Seisin. Under this covenant the grantor guarantees that he is seised of an absolute, perfect, and indefeasible estate in fee simple. Encumbrances do not breach this covenant, since they do not divest the grantor of his technical seisin. The seisin (possession claiming a freehold interest) will pass to the grantee subject to the encumbrances.

- (b) Covenant of Right to Convey. This covenant guarantees the grantee that the grantor has good right to sell the premises. It is usually cited with the covenant of seisin. An outstanding paramount title existing at the time the deed is delivered amounts to a breach of this covenant.

- (c) Covenant Against Encumbrances. This covenant guarantees that the premises are free from encumbrances. It is quite important that, if there are encumbrances subject to which the property is conveyed, they be stated in the deed. An encumbrance is "every right to or interest in the land granted, to the diminution of the value of the land, but consistent with the passing of the fee."

(2) Future Covenants

- (a) Covenant of Further Assurance. Under this covenant, the grantor agrees to voluntarily procure and deliver any instrument necessary to give the grantee the title he expected to receive, or which may be required to make the title good.

- (b) Covenant of Quiet Enjoyment. The quiet enjoyment covenant assures the grantee that he will not be disturbed in his possession of the property, or be ousted by anyone under a paramount title. To make the grantor liable for a breach, however, the grantee must show actual eviction.

- (c) Covenant of Warranty. This covenant is similar to, and is often considered with, the covenant of quiet enjoyment. This warranty is an absolute guarantee by the grantor to the grantee of title and possession of the property. The grantor, in effect, agrees to protect and defend the grantee against anyone.

b. Special Warranty Deed

In the special warranty deed, the grantor will defend the <u>title</u> against claims brought only by the grantee, his heirs, administrators, and those claiming by, through, or under him. Normally, the grantor assumes no other liability. He may, however, include the covenant against encumbrances which may have originated during the time he held title. This type of deed is most often used by fiduciaries, such as trustees, executors, or administrators, who are in title only for a limited time and have no other personal involvement.

The general warranty clause can be made into a special warranty by inserting the words, "by, from, through, or under him." If there is more than one grantor, the words "them, or any of them" would be used. A purchaser has no right to expect a covenant of general warrant in his deed unless he bargains for it in the agreement of sale. He cannot refuse to take the deed merely because it contains a special warranty.

2. Quitclaim Deeds

Under a quitclaim deed, the grantor makes no warranty as to the condition of the title. He simply releases whatever interest he has. On occasion, persons other than the grantor or grantee may appear to have some vague claim upon the property. Such a claim places a "cloud on the title." A quitclaim deed serves to clear "clouds" upon the title. The words of conveyance in the granting clause are "remise, release, and quitclaim." By using these words, the grantor does not warrant possession of any right of title whatsoever. It does pass to the grantee any title the grantor has. From the grantor's position, the quitclaim deed imposes a minimum degree of liability. Such deeds may be with covenants or without them.

   a. Quitclaim Deed With Covenant. In this type of deed, the grantor guarantees the title in a limited way only. He guarantees the title only against the claims of "persons claiming by, through, or under" him. He guarantees the title only against defects or claims arising since he acquired the land, but not against such defects or claims arising before that time. He covenants that he has done nothing to impair the title since he became connected with the land.

   b. Quitclaim Deed Without Covenants. This type of deed is sometimes called a release deed. It warrants nothing. The grantor merely releases whatever interest, if any, he may have at the time. In most states today, a quitclaim deed of either kind will convey whatever estate the grantor has in the land as effectually as a general warranty deed, even though it may lack the assurance and the personal backing of a warranty deed.

3. Bargain and Sale Deeds

The bargain and sale deed is an instrument adopted in many states to transfer real estate. Such a deed must recite a valuable consideration. The usual words of conveyance are "bargain and sell," "grant and release," or other equivalent words. Under the law, the use of these words places in the deed an implied covenant on the part of the grantor that he has possession and substantial title. A bargain and sale deed transfers full title to the property. If a bargain and sale deed contains a warranty of title, it becomes a warranty deed; if it merely conveys the grantor's interest in the property, it may be a quitclaim deed. If the grantor cannot warrant that he has substantial title or possession, he should not sign a bargain and sale deed.

To be effective, three elements are essential in the bargain and sale deed. It must be under seal, it must recite a valuable consideration, and it must be delivered. Bargain and sale deeds may be classified as either with or without covenants against grantor's acts.

    a. Bargain and Sale Deed With Covenants Against Grantor's Acts. This kind of bargain and sale deed covenants that the grantor has not done or suffered anything whereby the premises have been encumbered in any way whatsoever.

    b. Bargain and Sale Deed Without Covenants Against Grantor's Acts. This is one of the simplest forms of a deed. It carries with it no promises by the grantor. It is used to convey all the rights, title, and interest of the grantor, and nothing more, for a consideration.

D. THE INVESTIGATION OF TITLE

1. Assuring the Marketability of Title

Every purchaser of property should ascertain that the seller's title to the property is marketable. The real estate agent should be aware that all of his efforts to this point are to no avail, if the seller cannot convey a marketable (merchantable) title. Once the sales agreement is signed, the purchaser should make immediate arrangements to engage an attorney or conveyancer to commence an examination of the public records. The object of this examination is to determine whether or not the seller's title is marketable.

    a. Marketable Title

A marketable title is that which can be held without reasonable apprehension of being assailed. It is readily transferable in the market place. The term is used interchangeably with "merchantable title." Such a title is one that can be readily sold or mortgaged to a reasonably prudent purchaser or mortgagee, one acceptable to a reasonable purchaser, informed as to the facts and their legal meaning, willing to perform his contract, in the exercise of that prudence which business men usually bring to bear on such transactions. Marketable title is free from material defects or grave doubts, and reasonably free from litigation. Marketability does not demand a perfect title; nevertheless, it is not necessary for one to prove that a title is wholly bad in order to label it as not marketable. In most states, it is the purchaser's responsibility (between the date of signing the sales agreement and the agreed date of conveyancing) to conduct his examination of the seller's title and notify the seller of any defects within a reasonable time to allow such defects to be cured, if possible. In other states, the responsibility is the seller's to "bring down" or bring up-to-date the abstract of title which will then be reviewed by the attorney for the buyer. The purchaser cannot wait until the date of conveyancing and reject the title as unmarketable to avoid his contractual responsibilities.

b. Evidences of Title

The prudent buyer will want to know the exact state of the seller's title. The fact that the seller can produce a deed to the property, naming him as grantee, is not adequate proof. His deed may be defective, or the previous owner's title may have been defective. The seller may own a fee simple absolute title or he may have some lesser degree of ownership; his title may be technically free and clear, or it may be legally unmarketable, or, perhaps, his title may be heavily encumbered by liens and restrictions. Equally concerned about the seller's title is the lender who may accept a mortgage on the property as security for the repayment of the loan he makes. Evidence of title or proof of ownership is the primary objective of the first step in the conveyancing process . . . the investigation of title.

2. The Recording System

a. General

Covenant and warranties drafted into deeds are meaningless, if the warrantor (grantor) is insolvent or unwilling to live up to his covenants. Unknown title defects passed unwittingly through the medium of even a general warranty deed require litigation, unless the grantor willingly gives satisfaction. At best, however, the purchaser may be required to relinquish the land and settle for money damages. The recording system helps give the purchaser of land the assurance he wants, indicating that the seller has a marketable title which can be conveyed without difficulty and without threat of legal actions. The individual state recording acts were designed to apply to written or paper titles that depend for their proof on a continuous, connected chain of documents wherein interests in real estate are transferred. The acts prescribe the instruments which are authorized to be recorded. These would include contracts, deeds, mortgages, trust deeds, leases, assignments of mortgages, et cetera. In this manner, a public, official, and permanent record is created and perpetuated which can be examined by anyone wishing to buy land or lend money on it. Obviously, the effectiveness of such a system depends significantly on the completeness and accuracy of the records, coupled with meticulous indexing.

b. Systems of Indexing

There are two basic systems of indexing -- the tract system and the grantor-grantee system.

(1) The Tract System. The tract system of indexing sets aside a separate page of the tract index to each piece of property covered by the index. In investigating a title, one would simply locate the proper page in the index to find listed all recorded documents relating to the specific property.

(2) The Grantor-Grantee System. Many states have a number of indexes. Some have a separate index for each type of instrument. The trend is to reduce the number of indices and use only one grantor-grantee index. Naturally, the person searching this index must have some point in time to mark the beginning of his search.

c. The Abstract of Title

Originally, attorneys examined the county records of land transactions and issued their opinions of title based upon their own examination of the title records. In the course of time, it became necessary for the attorneys to prepare abstracts of the records containing copies of the various instruments and court proceedings which they examined to write their opinions. In some parts of the country, attorneys still make their own abstracts. Today, however, abstracts are usually prepared by qualified companies which specialize in this work. The preparation of abstracts by abstract companies, and the examination of them by attorneys, is still the pattern in some parts of the United States. To the average, unskilled purchaser, the receipt of an abstract affords him no knowledge of the state of the title to the real estate. In addition to the abstract, the opinion of an attorney is required to inform him of the nature of the seller's title and of any defects, liens, encumbrances, or other rights which might be disclosed by the abstract.

Under provisions of the recording acts, the public has constructive notice of all property recorded and of all filed papers. That is, one is presumed to know the existence and legal effect of every paper affecting title to land which has been properly recorded or filed in the office of record.

In order that one may examine the title to a parcel of land, to determine ownership and condition of the title, it is necessary that a search be made of these public records. Further, one must know the contents of all the instruments disclosed by such search. This implies the reading of all of these records in their entirety.

Abstracting is the "briefing" or "digesting" of the particular records affecting a given parcel of land. An Abstract of Title contains a digest of every instrument or event brought out by the search, arranged in chronological order, to enable an examiner to determine the ownership and condition of title. Every fact and element in the records bearing in any way on the title to such parcel of land must be included in the Abstract of Title.

An Abstract of Title is often referred to as a "History of Title." It must necessarily show each transfer of ownership, whether by deed, descent, devise, or foreclosure, as well as any mortgage, lien, encumbrance, or other matter, in any way affecting the title. Consequently, most Abstracts of Title are voluminous.

It must be stressed that an Abstract of Title is merely the history of happenings to a particular parcel of land, as shown by the records. Thus, one may have a perfectly good abstract and a very poor title. The Abstractor's certificate covers only the completeness of his work in showing a digest of the records. An Abstract of Title must be thoroughly examined by a competent attorney, familiar with real estate law, in order that the persons interested in the land may know the ownership and condition of the record title. Of course, no Abstract of Title can cover unseen hazards such as missing heirs, forged deeds, transactions by a minor or incompetent, et cetera.

The voluminous procedure necessary in the use of Abstracts of Title in the closing of real estate transactions has practically eliminated their acceptance by money lenders and most buyers of real estate. Other inadequacies of an Abstract of Title, such as limitation of liability, additional examination costs, with consequent delay in closing of a transaction, and the duplication when land is divided, have resulted in the Abstract of Title becoming obsolete in many parts of the country.

(1) Abstractor's and Attorney's Liability. The abstractor is in no way a guarantor of the title to the real estate. The law imposes upon him only the duty to exercise due care in the preparation of the abstract. If the abstractor negligently omits a document from the abstract or incorrectly summarizes the content of such instrument, he can be held liable for any loss caused the purchaser. Likewise, an attorney can only be held liable for damages which are caused by his negligence in the examination of the abstract. As an example, the attorney is liable for any loss caused by his failure to discover an existing, recorded lien contained in the abstract.

(2) Risks Involved. It has been said that no evidence of title can completely and conclusively reveal the exact state of the title to real property. For instance, an abstract may indicate that the seller has clear title, but the chain of title may contain a forged deed. There is no way of knowing from the abstract whether a deed is forged or not, and, of course, such a deed passes no title. Also, an abstract will not reveal the rights of parties in possession. The abstract may show title in one person, but another may possibly have superior right through adverse possession. Fortunately, such things rarely happen. With an abstract and opinion, together with an examination of the property itself, the buyer can be reasonably certain that he will obtain a good title.

3. Title Insurance

   a. General

   Title insurance is a contract which protects the insured against loss occurring through defects in title to real property. The risk of loss, as in other policies of insurance, is transferred from the property owner to a responsible insurer. A title company will not insure a bad title, any more than a life insurance company will insure a dying person.

   Title insurance is completely dependent upon the recording system and involves a search of the records in much the same manner indicated in the preceding paragraphs. The principal advantage lies in the investigation of title by a group of specialists whose work is then insured by a reputable institution.

   The date of the title policy is very important. The title insurance company guarantees against loss occurring because of defects existing at or before the date of the policy. Defects which come into existence subsequent to the date of insurance of the title policy are not covered.

   b. Title Insurance Coverage

   Usually title insurance covers the following:

   (1) Defects in the title of record,
   (2) Defects not disclosed by the record, and
   (3) Costs of defending the title against attack.

   c. Exclusions

   Examples of typical standard exclusions which the title policy does not insure against are:

(1) Rights or claims of parties in possession not shown of record, including unrecorded easements.
(2) Any state of facts an accurate survey would show.
(3) Mechanics' liens, or any right thereto, where no notice of such liens or rights appears of record.
(4) Taxes and assessments not yet due or payable, and special assessments not yet certified to the Treasurer's office.

d. Owner's and Mortgagee's Policies

Title insurance companies will issue policies to both the owner and the mortgagee. The fee or premium for the title policy, unlike other insurance, is paid only once and the policy continues in force without further payment. The fee, as with other insurance, is based upon the amount of insurance purchased. The owner's policy is not transferable; therefore, when the property is resold, the new purchaser should obtain a reissue title policy. The mortgagee's policy is normally transferable, so that if the note and mortgage are sold, the new mortgagee need not obtain a reissue policy.

It should be remembered that a "Mortgagee's Policy" does not protect the owner's equitable interest in the property; a mortgagee's policy will protect only the mortgagee and only to the extent of the mortgagee's interest, whatever that may be; the equity of the owner is protected only by an "owner's policy."

4. The Torrens System of Title Registration

a. General

The basic principle of the Torrens System is the registration of the title instead of recording of the evidence of title as under the recording system. Under the Torrens System, the ultimate fact that a certain named party has title to a particular tract of land is registered, and a certificate thereto is delivered to him. Under the Recording System, the entire evidence is recorded from which proposed purchasers must draw their own conclusions, at their peril.

The Torrens System of title registration of real estate was developed by Sir Robert Torrens, a British businessman, who successfully urged in 1857 that the principle of registration of titles of ships be applied to land. The registry of ships showed the name of the ship's owner and all liens and encumbrances against it. It revealed briefly and simply the condition of the ship's title. A modern comparison would be the registered title to an automobile, which on one document shows the name of the owner and any existing liens or encumbrances.

b. Methods of Registration

To register title to land under the Torrens System, the owner files a written application with the appropriate court for the county in which the property is located. The court then holds proceedings to inquire into the state of the title. All persons known to have an interest or claim in the property are served personal notice of the registration proceedings. All other persons are given notice through newspaper publication. The registration proceeding is, in essence, a quiet title lawsuit. After the hearing, the court issues its decree of confirmation of title and registration. When the court's decree is filed with the registrar of titles, he makes an original certificate of title setting forth the court's findings as to the owner, his interest, and all liens, claims, encumbrances, and other rights, if any, against the property. The registrar then issues an <u>exact</u> <u>duplicate</u> to the owner, called an "owner's duplicate certificate of ownership." Usually, after a statutory period following the issuance of the decree, no person may maintain any action that challenges the findings set forth in the decree. After that time, the owner of the real estate is conclusively presumed to have title as decreed.

c. Transferring Title

An owner of registered land conveying the same or any portion thereof, in fee, shall execute a deed of conveyance which the grantor shall file with the registrar of titles in the county where the land lies. The owner's duplicate certificate shall be surrendered at the same time, and shall be by the registrar marked "cancelled." The original certificate of title shall also be marked "cancelled." The registrar of titles shall thereupon enter in the register of titles a new certificate of title to the grantee, and shall prepare and deliver to such grantee an owner's duplicate certificate. All encumbrances, claims or interests adverse to the title of the registered owner shall be stated upon the new certificate or certificates, except insofar as they may be simultaneously released or discharged. When only a part of the land described in a certificate is transferred, or some estate or interest in the land is to remain in the transferor, a new certificate shall be issued to him for the part, estate, or interest remaining to him.

E. DRAFTING OF THE CONVEYANCE

In Paragraph B. 2. of this Chapter, the elements of a valid deed were enumerated. This paragraph will explore in more depth each of these elements:

1. The Premises

a. Names of the Grantor and Grantee

To be valid, a deed must be from a party, identified as the grantor, who is competent to convey to one, identified as the grantee, who is capable of receiving the grant or title to the property. The names of the seller and buyer are set forth in that order. Where a party customarily uses a middle initial, it should be reflected. Any uncertainty as to the identity of the persons intended would render the deed void. For purposes of further identification, therefore, each name should be followed by the address of the party. The marital status of the grantor should be indicated. If the spouse is to sign the deed, the name of the spouse should be included in the body of the deed. Parties to the deed may also be termed "party of the first part" and "party of the second part" for grantor and grantee, respectively. In states still recognizing dower rights, the wife must release her dower rights. If homestead rights are to be relinquished, the name of the spouse is also required as a grantor. Finally, a deed must be made to a certain person or it is void.

Note: In some jurisdictions, a deed by a married woman for real estate held in her own name is void unless her husband joins in the conveyance or unless she has been declared a feme sole (single woman).

b. Operative Words of Conveyance

Any words indicating an intention to convey will operate to transfer title. The words used to effect the conveyance are known as the "operative words." The operative words must be carefully chosen as they reflect the type of deed used. Insertion in the granting clause of the words "remise, release, and quitclaim" reflect a quitclaim deed. Such words as "grant and release" would indicate a bargain and sell deed. If the granting clause "conveys and warrants," such words are indicative of a warranty deed. They usually follow the recital of the consideration in the deed as in the example, "do hereby grant and release unto the party of the second part _____ and assigns forever." Care must also be exercised to insure that this "granting clause" is carefully worded since the quantity of the estate conveyed is affected. If, for example, the interest to be conveyed is an estate in fee simple, the words "heirs and assigns" will ordinarily be used as in the phrase "to the grantee, his heirs or assigns forever." If the interest to be conveyed is for a life estate, the word "heirs" would be omitted. The word "heirs" is said to be a word of limitation. It indicates a complete title of perpetual duration with power to sell to anybody. The operative words in a deed, "grant and convey," or either, will usually be held today to effectively convey a fee simple title, if the grantor had such title. Any instrument under consideration is always construed against its maker. In the case of a deed, the grantor is presumed to intend to grant a fee simple estate unless he expressly limits it either by the granting clause or the habendum clause (sub-paragraph 2, below). To be operative as a deed, the written instrument must convey a present interest in land. If it postpones the passing of title, the instrument is invalid as a deed.

c. Consideration

The statement of consideration is expressed next. There are different types of consideration, each of which may differently affect the title conveyed and the rights of the purchaser or grantee. Generally, consideration is divided into three categories; good, valuable, and illegal. Good and valuable consideration technically are not synonymous -- each gives the purchaser different rights.

(1) Good Consideration. Good consideration is not measurable in terms of money or money's worth. It usually bears no relation to the value of the property conveyed. Good consideration may be based on a relationship of blood or marriage or be founded on motives of generosity, prudence, love, affection, or natural duty. While good consideration may be sufficient to support a deed between seller and purchaser, it may be regarded as in fraud against creditors of the sellers, and they may be able to set the deed aside.

(2) Valuable Consideration. Valuable consideration is a class of consideration upon which a promise may be founded which entitles the promisee to enforce his claim against an unwilling promisor. It is some right, interest, profit, or benefit accruing to one party, or some forbearance, detriment, loss, or responsibility given, suffered, or undertaken by the other. A gain or loss to either party is not essential; it is sufficient if the party in whose favor the document is made parts with a right which he might otherwise exert. Such consideration usually bears some fair relation to the property's value.

(3) Illegal Consideration. Illegal consideration would include an act or a promise which if done or enforced would be prejudicial to the public interest. This type of consideration may be viewed as a misnomer, since, being illegal, it cannot be consideration in the eyes of the law. In effect, it may be defined as "anything which the law prohibits."

Some expression of consideration should always be inserted in the deed, even though in some jurisdictions the seal at the end of the instrument imparts consideration . . . it might be omitted inadvertently. In other jurisdictions, even though the seal is required, statutes also require the actual consideration to be reflected in the deed.

d. Legal Description

To be sufficient for the deed, the description must unquestionably identify the property. While a description by street and number may be appropriate in a contract, since a contract is normally consummated within a short time, such description is not desirable in a deed which remains a permanent record and becomes an integral part of the chain of title which endures for many years. Use of street numbers which may change as buildings are altered or demolished is inadvisable. The various methods of arriving at a legal description of real property are explained in Chapter 12 - THE SALES CONTRACT. As a general rule, the form of description should never be changed. Much trouble has resulted from failure to observe this rule. The seller should invariably use the same description as that in the deed by which he took title.

2. The Habendum

Description of the Estate to be Taken

The habendum clause in a deed sets forth the duration of the grantee's ownership in the property granted. The clause commences with the words, "To have and to hold . . . ," and describes the estate being granted. It should be consistent with the granting clause (operative words of conveyance) in the premise. The habendum clause is not absolutely necessary. In the event of a contradiction between the granting clause and the habendum clause, the granting clause will usually prevail.

a. Encumbrances

The grantor is assumed to be conveying title free of all encumbrances except those specifically stated. If the property is being conveyed, subject to such encumbrances, it is usual to set them forth following the habendum clause. All encumbrances may be classified as follows:

(1) Pecuniary Charges on the Granted Premises. These would include mortgages, judgment liens, taxes, special assessments, and mechanics' liens.

(2) Estates or Interests Less than Fee Simple in the Premises. These would include leaseholds, life estates, or dower rights.

(3) Easements or Servitudes to which the Premises Are Subject. These would include restrictive covenants, rights of way, and easements.

b. Restrictive Covenants

As noted above, restrictive covenants technically are a classification of encumbrances. Nevertheless, such covenants are usually inserted in the deed following the enumeration of the other encumbrances. Relative to restrictive covenants, it is a recognized legal principle that the grantor has the right to restrain the use of the land he conveys and to limit its appropriation to purposes which would in any manner impair or lessen the value of that portion which he retains.

Restrictions must be reasonable and not contrary to public policy. The use of restrictions - usually called "deed restrictions" or "restrictive covenants" - is an old practice. The foundation of this practice arises out of the rights of property. The owner has the right of free alienation; that is, he may dispose of his estate in any manner he may elect. Once the deed restrictions are established, they run with the land and are limitations upon the use of all future grantees. Deed restrictions are most frequently encountered in the development of subdivisions wherein the limitation is for the benefit of all the landowners. Typical restrictions deal with the minimum size of the house, type of material that may be used, exclusion of commercial establishments. Well formulated deed restrictions have a stabilizing effect upon property values. A homeowner is protected against forbidden uses; he can rely in safety, knowing that a grocery store will not be his neighbor and that his neighbor's house must conform to certain minimum standards. Violations of deed restrictions can be enjoined through a court action brought by any party for whose benefit the restrictions were imposed.

3. The Execution Clause

a. Date

The date is not essential to the validity of a deed. However, when used it reflects the date that the deed was delivered. If a date is not inserted, the party accepting the deed would have the burden of proving that the deed was actually delivered. Incidentally, a deed dated on a Sunday, but delivered on a week day, is valid.

b. Signatures

The grantors must sign the deed by affixing their signatures, or marks, if they cannot write. A signature by mark must be witnessed. The deed may be executed by either the grantors or through their proxy under a power of attorney. In some states, such as Illinois, the grantor's marital status must be reflected and, if married, the signature of the spouse is required to release any possible homestead rights. Additionally, in several states, the names of the grantors must be typed below their signatures.

c. Seal

Historically, any instrument under seal was called a "deed." Except as a means of authentication, the legal effect of the seal has been abolished in most states and is no longer accepted as conclusive evidence of consideration. Furthermore, the seal does not extend the statute of limitation, except in a few eastern states. Use of the seal continues, nevertheless. In those states where the deed is to be executed under seal, it is good policy to recite this intention by including a clause that attests to this fact, e. g., "In witness whereof this instrument has been duly signed and sealed by the parties named above . . . " In some states, seals are not required on deeds executed by individuals, but are required on corporate deeds.

d. Witnesses

While some states require one or more witnesses, others, such as Massachusetts, require none. It is not necessary to have the deed witnessed in most states. In Georgia, for example, the law requires two witnesses in order to record a deed, but without witnesses, the deed is still valid between the grantor and the grantee. Even though not required, a witness is convenient as evidence of the signing, if such proof becomes necessary.

4. The Acknowledgement

The acknowledgement is a formal declaration by the grantor, made before a notary public, justice of the peace, or officer of a court, affirming the authenticity of his signature on the deed. In most states, a deed must be acknowledged before it can be recorded. In other states, such as Illinois, acknowledgement is not required, either to validate the deed or to enable it to be recorded, except where there is a homestead waiver. When acknowledged, however, the conveyance may be introduced as evidence in court without further proof of execution. In all but two states a deed is valid, although not acknowledged. If there is more than one grantor on the deed, acknowledgement by any one of them suffices.

The acknowledgement accomplishes two things: it establishes the deed as prima facie evidence in any legal proceedings, and it permits recording of the deed in those states where acknowledgement is a prerequisite for recording.

In some states - - Alabama, New Jersey, North Carolina, South Carolina, and Texas - - separate acknowledgements are necessary for husband and wife. The wife's acknowledgement must be taken apart from her husband as evidence that she signed the deed freely and voluntarily.

F. CONVEYING THE TITLE

1. Escrow

Any discussion revolving around the closing of a real estate transaction and the transfer of title from the vendor (grantor) to the vendee (grantee) would be incomplete without some reference to "escrows." In many states, an escrow has become an almost indispensable procedure for consummating real estate transactions.

    a. Definition

An escrow is a writing, or deed, delivered by the grantor, promisor, or obligor into the hands of a third person, to be held by the latter until the happening of a contingency or performance of a condition, and then by him delivered to the grantee, promisee or obligee. Escrow is also used in an adjectival form to describe any transaction wherein one person, for the purpose of effecting the sale, transfer, encumbering, or leasing of real or personal property to another person, delivers any written instrument, money, evidence of title to real or personal property, or other thing of value to a third person to be held by such third person until the happening of a specified event or the performance of a prescribed condition, when it is then to be delivered by such third person to the grantee, grantor, promisee, promisor, et cetera, or any agent or employee of any of the latter.

In strict technical interpretation the term "escrow" characterizes the instrument while it is being held by the third party. If such an instrument is a document for conveyancing real estate, it is not, precisely speaking, a deed while it is held on deposit, simply because it has not been completely delivered to the grantee. In this intermediate stage, the conveyancing document is more accurately called an "escrow." Consequently, an escrow differs from a deed only in respect to its delivery.

In a broader sense, the term "escrow" is used to describe the arrangement under which an instrument is deposited with a third person to be delivered upon the performance of a condition. Thus, we hear of an instrument being deposited either "as an escrow" or "in escrow."

    b. Essential Elements of a Valid Escrow

For an escrow to be valid, there must be:

(1) A valid and enforceable contract for the sale of land.
(2) A conditional delivery of transfer instruments to a third party. The conditional delivery is accompanied by instructions (the escrow agreement) to a third party to, in turn, deliver the

instruments upon the performance of the stipulated conditions.
   (3) A valid deed.
   (4) An escrow holder who is a disinterested third party.

c. Basic Steps in the Escrow Process

The basic steps in the escrow process usually include the following - -

   (1) Preliminary title search and report.
   (2) Lender's (beneficiary's) statement.
   (3) Mutual instructions and deposit of funds and instruments.
   (4) Adjustments and prorations.
   (5) Title run to date.
   (6) Transfer of fire policies.
   (7) Recordation.
   (8) Issuance of title policy.
   (9) Disbursement of funds
   (10) Preparation of the escrow statement.

d. Advantages of Escrow as a Closing Device

   (1) The transaction is less likely to "fall through" when the mechanical details are carried out through the instrumentality of the third-party escrowee.
   (2) An escrowee may, <u>notwithstanding the grantor's death</u>, properly deliver the deed in escrow upon performance of the conditions, and such deed will operate as a valid conveyance.
   (3) When an escrow is used, the concurrent acts involved in a sale of real estate can usually be performed in such a manner as to more adequately protect the interests of both vendor and vendee.
   (4) The escrow is particularly convenient in those complex transactions involving the interests of several parties where a clearing house is needed to sort out the diverse mechanical considerations.
   (5) For the real estate agent, the escrow serves to relieve him of the responsibilities he would otherwise be expected to accept, to include the clerical detail of maintaining the earnest money as a separate trust account.

e. Who May Act as Escrow Agent (Holder)?

Usually the law provides that escrow agencies must be licensed by the appropriate state authority. Normally, banks, trust companies, building and loan or savings and loan associations, insurance companies, licensed attorneys, and title companies are exempt from the licensing provisions. In some states, real estate brokers may, under certain conditions, serve as escrow agents.

In the usual real estate transaction, the function of the escrow agent will necessarily be very closely related to that of the title insurance company. The purchaser will usually be furnished with a preliminary report showing the condition of the title to the lands in question prior to the time the funds are deposited. The purchaser's instructions will usually enumerate the exceptions or encumbrances which will be permitted to remain on closing. In order to insure compliance with the purchaser's instructions, the escrow agent will find it necessary to cause the records to be re-examined at the time of closing and, after closing, to deliver the necessary title insurance policies provided for in the instructions. As a consequence, it is commonplace for title insurance companies to function as the escrow holder.

f. Duties of the Escrow Agent

The escrow agent's duties arise in the first instance from the written agreement between the parties stating the terms of the transaction, and are more fully defined and described in such written instructions as may be given by the parties, and by the terms of such documents relating to the transaction as may be deposited. The primary source of the escrow agent's duties and responsibilities is the written instructions of the parties. These instructions are usually incorporated in printed forms supplied by the escrow agent and completed to express the details of the particular transaction. Apart from securing the necessary legal documents required to complete the transaction in accordance with the written instructions and the agreement of the parties, one of the essential functions of the escrow agent is to assemble the necessary data from which the required financial adjustments between the parties can be made. This extremely important part of the escrow closing is essentially a matter of accounting detail and includes such matters as obtaining all pertinent information on mortgage balances, interest accruals, commissions, and other charges payable by the various parties; tax and insurance information, rental data, and a host of allied details. As this information is assembled, it is incorporated in a work sheet with adjustments made to the agreed or probable closing date. This information is then transferred to a settlement sheet for presentation to the parties in order that they may better visualize the financial results of the transaction. (Reference Appendix A).

When all necessary funds and documents have been deposited with the escrow agent and the transaction is ready to close, the escrow agent will set in motion the process of recording all documents which are to be recorded, secure the necessary assignments of fire insurance, transfer mortgages and loan reserves, and cause the necessary final title search to be made. Instructions will have authorized the escrow agent to disburse the funds at the proper time to the persons entitled thereto. After recording has been completed and the funds disbursed, a simple statement must be prepared which will disclose to each party in detail the exact result of the transaction. This statement should be as simple as the details of the transaction will permit and should briefly identify each item entered therein. After closing, it is the duty of the escrow agent to see that all documents described in the instructions are delivered to the party properly entitled thereto.

g. Who Should Designate the Escrow Agent?

When a vendor and vendee desire to close the sale by means of an escrow, one of their first concerns is the selection of an escrowee. The prudent course for both the vendor and the vendee should be to select a disinterested third party, as escrowee, who is neither the agent nor the attorney for either the vendor or vendee.

h. The Escrow Agreement

The escrow agreement is a three-party contract involving the seller, the buyer, and the escrow holder. Usually, the escrow holder is an attorney, a title insurance company, or a lending institution. In essence, at the time contracts are signed, what normally would be exchanged upon conveyancing of title (i. e., the purchase price by the buyer and the deed with related papers by the seller) are instead turned over to the escrow holder, by agreement, who, upon clearance of title, makes the necessary adjustments, records the deed, and remits the balance due to the seller. Such contracts ensure the seller that the provisions of the contract will be met, if his title is found to be marketable, even though he usually received no money at the time the contract was executed.

An escrow agreement should contain at least the following:

(1) Name and signatures of buyer and seller and name of escrow holder.
(2) Documents to be deposited by seller, such as deed, insurance policies, separate assignments of insurance policies, leases, assignments of leases, abstract or other evidence of title, tax bills, cancelled mortgage notes, notice to tenants to pay rent to buyer, service contracts, et cetera.
(3) Deposits to be made by buyer, such as purchase price, and purchase money mortgage, if any.
(4) When deed is to be recorded, whether immediately or after buyer's check clears, or after seller furnishes evidence of good title at date of contract.
(5) Objections to which buyer agrees to take subject.
(6) Type of evidence of title to be furnished.
(7) Time allowed seller to clear defects in title.
(8) How and when purchase price is to be disbursed with directions as to what items are to be prorated or apportioned,

if escrow holder is to do the prorating.
- (9) Directions to deliver deed, leases, insurance policies, assignments of policy, service contracts, et cetera, to buyer when title shows clear.
- (10) Return of deposits to the respective parties where title cannot be cleared.
- (11) Reconveyance by buyer to seller, if deed to buyer has been recorded immediately on signing of escrow agreement and examination of title thereafter discloses seller's title was defective and cannot be cured.
- (12) Payment of escrow, title and recording charges, the broker's commission, attorney fees, et cetera.

2. Matters of Concern At Closing

Although in some communities much of the burden in closing an escrow is assumed by the escrow department of the title companies, all efficient brokers and salesmen should be thoroughly acquainted with the matters to be considered. In closing, the following should be kept in mind by brokers or salesmen in order to fully protect the parties in the transaction:

a. Buyers should determine that title is clear of all except agreed objections. If by agreement seller is to clear certain objections, the buyer should retain part of the purchase price . . . usually to be the amount of lien . . . to insure performance of contract on part of seller.

b. The buyer should require the seller to produce the deed by which he acquired title. This affords some measure of protection against forgery and impersonation.

c. The buyer should determine that the seller's insurance premiums have been paid.

d. Prorations or adjustments should be computed and the closing statement prepared. (See sub-paragraph 9. below).

e. The balance due according to the closing statement should be paid, and documents to which each party is entitled delivered.

f. The broker's commission should be paid.

3. Preparation by Seller

The seller, upon closing of title, should be prepared to produce the following forms and figures at the title passing:

a. His copy of the sales contract.

b. Seller's last deed.

c. Estoppel certificates from the mortgagee showing balance due and date to which interest is paid.

d. Satisfaction pieces of liens, mortgages, or judgments that are to be paid at or prior to the closing.

e. Affidavit of title.

f. Latest receipted bills for water, taxes, and assessment.

g. Latest possible meter readings for water, gas, electricity.

h. Receipts for latest mortgage interest payments.

i. Originals of all insurance policies relating to premises.

j. Names of tenants and all information relating to rents, due dates, et cetera.

k. Assignment of leases.

l. Letters advising tenants to pay all subsequent rents to purchaser.

m. Bill of Sale for personal property sold and reflected in the sales contract.

n. All other subordinate agreements relating to the contract.

o. Agent's authority to execute the deed in the seller's absence.

p. Deed and other instruments that the seller is to deliver or prepare.

q. The seller's closing statement.

4. Preparation by Buyer

At the closing of title, the buyer should be prepared to do the following:

a. Provide his copy of the sales contract.

b. Obtain and examine abstract or report of title.

c. See that all liens are properly disposed of.

    d.   Obtain and examine estoppel certificate.

    e.   Obtain affidavit of title.

    f.   Make adjustments as called for in the sales contract.

    g.   Examine all insurance policies.

    h.   Secure names of tenants and all related information.

    i.   Secure assignment of leases and unpaid rents.

    j.   Obtain letters to tenants.

    k.   Obtain Bill of Sale for personal property covered by the sales contract.

    l.   Examine agent's authority to execute the deed in seller's absence.

    m.   Examine deed to ensure it conforms to the sales contract, properly describes the property, and is properly executed.

    n.   Examine survey if one was made.

    o.   Have sufficient cash or certified checks on hand to make necessary payments of closing costs and those required by the contract.

    p.   Examine any bond or note to be executed.

    q.   Examine purchase money mortgage and execute same, if applicable.

    r.   The buyer's closing statement.

5. **Documents to be Obtained by Seller**

    a.   Balance of purchase money.

    b.   If purchase money mortgage is given, the seller should receive mortgage note and deed.

    c.   Chattel mortgage on personal property sold, if applicable.

6. **Documents to be Obtained by Buyer**

    a.   Deed

    b.   Title Policy

c. Bill of Sale (for personal property).

d. Receipt for Purchase Price.

e. Survey

f. All paid notes on existing mortgages.

g. Statement by mortgagee showing amount due on existing mortgage.

h. Insurance policy and assignment thereof.

i. Leases and assignments thereof.

j. Letter by seller to tenants advising them to pay future rents to buyer.

k. Statement by seller as to name of tenants, rents paid and unpaid, et cetera.

l. Service contracts, such as exterminator contracts, et cetera.

m. Last receipt for taxes, special assessments, gas, electricity, et cetera.

7. <u>Examination of Instruments:</u> - - Normally, a number of instruments must be carefully examined to see that they are in accord with the purchase and sales agreement. Whenever a property is sold, there is a deed evidencing the conveyance. Frequently, there is a bond or a note supported with a mortgage. The deed instrument must be examined to ensure that the proper estate is conveyed in the manner agreed upon. The bond or note and the mortgage, if applicable, must be in consonance with the terms of the agreement. At this point, it is not unusual to have the seller execute an "affidavit of title" which assures the purchaser that there are no defects in the seller's title to the property. The affidavit of title <u>supplements</u> the title examination and <u>covers matters that may not be revealed by a title search.</u>

8. <u>Delivery and Acceptance of the Deed:</u> - - Legal title to the property passes only when the deed is delivered by the grantor and accepted by the grantee. (Reference paragraph B. 3., supra). As previously noted, the law prescribes no specific formality, except that both delivery and acceptance must be the voluntary and concurrent acts of the grantor and the grantee, respectively. According to some statutes, when a deed is acknowledged and recorded, the law presumes that there has been an effective delivery. <u>For delivery of a deed to be effective</u>, it generally <u>must be made during the lifetime of the grantor.</u> If the grantor executes a deed, retains it and directs that upon his death it is to be delivered to the grantee, such deed does not pass title. Delivery of the deed may be made to some third person for the benefit of the grantee, but, to be effective, <u>the grantor must surrender all right to control or recover the deed.</u>

There are two kinds of delivery:

a. Delivery absolute - when made to grantee or his agent without conditions or stipulations.

b. Delivery in escrow - when deed is delivered to a third person and will take effect only upon the performance of some condition by one of the parties or the happening of some event. In an escrow delivery, the grantor loses all control over the deed, and he is powerless to recall it.

9. The Closing Statements

At the time of closing there are various costs, charges, and adjustments for accrued or prepaid expenses which must be considered. At the time of closing, a closing statement for both the seller and the buyer is prepared which reflects the debits and credits to each. A more circumspect treatment of closing statements will be found in Appendix A to this text. For our immediate purposes, however, a general reflection of what is normally contained in the closing statement is listed below:

a. Credits Due Seller

(1) Full purchase price.
(2) Prepaid insurance premiums.
(3) Fuel on hand.
(4) Any items paid by seller in advance, such as water tax, prepayments of taxes made by seller to mortgagee under the terms of the mortgage where said mortgage is assumed by buyer.
(5) Prorata share of personal property taxes on personal property sold, if seller is to pay same.

b. Credits Due Buyer

(1) Earnest money.
(2) Existing mortgages.
(3) Interest accrued and unpaid on existing mortgages.
(4) Unearned rents which have already been collected.
(5) Deposits by tenants made as security for payments of rent.
(6) Taxes.
(7) Items based on Meter Readings.
(8) Wages and other charges accrued and unpaid, such as janitor's salary, et cetera.
(9) Amount of purchase money mortgage, since seller has agreed to receive such mortgage as part of the purchase price.
(10) Release and recording charge, where buyer will record or obtain re-

lease of mortgage which seller should have removed.

10. Matters of Concern After Closing

   a. Buyer should immediately record his deed and any release of mortgage obtained at closing.

   b. Have water, gas, electricity bills charged to his own name.

   c. Obtain consent of insurance company to assignment of policy.

   d. Have mortgagee loss clause attached to existing policy.

   e. Obtain Workmen's Compensation Insurance, if necessary.

G. RECORDING

1. General: - - The transfer of title is complete when the deed has been signed, sealed, and delivered. Nevertheless, by statute, no conveyance of an estate in fee simple or for life is valid as against any person, except the grantor, his heirs or devisees and persons having actual notice of it, unless it is properly recorded in the office of record for the county in which the land is located. Recording serves as constructive notice to all of one's ownership. It protects the owner by relieving him of the necessity of remaining constantly in possession, and it protects persons who, desiring to deal with the property, wish to determine the identity of the real owner. As a consequence, anyone dealing with real estate is bound by all recorded instruments.

2. Real Estate Transfer Revenue Stamp Tax: - - Prior to December 31, 1967, the federal government imposed a Federal Revenue Stamp Tax on all conveyances of real estate. Following the repeal of the federal tax, all but fifteen states enacted laws imposing an identical tax via revenue stamps to be affixed to deeds, other conveyances, or, as in Illinois, real estate transfer declarations which accompany each deed. The tax is usually payable at the time of recording of the deed and, normally, is a prerequisite to recording. These taxes are generally based on the selling price and are an expense to the Seller in most states. If the purchaser takes over the seller's existing mortgage, stamps are usually based on the price paid over the existing mortgage rather than on the selling price. In every state where a transfer tax has been enacted, the amount of the tax is specified as well as the procedures employed to determine the taxable base. Certain deeds exempted from the tax are also specified. In each of these areas, local statutes govern and should be consulted as applicable. A table of general information relative to this revenue stamp tax follows the end of this chapter on page 635.

CONVEYANCING

MAIN DIVISIONS

1. Investigation of Title

2. Drafting of the Conveyance

DEED OF CONVEYANCE

A formal written document by which title to, or an interest in, real property is conveyed from one person to another.

SECTIONS OF A VALID DEED

1. The Premises

2. The Habendum

3. The Execution Clause

4. The Acknowledgement

THE HABENDUM
(To Have and to Hold Clause)

1. Description of Estate to be Taken
2. Declaration of Trust, if Any
3. Conditions or Powers Affecting Grant
4. Covenants of Title

THE EXECUTION CLAUSE

1. **DATE**
2. **SIGNATURES OF GRANTOR[s]**
3. **SEAL**
4. **SIGNATURE OF WITNESSES**

ESSENTIAL ELEMENTS OF A VALID DEED

1. **A Written Instrument**
2. **Identification of Grantor[s] and Grantee[s]**
3. **Words of Conveyance**
4. **Description of the Land**
5. **Consideration**
6. **Signature of Grantor[s]**

(Delivery and acceptance
complete the conveyance)

COMMON TYPES OF DEEDS

1. **WARRANTY DEEDS:**
   a. General
   b. Special

2. **QUITCLAIM DEEDS:**
   a. With Covenants
   b. Without Covenants

3. **BARGAIN AND SALE DEED:**
   a. With Covenants Against Grantor's Acts
   b. Without Covenants Against Grantor's Acts

GENERAL WARRANTY DEED

COVENANTS

1. Seisin
2. Right to Convey } Present Covenants
3. Against Encumbrances

4. Further Assurance
5. Quiet Enjoyment } Future Covenants
6. Warranty

METHODS OF TITLE ASSURANCE

1. **THE RECORDING SYSTEM**
2. **TITLE INSURANCE**
3. **THE REGISTRATION SYSTEM**

DRAFTING OF THE CONVEYANCE

"Operative Words"

WARRANTY DEED:
    convey and warrant
    grant, bargain and sell
    warrant general

QUITCLAIM DEED:
    remise, release, and quitclaim

BARGAIN AND SALE DEED:
    grant and release
    bargain and sell

ENCUMBRANCES

1. **PECUNIARY CHARGES ON GRANTED PREMISES:**
    a. Mortgages
    b. Judgment Liens
    c. Taxes
    d. Special Assessments
    e. Mechanics' Liens

2. **ESTATES OR INTERESTS LESS THAN FEE SIMPLE:**
    a. Leaseholds
    b. Life Estates
    c. Dower Rights

3. **EASEMENTS OR SERVITUDES:**
    a. Restrictive Covenants
    b. Rights of Way
    c. Easements

ESSENTIAL ELEMENTS OF A VALID ESCROW

1. A valid and enforceable contract for the sale of land

2. A conditional delivery of transfer instrument to a third party

3. A valid deed

4. An escrow holder who is a disinterested party

CONVEYANCING

CERTIFICATE OF TITLE:
A title examiner's written and signed opinion that seller has good title.

ABSTRACT OF TITLE:
A summary of all deeds upon which the existing title depends.

AFFIDAVIT OF TITLE:
The seller's assurance to the buyer that there are no defects in the title.

REAL ESTATE TRANSFER REVENUE STAMP TAX RATES

Note: Consult specific state law for details

ALABAMA	$.50 per $500 or fraction thereof	MONTANA	None
ALASKA	None	NEBRASKA	$.55 per $500 or fraction thereof
ARIZONA	None	NEVADA	$.55 per $500 or fraction thereof
ARKANSAS	$1.10 per $1000 or fraction thereof	NEW HAMPSHIRE	$.15 per $100 or fraction thereof
CALIFORNIA	$.55 per $500 or fraction thereof	NEW JERSEY	$.50 per $500 or fraction thereof
COLORADO	$.01 per $100 in excess of $500	NEW MEXICO	None
CONNECTICUT	$.55 per $500 or fraction thereof	NEW YORK	$.55 per $500 or fraction thereof
DELAWARE	2 % of property value	NORTH CAROLINA	$.50 per $500 or fraction thereof
FLORIDA	$.30 per $100 plus $.55 per $500 or fraction thereof	NORTH DAKOTA	None
GEORGIA	$1.00 per first $1000, $.10 for each additional $100	OHIO	$.30 per $100 and/or $1.00, or $.10 per $100 whichever is greater
HAWAII	$.05 per $100	OKLAHOMA	$.55 per $500 or fraction thereof
IDAHO	None	OREGON	None
ILLINOIS	$.50 per $500 or fraction thereof	PENNSYLVANIA	1 % of value
INDIANA	None	RHODE ISLAND	$.55 per $500 or fraction thereof
IOWA	$.55 per $500 in excess of $500	SOUTH CAROLINA	$1.00 per $100 to $500; $1.00 additional for each $500
KANSAS	None	SOUTH DAKOTA	$.50 per $500 or fraction thereof
KENTUCKY	$.50 per $500 or fraction thereof	TENNESSEE	$.26 per $100
LOUISIANA	None	TEXAS	None
MAINE	$.55 per $500 or fraction thereof	UTAH	None
MARYLAND	$.55 per $500 or fraction thereof	VERMONT	½ of 1% of sales price
MASSACHUSETTS	$1.14 per $500 or fraction thereof	VIRGINIA	$.15 per $100; $.50 per $500 or fraction thereof
MICHIGAN	$.55 per $500 or fraction thereof	WASHINGTON	$.50 per $500 plus 1% of sales price
MINNESOTA	$2.20 per first $1000; $1.10 per each additional $500	WEST VIRGINIA	$1.65 per $500 or fraction thereof
MISSISSIPPI	None	WISCONSIN	$.10 per $100
MISSOURI	None	WYOMING	None

Chapter 14

REVIEW DEFINITIONS IN GLOSSARY OR TEXT OF FOLLOWING TERMS:

abstract of title
acknowledgement
affidavit
affidavit of title
appurtenance
certificate of title
closing title
cloudy title
constructive notice
conveyance
deed
delivery in escrow
delivery of deed
documentary stamps
encumbrance
escrow
execution
further assurance
grant
grantee

granting clause
grantor
habendum clause
marketable title
municipal lien certificate
passage of title
quitclaim deed
recording of deed
registered land
registered title
remise
restrictive covenant
sealing
seisin
signing
title insurance
title search
warranty
warranty deed

REVIEW QUESTIONS:

1. What are the two main divisions of the subject of conveyancing?

2. What are the essential elements of a valid deed?

3. What is a warranty deed?

4. What is a quitclaim deed?

5. When does legal title to property which is being conveyed by deed pass?

6. What are the six usual covenants made by the grantor in a general warranty deed?

7. Essentially, what is the Torrens System?

8. From the grantor's position, what type of deed imposes a minimum degree of liability?

9. Who executes the affidavit of title?

10. Give an example when a deed is not delivered directly to the grantee.

11. What is meant by "executing a deed?"

12. What are the usual sections of a deed?

13. What are the essentials of a valid escrow?

14. What are the three methods of title assurance?

FOR ANSWERS TO REVIEW QUESTIONS:

1.

2.

3.

4.

5.

6.

7.

8.

9.

10.

11.

12.

13.

14.

Chapter 15

Property Insurance

A.	INTRODUCTION		449
B.	WHAT IS RISK ?		449
	1.	Definitions	449
		a. Risk	449
		b. Peril	449
		c. Hazard	449
		(1) Physical	449
		(2) Moral	449
	2.	Classification of Financial Risk	449
		a. Speculative	450
		b. Pure	450
		c. Fundamental	450
		d. Particular	450
	3.	Classification of Financial Loss	450
		a. Liability Losses	450
		b. Personal Losses	450
		c. Property Losses	450
	4.	Approaching the Uncertainties of Financial Loss	451
		a. Risk Retention	451
		b. Risk Prevention	451
		c. Risk Insurance	451
	5.	Insurable Risks	451
C.	WHAT IS INSURANCE ?		452
	1.	General	452
	2.	The Function of Insurance	452
	3.	The Effect of Insurance	452

D.	BASIC INSURANCE CONCEPTS		452
	1. Indemnity Principle		452
		a. Insurable Interests	453
		b. Subrogation	453
		c. Other Insurance	453
	2. The Equity Principle		453
	3. The Large Loss Principle		453
	4. The Small Loss Principle		453
	5. The Concept of Insurance to Value		454
		a. The Tendency Towards Underinsurance	454
		b. The Predominance of Partial Losses	454
		c. The Problem of Rate Equity	454
		d. Coinsurance as a Solution	454
E.	THE INSURANCE BUSINESS		455
	1. Organization		455
	2. Types of Insurers		455
		a. Capital Stock Organizations	455
		b. Cooperative Enterprises	456
	3. Agencies		456
		a. Branch Office	456
		b. General Agency	456
	4. Legal Aspects of Agency		456
		a. Record Agents	456
		b. Survey Agents	457
	5. Agent and Broker Differentiated		457
		a. Agent	457
		b. Broker	457
	6. Types of Insurance		457
		a. Liability Insurance	457
		b. Personal Insurance	458
		c. Property Insurance	458

| | | 7. | When Protection Starts | 458 |
| | | 8. | The Insurance Claims Adjuster | 459 |

            a.   General   459
            b.   Adjusting Procedures   459

                  (1) Investigation of Claim   459
                  (2) Establishing Value of Loss   459
                  (3) Negotiating the Settlement   460

      9.   Insured's Recourse Against the Insurer   460

F.   TYPES OF PROPERTY LOSSES   460

      1.   Direct Losses   460
      2.   Indirect Losses   460

G.   TYPES OF PROPERTY COVERAGE   460

      1.   Specific Perils   460
      2.   All-Risks   461

H.   HOMEOWNERS' (HO) POLICIES   461

      1.   Introduction   461
      2.   General Coverage   461
      3.   Specific Perils   462
      4.   Specific Limits of Liability   462
      5.   Types of Homeowners' Policies   463

            a.   Home Owners   463
            b.   Condominium Owners   464
            c.   Renters   464

      6.   How Much Insurance is Enough ?   465

            a.   Real Property   465
            b.   Personal Property   465

      7.   Summary   465

I.   THE INSURANCE CONTRACT   466

      1.   Essential Elements   466

		a.	Mutual Assent	466
		b.	Legal Consideration	466
		c.	Competent Parties	466

                (1) Infants   467
                (2) Insane Persons   467
                (3) Drunkards   467

        d. Legal Purpose   467
        e. Legal Form   467

    2. <u>Distinctive Features of the Insurance Contract</u>   467

        a. Aleatory Contract   467
        b. Unilateral Contract   468
        c. Executory Contract   468
        d. Contract of Adhesion   468
        e. Non-assignable Contract   468
        f. Fiducial Contract   468
        g. Indemnification Contract   469

J. ORGANIZATION OF THE INSURANCE CONTRACT   469

    1. <u>Declarations</u>   469
    2. <u>Coverage</u>   469
    3. <u>Exclusions</u>   469
    4. <u>Conditions</u>   470
    5. <u>Endorsements</u>   470

Chapter 15
Property Insurance

A. INTRODUCTION

Property ownership entails the <u>possibility</u> of financial loss over which the property owner has absolutely no control. Efforts to control circumstances, minimize uncertainty and reduce <u>risks</u> have been a constant striving of man throughout history. Anyone directly or indirectly involved with real estate or with the owners of real estate should be familiar with methods which enable property owners to protect themselves against foreseeable but uncertain perils. To reduce the uncertainty of financial loss requires a fundamental knowledge of risk. One method of treating risk - i. e., insurance - is the subject matter of this chapter.

B. WHAT IS RISK ?

1. <u>Definitions:</u>

   a. Risk, as it relates to property risk, is the uncertainty of financial loss. Risk and peril are often used incorrectly but interchangeably.

   b. Peril - peril is defined simply as the source of loss. Perils, such as fires, hurricanes, floods, and earthquakes, are sources of loss which give rise to risk, although they are themselves not risks.

   c. Hazard - hazard also is often confused with both risk and peril. Hazard is a condition that increases the likelihood of loss. There are two classifications of hazard: physical and moral.

      (1) Physical Hazard. Hazards which arise from either the natural condition of property or from the impersonal surroundings are physical hazards. A building located in the frequent path of hurricanes or tornados is an example of a physical hazard.

      (2) Moral Hazard. Any characteristic of an insured person that might increase the severity or frequency of loss is a moral hazard.

2. <u>Classifications of Financial Risk:</u>

   Financial risk may be classified as speculative, pure, fundamental, and particular. The technique for treating risks depends upon an understanding of each classification.

    a.   Speculative Risks. Those risks which may be rewarded by gain or exposure to loss are speculative risks. The risks involved in gambling fall in this classification.

    b.   Pure Risks. Pure risks afford one the prospect of only loss or no loss. The uncertainty concerning the destruction of property by fire is a pure risk. Since no gain is possible, this type of risk can be treated by the technique of insurance.

    c.   Fundamental Risks. The impact of losses from fundamental risks affect an entire group. These risks arise from losses that are <u>impersonal</u> in both origin and consequence. Floods, earthquakes, war, inflation are sources of fundamental risk. Losses from fundamental risks often cannot be prevented and frequently are catastrophic in their results.

    d.   Particular Risks. Particular risks, conversely, result from losses that originate in individual events. The impact of particular risks is felt in consequences that are localized. Risks may shift from fundamental to particular. Automobile accidents, long believed to be caused by the failure or negligence of a particular driver, are recently being viewed as the result of a combination of circumstances, many of which are beyond the control of any person. Those embracing this view suggest that it is inappropriate to impose the burden of cost by way of the liability system and feel that all involved in automobile accidents, regardless of fault, are victims of a fundamental risk. The emerging concept of "no - fault" insurance supports this position.

3.   <u>Classifications of Financial Loss</u>:

The definition of risk as it relates to persons or property is the uncertainty of financial loss. Financial <u>losses</u> may be classified in three ways: liability, personal, and property losses.

    a.   Liability Losses. Liability losses result from legal judgments that take one's property lawfully, or as the result of a relinquishing of property voluntarily under threat of a suit.

    b.   Personal Losses. Premature death, sickness, accident, unemployment are examples of personal losses. Personal losses <u>directly</u> affect an individual.

    c.   Property Losses. Property losses include the <u>direct</u> damage, destruction, or wrongful taking by others of one's property. Property losses also include the adverse effect on one's financial position by some occurrence.

4. Approaching the Uncertainties of Financial Loss:

There are three major areas begging our consideration once the uncertainties of financial loss have been identified. These considerations are risk retention, risk prevention, and insurance.

   a. Risk Retention. Risk retention or "self-assumption of risk" is simply the acceptance of the risk. No action is taken to counter the uncertainties of possible loss. Risk retention, then, is the assumption of the property risk by the individual or business.

   b. Risk Prevention. Risk prevention is a method of reducing or eliminating the uncertainty of financial loss arising out of the many perils to property. Positive prevention activities and programs are ideally adaptable to property risk. Flood control measures serve as an excellent example.

   c. Risk Insurance. The most widely accepted method of dealing with the uncertainty of financial loss related to property is property insurance. By property insurance we refer to that type of insurance which indemnifies the person with an insurable interest in the property for its direct loss or for consequential losses.

5. Insurable Risks:

Before a risk can be insured, all of the following conditions must exist:

   a. Risk Must Be Economic in Character. To be insurable, the risk must lend itself to expression in financial terms relating to that which may be lost or stolen.

   b. Risk Must Be Subject to Appraisal in Monetary Terms. Any risk which cannot be appraised in monetary terms because of lack of sufficient data regarding the loss is generally uninsurable. For example, moral hazards are uninsurable.

   c. Units of Risk Must Represent Large Numbers. Insurance generally is a mass arrangement into which small numbers of individuals are incapable of entering. Moreover, the larger the number of insureds, the more predictable the total amount of loss for the group.

d. Risk Must Relate to Fortuitous Events. The events insured against must not be predictable. They must be random happenings, or they must develop according to the law of chance.

C. WHAT IS INSURANCE?

1. General

Insurance is a plan for cooperatively sharing risks with a group so that the consequences of severe loss will not fall too heavily on any individual. Everyone is continually exposed to the risk of accident and disaster. It is difficult for most, and impossible for some, to bear the cost of serious or extensive damage to their property. The concept of insurance was developed because of this specific reason. The principle of insurance is not complex. Those who are exposed to the same type of hazards pay into a general fund certain set sums of money called premiums. Since a large number of people contribute to the general fund, while only a relatively small number suffer a loss within a given period, the premium payment is not great. When any of the insured suffers a misfortune, money is drawn from the general fund to indemnify him. Thus, it can be seen that insurance is a cooperative or group undertaking. Members of the group are bound by contractual obligations. Under their contract, or policy, they agree to make periodic premium payments in exchange for the promise to indemnify the group member who suffers any of the misfortunes covered by the policy.

2. Function of Insurance

The function of insurance is to substitute certainty in the form of a known premium payment for uncertainty in the form of a large expense which might befall one not insured.

3. The Effect of Insurance

Insurance has the effect of spreading a loss which normally would be borne by one individual over a large group of individuals exposed to the same risk of loss. Insurance serves to "indemnify" the insured. This means that the insured is restored to about the same economic position he enjoyed before the loss occurred. The possibility of gain never enters into the concept of insurance.

D. BASIC INSURANCE CONCEPTS

1. Indemnity Principle:

The possibility of the insured to realize a gain from insured losses might encourage the intentional destruction of property which would be socially undesirable. Thus, the principle of indemnity may be considered as the cardinal principle of insurance. This principle, in essence, holds that the insurer is not liable for more than the actual value of the loss sustained. Enforcement of this principle involves consideration of three corollaries: insurable interest, subrogation, and other insurance.

    a. Insurable Interest. Since the purpose of insurance is to indemnify for loss, only those persons subject to loss are entitled to recovery. Any person who stands to suffer a loss which can be expressed in monetary terms has an insurable interest.

    b. Subrogation. Subrogation is the transfer of one party's legal right or claim to another. When, for example, an insurance company pays an insured for property damage in a fire caused maliciously by another, subrogation allows the company to proceed aganst the wrongdoer. Subrogation is a legal doctrine which supports the concept of insurance as a contract of indemnity.

    c. Other Insurance. An insured cannot obtain a double recovery. If, for example, the insured insures his home for $40,000 with two different insurance companies for $40,000 each, he could only collect $40,000. Double recovery would violate the principle of indemnity.

2. The Equity Principle

The equity principle holds that the rate charged the insured generally depends upon both the nature of coverage purchased and the rate class in which the insured person or insured property belongs. This principle recognizes the unfairness of charging all those insured the same rate - even for the same coverage. Fire insurance rates, for example, would vary according to building construction, location, occupancy, et cetera. The principle of equity holds that the premium rate reflects the insured's expectation of loss. The insurance laws of all states recognize the frailties of this principle. They, consequently, remind insurers continuously that they must avoid discrimination among policyholders of the same class.

3. The Large Loss Principle

The large - loss principle holds that priority be given to the purchase of insurance coverage of those sources of loss (perils) that could cause substantial financial loss. Most persons have only a limited amount of money to allocate to all forms of insurance. The expenditure of premium dollars for protection against relatively inconsequential losses precludes coverage in areas where more significant losses may be suffered.

4. The Small Loss Principle

The small - loss principle eliminates small claims by a deductible concept relative to sources of losses which might cause substantial losses, but also cause frequent small losses. By use of the deductible, many small claims are eliminated along with the disproportionately high administrative expenses involved. This, of course, results in the reduction of the insured's premium. While the use of deductible is frequently used in ocean marine cargo insurance, automobile collision policies and health insurance, it is seldom used in fire and liability insurance with some exceptions in commercial and industrial coverages.

5. The Concept of Insurance to Value:

   a. The Tendency Toward Underinsurance. Most people are insufficiently covered by insurance. For example, few insureds continually keep abreast of inflationary trends or appreciation rates on their real and personal property. Their insurance coverage, almost universally, is considerably less than the actual value of the property.

   b. The Predominance of Partial Losses. Significant, too, is the fact that partial losses predominate. Rarely, for example, do fire losses result in the total destruction of property. Property insurance policies are contracts of indemnification. As such, the insurer is only responsible for the actual cash value of the loss, regardless of the face amount of the contract.

   c. The Problem of Rate Equity. The tendency towards underinsurance, coupled with the preponderance of partial losses, creates a problem of rate equity in some types of insurance. Assume two persons own homes comparable in all respects, each valued at $50,000. Assume further that owner A purchases a fire insurance policy for $40,000 while owner B has coverage for $20,000. Obviously, A's coverage would be about twice that of B's. The problem crystallizes when both A and B suffer a partial fire loss of $10,000. True, if the houses were totally destroyed, A would recover twice the amount that B would recover. Why, then, should B be indemnified in the same amount as A in the event of an identical partial loss?

   d. Coinsurance As a Solution. The principle involved in "coinsurance" is universally misunderstood, even though it is one of the most important in the area of general insurance. The necessity for coinsurance stems from the fact that rate-making proceeds on the assumption that the total value of a risk property will be insured despite the fact that the vast majority of losses are only partial. Coinsurance has the effect of making the insured a "coinsurer" for the difference between a specified percentage of the insured's property and the amount of insurance actually carried. For example, if A, the insured, was advised to purchase insurance on his property in an amount equal to 80% of the value of it, his policy on a

$50,000 home would be written in the face amount of $40,000. A $10,000 partial fire loss would be completely covered. Homeowner B, however, has purchased insurance in the face amount of only $20,000. His indemnification for a $10,000 partial fire loss under the coinsurance concept would be $5,000, the difference between the specified percentage of the insured's property (80% of $50,000 or $40,000) and the amount of insurance actually carried ($20,000 or 50% of the amount specified). Owner B would be entitled to 50% indemnification of the actual loss suffered.

E. THE INSURANCE BUSINESS

1. Organization:

The insurance business, for the conduct of its commercial activities, requires a structure consisting essentially of four organizations:

   a. Insurers. Organizations called insurers perform the function of assuming and carrying the risk.

   b. Agencies. Agencies represent the field organizations necessary to establish and maintain contacts with the public for both the writing of insurance and the settlement of losses.

   c. Associations and Bureaus. These inter-company organizations establish standards, determine rates, and are involved in activities, such as institutional advertising, research, and such other activities, which promote the interests of the insurers.

   d. Agent Associations or Boards. Organizations of agents are formed principally to promote the interest of agents.

2. Types of Insurers:

Organizations referred to as insurers fall into two categories: those organized on a capital stock basis; and those organized as cooperative enterprises.

   a. Capital Stock Organizations. Those who insure obviously must have funds with which to pay the promised indemnity. In capital stock organizations, the contributions of capital in exchange for stock serve as the basis from which losses may be paid in the event collected premiums are insufficient. The inducement offered to those who must bear the risk is the dividends on the capital stock purchased, assuming, of course, that the business operation is successful. The public benefits by being assured that losses will be met, since state laws closely guide and govern the organization and monitor the safeguards felt necessary to protect the public interest.

    b.   Cooperative Enterprises. Cooperative enterprises, including mutual associations, are organized without the use of subscriptions for capital stock. Funds to meet the payment of claims must, of necessity, be derived from premiums paid. To assure the public that sufficient resources exist to meet nominal losses, state laws often require that a certain number of policies be written, and premiums collected, before such cooperative organizations can do business.

3.   <u>Agencies</u>:

The agency system is established for maintaining contact with the public. Its primary function is to produce "sales." Two general types of agency organization exist . . . the branch office type operation and the general agency system.

    a.   Branch Office. When the company wishes to maintain tight control over its operations, branch offices may be established in each of a number of districts. The branch office is in charge of a manager who is an employee of the company.

    b.   General Agency. The general agency is established when the company does not wish to incur the expense or assume the responsibility of maintaining branch offices. In the general agency system, the company may designate an established agency to act as its representative for the district. In the field of property insurance, it is common practice for such local agents to represent a number of insurance companies. A significant amount of property insurance, however, is sold on a brokerage basis which, in some important respects, differs from the agency system.

4.   <u>Legal Aspects of Agency</u>:

The principal - agent relationship is covered in some detail in Chapter 3. In the agency system, contract negotiations between the insurer and the insured through an agent of the company (insurer) is governed by the authority granted the agent by his contract with the insurer. There are two types of local agents associated with insurance underwriting - record agents and survey agents.

    a.   Record Agents. The authority of record agents and survey agents is the same. The record agent, however, may write his own policies.

b. Survey Agents. Survey agents must submit applications for insurance to the home office where the policies are written.

5. Agent and Broker Differentiated:

   a. Agent. An insurance agent is generally defined as a representative of his principal, the insurer. He is normally compensated by means of commissions based on the business he writes. The agent in property insurance has the distinguishing authority to bind the company on many insurance contracts. In spite of the agent's legal obligations to his principal, the insurance company, there is a natural tendency to cater to the interests of his customers, the insureds. If the agent leans towards his customers too much, he may jeopardize his company contacts.

   b. Broker. An insurance broker represents the applicant for insurance, not the company. The applicant is the broker's principal, even though the broker's compensation usually comes from commissions paid directly to him by the insurance company or through the company's agent. The broker usually deals through the company's agent although he may work directly with the insurer.

6. Types of Insurance:

Insurance is an important technique of dealing with the uncertainty of financial loss as it relates to liability, personal, and property risks. These three areas of possible financial loss give rise to the three general categories of insurance coverage - liability, personal and property.

   a. Liability Insurance. Liability insurance developed as a consequence of and a response to tort law. Initially, liability policies indemnified the insured against loss rather than against liability. The later shift from indemnity against loss to indemnity against liability reflects the purpose of the liability policy to protect the public interests as well as the parties to the contract. Generally, liability insurance can be categorized as:

   (1) Automobile insurance, and
   (2) Miscellaneous.

   Included under miscellaneous insurance are . . .

   (a) Employer's Liability coverage which is written with the Workmen's Compensation Policy;

(b) Public liability coverage which is designed to protect the insured against liability to members of the public generally;

(c) Comprehensive liability coverage relates to both general and personal liability. It provides protection against most of the important hazards in a single policy, such as Owner's, Landlord's, and Tenant's Form (O. L. & T.) and the Manufacturer's and Contractor's Form (M. & C.);

(d) Contractual liability coverage protects the insured from risk of tort loss assumed by contract;

(e) Independent contractor's liability coverage (also known as contingent or protective liability insurance) protects the insured from losses due to operations of independent contractors or others for whom there may be secondary liability;

(f) Professional liability coverage recognizes that the reputation of a professional man is at stake;

(g) Business liability coverage ordinarily tends to be more complex and involves more than one limit of liability which requires individual tailoring by endorsement to meet the needs of the insured;

(h) Personal liability coverage usually contains only one limit of liability and is more likely to afford coverage on an occurrence than on an accident basis.

b. Personal Insurance. Personal risks covered by insurance focus on disability, excessive longevity, and premature death.

c. Property Insurance. Property insurance is involved with covering those risks of financial loss arising out of the damage or destruction of physical property from either the actions of individuals or from the forces of nature. A complete listing of all the perils to which a property is exposed is beyond the scope of this chapter. However, the general types of property losses and the coverage designed to indemnify insureds against such loss are of importance to the real estate agent and are explored in the following pages.

7. When Protection Starts

The effective date of an insurance policy depends on the specific type of insurance and on the provisions of the insurance contract. Casualty and fire insurance are effective immediately upon issuance of a memorandum or binder which summarizes the coverage you have agreed to purchase. Frequently, a binder is issued even before a payment is made by the insured. Nevertheless, the insured is protected while the company checks on the applicant's insurability. If the company does not give the applicant a binder or issue an oral acceptance advising that the applicant is temporarily protected, the policy usually does not go into effect until it is delivered. This does not mean that the policy must be in the applicant's hands. The moment the insurance contract is addressed either to the applicant or the insurance agent for forwarding to the applicant, it is generally considered as having been constructively delivered.

8. The Insurance Claims Adjuster:

   a. General

   Upon notification of a claim made against it, the insurance company must determine the extent of its liability to the insured by carefully investigating the circumstances of the reported loss. The person responsible for this investigation is often the company's agent, when the claim is small. When acting in this capacity, he may be referred to as an investigator, examiner, or claims adjuster.

   b. Adjusting Procedures:

   The kind of insurance and the specific type of claim normally will determine the procedure in settling or adjusting a claim. Certain basic functions must be performed by all claims adjusters: claims must be investigated, value of loss must be established, and a settlement must be negotiated.

   (1) Investigation of Claim. If the claim is a minor one and there is no question as to coverage under the policy provisions, little difficulty is likely in reaching a settlement. Insurance claims may be fraught, on the other hand, with many complexities which the uninitiated would not anticipate. In these instances, the services of an experienced attorney retained by the insured may be advisable in handling negotiations with the claims adjuster.

   (2) Establishing Value of Loss. Understandably, establishing the value of loss which is acceptable to both the insurer and the insured may result in protracted negotiations. Again, the guidance of a seasoned attorney may save the insured a considerable amount of money.

(3) Negotiating the Settlement. When a settlement is agreed upon, the insurance company will request that the insured sign a paper indicating satisfaction with the settlement and agreement that subsequent suit will not be brought against the insurer. This paper is known as a release. Should another party be legally liable for the loss, the insurance company may wish to proceed against this party in an effort to be reimbursed for the money paid to the insured. In this event, the claims adjuster will ask the insured to sign a paper authorizing the company to proceed against this party. This action is called subrogation. (Reference Paragraph D. 1. b.)

9. Insured's Recourse Against the Insurer

An insurance policy is a contract. Refusal by the insurer to pay a just claim is a breach of contract which gives the insured a right to bring legal action against the insurer. The principle of insurance is to restore the insured's property to him in its condition at the time of loss. The insured can never recover more than the actual amount of loss up to the face value of the insurance policy. The company must pay the insured the actual value of the lost, damaged, or stolen property, less depreciation.

F. TYPES OF PROPERTY LOSSES

Property losses may be categorized as either direct or indirect.

1. Direct Losses

A direct loss is the recognized loss sustained as a result of a peril in terms of the value of damage to physical property. For example, if a home is partially or totally destroyed by fire, a direct loss results. The major problems relative to direct losses revolve around the determination of the actual value of the loss.

2. Indirect Losses

Indirect or consequential losses frequently far exceed the value of direct losses. Indirect property losses may be broken down into two subdivisions: decrease of income and increase of expenses. As an example, if an apartment complex was destroyed by fire, the landlord not only suffers a direct loss caused by fire damage to his building, but consequential or indirect loss of rental income, and most probably increased expenses soliciting new tenants to replace those who may have been released from their contractual obligations under the lease because of the fire.

G. TYPES OF PROPERTY COVERAGE

1. Specific Perils

Property risks may be covered by two general types of policies, specific perils and all-risks. Generally, property insurance is written to cover specific perils. In this type of a policy, the particular cause of loss for which the insured may be indemnified is clearly stipulated. The typical fire insurance policy is an example of a specific perils contract. With the many perils facing us today, it is apparent that the issuance of a single peril policy is inadequate. Coverage from other perils, therefore, is affected by endorsements to the basic policy.

2. All - risks

Unlike the specific risks policy, the all-risk policy affords the insured protection against all sources of fortuitous loss to the property covered except that which is specifically excluded. A property insurance policy which assures comprehensive coverage is to be favored over specific-risk policies which may not cover the "holes" in one's insurance program that is based on several separate policies. The wide coverage suggested by the term "all-risk" should be qualified by the term "fortuitous," since risk is defined as the uncertainty of financial loss. The intentional destruction of property or anticipated losses due to fair wear and tear or depreciation are, therefore, not perils covered by an all-risk policy.

H. HOMEOWNERS' (HO) POLICIES

1. Introduction

The rapid rate of inflation we have experienced over the past few years has significantly increased the value of everything we own. Now, most emphatically, is the time to re-evaluate our home and belongings. This is the most difficult task . . . determining how much insurance we need. Selecting the type of insurance to meet this need has been greatly facilitated by a group of all-purpose packages of protection developed by insurance companies. Any of these packages can be purchased at one time and tailored to fit your particular needs.

2. General Coverage:

Homeowner policies are not designed to cover all losses of all descriptions of any amount. These policies, like other property policies, incorporate limits, exceptions, and restrictions which the insured may wish to cover with "floater" policies for an extra premium. Nevertheless, these all-purpose homeowner policies will pay for:

    a. Damage to your house and anything attached to it from the perils listed in sub-paragraph 3 below.

    b. Damage from the perils listed below to detached structures, such as toolsheds, garage, and similar outbuildings.

    c. Damage to or losses from theft of personal property both on and away from the premises.

d. Additional living expenses incurred while your house or apartment is being repaired or until you settle in permanent quarters.

e. Personal liability claims against you and your family and others living with you under 21 years of age.

f. Medical expenses of those injured by you and others covered by the policy, even though you may not be legally liable.

3. <u>Specific Perils</u>:

As you will note in subsequent paragraphs, the insurance for several types of specific losses is a percentage of the amount of insurance on the house, or a percentage of the amount of personal property in the case of renters. These limits can usually be increased by paying extra premiums. However, the only item that usually can be reduced is the personal property coverage which can be cut to 40% of the amount of insurance on the house. The specific perils covered by the six varieties of homeowner policies encompass

a. fire, lightning
b. damage to property removed from premises endangered by fire
c. windstorm, hail
d. explosion
e. riots
f. damage by aircraft
g. damage by vehicles not owned or operated by those covered by the policy
h. damage from smoke
i. vandalism, malicious mischief
j. glass breakage
k. theft
l. falling objects
m. weight of ice, snow, sleet
n. collapse of the building or any part of the building
o. bursting, cracking, burning, or bulging of a steam or hot water heating system, or of appliances for heating water
p. leakage or overflow of water or steam from a plumbing, heating, or air-conditioning system
q. freezing of plumbing, heating, and air-conditioning systems and domestic appliances
r. injury to electrical appliances, devices, fixtures, and wiring (excluding tubes, transistors, and similar electronic components) from short circuits or other accidentally generated currents.

4. <u>Special Limits of Liability</u>:

The special limits of liability prescribe the maximum amounts the policy will pay for the specific types of personal property listed below. These items must be insured separately to obtain greater coverage . . .

    a. money, bullion, numismatic property, bank notes - $100;
    b. securities, bills, deeds, tickets, et cetera - $500;
    c. manuscripts - $1,000;
    d. jewelry, furs - $500;
    e. boats, including trailers and equipment - $500;
    f. trailers - $500.

5. <u>Types of Homeowners' (HO) Policies:</u>

Homeowners' policies have been developed to meet the needs of those who own their own homes, those who own condominium units, and those who rent an apartment or house. State requirements and company policies may reflect slight variations. In most instances, additional premium payments would also increase insurance provided for specific categories, such as personal property and comprehensive personal liability. Normally, items subject to special limits (e. g., furs, jewelry) have to be insured separately to obtain greater coverage.

a. TYPES of HOMEOWNERS' POLICIES:

	HO - 1	HO - 2	HO - 3	HO - 5
PERILS COVERED: (see sub-paragraph 3, above)	a thru k	All	Personal Prop. except glass breakage. Building: All risks except those specifically excluded.	All risks except those specifically excluded.
STANDARD AMOUNT OF INSURANCE ON:				
House, attached structures	\$8,000	\$8,000	\$8,000	\$15,000
	Based on Property Value; Minimum			
Detached structures	10% of amount of insurance on house			
Trees, shrubs, plants	5% of amount of insurance on house; $250 maximum per item			
Personal property on premises	50% of amount of insurance on house			
Personal property off premises	10% of personal property insurance; Minimum $1,000			50% of insurance on house
Additional living expense	10%	20%	20%	20%
SPECIAL LIMITS OF LIABILITY	Standard (see sub-paragraph 4, above)			
COMPREHENSIVE PERSONAL LIABILITY	$25,000			
DAMAGE TO PROPERTY OF OTHERS	$ 250			
MEDICAL PAYMENTS	$500 per person, up to $25,000 for all injured in the same accident			

b. Condominium Owners:

The HO-6 insurance policy which was recently developed for owners of condominium units insures only the interior of the owner's unit. The policy does not cover the exterior structure of which the individual unit is a part. The principal features of the standard HO-6 policy are listed below:

Perils Covered: all except glass breakage (see sub-paragraph 3, above)
Standard Amount of Insurance on:

(1) House, attached structures: $1,000 on owner's additions and alterations to unit.
(2) Trees, shrubs, plants: 10% of personal property insurance: $250 maximum per item.
(3) Personal property on premises: based on value of property; minimum $4,000.
(4) Personal property off premises: 10% of personal property insurance; minimum $1,000.
(5) Additional living expense: 40% of personal property insurance.

Special Limits of Liability: Standard (see sub-paragraph 4, above)
Comprehensive Personal Liability: $25,000
Damage to Property of Others: $250
Medical Payments: $500 per person, up to $25,000 for all injured in same accident.

c. Renters:

The HO-4 insurance policy is tailored for those who rent a house or an apartment. The principal features of this policy are reflected below:

Perils Covered: all except glass breakage (see sub-paragraph 3, above)
Standard Amount of Insurance on:

(1) House, attached structures: 10% of personal property insurance on additions and alterations to unit.
(2) Trees, shrubs, plants: 10% of personal property insurance; $250 maximum per item.
(3) Personal property on premises: based on value of property; minimum $4,000.
(4) Personal property off premises: 10% of personal property insurance; minimum $1,000.
(5) Additional living expenses: 20% of personal property insurance.

Special Limits of Liability: Standard (see sub-paragraph 4, above)
Comprehensive Personal Liability: $25,000
Damage to Property of Others: $250
Medical Payments: $500 per person, up to $25,000 for all injured in same accident.

6. How Much Insurance Is Enough ?

   a. Real Property

   Keeping abreast of inflationary trends and their effect on property values is but one aspect in determining "how much insurance is enough." We must also clearly understand what the insurance company will actually pay should you suffer a loss. For example, the standard amount of insurance on your house and attached structures is based on the property value. You will realize full replacement cost only if the total amount of insurance on the house equals at least 80% of the cost of replacing the entire house. If the amount of insurance carried is less than 80%, the company will usually pay a portion of the replacement cost based on the ratio of the amount for which the house is insured to the amount for which it should have been insured to meet the 80% rule. It is important to realize that insuring one's property at 80% of value does not obligate the insurer to rebuild a structure which is 100% destroyed. The insurer's liability is limited to the face amount of the policy. Only coverage for 100% replacement value would guard the insured against complete loss.

   b. Personal Property

   A claim for a personal property loss under a Homeowners' policy is paid by the insurance company based on "actual cash value" which usually is defined as the item's replacement cost minus depreciation.

7. Summary

Homeowners' policies are available in six packages. Four (HO - 1, 2, 3, 5) are designed for those who own their own homes. HO - 6 has been recently developed especially for condominium owners. HO - 4 is available for those who rent. For those who own their home, HO - 1 provides the least coverage, while HO - 5 (an all-risk policy) provides the most coverage. HO - 3 is an all-risk policy as far as damage to the house is concerned. The premiums charged depend on the breadth of coverage selected, the company, the construction of the house, the locality, and the amount of insurance desired. Many companies providing Homeowners' policies now offer special plans which periodically raise the house insurance by fixed percentages or in step with a construction cost index. These plans would assure property owners that their insurance coverage is kept abreast of increasing values. Advising property owners accordingly, especially those who hire the real estate practitioner as their agent, would fall within the professional agent's responsibilities of protecting and promoting his client's interests.

I. THE INSURANCE CONTRACT

1. <u>Essential Elements</u>:

The law of contracts, discussed previously in Chapter 4, sets forth the rules that govern the drafting and performance of any contractual agreement. In this light, the essential elements of an insurance contract reflect those of any contract, i. e., mutual assent (the offer and acceptance), legal considerations, competent parties, legal purpose, and legal form. In subsequent paragraphs, each of these essential elements will be reviewed as they specifically relate to property and liability insurance.

    a. Mutual Assent

The offer and acceptance embodied in the essential element of mutual assent is usually not complicated in property and liability insurance. Normally, the insurance agent has complete authority to enter into a binding contract for his principal, the insurer. If a buyer were to call his insurance agent and state, "I would like to insure a home that my wife and I just purchased at 1055 Washington Street. I want it insured against fire for $30,000." This constitutes the offer. The agent would accept by simply advising the buyer, "O. K., you're insured with the Acme Insurance Company." At that moment, the element of mutual assent is provided.

    b. Legal Consideration

The insurance policy is a contract, and like all other simple (informal) contracts, must be supported by an exchange whereby each party undertakes to surrender or promises to surrender a legal right at the request of the other. When each party to the contract is obligated and each receives what he bargained for, consideration is present. The consideration provided by the insurer is the promises reflected in the insurance policy. The consideration furnished by the insured is usually the actual premium payment, but could be only the promise to pay the premium.

    c. Competent Parties

Any legal contract carries with it the implication that the contracting parties have the capacity to enter into an agreement. Generally, relative to insurance, all persons are viewed as competent, with the notable exceptions of infants (minors), insane persons, and drunkards.

(1) Infants. An infant, in most states, may contract for insurance and later repudiate his obligations and receive full refund of all premiums paid. A few states have enacted statutes which view infants as competent for insurance purposes. While an infant may be compelled to pay for the value of the necessaries of life, insurance, to date, has not been viewed as such a necessary.

(2) Insane Persons. Persons legally judged insane have no contractual capacity; their contracts are void. Contracts of those not legally declared insane are voidable.

(3) Drunkards. Only when intoxication is to such an extent as to render one incapable of understanding the effects of his actions are his contracts voidable. Simply being "high" will not render the person incompetent.

d. Legal Purpose

A contract which has an illegal purpose is unenforceable. Insurance against gambling losses, for example, is illegal. The "pure risk" aspect of insurance, where loss or no loss only is insured and there is no promise of gain, severs insurance from covering gambling losses.

e. Legal Form

Some states prescribe a standard form for various insurance contracts. Use of some other form by the insurer would be illegal in such an instance. Some states require that insurance contracts be in writing to be enforceable. Most states recognize, however, the legality of oral contracts to include oral insurance contracts. <u>Temporary</u> oral contracts are frequently used in the field of property and liability insurance. Finalized insurance contracts, universally, are almost always reduced to writing.

2. <u>Distinctive Features of the Insurance Contract:</u>

Insurance contracts are generally further described as embodying some or all of the following characteristics. It will be noted that many of these characteristics are not exclusively related to contracts of insurance.

a. Aleatory Contract. An aleatory contract is a contract in which the promise of one party is conditioned on an uncertain event. Insurance contracts are contracts of chance which are payable upon the happening of a fortuitous event. Should this event happen, the insurer will be called upon to pay to the insured a sum far in excess of that paid by the insured in premiums. For this reason, the insurer must be able to appraise correctly the risks involved.

b. Unilateral Contract. A unilateral contract exists whenever a promise is exchanged for an act. Most insurance policies are unilateral contracts. The insured makes premium payments for the promise of the insurer to fulfill the terms of the insurance contract upon the happening of the fortuitous event against which the insured is covered.

c. Executory Contract. An insurance contract is an executory contract in that it has not been fully performed by the insurer. The insurer is only expected to perform upon the happening of the event insured against.

d. Contract of Adhesion. An insurance contract is usually drafted by the insurer, leaving little opportunity for negotiation by the insured. Either the insured may "adhere" to or reject the offer of insurance. Contracts of this type obviously would be drafted to benefit the insurer. In the event of any ambiguities or contradictions, the court will usually find in favor of the insured.

e. Non-assignable Contract. When parties to a contract enter a contractual relationship predicated on the character, reputation, credit, et cetera, of the other, such resultant contract is viewed as being personal. As such, contracts of this nature are not ordinarily assignable without consent. Property and liability insurance contracts are not usually assignable without the consent of the insurer. Because undesirable insureds who may represent excessive risks cannot be grouped with desirable insureds, the insurer has the right to exercise control over who is to be insured. It is important for the real estate agent to realize that property and liability insurance contracts are contracts of a personal nature made by the insurer with a _particular_ insured. The contract does not run with the property insured. After a loss occurs, however, the right to collect the insurance covering the loss may be assigned without restriction.

f. Fiducial Contracts. An insurance contract establishes a fiduciary relationship between the contracting parties. This relationship holds that each party must repose _trust_ and _confidence_ in the other, and each must exercise a corresponding degree of fairness and good faith. In order to determine equitable rates, the insurer must rely upon full disclosure and truthfulness by the insured, while the insured must rely on his trust and confidence in the insurer that certain conditions relating to the risk are fulfilled.

g. Indemnification Contracts. Insurance contracts are designed to cover pure risks. . . risks in which there are no promises of gain. The law requires every insured to have an <u>insurable interest</u> in the subject matter to be insured. For example, a mortgagee (lender) holding a mortgage on the mortgagor's (borrower's) property has an insurable interest. Under the standard mortgagee clause, the insurance company agrees to make any payment for loss to the lender named in the policy up to the amount of the mortgage. In property and liability insurance, the insurable interest need not exist at the inception of the contract, but must exist at the time of loss. Insurance contracts, whether or not provided for in the policy, give the insurer the <u>right of subrogation.</u> This right enables the insurer to substitute himself for the insured for the specific purpose of claiming indemnity from a third person for a loss covered by the insurer.

J. ORGANIZATION OF THE INSURANCE CONTRACT

An analysis of the organization of an insurance policy is one way to unravel the seemingly complex provisions of the contract. The form of the insurance policy normally sets forth standard provisions which are usually modified or amplified by endorsement to tailor the policy to meet the specific needs of the insured or the underwriting demands of the insurer. The elements or sections of an insurance contract are frequently labeled in the policy as declarations, coverage, exclusions or limitations, conditions, and endorsements or riders. Essentially, however, a property insurance contract is made up of the basic policy supplemented by a form with applicable endorsements.

1. <u>Declarations</u>. Declarations are that part of the policy containing the blanks which must be filled in. It, in effect, individualizes the policy for the insured. The declarations of the insured in this section are used by the insurer to determine premiums.

2. <u>Coverage.</u> The coverage afforded by the policy is set forth in this section. Caution must be exercised that the coverage reflected is considered in conjunction with the section on exclusions or limitations which may significantly alter the coverage assumed if this section - sometimes referred to as the insuring agreement - is read alone.

3. <u>Exclusions or Limitations</u>. Exclusions and limitations in a policy are too frequently read and understood only after a loss has been suffered by an insured for which he assumed erroneously that his policy covered him. The reasons for exclusions are diverse and yet are often interrelated. A hazard may be excluded because it is not insurable. Perhaps the exclusion relates to a specialized coverage which the insured may not want or which the insurer is not qualified to write. The exclusion may also be an attempt to eliminate controversial losses. Whatever their reason,

exclusions or limitations often represent weaknesses in the insured's overall insurance program which should be considered and, if found necessary, eliminated by obtaining a special policy to cover the exclusion, by having the exclusion or limitation deleted by appropriate endorsement, or by seeking a different form of policy which does not contain the exclusion or limitation.

4. <u>Conditions</u>. Conditions may contain the general tenor of the policy, method of premium payment, definitions, and most important, a description of the insured event and obligations of the insured in the event of loss. In property and liability insurance, from the insured's position, conditions are as important as the coverage or the exclusions and limitations sections. Nonfulfillment of a condition by the insured may relieve the insurer of liability.

5. <u>Endorsements</u>. Any attempt to specifically tailor the insurance policy to meet the insured's need may be considered an endorsement. An endorsement is often called a rider. Its purpose is to amend the policy by amplification, modification, contraction, or expansion. Restrictive amendments cannot be added without the insured's consent. Otherwise, amendments can be added at any time a change in circumstances warrants it.

WHAT IS RISK?

DEFINITIONS

RISK   The uncertainty of financial loss

PERIL   The source of loss

HAZARD   A condition that increases the likelihood of loss

CLASSIFICATION of FINANCIAL RISK

1. Speculative

2. Pure

3. Fundamental

4. Particular

BASIC INSURANCE CONCEPTS

1. Indemnity Principle

2. Equity Principle

3. Large Loss Principle

4. Small Loss Principle

5. Insurance to Value Concept

THE CONCEPT of INSURANCE TO VALUE

1. The tendency towards underinsurance

2. The predominance of partial losses

3. The problem of rate equity

4. Coinsurance as a solution

TYPES OF INSURANCE

1. **Liability**

2. **Personal**

3. **Property**

DISTINCTIVE FEATURES
of the
INSURANCE CONTRACT

1. **Aleatory**

2. **Unilateral**

3. **Executory**

4. **Adhesion**

5. **Non-assignable**

6. **Fiducial**

7. **Indemnification**

ORGANIZATION
of the
INSURANCE CONTRACT

1. **Declarations**

2. **Coverage**

3. **Exclusions or Limitations**

4. **Conditions**

5. **Endorsements**

Chapter 15

REVIEW DEFINITIONS IN GLOSSARY OR TEXT OF FOLLOWING TERMS:

  aleatory contract   insurance
  coinsurance   particular risk
  fundamental risk   peril
  hazard   pure risk
  indemnification contract release
  insurable interest   speculative risk
  insurable risk   subrogation

REVIEW QUESTIONS:

1. What is risk, as it relates to property ?

2. What is the difference between a peril and a hazard ?

3. Define a pure risk.

4. Name four classifications of financial risk.

5. What conditions must exist before a risk can be insured ?

6. What is insurance ?

7. What principle of insurance holds that the insurer is not liable for more than the actual value of the loss sustained ?

8. What principle of insurance holds that the rate charged the insured generally depends upon both the nature of coverage purchased and the rate class in which the insured person or property belongs ?

9. The idea of making the insured responsible for the difference between a specified percentage of his property and the amount of insurance actually carried is referred to by what term ?

10. What is the difference between a record agent and a survey agent ?

11. Who does the insurance agent represent ?

FOR ANSWERS TO REVIEW QUESTIONS:

1.

2.

3.

4.

5.

6.

7.

8.

9.

10.

11.

12.

13.

14.

15.

16.

17.

12. Who does the insurance broker represent ?

13. Name the three general categories of insurance coverage.

14. What three functions are performed by the claims adjuster ?

15. Name the two general types of property coverage.

16. Name three distinctive features of an insurance contract.

17. What are the five major sections of an insurance contract ?

Chapter 16

Mathematics in Real Estate

A.	INTRODUCTION	479
B.	MEASURES	479
	1. Linear Measures	479
	2. Square Measures	479
	3. Surveyors' Measures	480
	4. Cubic Measures	480
C.	AREA PROBLEMS	480
	1. General	480
	2. Units Must Be the Same	480
	3. Conversion to Decimal	480
	4. Finding Area of Rectangle or Square	480
	5. Finding Area of a Triangle	481
	a. General	481
	b. Equilateral Triangle	481
	c. Isosceles Triangle	482
	d. Right-angled Triangle	482
	e. Obtuse-angled Triangle	482
	f. Scalene Triangle	482
D.	CUBIC VOLUME	482
E.	PERCENTAGE PROBLEMS	483
F.	TAX ASSESSMENT PROBLEMS	486
G.	EXCISE STAMPS AND SURCHARGE	486
REVIEW PROBLEMS		488

Chapter 16
Mathematics in Real Estate

A. INTRODUCTION

This section is devoted to that segment of mathematics most frequently encountered in the practice of real estate brokerage. Mathematics to many persons is regarded as a rather difficult subject. Actually, however, the most difficult aspect of any particular math problem is not in the actual calculation but in defining the problem, listing all the pertinent information, and then selecting the proper formulae or rules required to arrive at the correct solution. FOREWARNED: The most basic errors occur as a consequence of incorrect interpretation of the problem. It is suggested that in all problems, calculations be carried out to three decimal places and then rounded off.

B. MEASURES

1. Linear Measures

12 inches	=	1 foot
3 feet	=	1 yard
5 ½ yards	=	1 rod
40 rods	=	1 furlong
320 rods	=	1 mile
8 furlongs	=	1 mile
5,280 feet	=	1 mile
3 miles	=	1 league

2. Square Measures

144 sq. inches	=	1 sq. foot
9 sq. feet	=	1 sq. yard
30¼ sq. yards	=	1 sq. rod
40 sq. rods	=	1 rood
4 roods	=	1 acre
160 sq. rods	=	1 acre
4,840 sq. yards	=	1 acre
640 acres	=	1 sq. mile

479

3. Surveyors' Measures

7.92 inches	=	1 link
25 links	=	1 rod
4 rods (100 links)	=	1 chain
66 feet	=	1 chain
10 sq. chains	=	1 acre
1 sq. mile	=	1 section
6 miles square	=	1 township
36 sq. miles	=	1 township
24 miles square	=	1 quadrangle, check, square

```
MEMORIZE - 43,560 square feet equal 1 acre
```

4. Cubic Measures

1,728 cu. inches	=	1 cu. foot
27 cu. feet	=	1 cu. yard
128 cu. feet	=	1 cord

C. AREA PROBLEMS

1. General: - - The area of any figure is the measure of a two dimensional surface expressed in a "squared" term, e. g., 24 square feet (also written 24 ft.^{2}).

2. Units Must Be the Same: - - When calculating areas, the units used in the calculation must be the same. Inches cannot be multiplied by feet, nor can feet be multiplied by inches. Either change inches to feet, or feet to inches, so that the resulting answer will be either square feet or square inches respectively. To change one unit to another, refer to the measures given in Paragraph B, above. For example, to change 6 inches to feet, divide by 12 (6 ÷ 12 = .5 ft.). To change yards into feet, multiply the number of yards by 3. For example, 2.3 yards = 6.9 feet (2.3 x 3 = 6.9).

3. Conversion to Decimal: - - The conversion of fractions to the decimal form often eliminates many common errors. To convert any fraction to a decimal, simply divide the numerator (top number) by the denominator (bottom number).
Example: 6/12 feet becomes 0.5 feet.
   5 feet, 3 inches becomes 5 3/12 feet or 5.25 feet.

4. Finding Area of a Rectangle or Square: - - Formula: Area = Length x Width. To find the area of a rectangle or a square, simply multiply the length by the width.
Example:

Area = Length x Width
Area = 5 ft. x 3 ft. or 15 square feet

Remember, the area is expressed in squared units.

5. Finding Area of a Triangle

   a. General. Formula: Area = ½ Base x Height. Any side may be taken as the base, but then the height must be taken from that side (base). The height is measured along a line which must be perpendicular to the base to the top of the triangle, i. e., the angle formed must be 90 degrees.

   Example #1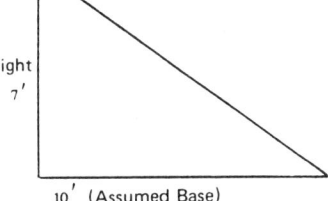

   Area = ½ Base x Height
   Area = ½ x 10 x 7 or 35 square feet
   Note: The area is always expressed in squared units.

   Example #2

   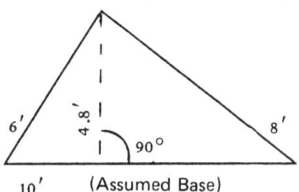

   In this example, the 10 ft. length is taken as the assumed base (any side could be taken as the assumed base). The height is measured along the dotted line which must be perpendicular (i.e., at a 90 degree angle) to the base line. This perpendicular line measures 4.8 feet. Thus we have:

   Area = ½ Base x Height
   Area = ½ x 10 x 4.8 or 24 square feet

   Once again, remember that all units in the calculation must be the same. In the above example, 4.8 ft. is 4 feet and 8/10 of a foot and not 4 feet, 8 inches. Also remember that the answer must reflect a squared unit.

   NOTE: The same formulae apply regardless of the type of triangle. In the examples given below, the assumed base is identified from which the height (dotted line) is drawn.

   b. Equilateral Triangle: (All sides equal)

   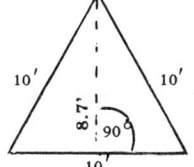

   Area = ½ Base x Height
   Area = ½ x 10 x 8.7 or 43.5 square feet

c. Isosceles Triangle: (Two sides equal)

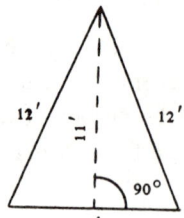

Area = ½ Base x Height
Area = ½ x 10 x 11 or 55 <u>square feet</u>

d. Right-angled Triangle: (One with a 90 degree angle)

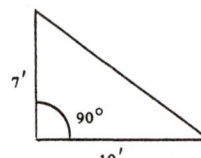

Area = ½ Base x Height
Area = ½ x 10 x 7 or 35 <u>square feet</u>

e. Obtuse-angled Triangle: (One with angle over 90 degrees)

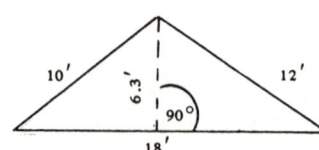

Area = ½ Base x Height
Area = ½ x 18 x 6.3 or 56.7 <u>square feet</u>

f. Scalene Triangle: (All sides and angles unequal)

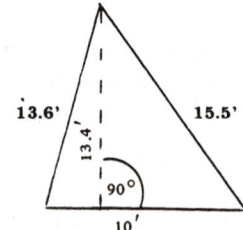

Area = ½ Base x Height
Area = ½ x 10 x 13.4 or 67 <u>square feet</u>

D. CUBIC VOLUME

1. <u>General</u>: - - Cubic volume equals area times height. Cubic footage is a measure of <u>volume</u> which is equal to the <u>area</u> times the height. The unit is a cubed term, such as 36 cubic feet, sometimes written 36 ft.^{3}.

2. <u>Example #1</u>. Find the cubic footage of the figure below.

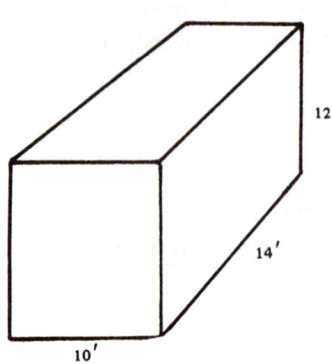

Cubic Volume = Area x Height
Cubic Volume = 10 x 14 (area) x 12 or 1,680 <u>cu. ft.</u>

<u>Note</u>: The answer is reflected in CUBIC units. Also remember, as in the case of area calculations, the units used in calculating cubic content must be the same.

3. Example #2. To find the cubic footage of the figure below:

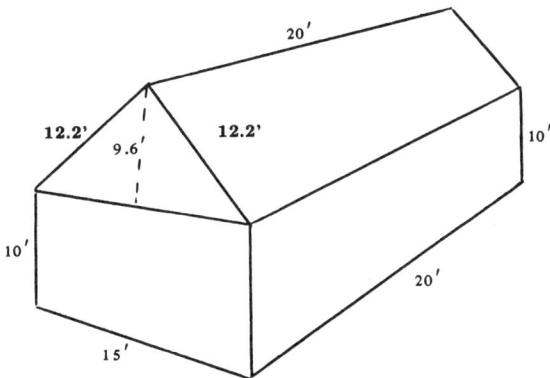

Apply the formulae presented in previous paragraphs.

Cubic footage of triangular portion of figure equals
   Area (½ x Base of 15 ft. x Height of 9.6) x Height (20 ft. is used)
   = 1,440 cubic feet.

Cubic footage of triangular portion of figure equals
   Area (½ x Base of 15 ft. x Height of 9.6 ft.) x Length (20 ft. is used)
   = 1,440 cubic feet.

Combine two calculations to arrive at total cubic footage of

4,440 cubic feet

E. PERCENTAGE PROBLEMS

1. <u>Terms Used</u>: -- When working in percentage problems there are three basic terms to consider: the whole, the part, and the rate.

   a. Whole. The whole is the quantity to which the rate (a percent) is applied to obtain the part.

   b. Part. The part is that portion of the whole determined by the rate.

   c. Rate. The rate is the percent (%).

2. <u>Equations</u>: -- The relationship between the terms mentioned above is best expressed by the following equations.

WHOLE = PART ÷ RATE
PART = WHOLE x RATE
RATE = PART ÷ WHOLE

3. <u>Changing Rate to Decimal Form:</u> - - When working with a rate as a percent, it must first be changed to a decimal form. To change a percent to a decimal form, simply move the decimal point two places to the left. To change a decimal back to a percent, the reverse is done.

    a.   Percent to Decimal - Examples

        5% becomes 0.05
        6½% becomes 0.065
        114% becomes 1.14

    b.   Decimal to Percent - Examples

        0.34 becomes 34%
        1.50 becomes 150%

4. <u>Problem #1:</u> - - $95 of a total monthly payment of $160 is interest. The interest rate is 6%. What is the principal amount on which the payments are being made?

    <u>Solution</u>: The problem asks for a whole of which a part is given. To determine the whole when a part and the rate are given, we employ the equation WHOLE = PART ÷ RATE.

The monthly interest payment	- $95
The yearly interest payment	- $95 x 12 or $1,140
Now fill in the equation	- <u>WHOLE = PART ÷ RATE</u>
	WHOLE = $1,140 ÷ .06
	WHOLE = $19,000
ANSWER..............	Principal Amount = $19,000

NOTE: As indicated in Paragraph A, supra, the most difficult aspect of any math problem is defining the problem, extracting the pertinent information, and selecting the correct formula. In this example, the $160 total monthly payment is extraneous information.

5. <u>Problem #2:</u> - - A house sold for $25,000, and the broker received a commission of $1,375. What was the commission percentage?

    <u>Solution</u>: In this problem we have the whole and the part; we are searching for the rate. Consequently, we select the equation RATE = PART ÷ WHOLE. Now we simply fill in the equation.

                    RATE = PART ÷ WHOLE
                    RATE = $1,375 ÷ $25,000
                    RATE = 0.055 or 5½%
ANSWER . . . . .   Percentage of Commission = 5½%

6. <u>Problem #3</u>: - - A house is assessed for $6,250 which is 40% of the market value. What is the market value of the house ?

<u>Solution</u>: In this problem we have the part and the rate; we are searching for the whole. Our equation, therefore, is WHOLE = PART ÷ RATE. Once again, we fill in the equation with known figures.

                    WHOLE = PART ÷ RATE
                    WHOLE = $6,250 ÷ 0.40
                    WHOLE = $15,625
ANSWER . . .   Market value = $15,625

7. <u>Problem #4</u>: - - Mr. Duncan owns a tract of land worth $25,000. He sells 3/5 of it to Mr. Smith and 1/3 of the remaining land to Mr. Jones. Mr. Duncan retains 15 acres. How many acres had he originally ?

<u>Solution</u>: The amount we are looking for is the whole figure. Logically, then, let us select the proper equation and proceed to attach the problem with the information provided. Our equation is WHOLE = PART ÷ RATE. We know that Mr. Duncan now owns 15 acres, which represents 2/3 of what he had left after selling 3/5 of his original holdings to Mr. Smith. We must first determine how much land he had left after the sale to Mr. Smith.

                    WHOLE = PART ÷ RATE
                    WHOLE = 15 acres ÷ .667 (2/3 or 66.7%)
                    WHOLE = 22.5 acres

The 22.5 acres represents what Mr. Duncan had left after selling 3/5 of what he originally had to Mr. Smith. The equation we use is the same as we are still searching for the whole figure. Now, if the 22.5 acres is what Mr. Duncan had left after selling 3/5 of his original tract to Mr. Smith, it is obvious that the 22.5 acres represents 2/5 of what he originally had. Thus, our equation:

                    WHOLE = PART ÷ RATE
                    WHOLE = 22.5 ÷ 0.40 (2/5 or 40%)
                    WHOLE = 56.25
ANSWER . . . .   Original Tract = 56.25 acres

F. TAX ASSESSMENT PROBLEMS

1. <u>Terms Used</u>: - - The same equations used in percentage problems can be applied to tax assessment problems also by simply redefining the definitions.

    a. Whole. The whole is represented by the value of the property to which the rate is applied.

    b. Part. The part is the amount of the tax in dollars.

    c. Rate. The rate is the tax rate changed to a <u>fractional form</u>.

2. <u>Problem</u>: - - A property valued at $20,000 is assessed at $55 per thousand. What is the amount of the annual tax? What is the amount of the monthly payments?

<u>Solution</u>: The amount $55 per thousand is more easily understood when the per thousand term is expressed as a fraction. For example, $55 per thousand = 55 ÷ 1,000 (or 55/1,000). The rate has been changed to its fractional form. The problem provides the <u>whole</u> and the <u>rate</u>. We need only select the proper equation to arrive at the solution.

<u>PART = WHOLE x RATE</u>

PART = $20,000 x 55/1,000
PART = $1,100
ANSWER ... Annual Tax = $1,100
Monthly Tax = $1,100 ÷ 12 or $91.67

G. EXCISE STAMPS AND SURCHARGE

1. <u>General</u>: - - Assume that on January 1, 1971, all deeds in your state when recorded must have Excise Stamps affixed. For every $500 or <u>part thereof</u> of the selling price, $1.00 worth of stamps is required. Normally, these stamps are purchased by the seller. On August 1, 1971, an additional surcharge was imposed. The surcharge is 14% of each $1.00 worth of stamps purchased. In effect, stamps now cost $1.14 per every $500 or part thereof of the selling price. <u>NOTE</u>: when the seller allows the buyer to take over the existing mortgage, the amount of excise stamps required is based on the <u>difference</u> between the existing balance of the seller's mortgage and the selling price and <u>not</u> on the entire selling price.

2. <u>Problem #1</u>: - - How much would excise stamps cost (to include surcharge) on a piece of property which sold for $32,250?

<u>Solution</u>: Since stamps cost $1.14 for each $500 or fraction thereof, we must determine how many $500 there are in the selling price. We divide the $32,250 by $500 and arrive at the figure 64.5. To account for the "fraction thereof", the figure 64.5 must be taken as 65. Our multiplier is 65, representing that number of 500 increments (or fraction thereof) that make up the $32,250 selling price. The cost

of excise stamps is determined by simply multiplying the $1.14 per $500 by the multiplier 65 to arrive at the answer of $74.10.

3. Problem #2: -- Assume that the seller of the above property allowed the buyer to take over his existing mortgage in the amount of $24,300.

Solution: In this instance, the seller is required to affix excise stamps of $1.14 per $500 or fraction thereof of the difference between the selling price ($32,250) and the balance of the existing mortgage ($24,300). $32,250 − $24,300 = $7,950. $500 can be divided into $7,950 15.9 times ... which we must regard as 16. This, then, becomes our multiplier which when applied to the $1.14 gives us the amount of the required excise stamps of $18.24 ($1.14 x 16).

Chapter 16

REVIEW PROBLEMS:

1. How many acres are contained in a rectangular tract of land 864 x 605 feet?

2. If you purchased a house for 25% less than the list price and sold it for the list price, what percent of profit on your investment would you make?

3. You negotiate a five year lease on a building which rents for $300 per month. Your commission is to be 5% of the annual rental for the first year, 4% of the annual rental for each of the next three years, and 3% of the annual rental for the last year. What is your total commission?

4. Mr. VENDOR owns a tract of land. He sells one third of it to Mr. VENDEE and one half of what is left to Mr. BYER. Mr. VENDOR, after both sales, still had 640 acres left. How many acres were in the original tract?

5. Company policy states that 20% of the commission received on a listed property will go to the listing broker. 50% of the commission received will go to the broker - owner, and the balance will go to the selling broker. The listed property sells for $40,000 at a 6% commission. How much will each receive?
Listing broker _____; owner _____; selling broker _____ .

6. A builder is subdividing a 4½ acre tract into 50' x 100' lots after allowing 71,020 square feet for the necessary streets. Into how many lots can the tract be divided?

7. A broker receives half the first month's rent for leasing an apartment and 5% of each month's rent thereafter for collecting the rent of $125 per month. What would his total commission be after 18 months?

8. What is the quarterly interest payment on a mortgage loan with a balance of $14,000 with interest at 6½% per year?

9. If a house sold for $38,000, how much in Excise Stamps would the seller have to pay?

10. If the rate of interest is 8% per annum, and the monthly interest payment is $80, on what principal are you paying?

11. The zoning in a particular town requires one acre with 150 foot frontage. A builder is going to subdivide 52 acres. Figuring 20% of his total area will be

used for easements, streets, et cetera, how many building lots will he have?

12. Jones, a salesman, is working for Smith, a broker, on a 60/40 commission split; 60% to Smith, 40% to Jones. Jones sells 100 acres of land at $300 per acre. The commission earned calls for 10% of the first $20,000, 5% on the next $15,000, and 2% on the balance. What will Jones' commission be?

13. A note is dated January 15, 1970. The amount of the note is $1,700 with interest at 5%. How much interest will have accrued by September 15, 1971.

14. What was the selling price (to the nearest $1,000) of a parcel of property if the seller had to purchase $25.08 worth of Excise Stamps?

15. The size of a lot is 60 feet and 4 inches by 122 feet. The sales price is 16 cents per square foot. What is the sales price of the property?

16. If a tract of land comprising 108,900 sq. ft. was sold for $1,250 per acre, what is the total amount realized from the sale?

17. The net amount received by a seller for his property - after the broker had deducted his commission of 5% and an allowance of $110 for reimbursement of other expenses - was $27,500. What was the selling price?

18. A sales contract calls for a monthly payment of $150 of which $100 is interest. The interest rate is 8%. What is the principal amount owing on the contract?

19. Joe Jones sells his home for $22,000 allowing buyer to take over his mortgage of $18,000. What amount of state excise stamps would be placed on the deed?

20. Mr. Scott built a house on a lot measuring 100 ft. wide and 120 ft. deep. The lot cost him $30 per front foot. The house cost him $14,000. He had a down payment of $3,400 and was able to obtain a loan for the balance at an annual interest rate of 8% payable semi-annually. What was the amount of his first semi-annual interest payment?

21. The size of a lot is 58 feet 9 inches on the street and 120 feet deep to the end of the lot. The sales price is 16 cents per square foot. What is the selling price?

22. The commission rate for selling an apartment house is 5% on the first $15,000, 3% on the next $20,000, and 1½% on the balance. The broker received a commission of $1,710. What was the selling price of the property?

23. A house can be rented for $50 a month or purchased for $6,800 ($6,200 for the house, $600 for the lot). The annual cost of owning and living in the house is as follows: interest, 3%; painting house, 2½%; taxes, $24 per $1,000 on 75% value of house and lot; insurance, $4.50 per $1,000 based on the value of the house; 5% for care of the lot. How much less per month would it cost to buy the property and live in it than to rent it?

24. What amount of excise stamps are required to be affixed to a deed, and by whom, for the following transaction; purchase price - $19,750; buyer to assume seller's mortgage of $14,000; cash payment of $2,000; balance to be paid by promissory note to be secured by a second mortgage ?

25. A contract requires a monthly payment of $150.56, of which $120 is interest at a rate of 8%. What is the principal amount owing ?

26. 100 ft. x 200 ft. is approximately what fraction of an acre ?

27. A house sold for $32,000, and the total commission paid to the broker was $1,920. What was the commission percentage ?

28. If 5¼% is the annual interest rate, and the monthly interest payment is $58.45, what is the principal amount ?

29. An apartment house had a gross income of $1,400 per month with annual expenses of $8,000. What price must a buyer pay to show a net return on his investment of 8%.

30. A bank lends a homeowner a sum equal to 70% of the appraised valuation of his home at an interest rate of 8% per annum. The first year's interest is $1,232. What is the full appraised value of the house ?

31. Mr. Newman is building a 24' x 44' house on a lot measuring 120 ft. wide and 200 ft. deep. The assessed value of the lot is $20 per front foot. The house is assessed at $18,000. The tax rate is $30 per $1,000. What are the annual taxes ?

32. A builder is subdividing a 6 acre tract into 132' x 330' lots after allowing 43,560 square feet for necessary streets. Into how many lots can the tract be divided ?

33. Mrs. White's annual expenses are 65% of her gross income which is $1,400 per month. What is her net income per year ?

34. How many excise stamps are required on a deed for a lot selling for $1,501 ?

35. Mr. Grimes has a house which is assessed at $9,520 which represents 40% of its actual value. What is the actual value of Grimes' house ?

36. A percentage lease calls for a minimum rent of $400 per month and 4% of the gross annual business over $200,000. If the total rent paid at the end of the year was $8,000, how much business did the tenant do over the year ?

37. Mr. Dooley bought a home for $22,000. Five years later he sold it for 25% more than he paid for it. The broker's commission was 6% of the sales price. How much did Mr. Dooley net on the sale ?

38. The schedule of commissions for negotiating a 20 year lease was 6% for the first year, 3% for the next 4 years, 2% for the next 5 years, and 1% for each year thereafter. What was the total commission earned if the yearly rent was $7,200?

39. What is a property worth if the net return is $600 per month, and the annual earning is to be 8% on the investment?

40. The value of a house at the end of 8 years was estimated to be $32,000. What was the original cost of the house if it appreciated in value 3% (always based on the original cost) a year?

41. Mary Elliot, a broker, sold three lots at $1,200 each, five at $1,800 each, and seven at $2,500 each. Her commission rate is 5%. What was her total commission?

42. Company policy states that all commissions are to be divided as follows: listing broker, 20% of gross commission; company, 50% of gross commission; selling broker, the balance. On a $38,000 sale with a commission rate of 6%, how much does the selling broker receive?

43. Monthly payments in a mortgage note are $201.40 of which $152.25 represents interest at a rate of 7½%. What is the principal amount owing on the note?

44. The tax rate is $44 per $1,000 of assessed value. What is the tax on a piece of property which cost $56,000 and is assessed at 80% of that figure?

45. What is the width of a rectangle containing 43,560 square feet if its length is 132 feet?

46. The commission received by a broker for the sale of a $123,456 parcel of land was $6,172.80. What was the rate of commission?

47. What is the cost of a lot measuring 80 feet wide by 120' long if it is priced at $20 per front foot?

48. Mr. Sharp sold a piece of property at list price which he purchased some months before at 80% of the list price. What percent of profit did he make on the sale?

49. Mrs. Falcione sells one fifth of her land to her neighbor, Mr. Clark. She sells three fourths of the remainder to Mr. Dourlet. She then donates one half of what remains to the church. How many acres does she retain if the original tract contained 240 acres?

50. How much in excise stamps is required to be purchased by the seller on the sale of his property for $36,000 where the buyer takes over the $28,999 mortgage balance?

ANSWERS TO REVIEW PROBLEMS:

1.

2.

3.

4.

5.

6.

7.

8.

9.

10.

11.

12.

13.

14.

15.

16.

17.

18.

19.

20.

21.

22.

23.

24.

25

26.

27.

28.

29.

30.

31.

32.

33.

34.

35.

36.

37.

38.

39.

40.

41.

42.

43.

44.

45.

46.

47.

48.

49.

50.

APPENDIX A

CLOSING STATEMENTS

A.	SAMPLE REAL ESTATE TRANSACTION	500
B.	COMPLETING THE WORKSHEET	500
C.	FINAL SETTLEMENT THROUGH A LENDING INSTITUTION	507
	1. Lender's Loan Statement	509
	2. Reconciliation by Broker	510
	3. Use of Worksheets	510
D.	FINAL SETTLEMENT WHEN LOAN IS ASSUMED	511
	1. General	511
	2. The Assumption Statement	511
E.	EXPLANATION OF OTHER CHARGES AND ADJUSTMENTS	512
F.	DISPOSITION OF CLOSING STATEMENTS	515

APPENDIX A

CLOSING STATEMENTS

A. SAMPLE REAL ESTATE TRANSACTION

You, the broker for Booth Realty Company, secured an exclusive listing from John R. and Mary Poe on a property located at 1726 Melbourne Road, at a price of $22,500. This property is presently encumbered by a note and trust deed for the benefit of the XYZ Loan Company and a balance of $9,450 is still owing.

On April twenty second, you secure a written offer from Arthur T. and Martha Lowe with a deposit of $1,500. The buyers agreed to purchase at the listed price, if they are able to secure a loan on the property in the amount of $16,900 and if the Sellers would accept a subordinate or second note and trust deed in the amount of $2,000.

The offer was accepted by the Sellers, and the Sellers authorized you to procure the abstract from the XYZ Loan Company. You delivered the abstract to the Buyers' attorney who found the title marketable. The abstract was then delivered to the Acme Loan Company, and its loan committee approved a loan application from the Buyers in the amount of $16,900 at 8% per year amortized monthly over a period of 20 years.

Both Buyers and Sellers and their respective attorneys authorize you to collect all moneys and to make disbursements. The closing was held in your office on May tenth.

B. COMPLETING THE WORKSHEET

From the contract between the parties, and from other sources, you gathered all information necessary for final settlement. Following is an itemization of all the information secured and an explanation of how it is charged and adjusted on the worksheet on page 717 . Each numbered item is equivalently numbered on the worksheet and on the statements given to Buyer and Seller. Numbered items on the worksheet which are not listed below are not pertinent to this transaction.

1. <u>Selling Price</u> - - $22,500. The full amount is credited to the Seller and the full amount is debited to the Buyer. Take note of the fact that the sum of the Seller's credits must all be paid for by the Buyer in some manner.

2. <u>Deposit</u> - - $1,500. This amount is credited to the Buyer and is debited to the Broker. Note that each debit to the Broker is money that he has or will collect.

3. <u>Trust Deed</u> - - payable to Acme Loan Company to secure its note in the amount of $16,900. This amount is a credit to the Buyer, since it will be applied to the purchase price of the property. This amount will be debited to the Broker, since

he is collecting the money.

4. <u>Second Trust Deed</u> - - payable to John R. and Mary Poe to secure a note in the amount of $2,000. This amount is credited to Buyer as with the first trust deed and will be debited to the seller.

5. <u>Existing Trust Deed</u> - - pay off to the XYZ Loan Company in the amount of $9,450. This amount is the credit to the Broker, since he must pay it and a debit to the Seller, because it is his obligation. In order to determine the amount of the payoff, the Broker requested a payoff statement from the XYZ Loan Company. This statement shows the final balance after adjustments of interest, penalty, and credits the Seller may have in the way of tax or insurance reserves.

8. <u>Abstracting Before the Sale</u> - - $34.00. Since it is the Seller's duty to perfect title, he must pay for all abstracting before the sale. Therefore, the total amount of $34.00 is debited to the Seller and credited to the Broker who must pay the abstractor.

9. <u>Abstracting After the Sale</u> - - $4.00 and $22.00. The loan company will insist that the Release of Trust Deed be recorded on the abstract after the sale. The charge for this entry is $4.00 and, since it is the Seller's duty to perfect title, the Seller is debited for this amount and the Broker who will pay the abstractor is credited. The loan company will also require that after the sale the Buyer's deed, both trust deeds, and the abstractor's certificate be shown on the abstract. This charge of $22.00 is debited to the Buyer and credited to the Broker who must pay the abstractor.

10. and 37. <u>Title Examination by the Buyer's Attorney</u> - - $50.00. Title examination by the Acme Loan Company's attorney - - $40.00. Both of these amounts must be paid by the Buyer and, therefore, debited to him and credited to the Broker who is making all payments for both parties.

11. <u>Warranty Deed</u> - - $2.00. It is the Seller's obligation to furnish the deed, but it is the obligation of the Buyer to record his own deed. Therefore, this fee is debited to the Buyer and credited to the Broker who will pay it.

12. and 14. <u>Recording: Trust Deeds</u> - - the fee for recording the first trust deed is $6.25 and the fee for recording the second trust deed is $3.50. Both are obligations of the Buyer. Therefore, each amount is debited to the Buyer and each amount is credited to the Broker who will pay the fees.

13. <u>Recording: Release of Trust Deed</u> - - $3.75. This is the release of the original loan with the XYZ Company and, since it is a document which corrects title, this amount is chargeable or debited to the Seller and credited to the Broker who will pay the recording fees for the parties.

15. <u>Documentary Fee</u> - - $2.25. State Law requires that a documentary fee be paid by the person recording an instrument of conveyance. This fee is paid to the clerk and recorder and is in the amount of one cent for each one hundred dollars of considera-

tion, inclusive of any loan. If the total consideration is $500 or less, there is no fee. The Seller has no further obligation after delivery of the deed, but the Buyer wishes to protect himself by recording his deed; therefore, the documentary fee is debited to the Buyer and credited to the Broker.

16. Tax Certificate - - $3.00. This certificate is the Buyer's future insurance that the county may not at a later date lay claim for any taxes other than taxes due as stated on the certificate. Therefore, this $3.00 cost is charged or debited to the Buyer and credited to the Broker.

17. Taxes for Preceding Year - - $480.24 were paid. Taxes for preceding years which have been paid are not entered on the closing statement. If they had not been paid, they would, of course, be chargeable to the Seller.

18. Taxes for Current Year to Date - - $173.42. This amount is pro-rated. The current year's taxes are not due until January 1, of the following year, so the preceding year's taxes are used as a basis for the adjustment. The Seller was the owner of the property from the first of the current year to date, May tenth. Therefore, he is chargeable for 4 1/3 months' taxes or $173.42. This amount is debited to the Seller and credited to the Buyer. This is an adjustment between the parties and not a payment that the Broker must make.

19. Tax Reserve - - $200.10. The Acme Loan Company will collect its loan in monthly installments. With each installment, they will also collect one month's taxes and hold this in reserve so that sufficient funds are on hand to pay the yearly taxes when they become due. It will require five months' tax reserve at $40.02 per month, because the first installment is not due until June first.

23. Premium for New Insurance - - $96.00. The Acme Loan Company requires that a one year hazard insurance policy be purchased. Since this policy is for the benefit of the Buyer, the cost of it is debited to Buyer. The same amount is credited to the Broker.

24. Hazard Insurance Reserve - - $16.00. The Acme Loan Company, as with the tax reserve, requires that a two month reserve be maintained by the Buyer. This amount is debited to the Buyer and credited to the Broker.

27. Loan Commission - - $169.00. This is the Acme Loan Company's commission or service fee for making the loan. This amount is debited to the Buyer and credited to the Broker.

29. Interest on New Loan - - $75.11. Since the Buyer's first installment on the new 8% loan will not be due until the first of the month and the loan was made on the tenth, the closing date, the loan company requires that this interest be paid in advance up to the first of the month. This amount is debited to the Buyer and credited to the Broker.

30. Survey - - $17.50. Both the Buyer and the Loan Company desired a survey of the property. This amount is debited to the Buyer and credited to the Broker.

32. Water Rent - - $18.75. The Sellers paid $33.75 in advance on April first for 3 months. Since the closing date is May tenth, the Seller has used 40 days of the 90 day period. Therefore, the Buyer is debited $18.75 and the Seller is credited with $18.75. The Broker makes no payment here; it is merely an adjustment between the parties.

36. Sales Commission - - $1,350.00. This amount is debited to the Seller and credited to the Broker.

Sub-totals. The totals of each column of debits and the totals of each column of credits are made only for the convenience of the calculator in determining the balances or differences between the debits and credits of each party.

Balance Due to/from Seller - - $9,503.58. This amount is the difference between the total of the Seller's credits and the total of the Seller's debits. It is also the amount which is the difference between the total of debits and total of the credits in the Broker's statement on the worksheet. This is the amount the Seller will actually receive in cash for his home. He will actually receive a $2,000 note and other benefits, but this amount represents the amount that he will actually receive in cash. There are instances in which the Seller must actually pay cash in order to accomplish the sale and closing, but these instances are the exception.

Balance Due to/from Buyer - - $2,648.04. This amount is the difference between the total of the Buyer's credits and the Buyer's debits. This is the amount of cash that the Buyer must have to accomplish his purchase at the time of final settlement. This amount is also recorded as a debit to the Broker, since he will collect all money and disburse all money.

Totals. The total of the debits and the total of the credits, as they pertain to each party, must equal each other.

WORKSHEET FOR REAL ESTATE SETTLEMENT

SELLER: John R. and Mary Poe
BUYER: Arthur T. and Martha Lowe
PROPERTY ADDRESS: 1726 Melbourne Road
SETTLEMENT DATE:
LEGAL DESCRIPTION: Lots 6 and 7, Block 14, Graham Heights, Denver

		SELLER		BUYER		BROKER	
		Debit	Credit	Debit	Credit	Debit	Credit
1.	Selling Price		22,500 —	22,500 —			
2.	Deposit, paid to Broker				1500 —	1500 —	
3.	Trust Deed, payable to Acme Loan Co.				16,900 —	16,900 —	
4.	Trust Deed, payable to Seller	2,000 —			2,000 —		
5.	Trust Deed, payoff to XY Loan	9,750 —					9,750 —
6.	Interest on Loan Assumed						
7.	Title Insurance Premium						
8.	Abstracting: Before Sale	34 —					34 —
9.	After Sale	4 —		22 —			26 —
10.	Title Exam, by Buyer's Attorney			50 —			50 —
11.	Recording: Warranty Deed			2 —			2 —
12.	Trust Deed 1st			6 25			6 25
13.	Release	3 75					3 75
14.	Other 2nd TD			3 50			3 50
15.	Documentary Fee			2 25			2 25
16.	Tax Certificate			3 —			3 —
17.	Taxes for preceding year(s)						
18.	Taxes for current year	173 42			173 42		
19.	Tax Reserve			200 10			200 10
20.	Special Taxes						
21.	Personal Property Taxes						
22.	Hazard Ins. Premium Assumed						
23.	Premium for New Insurance			96 —			96 —
24.	Hazard Insurance Reserve			16 —			16 —
25.	FHA Mortgage Ins. Assumed						
26.	FHA Mortgage Ins. Reserve						
27.	Loan Commission (Buyer) 1%			169 —			169 —
28.	Loan Discount Fee (Seller)						
29.	Interest on new loan based on 30 days mo.			75 11			75 11
30.	Survey			17 50			17 50
31.	Appraisal Fee						
32.	Water Rent		18 75	18 75			
33.	Rental Income						
34.	Loan Transfer Fee						
35.	Loan Payment Due						
36.	Sales Commission 6%	1,350 —					1,350 —
37.	Title Exam. by Loan Co Attorney			40 —			40 —
	Sub-totals	13,015 17	22,518 75	23,221 46	20,573 72	18,400 —	11,544 46
	Balance due to seller	9,503 58					9,503 58
	Balance due from buyer				2,648 04	2,648 04	
	TOTALS	22,518 75	22,518 75	23,221 46	23,221 46	21,048 04	21,048 04

It is important that the veteran obtain a Certificate of Eligibility so that, if he is applying to a lender for a guaranteed loan, the lender will know he is eligible.

If the veteran sells his house and the loan has been paid in full, his eligibility may be restored.

Legislation enacted in 1970 eliminated the expiration date of the entitlement and it is now available until used.

STATEMENT OF SETTLEMENT

ADDRESS: 1726 Melbourne Road
DATE: May 10 (Current Year)
SELLER: John R. and Mary Poe
PURCHASER: Arthur T. & Martha Lowe
LEGAL DESCRIPTION: Lots 6 & 7, Block 14, Graham Heights, City and County of Denver

BUYERS	Debit		Credit	
1. Selling Price	22,500	-		
2. Deposit Paid To *Booth Realty Co.*			1,500	-
3. Trust Deed, payable to *Acme Loan Co.*			16,900	-
4. Trust Deed, payable to *John R. and Mary Poe (2nd T.D.)*			2,000	-
5. Trust Deed, payoff to				
6. Interest on Loan Assumed				
7. Title Ins. Premium				
8. Abstracting Before Sale				
9. After Sale	22	-		
10. Title Exam by *Buyer's attorney*	50	-		
11. Recording Warranty Deed *after close*	2	-		
12. Trust Deed *(First)*	6	25		
13. Release				
14. Other *(2nd Trust Deed)*	3	50		
15. Documentary Fee	2	25		
16. Tax Certificate	3	00		
17. Taxes for preceding year(s) *$480.24 Paid*				
18. Taxes for current year *prorated - based on previous year*			173	42
19. Tax Reserve *Buyer's reserve account*	200	10		
20. Special Taxes				
21. Personal Property Taxes				
22. Hazard Ins. Prem. Assumed Policy No. Company				
23. Premium for New Insurance *(1 year policy effective May 10)*	96	-		
24. Hazard Ins. Reserve	16	-		
25. FHA Mortgage Ins. Assumed				
26. FHA Mortgage Ins. Reserve				
27. Loan Commission (Buyer) *1%*	169	-		
28. Loan Discount Fee (Seller)				
29. Interest on new loan *20 days (based on 30 day month)*	75	11		
30. Survey	17	50		
31. Appraisal Fee				
32. Water Rent	18	75		
33. Rental Income				
34. Loan Transfer Fee				
35. Loan Payment Due				
36. Sales Commission				
37. Title Examination by Loan Co. Attorney	40	-		
Sub Total	23,221	46	20,573	42
Balance Due to Seller				
Balance Due from Buyer			2,648	04
TOTALS	23,221	46	23,221	46

APPROVED AND ACCEPTED
Arthur T. Lowe   Martha Lowe
Booth Realty Co. - Paul T. Broker

STATEMENT OF SETTLEMENT

ADDRESS: 1726 Melbourne Road
SELLER: John R. and Mary Poe
LEGAL DESCRIPTION: Lots 6 & 7, Block 14, Graham Heights, City and County of Denver
DATE: May 10 (Current Year)
PURCHASER: Arthur T. & Martha Lowe

	SELLERS	Debit	Credit
1.	Selling Price		22,500 —
2.	Deposit, paid to		
3.	Trust Deed, payable to *John R. and Mary Poe*	2,000 —	
4.	Trust Deed, payable to		
5.	Trust Deed, payoff to *XYZ Loan Co.*	9,450 —	
6.	Interest on Loan Assumed		
7.	Title Ins. Premium		
8.	Abstracting Before Sale *Certification to date of closing*	34 —	
9.	After Sale *Release entry existing 1st Trust Deed*	4 —	
10.	Title Exam by		
11.	Recording Warranty Deed		
12.	Trust Deed		
13.	Release *Existing Trust Deed*	3 75	
14.	Other		
15.	Revenue Stamps		
16.	Tax Certificate		
17.	Taxes for preceding year(s) *$480.24 — paid*		
18.	Taxes for current year *prorated — based on previous year*	173 42	
19.	Tax Reserve		
20.	Special Taxes		
21.	Personal Property Taxes		
22.	Hazard Ins. Prem. Assumed Policy No. Company		
	$ Yr. Term Expires		
	Premium $ Days Unused at per day		
	Policy No. Company		
	$ Yr. Term Expires		
	Premium $ Days Unused at per day		
23.	Premium for New Insurance		
24.	Hazard Ins. Reserve		
25.	FHA Mortgage Ins. Assumed		
26.	FHA Mortgage Ins. Reserve		
27.	Loan Commission (Buyer)		
28.	Loan Discount Fee (Seller)		
29.	Interest on new loan		
30.	Survey and/or Credit Report		
31.	Appraisal Fee		
32.	Water Rent		18 75
33.	Rental Income		
34.	Loan Transfer Fee		
35.	Loan Payment Due		
36.	Sales Commission	1,350 —	
	Sub Total	13,015 17	22,518 75
	Balance due to Seller	9,503 58	
	Balance due to from Buyer		
	TOTALS	22,518 75	22,518 75

APPROVED AND ACCEPTED *John R Poe   Mary Poe*
Booth Realty Co.   Paul T. Broker

C. FINAL SETTLEMENT THROUGH A LENDING INSTITUTION

The worksheet which you have previously completed will provide you with all the necessary itemized dollar amounts to copy on the preceding final statements of settlement. However, in the event that the closing is held in a financial institution pursuant to a Loan Statement (which is the more usual practice), the Broker's debits and credits would appear differently on the worksheet as indicated on the opposite facing page. The reader, in this circumstance, should study the following portion of this appendix.

WORKSHEET FOR REAL ESTATE SETTLEMENT

SELLER: John R. and Mary Poe
BUYER: Arthur T. and Martha Lowe
PROPERTY ADDRESS: 1726 Melbourne Rd.
SETTLEMENT DATE: _____
LEGAL DESCRIPTION: Lots 6 & 7, Block 14, Graham Heights, Denver

		SELLER		BUYER		BROKER	
		Debit	Credit	Debit	Credit	Debit	Credit
1.	Selling Price		22,500 —	22,500 —			
2.	Deposit, paid to Broker				1,500 —	1,500 —	
3.	Trust Deed, payable to Acme Loan Co				16,900 —		
4.	Trust Deed, payable to Seller	2,000 —			2,000 —		
5.	Trust Deed, payoff to XYZ Loan	9,450 —					
6.	Interest on Loan Assumed						
7.	Title Insurance Premium						
8.	Abstracting: Before Sale	34 —					34 —
9.	After Sale	4 —		22 —			
10.	Title Exam, by Buyer's Atty			50 —			50 —
11.	Recording: Warranty Deed			2 —			
12.	Trust Deed 1st			6 25			
13.	Release	3 75					
14.	Other 2nd TD			3 50			3 50
15.	Documentary Fee			2 25			
16.	Tax Certificate			3 00			3 —
17.	Taxes for preceding year(s)						
18.	Taxes for current year	173 42			173 42		
19.	Tax Reserve			200 10			
20.	Special Taxes						
21.	Personal Property Taxes						
22.	Hazard Ins. Premium Assumed						
23.	Premium for New Insurance			96 —			96 —
24.	Hazard Insurance Reserve			16 —			
25.	FHA Mortgage Ins. Assumed						
26.	FHA Mortgage Ins. Reserve						
27.	Loan Commission (Buyer) 1%			169 —			
28.	Loan Discount Fee (Seller)						
29.	Interest on new loan, based on 30 day mo.			75 11			
30.	Survey			17 50			
31.	Appraisal Fee						
32.	Water Rent		18 75	18 75			
33.	Rental Income						
34.	Loan Transfer Fee						
35.	Loan Payment Due						
36.	Sales Commission 6%	1350 —					1350 —
37.	Title Exam by Loan Co Atty			40 —			
38.	Proceeds from Acme Loan Co					6892 04	
	Sub-totals	13,015 17	22,518 75	23,221 46	20,573 42	8392 04	1536 50
	Balance due to seller	9,503 58					9503 58
	Balance due from buyer				2,648 04	2648 04	
	TOTALS	22,518 75	22,518 75	23,221 46	23,221 46	11,040 08	11,040 08

1. Lender's Loan Statement

The Worksheet for Real Estate Settlement on two previous pages indicates that all payouts are made by the broker. In practice, this may not always be true. When a new loan is secured, the lending institution may make some of the payouts in order to protect itself. The lending institution in such a case will provide a loan statement showing the amount of the loan and the payouts it has made or will make. These payouts are deducted from the amount of the loan and a balance is shown which is called the loan proceeds. The check on the loan company will be drawn in this amount and made payable jointly to broker and purchaser.

The various charges that a lending institution will make to protect its interest will vary from lender to lender. A loan statement from the Acme Loan Company in the sample problem would probably appear as follows:

Loan Statement

Loan		$16,900.00
Payoff on existing note	$9,450.00	
Loan Service Charge	169.00	
Title Exam by XYZ Loan Company Attorney	40.00	
Recording Fees		
Warranty Deed	2.00	
Trust Deed (1st)	6.25	
Release	3.75	
Abstracting After Sale	26.00	
Documentary Fee	2.25	
Survey	17.50	
Tax Reserve	200.10	
Hazard Insurance Reserve	16.00	
Interest on Loan May 10 to May 31 (based on 30-day-month)	75.11	
Total Charges		$10,007.96
LOAN PROCEEDS		$ 6,892.04

2. <u>Reconciliation by Broker</u>

The Loan Statement in no way relieves the broker of his responsibility to prepare and provide a closing statement for his clients. The loan company has made these payouts by deducting them from the amount of the loan regardless of whether such payouts are chargeable to the buyer or chargeable to the seller. The loan companies may also vary as to which of the costs they wish to pay. The broker must balance the loan proceeds shown on the loan statement with the final payment due from the buyer and the final payment due the seller as shown on the closing statement. This may be done in the following manner:

Reconciliation

Loan Proceeds	$6,892.04	
Deposit in Escrow	1,500.00	
Money due from Buyer	2,648.04	
Payouts made by broker:		
Examination of title by Purchaser's Attorney		50.00
Commission		$1,350.00
Recording Trust Deed (second)		3.50
Bringing abstract to date		34.00
Hazard Insurance		96.00
Tax Certificate		3.00
Amount due Seller		9,503.58
Totals	$11,040.08	$11,040.08

This reconciliation may be made on the Broker's debit and credit portion of the second worksheet as shown on a previous page earlier in this section. The theory behind the itemization is the same as in the first worksheet. The Broker's debits are a listing of all the money actually collected by the Broker. The Broker's credits are an itemization of all the money that the Broker actually disburses, including his own commission. When the closing is performed through a lending institution, he will not be collecting the full amount of the loan, but only the loan proceeds which are shown on line 38 of the worksheet. Consequently, the broker will not actually disburse all the money involved in the transaction. The loan company will pay many of the obligations of the Buyer and Seller.

The items paid for by the Acme Loan Company, which was not concerned as to which of the parties was obligated to pay a particular item, are appropriately debited or credited by the broker as he did on the first worksheet.

3. <u>Use of Worksheets</u>

There is, of course, no necessity to prepare both worksheets. The first one is in the event the broker collects all the money, and the second worksheet is in the event the loan company makes some of the payments on behalf of the Buyer and the Seller. Most loan companies will insist that they make certain payments from the proceeds of the loan.

If the broker is sufficiently familiar with closing statements, he may omit the worksheet and prepare the Seller's and Buyer's Statements of Settlement directly from the Loan Statement, the contract, and other information he has gathered. However, if he does it by short-cutting the worksheet, he should be careful to prepare for himself a reconciliation as shown on the preceding page. The reconciliation is important to the closing broker because he has taken upon himself the responsibility for the accuracy of statements of settlement given to each of the parties. Among other possible errors, the reconciliation is a check on the accuracy of the loan company in tendering its loan proceeds. The reconciliation also insures the broker that there are sufficient funds to pay the commission.

D. FINAL SETTLEMENT WHEN LOAN IS ASSUMED

1. General

The proposed real estate transaction in this appendix involves a new loan which the purchaser secures. Often, for various reasons, the purchaser, with the consent of the seller, may agree to assume and pay the existing loan. This agreement to assume and pay the existing loan should be written in the preliminary agreement to sell (offer and acceptance) and should also be written in the deed.

2. The Assumption Statement

The assumption statement prepared by the lending institution holding the existing trust deed or mortgage will contain the following information from which you, the broker, may prepare your closing statement. All of this information will be as of a certain date, the date being requested by the broker.

    a. The loan balance and term.

    b. The rate of interest and the amount of interest paid in advance or the amount of interest earned but not yet due.

    c. The due date of the next payment or the amount of the delinquent payments.

    d. The amount of the tax account escrowed for the benefit of the mortgagor.

    e. The amount of the insurance account escrowed for the benefit of the mortgagor.

f. The face amount of the existing insurance policy, the date of the policy, the term of the policy, and premium of the policy.

g. The amount of the loan transfer fee, if any, and a statement of what record evidence the lender requires before transferring the loan, e. g., a true copy of the contract or a certified copy of the deed or abstracting to date after conveyance.

h. New owner's monthly payment, including principle, interest, taxes, and hazard insurance.

E. EXPLANATION OF OTHER CHARGES AND ADJUSTMENTS

No single real estate transaction will contain every type of charge or adjustment. All closings are similar, but each is different. The following will explain some of the more common types of charges and adjustments that a broker will encounter in practice.

It should be remembered that although this entire Appendix on Closing Statements refers to the obligations of the Buyer and the obligations of the Seller, any of these obligations may be reversed or changed by contract.

The numbering below will conform to the worksheets and statements of settlement.

7. <u>Title Insurance Commitment and Policy</u>. In the larger metropolitan areas, use of a title insurance policy as evidence of good and marketable title is commonplace today. This is especially true among new dwellings and larger subdivisions, because many lending institutions insist on a title policy before making a loan. Unless the contract provides otherwise, the cost of the owner's policy is a charge or debit to the Seller and a credit to the Broker, if he pays it. If the Buyer should retain an attorney to examine the title insurance commitment because of exceptions thereon, the attorney's fee is debited to the Buyer and credited to the Broker. Many lending companies will demand a mortgagee's policy which is an additional fee. This is a charge or debit to the Buyer and would probably be shown on the loan statement as having been deducted from the loan by the loan company.

18. <u>Taxes for Current Year</u>. In the previous example of a real estate transaction, the previous year's taxes were used as a base from which to prorate the current year's taxes. This is the customary method of pro-rating for vacant land and for those improvements (houses) which have been in existence long enough to have been included in the previous year's tax bill. If the following situation is involved, then the preliminary contract should be written so that you may accomplish another method of pro-rating. If the improvements were made recently, but have been appraised for tax purposes for the year of the closing, the pro-rating should be done in this manner. The amount of the assessed valuation may be determined by calling the county treasurer's office; although the treasurer will be unable to provide you with a "Certificate of Taxes Due" which reflects the taxes on the improvements, this office will also tell you what the mill levy was

for the previous year; thus, the previous year's mill levy applied to the current assessed valuation will give you the fairest estimate of the general property taxes for the current year; upon this amount of taxes you will prorate at the time of transfer of title. This will also enable the lending company to make proper charges for the tax escrow account.

19. and 24. <u>Tax Insurance Trust Account</u>. On home loans practically all lending institutions today require that a sum equal to one month's taxes and insurance be paid with each monthly installment. This is to be placed in the mortgagor's trust account to insure that moneys will be available for payment of taxes and insurance when due. In a transaction where the existing loan is being assumed and there is a Tax Insurance Trust Account, this amount is credited to the Seller and debited to the Buyer.

20. <u>Special Taxes.</u> These special assessments on property improvements, such as street paving, storm sewers, et cetera, are paid for by the Seller if they were installed at the time of sale, even though not yet assessed. The estimate of this amount of taxes may be secured from the county treasurer's office, if the improvements are already installed. If the special taxes have been assessed, the reason for debiting the Seller is obvious, when it is realized that the Buyer has contracted for clear title other than named exceptions. Special taxes are often amortized and paid in installments with the continuing ad valorem taxes, and, therefore, it is not unusual for the Buyer to agree and contract to assume the balance of taxes due for special improvements.

21. <u>Personal Property Taxes</u>. Personal property taxes will not be involved unless the property was used for business purposes or income producing purposes. If such personal property is included in the sale, these taxes are prorated as ad valorem taxes would be prorated. When title passes, the responsibility passes from Seller to Buyer. Personal property tax situations are more frequently encountered in business opportunity transactions. The county will demand advance payment of these taxes for the current year and, therefore, prorated to date of settlement, with the whole year's taxes paid to treasurer.

25. <u>FHA Mortgage Insurance Premium</u>. This item is involved only when an FHA Loan is assumed. The premium is paid by the loan company to FHA for FHA's charge to insure the lender against loss in the event the borrower defaults on the loan. The money for the premium is first paid by the borrower to the lender. On FHA loans originated after August 5, 1957, the premium is payable annually in arrears. Prior to that date, premiums were payable annually in advance.

If the premium was paid in arrears, the seller would be debited pro-rata for the part of the premium accruing from the date of the last premium to the date of settlement. The buyer would be credited this amount.

If the premium was paid in advance, the seller would be credited pro-rata for the unearned part of the premium paid in advance beyond the date of settlement.

26. <u>FHA Mortgage Insurance Reserve</u>. This item is involved when a new FHA loan is obtained and when an FHA loan is assumed. In the case of a new FHA loan,

the lender will hold a one or two month reserve. This is a debit to the buyer and is withheld from the loan by the lender.

In the case of an assumption, the reserve amount currently held by the lender is a debit to the buyer and a credit to the seller.

28. Loan Discount Fee. This fee is payable by a Seller to the Lending Company and usually occurs in government insured or government guaranteed loans. The term discount fee is probably a misnomer, but is in common usage, since it is truly neither a discount nor a fee. It is a charge made by the loan company to increase its "yield" on the investment. The loan company's yield is provided by its interest charge. Government insured or guaranteed loans are "pegged" or have a set maximum interest that a borrower may pay. If the interest rate set by the government is lower than the interest which could be secured if the loan company made a conventional loan without government restrictions, insurance, or guarantee, then, the loan company may refuse to make the loan unless it is paid a premium. This premium is expressed as a percentage of the total loan, e. g., 2% of $15,300. Federal law prohibits the Buyer from paying this fee, because it is in truth "interest" which adds to the lenders' "yield." Although anyone except the Buyer may pay this discount fee to the lender, it is usually the Seller who pays it, if he wishes to sell his property to a Buyer seeking a government insured or guaranteed loan. The competent broker will be sure that the Seller understands his position before he signs a contract obligating him to pay it. In such a case, the Seller would be debited with this fee, and the lender usually withholds it when he makes the loan.

29. Interest on Existing Loan. When a sale is made subject to an existing loan which is to be assumed by the Buyer, then any earned interest on the loan from date of last payment to date of settlement should be charged to Seller as a debit and credited to Buyer. However, in many instances, a lending institution will require that the monthly payment reflect interest paid one month in advance. If such is the case, the interest paid beyond the date of settlement should be a debit to the Buyer and a credit to the Seller.

31. Appraisal. When an appraisal fee is involved in closing a transaction, a rule of thumb calls for the fee to be chargeable to the party who benefits from it . . . normally, the Buyer. However, in many instances, the Seller will ask you to order an appraisal to determine a fair market value and/or to receive a firm loan commitment. If such is the case, the broker should ascertain in advance and enter into a mutual agreement as to who shall pay the appraisal fee. If the broker has paid the appraisal fee and expects reimbursement from either Buyer or Seller, such provisions should be included in the sales contract.

33. Rental Income. Adjustment should be made on any rental paid by a tenant in advance, and a prorated share for the rental period credited to the Buyer and debited to the Seller. Delinquent rents should not be prorated.

F. DISPOSITION OF CLOSING STATEMENTS

The student will note that the statements of settlement given to the Seller and Buyer are more complete and informative than the worksheets. Dates of adjustments, names of payees of notes, et cetera, are shown on the final statement of settlement. Each statement of settlement must be prepared in conformance with the rules set forth by the Real Estate Commission, where applicable.

The real estate broker should furnish to each buyer and to each seller in every real estate or business opportunity transaction wherein he acts as broker, at the time such transaction is consummated, a complete, detailed closing statement as it applies to said Buyer and a complete, detailed closing statement as it applies to said Seller:

1. The broker should retain a copy of all closing statements approved by the respective buyers or sellers for future use or for inspection by an authorized representative of the Real Estate Commission.

2. The closing statement or statements of all real estate or business opportunity transactions in which a real estate broker participates shall show the date of closing, the total purchase price of the property, an itemization of all adjustments, money, or things of value received or paid, showing to whom each item is credited and/or to whom each item is debited, the dates of the adjustments shall be shown if not the same as the date of closing; also shown shall be the balances due or due from the respective parties to the transaction, and the names of the payees, makers and assignees, of all notes paid or made or assumed; the statements furnished to each party to the transaction shall contain an itemization of such credits and an itemization of such debits as pertain to each respective party.

3. Closing statements should be delivered to the respective parties at the time of the delivery and acceptance of the title, whether such delivery and acceptance be effected by bill of sale, deed or by an installment contract to give a deed at a future date.

The recommended procedure on settlement date is to have the Buyer furnish a certified check, cashier's check, or bank draft for the amount due. The Buyer may make this instrument payable to the Broker, jointly to Broker and Seller, or payable to himself. Many brokers prefer the latter method because proper endorsement provides for more flexibility at the closing. The broker should sign the statements of settlement given to Buyer and Seller. The broker should also secure the signed approval and acceptance of the Buyer and the Seller on a copy of their respective statements for his own protection and for future use or inspection by the Real Estate Commission.

APPENDIX B

TRUTH-IN-LENDING

A.	GENERAL	518
B.	APPLICABILITY	518
C.	"ARRANGER" AND "CREDITOR"	519
D.	DISCLOSURE	519
	1. Purpose	519
	2. When Made	520
	3. Definitions	520
	a. Finance Charge	520
	b. Annual Percentage Rate	521
E.	THE DISCLOSURE STATEMENT	521
F.	LICENSEES' DISCLOSURE RESPONSIBILITIES	523
G.	ADVERTISING	524
H.	ENFORCEMENT AND PENALTIES	524
I.	RESCISSION	525
J.	EFFECT OF RESCISSION	527
K.	SAMPLE FORMS	529
	1. Real Estate Disclosure Statement (1st or 2nd Lien)	529
	2. Real Estate Disclosure Statement (Installment Land Contract)	531
	3. Notice of Right of Rescission	533

APPENDIX B

TRUTH - IN - LENDING

A. GENERAL

Title I of the National Consumer Credit Protection Act, which is commonly known as the Truth-In-Lending Act, became effective on July 1, 1969. The act authorized the Board of Governors of the Federal Reserve System to prescribe regulations pursuant to the Act, and, consequently, Regulation Z was published to implement truth-in-lending.

This section will only attempt to describe briefly the coverage and effect of this Act as it concerns real estate practice.

Essentially, TIL requires disclosure of certain information to a borrower, the most important of which is the Finance Charge and the Annual Percentage Rate. It also permits a borrower to rescind a credit transaction in certain instances. TIL applies only to an extension of consumer credit to a natural person and not to credit extended to corporations, partnerships, associations, government agencies, et cetera. The Act does not apply to business loans or commercial loans, such as construction loans to builders, but it will apply when the construction loan is converted to a consumer loan made to the purchaser of the house. The Act will apply only if payment of the loan is to be made in more than four installments, or if a Finance Charge is or may be made.

B. APPLICABILITY

All creditors must comply with the Act. Regulation Z defines a creditor as "a person who in the ordinary course of business regularly extends or arranges for the extension of consumer credit." (Reg. Z, Sec. 226.2 (m)). Of course a licensee may, in some cases, be an "extender of credit" but, in other cases, an "arranger of credit."

If the licensee is an operative builder, a subdivider, or even a broker selling property on his own account, he may be deemed to be a "creditor" and, therefore, the obligation of compliance would fall upon him.

Regulation Z defines the clause . . . "arrange for the extension of credit" as follows: "means to provide or offers to provide consumer credit which is, or will be, extended by another person under a business or other relationship pursuant to which the person arranging such credit receives or will receive a fee, compensation, or other consideration for such service, or has knowledge of the credit terms and participates in the preparation of the contract documents required in connection with the extension of credit." (Reg. Z, Sec. 226.2).

C. "ARRANGER" AND "CREDITOR"

Whether or not a licensee is an "arranger" of credit is a question which must be answered by an analysis of the circumstances surrounding the real estate transaction.

In the ordinary case of the licensee selling an owner-occupied house, the licensee would not receive any fee for securing the loan necessary to the purchase; neither would he prepare the credit documents. Although a licensee may direct the purchaser to a lending institution, he is not paid under any business or other relationship for doing so; and he should be careful not to assist in the preparation of credit instruments.

When a licensee prepares a contract of sale in which the seller has agreed to extend credit to the purchaser by way of taking back a first or second purchase money mortgage*, the broker usually prepares the instrument and has knowledge of the actual terms. However, if the seller is not a "creditor," the seller is exempt from the requirements of TIL. When the seller is not a "creditor," the licensee need not make TIL disclosures as an "arranger." An owner-occupant seller does not usually fall within the definition of a "creditor," and, therefore, the licensee need not make disclosures as an "arranger," unless he has arranged for the sale of the purchase money note and received a fee for its sale. However, most persons who are not owner-occupant sellers, but who sell and extend or arrange credit in the ordinary course of business, would be "creditors," and in such case the seller and the broker would each be required to give those disclosures within their knowledge and the purview of their relationship with the customer. (Reg. Z, Sec. 226.6 (d)).

The licensee is in the same position when he prepares an Installment Land Contract as when he prepares the contract of sale for the seller to take back a first or second purchase money mortgage. Owner-occupant sellers are not usually "creditors," but most others would be "creditors" and joint responsibility would result. Of course, even if the seller-client is an owner-occupant, the licensee would be an "arranger" if he sold the installment contract and collected a fee for its sale.

Assumptions of existing mortgage loans are subject to all requirements of TIL. If the purchaser assumes and agrees to pay an existing obligation and is accepted by the original creditor in a written agreement with the purchaser, disclosure would be necessary. If the purchaser is not accepted by the creditor, the seller must make TIL disclosures if he meets the definition of "creditor."

D. DISCLOSURE

1. Purpose

The primary purposes of TIL are to disclose to the consumer how much it is costing him to borrow money and to disclose what the terms and conditions are. To

---

*For the purpose of this Appendix, the word "mortgage" is used synonymously with "trust deed."

accomplish this, the "creditor" or "arranger" must provide the borrower with a statement of such information. The statement itself is required to be given "clearly, conspicuously, and in meaningful sequence." It must be printed on only one side of a single sheet of paper. The law also requires that: "such disclosures must be made before the (credit) transaction is consummated." This means that the disclosure must be made before a contractual relationship is created by the borrower and creditor, irrespective of the time of performance.

2. When Made

The disclosure must be made <u>before settlement</u> in the ordinary sale of residential real estate. In other words, disclosures would not have to be made before the signing of the preliminary contract between the seller and the buyer, insofar as the first mortgage is concerned. (The lending institution will probably provide the disclosure statement at the same time it provides the loan statement for the 1st loan). But, if a second mortgage is carried back by the seller, who is a "creditor" under TIL (such as an operative builder, a broker dealing on his own account, or a broker taking a second mortgage as a commission), then disclosure with respect to the second mortgage would have to be made no later than the time of the signing of the preliminary agreement of sale. This is true because the preliminary agreement establishes the contractual relationship, inasmuch as seller and "creditor" are one and the same person. This will also be true of the signing of an Installment Land Contract. Disclosure would be required immediately.

It should be remembered that whenever a licensee is an "arranger," even though the creditor is a lending institution, the licensee should make certain that his name and address clearly appear on the disclosure statement or else submit his own disclosure statement.

3. Definitions

Before studying the list of the specific disclosure required in the statement, the licensee should clearly understand two terms defined in Regulation Z, i. e., the Finance Charge and the Annual Percentage Rate.

    a. Finance Charge

        The Finance Charge is the <u>total of all costs</u> imposed, directly or indirectly, by the creditor and payable, either directly or indirectly, by the borrower or by another party on behalf of the borrower as an incident to the granting of credit.

        Included in the Finance Charge are:

        (1) Interest, loan fees, points, service charges, finder's fees, or similar charges;

(2) Insurance premiums for protecting the creditor against the customer's default; premium for credit, life, accident, health, or loss of income insurance, unless it is clearly stated in writing that such insurance is not a condition to obtaining the loan and the borrower gives specific, dated, and separately signed written indication that he desires such insurance coverage;

(3) Premiums for hazard insurance, unless the borrower receives a statement from the creditor showing the cost of such insurance, if obtained through him, and stating that the borrower has a free choice of obtaining such insurance elsewhere;

(4) Fees for appraisal, investigation or credit reports.

Excluded from the Finance Charge, in a real property transaction, if bona fide, reasonable in amount, and not for the purpose of evading the regulation are: charges for title examinations; premiums for title insurance; fees for surveys, preparation of deeds, settlements, or other documents; notary fees, appraisal fees, and charges for credit reports; and amounts required to be paid into an escrow or trustee account for future payment of taxes, insurance, et cetera.

b. Annual Percentage Rate

The Annual Percentage Rate, as used in Regulation Z, is not "interest" as it is usually understood. Interest is included in computing the Annual Percentage Rate, along with the other finance charges. The Annual Percentage Rate is the relationship of the total Finance Charge to the total amount to be financed, and must be computed to the nearest ¼ of 1%. The licensee may have to explain this differentiation to his customer. Thus, the Annual Percentage Rate will give to the customer a description of the total cost imposed by the lender for making the loan. Tables which may be secured from any Federal Reserve Bank for a nominal fee may be used to determine the Annual Percentage Rate. Since the Annual Percentage Rate will vary with the term of the loan and with the frequency of payments, computation is made much easier by use of the tables.

E. THE DISCLOSURE STATEMENT

The Disclosure Statement itself must disclose as follows:

1. The date on which Finance Charge begins to accrue, if that date is different from the date of consummation;

2. The Annual Percentage Rate (described earlier);

3. The number, amount, and due dates or periods of payments scheduled to repay the indebtedness, and the sum of all these payments using the term "Total of Payments" (except in the case of a loan secured by a first lien or equivalent security interest on a dwelling to finance the purchase or sale of that dwelling). If any payment is more than twice the amount of an otherwise regularly scheduled equal payment, the creditor shall identify the amount of such payment as a "balloon payment" and shall state the conditions, if any, under which that payment may be refinanced if not paid when due;

4. The amount, or method of computing the amount, of any default or delinquency charge payable in the event of late payment;

5. A description or identification of the type of any security interest held or to be retained or acquired by the creditor, and a clear identification of the property to which the security interest relates;

6. A description of any penalty charge that may be imposed by the creditor for prepayment of the principal sum remaining on the mortgage, including the method of computing such a penalty and the conditions under which it may be imposed;

7. Identification of the method of computing any unearned portion of the finance charge in the event of prepayment, and the amount or method of computation of any charge which may be deducted from any rebate which will be credited or refunded;

8. The Total Finance Charge and the composition of the Finance Charge, which must be individually itemized except in the case of a first mortgage lien given to finance the purchase or sale of a dwelling;

9. The total amount of credit which will be made available to the borrower, including all charges, individually itemized, which are included in the amount of credit extended, but which are not part of the finance charge, using the term "Amount Financed";

10. Any Finance Charges (points, et cetera), including those paid out of loan proceeds, such as a discount, and any deposit balance or investment which the creditor requires the borrower to make and which must either be paid by the borrower (or another) at settlement (or before proceeds are disbursed), using the terms "Prepaid Finance Charge" and "Required Deposit Balance," as applicable;

11. In the case of a credit sale (Installment Land Contract, or any other sale where the credit is extended or arranged by the seller), the cash price, total down payment (cash trade-in), and the unpaid balance of the cash price.

You will note from the above listed disclosure provisions that the Total of Payments (sum of all monthly payments) and the composition of the Finance Charge need not be disclosed in the case of a first mortgage (or equivalent, e. g., an installment land contract) to finance the construction or acquisition of a dwelling or an assumption of such first loan. All loans, secured or otherwise, to finance the acquisition of building lots or raw acreage must disclose the Total of Payments and the Finance Charge. Refinancings are also subject to disclosure requirements without exception, because these are not loans to finance the acquisition or construction of a dwelling. Second mortgage transactions that are covered by TIL are fully subject to disclosure, even if the first mortgage transaction is excluded from the provision that the total Finance Charge and Total of Payments must be set forth.

In addition to the above requirements, when a seller ("creditor") carries back a secured loan or uses an Installment Land Contract, the Disclosure Statement must also show the cash price, total down payment (cash or trade-in) and the unpaid balance of the cash price, although the statement need not show the total Finance Charge and the Total of Payments, because the security is a first mortgage lien (or its equivalent) to acquire a dwelling.

This Appendix contains two sample forms of disclosure statements, each for a particular type of transaction:

(1) 1st or 2nd lien to finance the purchase of a dwelling (also assumptions).

(2) Contract with 1st lien taken back by seller or sale by Installment Land Contract.

F. LICENSEES' DISCLOSURE RESPONSIBILITIES

Remembering that a seller-occupant, although he may be a lender, would rarely be a "creditor," we can summarize generally or by rule of thumb in the ordinary real estate transaction. A licensee has no personal disclosure responsibility under TIL unless:

(1) he prepares a sales contract in which the seller who is a "creditor" extends credit by way of taking back a mortgage or by way of an Installment Land Contract; or,

(2) with actual knowledge of the terms, he assists in the preparation of the credit instruments for the lender who is a "creditor"; or,

(3) receives a fee, compensation or other consideration from the "creditor" lender; or,

(4) he is selling on his own account in the ordinary course of business and takes payment by way of a mortgage on the property; or,

(5) he takes his commission by way of an installment note or

>   note and mortgage on the property; or,
>
>   (6) as a part of the sales transaction he arranges for the sale of his seller's contract or note and mortgage to a third party and receives a commission for such sale.

However, in any real estate transaction and in all of his negotiations, the licensee does have responsibility to his client under the Real Estate Broker and Salesman License Act. His client will expect him to be knowledgeable in matters concerning TIL and will expect the licensee to inform him about documents that he may receive pursuant to TIL. Consequently, the licensee must be concerned with more than his personal responsibility.

G. ADVERTISING

TIL does not prohibit the advertising of credit terms, but it does determine how credit terms may be advertised, and all agents must comply.

In general, you may advertise the cash price and the "Annual Percentage Rate" (not the interest rate), and you must use that term.

No other credit terms, such as down payment, the monthly payment, the dollar amount of the finance charge or the term of the loan may be advertised, unless the following information is set forth as well: the cash price or the amount of the loan, the required down payment, the number, amount and due dates of all payments, and the Annual Percentage Rate. The "Total of Payments" over the term of the mortgage must also be set forth, unless the credit advertised refers to a sale of a dwelling or a first mortgage on a dwelling to finance the acquisition of that dwelling.

This restriction will practically eliminate the advertising of down payments, et cetera, on properties listed for resale, because the financing terms are not usually known before the advertising begins. Sellers of new houses may find it easier to comply with full disclosure in advertising, because financing is usually prearranged.

However, TIL does not prohibit advertising in general terms, e. g., "excellent loan for assumption," "reasonable monthly payments," "FHA-VA financing available." Other generalized phrases would be permissible.

H. ENFORCEMENT AND PENALTIES

The Federal Trade Commission is responsible for the administration and enforcement of TIL insofar as most licensees are concerned. The Federal Home Loan Bank Board will administer and enforce TIL as it applies to Savings and Loan Associations. Commercial banks and other creditors will have their respective and appropriate Federal Agency to administer and enforce TIL as it concerns them.

Any "creditor" or "arranger" who willfully and knowingly gives false or inaccurate information, or fails to provide information he is required to disclose, is subject to criminal liability punishable by up to a $5,000 fine, or one year in jail, or both.

If there is a failure to disclose to a borrower any information required under TIL, one may become civilly liable to the borrower for as much as twice the finance charge, but in no case less than $100 or more than $1,000, and one may also become liable for court costs and reasonable attorneys' fees.

A "creditor" may avoid liability by correcting an error within 15 days of its discovery, providing that suit has not been brought and that he has not received written notice of the error. The creditor may successfully defend a civil action if he can show by a preponderance of the evidence that the error was not intentional, but resulted from a bona fide error notwithstanding the maintenance of procedures reasonably adapted to avoid any such error. No civil penalty may be imposed, unless the action is brought within one year from the date of the violation.

I. RESCISSION

The rescission rights given the borrower in the TIL Statute were undoubtedly intended to protect the homeowner from unscrupulous sellers of home improvements, appliances, furniture, et cetera, who secured the credit advance by taking a second mortgage on the purchaser's home. Questionable practices in this area have caused many low income families to lose their homes through default on the second mortgage. However, the rescission provision extends far into other areas which directly affect the broker and the salesman.

Whenever a customer has the right to rescind a transaction, the "creditor" must give notice according to the specifications given in Regulation Z. The notice must be printed in capitals or lower case letters of not less than 12 point bold-face type on one side of a separate statement which identifies the transaction. Two copies must be given to the customer, one of which he can use to cancel the transaction. The phraseology is also specified, and a sample copy is shown at the end of this section.

When rescission rights are applicable under the statute, the customer has the right to rescind the transaction until midnight of the third business day following the date of consummation of the transaction or the date of delivery of the Notice of Rescission and all other material disclosures, whichever is later. A transaction is consummated when a "creditor" is bound to lend and a customer agrees to borrow. During this rescission period, no money may be disbursed except in escrow.

The customer may modify or waive his right to rescind if money is needed to meet personal emergencies and the customer has determined that the delay will be harmful to natural persons, or endanger the customer's property. The customer must furnish the "creditor" with a separate, dated, and personally signed statement describing the situation, and waiving his rights of rescission. The use of printed forms for the purpose is prohibited.

The rescission provision of TIL permits the borrower, for any reason, to rescind "any credit transaction in which a security interest is or will be retained or acquired in any real property which is used or is expected to be used as the principal residence of the customer." (Reg. Z, Sec. 226.9 (a)).

The principal exemption to this general rule is when a first lien or equivalent security interest is taken to finance the acquisition of a dwelling in which the person resides or expects to reside. The assumption of an exempt first lien is also exempt. The Installment Land Contract, if given to acquire a dwelling, is the equivalent of a first lien, so it would also be exempt from the rescission provision.

Because the exemption applies only if the proceeds of the first lien are used to acquire or build a dwelling, the Notice must be given when raw land or vacant subdivision lots are sold on credit and a security interest is created. The phrase "used or expected to be used as the principal residence of the customer" is subject to interpretation. Certainly in most instances the purchaser of a vacant parcel intends to put a dwelling on it and reside there. A vacation home in a recreation area is no more than an extension of the principal residence, and an all year round dwelling could be built. If the lot is sold as a possible home site, there may be rescission rights*. Zoning may be the determining factor as to intention. A statement on the face of the contract to the effect that the purchaser is buying only as an investment cannot prevent rescission rights from attaching, if they are applicable. Neither can such a statement operate as a waiver. The law has provided a specific method by which rescission rights may be waived, and no other method will be effective. No firm criteria have been established by Regulation Z, and, therefore, this writer suggests that when in doubt, the Notice of Rescission should be given.

TIL does not exempt the extender of credit on a second mortgage from giving Notice of the right to rescind (remember that the usual seller-occupant who takes back a second mortgage is not affected by TIL). Regular lenders, whether institutional or natural persons, operative builders, and licensees acting in the ordinary course of business who take back second mortgages must give Notice of opportunity to rescind.

As was explained earlier, the time of consummation of the credit transaction is the time of signing the sales contract, if the seller is a "creditor." In such cases, the Notice could be given at the time of signing the contract. And, it would be advisable to have the contract provide the date of transfer of deed and occupancy at least three days (preferably a week) after signing the initial contract and giving Notice.

The same reasoning prevails if the seller is a "creditor" and an Installment Land Contract is used. Notice may be given at the time of signing the contract and if there is a dwelling on the property, provide for a delayed occupancy. There would be no

---

*The required Notice refers to "home" and, since the "creditor" on the sale of a vacant lot is referring only to an intended home on the lot, the Notice may carry a footnote to that effect, but the Notice may not be amended.

difficulty at all when a vacant building lot is sold by use of an Installment Land Contract.

When the "creditor" who takes back a second mortgage is a third party to the transaction, such as a private or an institutional lender, the money could not be disbursed until after the three-day period has elapsed and the creditor has reasonably satisfied himself that the customer has not rescinded. Therefore, in this case, it would probably be wise to prepare the credit instruments, secure the necessary signatures, and deliver the Notice three days (or better, a week), before the time scheduled for closing and delivery of deed. In this case, some type of escrow arrangement would have to be made for the period between the signing of the credit instrument and the time of closing when the money is disbursed.

J. EFFECT OF RESCISSION

In the event a disclosure was not properly made or the formal Notice of opportunity to rescind was not given to a borrower, the borrower's right to rescind continues indefinitely for months or for years. There is no statute of limitations on this right.

Regulation Z is quoted as to the effect or responsibility: "when a customer exercises his right to rescind under paragraph (a) of this section, he is not liable for any finance or other charge, and any security interest becomes void upon such a rescission. Within 10 days after receipt of a notice of rescission, the creditor shall return to the customer any money or property given as earnest money, down payment, or otherwise, and shall take any action necessary or appropriate to reflect the termination of any security interest created under the transaction. If the creditor has delivered any property to the customer, the customer may retain possession of it. Upon the performance of the creditor's obligations under this section, the customer shall tender the property to the creditor, except that if return of the property in kind would be impractical or inequitable, the customer shall tender its reasonable value. Tender shall be made at the location of the property or at the residence of the customer, at the option of the customer. If the creditor does not take possession of the property within 10 days after tender by the customer, ownership of the property vests in the customer without obligation on his part to pay for it." (Reg. Z, Sec. 226.9 (d)).

The effect of rescission on the lender and the real estate practitioner is probably greater than is at first apparent. If rescission does occur, consider these possible situations:

1. When the "creditor" of the second mortgage is a third party to the transaction, and rescission occurs before transfer of the deed, the credit transaction could probably be severed from the sales contract. This would leave the purchaser still responsible to purchase under the sales contract and under a legal compulsion to find the money elsewhere. If the rescission is made after transfer of the deed, only the second mortgage lender would suffer a loss.

2. When the seller is also a "creditor" and takes back a second mortgage, then the second mortgage is an integral part of the contract itself. If the purchaser rescinds before transfer of the deed, the entire contract fails, but no one is hurt.

But, if the rescission is made at any time after the time of transfer of deed and the disbursing of moneys, many complications arise. Consider this imaginary, but not unusual, transaction:

A "creditor" seller, such as an operative builder, sells a house for $30,000. The purchaser secures a first mortgage loan in the amount of $25,000. He makes a $3,000 down payment and gives a second note and mortgage to the builder in the amount of $2,000, which is really the builder's profit. Some time after closing, because of the builder's failure to disclose or give proper Notice, the purchaser rescinds. This will probably be the effect:

a. The security interest (second mortgage) is voided and finance charges are lost, but the builder still has an unsecured note for the balance due.

b. If the builder cannot return the down payment (he may have used it to pay off the construction loan or a mechanic's lien), the purchaser may retain title to the house and has no responsibility to pay the second note.

c. If the builder returns to the purchaser the $3,000 down payment and any other money paid, the customer must tender title to the house to the builder.

d. If the builder recovers title to the house, the first mortgage lender will still have a note signed by the original purchaser, but it will be secured by a mortgage on a house now owned by the builder who has not signed the note. In effect, the builder has taken title to the house subject to the first mortgage, but has not assumed and agreed to pay the first note. First mortgage lenders do not usually approve of a situation like this, and the result may be that first mortgage lenders will no longer make loans if a second mortgage is involved in the transaction*.

---

*It might be argued that, with the rescission, the entire transaction failed because the second mortgage was an integral part of the transaction, and that the deed to the customer was invalid, which would mean that the first mortgage lender had no security; however, this writer believes that since Regulation Z provided for a tender of the property by the customer that the intention was that the original deed of conveyance was valid.

K. SAMPLE FORMS:

REAL ESTATE DISCLOSURE STATEMENT
(1st or 2nd Lien Evidenced by Note and Trust Deed)

.... (Date of Transaction) .... (Date Disclosures made to Borrowers)

BORROWERS: ....
(Print FULL NAMES) (No. Street, or R.F.D.) (City) (State) (Zip)

LENDER: ....
(LENDER'S NAME) (Mailing Address, including Zip)

DISCLOSURES REQUIRED BY FEDERAL LAW:

PAYMENT TERMS: Payable:
....

after date; or Payable in ...., equal monthly payments of

$..............., commencing on

..............., 19......, and on the same day of the month thereafter, plus an irregular payment of $.......

due on ...., 19 ; (tax) (insurance) escrow deposits are called for in deed of trust and are in addition to above payments; (Delete payment terms inapplicable.); together with a delinquency or late charge of

....

Finance charge will begin to accrue on: ....

Further, upon Borrowers' Default, to collect OUTSTANDING BALANCE or otherwise to enforce NOTE and DEED OF TRUST; on default BORROWERS shall be liable for costs and

expenses and ....

.... as Attorneys' fees of LENDER. BALLOON PAYMENT, if any, and conditions (if any) for refinancing same, if not paid when due:

$ ....

BASIC TERMS OF LOAN CONTRACT:
1. LOAN PROCEEDS: $...............
2. OTHER CHARGES: (Total) $...............
   a. Premium, Credit Life: $...............
   b. Premium, Disability Insurance: $...............
   c. Premium, Property Insurance: $...............
   d. Title Exam. Fees: $...............
   e. Title Insurance: $...............
   f. Property Survey Fees: $...............
   g. Legal Fees, Drafting Documents: $...............
   h. Escrow Deposit for Taxes: $...............
   i. Escrow Deposit, Ins.: $...............
   j. Notary Fees: $...............
   k. Appraisal Fees: $...............
   l. Credit Reports: $...............
   m. Filing or Recording Fees: $...............
   n. Other: $...............
3. LESS:
   Prepaid Finance Charge: $...............
   Required Deposit Balance: $...............
   TOTAL PREPAID FINANCE CHARGE AND REQUIRED DEPOSIT BALANCE: $...............
4. AMOUNT FINANCED (No. 1 plus No. 2 minus No. 3): $...............
*5. **FINANCE CHARGE:** (Total) $...............
   a. Interest: $...............
   b. Loan Fee: $...............
   c. Other: $...............
*6. TOTAL OF PAYMENTS: $...............
7. **ANNUAL PERCENTAGE RATE:** ....%

*Not required for loans secured by first liens on dwellings, made to finance purchase of same.

PENALTY CHARGE ON PREPAYMENT OF PRINCIPAL

(Method of computation and conditions under which penalty may be imposed):

....

INSURANCE DISCLOSURES:

PROPERTY INSURANCE, if written in connection with this loan, may be obtained by BORROWERS through any person of their choice: subject only to LENDER'S right to refuse to accept any insurer offered by BORROWERS, for reasonable cause. If BORROWERS desire property insurance to be from or through LENDER, the cost will be $..............., per annum, based upon current rates and classifications. CREDIT LIFE AND/OR DISABILITY INSURANCE are not required to obtain this loan, purchase of such through LENDER being voluntary on BORROWERS' part. No charge is made for credit insurance and no such credit insurance is provided unless the BORROWER to be insured under such Credit Insurance Policy signs the appropriate Statement below: (a) The estimated cost for Credit Life Insurance alone will be $............... for the term of the credit. (b) The estimated cost for Credit Life and Disability Insurance will be $............... for the term of the credit.

I DESIRE CREDIT LIFE AND DISABILITY INSURANCE:

....
(Date)   (Signature of Borrower)

I DESIRE CREDIT LIFE INSURANCE ONLY:

....
(Date)   (Signature of Borrower)

SECURITY

Lender has a right of Set-Off against deposits or other sums which may be due Borrowers, as by law provided. The following security provisions are in addition to said right of set-off.   (Description)

☐ FIRST LIEN ....

on ....

☐ SECOND LIEN ....

☐ This property will Secure Future Advances or other Indebtedness

☐ The deed of trust will Cover after-acquired Property

ACKNOWLEDGMENT OF RECEIPT OF DISCLOSURES:

The undersigned BORROWERS do herewith acknowledge receipt of the DISCLOSURES contained herein. They further acknowledge that at the time they received a copy of this Statement it was complete and all blanks were filled in.

....
(WITNESS)   (Date Disclosures Received)   (Signature of Borrower)

NOTE: *If the 2nd lien is taken back by the seller (creditor) the cash price, total downpayment (cash or trade-in) and the unpaid balance must also be shown.*

NOTE: *This disclosure statement must be printed on only one side of a single sheet of paper.*

REAL ESTATE DISCLOSURE STATEMENT

[For Sale by Installment Land Contract or First Lien taken back by Seller]
[Proceeds used to acquire or build a dwelling]

Date of Transaction......................, 19......

Name of Lender ....

Address ....

Name of Borrower ....

Address ....

1. Cash Price $.............
2. Cash Down Payment $.............
   Trade-in $.............
   Total Downpayment $.............
3. Unpaid balance of $.............
   Cash Price (1 minus 2) $.............
4. Prepaid finance
   charge (if any) $.............
   Required deposit
   balance (if any) $.............
   Total prepaid finance
   charge and required
   deposit balance $.............
5. Amount financed
   (3 minus 4) $.............
6. ANNUAL PERCENTAGE RATE............ %

7. Payment Schedule
   .... equal ....
   payments of $.............. each commencing..........................., 19.......
   and continuing on the same day of each................... thereafter, except a final payment of $.................. due on .... 19..... and other irregular payments (if any) as follows:
   $......... due.......$......... due.......
   $......... due.......$......... due.......
   The payment(s) due........................
   is a (are) balloon payment(s) and may be refinanced if not paid when due on the following conditions: ....
   ....

8. Finance charge will begin to accrue on:
   ...., 19........... ...

	AMOUNT OR METHOD OF COMPUTATION	CONDITIONS FOR IMPOSING
9. Late payment charge (if any)		
10. Prepayment charge (if any)		
11. Refund - unearned Finance charge (if any)		

12. This transaction will be secured by a .... which will be a ....
    lien on the following described real property and on all after-acquired property becoming a part thereof: ....
    ....

13. This security interest ☐ will ☐ will not cover future advances.

14. Property insurance, if written in connection with this transaction, may be obtained by Customer through any person of his choice. If obtained through Creditor, the cost of such insurance will be $ .... for the term of this transaction.

15. Credit life/accident/health/loss of income insurance ☐is ☐is not required for this transaction. (Delete inapplicable provisions.) If not required, it will not be obtained unless Customer signs below.

I (We) desire _____ insurance at a cost of $_____ for the term of this transaction.

Date _____, 19_____ .   _____   _____
                                  (Insured Customer's Signature)   (Insured Customer's Signature)

16. Additional Provisions:_____
_____

I acknowledge receipt of a completely filled-in copy of this Disclosure Statement prior to the execution of the documents to be given in connection with this sale.

Dated _____, 19 _____ .   _____
                                                        (Customer's Signature)

NOTE: *The "Total of Payments" must be shown if the loan is not made to acquire the dwelling or if vacant land is sold.*

NOTE: *This disclosure statement must be printed on only one side of a single sheet of paper.*

NOTICE OF RIGHT OF RESCISSION

-- LOAN NO.------------
(Identification of Transaction)

Notice To Customer Required By Federal Law:

You have entered into a transaction on ....
(Date)
which may result in a lien, mortgage, or other security interest on your home. You have a legal right under federal law to cancel this transaction, if you desire to do so, without any penalty or obligation within three business days from the above date or any later date on which all material disclosures required under the Truth in Lending Act have been given to you. If you so cancel the transaction, any lien, mortgage, or other security interest on your home arising from this transaction is automatically void. You are also entitled to receive a refund of any downpayment or other consideration if you cancel. If you decide to cancel this transaction, you may do so by notifying

----
Name of Creditor

at --
Address of Creditor's Place of Business

by mail or telegram sent not later than midnight of

Date

You may also use any other form of written notice identifying the transaction if it is delivered to the above address not later than that time. This notice may be used for that purpose by dating and signing below.

I hereby cancel this transaction.

-----------------------------------   --------------------------------------
(Date)   (Customer's Signature)

NOTE: (The above notice must be reproduced in 12 point bold faced type as shown above)

EFFECT OF RESCISSION. When a customer exercises his right to rescind under paragraph (a) of this section, he is not liable for any finance or other charge, and any security interest becomes void upon such a rescission. Within 10 days after receipt of a notice of rescission, the creditor shall return to the customer any money or prpperty given as earnest money, downpayment, or otherwise, and shall take any action necessary or appropriate to reflect the termination of any security interest created under the transaction. If the creditor has delivered any property to the customer, the customer may retain possession of it. Upon the performance of the creditor's obligations under this section, the customer shall tender the property to the creditor, except that if return of the property in kind would be impracticable or inequitable, the customer shall tender its reasonable value. Tender shall be made at the location of the property or at the residence of the customer, at the option of the customer. If the creditor does not take possession of the property within 10 days after tender by the customer, ownership of the property vests in the customer without obligation on his part to pay for it.

Received Notice of Right of Rescission in duplicate this date --

---   ---
(Signature)   (Signature)

APPENDIX C

FEDERAL ANTI-DISCRIMINATION LAW

A.	THE CIVIL RIGHTS ACT OF 1968	536
	1. Prohibited Discriminatory Activities	536
	2. Limited Exemptions or Exceptions in the Act	537
B.	THE U. S. SUPREME COURT AND THE 1866 CIVIL RIGHTS ACT	538
	1. Introduction	538
	2. Areas Where 1968 Act Goes Beyond The Jones Case	538
	3. Areas of the 1968 Act Substantially Nullifed by The Jones Case	539
C.	SCOPE OF THE FEDERAL LAW	539

APPENDIX C

FEDERAL ANTI-DISCRIMINATION LAW

A. THE CIVIL RIGHTS ACT OF 1968

1. Prohibited Discriminatory Activities

After several years of discussion and controversy, Congress enacted an open housing law as Title VIII of the 1968 Civil Rights Act. The "discrimination" against which the Act is directed is discrimination based on race, color, religion, or national origin. Certain types of discriminatory activities are prohibited, including:

a. Discriminatory Refusal to Sell or Rent. For example, a seller who refuses a buyer's offer because the buyer is Catholic violates the Act.

b. Discriminatory Refusal to Negotiate for Sale or Lease. For example, an owner who refuses to discuss possible sale terms with a prospective buyer because the buyer is Italian violates the Act. On the other hand, an owner who refuses to discuss possible sale terms with anyone, because the property is simply not for sale, does not violate the Act.

c. Discrimination in the Furnishing of Housing Services or Facilities. For example, a Negro landlord who refuses garage space to white tenants, but provides it for his black tenants, violates the Act. So does the broker who refuses his services to a man because the man is Puerto Rican.

d. Discrimination in Setting Terms of Sale or Lease. For example, a Jewish landlord who charges Protestants higher rents than he charges Jews for the same type of apartment violates the Act.

e. Discriminating by Falsely Stating that Housing Is Not for Sale or Rent. For example, a landlord with an apartment for rent who falsely told a Negro applicant the apartment was already rented would violate the Act.

f. Discriminatory Advertising in a Newspaper or Posting Notices on Property. For example, a "Whites Only" sign at a new subdivision would be a violation of the Act.

g. Discrimination in Providing Financial Assistance for the Purchase of Housing. For example, a bank controlled by Negroes which enforced a policy of refusing to lend to white borrowers would violate the Act.

h. Discriminatory Refusal to Admit a Real Estate Broker to Membership in a Real Estate Organization or Multiple Listing Arrangement. For example, a local brokers' organization would violate the Act if it excluded black brokers in the community.

i. Block-busting. Block-busting is persuading or trying to persuade a person to sell by creating or exploiting fears of racial change in a neighborhood. For example, a broker who, after one black family bought a home in a particular neighborhood, contacted other owners and urged them to sell before more black families began to move in would violate the Act.

NOTE: Purely commercial or industrial property is not covered. These prohibitions against discriminatory acts apply only to housing. Dwellings, such as single-family homes, duplexes, small and large apartment buildings, residential cooperatives, and condominiums are covered, as is vacant land on which dwellings are to be constructed.

2. Limited Exemptions or Exceptions in the Act

There are certain very limited exemptions or exceptions to the Act, including:

a. Sale or rental of a single-family house by its owner, provided he owns no more than three such houses and resides in the house or was its most recent resident, and also provided that he does not advertise the fact that the house is to be sold or rented on a discriminatory basis, and also provided that he does not use the sales or rental facilities or services of a real estate broker, agent, or salesman. Note that the exemption is not available if the owner is anyone other than a bona fide homeowner selling or renting his own home, or if he advertises in a discriminatory way, or if he uses a broker to help him sell or rent. Note also, this exemption may be largely nullified by the United States Supreme Court decision discussed in paragraph B, following.

b. The Act does not apply to "rooms or units in dwellings containing living quarters occupied or intended to be occupied by no more than four families living independently of each other, if the owner actually maintains and occupies one of such living quarters as his residence." For example, this would allow the owner of a fourplex apartment building who lived in one of the four units to discriminate in the rental of the other three. But again, refer to the discussion in paragraph B, following.

c. A religious or church-related non-profit organization may limit the sale, rental, or occupancy of dwellings which it owns or operates for other than a commercial purpose to persons of the particular religion, or may give preference to persons of that religion, unless membership in the religion is restricted on account of race, color, or national origin.

    d.   A private club, if it is really private and not open to the public, which, as a mere incident to its primary purposes, provides lodgings which it owns or operates for non-commercial purposes, may limit the rental or occupancy of such lodgings to club members, or may give preference to members.

B.   THE U. S. SUPREME COURT AND THE 1866 CIVIL RIGHTS ACT

    1.   <u>Introduction</u>

For more than 100 years, our national statutory law has contained essentially this statement:

> All citizens of the United States shall have the same right, in every State and Territory, as is enjoyed by white citizens thereof, to inherit, purchase, lease, sell, hold, and convey real and personal property.

In 1965, a Negro from St. Louis, Joseph L. Jones, brought suit in federal court, complaining that the Alfred H. Mayer Company had refused to sell him a home in a St. Louis County subdivision for the sole reason that Jones was black. The federal district court dismissed the complaint, in effect throwing the suit out of court. Jones appealed, but the intermediate appeals court upheld the district court and said that the language quoted above, originally from the Civil Rights Act of 1866, applies only to "State Action" and does not cover private refusals to sell. Jones appealed again, and in the Supreme Court of the United States he won. The Court said:

> We hold that Sec. 1982 (the statute quoted above) bars <u>all</u> (emphasis is the Court's) racial discrimination, private as well as public, in the sale or rental of property, and that the statute, thus construed, is a valid exercise of the power of Congress to enforce the Thirteenth Amendment (to the United States Constitution).

This means that every refusal, by any person, to sell or rent any real property is unlawful and prohibited, if such refusal is motivated by racial discrimination. In some ways, this interpretation goes beyond the open housing portion of the 1968 Civil Rights Act. Conversely, the 1968 Act goes beyond the Jones Case in many respects.

    2.   <u>Areas Where 1968 Act Goes Beyond The Jones Case</u>

        a.   The 1968 Act covers discrimination based on religion or national origin; the Jones Case does not.

b. The 1968 Act provides for enforcement responsibilities in the Attorney General of the United States and in the federal Department of Housing and Urban Development in certain situations; the rights given in the Jones Case can be enforced only by a private lawsuit brought by the person discriminated against.

c. The 1968 Act prohibits discrimination in setting terms of sale or rental and in providing facilities or services, matters which the Jones decision does not reach.

d. The 1968 Act prohibits discrimination in real estate financing arrangements, while the Jones Case does not.

3. Areas of the 1968 Act Substantially Nullified by the Jones Case

The Jones decision substantially nullifies two of the potentially significant exemptions in the 1968 Act. Under the Act, a homeowner who did not use discriminatory advertising and did not use a broker's services was permitted to discriminate in sale or rental of his own home. But under the Jones Case, if the discrimination is on racial grounds, it is unlawful. Similarly, under the Act, the owner who owns a building with four or less apartments and lives in one of them can discriminate in renting the others. Under the Jones Case, however, this is disallowed if the discrimination is on racial grounds.

C. SCOPE OF THE FEDERAL LAW

Even disregarding state law and municipal ordinances, federal law has clearly outlawed the basic sorts of discrimination in housing which have been relatively widespread in some areas in the past, and in which real estate brokers or salesmen might become involved.

APPENDIX D

UNIFORM COMMERCIAL CODE

A.	INTRODUCTION	542
B.	SCOPE	542
	1. General	542
	2. Applicability to Real Estate	542
C.	PROCEDURES	542
	1. Filing Financial Statement	542
	2. Creation of Lien	542
D.	BULK TRANSFER LAW	543
	1. Purpose	543
	2. Responsibilities	543
	a. Buyer	543
	(1) Demand and Receive Affidavit from Seller	543
	(2) Give Notice to Seller's Creditors	543
	b. Seller	544
	c. Broker	544
	3. Personal Property	544
	4. Statute of Limitations	544

APPENDIX D

UNIFORM COMMERCIAL CODE

A. INTRODUCTION

The law of contracts over the years has adjusted to the needs of business and society. Many of these changes have been brought about by legislation; other changes are the results of court interpretations. Perhaps the most significant legislation affecting the law of contracts is the Uniform Commercial Code which has been adopted by forty-nine states, the District of Columbia, and the Virgin Islands. Louisiana has not adopted the entire Code, but has adopted Article 2 - Sales. It should be remembered that the Code provisions discussed in this appendix are only applicable to contracts for the sale of goods. Its provisions are not applicable to contracts involving the sale of real property, to contracts for personal service, or to contracts involving intangible personal property not classified as collateral.

The Code was promulgated by the National Conference of Commissioners on Uniform State Laws and the American Law Institute with the endorsement of the American Bar Association in 1951.

B. SCOPE

1. General: -- As noted above, the Code is restricted to transactions involving various aspects of the sale, financing, and security in respect to personal property ... tangible and intangible.

2. Applicability to Real Estate: -- The Code relates only indirectly to real property. Real estate practitioners have an interest in the Code, because security agreements will be used when "fixtures," "growing crops," or "standing timber" and other "goods" are used as security for a loan.

C. PROCEDURES

1. Filing Financial Statement: -- A person claiming security upon such goods must file a "financing statement" with the appropriate office of record. The parties to the financing statement are the "debtor" and the "secured party." If growing crops, timber to be cut, or goods which are, or are to become, fixtures are involved, the financing statement must contain a description of the real estate concerned.

2. Creation of Lien: -- The lien created by the filing, if for six years or less, is effective until the maturity date, and thereafter for a period of 60 days. If no maturity date is given, the lien is effective for a period of six years. The execution and filing of a "continuation statement" will extend the lien for an additional six-year period.

D. BULK TRANSFER LAW

1. Purpose: - - Real estate brokers may have occasion to make sales which involve the sale of a going business. Those brokers who do this only occasionally are not apt to be familiar with the procedure required by the Bulk Transfer section of the Uniform Commercial Code. The purpose of the Bulk Transfer law is to prevent fraud, to protect creditors, and to make the matter of the sale known to creditors. In the event of a violation, the sale is presumed to be fraudulent and void as to existing creditors.

2. Responsibilities

    a. Buyer

        (1) Demand and Receive Affidavit from Seller. The Bulk Transfer Law provides that it is the duty of every person buying any commercial business or establishment, including restaurants and other food dispensing establishments, or of all, or substantially all, of the furniture, fixtures, supplies, or equipment of any such business or establishment, to demand and receive from the seller an affidavit containing the names and addresses of all of the creditors of the seller, together with the amount of the indebtedness due to each creditor.

        The buyer must preserve the affidavit for six months following the sale and permit inspection by any creditor of the seller, or he may file the affidavit in the office of the county recorder in the county in which the seller's place of business is located.

        (2) Give Notice to Seller's Creditors. The law further provides that after a purchaser receives the affidavit, and at least 10 days before the closing of the sale, the purchaser must notify personally or by registered letter each of the creditors of the seller named in the affidavit of the proposed purchase. The contents of the notice are prescribed by law. The reason for this notice is to give to all such creditors listed the opportunity to attach the assets of the business prior to the consummation of the sale.

        If the intended sale is to be made at public auction, in addition to information required for ordinary bulk transfer, the notice must state that the sale is to be by auction, the name of the auctioneer, and the time and place of the auction.

        In an auction sale, the responsibility for giving the statutory notice is the auctioneer's. A sale which violates the requirements does not render the transfer fraudulent and void, but the auctioneer becomes personally liable to the transferor's creditors.

    b.   Seller

It is the duty of the Seller to furnish to the buyer the affidavit demanded.

    c.   Broker

It is quite obvious that in the event any business establishment is being sold, regardless of the nature of the business which is being conducted, the law should be strictly complied with; and if a broker is closing a transaction, even though there is included in the transaction, in addition to the assets of the business, the real property on which the business is located, it is the duty of the broker to see to it that this law is strictly complied with.

3.   <u>Personal Property</u>: - - The law further provides that, in any case where there is a purchase of personal property coming within the purview of the Act, without receiving such affidavit and without notifying the creditors listed in the affidavit, if any are listed, the purchase shall be ineffective as to any creditor who has not been notified. In other words, unless this procedure is followed as required by law, the purchaser does not acquire good title to the assets of the business, and the assets of the business are subject to being attached for the payment of debts owed by the seller.

4.   <u>Statute of Limitations</u>: - - No action shall be brought nor levy made under the Bulk Transfer Law more than six months after the date on which the buyer took possession of the goods, unless the sale has been concealed. If the transfer has been concealed, actions may be brought or levies made within six months after its discovery.

APPENDIX E

Addresses of Real Estate License Law Officials

APPENDIX E

ADDRESSES OF REAL ESTATE LICENSE LAW OFFICIALS

ALABAMA
 Chairman, Real Estate Commission
 562 State Office Building
 Montgomery 36104

ALASKA
 Chairman, Real Estate Commission
 c/o Division of Occupational Licensing
 Pouch D
 Juneau 99801

ALBERTA
 Commissioner of Real Estate
 Main Floor, Madison Building
 9919-105 Street
 Edmonton

ARIZONA
 Chairman, State Real Estate Commission
 c/o Real Estate Department
 1645 West Jefferson Street
 Phoenix 85007

ARKANSAS
 Chairman, Real Estate Commission
 1311 W. Second, P. O. Box 3173
 Little Rock 72201

BRITISH COLUMBIA
 Chairman, Real Estate Council
 608-626 West Pender Street
 Vancouver V6B 1W3

CALIFORNIA
 Chairman, State Real Estate Commission
 714 P Street
 Sacramento 95814

COLORADO
 Director, Real Estate Commission
 110 State Services Building
 Denver 80203

CONNECTICUT
 Chairman, Real Estate Commission
 90 Washington Street
 Hartford 06115

DELAWARE
 Chairman, Real Estate Commission
 State House Annex
 Dover 19901

DISTRICT OF COLUMBIA
 Chairman, Real Estate Commission
 614 "H" Street, N. W.
 Washington 20001

FLORIDA
 Chairman, Real Estate Commission
 State Office Building
 Winter Park 32789

GEORGIA
 Chairman, Real Estate Commission
 166 Pryor Street, S. W.
 Atlanta 30303

HAWAII
 Chairman, Real Estate Commission
 1010 Richards Street, P. O. Box 3469
 Honolulu 96801

IDAHO
 Chairman, Real Estate Commission
 State Capitol Building
 Boise 83720

ILLINOIS
 Commissioner of Real Estate
 77 W. Washington Street
 Chicago 60602

INDIANA
    Chairman, Real Estate Commission
    1022 State Office Building
    100 N. Senate Avenue
    Indianapolis 46204

IOWA
    Chairman, Real Estate Commission
    State Capitol Building
    Des Moines 50319

KANSAS
    Chairman, Real Estate Commission
    535 Kansas Avenue, Room 1212
    Topeka 66603

KENTUCKY
    Chairman, Real Estate Commission
    100 E. Liberty Street, Suite 204
    Louisville 40202

LOUISIANA
    Chairman, Real Estate Commission
    P. O. Box 52304
    Lafayette 70501

MAINE
    Chairman, Real Estate Commission
    Capitol Shopping Center
    Western Avenue
    Augusta 04330

MARYLAND
    Chairman, Real Estate Commission
    c/o Department of Licensing and Regulation
    One South Calvert Street, Sixth Floor
    Baltimore 21202

MASSACHUSETTS
    Chairman, Board of Registration of Real
        Estate Brokers and Salesmen
    State Office Building
    100 Cambridge Street
    Boston 02202

MICHIGAN
    Director, Department of Licensing
        and Regulation
    1033 S. Washington Avenue
    Lansing 48926

MINNESOTA
    Real Estate Licensing Director
    Department of Commerce
    Real Estate Section of Securities
        Division
    2nd Floor, State Office Building
    St. Paul 55155

MISSISSIPPI
    Chairman, Real Estate Commission
    505 Woodland Hills Building
    3000 Old Canton Road
    Jackson 39206

MISSOURI
    Chairman, Real Estate Commission
    222 Monroe Street
    Jefferson City 65101

MONTANA
    Board Director, Board of Real Estate
    42-½ N. Main
    LaLonde Building
    Helena 59601

NEBRASKA
    Chairman, Real Estate Commission
    2300 State Capitol Building
    Lincoln 68509

NEVADA
    Administrator, Department of
        Commerce, Real Estate Division
    111 W. Telegraph Street, Suite 200
    Carson City 89701

NEW HAMPSHIRE
    Chairman, Real Estate Commission
    3 Capitol Street
    Concord 03301

NEW JERSEY
President, Real Estate Commission
201 E. State Street
Trenton 08625

NEW MEXICO
President, Real Estate Commission
Room 1031, 505 Marquette, N. W.
Albuquerque 87102

NEW YORK
Director, Division of Licensing Services
270 Broadway
New York 10007

NORTH CAROLINA
Chairman, Real Estate Licensing Board
813 BB & T Building
P. O. Box 266
Raleigh 27602

NORTH DAKOTA
Chairman, Real Estate Commission
410 E. Thayer Avenue, Box 727
Bismarck 58501

OHIO
President, Real Estate Commission
33 North Grant Avenue
Columbus 43215

OKLAHOMA
Chairman, Real Estate Commission
4040 N. Lincoln Boulevard
Oklahoma City 73105

ONTARIO
Registrar, The Real Estate and Business
 Brokers' Act
Ministry of Consumer and Commercial
 Relations
555 Yonge Street
Toronto M4Y1Y7

OREGON
Commissioner, Department of
 Commerce, Real Estate Division
Commerce Building
Salem 97310

PENNSYLVANIA
Chairman, Real Estate Commission
Room 300, 279 Boas Street
Harrisburg 17120

QUEBEC
Superintendent, Real Estate Brokerage
 Branch
Department of Financial Institutions,
 Companies, and Cooperatives
800 Place D'Youville
Quebec GIA IL7

RHODE ISLAND
Director, Real Estate Division
Department of Business Regulation
169 Weybosset Street
Providence 02903

SOUTH CAROLINA
Chairman, Real Estate Commission
900 Elmwood
Columbia 29201

SOUTH DAKOTA
Chairman, Real Estate Commission
P. O. Box 638
Pierre 57501

TENNESSEE
Chairman, Real Estate Commission
215 Stahlman Building
Nashville 37201

TEXAS
Chairman, Real Estate Commission
P. O. Box 12188, Capital Station
Austin 78711

UTAH
> Director, Real Estate Division
> Department of Business Regulation
> 330 East Fourth South
> Salt Lake City 84111

VERMONT
> Chairman, Real Estate Commission
> 7 East State Street
> Montpelier 05602

VIRGINIA
> Chairman, Real Estate Commission
> Department of Professional and
>   Occupational Registration
> Ninth Street Office Building
> P. O. Box 1 - X
> Richmond 23202

VIRGIN ISLANDS
> Chairman, Real Estate Commission
> Division of Licensing
> Department of Finance
> P. O. Box 2515
> St. Thomas 00801

WASHINGTON
> Chairman, Real Estate Division
> P. O. Box 247
> Olympia 98501

WEST VIRGINIA
> Chairman, Real Estate Commission
> 402 State Office Building, No. 3
> Charleston 25305

WISCONSIN
> Chairman, Real Estate Examining Board
> 819 North 6th Street
> Milwaukee 03203

WYOMING
> Commissioner, Real Estate Commission
> 2219 Carey Avenue
> Cheyenne 82002

APPENDIX F
CODE OF ETHICS
NATIONAL ASSOCIATION OF REALTORS
As Amended at the Annual Convention, 1974

APPENDIX F

CODE OF ETHICS

NATIONAL ASSOCIATION OF REALTORS

PREAMBLE...

Under all is the land. Upon its wise utilization and widely allocated ownership depend the survival and growth of free institutions and of our civilization. The REALTOR should recognize that the interests of the nation and its citizens require the highest and best use of the land and the widest distribution of land ownership. They require the creation of adequate housing, the building of functioning cities, the development of productive industries and farms, and the preservation of a healthful environment.

Such interests impose obligations beyond those of ordinary commerce. They impose grave social responsibility and a patriotic duty to which the REALTOR should dedicate himself, and for which he should be diligent in preparing himself. The REALTOR, therefore, is zealous to maintain and improve the standards of his calling and shares with his fellow-REALTORS a common responsibility for its integrity and honor. The term REALTOR has come to connote competency, fairness, and high integrity resulting from adherence to a lofty ideal of moral conduct in business relations. No inducement of profit and no instruction from clients ever can justify departure from this ideal.

In the interpretation of his obligation, a REALTOR can take no safer guide than that which has been handed down through the centuries, embodied in the Golden Rule, "Whatsoever ye would that men should do to you, do ye even so to them."

Accepting this standard as his own, every REALTOR pledges himself to observe its spirit in all of his activities and to conduct his business in accordance with the tenets set forth below.

ARTICLE 1

The REALTOR should keep himself informed on matters affecting real estate in his community, the state, and nation so that he may be able to contribute responsibly to public thinking on such matters.

ARTICLE 2

In justice to those who place their interests in his care, the REALTOR should endeavor always to be informed regarding laws, proposed legislation, governmental regulations, public policies, and current market conditions in order to be in a position to advise his clients properly.

ARTICLE 3

It is the duty of the REALTOR to protect the public against fraud, misrepresentation, and unethical practices in real estate transactions. He should endeavor to eliminate in his community any practices which could be damaging to the public or bring discredit to the real estate profession. The REALTOR should assist the governmental agency charged with regulating the practices of brokers and salesmen in his state.

ARTICLE 4

The REALTOR should seek no unfair advantage over other REALTORS and should conduct his business so as to avoid controversies with other REALTORS.

ARTICLE 5

In the best interests of society, of his associates, and his own business, the REALTOR should willingly share with other REALTORS the lessons of his experience and study for the benefit of the public, and should be loyal to the Board of REALTORS of his community and active in its work.

ARTICLE 6

To prevent dissension and misunderstanding and to assure better service to the owner, the REALTOR should urge the exclusive listing of property unless contrary to the best interest of the owner.

ARTICLE 7

In accepting employment as an agent, the REALTOR pledges himself to protect and promote the interests of the client. This obligation of absolute fidelity to the client's interests is primary, but it does not relieve the REALTOR of the obligation to treat fairly all parties to the transaction.

ARTICLE 8

The REALTOR shall not accept compensation from more than one party, even if permitted by law, without the full knowledge of all parties to the transaction.

ARTICLE 9

The REALTOR shall avoid exaggeration, misrepresentation, or concealment of pertinent facts. He has an affirmative obligation to discover adverse factors that a reasonably competent and diligent investigation would disclose.

ARTICLE 10

The REALTOR shall not deny equal professional services to any person for reasons of race, creed, sex, or country of national origin. The REALTOR shall not be a party to any plan or agreement to discriminate against a person on the basis of race, creed, sex, or country of national origin.

ARTICLE 11

A REALTOR is expected to provide a level of competent service in keeping with the Standards of Practice in those fields in which the REALTOR customarily engages.

The REALTOR shall not undertake to provide specialized professional services concerning a type of property or service that is outside his field of competence unless he engages the assistance of one who is competent on such types of property or service, or unless the facts are fully disclosed to the client. Any person engaged to provide such assistance shall be so identified to the client and his contribution to the assignment should be set forth.

The REALTOR shall refer to the Standards of Practice of the National Association as to the degree of competence that a client has a right to expect the REALTOR to possess, taking into consideration the complexity of the problem, the availability of expert assistance, and the opportunities for experience available to the REALTOR.

ARTICLE 12

The REALTOR shall not undertake to provide professional services concerning a property or its value where he has a present or contemplated interest unless such interest is specifically disclosed to all affected parties.

ARTICLE 13

The REALTOR shall not acquire an interest in or buy for himself, any member of his immediate family, his firm or any member thereof, or any entity in which he has a substantial ownership interest, property listed with him, without making the true position known to the listing owner. In selling property owned by himself, or in which he has any interest, the REALTOR shall reveal the facts of his ownership or interest to the purchaser.

ARTICLE 14

In the event of a controversy between REALTORS associated with different firms, arising out of their relationship as REALTORS, the REALTORS shall submit the dispute to arbitration in accordance with the regulations of their board or boards rather than litigate the matter.

ARTICLE 15

If a REALTOR is charged with unethical practice or is asked to present evidence in any disciplinary proceeding or investigation, he shall place all pertinent facts before the proper tribunal of the member board or affiliated institute, society, or council of which he is a member.

ARTICLE 16

When acting as agent, the REALTOR shall not accept any commission, rebate, or profit on expenditures made for his principal-owner, without the principal's knowledge and consent.

ARTICLE 17

The REALTOR shall not engage in activities that constitute the unauthorized practice of law and shall recommend that legal counsel be obtained when the interest of any party to the transaction requires it.

ARTICLE 18

The REALTOR shall keep in a special account in an appropriate financial institution, separated from his own funds, monies coming into his possession in trust for other persons, such as escrows, trust funds, clients' monies and other like items.

ARTICLE 19

The REALTOR shall be careful at all times to present a true picture in his advertising and representations to the public. He shall neither advertise without disclosing his name nor permit any person associated with him to use individual names or telephone numbers, unless such person's connection with the REALTOR is obvious in the advertisement.

ARTICLE 20

The REALTOR, for the protection of all parties, shall see that financial obligations and commitments regarding real estate transactions are in writing, expressing the exact agreement of the parties. A copy of each agreement shall be furnished to each party upon his signing such agreement.

ARTICLE 21

The REALTOR shall not engage in any practice or take any action inconsistent with the agency of another REALTOR.

ARTICLE 22

In the sale of property which is exclusively listed with a REALTOR, the REALTOR shall utilize the services of other brokers upon mutually agreed upon terms when it is in the best interests of the client.

Negotiations concerning property which is listed exclusively shall be carried on with the listing broker, not with the owner, except with the consent of the listing broker.

ARTICLE 23

The REALTOR shall not publicly disparage the business practice of a competitor nor volunteer an opinion of a competitor's transaction. If his opinion is sought and if the REALTOR deems it appropriate to respond, such opinion shall be rendered with strict professional integrity and courtesy.

ARTICLE 24

The REALTOR shall not directly or indirectly solicit the services or affiliation of an employee or independent contractor in the organization of another REALTOR without prior notice to said REALTOR.

NOTE: Where the word REALTOR is used in this Code and Preamble, it shall be deemed to include REALTOR-ASSOCIATE. Pronouns shall be considered to include REALTORS and REALTOR-ASSOCIATES of both genders.

GLOSSARY OF TERMS
used in
REAL ESTATE BROKERAGE

GLOSSARY OF TERMS USED IN REAL ESTATE BROKERAGE

Terminology used in real estate brokerage is specialized to a degree and often incorporates legal and economic terms which in ordinary usage take on a meaning quite distinct from that used in the practice of real estate. The definitions given are those to which usage in the specialized fields generally ascribes.

Some of the definitions reflected in this glossary are more detailed than those found in preceding chapters; some are condensations. Included, also, are terms not previously expressed, but which may be encountered in your practice of real estate brokerage.

GLOSSARY

ABANDONMENT OF LEASED PREMISES. Leaving of premises by the lessee prior to termination of the lease and without the lessor's consent. 169

ABATEMENT. (Of taxes.) A reduction of taxes authorized by the tax authority upon petition of taxpayer. 198

"ABILITY TO PAY" PRINCIPLE. Relative to taxation, the "ability to pay" principle holds that taxes should be progressive to income rather than proportional or regressive. 187

"ABLE." Used in commercial sense, it means that the customer must have the required cash at the time title passes. "Able" infers one's ability to command the necessary funds to meet contractual obligations within the time required even though part of the money must be obtained by mortgaging the property being purchased. 240

ABROGATION. The annulment, repeal, or abolishment of a law.

ABSOLUTE TITLE. Title which is exclusive to the person who has it. No one else has any right, interest, or claim in the same property. 123

ABSTRACT OF TITLE. A summary of all the deeds upon which title to real property depends... and of all the charges (mortgages and liens) affecting said property. 414

ABUTTING LAND. Adjoining land with a common boundary.

ACCELERATION CLAUSE. A clause in a written contract which provides that if the contract is breached in any way, as when an installment is not paid when due, the entire debt becomes payable at once. 341

ACCEPTANCE. An indication of willingness to be bound by the terms of an offer. 70

ACCESS. The right of ingress or egress to a parcel of real estate over property held by another. 143

ACCESSIBILITY. Easiness or ability of access or approach.

ACCESSION. Additions to, or increases in, the value of property, either by natural or artificial process. 138

ACCOMMODATION PARTY. One who signs an instrument as a maker, drawer, endorser, or acceptor for the purpose of lending his credit to the instrument or as a means of securing credit for another. 341

ACCORD AND SATISFACTION. A method of discharging a contract. The "accord" is the agreement of the contracting parties whereby one is to do something other than what is stipulated in the terms of the contract. "Satisfaction" results when the new terms are fully performed. 81

ACCRETION. The gradual and imperceptible increase in real property through natural causes, e. g., additional land created by alluvial deposits from a stream or river (or additional land created when the sea shrinks below the usual level). Such increases of land through accretion become the property of the owner of the land to which they have been added. 138

ACCRUE. To augment or to increase. 218

ACCRUED DEPRECIATION. The difference between the cost of the reproduction cost of a building as of the date of the appraisal and the value of the buildings as of the same date. It is all the depreciation up to the date of the appraisal caused by physical deterioration, functional obsolescence, and economic obsolescence. 218

ACKNOWLEDGEMENT. The act by which a person who has executed an instrument goes before an authorized officer, such as a Justice of the Peace or a Notary Public, and acknowledges the same as his genuine and voluntary act and deed. 405

ACRE. 43,560 square feet; 4,840 square yards; 160 square rods. 480

ACTUAL EVICTION. When a landlord forces a tenant to leave the leased premises either by physical force or by way of legal action. 172

ADJACENT. Near or close to.

ADJOINING. Joining or touching.

ADMINISTRATOR. A legal representative of a deceased person's estate, appointed by a court when the individual dies without a will or without naming someone as the executor of his estate in a will. 139

AD VALOREM. A tax or duty based on value and levied as a percentage of that value, e. g., 30 mills per dollar (3.0%) of property value. 192

ADVERSE POSSESSION. To acquire by adverse possession the legal title to another's land, the claimant must be in continuous possession during the period prescribed in the statute. This possession must be actual, visible, known to the world, with an intention by the possessor to claim the title as owner as against the rights of the true owner. 137

AFFIDAVIT. A written, voluntary statement signed and sworn to before some person authorized to take an oath.

AFFIDAVIT OF TITLE. An affidavit executed by the seller upon a sale of real property to assure the purchaser that there are no defects in the seller's title to the property. It supplements a title examination and covers matters that may not be revealed by a title search. 431

AFFILIATE BROKER. An individual who performs any act or engages in any transaction performed by a broker except the completion of the negotiation of any agreement or transaction. He is employed by and is under the direction and supervision of a broker or a regular employer engaged in the real estate business. 19

AGENCY. A legal relationship whereby one person (the agent) is employed to represent another (the principal) in business or legal affairs with third persons. 43

AGENCY BY ESTOPPEL. (See Ostensible Agency.) 46

AGENCY BY NECESSITY. An agency created by force of law when circumstances make such an agency necessary. This type of agency requires neither the voluntary consent of the principal nor the agent. 46

AGENT. One who is employed to represent another (a principal) in business and legal affairs with third persons. 44

AGREEMENT OF SALE. (See Purchase and Sale Agreement.) 294

AGRICULTURAL PROPERTY. A subclassification of income property relating to land devoted to, and especially suited for, the raising of crops or livestock. 25

AIDS. An incident of tenure in feudal England represented by those financial contributions of the tenant to his lord during times of stress. 109

AIR RIGHTS. The right of the owner of property to the space above his property which may be limited by statutes and zoning laws. 142

ALEATORY CONTRACT. One in which the promise of one party is conditioned on an uncertain event. 467

ALIENATION. The transfer of the owner's interest and title by the owner to another. 341

ALLODIAL. A term used in law to describe land held in absolute independence without being subject to any rent, service, or acknowledgement to a superior. 105

ALLUVION. An accession to land by the natural and gradual, imperceptible increase in earth at the shore or mouth or bank of a stream. Such addition belongs to the owner of the land to which it is added. (Also spelled alluvium.) 138

AMENITIES. An act, pursuit, feature, circumstance, or the like, that increases the value of real estate by enhancing the pleasantness or contributing to the enjoyment of the occupants.

AMORTIZATION. The process of gradually extinguishing a debt by a series of periodic payments to the creditor. The usual method of amortization calls for equal periodic payments made at equal intervals of time and is used principally in the liquidation of bonded indebtedness and mortgages. 352

ANNUITY. An amount, especially of money, payable yearly until death of the recipient.

ANTICIPATORY BREACH. The repudiation of a contractual obligation before the duty to perform arises. 84

APPARENT AUTHORITY. That which is conferred on an agent as a matter of law without the voluntary assent of either the principal or the agent. It is that authority which, though not actually granted, the principal knowingly permits the agent to exercise, or which he holds him out as possessing. 50

APPEAL. In general terms, an appeal is a resort to an upper court or tribunal. In civil practice, an appeal is the complaint to a superior court of an injustice done or error committed by an inferior one, whose judgment or decision the court above is called upon to correct or reverse. 190

APPRAISAL. An estimate or opinion of the value of a property as of a specific date. 214

APPRAISER. A person engaged in the procedures of estimating the value of property. This definition includes the professional appraiser who devotes the bulk of his time to appraising, either as a fee appraiser or as an employee of some agency. 214

APPROPRIATION. Relative to the process of taxation, appropriation is the decision of the taxing authority formally enacted into law to meet the expenditures forecast in the budget. 189

APPURTENANCES. Articles, interests, and rights which attach to and pass with real property, such as rights of way and other forms of easements. 143

ASSESSED VALUATION. The value placed upon real or personal property for taxation purposes by the appropriate governmental authority. 189

ASSESSMENT. The valuation of property to establish a basis for an ad valorem tax. The act of assessing, or the specific amount or value assessed. 189

ASSESSMENT ROLL. A list of all property and the owners thereof who are subject to taxation. 190

ASSESSOR. In the United States, the assessor is an elected official who evaluates property for the purpose of taxation. 190

ASSIGNEE. The one to whom a legal right is transferred. The assignee can acquire no greater rights than the assignor. 174

ASSIGNMENT. The transfer by one party to a contract (the assignor) of contract rights to another person (the assignee) who is not a party to the contract. 174

ASSIGNMENT OF LEASE. The transfer by a tenant of all his interest in a lease to another. If a tenant retains part of his term, the transfer is a sublease. 174

ASSIGNOR. The one who makes an assignment. 174

ATTACHMENT. The process by which a debtor's property (real or personal) is placed in the custody of the law and held as security pending the outcome of a creditor's suit. 146

ATTORNEY AT LAW. A person licensed to practice law.

ATTORNEY IN FACT. An agent whose authority to act for his principal is embodied in a written instrument called power of attorney. An attorney in fact may or may not be an attorney at law. 310

ATTRACTIVE NUISANCE DOCTRINE. A legal doctrine holding a property owner liable for maintaining an object or condition dangerous to children in a place where he knows or should know that children are likely to trespass. It is important to note that the dangerous condition of the property must be an artificial one, not natural, and must be reasonably recognized as dangerous to a child.

AUCTION. A public sale of property to the highest bidder. 355

AVULSION. The sudden and perceptible removal of land from the estate of one person to that of another, as by a sudden change in the course of a river. 138

BANK DRAFT. A check drawn by one bank upon another bank, payable to a third party upon demand. This form of check is often used in situations where a personal check is unacceptable.

BANKRUPT. One whose property has been taken over by a bankruptcy court under the National Bankruptcy Act. 54

BANKRUPTCY. A legal proceeding in which a debtor's property is taken over by a receiver or trustee in bankruptcy for the benefit of the creditors. 54

BARGAIN AND SALE. A type of deed in which title is transferred, but no warranties are made respecting title to or use of the property. 406

BARON. In English history, originally, a tenant holding immediately of the King or other feudal superior. If holding immediately of the King, he was known as a tenant-in-chief. 105

BASE LINES. As used in the Rectangular Survey System, base lines are east-west lines, running at right angles to meridian lines. 299

BENCH MARK. A mark affixed to a permanent object used to measure elevations by surveyors.

BENEFICIARY. One entitled to the income or enjoyment of property, the title to which is held by another as trustee; a person who receives a gift under a will; one to whom a life insurance policy is payable. 357

"BENEFIT" PRINCIPLE. Relative to taxation, the benefit principle holds that the tax liability of the taxpayer is more or less in direct proportion to benefits accruing to him. Gasoline taxes and social security employment taxes illustrate this principle. 187

BEQUEST. A provision in a will giving personal property.

BETTERMENTS. Improvements of an estate which render it better than mere repairing would do, i. e., sidewalks, roads, et cetera, by the government.

BILATERAL CONTRACT. One wherein a promise is exchanged for a promise, with each party being both a promisor and promisee. 66

BILL OF SALE. A written contract transferring personal property from one person to another. 297

BINDER. A preliminary agreement for the purchase of real estate accompanied by a down payment as evidence of good faith on the part of the purchaser. Also, a temporary agreement given by an insurance company to one who desires insurance coverage, "binding" the company to pay the loss should such occur before the insurance application is approved.
294

BLANKET MORTGAGE. One mortgage on a number of parcels of Real Property. 351

BLIGHTED AREA. A geographical area in which the value of real estate has appreciably decreased.

BLIND ADVERTISING. Relative to real estate brokerage, blind advertising is the insertion of an advertisement in any publication where only a post office box number, telephone number, or street address appears. Blind advertising is that which fails to disclose that the party advertising is a real estate broker and not a private party. Prohibited by many state license laws.

BLUE LAWS. Criminal laws originally enacted in many states making it a criminal act to conduct business activity on Sunday. These criminal laws have been repealed in many states.

BOARD OF EQUALIZATION. An appointed or elected board whose purpose is to equalize the assessments of the various taxing jurisdictions. 190

BONA FIDE. In good faith.

BOND. An agreement under which a person or corporation becomes surety to pay, within the stated limits, for financial loss caused to another by the act of default of a third person or by some contingency over which the principal may have no control. 147

BOUNDS. Artificial and natural boundaries containing land within fixed limits. 298

BREACH OF CONTRACT. Unexcused non-performance of a contract. The injured party has the right to collect damages and, in addition, may sometimes be excused from performing his part of the contract. 82

BROKER. Generally, a special agent who acts as an intermediary between other parties and assists in negotiating agreements between them. 18

BUDGET. Relative to the process of taxation, the budget is the forecast by a government of all expenditures that it will have to cover during a financial year and of the revenue that it will have to raise in order to so cover, after considering and allowing for governmental borrowing. 189

BUILDING CODE. The statutory rules and regulations of a local government which stipulate the materials and methods of construction of buildings within its jurisdiction. 142

BUILDING LINE. A line set by local ordinance drawn parallel to and a specific distance from the curb, beyond which no building can be erected.

BULKHEAD LINE. A line near the shore of a body of water, beyond which one cannot build.

BUNDLE OF RIGHTS. The rights of an owner of realty to possession, quiet enjoyment, disposition, and control of his property. 140

BUSINESS OPPORTUNITY. A business opportunity means and includes the sale or lease of a business and goodwill of an existing business enterprise or opportunity. Also called Business Chance. 26

BUSINESS TAX. A tax resulting from the ownership and operation of a business. Such a tax bears no relationship to the personal status of the business owner. 193

CAPACITY. In a legal sense, capacity (or competency) means legal competency or capacity as distinguished from either physical or mental and relates to competency to contract. Presumably, all persons are competent to contract <u>without</u> <u>restriction</u>, except infants, insane persons, drunkards, married women (in certain states), convicts, spendthrifts, or aged persons and corporations. 72

CAPITAL GAINS. Gains from the sale of capital assets in excess of appraisal values or costs. The special tax treatment for capital gains was originally enacted to limit the taxing of the property in a single year that may have appreciated in value over a longer period. It gave relief to those taxpayers with fluctuating or bunched income. It also provided an incentive to businesses and private investors. 195

CAPITAL GAIN TAX. A tax applied to gain or profit realized on the sale or exchange of a capital asset. A principal capital asset is a property held for investment or for personal use. 195

CAPITALIZATION. Relative to real estate income, it is the estimation of present value which is determined by future income from the property. A process of converting income into value. 219

CAPITALIZATION APPROACH. (See INCOME APPROACH.) 219

CASHIER'S CHECK. A bill of exchange drawn by a bank upon itself as drawee. Since the drawer and the drawee are one and the same, it is equivalent to a promissory note by the bank. (See BANK DRAFT.)

CAVEAT EMPTOR. Latin for "let the buyer beware." Legally, it indicates that the buyer takes the risk as to the quality of goods in a contract of sale and usually applies where the buyer has an opportunity to examine goods before purchasing.

CERTIFIED CHECK. A check on which the drawee bank guarantees that the drawer has sufficient funds on deposit to cover the amount reflected and that such funds are set aside for the purpose of payment. 306

CERTIFICATE OF ESTOPPEL. An instrument, commonly used when a mortgage is assigned, showing the unpaid principal and interest due on a mortgage. It may be executed by a mortgagee or holder of a lien and bars the signer from making a claim inconsistent with the instrument. 429

CERTIFICATE OF REGISTRATION. (See REGISTERED TITLE.) 417

CERTIFICATE OF TITLE. A document, written and signed by a title examiner, stating that in his opinion the seller has good title to property to be conveyed. 417

CHATTEL. Any tangible, movable or immovable personal property - as distinguished from intangible personalty and real property. Any species of property not amounting to a freehold. 102

CHATTEL INTEREST. An interest in corporeal hereditaments less than a freehold.

CHATTEL MORTGAGE. A mortgage on tangible personal property used primarily to give sellers security for the purchase price of goods bought on the installment plan. The buyer is generally given possession while title to the goods remains with the seller as security.

CHATTEL PERSONAL. Movable things. 102

CHATTEL REAL. Estate in land of less than freehold (e. g., estate for years) which descends under the rules of personal property. 164

CHECK. A quadrangle measuring 24 miles on each side and representing the largest unit of measure in the Rectangular Survey System. 299

CHOSE IN ACTION. An intangible personal property in the form of a right to receive or recover a debt or damages in an action on a contract or in a tort action.

CIVIL LAW. The laws concerned with protecting private rights and enforcing the duties that individuals owe to each other. The laws dealing with contracts, agency, real property, torts, and the like, are civil laws.

CLAIMANT. One who asserts a right or a title.

CLEAR RECORD TITLE. Title, which according to records in the registry of deeds, is clear and stands in the name of the owner claimed. 416

CLOSING DATE. The date established by contractual agreement for the transferring of title.

CLOSING STATEMENT. A final recapitulation of cash requirements for the purchase of property and for the disposition of the proceeds. 500

CLOSING TITLE. The transaction in which the formalities of a sale of real property are executed. 428

CLOUDY TITLE. A title affected by an attachment, a lien, judgment, et cetera. 411

COINSURANCE. Coinsurance is a concept which, in effect, makes the insured a "co-insurer" for the difference between a specified percentage of the insured's property and the amount of insurance actually carried. 454

COLLATERAL. Something of value, easily converted into cash, deposited as a pledge with a lender to secure the repayment of a loan. 361

COLLATERAL NOTE. A promissory note containing a clause stating that the maker gives the payee said note as security. In the event of default or dishonor, the payee has authority to sell the security and apply the proceeds to the payment of the note. 361

COLLATERAL SECURITY. (See SECURITY.) A security given in addition to the direct security. 361

COLLUSION. A secret agreement between two or more persons to take advantage of another with the object of depriving him of a legal right or property.

COLORABLE TITLE. (See TITLE.) A claim of title which, though it appears to be valid, actually is not, because some conditions necessary to the acquisition of title are missing.

COMMERCIAL BANK. A bank whose principal functions include making short-term loans and term loans, maintaining checking accounts, receiving time deposits, and discounting negotiable instruments. 333

COMMERCIAL PROPERTY. A type of income property, as distinguished from industrial or agricultural properties, which is normally zoned for business purposes. Property held for the production of income through rental to one or more tenants is also included in the subclassification of commercial properties. 22

COMMINGLING. When used in connection with real estate brokerage, commingling refers to the mingling of the money or other property of his principal with that of the broker's own. Commingling by the real estate broker may be cause for the Licensing Board to suspend, revoke, or refuse to renew a license of one guilty of such an unauthorized procedure. 48

COMMISSION. The amount due to a broker for services rendered, usually figured as a percentage of the total price. 308

COMMON LAW. A system of law, or a body of legal rules, derived from decisions of judges based upon accepted customs and traditions which were developed in England. Common law serves as the basis of the laws of every state in the United States except Louisiana, which based its laws upon the early laws of France. 99

COMMUNITY PROPERTY. Property owned jointly by a husband and wife by reason of their marriage. 135

COMMUTATION. Alteration; change; substitution; the act of substituting one thing for another.

COMMUTATION OF TAXES. The payment of a designated permanent or lump sum for the privilege of being exempted from taxes. Also, the settlement in advance of a specific sum in lieu of an ad valorem tax.

COMPARISON APPROACH. (See MARKET DATA APPROACH.) 217

CONDEMNATION. The taking of real property from an owner for a public purpose under a right of eminent domain upon the award and payment of just compensation. 141

CONDEMNATION PROCEEDINGS. Proceedings whereby the amount is determined to which an owner is entitled in compensation for his property taken under the right of eminent domain. 141

CONDITIONAL FEE. A fee simple interest in real property which continues while the condition exists. In effect, the estate begins on the happening of a contingency. 125

CONDITIONS. Facts or events which, by their occurrence or failure to occur, affect the rights and duties of parties to contracts. 82

CONDITION CONCURRENT. A stipulation or provision of a contract which requires the occurrence or non-occurrence of a specified event at the same time that the duty to perform arises. 82

CONDITION PRECEDENT. A condition that an event must occur, or not occur, before one or both of the parties is required to perform his part of the contract. 82

CONDITION SUBSEQUENT. A stipulation or provision in a contract which excuses a duty to perform a promise after that duty has arisen.

CONDOMINIUM. An apartment complex where individual apartments are purchased by the occupants rather than leased. 195

CONSIDERATION. The promise or conduct that each party to a contract gives in exchange for the promise or conduct of the other. Consideration supplied by each party is a necessary element in a valid contract, except in a formal contract. 71

CONSTRUCTION LOAN MORTGAGE. One made for the construction of a building on the mortgaged premises, whereunder installment advances are made by the mortgagee to the mortgagor as the construction progresses and usually upon completion of specific portions of the construction. 351

CONSTRUCTIVE EVICTION. When landlord makes it impossible or undesirable for the tenant to use the premises. (See EVICTION.) 172

CONSTRUCTIVE NOTICE. Notice arising from a legal presumption. The presumption is one of law and not of fact. Thus, when a mortgage is recorded with the proper public authorities, such is constructive notice of the mortgagee's (lender's) interest in the property. 354

CONTINGENCIES. That which is dependent on something that may or may not occur. A doubtful or uncertain future event. 378

CONTRACT. A promise or agreement, the performance of which is a legal duty, and the breach of which is actionable at law. 65

CONTRACT OF ADHESION. Relative to insurance, a contract drafted by the insurer, leaving little opportunity for negotiation by the insured. The insured may either "adhere" to or reject the offer of insurance. 468

CONSUMPTIVE TAX. A "hidden" tax passed on to the consumers and reflected in higher product prices, even though they initially were levied on the producers and distributors. 193

CONVENTIONAL MORTGAGE. One that is neither insured by the Federal Housing Administration nor guaranteed by the Veterans' Administration. 352

CONVERSION. Unauthorized control or use of another person's personal property.

CONVERSION FACTOR. (See GROSS RENT MULTIPLIER.) 220

CONVEYANCE. (See DEED.) A written instrument that transfers interest or title in real property from one person to another. 404

COOPERATIVE APARTMENT. An apartment in which the tenant buys stock in the corporation that owns the building rather than simply renting his apartment. 195

COOPERATIVE SALE. One where the seller is represented by one broker while the buyer is represented by a competing broker. 248

CORPOREAL PROPERTY. In describing real property, the actual land and all physical items affixed to it. 103

CORRECTION LINES. In Rectangular Survey Systems of land descriptions, correction lines are adjustments made to compensate for the curvature of the earth's surface. 305

COST. Cost is that amount which relates to past expenditures to produce or acquire a commodity. 211

COST APPROACH. An appraisal technique whereby the appraiser obtains an indication of value by adding to his estimate of the land's value his estimate of the depreciated reproduction cost of the building and other improvements. Also known as the "Reproduction Cost Approach," "Replacement Cost Approach," and the "Summation Approach." 218

COUNTER-OFFER. A counter-offer is a rejection of the original offer by proposing a new offer, thus terminating the original offer. (See REJECTION.) 69

COURSE. The direction of a boundary line relative to true or magnetic North. 298

COVENANT. A promise in writing under seal often used as a substitute for the verb "contracts." 349

COVENANTS OF TITLE. Guarantees made by a grantor when real property is conveyed by a warranty deed. These covenants are usually of seizin, quiet enjoyment, and against encumbrances. 409

CRIME. An act or omission, prohibited by the public law for the protection of the public, and punishable by the state in a judicial proceeding in the name of the state. 306

CUBAGE. The entire interior space of a building. Measured by multiplying the width by the depth by the height, figured from basement floor to the outer surfaces of the walls and roof. 482

CUBIC CONTENT. (See CUBAGE.) 482

CURTESY. The interest that a husband acquires by operation of law in any separate property of his wife. 129

DAMAGES. The sum allowed by law as compensation for an injury or loss caused by another. 84

DECEDENT'S DEBT LIEN. The right given by law to a creditor to establish a lien against the real and personal property of a deceased person which has been left to another. 145

DEED. A formal document by which title to real property is conveyed from one person to another. 404

DEED - POLL. A deed in which only the party making it executes it. Virtually all deeds to property are deeds poll. 406

DEFAULT. Failure of a party to fulfill a contractual obligation or to perform some duty. 84

DEFEASANCE CLAUSE. In "title theory" states where a mortgage conveys legal title subject to a condition, a defeasance clause provides for the automatic revestment of the title to the mortgagor upon payment of the secured obligation. 348

DEFICIENCY. That portion of a debt secured by a mortgage which is not satisfied from the sale of the mortgaged property. 356

DEFICIENCY JUDGMENT. A judgment entered against the mortgagor when the amount realized at a foreclosure sale is less than the sum due on the foreclosed mortgage. 356

DELIVERY IN ESCROW. A conditional delivery of something to a third person to be held until the happening of some event or the performance of some act. 424

DELIVERY OF DEED. The final act by which one who has signed and sealed an instrument signifies his intention that it shall have legal operation as his deed. Delivery by the grantor is requisite to the validity of this deed. 405

DEMAND MORTGAGE. One in which the repayment is at the demand of the mortgagee. Also, a mortgage which is outstanding after its maturity date is said to be "on demand" or "open." 352

DEMISE. The conveyance of an estate, chiefly by lease. 164

DEPRECIATION. The decline in value of an asset due to physical deterioration, functional obsolescence, and economic obsolescence. It is a term used in the Cost Approach of appraising. 218

DEVISE. A provision in a will giving real property or a right in real property to the beneficiary of a will. 139

DEVISEE. One who receives a devise. 139

DIRECT PROPERTY LOSS. The recognized loss sustained as a result of a peril in terms of the value of damage to physical property. 460

DIRECT REDUCTION MORTGAGE. One which calls for constant periodic payments of principal and interest which will pay off the principal sum loaned at the maturity date of the loan. 352

DIRECT SALES COMPARISON APPROACH. (See MARKET DATA APPROACH.) 217

DIRECT TAX. That borne by the person upon whom the government levies the tax. 192

DISCHARGE. (See SATISFACTION PIECE.) The word has many meanings. A person who is released from any legal obligation is discharged. 342

DISCLOSED PRINCIPAL. The principal in an agency relationship whose identity is made known to third persons dealing through the agent. 44

DISPOSSESS. A summary proceeding on a legal action brought by the landlord against the tenant to exclude him from occupancy of the real property for failure to pay rent.
173

DISSEISIN. A landlord's wrongful and injurious ousting of a tenant from possession of real property.

DISTANCES. The actual measurement between the terminal points of boundaries. 298

DISTRAIN. The taking for rent of property on the premises by the landlord. 176

DISTRESS. The taking of personal chattel out of the possession of a wrongdoer into the custody of the party injured, to procure a satisfaction for a wrong committed. 176

DISTRESS WARRANT. A common-law remedy by which the landlord may seize the personal property of the tenant to force payment of rent. 176

DOCTRINE OF ESTATES. The doctrine under the English law of real property which defined the relationship of the parties to the land, the person to the thing, as opposed to the person - to - person relationship reflected by the Doctrine of Tenures. 110

DOCTRINE OF TENURES. The doctrine under the English law of real property which explores the feudal relationship between the lord and vassal. 105

DOCUMENTARY STAMPS. State revenue stamps required to be affixed to a deed, with the amount required determined by the sale price of the property. 433

DOMICILE. A fixed and permanent home to which a person, if he is absent therefrom, intends to return. A person can have several residences at a time, but only one domicile. Domicile is not synonymous with residence. (See RESIDENCE.)

DOMINANT ESTATE. The right in the owner of one parcel of land by reason of such ownership to use the land of another (servient owner) for a specific purpose.   143

DOWER. The interest that a wife acquires by operation of law in any separate property of her husband.   129

DUPLEX. A house accommodating two families either side by side or one above the other on two or more floors.

DURESS. Physical violence, or the threat of it, done to a person or his goods to force him to perform some act that he otherwise would not perform.   77

EARNEST (EARNEST MONEY). Money paid as evidence of good faith or actual intent to complete a transaction, usually forfeited by willful failure to complete the transaction. Earnest money is often referred to as the amount paid by the purchaser as a deposit to the seller.   307

EASEMENT. A right or privilege to use the Real Property of another for a specific purpose. An easement is an encumbrance against the property.   143

EASEMENT APPURTENANT. An easement expressly granted in a deed conveying the property.   143

EASEMENT BY NECESSITY. Also known as an implied easement. An easement created by operation of the law where the easement is necessary and its prior use has been obvious.   143

EASEMENT BY PRESCRIPTION. An easement acquired through the open, continuous, adverse use of real property for a specified time period. The time required is usually the same as that necessary to obtain title by adverse possession.   143

ECONOMIC LIFE. The period for which a property can be used profitably.

ECONOMIC OBSOLESCENCE. A depreciation loss which results from external causes as of the date of the appraisal from the cost of the property new. Changes in character of a neighborhood or environmental changes may cause economic obsolescence. It is a term used in the Cost Approach to appraising.   218

ECONOMIC RENT. The rent a property on the open market would command if it were available for rental.   219

EFFICIENT AND PROCURING CAUSE. The words used to describe the requirements in determining if a broker is entitled to a commission. The broker must be the procuring cause of the consummated transaction, and his services must have been the effective cause by which the transaction was brought about.   247

EJECTMENT. A legal action brought to regain possession of real property and to obtain damages for its unlawful retention. (See DISPOSSESS.)

EMBLEMENTS. Certain annual crops that the tenant has the right to harvest after his tenancy has ended, provided that they are the result of his own care and labor. 25

EMINENT DOMAIN. The power of the federal, state, and local governments to appropriate private property for public use or for the public welfare. 141

ENCROACHMENT. Illegal infringement upon the property of another. It may consist of a wall, cornice, casement windows, or garage doors that extend upon adjoining property when opened, et cetera.

ENCUMBRANCE. A lien, charge, or claim against real property which diminishes the value of the property, but does not prevent the passing of title. An existing mortgage on a property is the usual encumbrance. 421

EQUITABLE TITLE. A person's right to obtain absolute ownership of property to which another has title under the law. A present right, created at the time of signing the sales agreement, which may ripen into ownership upon performance of conditions subsequent, i. e., conveyancing of title. 310

EQUITY. The owner's interest in the value of real property usually reflected as the difference between the market value and the balance owed on the mortgage.

EQUITY OF REDEMPTION. The right of a mortgagor (borrower) to recover (redeem) the property and regain legal title to it after default and before foreclosure sale by paying the amount due in full with interest. A clause in a mortgage waiving the equity of redemption has no legal effect, as this equity is extinguished only by foreclosure. (See REDEMPTION.) 354

EROSION. Wearing away of land by forces of nature, e. g., rivers, rainfall.

ESCALATOR CLAUSE. A clause in a contract that permits an upward or downward adjustment of obligation should certain events occur. 176

ESCHEAT. The return to the state of real or personal property if the owner dies without legal heirs. 142

ESCROW. A conditional delivery of something to a third person to be held until the happening of some event or the performance of some act. 424

ESTATE. An interest or right in the use, enjoyment, and disposition of land. The term "estate" is often used synonymously with the word "interest." 110

ESTATE AT WILL. (See TENANCY AT WILL.) 163

ESTATE FOR YEARS. A lease for a definite time or term. (See TENANCY FOR YEARS.) 163

ESTATE IN REVERSION. The remainder of a grantor's estate which commences in possession after the termination of the estate granted by him. A lessor, for example, has the estate in reversion after the lease is terminated. 127

ESTOPPEL. A bar to one's alleging or denying a fact because of one's own private action by which the contrary has been admitted, implied, or determined. 46

ESTOPPEL CERTIFICATE. A certificate which provides a written statement signed by one, which, when acted upon by another, cannot be denied. 429

ET AL. Latin for "and another" or "and others."

ET UX. Latin for "and wife" - abbreviated from et uxor.

EVICTION. A forcible removal of a tenant by a landlord from possession of real property (actual eviction), or a violation by the landlord of an important provision of the lease amounting to an interference with the tenant's useful and peaceful enjoyment of the premises (constructive eviction). 172

EXCLUSIVE AGENCY. The appointment by the owner of one real estate broker as exclusive agent for the sale of his property during a specific period of time. The owner usually reserves the right to sell his property himself. 240

EXCLUSIVE RIGHT OF SALE. The appointment by the owner of one real estate broker with the exclusive right to sell his property. Regardless of who produces a customer or sells the property, the broker is entitled to his commission. 240

EXECUTED CONTRACT. One in which the terms of the contract have been fully performed by all parties thereto. 66

EXECUTION OF DEED. The signing, sealing, and delivery of a deed. Note, however, that to be completely effective, a deed should also be acknowledged and recorded.

EXECUTION OF JUDGMENT. A legal writ directing an officer of the law to carry out a judgment. Execution may be issued on the judgment to the county sheriff, who may make a compulsory collection (seizure and levy) against any property or money of the judgment debtor in his jurisdiction. 147

EXECUTOR. A person named in a will to be the legal representative of the testator's estate. 139

EXECUTORY CONTRACT. One wherein something remains to be done at some future time. 66

EXPRESS AGENCY. An agency resulting when the contract which creates the agency relationship explicitly describes the scope of the agent's authority to act for the principal. 46

EXPRESS AUTHORITY. The instructions of a principal to his agent that are explicitly described in the provision of the agency agreement between them. 50

EXPRESS CONTRACT. One wherein the terms are expressly or specifically stated by the parties, either orally or in writing. 66

EXTENSION OF MORTGAGE. An agreement between mortgagor (borrower) and mortgagee (lender) postposponing to a later date the time when payment of the principal amount of the mortgage is to become due.

FACE VALUE. The value of an instrument that is set forth in the instrument itself.

FALSE ADVERTISING. Advertising which is misleading in a material respect.

FEALTY. An incident of tenure in feudal England manifested by an oath taken by the tenant in which he promised to his lord his complete loyalty. 109

FEDERAL HOUSING ADMINISTRATION (FHA). The governmental agency which insures loans on homes which meet FHA standards. 373

FEE SIMPLE. The absolute ownership of real property giving to the owner and his heirs the unconditional power of disposition and other rights. 123

FEE SIMPLE ABSOLUTE. Synonymous with Fee Simple. 123

FEE SIMPLE DETERMINABLE. A fee simple in real estate that may be terminated by the grantor if the grantee violates the terms of the conveyance. 123

FEE SIMPLE LIMITED. (See FEE SIMPLE QUALIFIED.) 123

FEE SIMPLE QUALIFIED. One that may be determined upon the fulfillment of a contingent qualification or limitation, or the happening of a certain event. Sometimes referred to as "fee simple limited." Fee upon condition and fee simple determinable are two types of a fee simple qualified. 123

FEE TAIL. A freehold estate which endures so long as the tenant or any of his descendants live. 126

FEE UPON CONDITION. A conditional conveyance in fee simple by the grantor to the grantee. It is an optional right retained by the grantor and until it is exercised, the fee continues. 125

F. H. A. (Federal Housing Administration). A federal government agency that insures real estate loans. 373

FIDUCIAL CONTRACT. One which establishes a fiduciary relationship between contracting parties, such as an insurance contract. 468

FIDUCIARY. One who is in a position of trust or confidence with respect to another person. 47

FIDUCIARY RELATION. A broad term embracing both technical and informal relations wherein one trusts or relies upon another. It exists whenever a special confidence reposes in one who, in good conscience, is bound to act in good faith and with due regard to protecting the interests of the one reposing the confidence. 47

FIRST LIEN. A lien which takes priority over all other liens. A tax lien, for example, is a first lien and takes priority over all other liens . . . including the mortgage note. 191

FISCAL. Of or pertaining to the public treasury or revenue, of or pertaining to financial matters generally. 188

FIXTURE. An item of personal property that loses its identity as such and through its attachment to or association with real estate becomes real property. 238

FORECLOSURE. A proceeding against property which secures a debt. Foreclosure is brought upon default to cut off the mortgagor's equitable right to redeem the property. 354

FOREHAND RENT. Rent may be payable in advance by agreement between landlord and tenant.

FORESHORE. The land which lies between the high and low water marks and which is alternately wet and dry because of the flow of the tide.

FRANKALMOIGN TENURE. A spiritual type of agreement in feudal England involving the tenant who was always a priest or religious body who would provide the lord with a divine service. The word "frankalmoign" means "free alms." 106

FRAUD. Willful misrepresentation of a material fact which results in a person's assent to a contract in reliance upon it to his damage. The misrepresentation must be a statement of fact, not an opinion. 78

FREE TENURE. The holding of land for services rendered by those in the feudal pyramid down to, but not including, the workers of the field. 105

FREEHOLD. An estate in which the owner of real property retains title thereto for a period of indeterminate duration, such as an estate in fee simple or a life estate. 123

FRONT FOOT. A standard of measurement one foot wide along the property frontage.

FRONTAGE. The length of the boundary line which abuts the street.

FUNCTIONAL OBSOLESCENCE. A depreciation loss caused by overcapacity, inadequacy, unattractive styling, poor or inefficient design, et cetera, as of the date of the appraisal from the cost of the property new. Functional obsolescence is an inherent part of the property. This is a term used in the Cost Approach of appraising. 218

FUNDAMENTAL RISK. A risk arising from losses that are impersonal in both origin and consequence, such as floods, earthquakes, war, and inflation. 450

FURTHER ASSURANCE. A special warranty, called a covenant, contained in a warranty deed where the grantor agrees to obtain and give to the grantee and to his successors any legal documents that may be necessary to perfect the title. 410

FUTURE ESTATE. An estate in which the time for obtaining possession is deferred to some date in the future. (See ESTATE IN REVERSION.) 127

GENERAL AGENT. A general agent is one given broad authority to act on behalf of his principal in a number of acts. 45

GENERAL LISTING. (See OPEN LISTING.) 240

G. I. MORTGAGE. A mortgage guaranteed by the Veterans' Administration. 368

GOOD TITLE. A title free from encumbrances, such as mortgages and liens, as disclosed by a complete abstract of the title as taken from the records in the recorder's office.

GOODWILL. Every positive advantage accruing to a business or acquired by a proprietor, whether connected with the premises in which the business is conducted, or with the name under which it is managed, or with any other matter carrying with it the benefit of the business. The favor which the management of a business wins from the public. 27

GRANT. The transfer of title to real property by means of a deed. 404

GRANTEE. One to whom real property is conveyed by deed. 404

GRANTING CLAUSE. A required clause in the deed where the seller agrees to transfer the property involved. 404

GRANTOR. One who conveys his real property to another by deed. 404

GREAT PONDS. Natural ponds with a superficial area of more than ten acres. The state has title to such ponds. If more than ten, but less than twenty acres in area, owners of abutting land may control access to the pond. If over twenty acres in area, however, the public must be allowed access. May vary among states.

GROSS INCOME. Total income before deduction of expenses.

GROSS LEASE. A lease wherein all property charges regularly incurred through ownership, such as operating expenses, taxes, and insurance, are paid by landlord. 175

GROSS RENT MULTIPLIER. The number which reflects the ratio between the sales price of a property and its monthly unfurnished rental. It is a term used in the Income Approach of appraising, and it is sometimes called the Conversion Factor. 220

GROSS RENT MULTIPLIER APPROACH. (See INCOME APPROACH.) 220

GROUND LEASE. A lease of land only. 175

GROUND RENT. A price per year or term of years paid for the right to occupy and improve a piece of land. It is a rent reserved by a grantor for himself, his heirs and assigns in conveying land in fee.

GUARANTY. A contract whereby one party agrees to answer for the debt or default of another. 341

GUARDIAN. One who has legal custody of the person or property of a minor or other incompetent. 72

HABENDUM CLAUSE. The clause in a deed or mortgage which sets forth the extent or duration of the grantee's ownership in the property granted. 421

HAZARD. A condition that increases the likelihood of loss. 449

HEAD LEASE. The principal lease agreement between landlord and tenant, varyingly referred to as the original lease, the main lease, the master lease, and the underlying lease. 176

HEIR. One entitled to inherit realty in the case of intestacy in accordance with the statute of descent. 139

HEREDITAMENTS. Any property that may be inherited. 139

HIGHEST AND BEST USE. The most profitable likely use to which a property can be put. 213

HOLDING OVER. The act of retaining, without the landlord's consent, possession of leased property after the term of the lease has expired. 170

HOLDOVER TENANT. A tenant who remains in possession after his lease expires. 170

HOMAGE. An incident of tenure in feudal England whereby the tenant acknowledged himself as the vassal of the lord. 109

HOMESTEAD. Real estate occupied by the owner which is given certain exemptions from the laws of conveyance, descent, and attachment. 131

HOMESTEAD LAWS. State statutes protecting certain property belonging to a debtor from the claims of his creditors. 3

HUNDRED PERCENT LOCATION. That location best adapted to carrying on a given type of business.

ILLEGAL CONTRACT. An agreement unenforceable in court because of its object or because the manner in which it is to be performed is contrary to the law or to public policy. 73

IMMUNITY. A freedom on the part of one person against having a legal relation altered by a given act or omission to act on the part of another person. For every immunity, there is a corresponding disability. 139

IMPLIED AGENCY. An agency voluntarily created by the acts and conduct of the parties (the principal and the agent) indicating an intention to create an agency relationship. 46

IMPLIED AUTHORITY. That authority created by the acts or conduct of the principal in connection with the principal's conferring of express authority on the agent. That authority necessary to carry out the express authority. 50

IMPLIED CONTRACT. One wherein the terms are not stated but are implied from the conduct of the parties. 66

IMPLIED EASEMENT. An easement by necessity. 143

IMPROVEMENT. A valuable addition made to real property, intended to enhance its value or beauty or to adapt it for new or further purposes. 297

INCHOATE. "As yet not perfect." Incomplete situations out of which rights and duties may later arise as for example, a wife's dower is inchoate until her husband's death. Also, recently or just begun; being in the first stages; rudimentary. 130

INCIDENTS OF TENURE. In feudal England, incidents of tenure were those obligations owed to the lord by the tenant incidental to the tenant's right in holding for his lord. These obligations were in addition to the services rendered relative to security, subsistence, splendor, and spirit. Specifically, these incidents involved obligations incurred during the tenant's lifetime, such as, homage, fealty, and aids; and those incurred upon death of the tenant, such as, wardship, relief, escheat, and marriage. 109

INCOME APPROACH. An appraisal technique or method whereby the evaluation of real estate is estimated on the assumption that value is indicated by the present and anticipated income the real estate can reasonably be expected to command. The Income Approach is also known as the Capitalization Approach and the Gross Rent Multiplier Approach. 219

INCOME PROPERTY. A broad classification of property which produces income directly (e. g., rental property) or as a factor in the production of income (e. g., commercial property used in one's trade or business). 22

INCOME TAX. A tax relating to the product or income from property or from business pursuits. A tax on a person's income, emoluments, profits, and the like, or the excess thereof over a certain amount. 193

INCORPOREAL PROPERTY. Any interest in realty which cannot be considered physical and which is not apparent. Examples would be easements, rights of way, and licenses. 103

INDEMNIFICATION CONTRACTS. Relative to insurance, indemnification contracts are designed to cover pure risks . . . risks in which there are no promises of gain. 469

INDEMNITY. An agreement that one party will secure another against loss or damage due to the happening of a specified event. 51

INDENTURE. A sealed agreement between two or more parties. Also, a deed executed by both parties as distinguished from a deed executed only by the grantor (i. e., a deed - poll).

INDEPENDENT CONTRACTOR. A person, usually in business for himself, who contracts to do a complete job for another, being responsible to the latter for the finished product only, and not for the means by which that product is produced. 44

INDIRECT PROPERTY LOSS. The decrease of income and / or the increase of expenses caused by direct losses suffered. 460

INDIRECT TAX. That tax demanded in the first instance from one person in the expectation and intention that he shall indemnify himself at the expense of another.
192

INDUSTRIAL PROPERTY. "A combination of land, improvements, and machinery which has been synchronized and perfected into a functioning unit intended for the assembling, processing, and manufacturing of finished or partially finished products from raw material or fabricated parts ... industrial property includes property used for the production of natural resources, such as, minerals and oils."
American Institute of Real Estate Appraisers 23

INHERITANCE. A term used to describe a real property that is taken from the estate of a deceased person and given to his heirs under the Intestacy Laws. 139

INSURABLE INTEREST. An interest residing in an individual who is subject to realizing a loss as a consequence of his relationship to a property. Any person who stands to suffer a loss which can be expressed in monetary terms has an insurable interest. 453

INSURABLE RISK. One that is economic in character, subject to appraisal in monetary terms, relating to a fortuitous event, and where the units of risk are represented in large numbers. 451

INSURANCE. A plan for cooperatively sharing risks with a group so that the consequences of severe loss will not fall too heavily on any individual. 452

INTANGIBLE PROPERTY. Any interest in personal property is intangible property. Examples would be copyrights, royalties, et cetera, and are called "choses in action."
104

INTEREST. (See ESTATE.) An interest in real property is known as an estate which may involve anything from a fee simple estate which indicates absolute ownership to a leasehold which is the right to use property for a fixed term on payment of rent. An interest in real property must include its use, possession, and disposition. 103

INTESTACY. Death without making a will. 139

INTESTATE. A person dies intestate who has not made a will. 139

INTESTATE LAWS. State laws regulating the distribution and apportionment of a person's estate when that person dies without having previously executed a valid will.
139

INVALID. Having no legal force; void.
66

INVESTMENT PROPERTY. Investment property (as distinguished from income property) is real property acquired for the specific purpose of realizing a profitable return at some future date. It is property which is not held, as is income property, for the immediate and continuing production of income.
25

JOINT TENANCY. An estate held by two or more persons at the same time under the same title or source of ownership in which each has the same degree of interest and the same right of possession. Joint tenancy has the distinct character of survivorship.
133

JUDGMENT. An adjudication by a court after a trial or hearing of the rights of the parties.
147

JUDICIAL SALE. The sale of a defendant's property to secure money to pay a judgment secured by a successful plaintiff.
137

JUNIOR FINANCING. Financing real property by means of a mortgage which is a subordinate lien to an existing first mortgage.
352

JUNIOR MORTGAGE. A mortgage which is legally subordinate to the first mortgage, such as a second or third mortgage.
352

JUSTICE OF THE PEACE. A local magistrate empowered chiefly to administer summary justice in minor cases, to commit for trial, and to administer oaths and perform marriages.
423

LACHES. Unreasonable delay in bringing suit or seeking remedy in an equity court. For a defendant to plead laches as a defense to a suit, he must show that he suffered from the plaintiff's delay in bringing suit.

LAND. The solid part of the surface of the earth and everything annexed to it. Within the Statute of Frauds, land includes all rights and interests in the land as well.
103

LAND TRUST. In effect, a method for secret ownership. It provides a method for placing title of record in a trustee, thus concealing the actual owner's identity from exposure to the general public. Normally, the power to control and direct the property is vested not in the trustee, but in the owners.

LANDLORD. A person who rents real property to another. More specifically, one who owns real property and grants an estate less than freehold to a party known as the tenant.
164

LATERAL SUPPORT. The duty of an owner of real property not to use his land in such a manner as to undermine or cause the collapse of the land of an adjoining owner.

LAW DAY. The day prescribed in a bond, mortgage, or defeasible deed for payment of the debt secured thereby, or, in default of payment, the forfeiture of property mortgaged at foreclosure.

LEASE. A contract, written or oral, between the owner of real property (the lessor or landlord) and a tenant (the lessee) for the possession and use of lands and improvements in return for the payment of rent. In most states, a lease for more than one year must be in writing to be enforceable.
168

LEASEBACK. A simultaneous sale of property and a lease back to the seller by the buyer who becomes the landlord (lessor). It is sometimes referred to as a "sales-leaseback."
176

LEASEHOLD. An estate in real property granted for a definite and certain term of years under the condition of a lease.
166

LEASEHOLD MORTGAGE. A mortgage of the lessee's interest under a lease (which is obtainable normally only from insurance companies).
352

LEGACY. Personal property disposed of by a will.
139

LEGAL DESCRIPTION. A description of the boundaries of a parcel of property in sufficient detail to locate and identify the property and allow enforcement of the boundaries in a court of law.
297

LEGATEE. One who receives a bequest; the person to whom a legacy is given.
139

LESSEE. One to whom property is rented under a lease.
164

LESSOR. (See LANDLORD.) One who rents property to another.
164

LEVY. Relative to the process of taxation, a tax levy is the imposition of a tax by the legislative body on a specific source for a specific amount for a specific purpose.
189

LIABILITY INSURANCE. Liability insurance indemnifies the insured against liability and was developed as a consequence of and in response to tort law.
457

LIABILITY LOSS. A loss resulting from a legal judgment that takes one's property lawfully, or the result of a relinquishing of property voluntarily under threat of suit.
457

LICENSE. The right to do something on the land of another without possessing any real estate or interest therein that would otherwise be unlawful. A license is a purely personal right which terminates at the death of either the grantor or the grantee and is not transferred with title.
143

LIEN. A right, hold, or claim against specific property as security for a debt.
144

LIENEE. One whose property is subject to a lien.
144

LIENOR. One who has a right of lien upon the property of another.
144

LIFE ESTATE. An interest in real or personal property that lasts only during the owner's lifetime or the lifetime of some other person.
127

LIFTING CLAUSE. The clause in a second (junior) mortgage which specifically provides that the second mortgagee shall waive priority of his mortgage in favor of any subsequent mortgage made in refinancing the existing first mortgage. It allows the borrower to lift out the first mortgage and replace it without affecting the second mortgage.

LIQUIDATED DAMAGES. An amount, specified by parties to a contract, payable for breach of contract.
84

LIS PENDENS. Suit pending. A notice that a lawsuit affecting title to, or possession, use, and enjoyment of, real property is pending. Such notice is required by state statutes to be filed in a designated record office.

LISTING. An agreement between a property owner and a broker to sell or lease the property.
240

LITTORAL PROPERTY. Real property situated on the shore of a lake, sea, or ocean, as distinguished from riparian property which is property situated on the banks of rivers and streams.
138

LONG-TERM LEASE. A lease of real property for an extended period of time, as long as 99 years, with an obligation on the part of the tenant to improve the leased property with suitable buildings within a given period.

LORD. A titled nobleman. Applied formally in England to a baron and, less formally, to any temporal peer from baron to marquis. With reference to feudalism, the lord is he of whom a fee or estate is held; the proprietor of feudal land.
105

MAKER. The party in a promissory note who promises to pay a sum of money. 340

MALFEASANCE. The commission of an unlawful act, especially by a public official.

MARKETABLE TITLE. A title which a court would compel the purchaser to accept under the terms of his contract. A title of such character that no apprehension as to its validity would occur to the mind of a reasonable and intelligent person. 412

MARKET DATA APPROACH. An appraisal method to determine the estimated value of a property by comparing it with similar properties which have been recently sold, or which are currently on the market in the same or competing areas. Also known as the Sales Approach, the Comparison Approach, and the Direct Sales Comparison Approach. 217

MARKET PRICE. The price actually paid for a property. 211

MARKET VALUE. The price in terms of money for which a property if exposed for a reasonable time will sell in a competitive market at a particular time by a seller to a buyer, each acting prudently and without obligation to act, with knowledge of the uses to which the property can be adapted. 211

MARSHALLING. The arranging of conflicting claims or interest in such an order of sequence so as to be most equitable to all concerned.

MATURITY. The date on which an instrument becomes due.

MATURITY VALUE. The value at which a negotiable instrument is redeemed when it becomes due.

MECHANIC'S LIEN. The statutory lien of a laborer, contractor, subcontractor, or material-man who performs work or furnishes material for the permanent improvement of real property. Such lien has for its purpose to subject the land of an owner to a lien for material and labor expended in the construction of buildings, which buildings having been placed on the land become a part thereof by the law of accession. 146

MEETING OF THE MINDS. A mutual agreement between two or more parties to enter into a contractual relationship. 67

MESSUAGE. A dwelling house with the adjacent buildings and the adjoining lands.

METES. Lineal measurements (e. g., inches, feet, yards) determining the quantity of land. 298

METES AND BOUNDS. The boundary lines of real property, including termination points and angular direction. The description of the boundaries of real property. 298

MERCHANTABLE TITLE. Title not subject to such reasonable doubt as would create a just apprehension of its validity in the mind of a reasonable, prudent, and intelligent person. 412

MILITARY TENURE. An agreement (tenure) in feudal England between the King and Baron whereby the Baron would hold land in return for providing a certain quota of Knights for the King's army. 106

MILL. The measure used to reflect the property tax rate; one tenth of one cent. A property taxed at $55 per thousand of assessed valuation has a tax rate of 55 mills. 198

MINOR. One who has not reached the age of a majority which is 18 in most states. A minor has only a limited right to enter into a contract. His contracts, for the most part, are voidable. 72

MISFEASANCE. The wrongful and injurious doing of an act which one might do in a lawful manner; a trespass.

MISREPRESENTATION. A mis-statement of material fact, reliance upon which results in contractual agreement. Willful misrepresentation which results in a person's assent to a contract in reliance upon it, to his damage, is fraud. 78

MONTH-TO-MONTH TENANCY. A form of tenancy whereby no definite term is specified, and the rent is payable monthly. A month-to-month tenant is one who pays rent monthly and has no lease.

MONUMENT. A building, structure, or other object, given in the title as part of the boundary description. 298

MORAL HAZARD. Any characteristic of an insured that might increase the severity or frequency of loss. 449

MORTGAGE DEED. A written document evidencing the fact that the real property is given as security for the payment of a loan. 347

MORTGAGE FORECLOSURE. (See FORECLOSURE.) 355

MORTGAGE NOTE. A form of promissory note that is secured by a mortgage deed. 338

MORTGAGE REDEMPTION INSURANCE. A type of life insurance which allows the policy beneficiary to pay off a mortgage debt upon the death of the insured.

MORTGAGEE. The person to whom a mortgage is given (the lender of the money secured by the mortgage). 348

MORTGAGEE IN POSSESSION. A creditor who has taken over the income from mortgaged property when the owner (debtor) defaults on the mortgage.

MORTGAGOR. The person who gives a mortgage (the borrower of the money secured by the mortgagee). 348

MULTIPLE LISTING. An arrangement whereby member brokers bring their listing to the attention of other member brokers with the understanding that if a sale results, the commission therefrom will be split between the broker furnishing the listing and the broker responsible for the sale.

MUNICIPAL LIEN CERTIFICATE. A certification prepared by a municipality reflecting the liens or lack thereof placed on a specific property by the municipality.

NECESSARIES. A term frequently found in contract law relating to what constitutes the necessaries of life. Normally, food, clothing, shelter, medical attention, and some degree of education are included in the term. 72

NET. That remaining after deduction of all charges, outlays, losses, et cetera.

NET LEASE. One which requires, as consideration, the payment of rent to the lessor, plus the payment of part or all of the maintenance and operational costs of the property. 175

NET LISTING. A listing wherein a price is expressly agreed upon between the owner and the broker, below which the owner will not sell and at which price the broker receives no commission. The broker's commission is to be the amount over and above the net listing price. 240

NIREB. NATIONAL INSTITUTE of REAL ESTATE BROKERS. The educational arm of the NATIONAL ASSOCIATION OF REALTORS.

NONCONFORMING USE. The continuance in use of existing structures, even though the area has been zoned for different purposes. Rebuilding or replacing such structures, however, may be prohibited. 141

NON-RESIDENT. An individual whose principal place of abode is without the state, and a corporation, society, association, or partnership organized, formed, or existing under the laws of another state and which does not maintain a usual place of business within the state.

NOTARY PUBLIC. A public officer who has authority to attest and certify deeds and other writings, to take affidavits and other depositions, and to protest negotiable instruments. 423

NOVATION. The substitution of a new contract for the existing one. When a new party is substituted for one of the original parties, or when new contract terms are agreed upon, novation occurs. 81

NUISANCE. A tort which arises from an unlawful, unreasonable, or unjustifiable use by a person of his own property in such a way as to restrict others in the use and enjoyment of their property.

OATH. A solemn affirmation that statements made or to be made are true.

OBJECTIVE VALUE. (See VALUE IN EXCHANGE.) 209

OBSOLESCENCE. A loss in value brought about by functional inutility, economic, and other changes. 218

OFFER. An intentional, definite, and communicated proposal made by one party (the offeror) to another (the offeree) indicating a willingness to do or refrain from doing something on condition that the other party do or refrain from doing something. 67

OFFEREE. The person to whom an offer is made. 67

OFFEROR. The person making an offer. 67

OPEN LISTING. A listing with a broker by the owner which does not preclude other brokers from selling the property. 240

OPEN MORTGAGE. One which can be paid at any time. Building and Loan Associations usually permit such prepayment. Note: a mortgage which is still outstanding after its maturity date is also referred to as an "open" mortgage, or "on demand." 352

OPEN-END MORTGAGE. One which may be increased by subsequent advances of principal which do not in the aggregate exceed the amount by which the original principal loan was reduced by amortization. 352

OPERATIVE WORDS. Any words indicating an intention to convey title to real property. The words used to effect the conveyance are known as the "operative words." Such words must be carefully chosen as they reflect the type of deed used. The clause of the deed in which these operative words are found is referred to as the "granting clause." 419

OPTION. The right given by the owner (optionor) to another (the optionee) to purchase or lease a property at a specific price within a set time for which the optionor is paid by the optionee a consideration for releasing this right. 69

OPTIONEE. The person receiving an option. 69

OPTIONOR. (See OPTION.) The person giving the option. 69

ORDINANCE. A law, regulation, or rule passed by a municipality. 142

ORIGINATION FEE. A charge by a bank for taking a mortgage, usually a percentage of the mortgage. 371

OSTENSIBLE AGENCY. One created by force of law and which comes into existence without the voluntary assent of either the principal or the agent. Under certain circumstances, the law prevents (estops) the principal from denying that it exists. An ostensible agency is sometimes referred to as an agency by estoppel. It is created when the principal (either intentionally or for want of ordinary care) induces another to believe that a third person is his agent. 45

OVER-IMPROVEMENT. An improvement not in consonance with the "highest and best use"... or an improvement exceeding that justified by local conditions. 213

OWELTY. The money payment ordered by the court in a partition proceeding to be paid by the favored co-tenant to compensate the other co-tenants where there is a physical partition, but division into exactly equal shares is unattainable. 135

OWNERSHIP. Generally used interchangeably with the term "title" to indicate one's right to possess, use, and dispose of property. 100

PACKAGE MORTGAGE. A mortgage which covers both real and personal property. 353

PARTIALLY DISCLOSED PRINCIPAL. A principal is considered partially disclosed when the agent, in his dealings with third persons, reveals the existence of an agency relationship, but does not divulge the identity of his principal. 44

PARTICULAR RISK. A risk which results from losses that originate in individual events and whose impact is felt in consequences that are localized. 450

PARTY TO BE CHARGED. In the Statute of Frauds, it is the party against whom an action on a contract is brought. 74

PARTY WALL. A dividing wall between two buildings having separate ownership which is used as an exterior wall of each building. Also, a wall built along a common boundary for the common benefit of separate owners.

PASSAGE OF TITLE. The transfer of ownership from one to another. 402

PATENT. Conveyance of title to government land. 4

PAYEE. The party to whom an instrument is made payable. 340

PENALTY. Relative to the process of taxation, a penalty is the "interest" charged for non-payment of taxes on or before the due date. 191

PERCENTAGE LEASE. A lease wherein the amount of the rental is determined by a percentage of the business transacted on the leased property . . . usually a percentage of the tenant's gross sales. 175

PERCOLATION TEST. A test of the soil for drainage to determine rate of absorption.

PERFORMANCE. The fulfillment of contract obligations which terminates the contract. 81

PERIL. The source of loss. 449

PERIODIC TENANCY. A tenancy which gives the tenant the right to occupy property for an indefinite period of time which may be from week to week, month to month, or year to year. 166

PERMISSIVE WASTE. Omission or failure to act to prevent injury to the leased property which results in damage. 174

PERSONAL EASEMENT. An easement made separately by contract and binding only on the parties to the agreement. 143

PERSONAL INSURANCE. Personal insurance relates to personal risks associated with disability, excessive longevity, and premature death. 458

PERSONAL LOSS. That which directly affects an individual, such as those losses resulting from sickness or accident. 460

PERSONAL PROPERTY. Tangible and intangible things which are not real property, but which are capable of ownership. 102

PERSONALTY. (See PERSONAL PROPERTY.) 102

PHYSICAL DETERIORATION. A depreciation loss caused by an impairment of the physical condition of the property through action of the elements, age, and use. It is a term used in the Cost Approach of appraising. 218

PHYSICAL HAZARD. That which arises from either the natural condition of property or from the impersonal surrounding of property, such as a building located by the bank of a river which is susceptible to flooding. 449

PLAINTIFF. The complaining party or the one who commences an action at law. 147

PLAT. A map or plan of real property indicating its subdivision into smaller lots or parcels. 305

PLAT BOOK. A record showing the location, size, and name of the owners of each plot of real property in a given area. 305

PLOTTAGE VALUE. Increment in value occurring when several tracts of land are combined into one package.

POINTS. (See ORIGINATION FEE.) 371

POLICE POWER. The power which state and local governments have to protect the property, life, health, and well-being of their citizens by legislation. 142

PORTABILITY. The method of annexation approach which is a major factor in determining if an item is realty or personalty. If the item is attached permanently to the land or building, it is considered to be realty. If it can be carried by a person, it is considered personalty. 238

POST-DATED CHECK. One that bears a date later than the actual date on which it is written. The bank may not make payment before the date stated.

POSTPONEMENT OF LIEN. Giving first priority to another lien.

POWER. A power is an ability on the part of a person to produce a change in a legal relation by doing or not doing a given act. For every power, there is a corresponding liability. 139

POWER OF ATTORNEY. Written evidence of the authority to act in a representative capacity which the principal gives his agent in an agency relationship. 45

PREPAYMENT OF MORTGAGE LOAN. Payment of all or any part of the principal amount of a mortgage loan in advance of the time when payment is due. 340

PRESCRIPTION. A means of acquiring an easement through the open, continuous and adverse use of real property for a specified period of time. Usually, the time required is the same as that which is necessary to obtain title by adverse possession. 143

PRICE. A determinable quantity of money or personal property payable by the buyer to the seller for goods purchased. It is the consideration given by the buyer under a contract of sale. In an economic sense, it is the amount presently asked for a commodity and suggests that the commodity is for sale. 211

PRIME MERIDIAN. (See PRINCIPAL MERIDIAN.) 299

PRINCIPAL. In an agency relationship, one who employs another (his agent) to represent him in business and legal dealings with third persons. 44

PRINCIPAL MERIDIAN. As used in the Rectangular Survey System, the principal meridian is the main imaginary line running north and south from which other meridians (each 24 miles apart) are surveyed. Also called Prime Meridians. 299

PRINCIPAL NOTE. The promissory note secured by the mortgage deed or trust deed. 338

PRINTER'S INK STATUTES. Statutes, enacted in most states, that make a seller guilty of a misdemeanor for untrue, misleading, or deceptive advertising of a product.

PRIVILEGE. A legal freedom on the part of one person as against another to do a given act, or legal freedom not to do a given act. For every privilege, there is an absence of a right. 139

PRIVITY. A relationship between persons who successively have a legal interest in the same right or property: an interest in a transaction, contract, or legal action to which one is not a party arising out of a relationship to one of the parties. 175

PROCEEDINGS "A CERTIORARI." A court proceeding which reviews the action of a lower court or a public agency, such as tax officials. During these proceedings, the officials produce their records and certify them to the court in order for the court to render a determination relative to the legality of the process. 190

PROFIT. A right to take something from the land of another. For example, the right to take water from a well on someone's land. 144

PROGRESSIVE TAX. A tax which takes a greater percentage of one's income as that income increases. 192

PROMISSORY NOTE. A written promise by one party (the maker) to pay a sum of money to a second party (the payee). 338

PROPERTY. The right or interest a person has in land or chattels to the exclusion of others. 100

PROPERTY INSURANCE. Property insurance covers risks of financial loss arising out of the damage or destruction of physical property from either the actions of individuals or from the forces of nature. 458

PROPERTY LOSS. An adverse effect on one's financial position from some occurrence. Also, the direct damage, destruction, or wrongful taking by others of one's property. 460

PROPERTY TAX. An impersonal levy which focuses on both real and personal property. It is determined by the property's exchange value and is levied against the property owner. 193

PROPORTIONAL TAX. A tax which reflects a constant ratio between the tax liability and the net income or net worth. 192

PROSPECTUS. An advertisement or document published by a business stating the objects and nature of an offering to the public and inviting the public to purchase.

PUBLIC REAL ESTATE ACTIVITIES. Those activities associated with the various levels, departments, and agencies of the federal, state, and local governments relative to taxation, acquisition, disposal, management, control, regulation, and financing, usually on a non-profit basis. 17

PUBLIC TRUSTEE. A court appointed officer who acts as the trustee of a trust or estate. 357

PURCHASE AND SALE AGREEMENT. A written contract for consideration paid whereby one party agrees to sell and another party agrees to buy certain real estate under the provisions of the agreement. 294

PURCHASE MONEY MORTGAGE. A mortgage executed by the purchaser as part of the purchase price upon a sale of real property. 353

PURE RISK. One which affords the prospect of only loss or no loss. No gain is possible in pure risk. 450

QUASI-CONTRACT. Implied contract which does not have a promise as its base. Also known as a "contract implied in law." 67

QUIET ENJOYMENT. A clause inserted in a warranty deed or lease that gives the grantee or tenant the right of possession without disturbance caused by defects in title. It does not mean freedom from noise or turmoil. 141

QUITCLAIM DEED. A deed by which the grantor releases any interest he may have in the real property, without attempting to convey title. The grantor makes no warranty; if he has title, he conveys it; if he does not have title, he is not responsible for failure to convey a clear title, and the grantee has no right of action against him.
406

RANGE. In the Rectangular Survey System of describing property, a range is one of the north-south strips of land six miles wide. Range lines are designated as being so many "ranges" east or west of a Principal Meridian. 299

RATIFICATION. In agency law, the subsequent approval by a principal of an agent's unauthorized act which makes the approved act binding on the principal. 46

READY. Readiness of the buyer to meet the terms and conditions of the seller. Such readiness is not required when the offer is made, but when the sale is to take place.
246

REAL ESTATE. Any and every estate or interest in land and the improvements thereon. 6

REAL ESTATE BROKER. Generally, one who assists a seller and a buyer in negotiating the sale and purchase of real property, and also who leases and manages the property of another. 18

REAL ESTATE CLOSING. (See CLOSING TITLE.) 500

REAL ESTATE TAX. A tax which relates to the income generated through two of the three factors in production, i. e., land and capital . . . (labor being the third). Real estate taxes may include real property taxes, income taxes, and capital gain taxes.
194

REAL PROPERTY. Land, buildings, minerals, and other products of the soil and the air space above the land. 102

REAL PROPERTY TAX. A direct tax levied against individual parcels of land by the city, town, county, or village. Such a tax does not fall within the realm of the federal government. 195

REALTOR. A title which may be used only by members of an organization affiliated with the NATIONAL ASSOCIATION OF REALTORS. 8

REALTY. Synonymous with real estate and real property. 102

RECAPTURE CLAUSE. A clause in an agreement providing for the retaking or recovering of possession. A term often found in percentage leases.

RECEIVER. An officer of the court appointed on behalf of all parties to a litigation to take possession of, hold, and control the property involved in a suit . . . for the benefit of the party who will be determined to be entitled thereto.

RECORDING. The act of a public officer in recording an entry in a public docket, archive, or record, and by so doing, establishing evidence of a particular transaction, lien, or obligation . . . and in placing the general public on notice of the rights of the parties concerned. 413

RECORDING OF DEED. The filing of a deed in a public office designated by state law which is usually the county or town clerk's office where the property is located.
413

RECORDING OF LEASE. The filing of a copy of the lease with the proper official of the county where the leased property is located. As a practical matter, regardless of whether the law requires it, it is advisable to record a lease on property of any importance. It serves notice to everyone that the tenant holds possession of the premises for a specified term.

REDEMPTION. The right of the original owner of property to reclaim his property after default, upon payment of the amount of the debt with interest and costs. 354

REFORMATION. A remedy given by a court of equity to correct or reform written instruments in instances involving fraud and mistake.

REFUSAL OF OFFER. (See REJECTION.) 69

REGISTERED LAND. Land ... the title to which has been registered by a special Land Court in states using the Torrens System. 417

REGISTERED TITLE. A title which is certified by a Decree of the Land Court and which is usually accepted as unquestionable up to the date of the Decree. 417

REGRESSIVE TAX. A tax which reflects a declining ratio of tax liability as the income increases.

REJECTION. The refusal to accept an offer on the terms provided. After rejection, no acceptance is possible and an attempted acceptance operates as a new offer. Rejection terminates an offer. 69

RELEASE. An instrument freeing one or both parties from contractual obligations.
81
> Relative to insurance, a release is a signed acknowledgement by the insured of his satisfaction with the settlement, and his agreement that subsequent suit will not be brought against the insurer. 460

RELIANCE. Action or forbearance of a definite and substantial character prompted by the promise of another who makes the promise with the intent of having it acted upon. 79

RELICTION. The gradual increase of land by the permanent withdrawal or receding of water. 138

RELIEF. An incident of tenure in feudal England compelling a ward, upon reaching majority, to sue for possession of land and, additionally, pay for the privilege of gaining such possession. This incident may be likened to the inheritance tax of today.
110

REMAINDER. The estate that is left over at the termination of a life estate. 127

REMAINDER ESTATE. (See REMAINDER.) 127

REMAINDERMAN. The person to whom the remainder of an estate passes at the termination of a life estate. 127

REMAINING ECONOMIC LIFE. The period of time, in years, from the date of appraisal to the date when the structure becomes valueless.

REMISE. (See RELEASE.) Remise means discharge or release and is also synonymous with "quit claim." 419

RENT. Periodic payment made regularly by a tenant to a landlord for the use of real property. 169

REPLACEMENT COST. The cost of replacing a property on the basis of current costs and as of a specific date having equivalent utility to the property in question. While "reproduction" refers to the physical property, "replacement" relates to the utility of the property. Both are terms used in the Cost Approach of appraising. 219

REPLACEMENT COST APPROACH. (See COST APPROACH.) 219

REPLEVIN. Redelivery to the owner of the pledge or thing taken in distress. (See DISTRESS, DISTRAIN.) 117

REPOSSESS. The right of the landlord to take possession of his property at the end of the lease term or under other circumstances provided for in the lease. 170

REPRODUCTION COST. The cost of reproducing an exact replica of the property on the basis of current costs and as of a specific date. It is a term used in the Cost Approach of appraising. 219

REPRODUCTION COST APPROACH. (See COST APPROACH.) 219

RESCISSION. The rescinding, cancellation, abrogation, or nullification of a contract.
83

RESIDENCE. A permanent and fixed abode where one is personally present. It is not synonymous with domicile. (See DOMICILE.)

RESIDENTIAL PROPERTY. Residential property is generally construed to mean that property primarily acquired for use as a residence. In some parts of the country, the word "residence" refers exclusively to a one-family dwelling, while "residential property" implies two- to four-family houses, inclusive. 21

RESPONDEAT SUPERIOR. Latin words meaning that the master is liable for the acts of his agent.

RESPONDENT. A person who answers another's bill or pleading, particularly in an equity case. Similar to the defendant in law cases.

RESTITUTION. The return by each party to a contract of the consideration he received from the other party, or its equivalent in money. If, however, one of the parties breaks the contract, he may not be able to recover anything.

RESTRAINING ORDER. An order by a court of equity to hold matters in abeyance until parties may be heard, e. g., a temporary injunction.

RESTRICTIVE COVENANT. A clause in a deed placing a restriction on the use of the property conveyed for a specific period of time. 143

REVENUE. As applied to the income of a government, revenue is a broad and general term which includes all public moneys which the state collects and receives, from whatever source and in whatever manner, and places into its treasury and is appropriated for the payment of its expenses. 188

REVERSION. A future estate which is returned to a grantor. A reversion is distinguished from a remainder which is a future estate which goes to someone other than the grantor. 127

REVOCATION. The withdrawal of an offer before acceptance. Revocation is not possible after acceptance because a contract has already been formed. 69

RIGHT. A legally enforceable claim of one person against another, that the other shall do a given act or shall not do a given act. 139

RIGHT OF REDEMPTION. (See REDEMPTION.) 354

RIGHT-OF-WAY. A form of easement which gives one person the right to pass over the estate of another. 143

RIPARIAN PROPERTY. Land situated beside a stream of water, either flowing over or along the border of the land.

RIPARIAN RIGHTS. The rights to accretion, and the rights accruing to those who own property on the banks of a stream or river. (See ACCRETION.) 138

RISK. As it relates to property, risk is the uncertainty of financial loss. It is often confused with "peril."   449

RISK INSURANCE. The most widely accepted method of dealing with the uncertainty of financial loss.   451

RISK PREVENTION. Relative to insurance, risk prevention is a method of reducing or eliminating the uncertainty of financial loss arising out of the many perils to property.   451

RISK RETENTION. Relative to insurance, risk retention is the assumption of risk by an individual (or business) who takes no action to counter the uncertainties of possible loss.   451

ROD. A measurement of 16½ feet. An acre has 160 square rods.   479

RUNNING WITH THE LAND. A covenant which passes with the transfer or disposition of an estate to the new owner.   143

RURAL. Of or pertaining to the country, as distinguished from a city or town.   30

RUR-URBAN. Of or pertaining to rural areas within commuting range of urban centers.   30

SALE. The transfer of title to property from seller to buyer for a consideration called the price.   294

SALE AND LEASEBACK. The sale of buildings and land to an investor by a business, accompanied by a simultaneous leasing back of the property under a long-term contract.   176

SALES APPROACH. (See MARKET DATA APPROACH.)   217

SATISFACTION. In legal phraseology, it means the release and discharge of a legal obligation.   81

SATISFACTION OF MORTGAGE. A certificate issued by the mortgagee when the mortgage is paid in full. A satisfaction of a mortgage always carries an acknowledgement by an authorized person (e. g., notary public) and is known also as a "satisfaction piece."   342

SATISFACTION PIECE. A certificate describing a mortgage, where it is recorded, and certifying that it has been paid and that the mortgagee is willing to have it discharged of record. It is issued by the lender (mortgagee) when the mortgage is paid in full.   342

SEAL. A mark on a written contract indicating that the instrument was executed in a formal manner. In a few states, it makes a contract valid without consideration. Under most statutes, any stamp, mark, scroll, or impression is adequate. The printed word "seal" or the letters "L. S." (Latin for "locus sigilli," meaning "place of the seal") is sufficient. 65

SEALING. In many states, it is a recital in any written instrument that it is sealed or bears the seal of the person signing it or is given under the hand and seal of the person signing it, or that it is intended to take effect as a sealed instrument. 65

SEARCHING THE TITLE. The process by which a lawyer or searcher of titles investigates to determine whether the seller of property has title and if there are any claims against the property. 412

SECOND MORTGAGE. (See JUNIOR MORTGAGE.) 352

SECTION. As used in the Rectangular Survey System, a section is an area 1 mile square, containing 640 acres. 302

SECURITY. Property, tangible or intangible, given by a debtor to a creditor with power to sell if the debt is not paid. Often referred to in this respect as collateral security. 342

SECURITY DEPOSIT. A money deposit often required by the landlord as security for payment of the rent which frequently takes the form of an advance rent payment. 169

SEISIN. The actual possession of real property. In a warranty deed, the provision that the seller is "seized" of the property in fee simple and has good right to convey means that at the time of execution and delivery of the deed he is in lawful possession of the property and has lawful title. A covenant of seisin benefits only the immediate grantee.
409

SEPARATE PROPERTY. That property owned by a married person in his or her own right during marriage. The spouse has no present rights in such property. 129

SERGEANTY TENURE. An agreement in feudal England whereby the landholder would provide services ranging from those of a ceremonial nature to services as butlers, cooks, and a wide assortment of petty services. The word "sergeanty" derives from the medieval Latin work "serientia," meaning service. 106

SERVANT. One who is employed to render personal services to his employer, other than in the pursuit of an independent calling, and who, in such service, remains entirely under the direction and control of the master. 20

SERVIENT ESTATE. An estate of one person which is limited to a degree by the right of the owner of another parcel of land (dominant) by reason of such ownership to use the former's land for a specific purpose. As an example, by virtue of an easement in the dominant estate, the property of the owner of the servient estate is limited. 143

SETBACK. The distance from the curb to an established line within which no building may be erected.

SEVERALTY OWNERSHIP. Real estate which is owned by one person only. 132

SHORT-TERM LEASE. One for a limited number of years, usually less than ten.

SIGNING. A requirement for the execution of a deed. The grantor's signature is essential to a valid deed. An estate or interest in land created without a signed, written instrument by the grantor or his attorney has the force and effect of only an "estate at will."
422

SIMPLE LISTING. (See OPEN LISTING.) 240

SKY LEASE. Long-term lease of the space above a piece of real estate.

SOCAGE TENURE. An agreement in feudal England wherein tenants who held land of the king would annually furnish products of the soil essential for life as required by the king. 106

SPECIAL AGENT. One whose authority to act is confined to do a particular job or accomplish a specific task. Normally, a real estate broker acts in the capacity of a special agent. 45

SPECIFIC PERFORMANCE. A requirement by court order for one party to a contract to do as he promised. Such remedy applies to contracts involving unique goods, such as real property, or peculiar circumstances where damages for the breach of contract would prove inadequate. 83

SPECIFIC TAX. A tax or duty based on a physical measurement or quantity, e. g., per ton, per foot, per gallon. 192

SPECULATIVE RISK. One which may be rewarded by gain or exposure to loss. 450

SPECULATOR. One who buys or sells with the expectation of realizing a profit by a rise or fall in price. Also one engaged in hazardous business transactions for the chance of realizing unusually large profits. 30

SPOT ZONING. (See ZONING ORDINANCE.) The application of a different zoning status for certain property from that applied to the surrounding area in those areas which are being transformed from one general use to another. 142

SQUARE. In the Rectangular Survey System, it is an area measuring 24 miles by 24 miles, sometimes called a "check."

SQUATTER'S RIGHTS. (See ADVERSE POSSESSION.) 137

STATUTE. A law passed by the legislative body of a state.

STATUTE OF FRAUDS. A statute adopted in every state to prevent frauds and perjuries by providing that no legal protection shall be given to certain express contracts, unless they are evidenced by a memorandum in writing and signed by the party to be charged.
74

STATUTE OF LIMITATIONS. Statutes which prescribe a time limit within which suit must be started after a cause of action arises.
81

STEP LEASE. A lease which allows for the increase or decrease of rent payments at fixed intervals in accordance with the terms of the lease contract.
175

STOP PAYMENT ORDER. An order to a bank from a drawer not to make payment on a particular check drawn by him.

SUBAGENT. An agent appointed by one who is himself an agent. A person appointed by an agent to perform some duty, in whole or in part, relating to his agency. A person employed by an agent to assist him in transacting the affairs of his principal.

SUBORDINATION CLAUSE. A clause in any security instrument providing that such a lien will be subordinate in priority to any specified existing or anticipated lien. It converts original security instrument into a junior security instrument.

SUBDIVIDER. One who buys undeveloped acreage wholesale, segments it into smaller parcels, and sells it retail. A subdivider is usually not interested in extending his involvement into the intricacies and complexities of land development.
30

SUBDIVISION. The division of a parcel of land into house lots.
30

SUBINFEUDATION. In feudal law, subinfeudation was the granting of lands by a vassal lord to another to hold as vassal of himself.
106

SUBJECTIVE VALUE. (See VALUE IN USE.)
209

SUBLEASE. The transfer for a portion of the balance of the term of the lease of the whole or a part of the leased premises.
174

SUBLETTING. The leasing to a third person by the lessee of a whole or part of the premises for a portion of the lessee's unexpired term.
174

SUBPOENA. A writ or order commanding the person named to appear and testify in a legal proceeding. Failure to appear will constitute a contempt of court.

SUBROGATION. The substitution of one person in another person's place and the acquisition of the other person's legal rights and remedies.
460

SUBROGATION. Relative to insurance, the transfer of one party's legal right or claim to another. It is a legal doctrine which supports the concept of insurance as a contract of indemnity. 460

SUBURBAN. Blending the urban and the rural. Of or pertaining to the outlying parts of a city or town. A smaller place adjacent to a city or town with residential districts on the outskirts. 22

SUFFERANCE. (See TENANCY BY SUFFERANCE.) 167

SUMMONS. A legal notice requiring a person to answer a complaint within a specified time. A copy of the summons must be left personally with the person against whom it is directed. Failure to answer the summons will result in judgment against the plaintiff by default.

SUNDAY LAWS. The laws enacted by some states or localities which prohibit business activity on Sundays. Sunday statutes render contracts calling for performance on Sundays void. 73

SURETY. A person who has made himself liable for the payment of money or the performance of some act by another.

SURETY BOND. A contract to indemnify injured parties upon the failure of another to perform a particular act.

SURRENDER. The cancellation by mutual consent of the lessor and lessee of their lease agreement. When leased premises, for example, are abandoned by a tenant, and such abandonment is accepted by the landlord as a termination of the lease, a surrender has occurred.

SURVEY. A process which determines the boundaries of an area with distance and directions. 298

SURVIVORSHIP. The chief characteristic of a joint tenancy which automatically passes the interests of the deceased to the surviving tenants until there is but one survivor. 133

TANGIBLE. Property that is physical in character and capable of being moved. 103

TANGIBLE PERSONAL PROPERTY. The obvious type of personal property which consists of all items which are physical and have substance - such as furniture, et cetera. 103

TAX. A pecuniary burden laid upon individuals or property to support the government, a payment enacted by legislative authority. In a general sense, a tax is any contribution imposed by government upon individuals for the use and service of the state, whether under the name of toll, tribute, tallage, gabel, impost, duty, custom, excise, subsidy, aid, supply, or other name. 185

TAX DEED. One issued by public authority to convey title to property after a tax sale of property. (See TAX SALE.)

TAX LIEN. A claim against real property from assessed taxes against the property that accrues to the taxing agency (municipality, city, et cetera). If not paid when due, the taxing agency sells the property at a tax sale. 146

TAX LIST. (See ASSESSMENT ROLL.) 190

TAX SALE. The sale of property for non-payment of taxes, usually at auction. 137

TAX TITLE. The title acquired by the purchaser through the public sale of land owned by a delinquent taxpayer for the collection of unpaid taxes. 137

TENANCY. The period of time that a tenant is permitted to remain in possession of real property. Also, an interest in land, e. g., joint tenancy, tenancy in common, tenancy by the entirety, and tenancy in severalty. 132

TENANCY AT WILL. One that can be cancelled at any time by either party. Sometimes referred to as an Estate at Will. 166

TENANCY BY THE ENTIRETY. An estate held by husband and wife and limited to them by virtue of title acquired by them jointly after marriage. If either spouse dies, his or her interest passes automatically to the other by survivorship. This type of tenancy cannot be terminated without the consent of both parties. 133

TENANCY BY SUFFERANCE. A form of tenancy whereby the landlord permits the tenant to occupy the property for some special reason without obligation on the tenant's part to pay rent, or on the landlord's part to permit occupancy. 167

TENANCY FOR YEARS. A tenancy which gives the tenant a right to occupy property for a fixed period of time. A tenancy for years is synonymous with a leasehold. (See LEASEHOLD.) 165

TENANCY FROM YEAR TO YEAR. A tenancy that continues for a year and is then continued automatically for another year and from year to year thereafter, unless notice of termination is given. 166

TENANCY IN COMMON. Ownership by two or more persons by separate and distinct titles. Tenants in common may have different degrees of interest in the estate and may have acquired their titles at different times and from different sources, but their right of possession is common. Upon death, interest passes to the heirs or beneficiaries and not to the other tenants in common.   134

TENANCY IN SEVERALTY. One owner holds the entire estate.   132

TENANT. One who holds or possesses land. More commonly, a person who acquires the use of real property that belongs to another person known as the landlord for a limited period of time.   132

TENEMENT. Generally, it means an estate in land or some interest connected therewith, such as, rents, profits, rights, and houses, to which a holder of the title is entitled. It is often used with the word "hereditaments."   132

TENURE. The mode or system of holding lands or tenements in subordination to some superior, which, in feudal society, was the principal characteristic of real property. 105

TERM OF LEASE. The time period during which a lease is to be effective.   165

TERMINATION OF AGENCY. The termination of an agency relationship between the principal and his agent.   70

TERRE-TENANT. One who is in actual possession of real property as distinguished from the person who owns the property.

TESTATE. Having left a will. One who dies leaving a will is said to have died testate.
139

TESTATOR. The person making the will. If a woman, a testatrix.   139

TIER. As used in the Rectangular Survey System, a tier is an east-west row of townships.
301

"TIME IS OF THE ESSENCE." When a contract specifies that "time is of the essence," timely performance becomes a condition precedent and performance that does not occur at the time required can be rejected entirely. (See CONDITION PRECEDENT.)   83

TITLE. Evidence of ownership and often used interchangeably with the term "ownership" to indicate a person's right to possess, use, and dispose of property.

TITLE AGENCIES. Those organizations in the business of servicing the public with respect to the condition or quality of title to real property.

TITLE CLOSING. The meeting of parties to a sales contract at a designated place and time for the performance (or closing) of the contract.   500

TITLE INSURANCE. An insurance which protects the insured from loss or damage resulting from defects in title. It guarantees the authenticity of every recorded instrument and places an absolute guarantee behind the work of the title company. 416

TITLE SEARCH. A circumspect review of all documents and records in the local recorder's office pertaining to a property to determine if the seller has good title to the property. This service is usually performed by a lawyer or a title insurance company. 412

TORRENS SYSTEM. A system of registering title to real property that accurately determines the ownership of land and every lien and claim upon it. This system was established in Massachusetts by law in 1898. Under this system, the owner of land may apply to register his title with the Land Court. A certificate of registration is issued after certain legal requirements are met, and the registered owner has good title to the property. 417

TORT. A wrongful act committed by one person against the person or property of another. 48

TOWNSHIP. As used in the Rectangular Survey System of land description, a township is a 6 mile square area containing 36 sections, each 1 mile square. 301

TRESPASS. Unauthorized entry upon the land of another or unlawful and violent interference with the person or property of another. Trespass is a tort, even though unintentionally committed. Further, actual damages need not be shown to maintain an action for trespass. 143

TRESPASSER. One who enters unlawfully upon the land of another without consent of the owner. 143

TRUST. A legal relationship by which one person (the trustee) holds property for the use and benefit of another (the beneficiary) in accordance with the directions of the creator of the trust (the settlor). In general, a trust is a right of real or personal property held by one party for the benefit of another. It is any agreement whereby property is transferred with the intention that it be administered by trustee for another's benefit. It is a fiduciary relationship with respect to property, subjecting the person by whom the property is held (trustee) to equitable duties to deal with the property for the benefit of another (the beneficiary) in accordance with the directions of the creator of the trust (the settlor, also called the trustor). 356

TRUSTEE. In a trust relationship, one who holds property for the benefit of another person (the beneficiary). 357

TRUST DEED. A deed which conveys real estate to a third person to be held for the benefit of a beneficiary. 356

UNDISCLOSED PRINCIPAL. The principal in an agency relationship whose identity is not disclosed by the agent in dealing with third persons - or the fact that an agency relationship exists.   44

UNEARNED INCREMENT. An increase in the value of real estate due to no effort of an owner, but attributable to natural causes.

UNENFORCEABLE CONTRACTS. Valid contracts which will not be enforced by courts of law because of some special barrier, e. g., contracts barred by the Statute of Limitations or unenforceable because of the Statute of Frauds.   66

UNFREE TENURE. The holding of land by the tillers of the soil (villeins) for services which were specifically identifed as to quantity (e. g., so many hours per day, per week), but were indefinite as to quality.   107

UNILATERAL CONTRACT. One wherein a promise is exchanged for an act.   66

URBAN. Of or belonging to a city or town. Characteristic of, constituting, or pertaining to, a city or town.

USURY. Charging or taking more interest than that allowed by law.

V. A. MORTGAGE. A mortgage in which the repayment of the loan to the lending institution is guaranteed in part by the Veterans' Administration. Sometimes referred to as a V. A. Loan, V. A. Guaranteed Mortgage, G. I. Loan, or G. I. Mortgage.   368

VALUE. Value is any consideration sufficient to support a simple contract; value and consideration within this context are identical. In a business sense, value means market value. The money equivalent of property is value. In a strict economic sense, value relates to the present worth and the future anticipated benefits of a commodity.   209

VALUE IN EXCHANGE. The term used to express the value of a commodity relative to its power to purchase other goods. Value in exchange is sometimes referred to as "objective value" and "market value."   209

VALUE IN USE. The term used to express the value of a commodity relative to its utility. Value in use is sometimes referred to as "subjective value."   209

VARIANCE. An exception to the zoning ordinances authorized by a special board of appeals in the event of unusual hardship or special circumstances.   142

VASSAL. One who has placed himself under the protection of another as his lord and has vowed homage and fealty.   109

VENDEE. The purchaser of real property. The word "buyer" usually applies to the purchaser of tangible personal property (chattels).   306

VENDOR. The seller of real property. The word "seller" is usually applied to the seller of personal property. 306

VILLEIN. About the 13th Century, the term was applied to a class of unfree peasants, or serfs, who, as regards their lord, were slaves, but were free in their legal relations with others. 107

VOID CONTRACT. One which has no legal effect and is, therefore, unenforceable. 66

VOID TITLE. Title without legal force or binding effect, so that it is no title at all, in reality.

VOIDABLE CONTRACT. One which is valid until one party, who has the power of avoidance, exercises such power. An infant has the power of avoidance of his contract. 66

VOIDABLE TITLE. Title which is valid and legally effectual until nullified by the party who has a right to rescind or nullify it. Voidable title may result from the incapacity of one of the parties to contract because of being a minor.

VOLUNTARY WASTE. Any positive act by the tenant of an unreasonable nature which causes injury to the leased property and results in damage. 174

WAIVER. The intentional relinquishment or giving up of a known right.

WARDSHIP. An incident of tenure in feudal England entitling the lord to all profits from the land of a deceased tenant until his heir became of age. 110

WARRANTY. A word relating to title and quality. It is a promise or representation that a certain fact regarding the subject matter of a contract is now true or will be true. Warranty is not to be confused with guaranty, which means a promise by one to answer for the performance of another. 409

WARRANTY DEED. A deed, upon a sale of real property, under which the grantor formally agrees (covenants) that he will forever guarantee title to the conveyed real property. A warranty deed does not correct a bad title. It simply gives the grantee the right to sue the grantor for breach of warranty if someone later makes a claim against the property.

WASTE. Damage to real property which impairs its value as security. 173

WATER RIGHTS. The rights of an owner of land adjoining a stream which is not navigable to use the stream to a reasonable extent. 142

WILL. The formal legal declaration by which a person (testator) disposes of his property, to take effect after he dies. 139

"WILLING." A matter of state of mind. It infers a willingness to accept a seller's terms and conditions, both when the oral understanding is reached and when executing the written agreement. It indicates that the buyer has the desire to reach a meeting of the minds with the seller. 246

WRIT OF EXECUTION. A sealed instrument of the state directing an officer of the court to carry out the judgment or decree of the court. 148

ZONING ORDINANCE. An ordinance under which communities restrict the use of certain land areas and control the type, intensity, and volume of building construction in such areas. 141